THE AMERICAN YEARS

THE
AMERICAN
YEARS

A Chronology of United States History

ERNIE GROSS

CHARLES SCRIBNER'S SONS

An imprint of Macmillan Library Reference USA
NEW YORK

Editor: Sylvia K. Miller
Copy Editors: Salvatore Allocco, Juanita Galuska, Eric Haralson
Proofreaders: Carol Holmes, Vida Petronis, Faye Zucker
Illustration Researcher: Martin A. Levick
Designer: Kevin Hanek

Charles Scribner's Sons
Macmillan Library Reference USA
1633 Broadway
New York, NY 10019

10 9 8 7 6 5 4 3 2

Library of Congress Cataloging-in-Publication Data

Gross, Ernie.
    The American years : a chronology of United States history / Ernie
Gross.
      p. cm.
    Includes index.
    ISBN 0-684-80590-1 (alk. paper)
    1. United States--History--Chronology. I. Title.
E174.5.G753 1999
973'.02'02--dc21   98-46674
                                       CIP

This paper meets the requirements of ANSI Z39.48-1992 (Permanence of Paper).

CONTENTS

PREFACE

THIS BOOK IS AN EFFORT TO GIVE AN OVERview of life in the United States since it became an independent nation. Most U.S. histories tend to concentrate on the most visible events occurring during a year, which provides a rather narrow picture; other facets of American life are either glossed over or ignored completely.

This book is an attempt to show what U.S. governments were doing on the national, state, and local levels and the major events in business and industry. But there is much more to living in the United States. Also included are events of the year in the arts and sciences, education and religion, and literature as well as what kept Americans busy in their spare time—entertainment and sports.

To provide this kind of look at American life, the annual focus is divided into the following categories: International, National, Business/Industry/Inventions, Transportation, Science/Medicine, Education, Religion, Arts/Music, Literature/Journalism, Entertainment, Sports, and Miscellaneous. All the categories might not be presented in every year.

This book was written with the hope that it would enable students and readers to follow trends in these varied aspects of American life and make it possible to relate traditional history to the many other things that are important to everyday living.

A reader interested in tracing the development of one aspect of American life can do so readily by following a category through the years or by comparing years or decades to see the changes.

The book is written in a concise telegraphic style so as to be able to include as much factual material as possible and to do so in clear, understandable language. I have sought to include what I consider to be the most important events of each year, using a wide range of source material.

The author and the publisher wish to thank historians Joshua W. Lane, Eugene Leach, and Allan M. Winkler for their valuable advice during the preparation of this book for publication.

—ERNIE GROSS

ABBREVIATIONS

AAFC	All-American Football Conference	NAACP	National Association for the Advancement of Colored People
AAU	American Athletic Union	NASA	National Aeronautics and Space Administration
AEC	Atomic Energy Commission		
AFB	Air Force Base	NASCAR	National Association for Stock Car Auto Racing
AFL	American Federation of Labor		
AFL	American Football League	NBA	National Basketball Association
AIAW	Association of Intercollegiate Athletics for Women	NBC	National Broadcasting Co.
		NCAA	National Collegiate Athletic Association
ATT	American Telephone & Telegraph Co.	NFL	National Football League
BAA	Basketball Association of America	NHL	National Hockey League
CBS	Columbia Broadcasting System	NIT	National Invitational Tournament (basketball)
FBI	Federal Bureau of Investigation		
FCC	Federal Communications Commission	PBA	Professional Bowlers Association
		PGA	Professional Golfers Association
IBM	International Business Machines Corp.	TVA	Tennessee Valley Authority
		UCLA	University of California, Los Angeles
ICC	Interstate Commerce Commission	U.N.	United Nations
IC4A	Intercollegiate Association of Amateur Athletes of America	UNLV	University of Nevada, Las Vegas
		USFL	United States Football League
ITT	International Telephone & Telegraph Co.	USLTA	U.S. Lawn Tennis Association
		USO	United Service Organization
LPGA	Ladies Professional Golf Association	VFW	Veterans of Foreign Wars
MIT	Massachusetts Institute of Technology		

COLONIAL HISTORY
A Brief Overview

ALTHOUGH THE UNITED STATES OFFICIALLY began with the signing of the Declaration of Independence, a great many occurrences preceded that momentous occasion. The following is a summary of the events that led to transforming the British colonies into a major independent nation.

INTERNATIONAL

Almost 100 years before the English began to create the colonies that emerged as the United States, the Spanish explored Central America and the American coastal areas. Operating from the Caribbean islands that Columbus discovered, Spanish explorers headed north.

Ponce de León landed near what was to be St. Augustine, Fla. (1513), followed by Pánfilo de Narváez and Hernando de Soto, who explored much of what is now the Gulf States. Less concerned with establishing settlements, the Spanish looked for gold, although they did set up St. Augustine (1565).

Other Spanish explorers traversed the West Coast, including João Rodrigues Cabrilho, who traveled as far as Oregon, and Gaspar de Portola. Franciscan missionaries, such as Junipero Serra, who founded many California missions, around which cities later grew, followed Spanish explorers.

The Spanish effort was not without hazards as British warships, led by Sir Francis Drake, preyed on Spanish shipping. In New Mexico, the Native Americans revolted and drove out the Spanish settlers for a time.

French explorers also were active in the New World. Beginning with Giovanni da Verrazano, who arrived off the Carolinas in 1524, the French created settlements on the southeast coast (Fort Caroline at the present Florida-Georgia border), the Gulf Coast (Mobile, in present-day Alabama), in eastern Canada, and thanks to Sieur de LaSalle and Jacques Marquette, in the Mississippi Valley.

There also were Swedish settlers in Delaware and Dutch around New York City (then called New Amsterdam).

English colonization began with the ill-fated Roanoke Island (N.C.) Settlement (1584). Supplies to sustain the colony failed to arrive until seven years later, by which time the colony ("Lost Colony") had disappeared. The first permanent settlement came in 1607 with Jamestown, followed in 1620 by Plymouth (Mass.).

Early settlers had to contend with local Native American tribes for survival and for additional living space. Many of the colonial wars were the local expression of fighting among the powers in Europe. Between 1664 and 1673, the English and Dutch were at war, and New York City changed hands three times. From 1689 to 1697, England and France were at war, and the American version was King William's War. Five years later, the English warred against Spain and France; this war was Queen Anne's War in the colonies. The ensuing peace lasted 30 years, and then war broke out in what the Americans called King George's War.

The final European conflict of the period was the Seven Years' War (1755–1763), in American history the French and Indian War, which first brought George Washington into the picture as a military leader.

When that war ended, the stirrings for American independence were growing.

NATIONAL

In 1764 the British tried to extract more revenue from the colonies by tightening customs operations, forbidding local currencies; Britain passed the Quartering Act, which required barracks and supplies for their troops, and the Stamp Act, the first direct tax on the colonists (1765).

William Penn's Treaty with the Delaware Indians, 1682, granting Penn and his heirs land in southeastern Pennsylvania (in present-day Bucks County). THE GRANGER COLLECTION, NEW YORK

The colonial answer was refusal to import British goods, which hurt British merchants but stimulated the start of American business and industry.

Britain tried again with the Townshend Acts (1767), which met the same resistance; Massachussetts sent a circular letter to the other colonies, urging united action against the British (1768); then British troops arrived in Boston to help New England customs collectors; nonimportation continued, and by 1769 several colonies were protesting taxation without representation.

The first physical clash occurred in 1770 when the Sons of Liberty in New York City tangled with British troops; such skirmishes continued, dramatically emphasized by this incident, which came to be known as the Boston Massacre.

In 1772 a customs schooner, *Gaspé*, ran aground off Providence, and colonials set fire to the vessel after removing the crew. The Tea Act in 1773 led to more serious opposition, climaxed by the Boston Tea Party, versions of which were copied in New York, Annapolis, and New Jersey.

The movement toward independence gathered momentum, and the colonists created the First Continental Congress (1774), which criticized British actions and set forth colonists' rights to "life, liberty, and property." British troops seized cannon and powder in the Boston area and began to build fortifications.

The British Parliament rejected American petitions and passed the New England Restraining Act, forbidding trade with anyone but the British and the British West Indies.

The inevitable came to pass in 1775, when colonists faced British soldiers at Lexington and Concord (Mass.). The Second Continental Congress decided to put the colonies in a state of defense and named George Washington chief of their forces. Congress still hoped to avoid war and adopted a "Declaration of the Causes and Necessities of Taking Up Arms," which rejected independence but said Americans would rather die than be slaves.

All these efforts proved fruitless and were followed by the Declaration of Independence and the American Revolution.

The first slaves were brought into Virginia 12

years after the first settlement; in 1712, Pennsylvania forbade the importation of slaves.

BUSINESS/INDUSTRY/INVENTIONS

Colonists wasted little time in beginning to build their businesses and factories: Jamestown residents began to make glass artifacts right after their arrival; James Rolfe began to grow tobacco (1609), and by 1617 colonists exported 50,000 pounds to England; wheat first grew in Virginia (1618), and cattle were introduced in New England (1624). The first fire-insurance company operated in Charleston, S.C., in 1735, and first life-insurance company opened in 1759 in Philadelphia.

The first ironworks in the colonies were established in Virginia (1619), a saltworks in New Hampshire, and a sawmill near York, Me. (1623); the Dutch built the first colonial flour mill (1623). In Massachusetts, a brick kiln was created at Salem, a leather tannery at Lynn (1629), a woolen mill at Rowley (1643); a paper mill was founded near Philadelphia (1690) and a glass factory in New Jersey (1738).

TRANSPORTATION

Colonists had to rely on water for their earliest transportation; the first ferry route (Boston to Charlestown) was created in 1630.

By 1736 stagecoach service operated between Boston and Newport, R.I., and by 1756 between Philadelphia and New York.

SCIENCE/MEDICINE

Medicine got an early start in the colonies when the first doctor (Lawrence Bohne) arrived (1610); six years later a smallpox epidemic swept through New England. In later years, Indians suffered from other diseases to which they lacked immunity.

Cotton Mather, religious leader, told local physicians of inoculation experiments on smallpox made in Constantinople; Zabdiel Boylston used the technique with some success. The community was upset with this unorthodox and possibly impious practice, but by 1722 Boylston had successfully treated more than 200 patients.

Pennsylvania Hospital in Philadelphia opened in 1752; the first medical school (College of Phil-

"Give me liberty, or give me death!" Patrick Henry delivers his great speech on the rights of the colonies before the Virginia Assembly, 1775. His fiery conclusion became the war cry of the Revolution. THE GRANGER COLLECTION, NEW YORK

The Declaration of Independence. CORBIS

adelphia, Department of Medicine) was founded in 1765.

In 1752 the versatile Benjamin Franklin conducted his experiment with a kite to find out about electricity.

EDUCATION

Schooling was important to the colonists: the Boston Public Latin School opened in 1635; four years later Dorchester, Mass., created the first school to be maintained by a community, and by 1647 Massachusetts required every community with 50 households to maintain a school.

Higher education was not far behind as Harvard was founded in 1636, followed by William & Mary (1689), Yale (1701), Princeton (1747), William Penn Academy (later University of Pennsylvania) (1751), Columbia (1754), Rutgers (1766), and Dartmouth (1769).

Benjamin Franklin spearheaded the founding of a library in Philadelphia in 1732. Libraries got an early start in 1820s with founding of two New York City library associations.

RELIGION

Colonists brought their religion with them. Churches sprang up quickly after their arrival: the Spanish built the first Catholic church in St. Augustine, Fla. (1565). Later came the Church of England (1609) and Presbyterian Church (1611) in Virginia, Congregational in Plymouth (1620), Dutch Reformed in New York City (1628), Lutheran in Delaware (1638), Baptists in Philadelphia (1701), Jewish in New York City (1730), and Moravian in Pennsylvania (1735).

John and Charles Wesley arrived in Georgia for a brief visit (1736), and early Methodist societies were formed in New York City and the mid-Atlantic states.

Religious tolerance was relatively rare in the colonies. Connecticut and Massachusetts persecuted Baptists and Quakers; Maryland enacted a Toleration Act providing religious freedom (1649) but repealed it five years later. Rhode Island, which provided a haven for insurgents Roger Williams and Anne Hutchinson, was the first to grant complete religious freedom (1641).

George Whitefield, English evangelist and founder of Calvinist Methodism, strengthened the Great Awakening religious movement (1726), which had been launched by Jonathan Edwards, considered the greatest theologian of his time; he served Congregational Church in Northampton, Mass., 21 years.

Salem witchcraft trials (1692) resulted in executions of 20 alleged witches.

John Eliot, a missionary to Native Americans, published an Indian-language Bible (1663).

Congregational churches in their Cambridge Platform (1651) spelled out the relationship of church and state.

ART/MUSIC

Colonists were too busy trying to make a living and gaining their independence to devote much time to art and music. However, Charleston, S.C., founded a museum (1773) and was the site of the first opera in America (1735). An English troupe presented *The Merchant of Venice* in Williamsburg (1752). Early artists (among them John Singleton Copley) began to paint portraits and landscapes; their work emerged soon after the Revolution.

LITERATURE/JOURNALISM

The first newspaper *Public Occurrences* (Boston) lasted only one issue before it was suppressed (1690) but was quickly followed by the *Boston News-Letter* (1704). In 1730, Benjamin Franklin began 18 years of editing the *Philadelphia Gazette*. In 1733 John Peter Zenger began to edit the *New York Weekly Journal* but was arrested a year later for seditious libel. His subsequent trial and acquittal laid the groundwork for freedom of the American press. Other early newspapers, all named *Gazette*, published in Annapolis (1727), Charleston, S.C. (1732), and Williamsburg, Va. (1736).

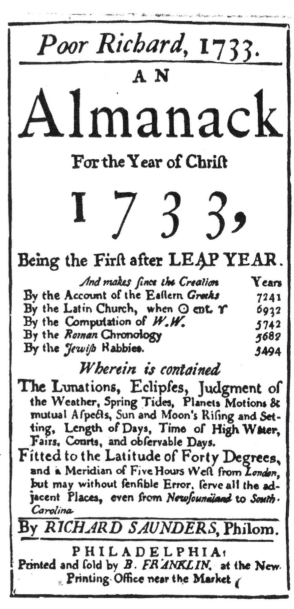

The 1733 issue of Poor Richard's *Almanack*, published by Benjamin Franklin. CORBIS

The first magazine, *The American Magazine*, appeared in 1741.

Book publishing began soon after settlement, an early work being Capt. John Smith's book about Virginia. One of the best-known early works was the *Bay Psalm Book* (1640). The first American best-seller was Michael Wigglesworth's long poem, *The Day of Doom*.

ENTERTAINMENT

A theatrical performance (*Ye Bare and Ye Cub*) was presented in Virginia as early as 1665, and one of the earliest New York theaters opened in 1732.

SPORTS

The playing of organized games came slowly to the colonies, beginning with a game of bowls (1611); then, in order, came something akin to miniature golf in New England (1652), horse racing on Long Island (1664), billiards in Charlestown, Mass. (1722), ninepins in New York City (1732), whist (1745), cricket (1751), and fox hunting in the Philadelphia area.

MISCELLANEOUS

The first public execution was that of John Billington, hanged for murder (1630) in Plymouth, Mass.

Slave revolts began in 1712 in New York City when a conspiracy led to the death of a white man and 27 slaves; in 1739, Cato's revolt at Stono, S.C., resulted in death of 25 whites and 50 slaves, and in 1741, New York City was scene of another revolt that ended with 35 deaths.

Indentured servants were numerous before slavery increased; in 1681, there were 6,000 indentured servants working out five-year contracts, compared to 2,000 slaves.

1776

INTERNATIONAL

American Revolution

George Washington announces formation of Continental Army; colonial flag flies for first time.

NORTH Boston is evacuated by 10,000 British troops (March 17); British land unopposed on Staten Island, N.Y. (July 2); Americans, defeated on Long Island (August 27), ferry to safety across East River to Harlem Heights, turn back British (September 16); British occupy New York City (September 15), capture Ft. Washington (October 28); Americans retreat to New Jersey, British capture Ft. Lee (November 20); Americans cross Delaware River (December 26), capture Trenton.

SOUTH Norfolk, Va., is burned for refusing provisions to British troops (January 1); Americans defeat British near Wilmington, N.C. (February 27), American troops on Sullivan Island, S.C., beat off British attack (June 28), delaying southern invasion for two years.

CANADA Americans abandon Canadian invasion in 1775 and begin retreat (May 6); Americans delay British invasion from north at Valcour Island in Lake Champlain until spring.

Congress names Benjamin Franklin and Catholic Bishop John Carroll to seek Canada's help; sends Silas Deane to Europe to buy war materials; France, Spain agree to help; Franklin, Deane, and Arthur Lee are named to represent U.S. in France.

John Paul Jones captures many prizes at sea; Americans successfully raid British naval station in Bahamas; British close American colonies to all commerce.

British-American peace talks on Staten Island fail (September 11).

The Sons of Liberty raise a Liberty Pole in 1776. THE GRANGER COLLECTION, NEW YORK

1776

Nathan Hale is captured; he is hanged as spy by British (September 21).

NATIONAL

Rhode Island (May 4) and New Hampshire (June 15) declare their independence; resolution for colonial independence is offered in Continental Congress by Richard Henry Lee of Virginia and John Adams of Massachusetts; committees are named to draft Declaration of Independence and Articles of Confederation.

Declaration draft is completed (June 28); final version, mostly written by Thomas Jefferson, is approved (July 4); Articles draft is finished (July 12).

Virginia adopts Bill of Rights drafted by George Mason; Patrick Henry becomes Virginia's first governor.

Congress adopts a national lottery to help pay for the war, grants land bounties to soldiers and British deserters, and approves pensions for disabled veterans.

Rhode Island convention adopts wage and price controls for New England to conserve scarce commodities.

State constitutions are adopted in New Hampshire, New Jersey, Pennsylvania, Delaware, Maryland, Virginia, North Carolina, South Carolina; Kentucky is established as a county of Virginia.

Presidio around which San Francisco will grow is founded; mission at San Juan Capistrano is dedicated.

Fire destroys most of the older section of New York City, including Trinity Church.

BUSINESS/INDUSTRY/INVENTIONS

David Bushnell invents one-man submarine, designed to attach mine to enemy hull.

First American engineering book is published, translated by Maj. Lewis Nicola from French book *L'Ingenieur de Campagne* by Louis André de Clairac.

SCIENCE/MEDICINE

John Bard, pioneer physician, helps introduce dissection of human bodies for instructional purposes.

EDUCATION

Harvard confers honorary Doctor of Laws degree on George Washington.

Phi Beta Kappa, first American fraternity, is created at College of William & Mary in Virginia.

RELIGION

Presbytery of Hanover petitions Virginia Assembly for religious liberty, removal of taxes to support Anglican Church; Virginia Bill of Rights calls for "free exercise of religion."

First Shaker "family" is formed in Watervliet, N.Y., by Ann Lee.

First Catholic chaplain, Rev. Louis E. Lotbinier, is named to Continental Army.

LITERATURE/JOURNALISM

Common Sense by Thomas Paine is published (January 9), calls for separation from Great Britain; first portion of his *American Crisis* and John Trumbull's *McFingal* are published.

Philip Freneau publishes his lyric poem, "The Beauties of Santa Cruz."

New York Packet newspaper begins publication.

MISCELLANEOUS

New Jersey becomes first state to grant women suffrage; repealed 1807.

1777

INTERNATIONAL

American Revolution

Americans capture Princeton, N.J. (January 3).

Gen. William Howe leads 15,000 British troops from New York to capture Philadelphia, takes Brandywine (September 11), occupies Philadelphia (September 19); Americans unsuccessful in assault on Germantown (October 4).

British begin three-pronged assault on New York state: Gen. John Burgoyne from the north, Gen. Howe from the south (most of his force goes to Philadelphia instead), and Gen. Barry St. Leger from the west. Burgoyne heads for Saratoga, takes Ft. Ticonderoga (July 6), is routed at Bennington, Vt. (August 16), is defeated at Bemis Heights (October 7), surrenders at Saratoga (October 17);

British force from Oswego, N.Y., takes Ft. Edward and Ft. Stanwix, fights bloody, indecisive battle at Oriskany (August 6); British return to Oswego, fearing American counterattack; British, heading north, burn Esopus (now Kingston), N.Y. (October 16); return to New York City.

British make three-day raid on Connecticut, burn Danbury (April 27), occupy Rhode Island (November 28).

General Washington and his troops set up winter quarters at Valley Forge, Pa.

Marquis de Lafayette and Baron Johann de Kalb arrive (July 27) to help American troops; Thaddeus Kosciusko is commissioned a colonel in Engineer Corps.

France recognizes American independence.

A New England kitchen of the Revolutionary War period, as depicted in a nineteenth-century lithograph. THE GRANGER COLLECTION, NEW YORK

1778

NATIONAL

Congress reconvenes in Philadelphia (March 4); oncoming British troops force removal to Lancaster, Pa. (September 19), then York (September 30); the Liberty Bell is moved from Philadelphia to Zion Reformed Church, Allentown, Pa.; Congress resolves (June 14) that American flag be 13 red and white alternating stripes, 13 white stars on blue field; Congress adopts Articles of Confederation and Perpetual Union (November 15).

Vermont convention adopts name, state constitution that forbade slavery, provides universal manhood suffrage regardless of property or wealth; New York and Georgia adopt state constitutions; Thomas Johnson is named first governor of Maryland.

First Thanksgiving Day is celebrated (December 18) to commemorate victory at Saratoga.

Massachusetts and Rhode Island outlaw distillation of spirits from grain because of need for corn and rye for food.

Cherokee give up all territory in South Carolina and western North Carolina.

DEATHS Button Gwinnett, Georgia legislator and Declaration of Independence signer; Samuel Prescott, who accompanied Paul Revere on his famous ride.

BUSINESS/INDUSTRY/INVENTIONS

Oliver Evans invents card-making machine for textile industry.

SCIENCE/MEDICINE

DEATH John Bartram, America's first important botanist.

EDUCATION

Episcopal rector James Madison begins 35-year presidency of College of William & Mary.

RELIGION

New Testament is published in English for the first time in U.S.

LITERATURE/JOURNALISM

New Jersey Gazette, first paper in state, begins publication in Burlington.

INTERNATIONAL

American Revolution

Battle of Monmouth, N.J. (June 28), ends with British return to New York City; Washington leads troops to White Plains; British evacuate Philadelphia, Liberty Bell is returned to city.

British capture Savannah, Ga. (December 29).

Loyalists and Native Americans raid New York and Pennsylvania; Cherry Valley (near Albany) massacre is climax (November 11).

U.S. and France sign treaties of amity, commerce, and alliance (February 5), which are ratified by Congress (May 4); Benjamin Franklin is named minister to France; French fleet sails to raid Newport, R.I., storm forces fleet to withdraw.

John Paul Jones leads raids on British shipping in harbor of Whitehaven, England (April 23).

George Rogers Clark leads American force to victory over British at Kaskaskia, Ill. (July 4).

British request for peace conference is refused, Congress says it would only negotiate for American independence, British withdrawal.

Capt. James Cook discovers Hawaiian Islands.

NATIONAL

South Carolina ratifies Articles of Confederation; adopts state constitution (March 19).

First military court-martial acquits Col. David Henley of conduct unbecoming an officer; Benedict Arnold, commander of American forces in Philadelphia, is court-martialed on charges of im-

Molly Pitcher at the Battle of Monmouth, New Jersey, in 1778. Mary Ludwig Hayes brings water to her husband and other soliders, who call her "Molly Pitcher." After her husband is killed, she helps fire the cannons. THE GRANGER COLLECTION, NEW YORK

proper conduct, is acquitted of most charges.

First secret service is organized (July 4) by General Washington; Aaron Burr is named head of "Department for Detecting and Defeating Conspiracies."

U.S. signs first treaty of peace and amity with Native Americans (the Delawares).

DEATH Pierre Lacléde, founder of St. Louis.

BUSINESS/INDUSTRY/INVENTIONS

New York printers go on strike, win $3-a-week raise.

SCIENCE/MEDICINE

William Brown publishes first American pharmacopoeia (official list of medicines).

EDUCATION

Phillips Andover and Phillips Exeter academies are founded.

ART/MUSIC

William Billings publishes the first American war song, "Chester."

John S. Copley completes the painting *Watson and the Shark*.

MISCELLANEOUS

Grand Lodge (Masonic) of Virginia is organized in Williamsburg.

Hoopskirts go out of fashion.

1779

INTERNATIONAL

American Revolution

British continue their successful campaign in the South, capture Sunbury, Ga. (January 6), Augusta, Ga. (January 29); occupy, then burn Portsmouth, Norfolk, Va. (May 10); Americans again fail to recapture Savannah; Count Casimir Pulaski is fatally wounded.

In the north, Americans defeat British–Native American force in Western New York and Pennsylvania, ending raids; capture Stony Point, N.Y. (July 15), and Paulus Hook, N.J.; British begin to attack Connecticut cities.

John Paul Jones in the *Bonhomme Richard* leads six ships in successful battle versus the *Serapis*, which was leading 39 merchant ships off England.

Spain, by the Treaty of Aranjuez, joins France in war against Great Britain but does not recognize American independence; Spain declares war (May 8), captures Baton Rouge, La.

NATIONAL

Massachusetts adopts state constitution.

Congress issues $10 million in paper money, bringing total to $242 million.

Thomas Jefferson becomes governor of Virginia.

SCIENCE/MEDICINE

Physicians in Connecticut, Massachusetts, and New York form the Sharon Medical Society.

EDUCATION

John Wheelock begins 37 years as president of Dartmouth College on the death of his father, Eleazar, founder of the college and of Hanover, N.H.

University of Pennsylvania (formerly College of Philadelphia) is chartered.

College of William & Mary introduces honor system in examinations, establishes modern language school, and law school with George Wythe the first American law professor.

RELIGION

Universalist Church of America is organized in Gloucester, Mass.

Thomas Jefferson drafts religious freedom bill, which is passed by Virginia legislature.

John Paul Jones, naval commander. The bottom panel illustrates the confrontation of the *Bonhomme Richard* and *HMS Serapis* in 1779. The Granger Collection, New York

ART/MUSIC

Ralph Earl paints portrait of William Carpenter.

LITERATURE/JOURNALISM

The House of Night by Philip Freneau is published.

SPORTS

Horse racing, two-horse quarter-mile sprints is held near Charlottesville, Va., for the first time.

INTERNATIONAL

American Revolution

British capture Charleston, S.C. (May 12), after 45-day siege; Johann de Kalb, German officer fighting with the Americans, is killed in effort to recapture Camden, S.C.; Americans defeat British at Kings Mountain, N.C.

British, checked in New Jersey, retreat to Staten Island, N.Y.; Americans fighting at Springfield, N.J., have to use hymnal pages from nearby church for gun wadding.

Treason of Benedict Arnold, who expected to command West Point, is revealed; Arnold meets with British Maj. John André near Haverstraw, N.Y. (September 21); André is captured (September 23); Arnold flees to British (September 25); André is hanged (October 2).

NATIONAL

Pennsylvania legislature passes law calling for

The Siege of Charleston, South Carolina, 1780. THE GRANGER COLLECTION, NEW YORK

gradual freeing of slaves; Massachusetts adopts state constitution outlawing slavery.

James Robertson leads settlers to what will become Nashville, Tenn.

Continental Congress establishes Court of Appeals.

Kentuckians ask Congress to form separate states of Virginia and Kentucky.

BUSINESS/INDUSTRY/INVENTIONS

Baker & Co., chocolate-making company, is founded with Dr. James Baker's purchase of John Hannan's mill in Dorchester, Mass.

TRANSPORTATION

Chaises (two-wheeled carriages) are introduced in Connecticut.

SCIENCE/MEDICINE

First astronomical expedition by four Harvard professors and six students travels to Penobscot Bay to watch sun's eclipse.

Humane Society of Philadelphia organizes to provide first aid.

EDUCATION

Harvard College, founded in 1636, becomes university.

RELIGION

First American Universalist church building, located in Gloucester, Mass., is dedicated.

ARTS/MUSIC

American Academy of Arts and Sciences is founded in Boston.

LITERATURE/JOURNALISM

Vermont Gazette, first Vermont newspaper, is published.

DEATH Jonathan Carver, author of first American travel book, *Travels in Interior Parts of America* (1778).

INTERNATIONAL

American Revolution

Americans defeat British at Cowpens, S.C. (January 17); British claim victory at Guilford Court House, N.C. (March 15), but weakened force retreats to Wilmington, N.C.; British burn Camden, S.C.; Americans defeat British at Eutaw Springs, S.C.

Gen. Charles Cornwallis leads British troops to Yorktown, Va. (August 1); French fleet with 3,000 troops arrives (August 30), inflicts heavy damage on British fleet (September 5); American and French troops encircle Yorktown (September 28), British surrender (October 19).

Spanish fleet besieges Pensacola, Fla.; British surrender city, all of West Florida (May 9).

Pennsylvania troops mutiny, begin march to Philadelphia; en route to Congress, problems are settled before their arrival.

Benedict Arnold leads 2,000-man British force in occupying Richmond, Va.

Benjamin Franklin, John Jay, and John Adams are named to negotiate peace with British.

Netherlands extends large loan to U.S.

NATIONAL

Virginia cedes western lands to federal government (January 2), paving way for Maryland to ratify Articles of Confederation, which is completed (March 1).

Robert R. Livingston is named Secretary of Foreign Affairs; Robert Morris, head of Finance Department; Congress issues additional $191 million in paper money; within months, it loses its value.

British troops (left) surrender to George Washington's army at Yorktown, Virginia, in 1781. THE GRANGER COLLECTION, NEW YORK

Congress charters Bank of North America, first central bank.

Los Angeles is founded.

Rebellious slaves in Williamsburg set fire to several buildings, including the capitol.

BUSINESS/INDUSTRY/INVENTIONS

Jeremiah Wilkinson begins to produce nails.

SCIENCE/MEDICINE

Medical Society of Massachusetts is incorporated.

EDUCATION

Yale University confers honorary degree on George Washington.

LITERATURE/JOURNALISM

Worcester (Mass.) *Gazette* is established.

Philip Freneau writes the poem "The British Prison Ship."

MISCELLANEOUS

New Jersey Society for Promotion of Agriculture, Commerce, and the Arts is established.

1782

INTERNATIONAL

American Revolution

Peace talks begin in Paris (April 12); formal negotiations (September 19), preliminary articles of peace are signed (November 30). British recognize American independence, Americans gain right to fish off Nova Scotia, Newfoundland.

British evacuate Savannah, Ga., which they occupied since 1778, and the Carolinas.

Netherlands recognize American independence, signs treaty of commerce and friendship (June 8).

NATIONAL

Bank of North America in Philadelphia begins operations.

Great Seal of America, designed by William Barton, is adopted.

SCIENCE/MEDICINE

Harvard Medical School is founded.

An early view of Harvard University, Cambridge, Massachusetts. CORBIS-BETTMANN

One of the first American dentists, Josiah Flagg, begins to practice in Boston.

EDUCATION

St. Mary's Church, Philadelphia, establishes first American parochial school.

John Witherspoon, president of College of New Jersey (later Princeton), reopens school.

RELIGION

Francis Asbury becomes leader of the then-unorganized American Methodist Church.

Robert Aitken prints first American Bible in Philadelphia.

LITERATURE/JOURNALISM

Thomas Jefferson's *Notes on Virginia* is first published in France.

J. H. St. John de Crèvecoeur publishes *Letters from an American Farmer.*

New York Evening Post is published.

MISCELLANEOUS

Order of the Purple Heart is established for those with "military merit."

1783

INTERNATIONAL

Congress ratifies preliminary peace treaty (April 15); it is formally signed in Paris (September 3); British sign preliminary articles of peace with France and Spain; Britain proclaims end of hostilities (February 4).

Spain, Sweden, Russia, and Denmark recognize American independence.

Loyalists and British troops sail from New York.

NATIONAL

George Washington takes leave of his officers in New York; American army is disbanded.

Congress moves meeting place to Princeton, N.J. (June 24), then Annapolis, Md. (November 26).

Robert R. Livingston resigns as Secretary of Foreign Affairs.

New Hampshire ratifies its state constitution.

Massachusetts Supreme Court proclaims abolition of slavery in state (July 8); Virginia frees slaves who served in Continental Army.

DEATHS John Hanson, first presiding officer of Continental Congress; James Otis, colonial orator.

BUSINESS/INDUSTRY/INVENTIONS

Patents are issued to Benjamin Hanks for a self-winding clock.

Benjamin Franklin designs bifocal spectacles.

SCIENCE/MEDICINE

Massachusetts Medical School is founded.

EDUCATION

Transylvania Seminary, now in Lexington, Ky., is chartered; it is the first university west of Alleghenies.

RELIGION

Rabbi Gershon M. Seixas of Philadelphia wins lawsuit to lift Pennsylvania ban on Jews holding public office.

ART/MUSIC

Connecticut and Massachusetts pass copyright laws.

The negotiators of the Treaty of Paris, 1783. John Jay, John Adams, and Ben Franklin are on the left. The artist, Benjamin West, cannot finish the painting because the British negotiators refuse to pose for it. THE GRANGER COLLECTION, NEW YORK

LITERATURE/JOURNALISM

The last of 16 essays by Thomas Paine, *Common Sense*, is published; Noah Webster issues first part of *Blue-Backed Speller*.

New York Daily Gazette begins as *Independent Journal*, later publishes Federalist Papers.

Pennsylvania Evening Post is founded.

SPORTS

The Sportsman's Companion, first important sports book, is published.

MISCELLANEOUS

Society of the Cincinnati, a veterans organization, is founded.

INTERNATIONAL

Congress ratifies final peace treaty ending the American Revolution (January 14).

Spain closes Mississippi River to American navigation.

Russians establish first permanent settlement in Alaska.

1784

NATIONAL

Congress moves to New York City; names commissioners to lay out new federal district.

John Jay is named Secretary of Foreign Affairs; Robert Morris resigns as superintendent of finance; Treasury Board is organized.

Rhode Island legislature votes (February 23) that all blacks, mulattoes born in the state after March are free.

Treaty is signed with Iroquois Confederacy, which gives up lands in Western Pennsylvania and New York.

James Madison publishes *Remonstrances Against Religious Assessments*, advocating separation of church and state.

Settlers in western North Carolina form independent state of Franklin, which will never be recognized by the federal government.

BUSINESS/INDUSTRY/INVENTIONS

Trade with China begins as the *Empress of China* sails from New York (February 22), arrives in Canton (August 30).

David Landreth establishes first American seed business in Philadelphia.

Banks of New York and Boston are established; Mutual Assurance Co. is founded in Philadelphia.

Bremen Glass Manufactory is founded near Frederick, Md., produces Amolung glass.

TRANSPORTATION

James Rumsey invents a motorboat.

First American balloon flight is made in Baltimore by 13-year-old Edward Warren in Peter Carnes's balloon.

Curious spectators watch navigators prepare for a balloon flight. BALDWIN H. WARD/CORBIS-BETTMANN

1785

SCIENCE/MEDICINE

Manasseh Cutler studies New England botanical species.

EDUCATION

State legislature creates University of New York.

Tapping Reeve opens law school in Litchfield, Conn.

RELIGION

Dutch Reformed Church creates first American theological seminary; becomes Brunswick (N.J.) Theological Seminary.

American Methodist Church is organized; Francis Asbury and Thomas Cooke are named superintendents.

Samuel Seabury is consecrated as first American Anglican bishop.

Pope Pius VI names John Carroll superior of American Catholic missions.

John Ettwein becomes bishop and presiding officer of North American Moravian Church.

DEATHS Ann Lee, founder of American Shakers; Junipero Serra, Franciscan founder of California missions.

ART/MUSIC

John S. Copley completes the painting *Death of Major Peirson*.

LITERATURE/JOURNALISM

First successful American daily newspaper, *Pennsylvania Packet and Daily Advertiser*, is published; *New Haven* (Conn.) *Gazette* is established.

Poet Joel Barlow publishes first issue of the weekly *American Mercury*.

BOOKS *Compendium of Various Sects* by Hannah Adams (first professional woman author); *Geography Made Easy* by Jedidiah Morse (which will stay in print through 25 editions).

MISCELLANEOUS

New York Society for Promoting Manumission (freedom from slavery) is established.

Abel Buell, engraver, produces first map of independent U.S.

INTERNATIONAL

Negotiations with Spain to open Mississippi River to American navigation are unsuccessful; treaty of commerce is negotiated with Prussia.

U.S. calls on Great Britain to vacate posts on the Great Lakes.

John Adams is named minister to Great Britain; Thomas Jefferson to France.

NATIONAL

Continental Congress adopts decimal system for money (July 6); Vermont and Connecticut mint copper cents.

Henry Knox is named War Secretary.

Massachusetts legislature passes resolutions calling for a convention to revise Articles of Confederation; its delegates fail to introduce the resolutions.

BUSINESS/INDUSTRY/INVENTIONS

Philadelphia Society for the Promotion of Agriculture, first in U.S., is organized.

Isaac Underhill begins to quarry marble in Vermont.

Oliver Evans develops a flour mill with water-powered machinery; it is not put to use.

TRANSPORTATION

Regular stagecoach service between Boston, New York City, and Philadelphia begins.

An American stage wagon stops at a public house. THE GRANGER COLLECTION, NEW YORK

SCIENCE/MEDICINE

John Greenwood introduces porcelain artificial teeth.

Dr. Benjamin Rush founds Philadelphia Dispensary.

American systematic botany begins with publications by Humphry Marshall and Manasseh Cutler; David Rittenhouse first uses crosshairs in a telescope.

EDUCATION

Colleges and universities founded: Georgia University, first state university chartered; Charleston (S.C.), first American city college; Williams College.

Cornerstone is laid for first American Methodist college, Cokesbury, in Abingdon, Md.

RELIGION

Protestant Episcopal Church of America is formed; Southern and New England wings resolve differences; first American ordination is that of Rev. Ashbel Baldwin of Middletown, Conn.

First African Baptist Church opens in Savannah, Ga.

LITERATURE/JOURNALISM

Three newspapers founded: *Falmouth Gazette and Weekly Advertiser*, first in Maine; *New York Daily Advertiser*; *Pennsylvania Herald*.

MISCELLANEOUS

John Macpherson publishes first city directory (Philadelphia).

1786

INTERNATIONAL

U.S. concludes treaty with Morocco to halt piracy; unable to agree on treaty with Algiers, Tripoli, and Tunis.

NATIONAL

Convention in Annapolis, Md., discusses interstate commerce; only five states attend; another convention set for 1787.

Daniel Shays in Massachusetts leads debt-ridden farmers in demanding paper money or a stay on foreclosures; rebels capture Worcester (December 5).

An engraving depicting a scene from Shays' Rebellion, 1786. THE GRANGER COLLECTION, NEW YORK

Congress amends Articles of Confederation but does not submit them for ratification.

Revolutionary War veterans organize Ohio Company for settlement there.

Congress adopts coinage system: $10 gold piece, $1 silver, a tenth of a dollar in silver, a copper cent (designed by Benjamin Franklin); calls for establishment of U.S. Mint.

BUSINESS/INDUSTRY/INVENTIONS

Typographical Union, some of whose members go on strike, votes to pay strike benefits.

A Mr. Hall in New York City makes first commercially produced ice cream in U.S.

Hugh Orr manufactures spinning, carding, and roping machinery.

RELIGION

Virginia legislature enacts ordinance on religious freedom written by Thomas Jefferson.

Samuel Provoost becomes first Episcopal Bishop of New York.

Probably the first American Sunday school is organized in Hanover County, Va., by Francis Asbury.

ART/MUSIC

American Musical Magazine is published in New York.

First art museum is established by Charles Willson Peale in Philadelphia.

John Trumbull completes the painting *The Battle of Bunker Hill*.

Musical Society of Stoughton, Mass., is founded.

LITERATURE/JOURNALISM

Philip Freneau publishes lyric poem "To a Wild Honeysuckle."

Pittsburgh Gazette, first newspaper west of Alleghenies, is issued.

Mathew Cary founds *Columbian Magazine*.

SPORTS

First American golf club is organized in Charleston, S.C.

NATIONAL

Constitutional Convention opens (May 25) in Independence Hall, Philadelphia; George Washington presides over 55 delegates; Edmund Randolph, Virginia, proposes (May 29) plan for what amounts to a new government; William Paterson, New Jersey, proposes (June 15) proportional representation; Roger Sherman, Connecticut, proposes (July 16) proportional representation in a house of representatives, equal representation in a senate; Convention approves Connecticut compromise and the Constitution (September 17); Congress votes to submit Constitution (September 28) to colonies for ratification.

First of 85 Federalist Papers is issued (October 27); urges approval of Constitution; most is written by Alexander Hamilton, James Madison, and John Jay.

Delaware becomes first state to ratify Constitution (December 7), followed by Pennsylvania (December 12) and New Jersey (December 18).

Congress approves Northwest Ordinance to govern territory north of Ohio River; Arthur St. Clair is named first governor.

People of Maine vote to separate from Massachusetts.

Shays Rebellion ends; Daniel Shays is arrested, jailed.

John Fitch carries members of Congress across the Delaware River at three miles per hour, 1787. THE GRANGER COLLECTION, NEW YORK

BUSINESS/INDUSTRY/ INVENTIONS

Levi Hutchins of Concord, N.H., makes first American alarm clock.

Boston Crown Glass Factory, the first important window-glass maker, is chartered; begins to produce in 1792.

Oliver Evans invents noncondensing steam engine.

TRANSPORTATION

John Fitch successfully launches first steamboat.

American ship *Columbia* begins round-the-world trip, which will end in 1790.

James Rumsey demonstrates a boat propelled by jets of water forced from stern by steam engine; probably world's first jet-propelled vehicle; cannot get financial backing.

EDUCATION

What later becomes University of Pittsburgh is founded as Pittsburgh Academy; Franklin & Marshall College is established.

Columbia (formerly Kings) College names its first president, William S. Johnson.

RELIGION

King's Chapel, Boston, first Anglican church in New England, becomes first American Unitarian church with ordination of James Freeman, who was refused Anglican ordination because of his revisions of *Book of Common Prayer*.

DEATHS Henry M. Muhlenberg, founder of American Lutheranism; Charles Chauncy, a leader in theological liberalism.

ART/MUSIC

Charles Willson Peale completes the painting *Benjamin Franklin*.

LITERATURE/JOURNALISM

Joel Barlow publishes poem "The Vision of Columbus."

First Kentucky newspaper, *Kentucky Gazette*, is founded.

ENTERTAINMENT

An American professional company presents the first American play, Royall Tyler's *The Contrast*, at John St. Theater, New York City.

MISCELLANEOUS

Society for Alleviating the Miseries of Public Prisons is organized.

NATIONAL

Eight states ratify proposed Constitution: Georgia (January 2), Connecticut (January 9), Massachusetts (February 6), Maryland (April 28), South Carolina (May 23), New Hampshire (June 21), Virginia (June 25), and New York (July 26); Rhode Island voters reject the Constitution (March 24); with ratification by nine states (June 21), Constitution is adopted.

Congress picks New York City as site of government, fixes January 7, 1789, for states to name electors to elect first president, sets March 4, 1789, for beginning of congressional session.

Maryland cedes 10 square miles to Congress for future District of Columbia.

Daniel Shays, in jail for leading rebellion in Massachusetts, is pardoned.

Slave trade is forbidden in Massachusetts.

Rufus Putnam and party establish first settlement in Northwest Territory at what is now Marietta, Ohio; New Jersey colonists found Cincinnati (originally Losantiville).

Fire destroys much of New Orleans.

BUSINESS/INDUSTRY/INVENTIONS

Boston Sail Cloth Factory is established; Hartford Woolen Manufactory, operated by waterpower, is organized.

Manufacture of salt begins at Salina (now part of Syracuse), N.Y.

New Yorkers celebrating the ratification of the Federal Constitution on July 26, 1788. THE GRANGER COLLECTION, NEW YORK

Meatpacking industry first operates in Cincinnati.

Paul Revere establishes foundry to produce andirons in Boston.

RELIGION

First organized Shaker community is established in New (later Mt.) Lebanon, N.Y.

ART/MUSIC

Francis Hopkinson, self-proclaimed first native-born composer, publishes *Seven Songs for the Harpsichord*.

LITERATURE/JOURNALISM

William Perry of Edinburgh compiles first American dictionary.

Philip Freneau, leading poet of the time, publishes his works.

1789

Presidential electors are named by the states (January 7); they meet, cast ballots (February 4).

First Congress meets (March 4) but lacks quorum; House of Representatives organizes (April 1), elects Frederick A. Muhlenberg, Pennsylvania, the first Speaker; Senate organizes (April 6), names John Langdon first president pro tem; Senate counts electoral votes: George Washington receives all 69 votes for presidency; John Adams, with 34 votes, becomes vice president.

Washington leaves Mt. Vernon (April 16) for New York; he and Mrs. Washington move into "presidential mansion" (Franklin House, Franklin and Cherry Sts., April 23).

Washington is inaugurated president (April 30) on balcony of Federal Hall (Wall and Broad Sts.); first inaugural ball is held (May 7) in Assembly Rooms on Broadway.

New government begins to organize: War Department is created (August 7) with Henry Knox secretary; Treasury Department (September 2) headed by Alexander Hamilton; State Department (originally Foreign Affairs) is headed by Thomas Jefferson (September 15); Office of Postmaster General (September 22) with Samuel Osgood as Postmaster; Federal Judiciary Act (September 24) creates Supreme Court and Attorney General, with John Jay the first Chief Justice and five associate justices.

President Washington signs (June 1) first act of Congress, prescribing oaths of allegiance by Congress, federal and state officials.

First federal navigation act (July 20) imposes duty on vessel's tonnage; Customs Service is created (July 31); first tariff sets $8\frac{1}{2}$% tax on about 30 items.

Congress sets (September 22) federal salaries: President $25,000, Vice President $5,000, Supreme Court justices $4,000, State and Treasury secretaries $3,500, War Secretary $3,000, Congress $6 per day plus mileage.

House of Representatives, at

The Bill of Rights. THE GRANGER COLLECTION, NEW YORK

urging of James Madison, recommends (September 9) 12 amendments to Constitution; submits them to states (September 25) for ratification.

North Carolina ratifies Constitution (November 21) becoming 12th state; Georgia adopts state constitution.

President Washington proclaims November 26 as day of general thanksgiving for adoption of the Constitution.

Congress authorizes federal bond issue, creates 1,000-member army (September 30), appropriates $639,000 to defray expenses.

Oliver Phelps and Nathaniel Gorham create land office in Canandaigua, N.Y., to sell 2.6 million acres in "Great American Wilderness."

Virginia cedes 10 square miles to federal government for future District of Columbia; also separates Kentucky counties from its jurisdiction.

DEATHS Silas Deane, who helped get aid for the Revolution; Ethan Allen, head of Green Mountain Boys, who fought during the Revolution.

BUSINESS/INDUSTRY/INVENTIONS

Samuel Wethermill begins to manufacture white lead for paint; cotton mills are established in Beverly, Mass., and near Charleston, S.C.

SCIENCE/MEDICINE

First American pharmacy professor, Dr. Samuel P. Griffis, appointed by Philadelphia Medical School.

DEATH Dr. John Morgan, chief medical officer in Revolution.

TRANSPORTATION

Christopher Colles publishes first American road map.

EDUCATION

First American Catholic college, Georgetown, is founded in Washington, D.C. (opens 1791); University of North Carolina is chartered.

Massachusetts creates school districts.

RELIGION

First American Catholic diocese is established in Baltimore (April 6), with John Carroll the first American Catholic bishop; first Catholic magazine, *Courier de Boston*, is published.

Presbyterian Church holds first general assembly in Philadelphia (May 2); American branch of Anglican church becomes Protestant church; *Book of Common Prayer* is revised accordingly.

Church of the United Brethren in Christ meets in Baltimore (November 30); founded by Martin Boehm, Philip Otterbein, and others.

LITERATURE/JOURNALISM

First children's magazine, *Children's Magazine*, appears in Hartford; lasts four months.

First issue of *United States Gazette* is published.

BOOKS *The Power of Sympathy* by William H. Brown, the first American novel; *History of the American Revolution* by David Ramsay.

ENTERTAINMENT

Two plays are produced: *The Father* by William Dunlap and *The Politician Outwitted* by Samuel Low.

Pennsylvania legislature repeals law banning performance of stage plays.

President Washington attends performance of *Darby's Return* at John St. Theater in New York City; reportedly laughs during performance.

MISCELLANEOUS

Farmers of Litchfield, Conn., form temperance society.

John Jacob Astor buys first of many parcels of New York City real estate.

Society of Saint Tammany (name of a Delaware tribal chief), an anti-Federalist fraternal organization, is founded in New York City.

1790

NATIONAL

House of Representatives fixes future capital along the Potomac River on land ceded by Maryland and Virginia (July 16); Philadelphia is named capital until 1800; Congress begins sessions there December 6.

First census reports total population of 3,929,214; Virginia most-populous state with 691,737; New York City has 33,131, Philadelphia 28,522, Boston 18,320.

Supreme Court meets for first time (see National, 1789).

Rhode Island ratifies Constitution and becomes 13th state; South Carolina adopts state constitution.

First national patent law is passed (April 10); Congress passes Naturalization Act requiring two-year residency.

Revenue Cutter Service (later part of Coast Guard) is authorized.

Society of Friends (Quakers) presents first petition to Congress to free slaves (February 11).

National debt is reported to be $11,710,378.

DEATH Benjamin Franklin, writer, diplomat, and inventor.

BUSINESS/INDUSTRY/INVENTIONS

Samuel Slater starts cotton mill using power to spin yarn in Pawtucket, R.I. Samuel Hopkins patents process to make potash and pearl ash.

Jacob Perkins invents machine to cut and head nails in one operation.

Duncan Phyfe opens cabinet-making shop in New York City.

TRANSPORTATION

John Fitch establishes regular steamboat service from Philadelphia to Trenton.

Samuel Slater's textile mill at Pawtucket, Rhode Island, which begins operation in 1790. THE GRANGER COLLECTION, NEW YORK

Capt. Robert Gray sails *Columbia* into Boston harbor, completing the first American circumnavigation of the Earth.

First leg of 61-mile Philadelphia-Lancaster Turnpike opens.

SCIENCE/MEDICINE

John Greenwood invents foot-powered dental drill.

EDUCATION

Law lectures first delivered at University of Pennsylvania.

RELIGION

John Carroll is consecrated as first American Catholic bishop (August 15) at Lulworth Castle, Dorset, England; Order of Carmelite Sisters establishes nunnery in Port Tobacco, Md.; Carey, Stewart & Co. prints first Catholic Bible in U.S.

President Washington attends consecration of new Trinity Church in New York City.

Rev. James Madison becomes first Episcopal bishop of Virginia.

American Methodist churches are encouraged to start Sunday schools; Episcopal Bishop William White creates Sunday school in Philadelphia.

ART/MUSIC

Moller & Capron begins to publish music in Philadelphia.

LITERATURE/JOURNALISM

First federal copyright law is passed (May 31);

John Barry's *Philadelphia Spelling Book* is first to be registered (June 9).

The New England Farmer, an agricultural dictionary, is published by Samuel Deane.

General Advertiser (newspaper) is published in Philadelphia.

MISCELLANEOUS

Massachusetts Historical Society is organized in Boston.

New York City outlaws hogs running loose in the streets.

NATIONAL

Bill of Rights (first 10 amendments to Constitution) goes into effect (December 15) after ratification by the states.

President George Washington calls on Congress to set exact location of District of Columbia; it is established (March 3); Pierre L'Enfant is retained to plan new capital.

Congress establishes a national bank; Bank of the United States is chartered (February 25), opens December 12.

Vermont is admitted to Union as 14th state (March 4).

President Washington meets twice with department heads, establishing precedent for cabinet meetings.

Excise tax is placed on manufacture of distilled liquors.

National debt is $75,463,476.

Timothy Pickering becomes first Postmaster General (August 19); John Buckley is named Librarian of Congress, is paid $2 per day of necessary attendance.

Richard Carter III of Virginia voluntarily frees more than 500 slaves.

DEATH George Mason of Virginia, colonial statesman.

BUSINESS/INDUSTRY/INVENTIONS

First securities exchange opens in Philadelphia.

Antonio Mendez opens sugar refinery in New Orleans; William P. Sprague, a carpet mill in Philadelphia.

Anthracite coal is discovered in Carbon County, Pa.

TRANSPORTATION

John Fitch patents (August 26) steamboat, which he launched in 1787; James Rumsey also patents a steamboat.

Construction begins on Knoxville Road to connect Knoxville and Wilderness Road.

SCIENCE/MEDICINE

City Dispensary for the Medical Relief of the Poor opens in New York City.

Naturalist William Bartram in *Travels* describes his

1791

The Bank of the United States, Third Street, Philadelphia, established 1791. THE GRANGER COLLECTION, NEW YORK

botany expeditions in North and South Carolina.

DEATH Dr. John Jones, publisher of first American surgical textbook.

EDUCATION

University of Vermont is chartered; Georgetown College opens in Washington, D.C.

First public school opens in New York State (Clermont).

DEATH John Manning, founder and first president, Rhode Island (later Brown) University.

RELIGION

Philadelphia religious leaders organize First Day Society (or Sunday School Society).

ART/MUSIC

Samuel Holyoke publishes *Harmonia Americana*, a songbook.

LITERATURE/JOURNALISM

First American best-seller is published, *Charlotte Temple* by Susanna H. Rowson; a portion of Benjamin Franklin's autobiography is published in France.

National Gazette, edited by Philip Freneau, and *Knoxville Gazette*, first Tennessee newspaper, are published.

Benjamin Banneker, black mathematician and scientist, begins to issue his almanac.

ENTERTAINMENT

Théâtre de St. Pierre, first opera house in North America, opens in New Orleans; Chestnut Street Theater in Philadelphia opens.

MISCELLANEOUS

One-way streets originate on John Street in New York City to prevent traffic confusion before and after theater performances.

1792

INTERNATIONAL

Thomas Pinckney is named first U.S. minister to Great Britain.

NATIONAL

Electors name George Washington president with 132 votes, 3 abstentions; John Adams, vice president with 77 votes.

Congress passes Presidential Succession Act providing for Senate president pro tem and House Speaker to follow the President and Vice President.

Cornerstone is laid for White House; Benjamin Banneker becomes District of Columbia planner after Pierre L'Enfant is dismissed; L'Enfant takes plans with him, but Banneker completes plan from memory.

U.S. Mint is established (April 2) with David Rittenhouse director; silver coins are authorized; Post Office Act establishes rates from 6 cents for single-page letter going up to 30 miles to 25 cents for more than 450 miles.

Kentucky is admitted to Union as 15th state (June 1).

States are authorized to create militia of able-bodied, free, white citizens 18–45 years old.

President Washington issues first veto (April 5) on proposed reapportionment of House of Representatives; second reapportionment (April 14) raises House membership to 105, one seat for every 33,000 persons.

South Carolina bans importation of slaves (repealed 1818).

Peace treaty is signed with Wabash and Illinois Native American tribes.

Capt. Robert Gray on second round-the-world trip discovers Columbia River.

DEATHS John Paul Jones, naval hero; Arthur Lee, diplomat who arranged French help during American Revolution; Henry Laurens, president of first Continental Congress.

BUSINESS/INDUSTRY/INVENTIONS

New York Stock Exchange is organized by 24 merchants (May 17); Insurance Company of North America is organized in Philadelphia.

Theodore Pearson founds the first U.S. cracker bakery, in Newburyport, Mass.

Samuel G. Dorr invents rotary cloth shear.

TRANSPORTATION

Bridge is opened over Merrimack River at Newburyport, Mass.

John Fitch's steamboat, which makes regular trips between Philadelphia and Trenton, is destroyed in storm.

SCIENCE/MEDICINE

Baltimore establishes first local health board.

James Woodhouse founds Chemical Society of Philadelphia, first in world.

RELIGION

Russian Orthodox Church begins missionary work in Alaska; resident bishop arrives 1798.

Thomas J. Claggett becomes Episcopal bishop of Maryland.

DEATH August G. Spangenburg, founder and bishop of North American Moravian Church (1735–1762).

ART/MUSIC

Columbus Monument in Baltimore is dedicated.

Ralph Earl completes the painting *Chief Justice Oliver Ellsworth and Wife*; John Trumbull of *Alexander Hamilton*; Charles Willson Peale of *Colonel Charles Pettit*.

1793

LITERATURE/JOURNALISM

Robert B. Thomas founds annual *Farmer's Almanac*.

First of five parts of *Modern Chivalry* by Hugh H. Brackenridge is published.

INTERNATIONAL

France declares war on Great Britain, Spain, and Holland; President George Washington proclaims U.S. neutrality (April 22); French Minister Edmond Genet is told to stop arming privateers to raid British shipping off U.S. coast, to halt organizing armed bands to attack British, Spanish settlements; commerce with France is suspended.

NATIONAL

President Washington gives second inaugural

ENTERTAINMENT

Pickett's Circus opens in Philadelphia.

1793

address; at 135 words, it is shortest on record.

William Thornton's design of Capitol is approved; southwest cornerstone is laid by President Washington (September 18); District commissioners approve lottery to pay for improvements.

Supreme Court in *Chisholm v. Georgia* reaffirms jurisdiction of federal courts in disputes between a state and citizens of another state.

Thomas Jefferson resigns as Secretary of State because of differences over French policy.

DEATH Roger Sherman, only signer of all four major American colonial documents (Articles of Association and of Confederation, Declaration of Independence, and Constitution).

BUSINESS/INDUSTRY/ INVENTIONS

Eli Whitney invents cotton gin; Thomas Jefferson develops the moldboard plow.

Almy, Brown & Slater mill in Providence, R.I., marks start of modern American textile industry; John Harrison begins to produce sulphuric acid in Philadelphia; Hannah Wilkinson begins to make cotton thread in Pawtucket, R.I.

TRANSPORTATION

Two canals are built in Massachussetts: one around South

The cotton gin, invented by Eli Whitney in 1793. In this nineteenth-century engraving, African American slaves are depicted happily doing all the work, while elegantly dressed slaveowners inspect the results. THE GRANGER COLLECTION, NEW YORK

Hadley Falls in the Connecticut River, and the Middlesex Canal to connect Merrimack River with Woburn; the Santee Canal in South Carolina begins construction.

First hot-air balloon flight in U.S. (January 9) is made by Frenchman Jean Pierre Blanchard, from Philadelphia 15 miles into New Jersey.

SCIENCE/MEDICINE

Worst U.S. yellow fever epidemic strikes Philadelphia from August to October, killing 4,000.

EDUCATION

Hamilton College (N.Y.) is founded as Hamilton Oneida Academy.

Samuel Slater founds school to teach reading, writing, and arithmetic to children working in his Pawtucket, R.I., textile mill.

RELIGION

Stephen T. Badin becomes first Catholic priest ordained in U.S.

ART/MUSIC

Two songbooks are published: Oliver Holden's *The Union Harmony* and Jacob Kimball's *Rural Harmony*.

Gilbert Stuart completes the painting *Mrs. Richard Yates*.

LITERATURE/JOURNALISM

American Poems, an anthology by Elihu H. Smith, is published.

Noah Webster founds *American Minerva* magazine.

Two newspapers are published: *Centinel of the North-Western Territory*, first Ohio paper, in Cincinnati and *American Daily Advertiser* in Philadelphia.

MISCELLANEOUS

Slaves in Albany, N.Y., rebel, set series of devastating fires in city.

1794

INTERNATIONAL

Jay's Treaty (November 19) provides for British withdrawal from northwestern posts, opens West Indies trade to U.S. vessels, establishes a commission to study debts of pre-Revolutionary War.

Neutrality Act (June 5) forbids U.S. citizens from enlisting in service of foreign nation, prohibits outfitting foreign armed vessels in U.S.

John Quincy Adams is named minister to Holland (Netherlands).

NATIONAL

Eleventh Amendment to Constitution proposes to override Supreme Court decision in *Chisholm v. Georgia* case (1793).

Whiskey Rebellion erupts over excise tax on distilled liquors; President George Washington creates first presidential commission (August 7) to study problem; rebellion ends in September.

Springfield (Mass.) Armory is established to manufacture small arms.

Congress passes law forbidding slave trading with foreign nations by Americans; Senate debates are opened to public.

Letter carriers begin to appear in cities.

Congress authorizes creation of U.S. Navy.

Gen. Anthony Wayne leads U.S. to victory over 2,000 Native Americans in Battle of Fallen Timbers in Ohio.

DEATH Richard Henry Lee of Virginia, colonial leader.

1794

Tarring and feathering an excise officer during the Whiskey Rebellion, 1794. THE GRANGER COLLECTION, NEW YORK

BUSINESS/INDUSTRY/INVENTIONS

First fire-insurance policy is issued, marks start of Hartford (Conn.) insurance business; Insurance Company of North America becomes first to insure a building and its contents.

Eli Terry begins to manufacture clocks in Plymouth, Conn.

Federal Society of Cordwainers (shoemakers) is organized.

Josiah G. Pierson patents machine to make rivets.

City Hotel opens on Broadway in New York City.

TRANSPORTATION

Lancaster Pike, connecting Lancaster and Philadelphia, is completed.

SCIENCE/MEDICINE

William Peck publishes first U.S. paper on zoology; it deals with fish taken near Piscatauqua, N.H.

Dr. Jesse Bennett performs first successful cesarean operation on his wife in Edom, Va.

EDUCATION

Two colleges founded: Bowdoin (Brunswick, Me.) and University of Tennessee, which begins as Blount, the nation's first non-denominational college.

DEATH John Witherspoon, president, College of New Jersey (1768–1794). (College will become Princeton in 1896).

RELIGION

Free African Society builds church in Philadelphia, affiliated with Methodist Church, the nation's first black church.

ART/MUSIC

William Billings publishes *The Continental Harmony* songbook.

John St. Theater in New York City presents James Hewitt's opera *Tammany, or the Indian Chief*, the first American opera.

ENTERTAINMENT

Federal St. Theater in Boston and Holliday St. Theater in Baltimore open.

MISCELLANEOUS

Powdered hair for men goes out of fashion; hair is worn in queue (pigtail), tied with a black ribbon; soft, low-crowned, straight-brimmed hats are popular.

1795

INTERNATIONAL

Pinckney's Treaty (Treaty of San Lorenzo) with Spain sets western U.S. boundary at Mississippi River, southern boundary at 31st parallel; gives Americans freedom of navigation of Mississippi (October 27).

Peace treaty is signed with Algiers (September 5), ending years of piracy on high seas; U.S. pays $800,000 plus $25,000 annual tribute.

Senate ratifies Jay's Treaty (June 24), President George Washington signs it.

NATIONAL

Eleventh Amendment to Constitution, spelling out judicial powers, goes into effect (February 7).

Naturalization Act is passed (January 29), requiring five years' residence for citizenship.

President Washington issues first presidential pardon (July 10) for most participants in Whiskey Rebellion.

Treaty of Greenville ends Native American wars in Ohio; tribes cede what later becomes most of Ohio.

Cornerstone is laid for U.S. Mint in Philadelphia.

John Jay resigns as Supreme Court Chief Justice to become New York governor; Senate rejects Associate Justice John Rutledge's nomination to succeed him (December 15).

DEATHS William Prescott, commander at Bunker Hill; Josiah Bartlett, first New Hampshire governor; Francis Marion, Revolutionary War commander.

BUSINESS/INDUSTRY/INVENTIONS

First business weekly, *New York Prices Current*, is published.

Abel Buell builds cotton mill at New Haven.

Robert Fulton patents a power shovel for digging canals.

TRANSPORTATION

First primitive railroad in U.S. is built in Boston, an inclined railway on slope of Beacon Hill.

SCIENCE/MEDICINE

College of New Jersey (later Princeton) creates first chemistry chair for John Maclean.

Thomas Jefferson's followers burn an effigy of John Jay after the treaty with England of 1794. THE GRANGER COLLECTION, NEW YORK

1796

EDUCATION

Union College (Schenectady) is chartered; University of North Carolina, first state university, opens.

Jedidiah Morse compiles *American Universal Geography*, gazetteer; Lindley Murray's *English Grammar*, which will eventually sell nearly 2 million copies, published.

DEATH Ezra Stiles, Yale University president (1778–1795).

RELIGION

Episcopal Bishop Williams White of Pennsylvania begins 41 years as presiding bishop. Demetrius A. Gallitzin is ordained, the first Catholic priest to receive his training and orders in U.S.

ARTS/MUSIC

Charles Willson Peale completes the painting *The Staircase Group*; Gilbert Stuart completes portrait of George Washington.

LITERATURE/JOURNALISM

Thomas Paine's *The Age of Reason* is published.

The American Citizen (newspaper) is founded as the *New York Argus*.

ENTERTAINMENT

Susanna H. Rowson writes *The Volunteers*, a play about the Whiskey Rebellion; John Murdock writes *The Triumphs of Love*.

SPORTS

Charleston (S.C.) newspaper announces anniversary observance of South Carolina Golf Club.

MISCELLANEOUS

Women's dresses change from stiff brocades and rustling silks to soft, clinging material.

1796

INTERNATIONAL

Treaty of peace, friendship, and navigation is signed with Tripoli (November 4).

Senate ratifies Pinckney's Treaty with Spain.

NATIONAL

President George Washington's farewell address is published in Philadelphia's *American Daily Advertiser* (September 17) but is never delivered as speech; stated reasons for not seeking third term, deplored dangers of political-party system, urged public credit be maintained, warned against permanent alliances with foreign nations.

President electors give Vice President John Adams 71 votes for president, Thomas Jefferson 68, making Jefferson vice president (December 7).

Tennessee is admitted as 16th state (February 7); adopts state constitution, John Sevier becomes first governor.

Vermont adopts state constitution (November 2).

Congress passes first national game law (May 19).

Moses Cleaveland and party establish city of Cleveland; Jean Pierre Chouteau establishes first white settlement in Oklahoma.

Oliver Ellsworth becomes chief justice of Supreme Court.

Arsenal at Harpers Ferry, W. Va., is founded.

Supreme Court issues first ruling that upholds a congressional action (*Hylton v. United States*) (March 8).

DEATH David Rittenhouse, first U.S. Mint director.

A New England tea party, eighteenth-century style. All well-dressed men and women put white powder in their hair, following European fashion. THE GRANGER COLLECTION, NEW YORK

BUSINESS/INDUSTRY/INVENTIONS

First American architectural book, *Country Builder's Assistant*, is published by Asher Benjamin.

TRANSPORTATION

First American suspension bridge is built across

Jacob's Creek in Westmoreland, Pa.

Canal around Little Falls in Mohawk River opens.

RELIGION

First church called Unitarian (Society of Unitarian Christians) is organized in Philadelphia.

DEATH Samuel Seabury, first American Episcopal bishop (1784–1796).

ARTS/MUSIC

Gilbert Stuart, portrait painter, opens studio in Phladelphia.

The Archers, opera by William Dunlap and Benjamin Carr, is performed in New York City.

LITERATURE/ JOURNALISM

Joel Barlow publishes epic poem, *The Hasty Pudding*.

Aurelia Simmons publishes first American cookbook, *American Cookery*.

First Sunday newspaper (*Monitor*) is published in Baltimore; *Federal Gazette* also founded in Baltimore.

ENTERTAINMENT

Haymarket Theater in Boston opens.

1797

INTERNATIONAL

President John Adams sends first war message to Congress; recommends preparations in case of war with France; Congress creates an 80,000-member militia.

France interferes with U.S. shipping; refuses to receive U.S. envoy; U.S. negotiating commission fails to resolve dispute.

Export of military weapons is prohibited.

The *Constitution* ("Old Ironsides"), first launched in 1797, leads a flotilla of tall ships out of Boston Harbor in 1992. © 1992 DAVID SHOPPER/STOCK BOSTON

Treaty is signed with Tunis in effort to stop pirate attacks on U.S. shipping.

John Quincy Adams is named minister to Prussia.

NATIONAL

Tennessee Senator William Blount is expelled on charge of plotting to aid British to get control of Spanish Florida and Louisiana.

First vessel of new navy, the *United States*, is launched May 10. Another 44-gun frigate, the *Constitution* ("Old Ironsides"), is launched October 21.

BUSINESS/INDUSTRY/INVENTIONS

Salt production begins at Kanawha, W.Va.

Eli Terry patents equation clock, showing both mean and apparent time; Charles Newbold patents a cast-iron plow.

SCIENCE/MEDICINE

Medical Repository, quarterly magazine, is founded.

EDUCATION

Law lectures are first delivered at Columbia College.

RELIGION

Rev. Edward Bass becomes first Episcopal bishop of Massachusetts, which includes Rhode Island and New Hampshire.

LITERATURE/JOURNALISM

Hannah Foster writes novel *Coquette*; Ann Eliza Bleecker, *The History of Maria Kittle*; Royall Tyler, *The Algerine Captive*.

ENTERTAINMENT

John Daly Burke writes patriotic drama *Bunker Hill*.

SPORTS

First horse-race track in Kentucky is built outside Lexington.

MISCELLANEOUS

Thomas Jefferson is elected president of Philosophical Society.

Capital of New York State moves from New York City to Albany.

Elizabeth Ann Seton founds first charitable institution (Society for the Relief of Poor Widows with Small Children).

INTERNATIONAL

Undeclared war with France begins; U.S. consolidates defenses, names former President Washington commanding general; French capture U.S. schooner *Retaliation*; all commerce with France is suspended.

British naval force boards U.S. frigate *Baltimore*, takes several U.S. sailors, claiming they are British deserters.

Federal property tax is established in anticipation of war with France.

NATIONAL

Congress abolishes imprisonment of debtors.

A Republican cartoon in which the devil and the British lion urge the English political journalist and Federalist editor William Cobbett ("Peter Porcupine") to libel Republicans. THE GRANGER COLLECTION, NEW YORK

1799

Congress passes Alien and Sedition Acts: Naturalization Act changes residency from 5 to 14 years; Alien Act empowers president to order out all aliens regarded as dangerous; Alien Enemies Act gives president power to arrest, imprison, or banish enemy aliens; Sedition Act spells out acts punishable by the government. Virginia legislature claims acts are unconstitutional.

Mississippi Territory is established (April 7).

Navy Department is established (May 21) with Benjamin Stoddert as secretary; Marine Corps is established (July 11).

Andrew Jackson becomes a judge on Tennessee Supreme Court.

DEATH Joshua Clayton, first Delaware governor (1792–1796).

BUSINESS/INDUSTRY/INVENTIONS

Eli Whitney receives government contract for 10,000 muskets; they are manufactured in plant; interchangeable parts are used; Whitney invents jig for guiding operating tools.

Moses Austin builds furnace and shot tower to manufacture lead along Missouri River.

SCIENCE/MEDICINE

Yellow fever epidemic in New York City kills more than 2,000.

Public Health Service is established (July 16) as Marine Hospital Service.

EDUCATION

Abraham Baldwin is named first president of University of Georgia; University of Louisville is founded.

RELIGION

A Russian Orthodox bishop arrives at Sitka, Alaska.

ARTS/MUSIC

Joseph Hopkinson writes lyrics for "Hail Columbia"; music by Philip Pile.

ENTERTAINMENT

William Dunlop's play *André* and John D. Burk's *Female Patriotism* are produced.

Park Theater in New York City is completed.

INTERNATIONAL

U.S. ships capture two French vessels.

William V. Murray is named new envoy to France.

NATIONAL

John Fries leads uprising in Pennsylvania against federal property taxes; is convicted of treason, sentenced to death, then pardoned by President John Adams.

New York legislature passes law for gradual freeing of slaves.

Kentucky legislature adopts state constitution; condemns Alien and Sedition acts as unconstitutional.

Senate concludes first impeachment proceedings against a U.S. senator, William Blount of Tennessee; charges are dismissed for lack of jurisdiction.

First federal forestry legislation is passed, allowing government to acquire timberlands for navy.

James Monroe is elected governor of Virginia.

DEATHS Former President Washington; Patrick Henry, orator and first governor of Virginia; William Dawes, who rode with Paul Revere; Joseph Iredell, an original Supreme Court justice.

The American frigate *Constellation* (left) bears down on the French ship *L'Insurgent* off the island of Nevis in the West Indies on February 9, 1799. THE GRANGER COLLECTION, NEW YORK

BUSINESS/INDUSTRY/INVENTIONS

Journeymen Cordwainers (shoemakers) of Philadelphia reach agreement on contract after short strike, first such action in U.S.

Eliakim Spooner invents a seeding machine.

TRANSPORTATION

Practical Navigator by Nathaniel Bowditch, is published; will remain a standard mariner's reference into the twenty-first century.

LITERATURE/JOURNALISM

Charles B. Brown publishes *Osmond* and *Edgar Huntley*.

Register is published in Raleigh, N.C.; *American Review and Literary Journal*, a quarterly, is founded.

1800

INTERNATIONAL

Formal peace talks begin, with an aim to end undeclared war with France.

Secret Treaty of Ildefonso is signed in which Spain returns Louisiana to France (October 1).

Treaty of Morfontaine (Convention of 1800) releases U.S. from defensive alliance with France.

Senate ratifies 1797 treaty with Tunis.

NATIONAL

Congress moves capital from Philadelphia to Washington; Congress opens session (November 17).

President John Adams becomes first occupant of White House (November 1).

President Adams is defeated for reelection; Thomas Jefferson and Aaron Burr receive same number of electoral votes (Congress later requires separate ballots for president and vice president).

Indiana Territory is created by dividing Northwest Territory (May 7).

Second census reports population of 5,308,483.

Congress approves sale of public lands on credit (credit abandoned 1820).

Library of Congress is established (April 24) with purchase of $5,000 worth of books (740 volumes).

Portsmouth (N.H.) Navy Yard is established; Navy builds floating drydocks at Portsmouth and Pensacola, Fla.

DEATH John Rutledge, former Supreme Court justice.

The Capitol in Washington, D.C., around 1800. Watercolor by William Birch. THE GRANGER COLLECTION, NEW YORK

BUSINESS/INDUSTRY/INVENTIONS

Eli Terry, clockmaker, begins to use water-powered machinery to make parts; William Mann builds axe-making plant in Johnstown, N.Y.; Paul Revere opens mill to roll sheet copper.

Latrobe-Roosevelt waterworks in Philadelphia begin operating.

TRANSPORTATION

Robert Fulton, steamboat builder, invents a practical submarine.

Santee Canal, first to be completed in U.S., connects Santee and Cooper rivers in South Carolina.

SCIENCE/MEDICINE

Dr. Benjamin Waterhouse successfully vaccinates his son and household against smallpox with cowpox vaccine.

Dr. Philip S. Physick successfully washes a patient's stomach of poison with a tube or syringe.

EDUCATION

Middlebury (Vt.) College is founded; University of Vermont opens.

RELIGION

Jacob Albright founds Evangelical Church in Lebanon County, Pa., as "The Newly-Formed Methodist Conference."

Church of the United Brethren in Christ holds first conference; Martin Boehm and Philip W. Otterbein, church founders, are named bishops.

First Swedenborgian (or New Church) service is held in Baltimore.

ART/MUSIC

Painter Ralph Earl completes *Looking East from Leicester Hills*; Rembrandt Peale completes portrait of Thomas Jefferson.

Benjamin Carr publishes weekly *Musical Journal*.

LITERATURE/JOURNALISM

Parson Mason Weems publishes the *Life of George Washington*, to which he later adds the cherry-tree story.

National Intelligencer newspaper is founded in Washington.

Charles Brockden Brown publishes *Arthur Mervyn*, an account of the Philadelphia yellow fever epidemic.

ENTERTAINMENT

First summer theater in the U.S. opens at Mt. Vernon Gardens, New York City.

SPORTS

Boys using cricket balls, but not the bats, play a game that will later develop into baseball.

MISCELLANEOUS

John Chapman (Johnny Appleseed) begins to distribute young apple trees and seeds.

Thomas Jefferson prepares a parliamentary manual.

Four-tined forks begin to replace two- and three-tined forks.

Women begin to wear their hair shorter; wigs of short, close curls are fashionable; curly hair for children is popular.

1801

INTERNATIONAL

Tripoli declares war on U.S. after U.S. refuses to increase tribute payments (May 14); USS *Enterprise* seizes the corsair *Tripoli*.

NATIONAL

House of Representatives elects Thomas Jefferson president (February 17); he and Aaron Burr each receive 73 electoral votes; Burr becomes vice president; Jefferson's inauguration (March 4) is the first held in Washington.

Congress assumes jurisdiction over Washington, D.C.; mayor is to be named by president.

Judiciary Act (February 27) reduces from six to five the number of Supreme Court justices, creates 16 circuit courts; John Marshall becomes Supreme Court chief justice (January 31).

James Madison becomes Secretary of State.

President Jefferson sends annual message to Congress in written form (December 8); sets precedent that will be followed until 1913.

DEATH Benedict Arnold, American military hero turned traitor, in London.

Thomas Jefferson hitches his horse outside the Capitol before delivering his first inaugural address in 1801. THE GRANGER COLLECTION, NEW YORK

BUSINESS/INDUSTRY/INVENTIONS

Titus Pease and Thomas Rose begin to manufacture whips in Westfield, Mass.; Adam Seybert, chlorides and oxide pigment in Philadelphia.

Josiah Bent begins to produce hardwater crackers in Milton, Mass.

E. I. du Pont builds gunpowder plant near Wilmington, Del.

Robert Hare invents blowtorch using oxygen and hydrogen.

EDUCATION

University of Georgia opens; University of South Carolina is chartered as South Carolina College.

Episcopal Bishop Benjamin Moore becomes president of Columbia College.

RELIGION

Camp meeting near Cane Ridge Meeting House in Bourbon County, Ky., attracts estimated 20,000 persons; begins a revival of religion that will grow in subsequent years.

Rev. Benjamin Moore becomes Episcopal bishop of New York.

LITERATURE/JOURNALISM

American Company of Booksellers is organized in New York City.

Paul Allen publishes *Original Poems, Serious and Entertaining*.

New York Evening Post and *Port Folio*, a literary journal, are founded.

1802

INTERNATIONAL

U.S. declares war on Tripoli (February 6).

NATIONAL

Naturalization Act of 1798 is repealed, the 1795 Act is restored, requiring five years' residence for citizenship; Judiciary Act of 1801 is repealed, restoring to six the number of Supreme Court justices and setting up six (rather than 16) circuit courts.

New financial policy is adopted, reducing deficit from $83 million in 1801 to $57 million in 1809 despite Tripolitan War and Louisiana Purchase; Congress abolishes all excise duties, including controversial whiskey tax.

Washington, D.C., is incorporated as city.

U.S. Military Academy opens (July 4) at West Point, N.Y.

Army Engineer Corps is established as a permanent unit (March 16).

John J. Beckley is named Librarian of Congress;

Gabriel Duval becomes first Comptroller of the Treasury.

Ohio convention ratifies state constitution.

DEATHS Martha Washington, First Lady (1789–1797); Daniel Morgan, Revolutionary War general.

BUSINESS/INDUSTRY/INVENTIONS

Simon Willard patents the "banjo" clock; Loammi Baldwin designs, builds fire engine for Groton, Mass.; Oliver Evans begins to manufacture steam engines.

Abel Porter opens first brass-rolling mill in Waterbury, Conn.

Union Hotel is built in Saratoga, N.Y.

TRANSPORTATION

Nathaniel Bowditch publishes *New American Practical Navigator*, considered the seamen's "bible."

SCIENCE/MEDICINE

Benjamin Silliman becomes Yale's first professor of chemistry and natural history.

1803

During the war with Tripoli, Stephen Decatur recaptures the *Philadelphia*, clears it of the enemy, and burns it, 1803. CULVER PICTURES, INC.

EDUCATION

University of Ohio (Athens) is chartered as American Western University: Washington & Jefferson College (Washington, Pa.) opens as Jefferson Academy.

Rev. Joseph McKeen becomes first president of Bowdoin College.

RELIGION

Congregation Rodeph Shalom is founded in Philadelphia.

DEATH John Ettwein, presiding officer of Moravian Church of North America (1784–1802).

ART/MUSIC

Benjamin West completes the painting *Death on the Pale Horse*.

LITERATURE/JOURNALISM

Beaver St. Coffee House, New York City, hosts first American book fair.

SPORTS

Two sports books published: *Chess Made Easy* (author unknown) and Johann C. F. Muth's *Gymnastics for Youth*.

New York State prohibits public horse races; races held by private jockey clubs are permitted.

INTERNATIONAL

U.S. frigate *Philadelphia*, blockading Tripoli, runs aground and is captured.

James Monroe is named minister plenipotentiary to France.

Spain restores right of Americans to use the port of New Orleans.

1803

NATIONAL

U.S. purchases Louisiana for 60 million francs (approximately $15 million), doubling area of U.S. by adding 828,000 square miles between Mississippi River and the Rockies; Senate approves purchase (October 20); U.S. takes formal possession (December 20).

Twelfth Amendment approved by Congress (December 9); proposes separate balloting for president and vice president; is submitted to states for ratification.

Marbury v. Madison (February 24) is first Supreme Court decision that holds an act of Congress unconstitutional; establishes doctrine of judicial review.

Lewis and Clark Expedition begins trip down Ohio River to the Mississippi (August 31).

Ohio is admitted as the 17th state (March 1).

Treaty of Vincennes is signed with Kaskaskia nation, which cedes half of what is now Illinois.

Ft. Dearborn at Chicago is built.

John Quincy Adams is elected a senator from Massachusetts.

DEATHS Samuel Adams, colonial leader and

The American flag is raised over the city of New Orleans to replace the French flag after the Louisiana Purchase, 1803. LOUISIANA MUSEUM

Massachusetts governor (1794–1797); John Barry, first naval commander.

BUSINESS/INDUSTRY/INVENTIONS

Thomas Moore of Baltimore invents the refrigerator; Moses Coats of Downingtown, Pa., an apple corer; John Stevens patents a multitubular boiler.

TRANSPORTATION

Middlesex Canal, connecting Boston Harbor and Merrimack River, opens.

SCIENCE/MEDICINE

John Young conducts important experiments on digestion at University of Pennsylvania Medical College.

John Halsam, who will be the first veterinary surgeon to practice in U.S., arrives from England.

Benjamin S. Barton publishes *Elements of Botany*.

EDUCATION

Library of Youth, the first government-funded library, is built in Salisbury, Conn.

RELIGION

First Catholic church in Boston is dedicated.

Massachusetts Society for Promoting Christian Knowledge is founded in Boston.

Massachusetts Baptist Missionary Magazine is published; later becomes *American Baptist Magazine*.

DEATH Edward Bass, first Episcopal bishop of Massachusetts (1797–1803).

ART/MUSIC

Benjamin Crehorne of Milton, Mass., builds first American piano.

MISCELLANEOUS

New York City Hall is built.

1804

INTERNATIONAL

Americans led by Stephen Decatur recapture the frigate *Philadelphia* in Tripoli harbor (February 16).

NATIONAL

President Thomas Jefferson is reelected with 162 of the 176 electoral votes, defeating Charles Pinckney; George Clinton is elected vice president.

Alexander Hamilton is fatally wounded in duel with Aaron Burr in Weehawken, N.J. (July 11); dies the next day.

Twelfth Amendment is ratified (September 25); provides for separate ballots for president and vice president.

Lewis and Clark Expedition begins trip up the Missouri River.

Upper Louisiana is transferred to U.S. (March 10), William C. C. Claiborne is named Louisiana territorial governor (October 1).

Territory of Orleans is established.

New Jersey passes legislation for gradual freeing of slaves.

Senate in first judicial impeachment trial finds Federal Judge John Pickering guilty of improper conduct, removes him from the bench.

DEATH Michael Hillegas, first U.S. treasurer; William Bingham, founder of Bank of North America.

BUSINESS

Oliver Evans builds a steam-operated dredge for Philadelphia to dredge the Schuylkill River and clean city docks; has powered rollers and paddle so that it can move on land and water.

EDUCATION

Eliphalet Nott begins 62 years as president of Union College (Schenectady, N.Y.).

RELIGION

John M. Mason, Presbyterian clergyman, founds what becomes (1835) Union Theological Seminary.

First African Presbyterian church opens in Philadelphia.

DEATH Barbara Heck, a leader in founding American Methodism.

ART/MUSIC

Washington Allston completes the painting *The Rising of a Thunderstorm*.

LITERATURE/JOURNALISM

First Indiana newspaper, *Indiana Gazette*, is founded in Vincennes; *Enquirer* first publishes in Richmond, Va.

MISCELLANEOUS

New-York Historical Society is founded.

The guide Sacajawea with Lewis and Clark on their expedition. Painting by N.C. Wyeth. THE GRANGER COLLECTION, NEW YORK

1805

INTERNATIONAL

U.S. force captures Derna in Tripoli; leads to end of fighting (April 27); peace treaty is signed (June 4) ending four-year war.

NATIONAL

Exploration of West is accelerated: Lewis and Clark Expedition comes within sight of Pacific Ocean (November 7); Lt. Zebulon Pike explores source of Mississippi River (August 9); expedition is sent to lower Red and Ouachita rivers by territorial governor to check on Spanish in area.

Two territories are created: Michigan (July 1) and Louisiana-Missouri (March 3).

New Orleans is incorporated (February 17); fire levels much of Detroit (June 11).

Supreme Court Justice Samuel Chase, accused of improper trial conduct, is acquitted in Senate trial (March 1).

DEATH William Moultrie, led American defense of Charleston (S.C.) harbor against British.

BUSINESS/INDUSTRY/INVENTIONS

Robert Fulton builds first marine torpedo.

Frederick Tudor, New England merchant, begins to export ice to warmer climates.

Philadelphia court rules Cordwainers (shoemakers) strike (1799) was a criminal "conspiracy" of workers to gain wage increase.

SCIENCE/MEDICINE

Dr. Benjamin Waterhouse publishes popular book *Shewing the Evil Tendency of the Use of Tobacco.*

EDUCATION

Free (later Public) School Society of New York is established.

University of South Carolina opens at Columbia.

RELIGION

Thousands attend a Methodist camp meeting at Smyrna, Del.

German pietist group, Harmonists, led by George Rapp, founds communal settlement at Harmony, Pa., near Pittsburgh.

ART/MUSIC

Pennsylvania Academy of Fine Arts is established.

LITERATURE/JOURNALISM

New York State amends its constitution to guarantee freedom of the press; becomes model for other state constitutions.

Mercy Otis Warren publishes three-volume *Rise, Progress, and Termination of the American Revolution.*

Boston Atheneum, a literary club, is founded.

SPORTS

Bill Richmond, son of an African American slave, knocks out John Holmes in England for boxing title (July 8); loses to Tom Cribb (October 8).

1806

INTERNATIONAL

France and Great Britain blockade each other's coasts, cutting off U.S. trade shipping.

NATIONAL

Senate attacks British seizures of U.S. shipping as "unprovoked aggression"; Congress passes Non-Importation Act (April 18), excluding many British articles because of raids, impressment of seamen.

Zebulon M. Pike sights Pike's Peak in Colorado.

Lewis and Clark Expedition returns to St. Louis (September 26).

President Thomas Jefferson warns citizens against participating in an illegal expedition against Spanish territory (November 27); asks Congress to ban importation of slaves by 1808.

Andrew Jackson fights duel with Charles Dickinson, who made derogatory remarks about Mrs. Jackson; Dickinson is killed, Jackson wounded.

DEATHS George Wythe, colonial leader and first American law professor; Henry Knox, first War Secretary; Horatio Gates, Revolutionary War general; Moses Cleaveland, founder of Cleveland, Ohio.

BUSINESS/INDUSTRY/INVENTIONS

American Builder's Companion by Asher Benjamin, early classic of architecture, is published.

William Colgate founds what later will become Colgate Palmolive toiletries company.

TRANSPORTATION

Cumberland Road and Natchez Road construction is authorized.

Bridge over Delaware River at Philadelphia opens (February 1).

EDUCATION

Bell-Lancastrian school, using monitors to help with instruction, opens in New York City.

RELIGION

Cornerstone is laid for Baltimore Catholic cathedral, the first Catholic cathedral in the U.S.

General Theological Seminary begins as Protestant Episcopal Theological Seminary, in New York.

ART/MUSIC

Charles Willson Peale completes the painting *Exhuming the Mastodon*.

LITERATURE/JOURNALISM

Noah Webster publishes *Compendious Dictionary of the English Language*; he considers it preparation for larger work (which is to come in 1828).

ENTERTAINMENT

Park Theater, New York, presents John H. Payne's play *Julia, or the Wanderer*.

Pike's Peak, Colorado, 14,110 feet, named after Zebulon M. Pike, the first white man to see it (November 1806). © JOHN ELK III/STOCK BOSTON

SPORTS

The horse, Yankee, is first trotter to run a mile in under 3 minutes (2 min, 59 sec).

MISCELLANEOUS

James Madison Randolph, grandson of President Jefferson, is first child born in the White House (January 17).

David Melville puts up the first streetlights in front of his home in Newport, R.I.

1807

INTERNATIONAL

U.S. frigate *Chesapeake* is fired on by British vessel, which takes four men off the U.S. vessel, claiming them as deserters (June 22); British step up campaign of impressment of U.S. seamen.

NATIONAL

President Thomas Jefferson orders British warships out of U.S. territorial waters (July 2); Embargo Act virtually halts all seagoing trade (December 22).

President Jefferson signs act prohibiting importation of slaves after January 1, 1808.

Aaron Burr is arrested in Alabama for illegally forming an expedition against Spanish territory (February 19), is acquitted (September 1); Burr is tried on conspiracy charges in Richmond, is acquitted (October 20).

Coast Survey begins (February 10), later becomes Coast and Geodetic Survey.

Patrick Magruder becomes Librarian of Congress, serving until 1815.

New Jersey removes property requirements for voting.

DEATHS Supreme Court Chief Justice Oliver Ellsworth (1796– 1799); Comte de Rochambeau, French leader who served in American Revolution.

BUSINESS/INDUSTRY/ INVENTIONS

Copperthwaite & Sons, furniture dealer, introduces consumer installment purchases.

David Martin, a black man from Massachusetts, is one of the four crew members removed from the *Chesapeake* by the British. THE GRANGER COLLECTION, NEW YORK

1808

A glue factory is created in Boston, a vitriol factory in Strafford, Vt.; Jesse Read begins to manufacture tacks in Connecticut.

TRANSPORTATION

Robert Fulton's steamboat *Clermont* completes New York–Albany round-trip on the Hudson River in 62 hours (August 17).

William Raymond builds first lifeboat, in Nantucket, Mass.

SCIENCE/MEDICINE

Maryland College of Medicine is founded, to become part of University of Maryland in 1812;

College of Physicians and Surgeons is established in New York City, combines with Columbia University medical faculty.

Massachusetts Humane Society establishes first lifesaving station at Cohasset.

LITERATURE/JOURNALISM

Series of essays, *Salmagundi*, by Washington Irving and others, is issued.

ENTERTAINMENT

William Dunlap's play *Leicester* and James N. Barker's *Tears and Smiles* are produced in New York City.

INTERNATIONAL

Third Embargo adopted by Congress to strengthen prohibitions against trading with foreign countries; France orders seizure of U.S. vessels entering French ports.

NATIONAL

President Thomas Jefferson does not seek reelection; James Madison is elected with 122 electoral votes defeating Charles Pinckney; George Clinton is reelected vice president.

Importation of slaves into U.S. is forbidden (January 1); impoundment of ships carrying them is called for.

Osage Treaty is signed (November 10); Osage nation cedes lands in Missouri and Arkansas.

Dr. Billy J. Clark organizes first temperance society in U.S. at Moreau, N.Y.

BUSINESS/INDUSTRY/INVENTIONS

Judge Jesse Fell of Wilkes-Barre, Pa., discovers anthracite coal's use as stove fuel.

Osage scalp dance, painted by John Mix Stanley in 1845. The Osage nation signs a treaty with the United States on November 10, 1808. NATIONAL MUSEUM OF AMERICAN ART, WASHINGTON, D.C./ART RESOURCE, NEW YORK

John Jacob Astor forms American Fur Co.; in St. Louis, Missouri Fur Co. incorporates.

American Law Journal is founded in Baltimore.

RELIGION

Catholic Diocese of Baltimore is raised to archdiocese.

Andover (Mass.) Theological Seminary opens; later moves to Cambridge.

First Bible society in U.S., Bible Society of Philadelphia, is organized.

American Methodist church adopts a constitution.

DEATH Jacob Albright, a founder of Evangelical church.

ART/MUSIC

Harvard University organizes a college orchestra.

A popular song of the day is "Believe Me If All Those Endearing Young Charms."

LITERATURE/JOURNALISM

St. Louis Republican begins as the *Missouri Gazette*, the first paper west of the Mississippi.

ENTERTAINMENT

James N. Barker's play *The Indian Princess* (later called *Pocahontas*) is produced in Philadelphia.

An opera house, Théâtre d'Orleans, is built in New Orleans at a cost of $100,000.

1809

INTERNATIONAL

John Quincy Adams is named minister to Russia.

NATIONAL

Enforcement Act is passed (January 7), calls for severe penalties for violating the embargo; mercantile interests in New York and New England oppose embargo; Non-Intercourse Act repeals embargo against all nations except Great Britain and France (March 15), authorizes president to permit resumption of trade with Great Britain and France if they stop violating neutral rights; action is reversed in August.

Supreme Court in *United States v. Peters* sustains power of federal government over states (February 20).

Territory of Illinois is established by dividing Indiana Territory (March 1).

Gen. William Henry Harrison negotiates treaty with Native American tribes in which they cede 3 million acres in Indiana Territory (September 30).

DEATHS Thomas Paine, Revolutionary pamphleteer; Jonathan Trumbull, first Comptroller of Treasury; Meriwether Lewis of Expedition fame.

BUSINESS/INDUSTRY/INVENTIONS

Commercial production of gloves is begun by Talmadge Edwards of Johnstown, N.Y.

Abel Stowel of Massachusetts invents a screw-cutting machine.

Boston Crown Glass Co. is incorporated.

New York cordwainers tried for conspiracy in restraint of trade; convicted, charged token fine.

TRANSPORTATION

Steam vessel *Phoenix* uses screw propeller to become first steam vessel to navigate in the ocean (New York City to Philadelphia).

SCIENCE/MEDICINE

Dr. Ephraim McDowell performs an ovariotomy in Danville, Ky., the first American abdominal operation.

William Maclure publishes *Observations on the Geology of the United States*, which includes first geological map of America.

1809

"Ograbme," or, The American Snapping-Turtle. A commentary on the embargo against trading with foreign countries. Begun in 1807, the embargo is strengthened by legislation passed in 1809. THE GRANGER COLLECTION, NEW YORK

EDUCATION

Miami University at Oxford, Ohio, is chartered.

Elizabeth Ann Seton founds free Catholic elementary school in Baltimore, starting U.S. parochial school education.

RELIGION

Thomas Campbell organizes Disciples, a Christian sect, in Washington, Pa.

American Board of Commissioners for Foreign Missions is established.

ART/MUSIC

Charles Willson Peale completes the painting *The Family Group*.

LITERATURE/JOURNALISM

Washington Irving publishes *History of New York*, a comic work, under a pseudonym.

New Hampshire Patriot is founded in Concord.

ENTERTAINMENT

John H. Payne stars in play *Douglas* by John Horne.

SPORTS

Boston Cricket Club is founded.

1810

INTERNATIONAL

Southern expansionists revolt against Spanish rule, capture Baton Rouge; proclaim (September 26) independent state of West Florida; President James Madison issues proclamation (October 27) taking possession of West Florida from Mississippi River to the Perdido River as part of the Louisiana Purchase.

NATIONAL

Supreme Court in *Fletcher v. Peck* invalidates a state law as unconstitutional for first time.

Third census reports population of 7,239,881.

Maryland removes property requirements for voting.

DEATH William Cushing, first associate justice named to Supreme Court.

The County Fair, painted by John A. Woodside, depicts a scene that will become typical in the U.S. following the first annual agricultural fair in Pittsfield, Mass., 1810. THE GRANGER COLLECTION, NEW YORK

1811

BUSINESS/INDUSTRY/INVENTIONS

American Fire Insurance Co. is organized in Philadelphia.

Simeon Viets establishes cigar factory in West Suffield, Conn.

Henry Shreve takes large load of lead down Mississippi River from Galena (Ill.) mines to New Orleans, demonstrating the practicability of steam navigation on the river.

John Jacob Astor founds Pacific Fur Co., at what later becomes Astoria, Ore.

National cotton production is 171,000 bales.

TRANSPORTATION

A. R. Hawley and Augustus Post complete 1,173-mile balloon flight from St. Louis to Canada.

Cornelius Vanderbilt initiates ferry service between Manhattan and Staten Island.

SCIENCE/MEDICINE

Yale University medical faculty is established.

RELIGION

Elizabeth Ann Seton and four other women organize Sisters of Charity of St. Vincent de Paul and St. Joseph College at Emmittsburg, Md.

Alexander V. Griswold is named Episcopal bishop of the Eastern Diocese (most of New England).

Michael Egan is consecrated as first Catholic bishop of Philadelphia.

Cumberland Presbyterian church is formed when Presbytery of Eastern Tennessee/Kentucky breaks away from Presbyterian church.

ART/MUSIC

Gottlieb Graupner organizes Philharmonic Society in Boston, first regular U.S. concert orchestra.

John Vanderlyn completes the painting *Ariadne.*

LITERATURE/JOURNALISM

William Cullen Bryant writes poem "Thanatopsis."

Agricultural Museum, first American farm periodical, is published.

ENTERTAINMENT

George F. Cooke is first English actor of note to make New York debut.

American Museum in New York City opens; will later be acquired by P. T. Barnum.

SPORTS

Englishman Tom Cribb beats Tom Molineaux, an American, to retain heavyweight boxing title.

MISCELLANEOUS

Berkshire Cattle Show opens in Pittsfield, Mass.; launches American practice of holding annual agricultural fairs.

William Duane publishes *A Military Dictionary.*

INTERNATIONAL

U.S. renews nonintercourse policy against Great Britain; British blockade New York; British frigate *Guerrière* stops U.S. brigantine *Spitfire,* seizes one U.S. seaman; U.S. vessel disables British vessel off New York Harbor.

NATIONAL

John Jacob Astor and group of colonists found Astoria, Ore., first settlement in Pacific Northwest; Native American tribal confederacy forms in Northwest to resist settlements; Russian settlers found Ft. Ross, trading post and agricultural colony, at

Situated at the mouth of the Columbia River, Astoria is the first permanent settlement in the Oregon country (1811). THE GRANGER COLLECTION, NEW YORK

Bodega Bay, north of San Francisco.

William Henry Harrison leads a U.S. force in turning back tribal attacks led by Tecumseh at Battle of Tippecanoe (Ind.).

James Monroe is named Secretary of State.

Senate refuses to renew charter of Bank of the United States; leads to opening of many local banks.

BUSINESS/INDUSTRY/INVENTIONS

First alum works are established at Cape Sable, Md.

TRANSPORTATION

Construction begins on Cumberland Road between Cumberland, Md., and Wheeling, W. Va.

Steam-propelled ferryboat, *Juliana*, begins service between Hoboken, N.J., and New York.

Steamboat *New Orleans* completes trip from Pittsburgh to New Orleans; inaugurates regular service ($18 for downstream trip, $25 upstream) on the Ohio and Missouri rivers.

SCIENCE/MEDICINE

Caspar Wistar publishes first American anatomy textbook, *A System of Anatomy*.

RELIGION

First church building of Disciples is constructed at Brush Run, Pa.

LITERATURE/ JOURNALISM

Newspapers founded are *Mobile Centinel*, first paper in Alabama; *Ohio State Journal* in Columbus; and *Niles Weekly Register* in Baltimore.

Isaac Mitchell publishes *The Asylum*.

ENTERTAINMENT

Walnut St. Theater in Philadelphia opens.

SPORTS

Competitive rowing races become popular; thousands watch the *Knickerbocker* of New York City beat the *Invincible* of Long Island.

MISCELLANEOUS

Earthquake, centered near New Madrid, Mo., causes an area of 30,000 square miles to sink 5 to 15 feet.

1812

INTERNATIONAL

War of 1812

President James Madison recommends (April 4) and Congress approves general embargo for 60 days; president is empowered to call up 100,000 militia for six months' service (April 10); British note is received, unyielding in its position.

President Madison sends message to Congress (June 1) outlining reasons for war with Great Britain; House (June 4) and Senate (June 8) vote for war; war is declared (June 19).

The clash between the *USS Constitution* and *HMS Guerrière* on August 19, 1812. THE GRANGER COLLECTION, NEW YORK

War in Midwest goes badly: Americans surrender post at Mackinac (July 17) and Detroit without firing a shot (August 16) because Gen. William Hull fears Native American massacre of women and children; Ft. Dearborn (Chicago) is surrendered, massacre of garrison and destruction of fort follows (August 15); William Henry Harrison is put in charge of army in West.

In the East, Americans defeat British at Ogdensburg (October 4); campaign heads to Montreal, stops at Canadian border (November 19) when militia refuses to proceed.

At sea, U.S. vessels fare better: frigate *President* defeats British sloop off Sandy Hook; the *Essex* captures another sloop (August 13); the *Constitution* (Old Ironsides) destroys the British *Guerrière* off Nova Scotia, captures frigate *Java* off Brazil (December 29); the *Wasp* bests a British brigantine off Virginia (October 17); U.S. frigate *United States* subdues British frigate *Macedonia* off Madeira (October 25).

British blockade Chesapeake and Delaware bays.

NATIONAL

President Madison is reelected with 128 electoral votes defeating De Witt Clinton, and Elbridge Gerry becomes vice president; earlier (April 20) Vice President George Clinton dies, first vice president to die in office.

Congress incorporates West Florida into Mississippi Territory (May 14); Louisiana adopts state constitution, is admitted to Union (April 30) as 18th state; Territory of Missouri is created (October 1).

First war-bond issue (March 4) and first interest-bearing Treasury notes are authorized (June 30).

Massachusetts legislature redistricts state for political advantage; practice is later called "gerrymandering" after governor's name, Elbridge Gerry.

General Land Office is created (April 25).

Mrs. Lucy P. Washington, sister of President Madison, marries Supreme Court Justice Thomas Todd in first White House wedding.

BUSINESS/INDUSTRY/INVENTIONS

First life-insurance company, Pennsylvania Company for Insurance on Lives and Granting Annuities, is incorporated.

William Monroe establishes the first U.S. pencil factory, in Concord, Mass.

DEATH Aaron L. Dennison, known as the "father of American watchmaking."

SCIENCE/MEDICINE

New England Journal of Medicine begins as the *New England Medical Review and Journal.*

Dr. Benjamin Rush publishes *Diseases of the Mind,* pioneer work on mental disorders.

Academy of Natural Sciences organizes in Philadelphia.

EDUCATION

Hamilton College (Clinton, N.Y.) is chartered.

University of Maryland organizes a law faculty.

DEATH James Madison, president, College of William & Mary (1777–1812).

RELIGION

Presbyterian theological seminary is located at College of New Jersey (Princeton).

MISCELLANEOUS

Isaiah Thomas founds American Antiquarian Society in Worcester, Mass.

1813

INTERNATIONAL

War of 1812

British blockade extends from Delaware and Chesapeake bays, includes most of U.S. coast from New York to Mississippi River.

U.S. force raids, sets fire to York (later Toronto); U.S. Gen. Zebulon Pike is killed in raid (April 27); British capture Plattsburgh, N.Y. (July 31), Americans return to York, defeat British along Thames River in Canada, during which American Indian chief Tecumseh is killed, leading to the fall of the Native American federation and the end of its support of the British cause.

Americans capture Ft. George (May 27), forcing British to evacuate Ft. Niagara and Ft. Erie, Ontario; in surprise attack (December 18), British capture Ft. Niagara, burn adjoining villages; British move on to Buffalo, part of which they burn (December 19) in retaliation foer burning York.

U.S. frigate *Chesapeake* is defeated by British *Shannon* (June 1); in that battle, dying American Capt.

James Lawrence urges his crew, "Don't give up the ship!" U.S. brigantine *Enterprise* defeats an English brigantine off Maine (September 5).

First American blackout takes place at St. Michaels, Md., on word of impending British shelling; blackout causes British to overshoot town.

Naval war continues with mixed results, ending with Battle of Lake Erie (September 10) in which U.S. ships led by Oliver Hazard Perry defeat six British vessels near Sandusky, Ohio; Perry sends message to Gen William Henry Harrison stating: "We have met the enemy and they are ours." Loss on Lake Erie forces British to evacuate Detroit.

British send letter (November 4) offering peace negotiations.

In an unrelated military action, Americans capture (April 15) Spanish fort at Mobile, Ala.

NATIONAL

British blockade of U.S. coast is effective: it stimu-

1813

Tecumseh is mortally wounded in the Battle of the Thames on October 5, 1813. THE GRANGER COLLECTION, NEW YORK

lates domestic industry but also leads to widespread speculation, price increases.

Clash between settlers and Native Americans occurs near Pensacola, Fla. (July 27); Native Americans massacre 250 Americans (August 30) at Ft. Mims, north of Mobile, leading to start of Creek War; Americans led by Gen. Andrew Jackson defeat Creek nations at Talladega, Ala. (November 8).

DEATH Robert R. Livingston, first Secretary of Foreign Affairs (1781–1783).

BUSINESS/INDUSTRY/INVENTIONS

Boston Manufacturing Co. (also called Waltham Co.) establishes first textile factory converting cotton into cloth in one operation.

Simeon North is awarded government contract for 20,000 pistols using interchangeable parts.

TRANSPORTATION

John Stevens builds first ironclad vessel, in Hoboken, N.J.

SCIENCE/MEDICINE

Alexander Wilson completes nine-volume *American Ornithology*.

Gotthilf Muhlenberg issues catalog of 2,800 species of North American plants.

DEATH Benjamin Rush, author of first American chemistry textbook (*A Syllabus of a Course of Lectures on Chemistry*, 1770).

EDUCATION

Colby College (Waterville, Me.) is founded.

RELIGION

Christian Observer begins publication in Philadelphia as *The Religious Remembrancer.*

ART/MUSIC

Two popular songs are "The Minstrel Boy" and "'Tis the Last Rose of Summer."

LITERATURE/JOURNALISM

Albany (N.Y.) *Argus* and *Boston Daily Advertiser* are first published.

MISCELLANEOUS

Connecticut Society for the Reformation of Morals is organized to combat errant clergymen; Lyman and Henry Ward Beecher are charter members.

1814

INTERNATIONAL

War of 1812

British extend blockade to include New England.

Americans capture Ft. Erie, Ontario (July 3), defeat British at Chippewa, north of Ft. Erie (July 5); the Battle of Lundy's Lane near Niagara Falls, Ontario, ends in a draw, Americans withdraw (July 25); British attack on Ft. Erie (September 17) is turned back, but Americans abandon attempt to capture Canada, blow up Ft. Erie (November 5), withdraw across Niagara River.

Americans gain control of Lake Champlain (September 11); British withdraw to Canada.

British force lands at Benedict, Md., at mouth of Patuxent River (August 19), defeats a U.S. force at Bladensburg, Md. (August 24), goes on to Washington where it burns the Capitol, White House, and most government buildings (August 25); British fleet bombards Ft. McHenry in Baltimore Harbor (September 13). Ft. McHenry attack leads Francis Scott Key to write poem about the successful defense, which will later be set to music ("To Anacreon in Heaven," a British song); it becomes "The Star-Spangled Banner."

Gen. Andrew Jackson leads a U.S. force to victory at Pensacola, Fla. (November 7); goes on to defend New Orleans (December 1) (see 1815).

Peace discussions between U.S. and British commissioners begin (August 8) at Ghent, Belgium; peace treaty is signed (December 24).

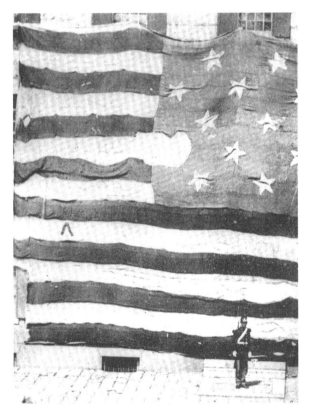

The actual "star-spangled banner" that inspired the song, photographed at Fort Henry. CORBIS-BETTMANN

NATIONAL

Gen. Andrew Jackson leads U.S. force to victory over Native Americans at Horseshoe Bend on Alabama River (March 27); peace treaty is signed (August 9) ending Creek War.

1814

Under the leadership of Major General Ross, the British Army overtakes the city of Washington on August 24, 1814. THE GRANGER COLLECTION, NEW YORK

Treaty of Greenville is signed with Northwest nation (July 22) bringing peace to that area.

Hartford Convention of representatives from five New England states (December 15), unhappy with British blockade and Madison's embargo, calls for revision of Constitution, creates committee to negotiate with federal government; New Orleans victory and peace treaty end work of convention.

Gen. William Hull is found guilty by court-martial for loss of Detroit without resistance (1812), is sentenced to death; penalty is waived because of his Revolutionary War record.

DEATH Vice President Elbridge Gerry (1813–1814), whose name is associated with politically drawn boundaries (gerrymandering).

BUSINESS/INDUSTRY/INVENTIONS

A. A. Lawrence Co. of Boston is founded, importers and merchants instrumental in developing New England textile industry.

David Melville invents a circular saw.

Francis C. Lowell establishes first factory to house power cotton spinning and weaving machinery in same building.

TRANSPORTATION

Demologos, a steam-propelled frigate built by Robert Fulton, is launched.

SCIENCE/MEDICINE

Jacob Bigelow publishes a botany manual, *Flora*

Bostoniensis, that will become longtime standard.

EDUCATION

Middlebury (Vt.) Seminary, women's college preparatory school, is founded by Emma Willard.

RELIGION

Baptist General Convention is established to support missionary work in Burma.

DEATH Thomas Coke, early American Methodist leader.

ART/MUSIC

Peale's Baltimore Museum and Gallery of Fine Arts opens; becomes Baltimore's first City Hall (1830).

LITERATURE/JOURNALISM

First Illinois newspaper, *Illinois Herald,* begins publication in Kaskaskia.

DEATH Mercy Otis Warren, colonial writer who aided the Revolution.

1815

INTERNATIONAL

Fighting breaks out around New Orleans (January 1), British attack is beaten back by American forces led by Jackson; British withdraw to their ships, sail away (January 8); battle is fought two weeks after signing of Treaty of Ghent which the New Orleans fighters do not know about.

Senate unanimously ratifies Treaty of Ghent (February 15); peace proclaimed (February 17).

Peace treaty is signed with Dey of Algiers after U.S. navy vessels defeat several Algerian vessels, sail into Algiers Harbor; treaty calls for end of attacks on U.S. shipping, return of all prisoners, end of tribute payments; similar treaties are signed with Tunis (July 26) and Tripoli (August 5).

John Quincy Adams is named minister to Great Britain.

NATIONAL

Library of Congress is restored after British attack (1814), purchases Thomas Jefferson's library; George Watterston is named librarian.

DEATH John Sevier, first Tennessee governor (1796–1801, 1803–1809).

TRANSPORTATION

Steamboat *Enterprise* sails from New Orleans to Louisville in 25 days.

John Stevens receives charter from New Jersey to build railroad across state; cannot get financial backing.

EDUCATION

Georgetown College, Washington, D.C., is chartered as university; Allegheny College (Meadville, Pa.) is founded.

RELIGION

Church of the United Brethren holds first general conference with elected delegates at Mt. Pleasant, Pa.

Boston Society for the Moral and Religious Instruction of the Poor is established.

DEATH John Carroll, first American Catholic bishop and archbishop of Baltimore.

ART/MUSIC

The Handel and Haydn Society, one of the earliest American choral groups, forms in Boston.

Cornerstone is laid for George Washington Monument in Baltimore.

DEATH John S. Copley, portrait painter.

LITERATURE/JOURNALISM

William Cullen Bryant publishes his poem "To a Waterfowl."

Western Journal (later *Enquirer*) is established in St. Louis.

1816

Andrew Jackson's victory in the Battle of New Orleans during the war of 1812 saves New Orleans and the Mississippi Valley from invasion by the British. UPI/CORBIS-BETTMANN

North American Review, edited by Jared Sparks, is published in Boston.

MISCELLANEOUS

New York Peace Society is organized to promote pacifism. Massachusetts Peace Society is organized; will later become the American Peace Society (1828).

1816

NATIONAL

James Monroe is elected president, receiving 183 electoral votes to 34 for Rufus D. King; Daniel D. Tompkins is elected vice president.

Congress creates Second Bank of the United States as a depository for federal funds (March 14).

Indiana is admitted as the 19th state (December 11).

Tariff of 25% is imposed on most woolen, cotton, and iron goods imports.

U.S. force destroys Ft. Apalachicola, Fla., touching off fighting with Seminole nation; by Treaty of Chickasaw Council House, Native Americans cede tribal lands on both sides of Tennessee River to U.S. in exchange for an annuity.

Ft. Dearborn (Chicago), destroyed by Native Americans in 1812, is rebuilt.

National debt exceeds $1 million for first time.

BUSINESS/INDUSTRY/INVENTIONS

One of the first American savings banks, Provident Institution for Savings, in Boston, is incorporated (see 1819).

Allaire Works, producing machinery, is founded in Jersey City, N.J.

TRANSPORTATION

Black Ball packet line begins regular monthly sailings between New York and Liverpool, England.

First iron wire-suspension bridge, built by Erskine Hazard and Josiah White, opens over Schuylkill River at Philadelphia.

EDUCATION

Infant school (children admitted at four years) is introduced in Boston; is included in public school system (August 8).

RELIGION

African Methodist Episcopal church is established in Philadelphia with Richard Allen as the first bishop.

American Bible Society organizes in New York City with Elias Boudinot as president.

Harvard Divinity School is founded.

Rev. John H. Hobart becomes Episcopal bishop of New York.

DEATHS Francis Asbury, leader of American Methodist church (1785–1816); Charles Inglis, first Anglican bishop in North America.

ART/MUSIC

Ananias Davisson publishes *Kentucky Harmony*, a music collection.

LITERATURE/JOURNALISM

John Pickering publishes *Vocabulary*, a dictionary of about 500 indigenous American words and phrases.

Ohio Monitor (later *Ohio Statesman*) is founded in Columbus.

SPORTS

Jacob Hyer claims U.S. heavyweight boxing title; no one disputes his claim.

MISCELLANEOUS

Manufacture of coal gas for street illumination begins in Baltimore.

Year of "no summer": ten-inch snowfall in Berkshire Mountains in Massachusetts, Vermont, and New Hampshire (June 6).

1817

INTERNATIONAL

U.S. and Great Britain sign Rush-Bagot Treaty, limiting armaments on Great Lakes, providing for unfortified U.S.–Canadian border.

NATIONAL

Second Bank of the United States begins operations in Philadelphia.

Mississippi is admitted as 20th state (December 10) after adopting a constitution (August 15); Territory of Alabama is established (March 3).

John Quincy Adams is named Secretary of State; John C. Calhoun, Secretary of War.

First Seminole War begins (November 20); Andrew Jackson is named commander of U.S. forces.

In treaty, Ohio nation gives up 4 million acres to U.S. in northwest Ohio.

President James Monroe makes goodwill tour of country north of Baltimore, west to Detroit.

New York adopts law forbidding slavery, effective 1827; also changes law on debtors, making $25 minimum for which one could be sued.

1817

John Tyler of Virginia begins four years' service in House of Representatives.

DEATH William C. C. Claiborne, first Louisiana governor (1812–1816).

BUSINESS/INDUSTRY/INVENTIONS

New York Stock Exchange (formed in 1792) is chartered.

Thomas Gilpin produces first machine-made paper in U.S., in a shop near Wilmington, Del.

Production of bar iron by puddling and rolling begins in Plumstock, Pa.

DEATH Francis C. Lowell, builder of first American cotton spinning, weaving mill.

TRANSPORTATION

New York legislature authorizes construction of Erie Canal (April 15); work begins July 4.

First steamer, designed by Henry Shreve, arrives in St. Louis, taking six weeks from Louisville; initiates regular service.

SCIENCE/MEDICINE

Philadelphia Medical Institute, first American postgraduate school, is established.

Lyceum of Natural History is founded, forerunner of New York Academy of Science.

First U.S. insane asylum opens at Frankford, Pa.

EDUCATION

Hartford School for Deaf, first such U.S. school, opens; is founded by Thomas Gallaudet; later becomes American Academy (1819).

College of Detroit is established; will later move to Ann Arbor (1837) to become University of Michigan.

Sylvanus Thayer becomes superintendent of the Military Academy.

Harvard Law School is founded.

DEATH Timothy Dwight, Yale president (1795–1817).

RELIGION

Catholic Bishop Ambrose Marechal becomes archbishop of Baltimore.

American Sunday School Union is formed.

Evangelical Church in New Berlin, Pa., first in the denomination, is dedicated.

First general convention of New Church (Swedenborgian) is held in Philadelphia.

DEATH John Murray, regarded as the father of American Universalism.

ART/MUSIC

Washington Allston begins to paint *Belshazzar's Feast*.

LITERATURE/ JOURNALISM

William Cullen Bryant's poem "Thanatopsis" is published in *North American Review*.

Publishing company J. & J. Harper is established in New York City; will later become Harper & Bros., HarperCollins.

Joseph E. Worcester publishes *Geographical Dictionary*.

Capture of the Seminole Indian chiefs in Florida by order of Andrew Jackson.
CORBIS-BETTMANN

Detroit Gazette is founded, first successful Michigan paper; *The Philanthropist*, first abolitionist newspaper, is published in Mt. Pleasant, Ohio.

ENTERTAINMENT

Noah M. Ludlow opens first showboat; it operates on the Cumberland, Ohio, and Mississippi rivers.

MISCELLANEOUS

American Colonization Society is organized to settle freed slaves in African colonies; soon to be criticized by abolitionists as a misguided effort at reform.

INTERNATIONAL

Convention of 1818 is signed in London, clarifying Treaty of Ghent, which has not set exact boundaries; convention sets northwest boundary along 49th parallel between Lake of the Woods and the Rockies; 10-year joint occupation of Oregon is set (October 20).

NATIONAL

U.S. control of East Florida is gained when Gen. Andrew Jackson leads American force in capture of St. Marks (April 7) and Pensacola (May 24) to end Seminole War; treaty is signed with Chickasaw nation (October 19).

Illinois is admitted as 21st state (December 3) after adopting a constitution (August 26).

Restored White House opens for public inspection (January 1); was burned by British in 1814.

U.S. flag is established with 13 red and white alternating stripes, a star for each state (April 4); is first flown over Capitol (April 12).

Congress sets its pay at $8 per day plus mileage, House Speaker and Senate President $16 per day (January 27); approves pensions for Revolutionary War veterans of $20 a month for officers, $8 for soldiers.

Tariff Act increases duty on iron manufactures, extends 25% duty on cotton and woolens to 1826 (April 20).

Connecticut voters ratify new state constitution, removing property qualifications for voting, limiting franchise to white voters, ending Congregationalist Church dominance over state government by putting all Christian sects on an equal basis.

South Carolina repeals 1792 law that forbade importation of slaves.

Ft. Nez Perce, Native American trading post, is established at junction of Columbia and Walla Walla rivers.

DEATHS Former First Lady Abigail Adams (1796–1800); George Rogers Clark, frontier leader and soldier; George Armistead, who led defense of Ft. McHenry.

BUSINESS/INDUSTRY/INVENTIONS

Gouverneur Kemble establishes foundry at Cold Spring, N.Y., which later manufactures Union Army artillery; Lambert Hitchcock establishes chair factory at Riverton, Conn.

Thomas Blanchard invents a profile lathe.

Suffolk Bank in Boston is founded.

The third flag of the United States, 1818. The five new stars are for Ohio, Tennessee, Louisiana, Indiana, and Mississippi. THE GRANGER COLLECTION, NEW YORK

1819

TRANSPORTATION

Cumberland Road from Cumberland, Md., to Wheeling, W.Va., is completed.

The *Walk-in-the-Water* sails from Buffalo to Detroit with 100 passengers; first steamboat to navigate Upper Great Lakes.

SCIENCE/MEDICINE

Army Medical Corps is organized with Joseph Lovell as surgeon general (April 14).

Insane asylums open in Boston and New York City.

American Journal of Science and Arts is founded, edited by Benjamin H. Silliman.

Edward Hitchcock publishes report on geology of New England.

EDUCATION

Academician, educational semimonthly, is published.

RELIGION

Methodist Magazine (later *Review*) is published.

Auburn Theological School is founded in Auburn, N.Y.

ART/MUSIC

Thomas Sully completes the painting *Lady With a Harp*; John Trumbull, *The Declaration of Independence*.

John Sweeney and other minstrel musicians develop the modern shape of the banjo.

SPORTS

First recorded trotting race is won by the horse Boston Blue.

INTERNATIONAL

Adams-Onis Treaty is signed (February 22) whereby Spain renounces all claims to West Florida, cedes East Florida to U.S.; claims to Texas are renounced by U.S., western limits are set for Louisiana Purchase.

NATIONAL

Supreme Court in *Dartmouth College v. Woodward* rules that a college charter cannot be changed by a state without consent of the college, holding that charter is a contract (February 2); Court upholds constitutionality of Second Bank of the United States.

Alabama is admitted as 22nd state (December 14) after adopting constitution (August 2); Arkansas Territory is created from part of Missouri Territory (March 2); convention in Maine adopts con-

stitution (October 29); it is ratified in town meetings (December 6).

DEATH Oliver Hazard Perry, leader of forces that won Battle of Lake Erie.

BUSINESS/INDUSTRY/INVENTIONS

Panic of 1819 begins as result of commodity inflation, speculation in western lands, contraction of credit; began economic recession.

First American savings banks—Bank for Savings in New York City, chartered March 26, and Provident Institution for Savings in Boston, incorporated in 1816—open; banks in New York, Philadelphia, and Baltimore begin paying interest on deposits.

Rodney and Horatio Hanks begin producing silk thread in Mansfield, Conn.; John J. Wood of Poplar Ridge, N. J., patents plow with inter-

The *Savannah* sails to London, 1819. THE GRANGER COLLECTION, NEW YORK

changeable parts; John Hall invents breech-loading flintlock; Seth Boyden develops process for manufacturing patent leather, opens first U.S. factory to make it.

American Farmer magazine begins publication.

DEATH Oliver Evans, builder of first American high-pressure steam engine.

TRANSPORTATION

The *Savannah*, sailing vessel with auxiliary steam power, sails from Savannah, Ga., to Liverpool, England, in 29 days.

A steamboat navigates the Missouri River for the first time.

SCIENCE/MEDICINE

American Geological Society is founded in New Haven.

DEATH John Greenwood, pioneer dentist, reputed inventor of foot-powered drill.

EDUCATION

Several colleges/universities founded: University of Virginia, with former President Jefferson as rector; University of Cincinnati; Centre College (Danville, Ky.); Colgate University; St. Louis University, first university west of the Mississippi.

Alden Partridge founds the first private military academy (American Literary, Scientific, and Military Academy) in Norwich, Vt. (August 6).

RELIGION

Rev. Thomas C. Brownell is named Episcopal bishop of Connecticut.

William E. Channing is named head of a group of Unitarian churches.

ART/MUSIC

Thomas Sully completes the painting *The Passage of the Delaware*; Washington Allston, *The Moonlit Landscape*.

English version of Rossini's *Barber of Seville* is performed in New York City.

LITERATURE/JOURNALISM

Washington Irving publishes *Sketch Book*, which introduces the characters Rip van Winkle and Ichabod Crane.

1820

First English-language newspaper in Texas (*Texas Republican*), the first Arkansas paper (*Arkansas Gazette*), and the *New York American* are founded.

ENTERTAINMENT

John H. Payne's play *Brutus* and Mordecai M. Noah's *She Would Be a Soldier* are produced.

INTERNATIONAL

New England missionaries arrive in the Hawaiian Islands.

NATIONAL

President James Monroe, unopposed, and Vice President Daniel D. Tompkins are reelected.

Missouri Compromise goes into effect (March 3), provides for entry of Maine as a free state, Mis-

MISCELLANEOUS

First Odd Fellows lodge is established in Baltimore, Md.

1820

souri, a slave state; excludes slavery from Louisiana Purchase territory north of 36°30′.

Maine is admitted as 23d state (March 15); Territory of Missouri adopts a constitution (July 19).

Fourth census reports population of 9,638,453.

Slave Trade Act (1820) passed by Congress makes slave trading piracy; punishment includes loss of ship and death penalty.

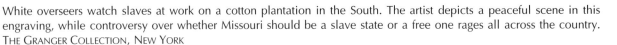

White overseers watch slaves at work on a cotton plantation in the South. The artist depicts a peaceful scene in this engraving, while controversy over whether Missouri should be a slave state or a free one rages all across the country.
THE GRANGER COLLECTION, NEW YORK

Public Lands Act reduces price from $2 to $1.25 per acre, abolishes credit buying.

Congress grants new charter to District of Columbia, provides for popular election of Washington mayor.

Moses Austin is granted land in Mexican Texas on which to settle 300 American families.

Daughter of President and Mrs. Monroe, Maria, becomes first presidential daughter to marry in White House.

DEATHS Commodore Stephen Decatur, in duel with James Barron; Daniel Boone, legendary frontiersman.

BUSINESS/INDUSTRY/INVENTIONS

Thomas R. Williams of Newport, R. I., invents mechanical process to manufacture felt; Merrimac Co., producer of textile machinery, is founded.

DEATH Benjamin H. Latrobe, architect who professionalized both American architecture and engineering.

SCIENCE/MEDICINE

U.S. Pharmacopoeia (official list of medicinal drugs) is founded.

New York Eye Infirmary opens on Chatham St.

American Journal of Medical Sciences is first published as the *Philadelphia Journal of Physical and Medical Sciences.*

John Gorham publishes *Elements of Chemical Science.*

EDUCATION

First U.S. high school (English Classical School) opens in Boston.

Society of Mechanics and Tradesmen opens Mechanics Library in New York City; Free Quakers open an apprentice library in Philadelphia; Mercantile Library Assn. opens library in New York City.

Alabama legislature charters state university at Tuscaloosa; Indiana University is founded.

RELIGION

General Synod of Lutheran Churches is founded.

Rev. John England is named first Catholic bishop of Charleston, S.C.

New York Port Society builds Mariners Church.

ART/MUSIC

Musical Fund Society of Philadelphia is established.

LITERATURE/JOURNALISM

National Gazette in Philadelphia and *Providence Journal* (Providence, R.I.) begin publication.

ENTERTAINMENT

Edwin Forrest, famous actor, debuts in Philadelphia in *Douglas*; Edmund Kean, English Shakespearian actor, makes U.S. debut in New York City as Richard III.

MISCELLANEOUS

Ship *Mayflower of Liberia* sails from New York to Sierra Leone with 86 free blacks who want to settle there; sponsored by American Colonization Society.

1821

INTERNATIONAL

American Colonization Society founds Republic of Liberia as a haven for freed American slaves.

Czar Alexander I of Russia claims all land north of 51st parallel on Pacific Coast.

NATIONAL

Missouri is admitted as 24th state (August 10).

New York and Massachusetts remove property qualifications for voting.

Santa Fe trail is opened by wagon train, led by William Becknell; trail stretches from Independence, Mo., to Santa Fe, N.M.

Men of U.S. shallop *Cecilia* make first documented landing on Antarctica (February 7).

Gen. Andrew Jackson is named governor of Florida Territory.

Boston is chartered as a city.

Martin Van Buren begins term as senator from New York.

BUSINESS/INDUSTRY/INVENTIONS

Zachariah Allen invents hot-air house heating system.

James Boyd of Boston patents fire hose made of rubber-lined cotton web.

TRANSPORTATION

First steamboat navigates Tennessee River.

SCIENCE/MEDICINE

Massachusetts General Hospital is founded.

Philadelphia College of Apothecaries (later Pharmacy) is established.

DEATH Samuel Bard, George Washington's physician and a founder, Columbia University medical school, New York Hospital.

EDUCATION

Emma Willard moves her female seminary from Middlebury, Vt., to Waterford, N.Y.; later to Troy, N.Y.

Amherst College opens; George Washington University in Washington is chartered as Columbia College.

Williams College is one of earliest to form an alumni organization.

RELIGION

Cathedral of the Assumption of the Blessed Virgin Mary in Baltimore, the first American Catholic cathedral, is dedicated by Archbishop Ambrose Marechal.

American frontiersman Davy Crockett, state legislator in Tennessee as of 1821. CORBIS-BETTMANN

Universalist Magazine (later *Leader*) is founded in Boston.

DEATH Elizabeth Ann Seton, who will become first American-born Catholic saint.

LITERATURE/JOURNALISM

James Fenimore Cooper publishes *The Spy.*

Saturday Evening Post is first published as newspaper, changes gradually to magazine by 1871.

ENTERTAINMENT

Junius B. Booth makes U.S. debut in Richmond, Va., as Richard III.

MISCELLANEOUS

A $1 tax on bachelors (21–50) is imposed in Missouri.

1822

INTERNATIONAL

U.S. recognizes newly independent Latin American nations: Colombia (June 12), Mexico (December 12).

NATIONAL

President James Monroe vetoes bill authorizing federal repairs for Cumberland Road, saying it is not a federal project, nevertheless urges national highway improvement program.

Territory of Florida is established (March 30).

Stephen Austin founds first legal settlement of Americans in Mexican Texas.

Nicholas Biddle becomes president of Bank of the United States.

Planned slave revolt in Charleston, S.C., blocked; Denmark Vesey, a freed slave, and five others are hanged July 2; leads to more violence and tightening of some Southern slave codes.

BUSINESS/INDUSTRY/INVENTIONS

Cotton mills are founded in Lawrence, Mass.

Peter Force of Washington patents press to print wallpaper.

Announcement in St. Louis asks for young men to "ascend Missouri River to its source" and work for Rocky Mountain Fur Co.; nearly 200 answer ad.

Daniel Treadwell of Boston builds steam printing press; William Church of Vermont patents machine for composing and casting printing type.

TRANSPORTATION

First section of Erie Canal, 280-mile stretch from Rochester, N.Y., to Albany, opens.

SCIENCE/MEDICINE

Charles M. Graham patents false teeth.

Yale Chemistry Professor Benjamin Silliman discovers that carbon vaporizes in an electric arc.

EDUCATION

Hobart College (Geneva, N.Y.) is founded as Geneva College.

RELIGION

Catholic Bishop John England founds seminary in Charleston, S.C.; founds *U.S. Catholic Miscellany*, first Catholic newspaper in U.S.

ART/MUSIC

Lowell Mason compiles collection of sacred music.

Charles Willson Peale completes self-portrait *The Artist in His Museum.*

LITERATURE/JOURNALISM

Washington Irving publishes *Bracebridge Hall.*

Mercury, leading secessionist newspaper, begins publication in Charleston, S.C.

ENTERTAINMENT

Charles P. Clinch writes his play *The Spy.*

1823

INTERNATIONAL

In annual message to Congress, President James Monroe enunciates what becomes known as the Monroe Doctrine, declaring that the American continents will no longer be open for European colonization, that the U.S. will consider any attempts to impose European systems in North or South America dangerous to its peace and safety (December 2).

U.S. notifies Russia that it does not recognize its claim of lands north of Oregon on the Pacific Coast.

U.S. recognizes Chile and Argentina (January 27).

NATIONAL

National Harbor Improvement Act is passed.

Treaties of St. Louis are signed with Osage and Kansa nations, which cede extensive land areas in what will become Kansas, Missouri, and Oklahoma.

Andrew Jackson begins term as senator from Tennessee.

BUSINESS/INDUSTRY/INVENTIONS

Rice production, nearly all in Louisiana, is 20,000 tons.

TRANSPORTATION

Steamboat *Virginia* arrives in Minneapolis, completing first navigation of Mississippi River north of St. Louis.

Champlain Canal opens, linking Lake Champlain and Hudson River.

John Stevens organizes a Pennsylvania railroad; it quickly fails because of lack of funds.

The birth of the Monroe Doctrine, 1823. James Monroe stands beside the globe; Secretary of State Adams sits at the far left, and War Secretary Calhoun sits third from the right. PAINTING BY CLYDE O. DELAND/CORBIS-BETTMANN

Delaware & Hudson Railroad is chartered as a canal company to build a railroad and canal to bring coal from Carbondale, Pa., to Rondout, N.Y., on Hudson River.

SCIENCE/MEDICINE

Yale Chemistry Professor Benjamin Silliman prepares hydrofluoric acid for first time in U.S.

Dr. George Frick publishes first American ophthalmology book.

EDUCATION

Samuel R. Hall opens first American normal school (for professional training of teachers) in Concord, N.H.

Kentucky opens special public school for the deaf.

St. Regis Seminary, first boys' school for Native Americans, opens in Florissant, Mo.

Trinity College is founded in Hartford as Washington College, with Episcopal bishop Thomas C. Brownell as president.

RELIGION

Christian Examiner is published in Boston.

Virginia Theological School is founded.

ART/MUSIC

Stewart & Chickering, piano manufacturers, established in Boston.

Asher B. Durand completes the painting *Declaration of Independence*.

LITERATURE/JOURNALISM

R. Hoe & Co., printing-press manufacturer, is founded.

Christmas poem by Clement C. Moore ("A Visit from St. Nicholas") appears anonymously in *Troy (N.Y.) Sentinel*.

Three newspapers begin publishing: *New York Mirror*, *New York Observer*, and *National Journal* (Washington).

BOOKS *The Pilot* and *The Pioneer* by James Fenimore Cooper; *Koningsmark* by James K. Paulding.

ENTERTAINMENT

John H. Payne's opera *Clari, or The Maid of Milan* opens in Park Theater, New York City; includes song "Home, Sweet Home" (lyrics by Payne and music by H. R. Bishop).

W. T. Moncrieff produces the play *Tom and Jerry*.

Ft. Clinton on the Battery in New York City is converted into an auditorium, Castle Gardens.

SPORTS

Match race between Southern horse, Henry, and Northern horse, American Eclipse, is won by Eclipse in two of three 4-mile heats.

1824

INTERNATIONAL

U.S. and Russia agree to set Pacific Northwest boundary at 54°40′ north latitude (April 17).

U.S. recognizes Brazil and the Federation of Central American States (August 4).

NATIONAL

No candidate in presidential election receives the majority of electoral votes required; election goes to House of Representatives (see 1825). John Quincy Adams receives 84 electoral votes (105,321 popular), Andrew Jackson 99 electoral (155,872 popular); John C. Calhoun is elected vice president.

First U.S. penitentiary opens in Auburn, N.Y.; includes cell blocks, group labor.

Bureau of Indian Affairs is created in War Department (June 17).

1824

James Bridger, American pioneer and scout, discovers the Great Salt Lake, 1824. THE GRANGER COLLECTION, NEW YORK

James Bridger, frontiersman and scout, becomes first white man to see Great Salt Lake.

Tariff increases protection for iron, lead, glass, hemp, and cotton bagging; 25% duty on cotton and woolens is raised to 33⅓%.

DEATH Charles Pinckney, colonial leader and South Carolina governor.

BUSINESS/INDUSTRY/INVENTIONS

William A. Hart discovers natural gas at Fredonia, N.Y.

First recorded strike by women workers (weavers) occurs in Pawtucket, R.I.

DEATH John Taylor, pioneer in crop rotation.

TRANSPORTATION

Supreme Court in *Gibbons v Ogden* upholds congressional power to regulate interstate commerce (March 2).

John Stevens builds first experimental steam locomotive to pull train on a track.

Work begins on Morris County Canal to link New York City with Delaware River.

SCIENCE/MEDICINE

Thomas Say publishes three-volume *American Entomology*.

EDUCATION

Rensselaer College (later Polytechnic Institute) is founded in Troy, N.Y., by Stephen Van Rensselaer; first private American technical school.

Catharine E. Beecher founds Hartford Female Seminary, an advanced school for girls; curriculum includes calisthenics as part of physical education.

African School Society in Wilmington, Del., is incorporated for education of blacks.

RELIGION

Sunday School Magazine is published.

ART/MUSIC

John Trumbull completes the painting *Surrender at Yorktown*.

LITERATURE/JOURNALISM

James A. Seaver publishes the best-selling story of Native American captivity *The Life of Mrs. Jemison*; Washington Irving publishes *Tales of a Traveler*.

Two newspapers are founded: *Springfield* (Mass.) *Republican* by Samuel Bowles and *Richmond* (Va.) *Whig*.

ENTERTAINMENT

Niblo's Gardens, New York City, are completed; become site for operas, concerts, plays.

PLAYS *Superstition* by James N. Barker produced in Philadelphia, *Charles the Second* by John H. Payne, *The Forest Rose* by Samuel Woodworth both produced in New York City.

MISCELLANEOUS

Historical Society of Pennsylvania is founded.

1825

INTERNATIONAL

Joel R. Poinsett is named first minister to Mexico.

NATIONAL

The 1824 presidential election is decided by House of Representatives (February 9) when 13 states vote for John Quincy Adams, 7 for Andrew Jackson, and 4 for William H. Crawford, making electoral vote Adams 87, Jackson 71, Crawford 54.

Marquis de Lafayette lays Bunker Hill Monument cornerstone

Hudson Bay Co. erects fort on site of present Vancouver, Wash.

Post Office dead-letter office is created.

John Tyler becomes governor of Virginia; James K. Polk begins 14 years representing Tennessee in the House; later Polk will serve as Speaker (1835–1839).

Robert Owen establishes socialist nonreligious settlement at New Harmony, Ind.

DEATHS Vice President Daniel D. Tompkins (1815–1824); Pierre L'Enfant, Washington city planner; John Chapman (Johnny Appleseed), planter; Mason L. (Parson) Weems, Washington biographer.

BUSINESS/INDUSTRY/INVENTIONS

Thomas Kensett patents tin-plated cans.

Boston carpenters strike to achieve 10-hour work-day.

TRANSPORTATION

Erie Canal opens between New York City and Buffalo; cuts travel time by a third, costs by 90%; Schuylkill Canal is completed; Chesapeake & Ohio Canal is chartered.

The Erie Canal, opened in 1825. THE GRANGER COLLECTION, NEW YORK

1826

Work begins on Miami Canal to connect Cincinnati and Dayton, is completed 1828.

SCIENCE/MEDICINE

Denison Olmstead issues report on North Carolina geology, the first official state geological survey.

American Journal of Pharmacy is founded.

EDUCATION

Kenyon College (Gambier, Ohio) is chartered as Episcopal Theological Seminary; Queens College (New Brunswick, N.J.) becomes Rutgers University.

RELIGION

American Unitarian Assn. is organized in Boston.

American Tract Society is organized in New York City.

Rev. Benedict J. Fenwick becomes Catholic bishop of Boston.

Princeton Review is first published as *Biblical Repertory*.

ART/MUSIC

Musical Fund Society is founded as music school in Philadelphia.

Thomas Cole establishes Hudson River School of landscape painting, the first American movement in painting.

LITERATURE/JOURNALISM

D. Appleton & Co., publisher, is founded.

James Fenimore Cooper writes *Lionel Lincoln.*

ENTERTAINMENT

Chatham Theater in New York City becomes first theater lighted by gas.

Samuel Woodworth's play *The Widow's Son* is produced in New York City.

SPORTS

New York Trotting Club establishes trotting course on Long Island; Screwdriver wins first race (May 16).

First American archery club, United Bowmen of Philadelphia, is formed.

INTERNATIONAL

U.S. recognizes Peru (May 2).

General Congress of South American States meets in Panama; two U.S. delegates, confirmed late, do not arrive on time.

Treaty of unity, commerce, and navigation is signed with Denmark (April 26).

NATIONAL

Two former presidents, Thomas Jefferson and John Adams, die the same day, July 4.

Naval Asylum (later Naval Home) opens in Philadelphia.

John Randolph and Henry Clay fight a duel over unsubstantiated charges that Clay made a corrupt bargain to become Secretary of State; neither man is hurt.

Maryland removes religious qualifications for voting.

DEATH Isaac Shelby, Revolutionary War general and first Kentucky governor (1792–1796).

BUSINESS/INDUSTRY/INVENTIONS

John Stevens develops a multitubular locomotive boiler.

Samuel Morey of Orford, N.H., patents an internal combustion engine.

Thomas Jefferson (1743–1826), in a painting by John Trumbull. THE GRANGER COLLECTION, NEW YORK

TRANSPORTATION

New York State grants charter to Mohawk & Hudson Railroad, which later becomes the New York Central.

A horse-drawn tramway becomes the first American chartered railroad (Granite Railway), making 3-mile trip from Quincy, Mass., to Neponset River.

SCIENCE/MEDICINE

Amasa Holcomb builds first American reflecting telescope.

EDUCATION

Western Reserve College (Hudson, Ohio) and Lafayette College (Easton, Pa.) chartered.

Former President James Madison named rector of University of Virginia.

RELIGION

Lutheran Theological Seminary founded at Gettysburg Seminary.

American Home Missionary Society established by Congregational Church to work on behalf of blacks in South.

ART/MUSIC

National Academy of Design organized in New York City by young artists unhappy with American Academy of Fine Arts; Samuel F. B. Morse first president.

LITERATURE/JOURNALISM

The Last of the Mohicans by James Fenimore Cooper is published.

John Adams (1735–1826), in a painting by Gilbert Stuart. THE GRANGER COLLECTION, NEW YORK

1827

Juvenile Miscellany, first children's magazine, founded in Boston by Lydia M. Child.

United States Telegraph is published in Washington.

ENTERTAINMENT

Three stage stars appear in New York City: Edwin Forrest (as Othello), James H. Hackett, and William C. Macready make their U.S. debuts.

Bowery Theater in New York City opens.

George P. Morris's play *Briar Cliff* is produced.

DEATHS Royall Tyler, whose play *The Contrast* was first American play produced professionally.

MISCELLANEOUS

American Society for the Promotion of Temperance organizes in Boston.

1827

INTERNATIONAL

U.S. and Great Britain renew agreement for joint occupation of Oregon, with stipulation that agreement can be terminated on one year's notice (August 6).

NATIONAL

Supreme Court rules in *Martin v. Mott* that the president has sole right to determine conditions for calling out the militia.

Slavery is abolished in New York State under terms of 1817 law.

Convention in Harrisburg calls for higher tariffs to protect U.S. industries.

Federal government authorizes construction of drydocks in Boston (completed 1833) and Norfolk, Va. (completed 1834).

John Tyler begins nine years as a senator from Virginia.

DEATH Henry Leavenworth, army officer for whom Kansas fort and city were named.

BUSINESS/INDUSTRY/INVENTIONS

First central labor union, Mechanics Union of Trades Assn., is created in Philadelphia.

Philadelphia Arcade, occupying a square block, is completed.

Cyrus Alger founds South Boston Iron Co., which will become largest in U.S.

Joseph Henry develops insulated wire.

TRANSPORTATION

Baltimore & Ohio Railroad is chartered in Maryland and Virginia.

Matthias W. Baldwin begins engine-construction works in Philadelphia; it becomes Baldwin Locomotive Works.

SCIENCE/MEDICINE

Cornerstone is laid for first naval hospital (Portsmouth, Va.) (August 2).

John James Audubon completes first of five volumes of *Birds of America*.

EDUCATION

Society for the Promotion of Public Schools is created in Philadelphia.

Lexington, Mass., establishes free public library for children.

First U.S. nursery school, Infant School Society, opens in New York City.

Massachusetts requires every community of 500 or more residents to have a high school.

ART/MUSIC

Carl Fischer establishes music publishing firm in New York City.

Popular song is "The Minstrel's Return from the War" by John H. Hewitt.

DEATH Charles Willson Peale, foremost American portrait painter.

LITERATURE/JOURNALISM

The Prairie by James Fenimore Cooper and *Tales of Peter Parley About America* by Samuel G. Goodrich, the first of 116 Peter Parley books, are published.

New newspapers: *New York Journal of Commerce, New York Morning Courier, Cincinnati Daily Gazette,* and *Baltimore Republican.*

Freedom's Journal, first African American newspaper, is founded in New York City by John B. Russworm and Rev. Samuel Cornish, and *El Redactor,* Hispanic paper, are published.

The Youth's Companion, popular children's magazine, is founded.

ENTERTAINMENT

Bowery Theater, New York City, presents first American ballet, *The Deserter.*

First Mardi Gras celebration is held in New Orleans; is launched by students who organized procession on Shrove Tuesday.

SPORTS

First U.S. swimming school opens, in Boston.

American Shooters' Handbook is published.

MISCELLANEOUS

Pennsylvania Horticultural Society organizes.

An American flamingo, from John James Audubon's *The Birds of America,* the first volume of which was published in 1827. THE GRANGER COLLECTION, NEW YORK

INTERNATIONAL

U.S. and Mexico sign treaty establishing common boundary along the Sabine River (January 12).

U.S. and Brazil sign treaty of peace and navigation (December 12).

NATIONAL

Andrew Jackson is elected president, receiving 647,231 popular and 178 electoral votes against President John Quincy Adams's 509,097 popular and 83 electoral votes; John C. Calhoun is elected vice president.

Tariff bill is signed, called the "tariff of abominations"; several Southern states (South Carolina, Georgia, Virginia, Mississippi) term the tariff unconstitutional and oppressive.

Congress authorizes construction of first post office building (Newport, R.I.).

1828

DEATH William Thornton, architect who designed the Capitol.

BUSINESS/INDUSTRY/INVENTIONS

Militia is called out at Paterson, N.J., to maintain peace during textile workers' strike.

Eliphalet Remington builds factory at Ilion, N.Y., to manufacture rifle barrels; Peter Cooper founds Canton Iron Works in Baltimore.

McLoughlin Co., producer of children's games and books, is organized in New York City.

First American labor paper, *Mechanics' Free Press*, is published in Philadelphia.

Physicist Joseph Henry invents the electromagnet.

TRANSPORTATION

Three canals are completed: Ohio Canal connects Cleveland and Portsmouth; Miami Canal connects Cincinnati and Dayton; Delaware & Hudson Railroad/Canal connects Honesdale, Pa., and Rondout, N.Y.

Baltimore & Ohio Railroad is instituted with laying of cornerstone in Baltimore; Pennsylvania legislature approves financial aid for the planned Pennsylvania Railroad.

A steamboat navigates the Illinois River for the first time.

SCIENCE/MEDICINE

John D. Godman produces three-volume *American Natural History*.

ART/MUSIC

Thomas Cole completes the painting *Expulsion from the Garden of Eden*; Chester Harding, the portrait of John Marshall.

DEATH Gilbert Stuart, renowned portrait painter.

LITERATURE/JOURNALISM

Noah Webster's *American Dictionary of the English Language* is published after more than 20 years' work.

First Native American newspaper, *Cherokee Phoenix*, is published.

BOOKS *Fanshawe* by Nathaniel Hawthorne, *The Red Rover* by James Fenimore Cooper, *Guido* by Emma C. Embury.

ENTERTAINMENT

William Chapman and his family of six operate an early showboat, a small floating theater that tours the Ohio and Mississippi rivers.

Thomas D. Rice introduces minstrel character and song "Jim Crow" in Louisville.

Arch St. Theater in Philadelphia opens.

William Dunlap's play *A Trip to Niagara* is produced in New York City.

SPORTS

New horse-race track is built at Lexington, Ky.

MISCELLANEOUS

American Peace Society, which will continue until formation of United Nations, is founded; promotes formation of a congress of nations and world court.

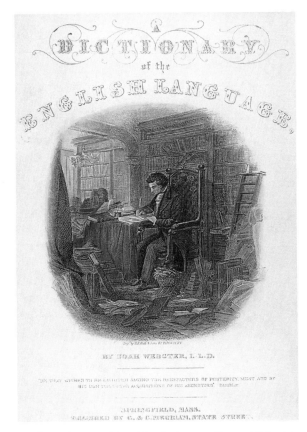

Noah Webster writing his dictionary, first published in 1828, as depicted on the title page of a nineteenth-century edition of *Webster's Dictionary of the English Language*. THE GRANGER COLLECTION, NEW YORK

1829

NATIONAL

President Andrew Jackson suspends regular cabinet meetings, relying instead on advice from "kitchen cabinet" made up of political confidants.

Postmaster General becomes member of the cabinet.

Eastern State Penitentiary in Pennsylvania opens; features solitary confinement, solitary labor, in contrast to Auburn system (see 1824).

Martin Van Buren begins term as New York governor; resigns after three months to become Secretary of State.

DEATHS John Jay, first Supreme Court chief justice; René Chouteau, a founder of St. Louis.

BUSINESS/INDUSTRY/INVENTIONS

Workingmen's Party organizes in Philadelphia, calls for free public education, protection of mechanics from prison labor; *Working Man's Advocate* is published in New York City.

Tremont House hotel opens in Boston.

William A. Burt patents "typographer," a predecessor of the typewriter.

Broadmeadow & Co. (Pittsburgh) begins manufacture of hand-operated cutting files.

TRANSPORTATION

Three canals open: first Welland Canal connects

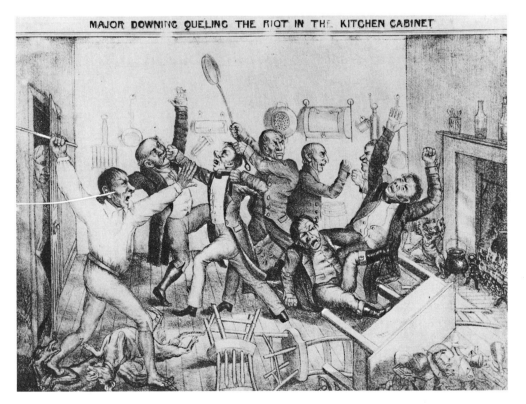

Critics of newly inaugurated president Andrew Jackson dub his political advisers the "kitchen cabinet," 1829. Major Jack Downing is a fictional character created by writer Seba Smith. THE GRANGER COLLECTION, NEW YORK

1829

Lakes Erie and Ontario; Delaware River–Chesapeake Bay Canal; Lehigh Canal connects Lehigh and Delaware rivers.

Cornelius Vanderbilt forms steamship company to operate on Hudson River.

First locomotive to operate in U.S. pulls a train at Honesdale, Pa., the Stourbridge Lion, built in England.

First stone-arch railroad bridge, Carrollton Viaduct, is designed to carry Baltimore & Ohio Railroad over Gwynn's Falls in Baltimore.

SCIENCE/MEDICINE

William E. Horner publishes first American pathology textbook.

New England Asylum for the Blind incorporates; will become Perkins Institution.

DEATH Dr. Nathan Smith, pioneering surgeon and founder, Yale Medical School.

EDUCATION

Jacob Abbott founds Mt. Vernon School for Girls.

RELIGION

First Catholic Provincial Council meets in Baltimore.

Baltimore sanctions use of parochial schools.

Seamen's Bethel, a mission in Boston is founded, with Rev. Edward T. Taylor as chaplain.

ART/MUSIC

George Washington Monument in Baltimore is completed.

LITERATURE/JOURNALISM

Encyclopedia Americana issues first of 13 volumes (13th will be issued in 1833).

The Frugal Housewife by Lydia M. Child is published.

Carey & Hart, publishing company, is founded in Philadelphia.

Poet William Cullen Bryant becomes editor of *New York Evening Post*; the *Philadelphia Inquirer* is published; Seba Smith founds first daily newspaper in Maine, *Portland Courier*.

Edgar Allan Poe anonymously publishes his first work, *Tamerlane and Other Poems*.

ENTERTAINMENT

PLAYS *Eighth of January* by Robert Penn Smith; *Metamora* by John A. Stone; *The Times* with James H. Hackett.

SPORTS

First international horse race takes place in England; the American horse Rattler beats the Welsh mare Miss Turner by nearly 60 yards.

American Turf Register and Sporting Magazine begins publication.

MISCELLANEOUS

Joel R. Poinsett, first U.S. minister to Mexico, brings back a subtropical plant that is named in his honor, the poinsettia.

1830

INTERNATIONAL

Mexico prohibits further settlement of Texas by U.S. citizens.

U.S. trade with British West Indies reopens.

NATIONAL

First U.S. warship to circumnavigate the globe, the *Vincennes*, returns to New York City.

Godey's Lady's Book, established in 1830, will have a major influence on fashion, etiquette, home economics, and standards of propriety for decades to come. These fashion illustrations are from an 1842 issue of the magazine. THE GRANGER COLLECTION, NEW YORK

Fifth census reports national population of 12,860,702.

Former President John Quincy Adams is elected to House of Representatives from Massachusetts.

Various Native American tribes sign treaty to cede most of what will become Iowa, Missouri, and Minnesota; Choctaws cede nearly 8 million acres in Mississippi in return for Oklahoma land.

DEATH Former First Lady Elizabeth K. Monroe (1817–1825).

BUSINESS/INDUSTRY/INVENTIONS

New York Life Insurance & Trust Co., organized by William Bard and first to specialize in life insurance, is chartered.

Samuel Colt develops pistol with a revolving barrel.

Jesse Oakley of Newburgh, N.Y., begins to produce soap in individually wrapped cakes of equal weight.

Rocky Mountain Fur Co. is organized.

National cotton production is 731,000 bales.

TRANSPORTATION

First American railroad, Baltimore & Ohio, begins operation, with first passengers carried in single cars drawn by horses; first American locomotive, "Tom Thumb," manufactured by Peter Cooper, is tested.

South Carolina Canal & Railroad Co. begins scheduled service on 6-mile stretch near Charleston, S.C., with a steam locomotive, the first in U.S. to pull train of cars.

Charles F. Durant, first professional balloonist, makes flight from New York City to South Amboy, N.J.

Louisville & Portland Canal around the falls of the Ohio River opens.

1830

The Baltimore and Ohio Railroad's "Tom Thumb" locomotive races a horse-drawn car in 1830. THE GRANGER COLLECTION, NEW YORK

Robert L. Stevens invents the T-rail for trains, which will remain in use into the 1990s; also a balance valve for steam engines.

SCIENCE/MEDICINE

First naval observatory, U.S. Naval Observatory, is established in Washington.

Charles C. Grice opens first U.S. veterinary hospital, in New York City.

Boston Society of Natural History is founded.

EDUCATION

American Institute of Instruction, first national education association, organizes in Boston, with Francis Wayland, Brown University president, as first chairman.

University of Richmond (Va.) and Randolph-Macon College (Ashland, Va.) are founded.

James Kent publishes first major work on Anglo-American law, *Commentaries on American Law.*

RELIGION

Joseph Smith founds Mormon Church (Church of Jesus Christ of Latter Day Saints) at Fayette, N.Y.

John Winebrenner forms Church of God.

Methodist Protestant church is founded in Baltimore after failure to achieve reforms in Methodist Episcopal church.

ART/MUSIC

Horatio Greenough completes marble statuary group *The Chanting Cherubs*; Thomas Doughty paints *The Raft.*

SONGS (popular): "Cape Cod Girls," "Old Colony Times," "Jim Crow."

LITERATURE/JOURNALISM

The poem "Old Ironsides" by Oliver Wendell Holmes appears in the *Boston Daily Advertiser.*

Joseph E. Worcester publishes original dictionary, touching off war with Noah Webster, which Worcester eventually loses.

New newspapers: *Washington Globe*; *Albany Evening Journal*; *Evening Transcript* (Boston); *Louisville* (Ky.) *Journal*, which becomes the *Courier-Journal*; *Daily Sentinel*, a labor paper (New York City).

BOOKS *The Lion of the West* by James K. Paulding; *Poems For Our Children* by Sarah J. Hale (including "Mary had a little lamb...");*The Water Witch* by James Fenimore Cooper.

ENTERTAINMENT

Robert Penn Smith writes play *The Deformed*; Richard P. Smith, *The Triumph at Plattsburgh*. Both plays are produced in Philadelphia.

SPORTS

Several teams in Boston begin to play "town ball," a version of English rounders.

MISCELLANEOUS

New York has 52 lottery drawings during year, with prizes totaling $9,270,000.

Women began to wear their hair very high; use of hair dye is very popular.

1831

INTERNATIONAL

U.S. and France agree on six annual payments for damages inflicted during Napoleonic Wars: France to pay 25 million francs for damage to U.S. shipping, U.S. to pay 1.5 million francs for alleged commercial violations of Louisiana Purchase (July 4).

NATIONAL

New England Anti-Slavery Society founded.

Nat Turner, a black preacher, leads a slave rebellion in Southampton County, Va., in which 57 whites are killed; Turner is captured after 10 days and is executed along with 19 other blacks.

Supreme Court in *Cherokee Nation v. Georgia* rules that Cherokees are a "domestic dependent" nation rather than a foreign state.

President Andrew Jackson vetoes bill renewing charter of Second Bank of the United States.

DEATHS Former President Monroe (1817–1825);

James Hoban, architect who designed White House and its replacement after being burned by the British.

BUSINESS/INDUSTRY/INVENTIONS

First U.S. building-and-loan association (Oxford Provident Loan Assn.) is organized in Thomas Sidebotham's Tavern, Frankford, Pa.; first loan is $500 (January 3).

Erastus and Thaddeus Fairbanks patent platform scale.

Joseph Henry invents electric bell, develops small motor, powerful electromagnets capable of lifting up to 3,600 pounds.

First recorded U.S. clothing factory opens in New York City.

Cyrus H. McCormick invents grain reaper.

TRANSPORTATION

New railroads include Pontchartrain Railroad, first west of the Alleghenies, from New Orleans to Lake Pontchartrain; Boston & Providence; New York & Harlem; Mohawk & Hudson.

A steamboat, *Yellowstone*, makes trip on upper Missouri River for the first time.

SCIENCE/MEDICINE

Dr. Samuel Guthrie distills chloroform, calling it chloric ether.

EDUCATION

University of Alabama, New York University, and Wesleyan University (Middletown, Conn.) are founded.

Prudence Crandall opens private girls' academy in Canterbury, Conn.; it is forced to close

Nat Turner, American slave leader (1800–1831). THE GRANGER COLLECTION, NEW YORK

1832

after she proposes to turn it into a school for black girls.

DEATH Stephen Girard, endower of Girard College.

RELIGION

Joseph Smith selects Independence, Mo., as the Mormon Holy City of Zion.

DEATH Richard Allen, a founder and bishop of the African Methodist Episcopal (AME) church.

ART/MUSIC

Daniel D. Emmett writes minstrel song "Old Dan Tucker."

"America," with words by Rev. Samuel F. Smith to the tune of the British "God Save the King," is first performed in Park St. Church, Boston.

LITERATURE/JOURNALISM

R. Hoe & Co. manufactures a cylinder printing press.

James K. Paulding's book *The Dutchman's Fireside* is published.

The Liberator, abolitionist paper, is founded by William Lloyd Garrison in Boston; *Boston Morning Post* begins publication.

New copyright law liberalizes protection for authors.

ENTERTAINMENT

Edwin Forrest stars in both *The Gladiator* by Robert M. Bird and *Caius Marius*; *The Dumb Belle* by William B. Bernard is produced.

SPORTS

Town ball, a version of English rounders and predecessor of baseball, is introduced in Philadelphia.

First U.S. curling club, Orchard Lake, organizes near Pontiac, Mich.

Spirit of the Times, a weekly racing sheet, is published.

MISCELLANEOUS

First American bank robbery occurs when burglars use duplicate keys to enter City Bank in New York City; robbers make off with $245,000 but are apprehended.

INTERNATIONAL

U.S. signs treaty of peace and commerce with Chile.

U.S. and Russia sign treaty for commercial agreements, setting 54°40′ as the southern limit of Russian occupation on West Coast.

NATIONAL

Convention in Charleston, S.C., votes to nullify the 1828 and 1832 tariffs; state legislature ratifies action, stating that federal use of force would be cause for secession (November 19). In proclamation to South Carolinians (December 10), President Andrew Jackson calls nullification an "impractical absurdity," asserts the supremacy of the federal government, says no state can refuse to obey the laws of the land or leave the Union.

Vice President John Calhoun resigns over tariff dispute; returns to South Carolina, which elects him to the Senate the next year.

Black Hawk War breaks out along Upper Mississippi Valley as the Sac and Fox nations try to retain their lands (April 6); Battle of Red Axe (August 2) virtually ends fighting; Chief Black Hawk is surrendered to federal officials (August 27).

First Democratic convention meets in Baltimore, unanimously endorses President Jackson for reelection, nominates Martin Van Buren for vice president; earlier in year, Senate by 24–23 vote rejects Van Buren for minister to Great Britain.

An American army of militia and regular infantry, led by General Henry Atkinson, defeat the Sauk and Fox Indians under Black Hawk at the mouth of the Bad Axe River, Wisconsin, 1832. THE GRANGER COLLECTION, NEW YORK

President Jackson is reelected, receiving 219 electoral votes (687,502 popular) to 49 for Whig candidate Henry Clay (530,189 popular); William Wirt, Anti-Masonic Party candidate, carries Vermont and 7 electoral votes.

Creek nation cedes all its lands east of the Mississippi to the U.S.; 15 Seminole chiefs do likewise with Florida land; President Jackson is named first Commissioner of Indian Affairs.

Capt. Benjamin de Bonneville begins three-year exploration of the West; Bent's Fort, near present LaJunta, Colo., is completed, becoming West's most famous trading post; Henry Schoolcraft leads exploring party to source of Mississippi River at Lake Itasca, Minn.

Mississippi convention approves state constitution, which is approved by popular vote; Delaware convention revises state constitution.

DEATH Mary L. H. Macauley, Revolutionary War heroine better known as Molly Pitcher.

BUSINESS/INDUSTRY/INVENTIONS

Baldwin Locomotive Works is founded in Philadelphia.

John I. Howe of Derby, Conn., patents machine to make pins.

Obed Hussey develops grain reaper similar to Cyrus McCormick's (1831).

DEATH Pliny Earle, inventor of wool-and-cotton carding machinery.

TRANSPORTATION

First streetcars (horse-drawn) begin to carry passengers on lower Fourth Avenue, New York City.

First American railway accident occurs near Quincy, Mass., when the cable on an incline snaps; the car goes over a cliff, killing one.

First clipper ship, *Ann McKim*, is built in Baltimore.

SCIENCE/MEDICINE

First cholera case is discovered in New York City (June 28), by end of August, there are 5,835 cases, 2,251 deaths; also hits Philadelphia and New Orleans.

Robley Dunglison writes *Human Physiology*; sells nearly 100,000 copies.

Samuel G. Howe converts blind asylum in Boston to Perkins Institute, first major U.S. school for blind.

RELIGION

Revs. Thomas and Alexander Campbell and Barton W. Stone found Disciples of Christ church (or Churches of Christ); originally the Disciples (see 1809).

1833

Lyman Beecher becomes first president of Lane Theological Seminary in Cincinnati.

Three Episcopal bishops are named: John H. Hopkins, first Vermont bishop; George W. Doane, New Jersey; Charles P. McIlwaine, Ohio.

First national convention of Sunday-school workers is held in New York City.

ART/MUSIC

Horatio Greenough is commissioned to sculpt statue of George Washington for Capitol Rotunda.

Thomas Sully completes the painting *Col. Thomas H. Perkins*.

Yale University Art Gallery opens.

Popular song of the year is "Rock of Ages."

LITERATURE/JOURNALISM

G. & C. Merriam Co., publisher, is founded.

James Gordon Bennett launches two-cent morning paper, *New York Globe*; the *Pennsylvanian* is founded in Philadelphia.

BOOKS *The Alhambra* by Washington Irving; *Moll Pitcher* by John Greenleaf Whittier; *Poems* by William Cullen Bryant; *The Young Christian* by Rev. Jacob Abbott.

ENTERTAINMENT

Edwin Forrest stars in Robert M. Bird's *Oralloosa*.

William Dunlap writes *A History of the American Theater*.

SPORTS

Philadelphia Union Cricket Club is founded.

MISCELLANEOUS

Imprisonment for debt is banned by New York State.

INTERNATIONAL

Convention of Texans resolves to separate from Mexico (April 3).

Treaty with Siam (which becomes Thailand) is signed, first with a Far East nation (March 20).

NATIONAL

The Force Bill, which empowers President Andrew Jackson to use force if necessary to execute revenue laws, passes in Congress (January 16); compromise tariff bill amends 1828 and 1832 tariffs; South Carolina legislature repeals its nullification measure.

Funds withdrawn from the Bank of the United States are deposited in state banks, ending a year-long battle that began with President Jackson's veto of a bill to renew the bank's charter.

Fire destroys Treasury Building in Washington, D.C.

1833

New York and New Jersey sign an interstate crime pact.

American Anti-Slavery Society forms with Arthur Tappan president; Lucretia Mott helps organize Female Anti-Slavery Society.

Federal drydock is built in Boston.

Abraham Lincoln is named postmaster of New Salem, Ill.; Franklin Pierce begins to serve first of two terms in House of Representatives from New Hampshire.

BUSINESS/INDUSTRY/INVENTIONS

Orlando Montague and Austin Granger open plant in Troy, N.Y., to produce men's linen collars and shirt bosoms; Roxbury (Mass.) India Rubber Co. incorporates as first U.S. rubber company; John Lane begins to manufacture steel-blade plows.

President Andrew Jackson slays the many-headed monster of the Bank of the United States. The cartoon refers to the president's battle against the bank that led to the withdrawal of government deposits in 1833. THE GRANGER COLLECTION, NEW YORK

Charles A. Gayler of New York City patents a fireproof safe; Samuel Preston invents machine to peg shoes.

Journeymen shoemakers win raise after a strike in Geneva, N.Y.

New York trade unions form General Trades Council.

TRANSPORTATION

First interstate railroad begins to operate from Petersburg, Va., to Blakely, N.C. (59 miles); Bangor & Piscatauqua Railroad, the first in Maine, is chartered.

Isaac Dipps invents locomotive cowcatcher; is first used on Camden & Amboy Railroad.

SCIENCE/MEDICINE

Hahnemann Society, a homeopathic medical group, organizes in Philadelphia.

Robley Dunglison prepares *New Dictionary of Medical Sciences and Literature*, which becomes standard of American medicine.

Dr. William Beaumont publishes study on digestion based on his observations while treating a man's open gunshot wound in his stomach.

EDUCATION

Harvard confers honorary degree on President Jackson over protest of an alumnus, former President John Quincy Adams.

Oberlin (Ohio) Collegiate Institute opens as first American coeducational college; Mercer Institute (later University) opens in Macon, Ga.

First evening public schools in U.S. open in New York City.

Peterborough, N.H., is first town in U.S. to establish a tax-supported library.

1834

RELIGION

Mormon Church creates permanent home at Kirtland, Ohio; adopts name of Latter Day Saints.

Mary Francis Clarke founds Sisters of the Blessed Virgin Mary in Philadelphia.

Massachusetts severs ties with Congregational church, becoming last state to separate church and state.

ART/MUSIC

Lowell Mason founds Boston Academy of Music.

Italian Opera House is built in New York City.

Thomas Cole completes the painting *The Titan's Goblet*; Asher B. Durand paints *The Capture of Major André*.

A popular song of the year is "Long, Long Ago."

LITERATURE/JOURNALISM

New newspapers include Benjamin H. Day's *New York Sun*, first successful penny daily; *Green Bay Intelligencer*, first Wisconsin paper; *Mercantile* (later *Evening*) *Journal* in Boston.

Knickerbocker Magazine, first popular monthly, is founded.

William G. Simms publishes the novel *Martin Faber*.

ENTERTAINMENT

William B. Bernard's play *The Kentuckian* is produced in New York City.

SPORTS

Olympic Town Ball Club organizes in Philadelphia.

MISCELLANEOUS

Pennsylvania and Massachusetts pass antilottery laws.

INTERNATIONAL

Stephen Austin travels to Mexico City to present complaints of Texans; is arrested, held for eight months.

Claims of U.S. and Spain are settled by the Van Ness Convention.

NATIONAL

Senate censures President Andrew Jackson for actions on the second Bank of the United States; House of Representatives upholds Jackson's actions.

Senate rejects nomination of Roger B. Taney for Treasury Secretary; first rejection of a cabinet appointee.

Congress establishes special Indian territory in Arkansas; also establishes Department of Indian Affairs.

President Jackson's annual message to Congress reports elimination of national debt.

Anti-abolition riots occur in New York City and Philadelphia.

Tennessee convention adopts state constitution; ratifies in 1835.

First settlement in Idaho is established at Ft. Hall on the Snake River.

DEATH William Wirt, Attorney General (1817–1829), handled many precedent-setting cases.

BUSINESS/INDUSTRY/INVENTIONS

Boston Stock Exchange opens.

Cyrus Alger begins to produce rifled guns, John Matthews begins to manufacture machinery to make carbonated beverages.

Cyrus Hall McCormick patents a grain reaper;

Isaac Fisher, Jr. of Springfield, Vt., patents sandpaper; and Thomas Davenport invents first commercially successful electric motor embodying now universal principles.

City central organizations form National Trades Union in Philadelphia.

Cultivator, first agricultural publication to achieve national circulation, is published.

Federal troops are used for first time to quell labor unrest when workers on Chesapeake & Ohio Canal riot in effort to achieve closed shop.

DEATH E. I. du Pont, founder of the du Pont family business.

TRANSPORTATION

First railway tunnel opens between Johnstown and Hollidaysburg, Pa.; railway from Philadelphia to Trenton, N.J., is completed.

Regular steamboat service begins between Chicago, Ill., and Buffalo, N.Y.

Delaware & Raritan Canal is completed.

SCIENCE/MEDICINE

Society of Surgeon Dentists of New York is organized.

DEATH Thomas Say, called the father of American descriptive entomology.

EDUCATION

Wake Forest University (Winston-Salem, N.C.) is founded.

Spectators are impressed with Cyrus Hall McCormick's invention, a reaping machine, patented in 1834. CULVER PICTURES, INC.

1835

RELIGION

Broadway Tabernacle is built in New York City; becomes a Congregational Church (1836).

James H. Otey becomes first Episcopal bishop of Tennessee.

Fire set by anti-Catholics destroys Ursuline convent in Charlestown, Mass.

Rev. Jason Lee establishes Methodist mission in Oregon.

ART/MUSIC

First U.S. music school is established in Chicago.

Popular songs are "The Old Oaken Bucket" and "Zip Coon" (later "Turkey in the Straw").

LITERATURE/JOURNALISM

George Bancroft issues first volume of *History of the United States*; Jared Sparks completes first volume of biography of George Washington.

Southern Literary Messenger is founded in Richmond.

Lorrin Andrews, Congregational missionary, publishes first newspaper in Hawaii.

New York *Staats-Zeitung*, the first U.S. German-language newspaper, is founded.

ENTERTAINMENT

Robert M. Bird's play *The Broker of Bogota* is produced.

SPORTS

First American steeplechase race is run at Washington (D.C.) Jockey Club Park.

Castle Garden Boat Club organizes in New York City.

Robin Carver writes *The Book of Sports*.

MISCELLANEOUS

Maine State Temperance Society is founded.

INTERNATIONAL

Armed clashes occur between Texans and Mexicans, lead to Texas declaring its independence from Mexico (November 13) and setting up provisional government; Mexico establishes military state in Texas (December 15), abolishes all local rights.

President Andrew Jackson's offer to buy Texas from Mexico is refused.

NATIONAL

Assassination of President Jackson is attempted when Richard Lawrence fires two shots at him; both shots misfire, Jackson is unharmed; assailant is adjudged insane, is committed to an asylum.

Second Seminole War begins, continues sporadically for eight years.

In treaty with U.S., Cherokee nation surrenders its lands east of the Mississippi in return for $5 million, land in Indian territory, and transportation costs paving the way for "removal" by Jackson administration.

U.S. mints are established in New Orleans, Charlotte, N.C., and Dahlonega, Ga.

Henry E. Ellsworth becomes first commissioner of Patents.

Convention adopts Michigan constitution, ratifies it (November 2).

Boatload of abolition tracts are seized and burned by mob in Charleston, S.C.; Kentucky Anti-Slavery Society is established.

James K. Polk, a Tennessee representative for 10 years, is elected House Speaker.

DEATH Supreme Court Chief Justice John Marshall, who served 34 years.

BUSINESS/INDUSTRY/INVENTIONS

Two insurance companies are founded: Manufac-

Colt's "revolver," a pistol with a revolving chamber patented in 1835. CORBIS-BETTMANN

Thomas McAuley, a founder, is named president (1836).

DEATH Rev. James Freeman, first American Unitarian clergyman.

ART/MUSIC

German Männerchor organizes in Philadelphia; is oldest German singing society in U.S.

Oliver Ditson begins to publish music in Boston.

Thomas Doughty completes the painting *In Nature's Wonderland*; William S. Mount paints *Bargaining for a Horse*.

LITERATURE/JOURNALISM

Edgar Allan Poe edits *Southern Literary Messenger*.

Jacob Abbott writes the first of 28 Rollo books for children.

BOOKS *The Partisan* and *The Yemasee* by William G. Simms; *Horse-Shoe Robinson* by John P. Kennedy; *The Monikins* by James Fenimore Cooper.

turers Mutual Fire Insurance Co. and New England Mutual Life Insurance Co.

Three inventions are reported: horseshoe manufacturing machine invented by Henry Burden of Troy, N.Y.; revolving breech pistol invented by Samuel Colt; electric commutator invented by Thomas Davenport.

Independence Sparks operates a laundry in Troy, N.Y.; Robert Wallace of Wallingford, Conn., manufactures nickel spools.

New York court holds that all combinations of employees to raise wages are illegal.

DEATH Samuel Slater, founder of American textile industry.

TRANSPORTATION

John Wise makes first ascent in balloon of his own design.

EDUCATION

Oglethorpe University (Milledgeville, Ga.) and Marietta (Ohio) College are instituted.

Academy in Canaan, N.H., is destroyed by mob because it has admitted 14 black students.

RELIGION

Union Theological Seminary opens in New York City;

Richard Lawrence attempts to assassinate President Andrew Jackson on the steps of the Capitol building in Washington D.C., 1835. THE GRANGER COLLECTION, NEW YORK

1836

Three new newspapers appear: *Morning Herald* (New York City); *Detroit Free Press*; *Kansas Weekly Herald* (Leavenworth), the first paper in the state.

ENTERTAINMENT

Robert T. Conrad produces his play *Jack Cade*.

National Theater in Washington, D.C., is completed.

SPORTS

Henry Standard wins ten-mile foot race (59 min, 44 sec) on Long Island.

Four-foot-high stakes, used in town ball for bases, begin to be replaced by flat stones, later by sand-filled sacks.

MISCELLANEOUS

Wood paving in hexagonal blocks is introduced in New York City.

Fire in New York City destroys 700 buildings in heart of city, causes $20 million in property damage.

INTERNATIONAL

Convention in Washington, Tex. (March 2), declares Texas independent; Sam Houston is named commander of army.

Siege of the Alamo in San Antonio begins (February 23): 145 men, led by William B. Travis, hold off 6,000–7,000 Mexican troops; ends March 6 with all Americans, including Davy Crockett, and 1,544 Mexicans killed.

Texas defeats 1,500 Mexicans at Battle of San Jacinto (April 21); captures Mexican Gen. Santa Anna who pledges independence for Texas, his pledge is repudiated by Mexican Government (May 14).

Sam Houston is installed as president of Republic of Texas (October 22).

NATIONAL

Democratic national convention nominates Vice President Martin Van Buren for president, Richard M. Johnson for vice president (May 20); Whig coalition cannot decide on candidate, name three: Daniel Webster, Hugh L. White, and John McLean.

Martin Van Buren is elected president with 170 electoral and 762,678 popular votes against 113 for the Whig candidates with 736,250 popular votes; no vice presidential candidate receives an

electoral vote majority; Senate (February 8, 1837) elects Johnson.

Congress calls for recognition of Texas, but President Andrew Jackson urges strict neutrality.

Arkansas is admitted as 25th state (June 15) after adopting state constitution (January 4); Territory of Wisconsin is established (April 20), territorial government is created (July 4).

Bureau of Indian Affairs is created.

Roger B. Taney is named Supreme Court chief justice (March 28).

Fire destroys Post Office and Patent Office buildings in Washington, D.C.

Patent law is completely rewritten.

Pensions are granted to widows of Revolutionary War soldiers.

Missionaries Marcus Whitman and H. H. Spaulding and their wives establish first white settlement in northern Oregon.

House adopts, over the strenuous objections of John Quincy Adams, "gag resolution" that automatically tables any petition involving slavery or abolition.

DEATHS Former President James Madison (1809–1817); Former Vice President Aaron Burr (1801–1805); Stephen F. Austin, colonizer of Texas.

Santa Ana's troops attack the Alamo, 1836. The Granger Collection, New York

Arms Manufacturing Co. of Paterson, N.J., revolvers.

Alonzo D. Phillips of Springfield, Mass., patents friction matches.

TRANSPORTATION

Illinois begins to build canal to connect Mississippi River and Lake Michigan.

First locomotive is built with cab for engineer and crew.

John Ericsson invents improved screw propeller for steamships.

SCIENCE/MEDICINE

John E. Holbrook prepares *North American Herpetology*, first major contribution to knowledge of American reptiles.

Asa Gray's *Elements of Botany* is published.

EDUCATION

William H. McGuffey prepares first two *Eclectic Readers*.

Emory University (Oxford, Ga., now in Atlanta) and Alfred (N.Y.) University are founded.

RELIGION

First Mormon temple is dedicated in Kirtland, Ohio (March 27).

The first Jewish congregation in Missouri holds its first service in St. Louis.

American and Foreign Bible Society is founded.

DEATH William White, a leader in creation of American Protestant Episcopal church.

ART/MUSIC

Thomas Cole completes five huge canvasses of *The Course of Empire*; Edward Hicks, *Peaceable Kingdom: The Cornell Farm*.

BUSINESS/INDUSTRY/INVENTIONS

Massachusetts passes labor law requiring children to attend school three months of year until age 15; manufacturers are not allowed to employ children for more than nine months of year.

Philadelphia Navy Yard establishes 10-hour workday.

Holmes & Hotchkiss of Waterbury, Conn., begins to manufacture hooks and eyes; Samuel Colt's Patent

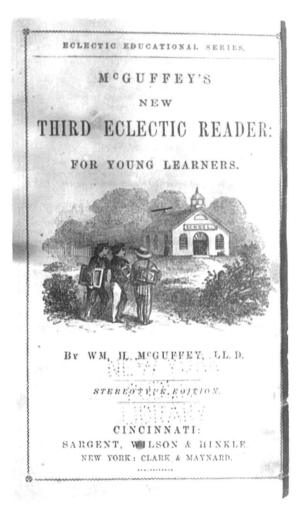

ECLECTIC EDUCATIONAL SERIES.

McGUFFEY'S

NEW

THIRD ECLECTIC READER:

FOR YOUNG LEARNERS.

BY WM. H. McGUFFEY, LL. D.

STEREOTYPE EDITION.

CINCINNATI:
SARGENT, WILSON & HINKLE.
NEW YORK: CLARK & MAYNARD.

One of the readers, or textbooks, first compiled by William Holmes McGuffey in 1836. Over the next 60 years, McGuffey's readers, which offer lessons in religion, morality, and patriotism, will help teach millions of American children to read. © CULVER PICTURES, INC.

LITERATURE/JOURNALISM

J. B. Lippincott & Co., publisher, is founded.

Three new newspapers publish: *Philadelphia Public Ledger*; *Picayune* (later *Times-Picayune*) in New Orleans; *DuBuque Visitor*, first Iowa paper.

BOOKS *Nature* by Ralph Waldo Emerson; *Awful Disclosures* by Maria Monk; *The Book of St. Nicholas* by James K. Paulding; *Poems* by Oliver Wendell Holmes; *Mellichampe* by William G. Simms.

ENTERTAINMENT

Charlotte Cushman debuts as Lady Macbeth in New York.

An early showboat, Henry Butler's boat on the Erie Canal, serves as "museum" by day, theater at night.

INTERNATIONAL

Senate recognizes independence of Texas (March 1); Republic of Texas petitions for annexation by U.S. (August 4), is refused (August 25).

Party of Canadian militia boards a U.S. steamboat, *Caroline*, on the American side, sets it afire, kills one American, because the *Caroline* was being used by Canadian rebels.

1837

NATIONAL

Panic of 1837 occurs after reckless speculation; price of cotton falls by almost half; there are demonstrations by New York City unemployed; mob breaks into New York City warehouse, sacks food supplies (February 12); banks suspend specie payments in New York, Baltimore, Philadelphia, and Boston; Congress votes $10 million to relieve economic distress; initiates economic depression that lasts until 1842.

Mob in Alton, Ill., destroys antislavery newspaper, editor Elijah P. Lovejoy is killed (November 7).

Michigan is admitted as 26th state (January 26).

Zachary Taylor leads U.S. force to victory over Seminole nation near Lake Okeechobee, Fla.

Senate, after nearly three years, expunges from its record its censure of former President Jackson for his actions involving the Bank of the United States.

Chicago incorporates as city, William B. Ogden as first mayor (March 4).

John H. Noyes and his followers form the Oneida (N.Y.) Community, which for nearly 40 years is the most successful of many utopian experiments.

Judiciary Act increases number of Supreme Court justices from 7 to 9.

Franklin Pierce becomes a senator from New Hampshire.

DEATH Joseph Anderson, first Comptroller of the Treasury (1815–1836).

BUSINESS/INDUSTRY/INVENTIONS

John Deere begins to manufacture steel plows in Grand Detour, Ill.

Erastus Bigelow of West Boylston, Mass., patents a carpet power loom; John A. and Hiram A. Pitts of Winthrop, Me., a threshing machine using steam; William Crompton, the first successful power loom for making fancy cotton fabrics.

Procter & Gamble Co. and Tiffany & Co., jewelers, are founded.

One of John Deere's steel hand plows, first manufactured in 1837. THE GRANGER COLLECTION, NEW YORK

Charles Goodyear receives a patent for manufacture of rubber tires.

TRANSPORTATION

Supreme Court in *New York v. Miln* upholds a New York law requiring masters of incoming vessels to provide complete information on passengers.

Railroad whistle first blown on Paterson & Hudson River Railroad October 6, 1837, on run from Paterson to New Brunswick, N.J.

SCIENCE/MEDICINE

James D. Dana completes *System of Mineralogy.*

DEATH Philip S. Physick, a pioneer of American surgery.

EDUCATION

Massachusetts creates state board of education, with Horace Mann as secretary.

Mary M. Lyon founds Mt. Holyoke Seminary (later College) in South Hadley, Mass.

First state school for blind, Ohio Institute for the Blind, opens in Columbus (July 4).

New colleges and universities include DePauw University (chartered as Indiana Asbury University), Knox College in Galesburg, Ill., and Davidson (N.C.) College.

ART/MUSIC

John S. Dwight leads organization of Members of the Pierian Sodality, later the Harvard Musical Association; Academy of Music Orchestra in Boston is established.

Painter George Catlin exhibits sketches of Native Americans.

Thomas Cole completes the painting *In the Catskills.*

LITERATURE/JOURNALISM

Sarah J. B. Hale, editor and author, becomes editor of *Lady's Book,* which soon becomes known as *Godey's Lady's Book.*

BOOKS *Twice-Told Tales* by Nathaniel Hawthorne; *Three Experiments of Living* by Hannah F. Lee; *Nick of the Woods* by Robert M. Bird, a forerunner of the "dime novel."

1838

Baltimore Sun is founded by Arunah S. Abell; *Milwaukee Sentinel*, the first Winconsin daily, publishes.

British authors request that the U.S. provide copyright protection.

ENTERTAINMENT

Nathaniel P. Willis writes play *Bianca Visconti*, which is produced in New York City; the ballet *The Maid of Cashmere* is produced.

First vaudeville show is presented in Niblo's Garden, New York City.

MISCELLANEOUS

Work begins on Croton Aqueduct for New York City water supply.

1838

INTERNATIONAL

President Martin Van Buren issues a neutrality proclamation in the *Caroline* affair (see 1837).

Canadian lumberjacks begin lumber operations in disputed area of Aroostook, Me.

Republic of Texas withdraws request to be annexed by U.S.; Mirabeau B. Lamar becomes second president of the republic.

NATIONAL

Territory of Iowa is established (June 12); Florida convention adopts state constitution.

Several states take steps to enforce temperance: Tennessee repeals all laws to license "tippling houses"; Massachusetts requires minimum sales of spirituous liquors to be 15 gallons; Maine Temperance Union is founded.

Between June 1838 and April 1839, federal and state troops force 15,000 Cherokees to emigrate to Indian Territory in Oklahoma.

Underground railroad, a network of escape routes for slaves, becomes a force in assisting slaves to reach the North or Canada.

DEATH William Clark, coleader of Lewis and Clark Expedition.

BUSINESS/INDUSTRY/INVENTIONS

Isaac Babbitt, while developing an improved housing bearing, prepares a material for the lining that becomes very widely used, Babbitt metal.

Chauncey Jerome develops an inexpensive, accurate one-day brass movement clock that soon floods the market.

Alfred Vail transmits telegraph message at Morristown, N.J., using the dot-dash code invented by Samuel F. B. Morse (January 6). The message is "A patient waiter is no loser."

Tredegar Iron Co., which later will make Confederate artillery during the Civil War, is established in Richmond, Va.

David Bruce Jr. patents pivotal typecaster that comes into general use by typefounders.

DEATH Loammi Baldwin, considered a leader in American civil engineering.

TRANSPORTATION

First oceangoing steamboat, *Great Western*, arrives in New York City from Bristol, England.

Wabash Railroad begins as the Northern Cross, the first Illinois railroad.

DEATH Nathaniel Bowditch, author of navigation manuals.

SCIENCE/MEDICINE

Naval scientific expedition to South Seas sets off with six ships commanded by Lt. Charles Wilkes; returns in 1842.

Charles A. Spencer constructs first American microscope.

EDUCATION

Common School Journal is founded by Horace Mann.

The removal of the Cherokee Indians to the West in 1838. THE GRANGER COLLECTION, NEW YORK

RELIGION

Mormons, led by Joseph Smith, move to western Missouri; friction with other settlers later forces them to move to Illinois.

Samuel S. Schmucker issues appeal to American churches to reunite.

Leonidas Polk is named Episcopal missionary bishop to the Southwest.

ART/MUSIC

Lowell Mason begins Boston public schools music instruction; 138 singing teachers from 10 states hold week-long meeting in Boston.

Thomas Cole completes the paintings *Schroon Lake* and *Dream of Arcadia*.

SONGS (popular) "Annie Laurie," "Flow Gently, Sweet Afton," "She Wore a Yellow Ribbon."

LITERATURE/JOURNALISM

Appleton Publishing Co. is founded.

BOOKS *Richard Hurdis* by William G. Simms; *Rob of the Bowl* by John P. Kennedy; *Burton, or the Sieges* by Joseph H. Ingraham; *Constance Latimer* by Emma C. Embury.

ENTERTAINMENT

James W. Wallack stars in *Tortesa, the Usurer* in New York City.

SPORTS

Edward Hoyle publishes handbook of card games.

MISCELLANEOUS

Fire in Charleston, S.C., causes $3 million in property damage.

Steamer *Moselle* explodes on the Ohio River; 100 killed.

1839

INTERNATIONAL

Maine names an agent, Rufus McIntire, to expel Canadians lumbering in Aroostook area; Canadians arrest McIntire, refuse to release him (February 2), which starts Aroostook "war."

Maine and Nova Scotia call out their militia (February 12); Gen. Winfield Scott arranges a truce; British agree to refer matter to boundary commission; Webster-Ashburton Treaty (1842) resolves matter.

Vessel *Amistad*, carrying captives for the American slave market, is taken over in mutiny near Cuba; captured by U.S. Navy in Long Island area. Mutineers are charged with piracy, but in 1841 the Supreme Court will set them free. Slaves are represented by John Quincy Adams; private charity will pay their passage to Africa.

Republic of Texas signs treaty with France, secures loan for commercial development.

NATIONAL

Russian settlers in California sell their fort to John A. Sutter for $30,000; leave U.S. in 1842.

"Helderberg War" breaks out in Albany (N.Y.) area when landowners (patroons) try to collect rents under the old perpetual leases; New York militia suppresses tenants' uprising.

James K. Polk becomes Tennessee governor.

Robert M. T. Hunter is elected House Speaker; at 30, is the youngest speaker.

BUSINESS/INDUSTRY/INVENTIONS

Charles Goodyear develops vulcanization process to make useable rubber products.

Two express companies are founded: William F. Harnden of Boston starts service between Boston and New York, Alvin F. Adams between Boston and Worcester, Mass.

William S. Otis of Philadelphia patents steam shovel.

First business periodical *Hunt's Merchants' Magazine* is published.

Jacob Sloat establishes cotton twine factory at Sloatsburg, N.Y.

Erastus B. Bigelow develops power loom to weave two-ply carpets; Thomas Davenport an electric printing press.

American Agriculturist magazine is published.

SCIENCE/MEDICINE

William C. Bond sets up private observatory at Harvard University, heads college observatory.

Charles Goodyear develops his vulcanization process for rubber, 1839. THE GRANGER COLLECTION, NEW YORK

American Journal of Dental Science, first of its kind, is published; Dr. Chapin A. Harris writes *The Dental Art*.

American Statistical Assn. is organized.

EDUCATION

Georgia Female (later Wesleyan) College in Macon is chartered; first in U.S. to grant degrees to women.

New colleges and universities include University of Missouri, Virginia Military Institute, State Normal School (Lexington, Mass.), Boston University.

William H. McGuffey, author of the famed *Readers*, is named president of Ohio University.

RELIGION

Concordia Seminary opens in Altenburg, Mo. (later moves to St. Louis).

Millerite (after William Miller), or Adventist, movement begins to gain national attention.

Joseph Smith and Mormon followers move to Nauvoo, Ill.

ART/MUSIC

Beethoven's opera *Fidelio* is presented in New York City.

SONGS (popular): "Kathleen Mavourneen," "Kemo-Kimo," "Rocked in the Cradle of the Deep."

LITERATURE/JOURNALISM

Edgar Allan Poe writes "The Fall of the House of Usher" in *Burton's Gentlemen's Magazine*.

Dodd, Mead & Co., publisher, is founded.

BOOKS *Voices of the Night* and *Hyperion* by Henry Wadsworth Longfellow; *Life of Washington* by Jared Sparks; *The Green Mountain Boys* by Daniel T. Thompson; *A New Home* by Caroline Kirkland.

ENTERTAINMENT

Joseph S. Jones produces *The People's Lawyer*, a play.

DEATH William Dunlap, playwright and writer on American art.

SPORTS

Abner Doubleday lays out first regular baseball diamond at Cooperstown, N.Y., establishes first set of rules for the game.

A trotter, Dutchman, sets record of 2 minutes 32 seconds for the mile.

Detroit Boat Club, oldest existing American boat club, is founded.

MISCELLANEOUS

Congress enacts law forbidding dueling in Washington.

1840

INTERNATIONAL

Republic of Texas concludes commercial treaties with Holland, Belgium, and Great Britain.

Hawaii's first written constitution is adopted.

NATIONAL

William Henry Harrison, a Whig, is elected president, defeating incumbent Democrat, Martin Van Buren, by 234 electoral votes to 60; popular vote is closer, 1,275,017 to 1,128,702; John Tyler is elected vice president.

Sixth census reports national population of 17,063,353.

Independent federal treasury system is created with subtreasuries in New York, Boston, Charleston, and St. Louis.

Lt. Charles Wilkes and his naval expedition sight the Antarctic continent.

BUSINESS/INDUSTRY/INVENTIONS

President Van Buren orders 10-hour day for all laborers and mechanics working on federal public works without reducing their pay; average daily hours of factory workers are estimated at 11.4.

Commercial production of graphite begins in Ticonderoga, N.Y.

David Thomas produces first pig iron using anthracite coal in blast furnace.

Plant is built in Marion, Conn., to manufacture nuts and bolts.

Joseph Gibbons of Adrian, Mich., patents a seeding machine.

TRANSPORTATION

Great National Pike (Cumberland Road) connecting Cumberland, Md., and Vandalia, Ill., is completed.

First American iron truss bridge is built over Erie Canal at Frankfort, N.Y.

SCIENCE/MEDICINE

Baltimore College of Dental Surgery, first dental school, incorporates.

Nehemiah Kenison opens first chiropodist's office in Boston.

DEATH William Maclure, who prepared first geological chart of U.S.

"Hurrah for Harrison and Tyler." An 1840 almanac cover promotes William Henry Harrison's candidacy for president. THE GRANGER COLLECTION, NEW YORK

EDUCATION

First class of women (11) graduates from Georgia Female College in Macon.

First college to complete a library building is University of South Carolina.

Bethany College is founded in Virginia (later W.Va.).

RELIGION

Catholic Bishop François N. Blanchet becomes first archbishop of Oregon City (later Portland).

Adin Ballou founds weekly paper, *Practical Christian.*

DEATH Demetrius A. Gallitzin, first Catholic priest wholly trained and ordained in U.S.

ART/MUSIC

Thomas Cole completes *Voyage of Life* series; *The Morning of Life* and *The Evening of Life* by Asher B. Durand.

LITERATURE/JOURNALISM

Henry Wadsworth Longfellow writes poem "The Village Blacksmith."

BOOKS *Two Years Before the Mast* by Richard H. Dana Jr.; *The Pathfinder* by James Fenimore Cooper; *Tales of the Grotesque and Arabesque* by Edgar Allan Poe.

SPORTS

Knickerbocker Alleys, New York City, sponsor first recorded U.S. bowling match.

MISCELLANEOUS

Steamboat *Lexington* catches fire near Eaton's Neck, N.Y.; 140 die.

INTERNATIONAL

U.S. brigantine *Creole*, en route to New Orleans with a cargo of slaves, is taken over by mutinous slaves who take ship to the Bahamas; Great Britain frees slaves, except for the active mutineers; pays no attention to U.S. demands for return of slaves (is resolved by arbitration 1855).

NATIONAL

President William Henry Harrison dies (April 4), a month after taking office; cause is a cold he catches at his inauguration when he speaks for 1 hour 45 minutes in cold, stormy weather; John Tyler becomes first vice president to assume the presidency when the chief executive dies in office.

Supreme Court in the *Amistad* case frees black passengers on a Spanish ship whose crew mutinied; the ship was captured by a U.S. warship in 1839.

1841

Independent Treasury Act, passed in 1840, provides for independent banks for federal deposits; Congress passes bills to set up a federal bank in Washington; President Tyler vetoes the bills and all but one member of his Cabinet resign, saying the president promised to support the bills.

First wagon train to head for California leaves Independence, Mo., with 47 persons on May 1; will arrive six months later.

Oregon settlers meet at Champoeg to organize territorial government.

First presidential-widow pension is authorized, $25,000 to widow of William Henry Harrison.

BUSINESS/INDUSTRY/INVENTIONS

Lewis Tappan founds Mercantile Agency, first rating organization for commercial credit; eventually becomes Dun & Bradstreet.

1841

Insurrection aboard the slave ship *Amistad*, off the coast of Cuba, 1839. The African prisoners are freed by the Supreme Court in 1841. THE GRANGER COLLECTION, NEW YORK

Volney B. Palmer of Philadelphia opens first U.S. advertising agency.

Samuel F. B. Morse receives a patent for the telegraph; Napoleon E. Guerin receives one for a cork life preserver.

John A. Roebling establishes plant to make wire rope for bridges; Wolcottville Brass Co. begins to manufacture brass wire.

Erastus Bigelow's perfected loom for weaving carpets revolutionizes the industry.

Frenchman Adrien Delcambre and James H. Young patent typesetting machine.

SCIENCE/MEDICINE

Alabama institutes licensing of dentists.

EDUCATION

St. John's College (which will become Fordham University) opens.

RELIGION

Hopedale Community, a religious society, is established near Milford, Mass.

Alfred Lee is consecrated as first Episcopal bishop of Delaware, Rev. William Meade as bishop of Virginia.

ART/MUSIC

Vose Art Gallery opens in Providence, R.I.

Horatio Greenough completes statue of George Washington.

Artist George Catlin writes book about life with Native Americans, *The Manners, Customs, and Conditions of the North American Indians.*

LITERATURE/JOURNALISM

Horace Greeley, its editor, founds *New York Tribune.*

Edgar Allan Poe publishes two stories: "The Murders in the Rue Morgue" and "The Masque of the Red Death."

BOOKS *The Destroyer* by James Fenimore Cooper, *Essays* by Ralph Waldo Emerson, *Ballads and Other Poems* by Henry Wadsworth Longfellow.

ENTERTAINMENT

P. T. Barnum purchases American Museum in New York City, which shows a collection of curious objects and people, including personal appearance of the little man Gen. Tom Thumb; museum is enlarged, is used for plays.

Boston Museum and Gallery of Fine Arts Theater opens.

SPORTS

Tom Hyer beats John McCluster in a boxing match, claims American heavyweight title.

MISCELLANEOUS

Steamboat *Erie* burns on Lake Erie; 175 perish.

1842

INTERNATIONAL

Webster-Ashburton Treaty, signed (August 9), fixes boundary between Maine and New Brunswick along present line, sets boundary westward to Lake of the Woods; is ratified by Senate.

Commodore Thomas Catesby, acting on mistaken belief U.S. and Mexico are at war, takes public buildings in Monterey, Calif., raises U.S. flag; apologizes the next day, lowers the flag, withdraws.

Group of Mexican soldiers invade Texas, capture San Antonio; for some years city is deserted because of constant Mexican raids.

NATIONAL

Rebellious Rhode Islanders, led by Thomas W. Dorr, demand equal voting rights (old constitution gave vote only to freeholders and their eldest sons); Dorr faction tries unsuccessfully to seize state arsenal (May 18); Dorr is sentenced to life in prison, is pardoned (1845).

Supreme Court upholds constitutionality of 1793 Fugitive Slave Law.

Tariff Act returns duties to 1832 levels, averaging between 23–35%.

Lt. Charles Wilkes and six ships return from four-year, 90,000-mile exploration of the Pacific and Antarctic oceans.

Reapportionment Act provides for district election of members of House of Representatives.

Start of federal fiscal year changes from January 1 to July 1.

A slaveowner offers a reward for the return of a slave. THE GRANGER COLLECTION, NEW YORK

1842

Adhesive postage stamps are used for first time.

John C. Frémont heads expedition to explore southern Wyoming, other Rocky Mountain areas.

Henry Clay retires after 40 years in Congress.

DEATH First Lady Letitia C. Tyler in the White House.

BUSINESS/INDUSTRY/INVENTIONS

Joseph Dart builds elevating apparatus to unload grain from vessels directly into waterfront warehouse; first American grain elevator to use the apparatus is built in Buffalo.

Samuel Colt builds armory in Hartford, Conn., uses assembly-line production techniques.

L. Candee Shoe Co. in Hamden, Conn., begins to manufacture rubber shoes; George H. Corliss patents a boot-stitching machine.

Massachusetts Supreme Court in *Commonwealth v. Nunt* rules that it is not unlawful for union members to strike to gain a closed shop; illegality depends on means used.

Merchants Vigilance Assn., credit protective group, forms in New York City.

J. J. Greenough receives patent for a sewing machine.

DEATH Benjamin Wright, chief engineer of Erie Canal.

TRANSPORTATION

Wire suspension bridge over Schuylkill River at Fairmount, Pa., opens.

SCIENCE/MEDICINE

First anesthesia (sulphuric ether) is used experimentally in a U.S. operation by Dr. Crawford W. Long in Jefferson, Ga. (March 30); Dr. Elijah Pope uses ether for a tooth extraction in Rochester, N.Y.

EDUCATION

Massachusetts passes law requiring minimum education for every child and a maximum workday of 10 hours for those under age 10.

New colleges and universities: Ohio Wesleyan University; Notre Dame; Villanova College; Oregon Institute (later Willamette University), first institute of higher education in Far West; The Citadel (Charleston, S.C.).

Kentucky Institute for the Blind in Louisville is chartered.

RELIGION

Chicago Sacred Music Society is founded.

Christian Metz leads 800 members of Protestant sect, the Community of True Inspiration, to U.S. from Germany; forms communal settlement at Ebenezer, N.Y., near Buffalo; eventually will move to Iowa and become Amana Community.

Coeur d'Alene Mission, a Catholic Indian mission, is established near Cataldo, Ida.

DEATH William Ellery Channing, a founder of Unitarian church.

ART/MUSIC

New York Philharmonic Society is founded; gives first concert (December 7).

A popular song is "We Won't Go Home Till Morning."

LITERATURE/JOURNALISM

Brother Jonathan, first illustrated weekly, begins publication in New York City.

BOOKS *Poets and Poetry of America*, an anthology, by Rufus W. Griswold; *Wing-and-Wing* by James Fenimore Cooper; *Twice-Told Tales* (second version) by Nathaniel Hawthorne. Short story "The Pit and the Pendulum" by Edgar Allan Poe is published.

ENTERTAINMENT

Edwin P. Christy organizes Virginia Minstrels (later the Christy Minstrels).

SPORTS

Large crowd at Union Course on Long Island sees Fashion, a Southern horse, beat Boston, a Northern horse, in 4-mile race for $20,000 purse.

Tom McCoy is knocked out in a fight at Hastings, N.Y.; he dies a short time later, becoming the first U.S. ring fatality.

MISCELLANEOUS

Mt. St. Helens volcano in Washington State erupts.

Charles F. E. Minnegeroude, a German immigrant, reportedly is first in U.S. to cut and trim a Christmas tree.

Croton Aqueduct begins to supply water to New York City.

INTERNATIONAL

President Santa Anna of Mexico notifies U.S. that incorporation of Texas into U.S. will be considered a declaration of war.

U.S. representatives attend World Peace Conference in London.

NATIONAL

Congress appropriates $30,000 to help Samuel F. B. Morse build telegraph line between Washington and Baltimore.

Rhode Island liberalizes voting rights in a new constitution, meeting some of the demands that led to earlier Dorr rebellion (see 1842).

Oregon settlers adopt constitution for a provisional government; Oregonians want boundary line at 49° moved northward to 54°40′.

A thousand Easterners leave Independence, Mo., to settle in Oregon, starting large westward migration; Ft. Bridger in Wyoming, a way station and supply point for emigrants, is built.

John Ericsson designs the *Princeton*, first warship to have propelling machinery below waterline.

Alexander D. Bache becomes head of U.S. Coast Survey, greatly expands its work.

Andrew Johnson from Tennessee begins first of five terms in House of Representatives.

DEATHS Isaac Hull, commander of USS *Constitution* (Old Ironsides); Stewart T. Mason, first Michigan governor (1835–1840).

BUSINESS/INDUSTRY/INVENTIONS

Mutual Life Insurance Co. of New York issues first policy.

Charles Thurber invents a typewriter; J. M. and L. Hollingsworth receive a patent for producing manila paper.

SCIENCE/MEDICINE

Cornerstone is laid for Adams Astronomical Observatory, near Cincinnati.

James P. Espy makes major contribution to meteorology with law of cooling of atmospheric air.

Great comet appears, stimulates interest in astronomy.

EDUCATION

Holy Cross College opens.

RELIGION

William Miller sets the year starting in March as the time for the Second Coming.

Mormon Leader Joseph Smith announces that a divine revelation sanctions the practice of polygamy.

B'nai Brith, Jewish fraternal society, is founded.

Catholic Rev. Michael O'Connor becomes first bishop of Pittsburgh.

Philander Chase, Episcopal bishop of Illinois, becomes presiding bishop.

ART/MUSIC

Bunker Hill Monument is dedicated in Boston, Mass.

Hiram Powers completes marble life-size sculpture *The Greek Slave*.

SONGS (popular): "Old Dan Tucker," "The Old

1843

Pioneers heading west call it a day and stop for dinner and some music. THE GRANGER COLLECTION, NEW YORK

Oaken Bucket," "I Dreamt I Dwelt in Marble Halls."

DEATHS John Trumbull, artist of historical scenes; Washington Allston, landscape artist.

LITERATURE/JOURNALISM

New Englander (later *Yale Review*) is founded in New Haven; *Cincinnati Commercial* is published.

BOOKS *Conquest of Mexico* by William H. Prescott, *The Wonders of the World* by Robert Sears, *Tales* by Edgar Allan Poe.

DEATH Noah Webster, lexicographer.

ENTERTAINMENT

Original Virginia Minstrels play at Chatham Theater, New York City.

New dance craze, the quickstep, is introduced.

SPORTS

Glumbalditch wins Peyton Stakes, the first futurity race.

Yale University becomes first school to feature rowing as a sport, with competition between classes and students.

Cricket club is founded at University of Pennsylvania.

MISCELLANEOUS

Mt. Rainier in Washington erupts.

1844

INTERNATIONAL

U.S. and Republic of Texas sign treaty calling for annexation of Texas (April 22); Senate rejects treaty (June 8).

Treaty of Wanghia is signed with China, a treaty of peace, amity, and commerce that opens five Chinese ports to American shipping (July 3).

NATIONAL

Democrat James K. Polk is elected president, defeating Whig candidate Henry Clay with 170 electoral votes to 105 (1,337,243 popular to 1,299,068). President John Tyler does not stand for reelection.

Secretary of State Abel P. Upshur, Navy Secretary Thomas W. Gilmer, and a senator are killed when a bow gun aboard the USS *Princeton* explodes during a Potomac cruise with President Tyler, his cabinet, and 350 guests aboard.

Widowed former President Tyler marries Julia Gardner in New York City.

New Jersey voters ratify state constitution that restricts vote to white male citizens; Iowa convention approves state constitution.

Thomas W. Dorr, who led Rhode Island rebellion, is sentenced to life imprisonment (see 1842).

John C. Calhoun becomes Secretary of State.

A twelve-inch cannon aboard the USS *Princeton* explodes, killing two cabinet members and six others accompanying President John Tyler on an inaugural cruise down the Potomac River in 1844. THE GRANGER COLLECTION, NEW YORK

1844

The telegraph key used by Samuel F. B. Morse to send the first commercial telegraph message in 1844. THE GRANGER COLLECTION, NEW YORK

BUSINESS/INDUSTRY/INVENTIONS

Government surveyors discover iron ore near Marquette, Mich.

Charles Goodyear receives patent for process to vulcanize rubber; Stuart Perry of New York, a patent for a gas engine.

New inventions are announced: Uriah A. Boyden's turbine operated by waterpower; Jerome I. Case's threshing machine; Moses G. Farmer's machine to print paper window shades.

Commercial telegraph service begins when Samuel F. B. Morse in Washington, D.C., sends message to Alfred Vail in Baltimore ("What hath God wrought?") on an experimental commercial line (May 24).

TRANSPORTATION

Steamer *J. M. White* sails from New Orleans to St. Louis in 3 days, 23 hours.

SCIENCE/MEDICINE

Dr. Horace A. Wells, dentist in Hartford, is one of first to use anesthesia.

American Psychiatric Assn. is founded; *American Journal of Psychiatry*, first specialized medical journal, is published.

James D. Dana, on return with Wilkes Expedition (1838–1842), describes for first time 230 species of 200 phytes and 636 of crustacea.

EDUCATION

Mississippi University and State of New York University are founded.

RELIGION

Joseph Smith, founder of Mormon Church, and his brother Hyrum are jailed in Carthage, Ill., as result of constant disagreement with non-Mormons; mob storms jail (June 27), kills the Smiths.

James J. Strang, when he fails to be named Joseph Smith's successor (above), forms a short-lived sect, the Strangites.

Baptist church cannot agree on question of slavery and splits into northern and southern branches.

William Miller and his Adventists set final date (October 22) for the Second Coming of Christ.

Native-born Protestants and immigrant Catholics clash violently on May 6–8 and July 5–8; approximately 100 injured, 20 killed.

Catholic Rev. John M. Henni becomes first bishop of Milwaukee.

DEATH Barton W. Stone, a founder of Disciples of Christ church.

ART/MUSIC

Mathew Brady opens a photo studio in New York City.

Wadsworth Atheneum, a public art museum, opens in Hartford.

SONGS (popular): "Buffalo Gals," "The Old Gray Goose," "Open Thy Lattice, Love," "Spring Song."

LITERATURE/JOURNALISM

R. Hoe & Co. begins to manufacture cylinder and flatbed printing presses.

Edgar Allan Poe publishes story "The Purloined Letter."

Brownson's Quarterly Review is founded.

Horace Greeley of the *New York Tribune* hires first U.S. book reviewer, Sarah Margaret Fuller.

BOOKS *The Monks of Monk Hall* by George Lippard, *Commerce of the Prairies* by Josiah Gregg, *Essays* by Ralph Waldo Emerson.

NEWSPAPERS *Louisville* (Ky.) *Courier*, *Springfield* (Mass.) *Republican* become dailies; first Oklahoma newspaper, *Cherokee Advocate*, is printed in English and Cherokee.

ENTERTAINMENT

Dan Rice, most celebrated clown of his day, begins his career.

Nathaniel H. Bannister's play *Putnam* is produced in New York City and W. H. Smith's *The Drunkard* in Boston.

SPORTS

New York Yacht Club is organized aboard the schooner *Gimcrack*.

Thomas Mathews produces *The Whist Players Handbook*.

1845

INTERNATIONAL

Congress approves annexation of Texas (February 28); Texas convention's call for annexation (July 4) is ratified by Texas voters (October 13); Mexico breaks off relations with U.S. (March 28).

Gen. Zachary Taylor, commander of Southwest U.S. troops, is ordered to locate "on or near" the Rio Grande; establishes base on bank of Nueces River near Corpus Christi.

U.S. emissary John Slidell arrives in Mexico City for talks with Mexican government, which refuses to meet because his appointment and mission are not confirmed by Congress (December 6).

Col. Stephen Kearny leaves Ft. Leavenworth, Kansas, to occupy New Mexico, California (June 5).

President James Polk claims Oregon for U.S. (December 1).

NATIONAL

Florida is admitted as 27th state (March 3); Texas convention approves a constitution, ratifies (October 13); Texas is admitted as 28th state (December 29).

Congress for first time overrides a presidential veto: outgoing President John Tyler vetoed a bill that would prohibit payment for some naval craft he ordered (March 3).

Uniform Election Day is set for first Tuesday after the first Monday in November (January 23), effective 1848.

Congress reduces postal rates to 5 cents for a half-ounce for up to 300 miles; contract system for hauling mail between post offices is authorized.

Irish potato famine causes a large migration to U.S. of impoverished Irish peasants; by 1850 about 1.5 million Irish had immigrated to U.S., expanding an already substantial Irish and Catholic presence concentrated in eastern states and especially in cities.

DEATH Former President Andrew Jackson (1829–1837).

BUSINESS/INDUSTRY/INVENTIONS

C. M. Bailey Sons & Co. begins to manufacture oilcloth in Winthrop, Me.; Benjamin T. Babbitt, soap powder, New York City; Abraham Miller of Philadelphia, wall and floor tiles.

New England Protective Union creates a central agency for retail stores.

DEATH Asher Benjamin, pioneer American architect.

TRANSPORTATION

Wire-cable suspension bridge over Allegheny River at Pittsburgh is completed; first iron railroad bridge is built at Manayunk, Pa.

John W. Griffiths builds and launches first U.S. clipper ship *Rainbow*.

SCIENCE/MEDICINE

Ohio College of Dental Surgery, second such school, is founded.

1845

EDUCATION

U. S. Naval Academy at Annapolis, Md., opens as the Naval School, with Commander Franklin Buchanan first superintendent.

Millard Fillmore becomes chancellor of University of Buffalo.

Baylor University and Wittenberg College (Springfield, Ohio) are chartered.

RELIGION

Fourteen Methodist state conferences organize Methodist Episcopal Church South after dispute over slavery; similarly, Southern Baptist Convention is organized, with Dr. W. B. Johnson president.

First American Methodist seminary, Wesley Theological Seminary (Newburg, Vt.), is founded.

Millerites (after William Miller) meet in Albany to form Adventist Church.

A. A. Grabau founds Buffalo Synod, Lutheran Church.

Alonzo Potter becomes Episcopal bishop of Pennsylvania.

DEATH Jason Lee, Methodist missionary who helped settle Oregon.

ART/MUSIC

George C. Bingham completes the painting, *Fur Traders Descending the Missouri*; William S. Mount paints *Eel Spearing at Setauket*.

Opera by Joseph R. and William H. Fry, *Leonora*, is performed in Philadelphia.

SONGS (popular): "Blest Be the Tie That Binds," "Scenes That Are the Brightest."

LITERATURE/JOURNALISM

Cleveland Plain Dealer is founded.

National Police Gazette, a weekly, and *Scientific American* are published.

A nineteenth-century baseball game at Elysian Fields, Hoboken, New Jersey. Lithograph by Currier & Ives. THE GRANGER COLLECTION, NEW YORK

BOOKS *The Raven and Other Poems* by Edgar Allan Poe, *Scarlet Feather* by Joseph H. Ingraham, *Women in the 19th Century* by Margaret Fuller, *Margaret* by Sylvester Jud.

ENTERTAINMENT

Anna C. O. Mowatt writes and produces two plays *Fashion* and *The Lady of Lyons*, in which she stars.

SPORTS

"New York Game" of baseball, an Americanized form of English rounders, began to be played in New York in 1842; first team organized by Alexander J. Cartwright (September 23, 1845).

New York Yacht Club stages its first regatta.

First American chess column appears in the newspaper *Spirit of the Times*.

MISCELLANEOUS

Fire in New York City causes $16 million property loss; Pittsburgh is almost completely destroyed by fire.

A Boston ordinance makes use of bathtubs unlawful, except on advice of a doctor.

1846

INTERNATIONAL

Mexican War

Mexico reaffirms its claim to Texas and its intention to defend its territory (January 4); Mexicans burn Port Isbel at mouth of Rio Grande (March 23), attack Matamoras (April 24), besiege Ft. Texas (May 1); U.S. force routs 6,000 Mexicans at Palo Alto (May 8), pursues and defeats them at Resaca de la Palma (May 9). Mexicans evacuate Matamoras (May 17), which becomes U.S. headquarters.

President James K. Polk delivers war message to Congress (May 11); Gen Winfield Scott takes command of U.S. troops, which capture Tampico (November 15), occupy Saltillo (November 16); take El Brazio, occupy El Paso, and move into Chihuahua Province.

Fighting in West and Southwest: Stephen W. Kearny, now a general, moves into New Mexico, then to California (May 13); Commodore John D. Sloat blockades Mexican ports on the Pacific, holds San Francisco Bay (June 3). U.S. occupies Santa Fe, proclaims New Mexico part of U.S. (August 15); Tucson is captured (December 16) by Mormon Battalion en route to California.

"Bear Flag" settlers seize Sonoma, Calif., raise flag of Republic of California (June 14); Commodore Sloat lands troops at Monterey (July 7), proclaims California part of U.S.; San Francisco and Sonoma are taken (July 9), followed by Santa Barbara and Los Angeles (August 13); Mexicans fight back, regain most of lost ground (September 22); U.S. forces retake Monterey (September 25) and much of lost territory by December 29.

Congress empowers President Polk to give Great Britain required year's notice on occupation of Oregon (April 27); British submits a draft treaty (June 6), setting north boundary along 49th parallel; treaty goes into effect (June 15).

U.S. signs commercial treaty with New Granada (Colombia) (December 12), in which U.S. receives right of way acros Panama Isthmus, guarantees its neutrality and the sovereignty of New Granada.

NATIONAL

Congress again passes Independent Treasury Act with its subtreasuries (August 6) (see 1840).

Walker Tariff is enacted (July 30) substituting specific for *ad valorem* (value) duties; few commodities are left duty freee.

Iowa state constitution is ratified (August 7); Iowa admitted as 29th state (December 28).

New York adopts new state constitution that elim-

1846

U.S. soldiers on the attack in the Battle of Resaca de la Palma in Texas on May 1, 1846. THE GRANGER COLLECTION, NEW YORK

inates the perpetual leases that touched off 1839–1840 riots by upstate tenant farmers; Maine passes first statewide prohibition law; Michigan becomes first state to abolish the death penalty.

Solomon L. Juneau, who becomes its first mayor, founds Milwaukee.

BUSINESS/INDUSTRY/INVENTIONS

Elias Howe patents first practical sewing machine.

Royal E. House invents teletype; Richard M. Hoe, rotary printing press.

Erastus B. Bigelow opens Lancaster Mills in Clinton, Mass., to produce gingham.

TRANSPORTATION

John A. Roebling builds suspension bridge, using wire rope instead of chain cable, over Monongahela River at Pittsburgh.

Pennsylvania Railroad is chartered.

Augusta (Ga.) Canal opens.

Sailing vessel *Yorkshire* arrives in New York City from Liverpool after 16-day voyage.

SCIENCE/MEDICINE

Smithsonian Institution is founded (August 10) with a bequest from English chemist John Smithson; Joseph Henry named first director (September 7).

George Hayward becomes first U.S. surgeon to use ether in major operation; William T. G. Morton completes painless tooth extraction using ether.

Joseph Leidy, anatomist, discovers the *Trichinella spiralis*, a pork parasite.

American Association for the Advancement of Science is founded.

DEATH Benjamin Waterhouse, physician who pioneered in the field of vaccination.

EDUCATION

Bucknell University (Lewisburg, Pa.) is founded as Lewisburg University; Grinnell College chartered as Iowa College in Davenport (later moved to Grinnell, IA).

RELIGION

Mormons led by Brigham Young leave Illinois for the West, to escape persecution.

Cornelia Connelly founds order of teaching nuns, Society of the Holy Child Jesus.

New Trinity Church in New York City is dedicated.

Elling Eielson founds Norwegian Evangelical Lutheran Church of North America; Evangelical Lutheran Church of America is founded; Seventh Day Adventist Church splits from the Adventist church.

American Missionary Assn. is founded as an outgrowth of *Amistad* cases to provide educational opportunities for minorities.

ART/MUSIC

Daniel D. Emmett writes song "Blue Tail Fly" (or "Jimmy Crack Corn").

Thomas Doughty completes the painting *Landscape After Ruisdael.*

DEATH Henry Inman, portrait painter.

LITERATURE/JOURNALISM

Charles Scribner's Sons, publisher, is founded in Boston as Baker & Scribner.

BOOKS *Typee* by Herman Melville, *Voices of Freedom* by John Greenleaf Whittier, "The Cask of Amontillado" by Edgar Allan Poe, *Mosses From an Old Manse* by Nathaniel Hawthorne, *The Redskins* by James Fenimore Cooper.

Two newspapers are founded: First Oregon newspaper, *The Spectator*, in Oregon City; *Californian*, first paper in state at Monterey.

SPORTS

New York Knickerbockers officially open first baseball season (April 10); first recorded game is played in Hoboken, N.J. (June 19), when Knickerbockers lose to "New York Nine."

INTERNATIONAL

Mexican War

Americans turn back Mexicans at Buena Vista, ending war in northern Mexico (February 24); Gen. Winfield Scott leads invasion force of 2,595 troops onto beaches 12 miles south of Veracruz in first U.S. amphibious landing (March 9), Veracruz is taken (March 27), then Cerro Gordo (April 18), Jalapo (April 19), and Puebla (May 15), 80 miles south of Mexico City.

Americans take Contreras and Churubuscu (August 20); Mexicans request an armistice that takes effect (August 27); peace negotiations break down (September 6), armistice ends (September 7).

Americans attack Chapultepec (September 13), storm through walls into Mexico City (September 14).

Meanwhile in California, U.S. troops defeat rebellious Californians at San Gabriel River (January 8), recapture Los Angeles (January 10); Treaty of Cahuenga is signed, ending hostilities in California.

Gen. Stephen Kearny is instructed to establish new government in California; conflicting instructions lead to dispute between Kearny and John C. Frémont, ending in Frémont's court-martial and resignation from Army.

NATIONAL

Irrigation on large scale in U.S. begins by Mormons a day after they arrive in Utah (July 23); they divert waters of City Creek onto present site of Salt Lake City to soften the ground for plowing.

First adhesive postage stamps go on sale (July 1), a 5-cent Benjamin Franklin, 10-cent George Washington.

1847

General Winfield Scott and his army enter Mexico City on September 14, 1847. THE GRANGER COLLECTION, NEW YORK

Illinois convention approves state constitution, ratifies 1848.

Abraham Lincoln begins two-year term as Representative from Illinois.

DEATH James Kent, jurist whose decisions helped create U.S. system of equity.

BUSINESS/INDUSTRY/INVENTIONS

Rogers Bros. establishes a silver-plating factory in Hartford, Conn.; Magnetic Telegraph Co. is incorporated; Remington Co. in Ilion, N.Y., manufacturer of rifles, introduces pistol.

New Hampshire legislature limits workday to 10 hours.

S. Page invents revolving disc harrow.

Massachusetts Health Insurance Co. is founded.

TRANSPORTATION

Robert W. Thomson, an Englishman, patents a rubber tire.

Chicago, Rock Island & Pacific Railroad is incorporated.

Suspension bridge across Niagara River below the Falls is completed.

SCIENCE/MEDICINE

Buffalo (N.Y.) Medical College is founded.

Cornerstone is laid for Smithsonian Institution.

Sheffield Scientific School is founded at Yale University; Lawrence Scientific School at Harvard.

Bellevue Hospital in New York City is founded.

American Medical Assn. is founded with Nathaniel Chapman president.

Matthew F. Mauray begins to issue "wind and current charts" that aid worldwide exploration, speed sailing time.

EDUCATION

State law for Akron, Ohio, provides for an elected

First United States general issue of postage stamps, 1847.
THE GRANGER COLLECTION, NEW YORK

school board, a single school district for the city, free admission for all students, local taxation to finance schools; this model spreads throughout the state.

COLLEGES/UNIVERSITIES Tulane is chartered as Louisiana University; Rockford (Ill.) College founded; University of Iowa is chartered as Iowa State University; Otterbein College (Westerville, Ohio) founded; City College of New York is founded as the Free Academy.

RELIGION

Missouri Synod of Lutheran Church forms with Carl F. W. Walther president.

Brigham Young is named head of Mormon church.

Rev. William A. Muhlenberg of New York City establishes a vacation fund to send poor children to the country.

Marcus Whitman and other missionaries are killed by Native Americans in Oregon.

Rev. John McCloskey becomes first Catholic bishop of Albany; Catholic bishop Peter A. Kenrick becomes archbishop of St. Louis.

Rev. George Burgess becomes first Episcopal bishop of Maine.

DEATH (Johann) George Rapp, founder of Harmonite sect.

ART/MUSIC

George C. Bingham completes the painting *Raftsmen Playing Cards*.

LITERATURE/JOURNALISM

Richard M. Hoe's rotary press is first used in newspaper printing.

Little, Brown publishers is founded in Boston.

Two newspapers begin publication: *Chicago Tribune* and *Santa Fe Republican*; two antislavery publications are started: *National Era* and *North Star*.

BOOKS *Poems* by Ralph Waldo Emerson, *Omoo* by Herman Melville, *Conquest of Peru* by William H. Prescott, *Evangeline* by Henry Wadsworth Longfellow.

ENTERTAINMENT

Astor Place Opera House in New York City opens.

Christy Minstrels begin 10-year engagement in Mechanics Hall on Broadway.

James E. Murdoch's play *Witchcraft* is produced in New York City.

MISCELLANEOUS

Gas lighting is approved for Capitol grounds in Washington, D.C.

The *Phoenix* sinks off Sheboygan, Wis., taking 148 lives, 127 of them immigrants arriving from Holland.

★ *1848* ★

INTERNATIONAL

Treaty of Guadelupe Hidalgo ends Mexican War (February 2), results in Mexico giving up claim to Texas, New Mexico, and California; 1,193,061 square miles are added to U.S.; Mexico ratifies treaty (March 25), Senate ratifies (July 4); U.S. has lost during Mexican War 1,721 men in battle and 11,155 from disease, 4,102 are wounded; military expenditures are $97.5 million.

Treaty of New Granada (Colombia), signed in 1846, is ratified by Senate (June 3); gives U.S. right of way across Isthmus of Panama.

NATIONAL

James W. Marshall discovers (January 24) gold on American River near Coloma, Calif., touching off gold rush that will bring 200,000 persons to California over the following four years.

First election on uniform Election Day (see 1845) is won by Zachary Taylor, Whig Party candidate, by 163 electoral votes (1,360,101 popular) over Lewis Cass, Democratic candidate; Cass receives 127 electoral and 1,220,544 popular votes; Millard Fillmore is elected vice president.

First women's rights convention opens in Seneca Falls, N.Y. (July 19), organized by Lucretia Mott and Elizabeth Cady Stanton; advocates women's suffrage, issues declaration modeled on Declaration of Independence.

Wisconsin is admitted as 30th state (May 29); adopts constitution (March 13) that forbids slavery.

Oregon Territory is established (August 14); Illinois voters ratify their constitution (March 5).

President James K. Polk lays cornerstone for Washington Monument; work is delayed for years by lack of funds.

Failure of a revolution in Germany starts great German migration to U.S.; nearly 600,000 will immigrate to the U.S. between 1851 and 1855.

Former President John Quincy Adams (1825–1829), a member of House of Representatives,

Fortune seekers searching for gold in California. THE GRANGER COLLECTION, NEW YORK

suffers cerebral stroke on House floor (February 21); dies two days later.

BUSINESS/INDUSTRY/INVENTIONS

Chicago Board of Trade is organized.

Antoine Zarega establishes macaroni factory; Oliver F. Winchester opens shirt factory in New York City.

DEATH Simon Willard, clockmaker who developed "banjo" clock.

TRANSPORTATION

Illinois Canal connecting Lake Michigan and Mississippi River opens.

U.S. Mail Steamship Co. begins regular service from New York to Charleston, S. C., New Orleans, Havana, and Panama; Pacific Mail Steamship Co., service between Panama, San Francisco, and Oregon.

Chicago & North Western Railroad is chartered as Galena & Chicago Union, first road to serve Chicago.

SCIENCE/MEDICINE

Congress passes Pure Food and Drug law to prevent import of adulterated drugs and regulate food and drug production.

Homeopathic Medical College, first such school, opens in Philadelphia.

First women's medical school in U.S. is organized in Boston (later merges with Boston University Medical).

Cholera epidemic strikes New York City; more than 5,000 die.

M. Waldo Hanchet patents a dental chair.

George F. and W. C. Bond discover Hyperion, eighth satellite of Saturn.

EDUCATION

New colleges/universities include Girard College (Philadelphia), University of Wisconsin.

Georgia School for the Deaf opens.

RELIGION

Rev. John M. Odin becomes first Catholic bishop of Texas.

ART/MUSIC

Stephen Foster writes songs "Old Uncle Ned" and "Oh! Susanna;" other popular songs include "Sweet Alice."

Musical Fund Society holds its first concert season in Boston's Tremont Temple.

DEATH Thomas Cole, a founder of Hudson River School of landscape painting.

LITERATURE/JOURNALISM

Associated Press is founded by a group of New York newspapers.

Toledo Blade is founded; first European edition of U.S. newspaper (*American Sun*) is established by Moses Yale Beach, publisher of *New York Sun*.

G. P. Putnam & Son, publisher, is established.

BOOKS *Biglow Papers* and *The Vision of Sir Launfal* by James Russell Lowell, *Life in the Far West* by George F. Ruxton, *Red Oak Openings* by James Fenimore Cooper.

ENTERTAINMENT

Benjamin Baker's play *A Glance at New York* and William E. Burton's *Toodles* are produced.

Broadway Theater, New York City, installs "air conditioning," promising 3,000 feet of cool air per minute.

SPORTS

First gymnastic organization in U.S., Cincinnati Turnegemeinde, is founded by German immigrants.

First rowing regatta is held on Hudson River at Peekskill, N.Y.

MISCELLANEOUS

Gaslights turn on for first time in White House (December 29).

Steamer *Seabird* catches fire at dock in Cape Girardeau, Mo., explodes, damages St. Vincent College buildings.

1849

NATIONAL

Department of the Interior is created as the Home Department (March 3); Thomas Ewing the first Secretary.

Temporary government is created in San Francisco area (February 12); convention held in Monterey (September 1) drafts constitution that prohibits slavery; is ratified by voters (November 13); temporary state government functions (December 20).

Mormons establish State of Deseret with Salt Lake City the capital, Brigham Young governor (March 4); lasts only a year until it becomes Territory of Utah; Minnesota territorial government is created.

New Kentucky state constitution is adopted.

Supreme Court rules unconstitutional New York and Massachussetts laws that call for a head tax on each alien brought into the state.

Ft. Worth, Tex., is established as a military outpost.

DEATHS Former President Polk (1845–1849); former First Lady Dolley Madison (1809–1817).

BUSINESS/INDUSTRY/INVENTIONS

Waltham Watch Co. is established in Roxbury, Mass., as American Horologe Co.; M. Heminway Sons in Watertown, Conn., begin to produce silk thread on spools.

Walter Hunt of New York City patents safety pin (sold rights for $100); Ichabod Washburn develops gauge to standardize size of drawn wire.

TRANSPORTATION

Chicago, Burlington & Quincy Railroad begins to operate.

Wheeling (W.Va.) Bridge over Ohio River opens, then world's longest (1,000+ feet).

Asa Whitney forms company to manufacture an improved cast-iron railroad-car wheel he invents.

SCIENCE/MEDICINE

Elizabeth Blackwell becomes first woman physician in U.S. (January 23) upon graduating from Geneva (N.Y.) Medical Institute.

St. Vincent's Hospital in New York City opens.

Yellow fever epidemic hits southern cities.

RELIGION

Disciples of Christ church holds first general convention; American Christian Missionary Society is organized.

DEATH William Miller, clergyman who predicted Second Coming (1843–1844), a founder of Adventist church.

ART/MUSIC

Mendelssohn Quintet Club, first U.S. chamber music group, gives first concert.

A new brass instrument, the saxophone, arrives from Belgium.

Asher B. Durand completes the painting *Kindred Spirits*.

SONGS (popular): "Nelly Bly" and "Nelly Was a Lady" by Stephen Foster; "What Was Your Name in the States?"

DEATH Edward Hicks, American primitivist painter.

LITERATURE/JOURNALISM

Amelia J. Bloomer founds *Lily*, a newspaper for women.

First Minnesota newspaper, *Minnesota Pioneer*, begins publication.

BOOKS *Poems* by John Greenleaf Whittier, *A Week on the Concord and Merrimack Rivers* by Henry David Thoreau, *The Oregon Trail* by Francis Parkman, *The Seaside and the Fireside* (poetry) by

Cartoon satirically proposing a device that will enable persons afflicted with Gold Rush fever to reach California in record time. Note the man at the right who will chop through the knot and cause the enormous rubber band to snap these eager fortune seekers right across the country to their destination. THE GRANGER COLLECTION, NEW YORK

Henry Wadsworth Longfellow, *Mardi* by Herman Melville, *Prairie Flower* by Emerson Bennett.

DEATH Edgar Allan Poe, author and poet.

ENTERTAINMENT

Astor Place (New York City) riot occurs (May 10) when partisans of American actor Edwin Forrest and English actor William C. Macready clash in outbreak of anti-British feeling; 22 die, 36 are injured when militia fires into crowd.

Edwin Booth debuts in *Richard III*; Joseph Jefferson in *Jonathan Bradford*.

Bella Union, a combination saloon, gambling house, and variety theater, opens in San Francisco.

SPORTS

Hambletonian, great sire of standardbred horses, is foaled; 95% of harness racehorses trace ancestry to him.

Tom Hyer, unofficial U.S. bare-knuckle champion, knocks out Yankee Sullivan; it is Hyer's final fight because no one challenges him.

Philadelphia Skaters Club is founded.

MISCELLANEOUS

Fire in St. Louis destroys 400 buildings, 27 ships; cholera epidemic follows.

Abraham Lincoln receives patent on inflatable cylinders to buoy vessels over shoals; is never used.

Two-day poultry show is held in Boston Public Garden; 1,423 specimens are displayed.

1850

INTERNATIONAL

Clayton-Bulwer Treaty is ratified (July 4); U.S. and Great Britain agree to a plan for a canal across Panama Isthmus; to be built by private enterprise.

NATIONAL

Vice President Millard Fillmore becomes president on the death of President Zachary Taylor (July 9) at 66 from coronary thrombosis.

Henry Clay engineers Compromise of 1850 to resolve differences over slavery; provides for admission of California as a free state, creation of territories of New Mexico and Utah; California is admitted as 31st state (September 9); territorial governments are formed in Minnesota, Michigan, and New Mexico.

Fugitive Slave Act is adopted, places fugitive slave cases under federal jurisdiction, designed to halt runaway slaves, requires return of slaves to owners, results in kidnappings and start of Underground Railway; slave trade in Washington, D.C., is abolished, effective January 1, 1851.

Week-long convention of nine slave states in Nashville calls for extending the Missouri Compromise line to Pacific Ocean; Southern Rights Assn. organizes in South Carolina to resist antislavery action.

Seventh census reports nation's population at 23,191,876.

National women's rights convention is held in Worcester, Mass.

First overland monthly mail route west of Missouri River between Independence, Mo., and Salt Lake City is first traveled.

Los Angeles, San Francisco, and San Diego are incorporated as cities.

DEATHS Two former vice presidents, John C. Calhoun (1825–1832) and Richard M. Johnson (1837–1841).

BUSINESS/INDUSTRY/INVENTIONS

American Express Co. is formed by merger of two smaller companies.

Allen Pinkerton founds National Detective Agency in Chicago.

New York Produce Exchange is established.

James H. Knapp begins to manufacture derby hats in South Norwalk, Conn.; Ichabod Washburn begins to manufacture piano wire in Worcester, Mass.; Henry Waterman builds first platform elevator in New York City.

INVENTIONS John E. Heath, an agricultural binder; D. D. Parmelee of New Paltz, N.Y., an adding machine; Abner Cutler of Buffalo, N.Y., a rolltop desk; Benjamin J. Lane, a gas mask with a self-contained breathing apparatus.

Henry Brown, a slave, has managed to escape from Richmond to Philadelphia in a box labeled "This side up with care." Frederick Douglass is shown second from left. THE GRANGER COLLECTION, NEW YORK

National cotton production is 2,133,000 bales.

TRANSPORTATION

Chesapeake & Ohio Canal, connecting Chesapeake Bay and Ohio River, is completed.

Louisville & Nashville Railroad is incorporated; Congress authorizes land grants in Midwest to stimulate railroad building.

Collins Line begins regular transatlantic service between U.S. and Great Britain; Donald McKay builds his first clipper ship, *Stag Hound*.

SCIENCE/MEDICINE

New York University Medical School is founded.

Elizabeth Blackwell, first American woman medical graduate, opens private clinic in New York City; clinic becomes New York Infirmary (1857).

Cholera epidemic sweeps through Midwest.

Astronomer William C. Bond photographs Vega, the first star to be photographed.

EDUCATION

University of Rochester, Dayton (Ohio), and Utah colleges open.

University of Pennsylvania creates first U.S. history chair.

Louisiana University (Tulane) offers first business course.

College of Charleston (S.C.) creates first college museum.

Public library is established in Wayland, Mass., the first to be established by a gift that is matched by town and is supported by regular tax funds.

RELIGION

American Bible Union is founded.

John Hughes becomes first Catholic archbishop of New York.

James Jesse Strang, founder of a Mormon sect, has himself crowned king.

DEATHS Adoniram Judson, Baptist missionary to Burma; Catholic Bishop Bernard J. Flaget, who served area between Alleghenies and Mississippi River (1810–1850).

ART/MUSIC

Boston Music School is founded.

George F. Bristow's opera *Rip van Winkle* opens in New York City.

Chicago Philharmonic Society is founded.

George C. Bingham completes the painting *Shooting the Beef*.

SONGS (popular): "Camptown Races," "Frankie and Johnny," "It Came Upon a Midnight Clear," "Sacramento," "Santa Lucia."

LITERATURE/JOURNALISM

Harper's New Monthly Magazine is founded; Timothy S. Arthur publishes *Arthur's Home Gazette*.

New newspapers include *Sacramento* (Cal.) *Transcript*, *Weekly Oregonian* in Portland.

BOOKS *The Scarlet Letter* by Nathaniel Hawthorne, *White Jacket* by Herman Melville, *The Wide, Wide World* by Susan B. Warner, *Representative Men* by Ralph Waldo Emerson.

DEATH Sarah Margaret Fuller, first woman professional journalist and foreign correspondent.

ENTERTAINMENT

Jenny Lind, the "Swedish nightingale," begins American tour arranged by P. T. Barnum; occasion brings on first ticket speculators.

Brougham Lyceum (later Wallack Theater) opens in New York City.

SPORTS

Six gymnastic societies create first national turner (gymnast) organization, Turnersbund, in Philadelphia.

Michael Phelan writes first American billiards book, *Billiards Without a Master*.

MISCELLANEOUS

First bathtub is installed in the White House.

Congress abolishes flogging in the navy.

Fire aboard the steamship *Griffith* on Lake Erie kills 300.

Brooklyn Institute imports eight pairs of English sparrows to kill caterpillars; by 1890 New York City will have to import starlings to prey on the sparrows.

1851

INTERNATIONAL

Southern volunteers, led by Narciso Lopez, leader of Cuban refugees in U.S., land about 60 miles from Havana (August 11) in an effort to spur an uprising against the government; uprising does not materialize; about 50 Southerners and Gen. Lopez are captured and later executed. Anti-Spanish riots occur (August 21) in New Orleans because of the episode.

NATIONAL

Three states approve new constitutions: Indiana (February 10), Ohio (March 10), and Maryland (June 4).

Treaty of Traverse des Sioux is signed with bands of Sioux; they cede about a third of land that will become Minnesota.

President Millard Fillmore lays cornerstone to south House extension of the Capitol.

Postal rates are reduced to 3 cents for a half-ounce for up to 3,000 miles; Congress authorizes issuance of silver 3-cent coin.

New York Navy Yard opens 307-foot dock.

U.S. Soldiers Home in Washington, D.C., is authorized.

BUSINESS/INDUSTRY/INVENTIONS

Isaac M. Singer patents an improved sewing machine; by 1860 is world's foremost sewing machine manufacturer.

William Kelly, an ironmaster, develops process for converting pig iron into steel by directing air on molten metal.

Commercial power laundry opens in Oakland, Calif.

Wells Fargo & Co. is founded to handle express business to California following the discovery of gold.

Western Union is organized as New York & Mis-sissippi Valley Printing Telegraph Co. in Mahwah, N.J.; will become Western Union in 1856.

TRANSPORTATION

Boston celebrates completion of railroads connecting it with Montreal, the Great Lakes, and 13 states.

Two railroads are completed: Erie, from Piermont to Dunkirk, N.Y.; Hudson River, from Albany to New York City.

Wire suspension railroad bridge over Kentucky River at Frankfort is completed.

Clipper ship *Flying Record* sets record of 89 days from New York to San Francisco via Cape Horn.

Charles G. Page of Washington develops motors that propel an experimental locomotive up to 20 miles per hour.

DEATH Henry M. Shreve, established praticability of steam navigation on Mississippi River; Shreveport, La., named for him.

SCIENCE/MEDICINE

John Allen, a dentist, perfects a type of denture still in use.

American Veterinary Journal is founded.

DEATH Sylvanus Graham, food reformer and advocate of whole wheat; developed graham cracker.

EDUCATION

Boston Public Library is founded; Massachusetts passes law that permits towns to levy taxes to support libraries.

New colleges include Northwestern University (Evanston, Ill.), Westminster College (Fulton, Mo.), University of Minnesota, and Santa Clara University.

DEATH Thomas Gallaudet, educator of the deaf.

RELIGION

Rev. Christian B. Willerup organizes Scandinavian Methodist Episcopal church in Cambridge, Wis.

In Herman Melville's famous novel, first published in 1851, Captain Ahab is determined to capture Moby-Dick, a great white whale that tore off his leg years ago. Rockwell Kent's classic illustrations capture the power of the story. Courtesy of the Rockwell Kent Legacies. THE GRANGER COLLECTION, NEW YORK

Bishop Francis P. Kenrick is named Catholic archbishop of Baltimore.

ART/MUSIC

Emanuel Leutze completes the painting *Washington Crossing the Delaware*.

SONGS (popular): "Arkansas Traveler," "Ring de Banjo," and "Old Folks at Home" ("Swanee River"), all by Stephen Foster; "Wait for the Wagon." (Foster's "Old Folks" sold 130,000 copies of sheet music in 1851.)

LITERATURE/ JOURNALISM

Harriet Beecher Stowe's anti-slavery novel *Uncle Tom's Cabin* begins to appear in serial form in the *National Era* (Washington, D.C.); other books are Nathaniel Hawthorne's *The House of Seven Gables* and Herman Melville's *Moby-Dick*.

Henry J. Raymond founds *The New York Times*, Joseph Medill the *Cleveland Leader*.

DEATH James Fenimore Cooper, author.

SPORTS

John C. Stevens's yacht *America* wins first America's Cup race, beating 17 British boats around the Isle of Wight, England (August 22).

In second baseball game of record, New York Knickerbockers are first to wear uniforms: straw hats, white shirts, full-length blue trousers.

Union Boat Club of Boston is founded.

James Lee and William Decker have a 5-mile sculling race around Bedloe's Island (New York Harbor); an estimated $100,000 is bet on the outcome; Decker wins $900 purse.

MISCELLANEOUS

Young Men's Christian Assn. is organized in Boston.

Three major fires occur: San Francisco (May 3), 1,500 homes are destroyed; large part of St. Louis is destroyed (May 4); 35,000 of 55,000 books in Library of Congress are destroyed.

Soft felt hats for women are introduced.

1852

INTERNATIONAL

Plan is approved to send Commodore Matthew C. Perry to Japan in effort to promote trade.

NATIONAL

Franklin Pierce is nominated on 49th ballot of Democratic convention; is elected president defeating Whig candidate Winfield Scott by 254 electoral votes to 42 (1,601,474 popular votes to 1,386,578).

Vermont, Rhode Island, and Minnesota Territory pass statewide prohibition laws.

Louisiana residents ratify their constitution.

DEATHS Two former first ladies, Margaret S. Taylor (1849–1850) and Louisa C. Adams (1825–1829); two noted legislators, Daniel Webster and Henry Clay; William King, first governor of Maine.

BUSINESS/INDUSTRY/INVENTIONS

Elisha G. Otis invents the first passenger elevator with a safety guard to keep it from falling.

Moses G. Farmer and W. F. Channing perfect an electric fire-alarm system that is installed in Boston.

Potter Palmer opens dry goods store in Chicago.

Ohio enacts law that sets a 10-hour maximum workday for women and children under 18.

National Typographical Union is organized.

National Society of Civil Engineers is founded in New York City.

Richard King in Texas starts what becomes the largest U.S. ranch (600,000 acres).

DEATHS Eli Terry, clockmaker; Amos Lawrence, textile manufacturer.

TRANSPORTATION

Clement Studebaker and his brothers found wagon company, which later becomes an automobile manufacturer.

First through-train from East arrives in Chicago; Pennsylvania Railroad is completed between Philadelphia and Pittsburgh.

SCIENCE/MEDICINE

American Pharmaceutical Assn. is organized in Philadelphia.

Mt. Sinai Hospital opens in New York City.

American Geographical Society is founded in New York City.

EDUCATION

Compulsory school attendance law is passed in

An American bookseller's announcement for *Uncle Tom's Cabin*, the novel by Harriet Beecher Stowe, published in 1852. THE GRANGER COLLECTION, NEW YORK

Massachusetts, requires 12 weeks of schooling annually for those between 8 and 14.

Three colleges are chartered: Tufts (Medford, Mass.); Antioch (Ohio); and Normal, which will later become Duke University (Durham, N.C.).

RELIGION

First session of Roman Catholic National Council is held in Baltimore.

Brigham Young, head of Mormon church, announces policy sanctioning multiple marriages, resulting in formation of a dissident group, Reorganized Church of Jesus Christ of Latter-Day Saints.

Antoinette L. B. Blackwell becomes first formally appointed American woman pastor when she is named by South Butler (N.Y.) Congregational church.

John H. Neumann becomes Catholic bishop of Philadelphia; Episcopal Bishop Thomas C. Brownell of Connecticut becomes presiding bishop.

DEATH Philander Chase, presiding American Episcopal bishop (1843–1852).

ART/MUSIC

New York Academy of Music opens.

Journal of Music, edited by John S. Dwight, begins publication.

Frederick E. Church completes the painting *Catskill Mountains*.

Stephen Foster writes the song "Massa's in de Cold, Cold Ground"; another popular song is "Row, Row, Row Your Boat."

DEATH John H. Payne, who wrote lyrics for "Home, Sweet Home."

LITERATURE/JOURNALISM

Two publishing firms are founded: Houghton Mifflin and E. P. Dutton.

BOOKS *Uncle Tom's Cabin* by Harriet Beecher Stowe, which will sell 300,000 copies in the first year; *The Curse of Clifton* by E. D. Southworth; *Pierre* by Herman Melville.

St. Louis Globe-Democrat begins publication as the *Missouri Democrat; Columbia*, first newspaper in Washington State, is founded.

ENTERTAINMENT

The play *The Silver Spoon* by Joseph S. Jones is produced.

The *Floating Palace*, a Mississippi River showboat, begins to operate.

DEATH Junius B. Booth, Shakespearean actor.

SPORTS

Harvard beats Yale in first eight-oared intercollegiate boat race.

John C. Morrissey claims heavyweight boxing title.

New York Gothams baseball club is formed.

MISCELLANEOUS

Frank H. T. Bellow draws first cartoon of Uncle Sam as the symbol of the nation; it appears in the comic weekly, *Lantern*.

1853

INTERNATIONAL

James Gadsden, minister to Mexico, completes U.S. purchase from Mexico of 29,640 square miles of what becomes southern Arizona and New Mexico for $15 million (later reduced to $10 million) (December 30).

Commodore Matthew C. Perry arrives in Edo (Tokyo) Bay, delivers to Japanese officials a letter from President Millard Fillmore who seeks to open trade with Japan (July 14).

NATIONAL

William R. de Vane King, vice president–elect, is sworn in at Havana where he goes for his health (March 4); dies at his home in Alabama (April 17) before assuming office.

First U.S. world's fair, Exhibition of Industry of All Nations, opens in New York City's Crystal Palace (July 4).

Washington Territory is created out of northern Oregon.

Michigan enacts a prohibition law.

Salary of vice president increases from $5,000 to $8,000.

Andrew Johnson begins first of two 2-year terms as Tennessee governor.

DEATH Former First Lady Abigail P. Fillmore.

BUSINESS/INDUSTRY/INVENTIONS

New York Clearing House is organized by 38 New York City banks, the first U.S. bank clearing house.

Seth Thomas Clock Co. is organized; Bausch & Lomb Optical Co. is established.

Elisha G. Otis installs a safety elevator in New York City, begins to manufacture elevators.

E. E. Matteson perfects sluicing process in mining.

Edward Clark and Isaac M. Singer open sewing-machine factory in New York City.

Alexander B. Latta of Cincinnati develops a practical fire engine.

Gail Borden develops evaporated milk, various juice concentrates.

DEATH Anson G. Phelps, cofounder of Phelps-Dodge Copper Co.

TRANSPORTATION

New York Central Railroad is formed by merger of 10 roads and Lehigh Valley Railroad.

Steamer *Eclipse* sets record of 4 days, 9 hours, 30 minutes for trip from New Orleans to Louisville.

Indianapolis opens Union Station to serve five railroads.

SCIENCE/MEDICINE

Dudley Observatory is established in Albany, N.Y.

Yellow fever epidemic hits New Orleans; more than 5,000 die in next two years.

EDUCATION

Four new colleges are founded: Manhattan (Riverdale, N.Y.); Washington University (St. Louis) as Eliot Seminary; Florida University; and Willamette University (Salem, Ore.).

Horace Mann becomes president of Antioch College.

RELIGION

Catholic Bishop Jose S. Alemany becomes first archbishop of San Francisco; Rev. James R. Bayley first Catholic bishop of Newark; Jean B. Lamy Catholic bishop of Santa Fe.

Thomas B. Atkinson becomes Episcopal bishop of North Carolina.

ART/MUSIC

Henry Steinway & Sons, piano manufacturers, is established in New York City.

George F. Root founds New York [City] Normal School to train music teachers.

Bronze equestrian statue of Andrew Jackson by Clark Mills is unveiled in Lafayette Park, Washington, D.C.; the first U.S. equestrian work.

SONGS (popular): "My Old Kentucky Home" by Stephen Foster, "Good Night Ladies," "Old Dog Tray," "Pop Goes the Weasel," "Sweet Betsy From Pike."

LITERATURE/JOURNALISM

Country Gentleman and *Putnam's Monthly* magazines are founded.

Sales of Harriet Beecher Stowe's *Uncle Tom's Cabin* reach 1.2 million copies.

ENTERTAINMENT

John Drew and wife, Louisa, found successful stock company at Arch St. Theater in Philadelphia.

Two new plays are produced: *Leonor de Guzman* by G. H. Boker and *Uncle Tom's Cabin* by G. L. Aiken.

Buckley's Serenaders, one of first professional American musical groups, make transcontinental tour.

SPORTS

First newspaper story about baseball appears in *New York Mercury*.

Upperville (Va.) Colt and Horse Show is inaugurated.

MISCELLANEOUS

Elisha Kent Kane and crew leave New York City in the *Advance* on an unsuccessful Arctic expedition.

Children's Aid Society is founded in New York City by Charles Loring Brace.

The Bloomer costume, popularized by Amelia Jenks Bloomer. Lithograph by Nathanial Currier. THE GRANGER COLLECTION, NEW YORK

Police in New York City are first to wear uniforms and official caps; police in Boston and Philadelphia are soon to do the same.

Large crowds come to hear Amelia Bloomer speak about women's rights in New York City and other towns in New York state, many curious to see the loose trousers she advocates as women's wear ("bloomers").

1854

INTERNATIONAL

Commodore Matthew C. Perry returns to Japan; signs Treaty of Kanagawa (March 31); ports of Shimoda and Hakodate are opened to U.S. trade.

Canadian Reciprocity Treaty is signed (June 5), grants the U.S. fishing privileges along Maritime Provinces and the British privileges along U.S. shores to 36th parallel.

Senate ratifies Gadsden Purchase (April 22) by which U.S. adds 29,640 square miles of territory in Arizona and New Mexico.

NATIONAL

Kansas-Nebraska Act is passed (May 22), creating two new territories; effectively repeals Compro-mise of 1820 by permitting them to decide on slavery when they reach statehood.

Republican Party is formed in Ripon, Wis.; be-comes national organization in 1856. Republicans oppose extension of slavery to the territories.

Massachusetts Emigrant Aid Society organizes to promote settlement of antislavery groups in Kan-sas.

Large-scale immigration of Chinese begins with arrival of 13,000; previous annual high was 42; most come to work on building railroad.

Abraham Lincoln makes his first public condem-nation of slavery in speeches in Springfield and Peoria, Ill.

Connecticut passes prohibition law.

Henry David Thoreau near Walden Pond. Painting by Tom Lovell. CORBIS-BETTMANN

BUSINESS/INDUSTRY/ INVENTIONS

Pennsylvania Rock Oil Co., first American oil company, is incor-porated.

Burleight Blanket Mills is estab-lished at South Berwick, Me.; first iron structural beams are built for fire-retardant build-ings; Ferdinand Schumacher founds German Mills American Oatmeal Co., first American oat-meal maker.

Aaron H. Allen of Boston pat-ents folding theater chair; Wal-ter Hunt invents disposable paper collar; J. Cutting of Bos-ton patents nitrocellulose film for photography.

Alvin Adams delivery service be-comes Adams Express Co., dominates delivery business in east and south 1840–1860.

Hat Finishers Union is organ-ized in Danbury, Conn.

Henry Smith and Daniel Wesson invent a revolver.

DEATH Duncan Phyfe, furniture maker.

TRANSPORTATION

Cornerstone is laid for first railroad bridge across Mississippi River (Rock Island, Ill., to Davenport, Iowa).

Illinois Central Railroad construction reaches Chicago; Chicago & Rock Island is first to reach Mississippi River from the east.

SCIENCE/MEDICINE

Nursery and Child's Hospital in New York City opens.

U.S. Inebriates Asylum in Binghamton, N.Y., is incorporated.

EDUCATION

New York's Astor Library opens.

RELIGION

Carl F. W. Walther, cofounder, becomes president of Concordia Theological Seminary; Rev. John Williams begins 45 years as dean of Berkeley Divinity School (Middletown, Conn.).

Two new Episcopal bishops are named: Horatio Potter of New York and Thomas M. Clark of Rhode Island.

First Protestant church (Baptist) in New Mexico is dedicated in Santa Fe.

Evangelical Lutheran Synod of Iowa is organized.

ART/MUSIC

Mason & Hamlin Organ Co. (also produced pianos) is founded in Boston.

George C. Bingham completes the painting *Stump Speaking*.

SONGS (popular): "Hard Times Come Again No More," "Jeannie with the Light Brown Hair," "Carnival of Venice."

LITERATURE/JOURNALISM

New newspapers include *Chicago Times*; *St. Paul (Minn.) Pioneer Press*; and *Nebraska Palladium* (Bellevue), the first paper in the state.

BOOKS *Ten Nights in a Barroom* by Timothy S. Arthur, *Maude Miller* (poetry) by John Greenleaf Whittier, *Leather Stocking and Silk* by J. E. Cooke; *Struggles and Triumphs* by P. T. Barnum, *The Lamplighter* by Marie S. Cummins, *Walden* by Henry David Thoreau.

DEATH Anne N. Royall, travel writer and journalist.

SPORTS

Knickerbocker Club and New York Gothams play to 12–12 tie, the first tie and first baseball game where record is kept by innings. Three new clubs are formed: the Eagles and Empires in New York City, the Excelsiors in South Brooklyn.

MISCELLANEOUS

First baby show is held in Springfield, Ohio, with 127 entries.

Worcester, Mass., creates first U.S. city park (Elm Park).

Philadelphia begins to use a street-cleaning machine.

First international convention of YMCA is held in Boston; first American YMCA is founded in Buffalo, N.Y.

Christian Metz leads members of his Community of True Inspiration from Ebenezer, N.Y., to a more spacious area in Iowa; it becomes the Amana Society.

Collins Line steamer *Arctic* sinks near Cape Race after collision, 300 perish; river steamer *Sultana* explodes, sinks near Memphis, 1,450 are killed.

1855

INTERNATIONAL

Arbitration awards U.S. $119,330 in 1841 *Creole* case.

NATIONAL

U.S. Court of Claims is established (February 24).

Kansas ratifies its state constitution, with the slavery issue still undecided.

Congress authorizes construction of telegraph line from Mississippi River to Pacific Ocean.

Law is passed to provide citizenship to children born abroad to U.S. citizens and to alien wives of U.S. citizens.

Massachusetts becomes first state to create an insurance department; New Hampshire enacts prohibition law.

Approximately 400,000 immigrants arrive in New York City during year; Castle Garden in New York is nation's immigration station (until 1892).

Frederick Douglass, author of *My Bondage, My Freedom*, published in 1855. LIBRARY OF CONGRESS

BUSINESS/INDUSTRY/INVENTIONS

Dr. Abraham Gesner patents process for manufacture of kerosene; James Oliver develops the chilled plow.

Dr. Samuel M. Kier of Pittsburgh builds small oil refinery; Sewell Newhouse of Oneida, N.Y., begins to manufacture steel animal traps.

Journeyman Stone Cutters Assn. is established.

Boston Clearing House opens.

TRANSPORTATION

Railroad makes first crossing over Mississippi River on the bridge that connects Rock Island, Ill., and Davenport, Iowa (April 21).

American Soo (Sault Ste. Marie) Canal is completed.

At Niagara Falls suspension bridge over gorge opens.

SCIENCE/MEDICINE

Women's Hospital in New York City opens.

Matthew F. Maury produces first work of modern oceanography, *Physical Geography of the Sea and Its Meteorology*.

Boston Veterinary Institute is incorporated.

DEATH John Gorrie, who developed mechanical refrigeration while trying to cure fevers.

EDUCATION

Mrs. Carl Schurz opens first German-type kindergarten in Watertown, Wis.

New colleges/universities include California College, which will become University of California; Michigan State; Iowa Wesleyan College; Pennsylvania State University (Penn State, originally Farmers' High School); Elmira (N.Y.) Female College.

American Journal of Education is founded and edited by Henry Barnard.

RELIGION

Garrett Theological Seminary (Evanston, Ill.) opens.

First Jewish rabbinical conference is held in Cincinnati.

ART/MUSIC

Joshua C. Stoddard patents a calliope, organizes American Steam Music Co.

Carl Zerrahu organizes Boston Philharmonic Orchestra.

George Inness completes the painting *The Lackawanna Valley*; Frederick E. Church, *Heart of the Andes*; John Quidor, *Ichabod Crane at the Ball*.

SONGS (popular): "Come Where My Love Lies Dreaming," "Listen to the Mocking Bird," "Londonderry Air."

LITERATURE/JOURNALISM

Former slave Frederick Douglass writes autobiography, *My Bondage, My Freedom*.

San Francisco Bulletin is founded.

BOOKS *Familiar Quotations* by John Bartlett, *The Age of Fable* by Thomas Bulfinch, *Leaves of Grass* (poetry) by Walt Whitman, *The Song of Hiawatha* (poetry) by Henry Wadsworth Longfellow, *The Prince of the House of David* by Joseph H. Ingraham.

ENTERTAINMENT

George H. Boker writes the popular play *Francesca Da Rimini*; John Brougham, the plays *The Game of Love* and *Pocahontas*.

Sanford's Minstrels begin to perform in Philadelphia.

SPORTS

Harvard beats Yale in a crew race on the Connecticut River.

New York Caledonian Curling Club is founded.

Eight new baseball clubs form in New York area.

MISCELLANEOUS

American Printing House for the Blind opens in Louisville, Ky.

NATIONAL

Kansas civil war breaks out over slavery; proslavery forces take Lawrence (May 21); in retribution, John Brown and a band of antislavery activists raid Pottawatomie, Kans., execute five proslavery settlers; guerrilla warfare follows. President Franklin Pierce appoints a territorial governor who, with federal troops, brings about temporary peace.

James Buchanan nominated by Democrats on 17th ballot, wins presidency over John C. Frémont, is selected by Republicans meeting in their first convention; Buchanan receives 174 electoral votes (1,927,995 popular), Frémont 114 electoral votes (1,391,555 popular), and former President Millard Fillmore, nominee of the American (Know-Nothing) Party, 8 electoral votes (874,534 popular).

1856

Senator Charles Sumner of Massachusetts denounces proslavery acts in Kansas, criticizes Southern senators, including Andrew P. Butler of South Carolina; Rep. Preston S. Brooks, Butler's nephew, attacks Sumner with his cane; Sumner never fully recovers from the beating; Brooks resigns from the House.

Use of adhesive postage stamps is made mandatory.

BUSINESS/INDUSTRY/INVENTIONS

Gail Borden receives patent for "the concentration of milk" (condensed milk); this launches development of instant foods such as juices and dried meat.

Sir Henry Bessemer's process for making steel is introduced in U.S.

1856

Iron and steel manufacturing in Pittsburgh. The Bessemer process, introduced in 1856, will enable factories to make steel from pig iron.
THE GRANGER COLLECTION, NEW YORK

Borax is discovered by Dr. John A. Veatch in Tehama County, Calif.; commercial production begins in 1864.

Five patents on various sewing machines are combined by Isaac Singer, Elias Howe, and Allen B. Wilson, allowing manufacture until patents expire in 1870s.

Charles E. Barnes of Lowell, Mass., patents a machine gun; Cullen Whipple of Providence patents a machine to make pointed screws; Abraham Gesner becomes first to market a coal-oil illuminant, "kerosine"; Hamilton L. Smith patents a tintype photograph process.

Corliss Steam Engine Co. is founded in Providence, R.I.

Bank clearing houses open in Philadelphia, Baltimore, and Cleveland.

United Cigarmakers Union is founded in New York City.

DEATH Cyrus Alger, designer of first rifled-barrel gun.

TRANSPORTATION

First street railroad in New England opens between Boston and Cambridge.

Illinois Central Railroad is completed from Cairo to Chicago.

DEATH Robert L. Stevens, inventor of T-rail for railroads.

SCIENCE/MEDICINE

Bellevue Hospital Medical College is established.

EDUCATION

New colleges include St. Lawrence University (Canton, N.Y.); Niagara University (Niagara Falls); and Auburn University.

RELIGION

Henry M. Dexter begins 34 years as editor-in-chief of *The Congregationalist.*

ART/MUSIC

Philadelphia Academy of Music opens.

Henry K. Brown completes bronze equestrian statue of George Washington; Clifton W. Tayleure, the painting *Horseshoe Robinson.*

Benjamin Hanby writes the song, "Darling Nelly Gray."

LITERATURE/JOURNALISM

Copyright law is enacted to protect dramatists' work from piracy.

Cyrus Chambers Jr. invents a machine to fold paper for books and magazines.

BOOKS *The Panorama* by John Greenleaf Whittier, *Arctic Explorations* by Elisha K. Kane, *Lena Rivers* by Mary Jane Holmes, *The Lost Hunter* by John T. Adams, *The Piazza Tales* by Herman Melville.

ENTERTAINMENT
Sidney F. Bateman's play *Self* is produced.

SPORTS
Chicago Unions, first baseball club in the city, is organized; four new clubs form in New York City area and Hoboken, N.J.

INTERNATIONAL
U.S. and Japan sign agreement to allow ships to use port of Nagasaki.

1857

Perforated postage stamps come into general use.

U.S. National Museum is established.

DEATH Elisha K. Kane, Arctic explorer.

NATIONAL
Supreme Court decides the landmark Dred Scott Case (March 6); Scott, a slave, sued for his freedom in Missouri courts (1846) on the grounds that his residence in a free state (Illinois) and territory (Wisconsin) made him a free man. Decision says that Scott is not a citizen and therefore is not entitled to sue in federal court, that his residence in a free state does not set him free, and that the Missouri Compromise, which forbids slavery in Wisconsin Territory, is unconstitutional.

Tariff is reduced to general level of 20%; list of free imports expands.

Residents of Minnesota and Oregon ratify their constitutions.

President James Buchanan declares Utah Territory to be in rebellion; names Alfred Cumming governor.

New House of Representatives chamber in Capitol is completed.

First overland stage arrives in San Diego, Calif., from San Antonio, Tex.

BUSINESS/INDUSTRY/INVENTIONS
Failure of New York City branch of Ohio Life Insurance Co. touches off commercial and financial panic (August 24), which is created by overspeculation in railroad securities and real estate.

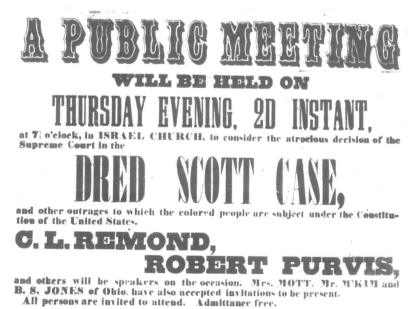

A PUBLIC MEETING
WILL BE HELD ON
THURSDAY EVENING, 2D INSTANT,
at 7½ o'clock, in ISRAEL CHURCH, to consider the atrocious decision of the Supreme Court in the
DRED SCOTT CASE,
and other outrages to which the colored people are subject under the Constitution of the United States.
C. L. REMOND,
ROBERT PURVIS,
and others will be speakers on the occasion. Mrs. MOTT. Mr. M'KIM and B. S. JONES of Ohio. have also accepted invitations to be present. All persons are invited to attend. Admittance free.

The decision in the Dred Scott case of 1857 provokes public outcry on behalf of the slave population. THE GRANGER COLLECTION, NEW YORK

1857

Gail Borden, developer of process to make condensed milk, founds New York Condensed Milk Co., which becomes Borden Co.; Saucona Iron Co., predecessor of Bethlehem Steel, is formed; Smith & Wesson Co. is founded to manufacture revolvers; Oliver F. Winchester organizes New Haven Arms Co.

William Kelly patents a "pneumatic process" to convert iron into steel, a refinement of Bessemer process.

Nation's first safety passenger elevator is installed by Elisha Otis in Haughmont Store in New York City.

James E. A. Gibbs patents a chain-stitch single-thread sewing machine; William F. Channing and Moses G. Farmer patent an electric fire alarm.

American Institute of Architects is founded.

DEATH William Colgate, founder of toiletries company.

TRANSPORTATION

Ohio & Mississippi Railroad, connecting Cincinnati and St. Louis, is completed.

SCIENCE/MEDICINE

New York College of Veterinary Surgery is founded.

EDUCATION

First state agricultural college opens in Lansing, Mich.

National Deaf Mute College is incorporated in Washington; is later named Gallaudet College.

Seton Hall College and Seminary, Florida State, San Jose, and University of the South (Sewanee) are founded.

National Teachers Assn. is organized; becomes National Education Assn. (1870).

RELIGION

Midwest Congregational churches organize Chicago Theological Seminary.

Christian Reformed Church forms in Zeeland, Mich.

Catholic Bishop John M. Odin becomes archbishop of New Orleans.

Samuel M. Isaacs founds *Jewish Messenger*.

ART/MUSIC

J. S. Pierpont writes the song "Jingle Bells."

Frederick E. Church completes the painting *Niagara Falls*.

DEATH Thomas Crawford, sculptor of *Liberty* statue atop the Capitol.

LITERATURE/JOURNALISM

Harper's Weekly and *Atlantic Monthly* are founded.

Hinton R. Helper writes *The Impending Crisis of the South*, sharpens differences over slavery, is banned in the South.

ENTERTAINMENT

Among the year's plays are *Love in '76* by O. Bunce and *Poor of New York* by Dion Boucicault.

Decorated floats make first appearance at New Orleans Mardi Gras.

SPORTS

First chess congress opens in New York City; American Chess Assn. is formed; Paul C. Morphy of New Orleans wins championship.

Prioress becomes first American-bred horse to win a major race abroad, the Cesarewitch Handicap at Newmarket, England.

MISCELLANEOUS

Frederick Law Olmsted and Calvert Vaux design New York City's Central Park.

1858

INTERNATIONAL

U.S. and China sign treaty of peace, friendship, and commerce (June 18).

Japan opens more ports to U.S. trade (see 1853, 1854).

NATIONAL

Voters in Kansas reject pro-slavery constitution (January 4) framed in fall of 1857 at Lecompton, Kans.; earlier vote (December 21, 1857) resulted in approval but widespread voting fraud was apparent. President James Buchanan recommends Lecompton constitution to Congress (February 2); Senate approves, House rejects. Kansans reject government land grant to Kansas in election held August 2, thereby expressing wish to postpone statehood and reject Lecompton constitution.

Abraham Lincoln, running for U.S. Senate in Illinois, speaks out on slavery question, declares that "this government cannot endure permanently half slave and half free." He and his Democratic opponent, Stephen A. Douglas, debate in seven Illinois cities; Lincoln wins popular vote but loses election in the legislature.

Minnesota is admitted as the 32nd state (May 11).

President Buchanan sends Col. Thomas L. Kane to Utah to put down rebellion against the federal government (April 10); rebellion ends in June.

First overland-mail stage arrives in St. Louis from San Francisco (October 9), takes 23 days, 4 hours; the opposite stage arrives in San Francisco (October 10) after 24 days, 20 hours.

DEATH James P. Henderson, first Texas governor (1846).

An early washing machine with built-in wringer on top. THE GRANGER COLLECTION, NEW YORK

1858

BUSINESS/INDUSTRY/INVENTIONS

Macy's department store in New York City is founded by Rowland H. Macy.

Fredonia (N.Y.) Gaslight and Waterworks is founded, one of first to market natural gas.

Richard Esterbrook establishes factory in Camden, N.J., to produce steel pens.

Patents are issued to Hyman L. Lipman for pencil with an attached eraser, Lyman L. Blake for shoe-stitching machine, Eli W. Blake for a stone crusher, Lewis Mill for a mower, Charles W. March for harvester that gathers grain into bundles. Several washing-machine inventions are patented during the decade.

Financial panic of 1857 results in failure of 4,222 businesses.

DEATH William A. Burt, inventor of a typographer, forerunner of typewriter.

TRANSPORTATION

Chicago & Milwaukee Railroad is completed.

George M. Pullman begins to produce railroad sleeping cars.

SCIENCE/MEDICINE

Harvard University opens chemistry laboratory for undergraduates.

St. Luke's Hospital in New York City is founded.

EDUCATION

Columbia University Law School is founded.

Boston College and Iowa State University open.

Francis Lieber, first American political scientist, becomes a professor at Columbia University.

RELIGION

Isaac T. Hecker and three other Redemptorist priests found the Paulist Fathers (Missionary Society of St. Paul the Apostle).

Construction begins on St. Patrick's Cathedral in New York City.

ART/MUSIC

William W. Story completes marble statue of Cleopatra.

SONGS (popular): "(Here We Go) Round the Mulberry Bush," "The Yellow Rose of Texas."

LITERATURE/JOURNALISM

Oliver Wendell Holmes writes *The Autocrat of the Breakfast Table* and a poem, "The Chambered Nautilus;" Henry Wadsworth Longfellow writes *The Courtship of Miles Standish.*

Charles F. Browne begins to write humorous sketches under pen name of Artemus Ward.

First Nevada newspaper, *Territorial Enterprise,* is published.

ENTERTAINMENT

PLAYS *Ten Nights in a Barroom* by William W. Pratt; E. H. Sothern stars in *Our American Cousin,* Dion Boucicault in *Jessie Brown.*

SPORTS

New York All-Stars win two of three games against Brooklyn for baseball championship of newly-formed National Association of Base-Ball Players; admission is charged (50 cents) for first time.

John Morrissey beats Tom Heenan to retain U.S. heavyweight boxing title.

Michael J. Phelan wins first American billiards championship.

MISCELLANEOUS

Former President Fillmore, a widower, marries a widow, Mrs. Caroline C. McIntosh.

Marble soda fountain is developed.

Mt. Vernon Ladies Assn. takes over the Mt. Vernon estate of George Washington.

Ladies Christian Assn. forms in New York City, eventually becomes YWCA (Young Women's Christian Assn.).

Explosion aboard steamer *Pennsylvania* on the Mississippi River near Natchez kills 160.

1859

INTERNATIONAL

Great Britain and U.S. sign treaty by which British give up any land in Central America that might cause friction with U.S. in developing a canal across Panama.

NATIONAL

John Brown leads 18 men on raid of federal arsenal at Harpers Ferry, then in Virginia, hoping to spark a slave insurrection (October 16); after two days of battle in which no slaves aid the attackers, Brown and his men are captured by military force led by Robert E. Lee; Brown and his group are convicted of criminal conspiracy to incite an insurrection (October 31); Brown is hanged (December 2), six others hanged later.

Oregon is admitted as the 33rd state (February 14); Kansas voters approve Wyandotte constitution that makes it a free state (October 4); Nevada convention approves a constitution that is ratified by voters (September 7).

Atlantic cable is completed (August 5); breaks down (September 1), is not restored until 1866.

Supreme Court upholds constitutionality of Fugitive Slave Act; states are forbidden to interfere with federal prisoners.

Senate moves into newly completed Capitol chambers.

Mail is carried by balloons for first time.

Southern Commercial Convention designed to develop South's economy meets in Baltimore; will continue in various cities with mission shifting to secession.

BUSINESS/INDUSTRY/INVENTIONS

First successful commercial oil well is drilled near Titusville, Pa.

Equitable Life Assurance Society founded.

Atlantic & Pacific Tea Co. is established; first store opens on Vesey St., New York City.

Comstock Lode, one of richest deposits of silver and gold, is discovered in Virginia City, Nev.

Direct steam pump is developed by Henry R. Worthington; William Goodale patents paper-bag-making machine.

Fifth Avenue Hotel in New York City opens; installs first passenger elevator.

National cotton production is 5,387,000 bales.

Three labor groups form national unions: iron-molders, machinists, and blacksmiths.

DEATHS Walter Hunt, inventor of steam table, safety pin; Seth Thomas, clockmaker; Alfred L. Vail, builder of first telegraph line.

TRANSPORTATION

First trip of a Pullman sleeping car (Bloomington, Ill., to Chicago) is completed.

Atchison, Topeka & Santa Fe Railroad is completed.

Merchants Grain Forwarding Assn. forms to move Midwestern grains more rapidly.

SCIENCE/MEDICINE

Edward R. Squibb establishes pharmaceutical laboratory.

Dr. Joseph C. Hutchison performs first mastoid operation in Brooklyn.

Louis Agassiz founds Museum of Comparative Zoology at Harvard; Missouri Botanical Garden is established in St. Louis.

EDUCATION

Cooper Union is founded in New York City to provide free public instruction.

DEATH Horace Mann, who revolutionized school organization, teaching.

RELIGION

Third Congregational Unitarian Society in New York City is organized.

1859

The Last Moments of John Brown, painting by Thomas Hovenden dramatizing Brown's execution on December 2, 1859. BETTMANN

Daniel D. Emmett's song "Dixie" is first sung publicly.

Adelina Patti, most popular singer of her time, makes opera debut in New York City.

LITERATURE/ JOURNALISM

Two newspapers are founded: *Rocky Mountain News*, the first Colorado paper; *Weekly Arizonan*, first in that state.

BOOKS *Beulah* by Augusta J. Evans, *The Hidden Hand* by E. D. Southworth, *The Minister's Wooing* by Harriet Beecher Stowe, *The Pillar of Fire* by Joseph H. Ingraham.

DEATHS Authors Washington Irving and William H. Prescott.

ENTERTAINMENT

The Octoroon, a play by Dion Boucicault, is produced.

SPORTS

Amherst beats Williams in first intercollegiate baseball game; Harvard wins first intercollegiate regatta.

Henry Hall begins to manufacture linen and silk fishing lines.

An All-England team wins international cricket tournament in Hoboken over New York's St. George's Club.

Josh Ward in a single scull wins Championship of America race.

MISCELLANEOUS

Frenchman Emile Blondin crosses Niagara Falls on a tightrope.

Henry B. Whipple becomes first Episcopal bishop of Minnesota.

ART/MUSIC

John Rogers completes group sculptures *The Slave Auction* and *Checkers Up at the Farm*; Randolph Rogers completes statue *The Blind Girl of Pompeii*; John Whistler completes the painting *At the Piano*.

1860

INTERNATIONAL

U.S. receives first Japanese diplomat to visit a foreign country.

NATIONAL

Abraham Lincoln, Republican, is elected president, receiving 1,866,352 popular and 180 electoral votes; defeating Stephen A. Douglas, Democrat who receives 1,375,157 popular and 12 electoral votes; remaining electoral votes go to John C. Breckenridge and John Bell, minor party candidates.

In response to election of Lincoln, who is against any extension of slavery and viewed in the South as an antislavery extremist, South Carolina legislature calls for convention to consider secession (November 10), adopts ordinance to secede from Union (December 20); Senator John J. Crittenden of Kentucky introduces resolution to recognize slavery south of 36°30′ (December 18); it fails. Federal troops in South Carolina move from Ft. Moultrie to Ft. Sumter (December 26); state troops occupy Ft. Moultrie; South Carolina demands withdrawal of federal troops from Charleston Harbor (December 28), President James Buchanan refuses; state troops seize federal arsenal in Charleston.

Eighth census reports national population at 31,443,321.

Pony Express service begins between St. Joseph, Mo., and Sacramento, Calif.

Government Printing Office and Secret Service are established.

Elizabeth Cady Stanton addresses New York legislature on women's suffrage.

Army Signal Corps is founded.

New York State enacts law that requires fire escapes for tenements.

DEATH Mirabeau B. Lamar, Texas president (1838–1841).

BUSINESS/INDUSTRY/INVENTIONS

Shoeworkers in Lynn, Mass., strike for higher wages: men received $3 per week, women $1, for a 16-hour workday; others join in New England; after six weeks, 10,000 workers win a raise.

Salt production in Michigan begins at East Saginaw.

Oliver F. Winchester introduces repeating rifle; Christopher M. Spencer patents self-loading repeating rifle.

Patent law is modified, copyright function is given to Library of Congress.

Washoe Gold & Silver Mining Co. forms near Virginia City, Nev.

Abraham Lincoln (1809–1865), sixteenth President of the United States. Photograph by Alexander Hesler. THE GRANGER COLLECTION, NEW YORK

1860

The Pony Express, which begins service in 1860. THE GRANGER COLLECTION, NEW YORK

National corn production is 838,793,000 bushels; cotton more than 2 billion pounds.

TRANSPORTATION

Albemarle-Chesapeake Canal system is completed.

EDUCATION

Elizabeth P. Peabody begins nation's first English-type kindergarten in Boston.

Louisiana State University opens; Bard College is chartered as St. Stephen's.

Cornerstone for Sewanee (University of the South) is laid by Episcopal Bishop Leonidas Polk; construction is delayed until after Civil War.

RELIGION

Joseph Smith, son of Mormon church founder, becomes president of Reorganized Latter-Day Saints Church, a nonpolygamous offshoot.

Free Methodist church forms with Benjamin T. Roberts, general superintendent.

Jonathan Cummings organizes Advent Christian church.

DEATHS Archbishop Antoine Blanc of New Orleans (1851–1860); John Winebrenner, founder of Church of God.

ART/MUSIC

Congress commissions Emanuel Leutze to paint *Westward the Course of Empire Takes Its Way* for U.S. Capitol stairway.

Rudolph Wurlitzer begins to make musical instruments.

James Whistler completes the painting *Blue Wave*.

SONGS (popular): "Old Black Joe" by Stephen Foster, "Annie Lisle," "I Was Seeing Nellie Home."

DEATH Rembrandt Peale, painter.

LITERATURE/JOURNALISM

Erastus F. Beadle publishes first "dime novel" (*Malaeska* by Ann S. Stephens); leads to hundreds of series of 10-cent paperbacks.

Des Moines Register and *New York World* are founded.

BOOKS *The Marble Faun* by Nathaniel Hawthorne, *The Conduct of Life* by Ralph Waldo Emerson, *Home Ballads* (poetry) by John Greenleaf Whittier, *Seth Jones* by Edward S. Ellis, "Paul Revere's Ride" by Henry Wadsworth Longfellow.

ENTERTAINMENT

Dion Boucicault produces the play *The Colleen Bawn*.

DEATH Thomas D. Rice, known as the father of American minstrelsy.

SPORTS

Harvard defeats Yale in first intercollegiate billiards match.

Cricket team is formed at University of Michigan.

Croquet, introduced from England, becomes very popular.

MISCELLANEOUS

Anti-Horse Thief Assn. is formed in Ft. Scott, Kans.

New York Police Department creates first traffic squad.

Excursion ship *Lady Elgin* collides with lumber ship in Lake Michigan; 300 die.

Beards become popular; Lincoln grows one for the election.

1861

INTERNATIONAL

Great Britain declares its neutrality in Civil War (May 13); forbids armed vessels from either side bringing prizes to British ports.

U.S. ship *San Jacinto* stops British steamer *Trent* (November 8), removes two Confederate commissioners, James M. Mason and John Slidell, en route to England; Britain protests; Mason and Slidell are released (December 26).

NATIONAL

Civil War

Following lead of South Carolina, other states secede: Mississippi (January 9), Florida (January 10), Alabama (January 11), Georgia (January 19), Louisiana (January 26), Texas (February 1), Virginia (April 17), Arkansas (May 6), Tennessee (May 7), North Carolina (May 10); western part of Virginia opposes secession, organizes a Union government (June 11); in Texas, legislature deposes Gov. Sam Houston (March 18) for refusing to take oath to support Confederacy.

A number of states vote against secession: Delaware (January 3); Tennessee originally votes against secession (February 9), then later secedes; Missouri (February 28), Maryland (April 27), Kentucky (May 20).

Secession sometimes accompanies direct action against federal installations: Georgia troops take over Ft. Pulaski (January 3) and arsenal at Augusta (January 24); Alabama troops seize Ft. Morgan in Mobile (January 4); Alabama and Florida troops take Ft. Barrancas and Pensacola Navy Yard (January 12); Louisiana troops seize arsenal and barracks at Baton Rouge (January 10) and mint and customs house in New Orleans (February 1); Texas troops seize arsenal at San Antonio (February 15).

An unarmed merchant ship, *Star of the West*, carrying supplies to Ft. Sumter, S.C., is fired on by shore batteries near fort, January 9, returns to New York.

President Abraham Lincoln in inaugural address (March 4) says there need be no violence unless it is forced on the nation; a month later (April 6), he notifies South Carolina that provisions are to be sent to Ft. Sumter; South Carolina calls on Major Robert Anderson to surrender fort (April 11); shore batteries begin to fire on fort (April 12); Sumter surrenders (April 13).

President Lincoln announces that an "insurrection" exists, calls for 75,000 three-month volunteers.

Delegates to a congress of Confederate states in Montgomery, Ala., frame a constitution, create a provisional government, elect Jefferson Davis president (February 8); capital of Confederacy is established at Richmond (May 21).

Union blockade of Southern ports begins (April

1861

19), shipbuilding program is authorized; Union forces capture a number of Southern naval bases: Fts. Clark and Hatteras, N.C., Ship Island in the Gulf, Ft. Royal, S.C.

First major land battle occurs at Manassas, Va. (Battle of Bull Run); begins as Union victory but Confederate reinforcements turn it into a rout (July 21).

Union troops occupy Newport News and Harpers Ferry, the Confederates burn Hampton, Va.; later, Confederates defeat Union forces at Balls Bluff, near Leesburg, Va.; Union force takes Paducah, Ky.

President Lincoln tells special session of Congress of steps being taken in conflict; requests additional powers; Congress calls for enlistment of 500,000 volunteers.

Kansas is admitted as 34th—and free—state (January 29); Colorado Territory (February 28) and Nevada and Dakota territories (March 2) are established.

Convention adopts constitution for West Virginia.

Issuance of paper money ($5, $10, $20) is authorized (July 17).

Income tax act goes into effect, 3% on incomes of more than $800.

Morrill Tariff returns to specific duties, which are raised 5–10%.

Last Pony Express trip is made between St. Joseph, Mo., and Sacramento, Calif.

National debt is reported at $90,380,874.

BUSINESS/INDUSTRY/INVENTIONS

Adolphus Busch founds Anheuser-Busch Co. in St. Louis

John Eberhard Faber opens first American pencil factory (New York City).

John Wanamaker and Nathan Brown open men's retail clothing store in Philadelphia; it later becomes department store.

Oliver Wendell Holmes, poet, invents stereoscope; Robert P. Parrott patents a rifled cannon, Linus Yale patents cylinder lock.

Union troops inside Fort Sumter try to defend the fort against Confederate cannon fire, April 12–13, 1861. THE GRANGER COLLECTION, NEW YORK

First transcontinental telegraph line is completed, connecting points from the Mississippi River to the Pacific Ocean.

Jay Cooke & Co., private investment bank, is established.

Illinois and Missouri coal miners form American Miners Assn.

Rice production is 270,000 tons.

DEATHS Elisha G. Otis, elevator manufacturer; Eliphalet Remington, firearms maker.

TRANSPORTATION

Central Pacific Railroad is established; Leland Stanford is president.

Thaddeus S. C. Lowe makes 9-hour, 900-mile trip by balloon.

SCIENCE/MEDICINE

School of Nursing of Philadelphia Woman's Hospital is chartered.

Bellevue Hospital Medical College is organized in New York City.

Dr. Erastus B. Wolcott successfully removes a kidney.

EDUCATION

Three new educational institutions are founded: Massachussetts Institute of Technology (MIT), Vassar Female College, Washington University (St. Louis).

Oswego (N.Y.) Training School for Primary Teachers opens.

Yale University organizes first American graduate department, awards nation's first Ph.D. degrees.

RELIGION

Presbyterian church in the Confederate States (later Presbyterian Church U.S.) is organized with 75,000 members.

DEATH Elijah C. Bridgman, first U.S. missionary to China.

ART/MUSIC

Theodore Thomas begins 30 years as conductor of the Academy of Music Orchestra in New York City.

George Inness completes the painting *The Delaware Water Gap*.

SONGS (popular): "Abide with Me," "The Bonnie Blue Flag," "John Brown's Body," "Maryland, My Maryland," "The Vacant Chair."

DEATH Anthony P. Heinrich, composer known as the Beethoven of America.

LITERATURE/JOURNALISM

David R. Locke begins to write "letters" as Petroleum V. Nasby in the *Findlay* (Ohio) *Jeffersonian*.

Ansell N. Kellogg of *Baraboo* (Wis.) *Republic* becomes first newspaper "syndicate" by providing "ready print" for local papers.

ENTERTAINMENT

Adah Menken stars in the play *Mazeppa*.

SPORTS

New York Sportsmen's Assn. holds first U.S. fly-casting tournament in Utica, N.Y.

MISCELLANEOUS

Sally Louisa Tompkins becomes only woman commissioned in Confederate Army so that she can operate military hospital in her Richmond home.

1862

INTERNATIONAL

U.S. and Great Britain sign treaty to suppress slave trade.

NATIONAL

Civil War

A most spectacular event is clash between ironclad vessels in Hampton Roads, Va. (March 9); the Confederate *Merrimac* and the Union's *Monitor* battle to a draw, but the *Merrimac* has to retire to Norfolk for repairs; *Merrimac* later (May 11) is blown up to prevent its capture; *Monitor* sinks in a gale off Cape Hatteras (December 30).

Land fighting is heavy in Virginia and the Carolinas, in the Ohio and Mississippi valleys.

VIRGINIA AND THE CAROLINAS Union forces capture Roanoke Island (February 8) and New Bern, N.C. (March 14), Ft. Pulaski, Ga. (April 11), and Ft. Macon, N.C. (April 26); after Confederates evacuate Yorktown, Va. (May 4), Union forces move in, capture Williamsburg and occupy Norfolk. Confederate troops under Gen. Stonewall Jackson begin campaign in Shenandoah Valley (March 23), capture Front Royal and Winchester. Confederates turn back Union troops at Battle of Cross Keys, near Richmond; Union wins seven-day battle near Richmond but withdraws; Confederates give up Peninsula Campaign and return to Richmond (June 25); a short-lived siege of Richmond ends when Union troops withdraw. Second Battle of Bull Run at Manassas (August 29) is another Union defeat, in which Gen. Philip Kearny is killed. Confederate troops take Harpers Ferry (September 15), defeat larger Union force at Fredericksburg, Va. (December 13); Battle of Antietam near Sharpsburg, Md., a bloody draw.

TENNESSEE AND OHIO VALLEYS Union troops win first victory in West at Mill Springs, Ky. (January 19); capture Ft. Henry and Ft. Donelson and Nashville in February; occupy Columbus, Ky. (March 3). In fierce two-day battle at Shiloh, Tenn. (April 6–7), Union loses 13,700 men, Con-

federates 11,000 including Gen. Albert S. Johnston; Confederates capture Murfreesboro, Tenn. (July 13).

MISSISSIPPI VALLEY Union victory at Pea Ridge, Ark. (March 5), breaks Confederate hold on Arkansas and Missouri; Union troops take New Madrid, Mo., 10 days later. Island #10 in the Mississippi falls to Union (April 7), Confederates evacuate Corinth, Miss. (May 30), and Union vessels defeat Confederate naval force, taking Memphis (June 6). Union naval force steams past New Orleans (April 18), which falls (April 29).

Actions related to the war include congressional approval of presidential power to take over railroads when necessary; presidential appointment of military governors for Louisiana, North Carolina, and Tennessee (Andrew Johnson), which later (May 7) votes to secede; President calls for 300,000 volunteers for three years' service. Confederate Congress passes bill (April 16) calling for compulsory military service for all white males 18–35, changes to 18–45 in September.

—⁊⁊⁊—

Department of Agriculture is created (May 15) with Isaac Newton the first commissioner; Bureau of Engraving and Printing begins operations.

Homestead Act passes (May 20) as does the Morrill Act to provide land for state colleges; Homestead Act grants free family farms of 160 acres to settlers who promise to stay five years (military service deductible)

President Lincoln signs bill abolishing slavery in District of Columbia (April 16), slavery is abolished in U.S. territories (June 19), and president tells cabinet (July 22) he will issue Emancipation Proclamation January 1 freeing slaves in Confederacy; a preliminary draft is approved (September 24) by 16 governors.

Congress passes an antipolygamy act.

George S. Boutwell becomes first commissioner of

The Antietam campaign. THE GRANGER COLLECTION, NEW YORK

internal revenue, as federal income tax (3% on incomes of more than $800) goes into effect.

DEATHS Former Presidents John Tyler (1841–1845) and Martin Van Buren (1837–1841).

BUSINESS/INDUSTRY/INVENTIONS

San Francisco Stock & Exchange Board, specializing in mining securities, and Gold Exchange in New York open.

Barrows & Co. of Oil Creek, Pa., builds first successful pipeline from an oil well to refinery 1,000 feet away; Greenway Pottery Co. of Trenton, N.J., begins to manufacture chinaware for restaurants; Alanson Dunham of Maine begins to produce snowshoes.

Richard J. Gatling patents a multiple-barreled rapid-fire gun, first practical machine gun.

Abram S. Hewitt produces first American steel using an open-hearth process he develops.

A. T. Stewart & Co. builds world's largest retail store on an entire square block in New York City.

Garment Cutters Union is formed.

Van Camp food packing company is founded.

TRANSPORTATION

Pacific Railway Act is passed, provides assistance for a northern transcontinental railroad that becomes the Union Pacific.

Cornelius Vanderbilt begins to buy New York & Harlem Railroad stock, gains control by 1863, initiates streetcar service in New York City.

Great Northern Railroad begins as the St. Paul & Pacific.

SCIENCE/MEDICINE

University of the City of New York opens Children's Clinic.

1863

James Dana publishes *Manual of Geology*.

EDUCATION

Congress passes law providing for education of black children in Washington, D.C.

University of South Dakota and Colorado State University are founded.

RELIGION

Two Episcopal bishops are named: Richard H. Wilmer of Alabama and John Johnson of Virginia.

ART/MUSIC

Albert Bierstadt completes the painting *Guerilla Scene–Civil War*.

Albright Art Gallery is founded in Buffalo, N.Y.

Three war songs become popular: "Battle Hymn of the Republic," "We Are Coming, Father Abraham," "Tenting Tonight."

LITERATURE/JOURNALISM

Julia Ward Howe's poem "Battle Hymn of the Republic" is published in *Atlantic Monthly*.

A best-seller of year is William G. Brownlow's *Parson Brownlow's Book*.

Thomas Nast becomes staff artist for *Harper's Weekly*.

DEATH Henry David Thoreau, author.

ENTERTAINMENT

Tony Pastor opens his first music hall in New York City.

Augustin Daly produces his play *Leah the Forsaken*.

Fifth Avenue Theater in New York City opens.

SPORTS

Oneida football team organizes in Boston.

Union Grounds in Brooklyn, first baseball enclosure, opens.

Two Union Army baseball teams play on Christmas Day at Hilton Head, S.C., before an estimated 40,000 spectators.

MISCELLANEOUS

Gen. Daniel Butterfield writes bugle call, "Taps."

INTERNATIONAL

Britain and France refuse to allow Confederate vessels constructed there to sail.

France intervenes in Mexican affairs, sends troops to occupy Mexico City.

NATIONAL

Civil War

Year is a turning point as two climactic battles are won by the Union forces.

Battle of Gettysburg has its beginnings in the Virginia fighting: Confederates win costly battle at Chancellorsville, losing many men, including Gen. Stonewall Jackson (May 2) who dies five days later; the Union loses Gen. Hiram Berry; Confed-erates drive north (June 13), capturing Winchester, Va., Chambersburg, Pa. (June 23), Carlisle and York (June 27); accidental meeting of Confederate and Union forces touches off Gettysburg battle (July 1). Two days of costly, heavy fighting end in Confederate defeat, including the famed Pickett's charge and death of Gen. Lewis A. Armistead; Union loses Gen. John W. Reynolds. Confederates withdraw to near Hagerstown, Md. Confederates had 2,592 killed, 12,706 wounded, 5,150 missing; Union Army had 3,070 killed, 14,497 wounded, 5,434 missing.

In the West, Gen. Ulysses S. Grant's Union forces move north from Memphis (March 29), make two futile assaults on Vicksburg, Miss.; in mid-May, settle down to siege. Union fleet sails past Confederate batteries during night. On July 4, Confeder-

This illustration of the meaning of the Emancipation Proclamation depicts the harsh treatment experienced by slaves.
BETTMANN

ate Gen. John C. Pemberton and his 30,000 men surrender Vicksburg; Confederacy loses control of the Mississippi River.

Following Vicksburg, the Union takes Port Hudson, La., to gain complete control of the Mississippi (July 9); Confederates evacuate Jackson, Miss.; Little Rock in September.

Meanwhile in the Tennessee Valley, Confederates win battle at Cedar Mountain, Ga.; a two-day battle at Chickamauga Valley, Ga., forces Union troops into Chattanooga (September 19). Three-day battle at Missionary Ridge (or Lookout Mountain) near Chattanooga ends in a Union victory, divides the Confederacy into northern and southern halves, and makes possible drive through Georgia.

Union men ages 20–45 are liable for military service or they can find a substitute or pay $300 (March 3); in New York City, rioting occurs July 13–16 as mobs damage buildings and lynch blacks; total dead estimated at 1,000; takes a dozen Union Army regiments to end rioting.

—∞—

President Abraham Lincoln formally issues the Emancipation Proclamation (January 1) freeing slaves in states currently in rebellion against the U.S.; calls for enlistment of black troops; delivers his immortal, two-minute speech at the Gettysburg Cemetery dedication (November 19); issues proclamation setting the fourth Thursday in November as Thanksgiving Day; calls for additional 100,000 volunteers; announces plans for Reconstruction (December 8).

West Virginia is admitted as the 35th state (June 20); Arizona (February 24) and Idaho (March 3) territories are established.

Free mail delivery begins in 49 larger cities (July 1), later extends to smaller ones.

1863

Supreme Court justices are increased from 9 to 10 (March 3).

Signal Corps is created as separate branch of Army.

Allan Pinkerton organizes Secret Service.

Comptroller of the Currency office is established.

James A. Garfield begins 17 years service in House of Representatives from Ohio.

DEATHS Former First Lady Jane M. Pierce (1853–1857); Sam Houston, Texas leader.

BUSINESS/INDUSTRY/INVENTIONS

First National Bank of Philadelphia becomes first chartered national bank.

First Bessemer steelmaking operation in U.S. begins in Troy, N.Y.

Bay (later California) Sugar Refining Co. founded by Claus Spreckels.

Travelers Insurance Co., first American accident-insurance company, founded in Hartford, Conn.

Gold seekers begin to arrive at Alden Gulch, Mon., where gold had been discovered; lead and silver are discovered in Little Cottonwood Canyon, Utah.

Brotherhood of Locomotive Engineers organized.

TRANSPORTATION

Ground is broken for Central Pacific Railroad at Sacramento, Calif.

George Pullman patents a folding upper berth in a railroad car.

SCIENCE/MEDICINE

National Academy of Sciences is chartered.

Private school for handicapped persons opened in New York City Hospital for Ruptured and Crippled.

Mary Harris Thompson becomes first American woman surgeon after graduating from New England Medical College.

U.S. Veterinary Medical Assn. founded.

EDUCATION

New colleges are University of Massachusetts, Kansas State University, and LaSalle University (Philadelphia).

RELIGION

First general conference held by Seventh Day Adventist church.

Augustana (Ill.) College and Theological Seminary founded.

ART/MUSIC

Albert Bierstadt completes the painting *Rocky Mountains*; James Whistler paints *The Little Girl in White*.

SONGS (popular): "When Johnny Comes Marching Home," "Just Before the Battle, Mother," "Sweet and Low."

LITERATURE/JOURNALISM

Gen. Ambrose E. Burnside orders closing of *Chicago Times*, an anti-Lincoln paper; three days later, the president rescinds the order.

Edward Everett Hale's classic story "The Man Without a Country" is published.

William Bullock patents printing press that uses a continuous roll of paper.

First Wyoming newspaper, *Daily Telegraph*, is published; *Army & Navy Journal* is founded.

BOOKS *Tales of a Wayside Inn* by Henry Wadsworth Longfellow, *The Fatal Marriage* by Emma D. Southworth.

DEATH Clement C. Moore, author of "A Visit from St. Nicholas" (popularly known as "'Twas the Night before Christmas...").

ENTERTAINMENT

Plays produced include *East Lynne* by C. W. Tayleure; *Rosedale* by Lester Wallack.

Ford's Theater in Washington, D.C., opens.

SPORTS

Saratoga racetrack opens.

Joe Coburn knocks out Mike McCoole for U.S. heavyweight boxing title.

Dudley Kavanaugh defeats seven others for American billiards championship.

James L. Plimpton, inventor of 4-wheeled skate, introduces roller-skating in U.S.

MISCELLANEOUS

Francis Lieber develops world's first code of military law and procedure; Union Army adopts code.

William Taylor, a missionary, sends eucalyptus seeds from Australia to California, starting the groves there.

Massachusetts Board of Charities, first in U.S., is established.

1864

INTERNATIONAL

France places Archduke Maximilian of Austria on throne as Emperor of Mexico.

NATIONAL

Civil War

Fighting is concentrated in Virginia, Tennessee, and Georgia. In Virginia, three days of indecisive, costly fighting in the Battle of the Wilderness, near Charlottesville (May 5), is followed by five bloody days at Spotsylvania, where the Union loses Gen. John Sedgwick, the Confederates Gen. J. E. B. Stuart (May 8), and three days at Cold Harbor. In all, the Union loses 60,000, the Confederacy 25,000–30,000, losses from which they cannot recover. At Petersburg, Confederates withstand four days of Union battering (June 15–18), then dig in to endure a nine-month siege. The Union besiegers miss an opportunity (July 30) when part of the Confederate defense is blown up in the Battle of the Crater and the Union does not follow through.

Confederate troops take Winchester, Va., and Martinsburg, W.Va. (July 2), then, led by Gen. Jubal A. Early, begin to raid the Shenandoah Valley (July 11), pushing to within 6 miles of Washington before falling back; reinforced Union troops drive Confederates back and under Gen. Philip H. Sheridan regain Winchester, Fisher's Hill, and Cedar Creek.

Starting from Chattanooga (May 17), Union troops led by Gen. William T. Sherman drive into Georgia to within 8 miles of Atlanta (July 17); Confederate troops evacuate Atlanta (September 1); Union troops take over the next day; Confederate Gen. James B. McPherson is killed.

In mid-November, Gen. Sherman leads 60,000 on a march through Georgia and South Carolina to the Atlantic Ocean, cutting a swath 300 miles long and 30 miles wide, destroying everything en route; reaches Savannah, Ga. (December 10), occupies the city (December 22).

In Tennessee, a two-day battle (December 15–17) at Nashville virtually destroys the Confederate Army in the state; in earlier fighting, Confederate Cavalry Gen. John H. Morgan is killed at Greenville (September 4) and Gen. Patrick A. Cleburne at Franklin (November 30).

Unsuccessful efforts to end war are made twice: Union representatives meet with Confederate President Jefferson Davis (July 17), and Horace Greeley meets with Southern representatives in Canada (July 18).

In the war at sea, a Confederate submarine sinks the USS *Housatonic*, then the sub with eight men also sinks; the Confederate raider *Alabama*, which preys on Union shipping, is destroyed off the French coast (June 19); Union Navy force under Farragut wins Battle of Mobile Bay.

Arlington National Cemetery is established; the first to be buried there is a Confederate prisoner.

—⚏—

President Abraham Lincoln, Republican, is re-elected, winning over Gen. George McClellan, Democratic candidate, by 212 to 21 electoral votes and a popular majority of 400,000 in the 4 million votes cast; Gen. McClellan resigns from the army.

President Lincoln vetoes a bill that calls for radical reconstruction of the South; is criticized by many for his liberality.

1864

Sherman (center) and his men burn the city of Atlanta, Georgia. From the painting *War Is Hell* by Mort Kunstler. © MORT KUNSTLER, INC. THE GRANGER COLLECTION, NEW YORK

Nevada is admitted as the 36th state (October 31); Montana Territory is established (May 26).

Arkansas constitution abolishing slavery is ratified (March 18); Louisiana convention approves new constitution (July 23), Missouri convention votes (July 1) to abolish slavery by 1870.

National Bank Act creates system of federally-chartered banks supervised by Office of the Comptroller of the Currency.

Federal income tax, which is 3% on incomes of more than $800, is raised to 5% on incomes of $601 to $4,999, 10% on incomes of more than $5,000 (June 30).

"In God We Trust" first appears on U.S. coins.

Salmon P. Chase becomes Supreme Court chief justice after death of Roger B. Taney.

Postal money-order system is established.

Ainsworth R. Spofford begins 33 years as Librarian of Congress.

DEATHS Former First Lady Anna T. Harrison (1841); former Vice President George M. Dallas (1845–1849).

BUSINESS/INDUSTRY/INVENTIONS

J. P. Morgan & Co. financiers, is established; Pratt & Whitney Co., toolmakers' firm, is founded; Stetson hat factory in Philadelphia opens; Milton Bradley Co., one of earliest game manufacturers, is founded; Nicholson File Co. opens plant to manufacture hand files mechanically.

John Thompson and John Ramsey develop a corn planter.

DEATH Thomas Blanchard, inventor of lathe.

TRANSPORTATION

First street railway line begins to operate in Louisville; first horse-drawn trolleys run on tracks in Wilmington, Del.

Northern Pacific Railroad is chartered; construction begins 1870.

George M. Pullman builds first specially constructed railway sleeper car.

SCIENCE/MEDICINE

Private medical school is founded in San Francisco by Hugh H. Toland; becomes part of University of California.

Army Ambulance Corps is created.

Lewis M. Rutherford builds an astronomical camera, photographs the Moon.

American Ophthalmological Society is founded.

DEATH Benjamin Silliman, a founder of Yale University Medical School.

EDUCATION

University of Denver is founded as Colorado Seminary; Swarthmore (Pa.) College established.

DEATH Platt R. Spencer, originator of penmanship style.

RELIGION

Catholic Bishop John McCloskey becomes archbishop of New York; Bishop Martin J. Spalding, archbishop of Baltimore.

Rev. Thomas H. Vail becomes first Episcopal bishop of Kansas.

John H. Vincent founds journal that becomes the *Sunday School Teacher*.

DEATHS John J. Hughes, first Catholic Archbishop of New York; Episcopal Bishop Leonidas Polk.

ART/MUSIC

Yale University founds its School of Fine Arts.

National Statuary Hall in the Capitol is established.

SONGS (popular): "Tramp, Tramp, Tramp"; "Father, Dear Father, Come Home with Me Now"; "Where Has My Little Dog Gone?"; "Beautiful Dreamer" by Stephen Foster.

DEATHS Stephen Foster, composer of many American classics; William H. Fry, composer of first publicly performed American opera (*Lenore*).

LITERATURE/JOURNALISM

First newspapers are published in North Dakota (*Frontier Scout*) and Montana (*Montana Post* in Virginia City); *St. Louis Dispatch* founded.

BOOKS *In War Time* (poetry) by John Greenleaf Whittier, *Our Burden and Our Strength* by David A. Wells, *Ishmael* by Emma D. Southworth, *The Maine Woods* by Henry David Thoreau.

DEATH Nathaniel Hawthorne, author.

SPORTS

Second Saratoga racetrack opens, features first running of Travers Stakes.

MISCELLANEOUS

Knights of Pythias is founded in Washington, D.C.

INTERNATIONAL

Civil War

1865

War winds down very quickly. Gen. William T. Sherman, who led Union troops through Georgia, swings north through the Carolinas. Confederates in Virginia are pinned down around Petersburg and Richmond; Gen.

Robert E. Lee's efforts to break out end in failure as the Southern forces are encircled by April.

Gen. U. S. Grant calls on Gen. Lee to surrender; the two meet at Appomattox Court House (April 9), quickly agree on terms of surrender. Confederate units in various locations surrender.

1865

The assassination of President Abraham Lincoln by John Wilkes Booth at Ford's Theatre, Washington, D.C., on April 14, 1865. Lithograph by Currier & Ives. THE GRANGER COLLECTION, NEW YORK

The war costs the Union 359,528 dead, 275,175 wounded; Confederacy 258,000 dead, about 150,000 wounded.

—⁓—

President Abraham Lincoln is fatally wounded (April 14) while watching a play in Ford's Theater in Washington; he dies the next morning; Vice President Andrew Johnson is sworn in three hours later. Actor John Wilkes Booth, Lincoln's assassin, is killed near Bowling Green, Va. (April 26).

A military commission is created to try the eight accused in Lincoln's assassination finds them guilty (June 30); four are hanged (July 7), the others are imprisoned.

One of President Johnson's first actions is to grant amnesty to most Southerners (May 29); provisional governments are established in most seceding states. Congress refuses (December 4) to accept President Johnson's actions, sets up joint committee to examine Southern rights to vote and to congressional representation.

Thirteenth Amendment, abolishing slavery, goes into effect on ratification (December 18).

Some seceding states act quickly to abolish slavery, approve new constitutions: Tennessee (February 22), South Carolina (September 15), Florida (October 28).

Freedmen's Bureau created (March 3) to assist blacks, primarily through education, in transition from slavery to freedom; Gen. O. O. Howard of Maine named commissioner; Bureau will end 1872.

Ku Klux Klan is founded as a social club by six young Confederate veterans in Pulaski, Tenn. (December 24).

Law is enacted that requires deposit of books and materials on which copyright is claimed in Library of Congress.

DEATH Edward Everett, Massachusetts governor (1841–1845) and Harvard University president (1846–1849).

BUSINESS/INDUSTRY/INVENTIONS

John D. Rockefeller founds Rockefeller & Andrews, an oil-refining company.

Thaddeus Lowe invents compression ice machine, which produces first American artificial ice; William Sheppard patents liquid soap.

Freedmen's Savings & Trust Co. is established for blacks in Washington, D.C.; Safe Deposit Co. of New York City opens first safe-deposit vault.

First oil pipeline, about 5 miles long, is completed between Oil Creek and Pithole, Pa.

Benjamin Altman opens dry-goods store in New York City (which becomes B. Altman & Co.): forerunner of Marshall Field's in Chicago is established.

Union Stock Yards in Chicago open.

Remington rifle company begins to produce agricultural equipment; Andrew Carnegie founds Keystone Bridge Co.

William Barbour & Sons establishes a linen-thread factory in Paterson, N.J.; sweet crackers are introduced by Belcher & Larrabee of Albany.

TRANSPORTATION

Oakes and Oliver Ames and T. C. Durant organize Crédit Mobilier of America to build and promote the Union Pacific Railroad; its scandalous operations are later uncovered.

W. R. Grace & Co. is established; will become a major shipping company in South American trade.

Southern Pacific Railroad is incorporated.

SCIENCE/MEDICINE

Chemist Oliver W. Gibbs introduces electronic analysis, a pioneer effort in spectroscopy which lay foundation for American chemistry.

Last major U.S. cholera epidemic spreads widely throughout the country.

Maria Mitchell becomes first American woman astronomy professor (Vassar).

The photographer Matthew Brady captures the scene in ruined Richmond. CORBIS

1866

EDUCATION

MIT introduces first U.S. college architectural course.

New colleges include Cornell University, which is chartered; Worcester (Mass.) Polytechnic Institute; University of Kentucky, and Lehigh University.

American Social Science Assn. is founded.

RELIGION

Cowley Fathers (Society of St. John the Evangelist) is founded; Harriet S. Cannon founds Episcopal order, Sisters of St. Mary.

Paulist Fathers begin to publish *The Catholic World*; Rev. Edward F. Sorin founds a magazine for Catholic laity, *Ave Maria*.

DEATHS Episcopal bishops Alonzo Potter of Pennsylvania (1860–1865) and Thomas C. Brownell of Connecticut (1819–1865).

ART/MUSIC

Boston Philharmonic Society is organized.

George Inness completes the painting *Peace and Plenty*.

SONGS (popular): "Johnny's My Darling," "Little Brown Church in the Vale," "Marching Through Georgia."

LITERATURE/JOURNALISM

William A. Bullock invents web printing press.

The Nation is founded by E. L. Godkin; *San Francisco Chronicle* is published.

Mark Twain publishes his first notable story, "The Celebrated Jumping Frog of Calaveras County."

BOOKS *Drum Taps* (poetry) by Walt Whitman (later incorporated in *Leaves of Grass*), *Hans Brinker, or the Silver Skates* by Mary M. Dodge.

DEATH Lydia H. H. Sigourney, most widely read American poet of her day.

ENTERTAINMENT

Joseph Jefferson stars in Dion Boucicault's *Rip van Winkle*.

Tony Pastor opens variety theater in New York City.

SPORTS

Convention of National Association of Baseball Players is attended by representatives of 91 baseball clubs.

MISCELLANEOUS

Editorial in *New York Tribune* states: "Go west, young man, go west!" Editor Horace Greeley later credits phrase to an Indiana editor.

Lydia Pinkham begins to produce the patent medicine Vegetable Compound to cure "woman's weakness" and other ills.

Steamship *Sultana* explodes on Missouri River, killing 1,700, most of them Union soldiers returning from Southern prisons.

New York City establishes first fire department with paid firefighters.

INTERNATIONAL

U.S. demands that France withdraw from Mexico; 50,000 U.S. troops are sent to Mexican border (February 12).

Several hundred Fenian secret-brotherhood members seeking Irish freedom cross Niagara River at Buffalo (May 31), briefly capture Ft. Erie but are driven out (June 2).

1866

NATIONAL

First Atlantic cable begins successful operation after years of failure.

Secretary of State William H. Seward negotiates purchase of Alaska from Russia ("Seward's Folly").

Joint Congressional Committee reports that Con-

Two elegant steamboats race on the Mississippi in this 1866 lithograph by Currier & Ives. The popularity of such races will reach its zenith with the famed race of the *Robert E. Lee* and the *Natchez* (see 1870). THE GRANGER COLLECTION, NEW YORK

gress rather than the president has control over Reconstruction; elections give radical Republicans control of Congress, which passes several bills over President Andrew Johnson's veto, including a Civil Rights Act, and forbids his naming new Supreme Court justices.

Congress enacts Fourteenth Amendment (June 13), guaranteeing that no person is to be deprived of life, liberty, or pursuit of happiness without due process of law.

Tennessee is readmitted to the Union (July 24); Georgia's secession resolution is repealed, slavery is abolished (November 4).

Several states adopt "black codes" to control freedmen and ensure they remain subordinate to whites (1865–1866).

Race riots occur in New Orleans and Memphis.

National debt, increased by Civil War, is $2,322,331,208.

Grand Army of the Republic (GAR), organization of Union army veterans, is founded by Benjamin F. Stephenson.

Fetterman Massacre occurs in Wyoming when 90

U.S. soldiers under Capt. William J. Fetterman are slain by the Oglala Sioux Indians led by Red Cloud.

Unique 40,000-volume collection of Smithsonian Institution is transferred to Library of Congress.

Henry Bergh founds American Society for the Prevention of Cruelty to Animals (ASPCA).

New 5-cent (nickel) coin is authorized.

DEATH Gen. Winfield Scott, Army general-in-chief (1841–1861).

BUSINESS/INDUSTRY/INVENTIONS

National Board of Fire Underwriters, with 75 companies, standardizes rates.

Competing steelmaking processes, Bessemer and Kelly, are combined into one.

National Labor Union is organized, calls for 8-hour workday.

Excelsior Needle Co. of Wolcottville, Conn., is established; Charles E. Hires begins to manufacture root beer.

John Abt invents wire-cutting machine and auto-

1866

matic wire straightener; Edson P. Clark invents an indelible pencil.

Copper is discovered in Montana (Butte and Anaconda).

American Law Review is founded.

TRANSPORTATION

First refrigerated railroad car is built.

SCIENCE/MEDICINE

New York City Metropolitan Board of Health is established.

Othniel C. Marsh becomes first American paleontology professor.

DEATH Horace Green, first American physician to specialize in diseases of the throat, air passages.

EDUCATION

Lincoln Institute (Jefferson City, Mo.) opens for freed blacks in community; Howard University (Washington, D.C.), University of New Hampshire, and University of Kansas are founded.

Raphael Pumpelly becomes first professor of mining at Harvard University.

RELIGION

Daniel Drew, Wall Street investor and speculator, endows Drew Theological Seminary (Madison, N.J.).

Catholic Publication Society is founded.

John B. Kerfoot becomes Episcopal bishop of Pittsburgh.

ART/MUSIC

Gustav Schirmer establishes music-publishing business.

Albert Bierstadt completes the painting *Merced River, Yosemite Valley*; Winslow Homer paints *Eight Bells* and *Prisoners from the Front*.

SONGS (popular): "Come Back to Erin," "Now I Lay Me Down to Sleep," "Tom Dooley," "When You and I Were Young, Maggie."

LITERATURE/JOURNALISM

Fireside Companion, a weekly is founded.

BOOKS *Snow-Bound* (poetry) by John Greenleaf Whittier, *A Rebel War Clerk's Diary* by John B. Jones, *Inside: A Chronicle of Secession* by George F. Harrington.

ENTERTAINMENT

The Black Crook by Charles M. Barras opens at Niblo's Garden, New York City; is sometimes considered first American musical.

SPORTS

First yacht race across the Atlantic begins in New York City with three boats; the *Henrietta* owned by James Gordon Bennett Jr. wins, making trip in 13 days, 22 hours.

Public roller-skating rink opens in Newport, R.I.

MISCELLANEOUS

Young Women's Christian Assn. begins as a local group in Boston.

Fire in Portland, Me., destroys 1,500 buildings.

1867

INTERNATIONAL

Napeoleon III withdraws French troops from Mexico after U.S. ultimatum.

U.S. formally purchases Alaska from Russia for $7.2 million (June 20); Senate ratifies purchase; formal transfer is made October 18; Midway Islands are occupied in name of U.S. by Capt. William Reynolds of USS *Lackawanna*.

Treaty to acquire Danish West Indies (Virgin Islands) for $7.5 million dies in Senate.

NATIONAL

Senate Judiciary Committee resolves that President Andrew Johnson "be impeached for high crimes and misdemeanors" (November 25);

In this newspaper cartoon, Secretary of State William H. Seward is mocked for having made a bad business deal in the Alaska Purchase. "I say, little boy, do you want to trade?" asks a "Russian Stranger." "I've got a fine lot of bears, seals, icebergs, and Esquimaux — They're no use to me, I'll swap 'em all for those boats you've got." THE GRANGER COLLECTION, NEW YORK

House votes down recommendation (108–57) for impeachment.

Congress passes the Reconstruction Act over presidential veto, requiring Southern states to call new constitutional conventions guaranteeing Negro suffrage and to ratify Fourteenth Amendment (March 2). In an earlier special session, Congress virtually deprives president of control of the Army, prohibits him from removing Senate-approved officials without Senate approval (Tenure of Office Act).

Mississippi gives blacks nearly full civil rights (February 13); Louisiana (March 2), Maryland (May 8), and Alabama (December 6) approve new constitutions.

Nebraska is admitted as 37th state (March 1).

Jefferson Davis, former Confederate president, is released on parole after nearly two years imprisonment.

Blacks receive right to vote in District of Columbia.

Congress approves $100,000 for Library of Congress purchase of major book collection.

BUSINESS/INDUSTRY/INVENTIONS

Christopher Sholes, Carlos Glidden, and Samuel W. Soulé build first practical typewriter.

First U.S. telegraph ticker is installed, at David Groesbeck & Co., New York City brokerage office.

National Grange (of the Patrons of Husbandry) is organized to protect farm interests.

Pullman Palace Car Co. is founded.

Averill Paint Co. of New York City produces ready-mixed paint.

Order of the Knights of St. Crispin, a shoemakers' national union, is founded.

Jacob Ruppert Brewery in New York City is founded.

DEATH Valcour Aime, builder of first American sugar refinery.

1867

TRANSPORTATION

Elevated railroad begins to operate on Greenwich St., New York City.

Bridge over Ohio River at Cincinnati is completed.

SCIENCE/MEDICINE

Harvard School of Dental Medicine is established.

Dr. John S. Bobbs performs first gallstone operation in Indianapolis.

American Entomological Society begins.

S. S. White Dental Manufacturing Co. introduces gas inhaler that covers nose and mouth.

American Naturalist is founded.

EDUCATION

Congress creates Department of Education; Henry Barnard first commissioner.

George Peabody endows Peabody Education Fund to help educational institutions in South.

New York State creates free public-education system. (Tuition was generally charged until this action.)

University of Illinois and West Virginia University are founded; University of Alabama is reestablished.

Clarke School for the Deaf is founded in Northampton, Mass.

RELIGION

First Greek Orthodox church in U.S., Holy Trinity in New Orleans, is founded.

Free Religious Assn. forms in Boston.

ART/MUSIC

Steinway Hall is built on 14th Street in New York City.

New England Conservatory of Music in Boston is founded.

Two popular songs are "I Was Seeing Nellie Home" and "Mary Had a Little Lamb."

LITERATURE/JOURNALISM

Harper's Bazaar, women's magazine, is published.

New York Evening Telegram is founded.

BOOKS *Ragged Dick*, the first of many books by Horatio Alger Jr.; *St. Elmo* by Augusta J. Evans; *May-Day and Other Poems* by Ralph Waldo Emerson; *Miss Ravenel's Conversion* by J. W. De Forest.

DEATH Thomas Bulfinch, author (*The Age of Fable*).

ENTERTAINMENT

Actress Lotta Crabtree is a sensation in *Little Nell and the Marchioness*.

Under the Gaslight by Augustin Daly opens in New York City.

SPORTS

Ruthless, ridden by J. Gilpatrick, wins first Belmont Stakes; winner's purse $1,850.

MISCELLANEOUS

Three national soldiers' homes go into operation at Taugus, Me., Dayton, Ohio, and Milwaukee, Wis.

1868

INTERNATIONAL

Burlingame Treaty is signed (July 28), provides for free immigration between U.S. and China.

NATIONAL

President Andrew Johnson begins test of constitutionality of Tenure of Office Act by removing War Secretary Edwin M. Stanton from office (February 21); House votes (126–47) to impeach Johnson for violating the act and "attempting to disgrace and ridicule the Congress."

Supreme Court Chief Justice Salmon P. Chase presides over Senate impeachment trial (March 13); Senate votes (May 16) on first impeachment article, 35–19 for impeachment, one vote short of required two-thirds; vote on other two articles the same; Secretary Stanton resigns.

Gen. Ulysses S. Grant, Republican, is elected president, receiving 214 electoral votes against 80 for his Democratic opponent, Horatio Seymour; Grant has a majority of only 306,000 in the 5,715,000 popular vote.

Fourteenth Amendment is ratified, guarantees citizens' rights (July 28).

Seven seceded Southern states are readmitted to the Union: Arkansas (June 22) and Alabama, Florida, Georgia, Louisiana, and North and South Carolina (June 25). Some states adopt new constitutions: Virginia, North and South Carolina, and Georgia.

Wyoming Territory is established (July 25); Alaska Territory is organized (July 27).

GAR (Grand Army of the Republic) begins Decoration (Memorial) Day observance.

Treason trial of Confederate President Jefferson Davis begins (December 3); charges are dropped (February 1869).

Uniforms for letter carriers are authorized.

U.S. and Oglala Sioux nation sign Treaty of Ft. Laramie.

Rutherford B. Hayes begins first of 2-year terms as Ohio governor.

DEATHS Former President Buchanan (1857–1861); Kit Carson, frontier guide and explorer; Thaddeus Stevens, Radical Republican leader.

BUSINESS/INDUSTRY/INVENTIONS

Patent for typewriter is issued to Christopher Sholes, Carlos Glidden, and Samuel Soulé; Thomas A. Edison develops a stock ticker (which leads to teletype machine); William H. Remington patents process for nickel plating; George Westinghouse patents an air brake.

Open-hearth furnace to make steel by Siemens-Martin process is built for Cooper Hewitt Co.

Federal government adopts standard system of screw threads.

Charles Fleischmann introduces compressed fresh yeast.

Eight-hour day is initiated for government laborers, mechanics.

Zion Cooperative Mercantile Institution, an early department store, opens in Salt Lake City.

Equitable Life Assurance Society Building in New York City is first office building with an elevator.

Brotherhood of Railway Conductors is established.

DEATH Linus Yale, lock manufacturer.

TRANSPORTATION

Eli H. Janney invents automatic railway-car coupler.

George Pullman introduces railroad dining car.

Henry V. Poor publishes *Manual of the Railroads of the United States*.

SCIENCE/MEDICINE

University of Michigan begins full training program for pharmacists.

American Journal of Obstetrics is published.

1868

A ticket to President Andrew Johnson's impeachment trial, March 13, 1868. CORBIS-BETTMANN

EDUCATION

Oregon State University and Hampton (Va.) Institute are founded.

First commercial high school is established in Pittsburgh.

Boston Public Library first to make facilities available for the blind.

American Philological Assn. is organized.

DEATHS Matthew Vassar, college benefactor; Walter L. Newberry, endower of Chicago reference library; Edwin A. Stevens, endower of technology institute.

RELIGION

"O Little Town of Bethlehem," the Christmas carol by Phillips Brooks, is first sung.

Three Catholic priests become bishops: William G. McCloskey of Louisville, Ky.; Bernard J. McQuaid, first bishop of Rochester, N.Y.; Michael Heiss, first bishop of La Crosse, Wis.

ART/MUSIC

Thomas's Symphony Orchestra is founded in New York City.

John La Farge completes the painting *Bishop Berkely's Rock*.

SONGS (popular): "The Daring Young Man on the Flying Trapeze," "Sweet By and By," "Whispering Hope."

DEATH Emanuel Leutze, historical painter.

LITERATURE/JOURNALISM

Atlanta Constitution and first New Mexico paper, *Daily New Mexico*, are founded; *Louisville Courier-Journal* is formed by merger; Charles A. Dana acquires the *New York Sun*.

Lippincott's Magazine, a literary monthly, and *Vanity Fair* are founded.

First volume of Louisa May Alcott's popular *Little Women* and first of 28 Elsie Dinsmore books by Martha Finley are published.

ENTERTAINMENT

George W. L. Fox produces first American burlesque, *Humpty Dumpty*.

Augustin Daly produces the play *A Flash of Lightning*.

SPORTS

New York Athletic Club is organized; stages first indoor amateur track-and-field meet.

General Duke, ridden by R. Swim, wins Belmont Stakes.

Harry (William H.) Wright organizes Cincinnati Red Stockings baseball team.

MISCELLANEOUS

Earthquake strikes San Francisco, causes $3 million damage.

Louisiana charters what was then the greatest lottery in U.S. history.

Sorosis, first women's professional club, is founded in New York City.

Benevolent & Protective Order of Elks is founded in New York City.

1869

NATIONAL

Congress passes Fifteenth Amendment, making it illegal to deprive a citizen of the right to vote on the basis of race, color, or previous condition of servitude.

Wyoming territorial legislature extends right to vote to women.

National Woman Suffrage Assn. is organized; American Equal Rights Assn. meets to discuss women's suffrage; first congressional hearing on women's rights hears Susan B. Anthony and Elizabeth Cady Stanton.

Maj. John Wesley Powell and nine men complete 900-mile trip down Colorado River.

First tunnel is built under a New York City street; a shield developed by Alfred E. Beach is used to protect operator of tunnel-digging machine.

Congress passes Public Credit Act calling for payment in gold of government obligations.

New York and Mississippi adopt new constitutions.

Postage stamps in two colors are issued.

Freedmen's Bureau goes out of operation.

DEATHS Former President Franklin Pierce (1853–1857); former First Lady Julia G. Tyler (1844–1845).

BUSINESS/INDUSTRY/INVENTIONS

Inventions reported include celluloid by John W. and Isaiah S. Hyatt, a suction-type vacuum cleaner by Ives W. McGuffey, and a coin farebox by Tom Johnson.

Jay Gould and James Fisk try to corner the nation's supply of gold, force price up to $162 per ounce; government sale of $4 million in gold drives price down to $135, ruining many speculators (September 24).

Knights of Labor, a national labor union, which begins as a secret society, is formed with Uriah S. Stevens as the leader; Daughters of St. Crispin, women shoemakers, is organized in Lynn, Mass.

James Oliver patents the chilled iron plow.

Sulphur is discovered in Calcasieu Parish, La.

DEATHS Jabez Gorham, founder of Gorham Silver; Deming Jarves, manufacturer of Sandwich glass; John A. Roebling, engineer who developed wire rope.

TRANSPORTATION

Central Pacific and Union Pacific railroads join at Promontory Point, Utah, completing first transcontinental railroad (May 10).

Women voting in Cheyenne, Wyoming, for the first time in 1888. Women's rights groups formed in 1869 played an important part in obtaining the vote for women. THE GRANGER COLLECTION, NEW YORK

1869

The Union Pacific and Central Pacific railroads meet at Promontory Point, Utah, completing the first transcontinental railroad. CORBIS-BETTMANN

Massachusetts enacts first state railroad law, sets up Board of Railroad Commissioners.

Inclined railway to top of Mt. Washington, N.H., is completed.

Work begins on Brooklyn Bridge.

New York Central and Hudson River railroads merge.

SCIENCE/MEDICINE

Professor Edward C. Pickering photographs solar eclipse at Mt. Pleasant, Iowa.

Massachusetts establishes Board of Public Health.

Cleveland Abbe initiates daily weather bulletins at Cincinnati Observatory.

EDUCATION

Charles W. Eliot begins 40 years as Harvard University president.

University of Nebraska and Southern Illinois and Purdue universities are founded.

Horace Mann School for the Deaf opens in Boston.

DEATH George Peabody, endower of an education fund, institutes, and museums.

RELIGION

"Chicago Protest" against Episcopal church results in formation of Reformed Episcopal church.

First Episcopal cathedral (Cathedral of Our Merciful Saviour) is built in Faribault, Minn.

Two Episcopal bishops are named: William C. Doane, first bishop of Albany, N.Y., and Abram N. Littlejohn of Long Island.

Rev. Kelly Lowe organizes first American Negro Sunday School in Springfield Baptist Church (Augusta, Ga.).

ART/MUSIC

Corcoran Gallery of Art in Washington opens.

SONGS (popular): "Little Brown Jug," "Now the Day Is Over," "Shoo Fly, Don't Bother Me," "Sweet Genevieve."

LITERATURE/JOURNALISM

The Agitator, a suffragist newspaper, merges with the *Woman's Journal* of Boston.

BOOKS *The Innocents Abroad* by Mark Twain, *The Outcasts of Poker Flat* by Bret Harte, *Oldtown Folks* by Harriet Beecher Stowe, *Ragged Dick* by Horatio Alger.

ENTERTAINMENT

Two new theaters are built in New York City: one by Edwin Booth, the other by Augustin Daly; California Theater opens in San Francisco.

John Brougham produces *The Dramatic Revue for 1868*.

SPORTS

Cincinnati Red Stockings, first professional baseball team, begins 12,000-mile tour (May 5); wins 66, ties 1.

Henry Chadwick begins to publish annual baseball handbook, which eventually becomes Spalding's *Official Baseball Guide*.

Tom Allen of England beats Bill Davis and claims world heavyweight boxing title; then Mike McCoole, U.S. champion, beats Allen.

Rutgers defeats Princeton 6–4 at New Brunswick, N.J., in first intercollegiate football game (November 6).

American Jockey Club holds steeplechase at Jerome Park with Oysterman the winner; Fenian, ridden by C. Miller, wins Belmont Stakes.

MISCELLANEOUS

National Peace Jubilee is held in Boston; features chorus of 10,000 and an orchestra of 1,000.

First modern apartment house, Stuyvesant Apartments, is built at 142 E. 18th St., New York City.

Ku Klux Klan is officially disbanded; its activities, however, continue for some time.

Coal-mine disaster in Avondale, Pa., takes 108 lives.

1870

Second Fenian attack (see 1866) is repulsed by Canadians; leaders of Irish independence movement are arrested on their return to U.S.

Treaty to annex Santo Domingo is rejected by Senate (June 30).

Fifteenth Amendment is ratified, declares that race is no bar to voting (March 30).

Justice Department, headed by attorney general, is created (September 24).

Four states are readmitted to the Union: Virginia

"A LIVE JACKASS KICKING A DEAD LION."

And such a Lion! and such a Jackass!

Cartoonist Thomas Nast depicts the Democratic Party as a donkey. The donkey will become a lasting symbol of the party. THE GRANGER COLLECTION, NEW YORK

(January 26), Mississippi (February 23), Texas (March 30), and Georgia (July 15).

Joseph H. Rainey of South Carolina becomes first African American to serve in House of Representatives; Hiram R. Revels of Mississippi in the Senate.

National debt is reported at $2.4 billion.

Ninth census reports national population of 38,558,371.

Immigration in year totals 387,203.

Utah Territory gives full suffrage to women.

Tariff Act places 130 articles, mostly raw materials, on free list; small reduction on other commodities.

Thomas Nast's cartoon of a donkey representing the Democratic Party appears in *Harper's Weekly.*

Congress authorizes $3,000 annual pension to widow of President Lincoln; increases in 1882 to $5,000 for all presidential widows.

Gov. William W. Holden of North Carolina is impeached and removed from office.

Grover Cleveland is elected sheriff of Erie County, N.Y.

DEATHS Gen. Robert E. Lee, Confederate general; Union Admiral David G. Farragut.

BUSINESS/INDUSTRY/INVENTIONS

Standard Oil Co. of Ohio incorporates; John D. Rockefeller president. Armour & Co. is founded.

Original Palmer House hotel opens in Chicago; destroyed by fire (1871).

Benjamin C. Tilgham patents a sand-blasting process.

Philadelphia Clearing House for stocks and bonds is organized; New York Cotton Exchange begins.

Beach Pneumatic Underground Railway in New York City opens.

Remington Co. begins to manufacture sewing machines.

E. H. Dyer establishes first successful American sugar-beet factory at Alvarado, Calif.

Annual livestock production is 24 million head of cattle, 8.9 million dairy cows, 25 million hogs, 7 million horses, 1 million donkeys.

TRANSPORTATION

Railroad bridge over Ohio River at Louisville, Ky., is dedicated.

The *Robert E. Lee* beats the *Natchez* in a widely followed steamboat race on the Mississippi.

SCIENCE/MEDICINE

Newly created Weather Bureau in Signal Corps makes first weather observations.

EDUCATION

John Eaton becomes U.S. commissioner of education.

New colleges are founded: Normal College (New York City) by Thomas Hunter, later named for him; Syracuse University; Wellesley (Mass.) College; Ohio State University.

Mt. Union College in Alliance, Ohio, one of first to have summer-school term.

Ada H. Kepley of Effingham, Ill., becomes first woman law graduate, earns her degree from Union College of Law, Chicago.

Lenox Library in New York City is founded.

DEATHS Emma Willard, pioneer in higher education for women; Sophia Smith, endower of Smith College.

RELIGION

Bishop Robert Paine establishes Colored Methodist Episcopal Church in Jackson, Miss.

The Outlook begins as the *Christian Union.*

DEATH Pierre Jean de Smet, Jesuit missionary among Native Americans.

ART/MUSIC

Metropolitan Museum of Art, New York City, and Boston Museum of Fine Arts open.

John La Farge completes the painting *The Muse of Painting*; Winslow Homer, *High Tide.*

DEATHS James M. Ives of Currier & Ives; Alexander Anderson, first American wood engraver.

1871

LITERATURE/JOURNALISM

Scribner's Monthly and *The Century* founded.

Lucy Stone founds *Woman's Journal* magazine, and sisters Victoria C. Woodhull and Tennessee Claflin, a women's rights weekly magazine.

BOOKS *The Luck of Roaring Camp* by Bret Harte, *Society and Solitude* by Ralph Waldo Emerson, *The Story of a Bad Boy* by Thomas B. Aldrich.

ENTERTAINMENT

PLAYS *Divorce* by Augustine Daly; *Saratoga* by Bronson Howard; *Fritz, Our German Cousin* by C. Gaylor; *The Twelve Temptations* by J. C. Foster.

SPORTS

U.S. yacht *Magic* defeats the English *Cambria* to retain America's Cup.

Brooklyn Atlantics end Cincinnati Red Stockings winning streak at 80; game features first double play, first switch hitter.

Kingfisher, ridden by W. Dick, wins Belmont Stakes.

MISCELLANEOUS

World's first boardwalk opens in Atlantic City (June 26).

First brick pavement in the U.S. is laid in Charleston, W.Va.

Kappa Alpha Theta, first women's Greek letter society, is founded at what is now DePauw University.

Esther H. Morris becomes first woman justice of the peace (South Pass City, Wyo.).

National meeting on prison reform is held in Cincinnati.

1871

INTERNATIONAL

Treaty between U.S. and Great Britain calls for arbitration of all damage claims against all British-built sea raiders of the Confederacy (*Alabama* et al.); Senate ratifies (May 24).

NATIONAL

First service pensions are granted to veterans of War of 1812.

George W. Curtis is named to head first Civil Service Commission.

Race riots against Chinese occur in Los Angeles; 15 are lynched.

The Tweed Ring, led by Tammany Boss William M. Tweed, which plundered the New York City treasury, is broken up by a combination of the New York City Committee of 70 and the *New York Times*. Tweed is arrested October 27.

U.S. Fish Commission, which will become Bureau of Fisheries, is created.

Chester A. Arthur is named collector of customs for Port of New York.

DEATHS Former President James Monroe (1817–1825); Robert Anderson, Union officer who commanded Ft. Sumter at start of Civil War.

BUSINESS/INDUSTRY/INVENTIONS

David A. Saylor patents Portland cement; Albert L. Jones patents process for making corrugated paper.

Frick & Co., producers of coke for steel mills, and Calumet Hecla Mining Co. (copper) are formed.

George Westinghouse at his Pittsburgh plant initiates Saturday half-holiday.

Stockyards in Kansas City, Mo., are completed.

TRANSPORTATION

The Cotton Belt (St. Louis & Southwestern) and Texas & Pacific railroads are founded.

Pilgrims of the Plains, an engraving showing a wagon train on its way west, halting for evening camp. THE GRANGER COLLECTION, NEW YORK

SCIENCE/MEDICINE

U.S. Weather Service is founded (January 3).

Foot-operated, cord-driven dental engine is introduced.

Harvard University creates the first American physiological laboratory for students, with Henry P. Bowditch in charge.

EDUCATION

University of Arkansas opened.

University of Michigan begins admission system based on secondary-school record rather than an entrance examination; James B. Angell begins 40 years as president of University of Michigan.

First black land-grant college (Alcorn University) is established at Rodney, Miss.

Francis E. Willard is named president of Evanston (Ill.) College for Ladies, first woman college president.

RELIGION

Boston University School of Theology is established by merger of Boston University and Boston Theological Seminary.

Celia C. Burleigh is ordained as Unitarian minister.

DEATH Edward T. Taylor, chaplain of Boston Seamen's Bethel (1829–1871).

ART/MUSIC

Winslow Homer completes the painting *New England Country Schoolhouse*; Thomas C. Eakins paints *Max Schmitt in a Single Scull*.

SONGS (popular): "Goodbye Liza Jane," "Reuben, Reuben, I've Been Thinking," "Sing a Song of Sixpence."

DEATH Henry E. Steinway, piano manufacturer.

LITERATURE/JOURNALISM

Henry M. Stanley, *New York Herald* correspon-

1871

Chicago after the devastating fire of 1871. UPI/Corbis-Bettman

dent, finds Dr. David Livingstone after a two-year search in Africa; on meeting, Stanley offers legendary greeting: "Dr. Livingstone, I presume."

Frank Leslie's *Lady's Journal* is founded.

BOOKS *Little Men* by Louisa May Alcott, *The Hoosier Schoolmaster* by Edward Eggleston, *Pacific Poems* by Joaquin Miller, *Wake-Robin* by John Burroughs.

DEATHS Alice and Phoebe Cary, poet sisters.

ENTERTAINMENT

Augustin Daly writes and produces the plays *Divorce* and *Horizon*; J. J. McCloskey produces *Across the Continent.*

SPORTS

National Association of Base-Ball Players organizes (March 4); first game is played (May 4) at Ft. Wayne, Ind., with Ft. Wayne beating Cleveland 2–0.

Two American boats, *Columbia* and *Sappho*, combine to beat the English boat *Livonia* to retain America's Cup.

Henry Bassett, ridden by W. Miller, wins Belmont Stakes.

Ira Paine wins trapshooting championship; then A. H. Bogardus takes title, holds it for 25 years.

Rowing Association of American Colleges is formed.

New York Canoe Club is organized.

MISCELLANEOUS

Two disastrous fires strike Midwest (October 8): the Chicago fire which starts in a barn, lasts 27 hours, kills 250, destroys 17,450 buildings, and leaves 100,000 homeless; and a week-long forest fire that roars through a large area of Michigan and Wisconsin, kills 1,200 persons, 600 of them in Peshtigo, Wis.

Mystic Shrine of the Masonic Order is founded; first temple, Mecca in New York City, is established 1872.

National Rifle Association is founded.

Women begin to pile their hair atop their heads and stop cutting it.

1872

INTERNATIONAL

An international tribunal awards U.S. $5.5 million for damage claims resulting from attacks by British-built Confederate sea raiders (see 1871).

Treaty is negotiated with Samoan Islands for a naval station at Pago Pago.

NATIONAL

President Ulysses S. Grant, Republican, is reelected with 286 electoral and 3,597,000 popular votes, defeating Liberal Republican/Democratic candidate Horace Greeley with 66 electoral and 2,834,079 popular votes.

Post Office Department becomes an executive, cabinet-level department (May 8).

Yellowstone National Park is created (March 1).

Amnesty Act forgives all but a few most prominent Confederates, made all individuals covered by it eligible to vote and hold office.

New York Sun exposé charges Vice President Schuyler Colfax and other prominent politicians with accepting stock in Crédit Mobilier, company that built Union Pacific railroad, in return for political influence.

Tariff Act reduces duties 10% on manufactured goods.

First Arbor Day celebration is held in Nebraska.

Civil Service Act goes into effect; first commission is created (January 1).

Federal fish hatchery to propagate Atlantic salmon is established at Buckport, Me.

William M. (Boss) Tweed is convicted of plundering New York City treasury.

Equal Rights Party, formed by women from National Woman's Suffrage Assn., nominates Victoria C. Woodhull for president, first woman presidential candidate.

DEATHS William H. Seward, Secretary of State (1861–1869); William H. Russell, founder of Pony Express; George G. Meade, Union general in command at Gettysburg.

BUSINESS/INDUSTRY/INVENTIONS

Francis M. Smith and William T. Coleman discover mineral containing borax; gain control of deposits, virtual world monopoly; organize Pacific Coast Borax Co.

Elisha Gray forms Gray & Barton Co.; it later becomes Western Electric.

Montgomery Ward opens a mail-order dry-goods business in Chicago; offers one-page catalog with 30 items.

Samuel K. Percy patents process to make dried milk; Luther C. Crowell, a machine to produce square-bottomed paper bags; Silas Noble and James P. Cooley, a machine to make wooden toothpicks; Edmund D. Barbour, an adding machine.

Illinois passes legislation providing equal employment opportunity for men and women.

Portrait of the Artist's Mother by James Abbott McNeill Whistler, completed in 1872. The Granger Collection, New York

1872

Bloomingdale's department store opens.

Walter Scott of Providence, R.I., introduces the lunch wagon.

Stockyards in St. Louis are completed.

DEATHS Samuel F. B. Morse, inventor of the telegraph; James Fisk, financier.

TRANSPORTATION

Railway from St. Louis to Joplin, Mo., is completed; stimulates mining of zinc and lead.

DEATH Erastus Corning, a founder and first president, New York Central Railroad.

SCIENCE/MEDICINE

American Public Health Assn. is founded.

Popular Science Monthly is published.

EDUCATION

Vanderbilt University and its seminary are chartered; University of Oregon is founded.

RELIGION

Charles Taze Russell founds International Bible Students Assn., later renamed Jehovah's Witnesses.

Russian Orthodox church establishes episcopal see (area headquarters) at San Francisco.

Catholic Bishop James R. Bayley becomes archbishop of Baltimore.

Rev. Edward G. Andrews is named Methodist bishop of Des Moines.

DEATH Peter Cartwright, Methodist clergyman who was a major influence in the Midwest.

ART/MUSIC

James Whistler completes his famous painting *Portrait of the Artist's Mother*; Winslow Homer, *Snap the Whip*; Frank Duveneck, *Whistling Boy*.

LITERATURE/JOURNALISM

Mark Twain writes *Roughing It*; William Dean Howells, *Their Wedding Journey*.

Publishers Weekly is founded.

Whitelaw Reid gains control of *New York Tribune*; Cyrus H. K. Curtis founds Boston's *People's Ledger*.

DEATH Horace Greeley, founder and editor, *New York Tribune* (1841–1872).

ENTERTAINMENT

Frank H. Murdock writes the play *Davy Crockett*.

Eadweard Muybridge designs the "zoopraxiscope," a crude predecessor of a motion picture projector.

DEATH Edwin Forrest, actor.

SPORTS

William Steinitz of Bohemia becomes world chess champion, holds title 22 years.

Joe Daniels, ridden by J. Rowe, wins Belmont Stakes.

Two lacrosse clubs are formed: New York University Club and Park Lacrosse Club of Brooklyn.

MISCELLANEOUS

World Peace Jubilee in Boston features Patrick S. Gilmore leading a 20,000-member chorus and a 2,000-piece instrumental combination.

Richest quarter of Boston burns; 13 die, 767 buildings are destroyed.

1873

INTERNATIONAL

Spanish gunboat captures steamer *Virginius*, illegally flying U.S. flag and carrying men and material to Cuban insurgents; eight Americans and eventually 53 crew and passengers are executed (October 31).

NATIONAL

U.S. temperance crusade begins (December 24) when Eliza Thompson of Hillsboro, Ohio, leads 70 women from a prayer meeting to the outside of a saloon, where they sing and plead for the owner to close; visit 12 other saloons in succeeding days; movement leads to formation (1874) of Women's Christian Temperance Union.

Congress approves doubling president's salary to $50,000; increases government officials, including members of congress, from $5,000 to $7,000 (March 3); public outcry at "salary grab."

Congressional investigation of Crédit Mobilier leads to censure of two congressmen, Oakes Ames of Massachusetts and James Brooks of New York.

First penny postcards are issued (May 1).

National Grange calls for laws fixing "reasonable maximum rates" for railroad freight and passengers, attacks "all chartered monopolies."

Coinage Act passes, making gold the sole monetary standard.

DEATH Salmon P. Chase, Supreme Court Chief Justice (1864–1873).

BUSINESS/INDUSTRY/INVENTIONS

Failure of Jay Cooke banking firm (September 18)

Cable-car service, beginning in 1873 and pictured here on Market Street, will become an important means of transportation in hilly San Francisco. THE GRANGER COLLECTION, NEW YORK

1873

touches off Panic of 1873, which results in sharp fall of security prices, substantial unemployment; New York Stock Exchange closes for 10 days.

American Linoleum Manufacturing Co. introduces linoleum; Remington & Sons begins to manufacture typewriters; Joseph F. Glidden starts to manufacture barbed wire he invented; Bethlehem Steel Co. begins operations.

New Palmer House hotel in Chicago opens.

Drover's Journal, livestock market paper, begins publication.

PATENTS Alfred Paraf for process to manufacture oleomargarine; Eli H. Janney for automatic railway coupler; Anthony Iske for meat-slicing machine.

Daniel H. Burnham and John W. Root form architectural firm that designs first U.S. skyscraper (Montauk Building, Chicago).

Brotherhood of Railway Firemen organizes.

TRANSPORTATION

San Francisco cable-car service begins on Clay St. hill; Providence, R.I., begins to use a gas-powered streetcar.

International Peace Bridge across Niagara River from Buffalo to Ft. Erie is completed.

Cornelius Vanderbilt completes first New York–Chicago rail system; orders construction of Grand Central Terminal in New York City.

Hoosac Tunnel at North Adams, Mass., completed.

SCIENCE/MEDICINE

New England Female Medical College merges into Boston University Medical School to create first coeducational medical school in U.S.

Bellevue Hospital in New York City establishes school of nursing.

Louis Agassiz founds pioneer marine station at Buzzard's Bay, Mass.

DEATHS Johns Hopkins, endower of university, hospital; Louis Agassiz, pioneer in glaciation studies, zoology.

EDUCATION

St. Louis Board of Education authorizes public-school kindergarten, started by Susan E. Blow.

Texas Christian University is founded.

DEATH William H. McGuffey, author of famed "readers."

RELIGION

Reformed Episcopal Church is formally organized.

Union of American Hebrew Congregations is founded in Cincinnati by Rabbi Isaac M. Wise.

ART/MUSIC

Leopold Damrosch founds Oratorio Society of New York.

SONGS (popular): "John Henry," "The Mulligan Guard," "Silver Threads Among the Gold," "Home on the Range."

LITERATURE/JOURNALISM

Henry Holt & Co., publisher, is established.

Women's (later *Ladies*) *Home Companion* and *St. Nicholas* magazine are founded.

Detroit Evening News and *New York Daily Graphic*, first illustrated daily, are published.

Thomas B. Aldrich writes *Marjorie Daw and Other People*, and William Dean Howells, *A Chance Acquaintance*.

ENTERTAINMENT

The play *Led Astray* by Dion Boucicault is produced.

SPORTS

Survivor, ridden by G. Barbee, wins first Preakness Stakes; Springbok wins Belmont Stakes.

Tom Allen beats Mike McCoole to reclaim world heavyweight boxing title.

Harvard, Yale, Princeton, Columbia, and Rutgers organize Intercollegiate Football Assn.

National Association of Amateur Oarsmen is formed.

MISCELLANEOUS

Society for the Suppression of Vice organizes in New York City.

1874

NATIONAL

Panic of 1873 leads to law that increases issuance of paper money to $400 million; is vetoed by President Ulysses S. Grant; Congress reduces figure to $382 million on greenbacks in circulation, proposes to resume specie payments later.

Congress bows to public outcry on Salary Act of 1873, repeals the law except for the increase for the president and vice president.

Tompkins Square riot occurs in New York City when police charge a radical labor meeting.

Morrison R. Waite becomes Supreme Court Chief Justice (January 21).

Chautauqua Movement originates in an assembly for Sunday school teachers at Chautauqua Lake, N.Y., designs a course of meetings for Sunday school operations and Bible subjects; these become so popular that meetings on many other subjects are sponsored.

Women's Christian Temperance Union (WCTU) is organized in Cleveland; first president is Mrs. Anna Wittenmeyer.

Cartoon by Thomas Nast using elephant as symbol for Republican Party appears in *Harper's Weekly*.

Men, women, and children head for work in a New England factory. Factory work has become a way of life for many American families. Drawing by Winslow Homer. THE GRANGER COLLECTION, NEW YORK

1874

Blanche Kelso Bruce becomes first black man to serve full term in Senate; represents Mississippi.

DEATH Former President Millard Fillmore (1850–1853).

BUSINESS/INDUSTRY/INVENTIONS

Pillsbury-Washburn flour mill is founded; Chester Greenwood begins to manufacture earmuffs, which he invented; Sargent & Greenleaf manufactures bank time lock; Rogers & Burchfeld open tin factory in Leechburg, Pa.; L. Straus & Son takes over pottery and glassware department at Macy's store.

Massachusetts enacts 10-hour workday for women.

Montgomery Ward issues an eight-page catalog (see 1872).

Henry S. Parmelee patents sprinkler head; Joseph F. Glidden patents barbed wire.

Stockyards in Cincinnati open.

Cigar Makers International Union is first to adopt union label.

TRANSPORTATION

Eads Bridge over Mississippi River at St. Louis opens (July 4).

SCIENCE/MEDICINE

Physiological laboratory is established in Sheffield Scientific School at Yale University.

EDUCATION

University of Nevada at Reno is founded.

DEATHS Ezra Cornell, cofounder of Cornell University and organizer of Western Union; Franklin Buchanan, first superintendent, Naval Academy.

RELIGION

Two Episcopal bishops are named: William H. Oldenheimer, first bishop of Newark; William E. McLaren of Illinois.

LITERATURE/JOURNALISM

Edward P. Roe publishes *Opening a Chestnut Burr*; Sidney Lanier, the poem "Corn."

Joseph Medill acquires control of *Chicago Tribune*; Edward W. Scripps founds *The Penny Press* (later *Cleveland Press*).

ENTERTAINMENT

PLAYS *The Shaughran* by Dion Boucicault, *Evangeline* by J. C. Goodwin and E. E. Rice, *Two Orphans* stars Kate Claxton.

The Lambs, a club for theater people, is founded in New York City.

SPORTS

Football goalposts are used for first time in game between McGill University and Harvard; the game introduces rugby to U.S. and is first to which admission is charged.

Mary E. Outerbridge introduces lawn tennis to U.S.

First international rifle tournament matches U.S. and Irish teams; U.S. wins 934 to 931.

Culpepper wins Preakness Stakes; Saxon, the Belmont Stakes.

Tennessee State Sportsmen's Assn. puts on first public field trials for setters, pointers.

MISCELLANEOUS

Philadelphia Zoological Garden, first U.S. zoo, opens.

Young Men's Hebrew Assn. (YMHA) opens in New York City.

First engraved Christmas cards are issued by Louis Prang in Roxbury, Mass.

Philadelphia soda-fountain operator puts ice cream in soda water, originating ice-cream soda.

Juliet Corson opens New York Cooking School in her New York City home.

Ashfield Reservoir dam near Williamsburg, Mass., collapses; 100 die.

1875

INTERNATIONAL

Commercial treaty is signed with Hawaii, is ratified by Senate.

U.S. becomes member of Universal Postal Union.

NATIONAL

Congress passes civil rights bill that guarantees all citizens equal access to public accommodations; forbids exclusion of blacks from jury duty.

George W. Curtis resigns as first Civil Service Commission chair when group's recommendations are ignored; Commission is disbanded.

St. Louis Democrat uncovers conspiracy among federal officials and distillers to defraud government; results in indictment of 238 persons (May 10); President Ulysses S. Grant's secretary, Gen. O. E. Babcock is indicted (December 9).

Missouri state constitution is ratified by popular vote.

Boss (William M.) Tweed, convicted swindler, escapes from jail, flees to Cuba (see 1871, 1872).

First state agricultural experiment station is established in Middletown, Conn., by Wesleyan University.

Second Sioux War begins; lasts a year.

Gold is discovered in Black Hills of South Dakota.

Tariff Act restores cuts made in 1872 act.

Former President Andrew Johnson becomes a senator from Tennessee.

Rutherford B. Hayes is elected governor of Ohio.

DEATHS Former President Andrew Johnson (1865–1869); Vice President Henry Wilson (1873–1875); former Vice President John C. Breckenridge (1857–1861); Confederate Gen. George E. Pickett, who led Gettysburg charge.

BUSINESS/INDUSTRY/INVENTIONS

Alexander Graham Bell sends first barely audible message on his "harmonic telegraph" (telephone) to his assistant, Thomas A. Watson (June 3).

John F. Dryden founds Prudential Insurance Co. as Prudential Friendly Society.

American Express Co. begins first retirement program in private industry.

Thomas A. Edison develops mimeograph machine, ushering in reproduction machinery.

American Bankers Assn. is organized.

More than 100 million acres in U.S. are devoted to agricultural crops: 40 million in corn, 22 million in wheat, 11 million in oats, 9 million in cotton, 20 million in hay.

TRANSPORTATION

Railroad chair car, refrigerated railway car are introduced.

SCIENCE/MEDICINE

George F. Green patents an electric dental drill.

Dr. Andrew T. Still develops osteopathy in Kirkville, Mo.

American Veterinary Review is founded.

DEATH Edward Delafield, founder, American Ophthalmological Society.

EDUCATION

Two women's colleges open: Smith and Wellesley; Brigham Young University, founded as Provo University

Towne Scientific School is added to University of Pennsylvania.

RELIGION

Mary Baker Eddy, founder of Christian Science Church, issues first version of *Science and Health*, which outlines the church's doctrine.

Catholic Archbishop John McCloskey is first American elevated to cardinal (March 15); Bishop

1875

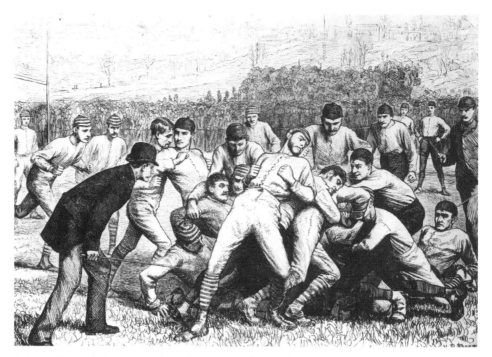

A football match between Yale and Princeton during the 1870s. CORBIS-BETTMANN

Jean B. Lamy of Santa Fe, N. Mex., is named archbishop.

Rev. James A. Healy becomes first black Catholic bishop when consecrated as bishop of Portland, Me.

Hebrew Union College for training rabbis is established in Cincinnati, Ohio.

Dwight L. Moody of Northfield, Mass., begins his revival meetings.

ART/MUSIC

Daniel C. French's sculpture *The Minute Man* is unveiled in Concord, Mass., at 100th anniversary of the start of American Revolution.

Thomas Eakins completes the painting *The Gross Clinic*; George Inness, *Autumn Oaks*.

James A. Bland writes the song "Carry Me Back to Old Virginny."

LITERATURE/JOURNALISM

First U.S. newspaper cartoon strip, "Professor Tigwissel's Burglar Alarm," appears in *New York Daily Graphic* (September 11).

Chicago Daily News is founded.

BOOKS *A Foregone Conclusion* by William Dean Howells, *The Masque of Pandora* (poetry) by Henry Wadsworth Longfellow, *A Passionate Pilgrim and Other Tales* by Henry James, *Sevenoaks* by J. G. Holland.

DEATH John Harper, cofounder of Harper Bros. publishers.

ENTERTAINMENT

Two Augustin Daly plays are produced: *Pique* with Maurice Barrymore and *The Big Bonanza*.

Baldwin Theater in San Francisco, Calif., opens.

SPORTS

First Kentucky Derby winner is Aristides, ridden by Oliver Lewis; Tom Ochiltree wins Preakness Stakes; Calvin, the Belmont Stakes.

Joe Borden of Philadelphia Nationals pitches first no-hit game in baseball (July 28).

Westminster Kennel Club is organized.

Frank Shaw claims national bicycle record after winning mile race in Brooklyn, N.Y.

Harvard beats Yale 4–0 in their football game.

Intercollegiate Association of Amateur Athletes of America (IC4A) is established.

Representatives of nine bowling clubs in New York and Brooklyn form National Bowling Assn.

MISCELLANEOUS

Lincoln Park (Chicago, Ill.) and Cincinnati (Ohio) zoos open.

Sons of the American Revolution (SAR) organize.

American Forestry Assn. is established in Chicago.

Helena P. Blavatsky and Henry S. Olcott found American Theosophical Society.

Fire destroys French Catholic church in South Holyoke, Mass., 120 are killed; steamer *Pacific* sinks after collision off Cape Flattery, 236 perish.

1876

NATIONAL

Presidential election is indecisive; Democrat Samuel J. Tilden wins popular vote by 250,000 over Republican Rutherford B. Hayes; however, electoral votes for Tilden in four states (Florida, Louisiana, South Carolina, Oregon) are disputed. Without these votes, Tilden is 1 vote short of election; on December 6, two sets of electoral votes are reported and election is sent to Congress for decision.

Colorado is admitted as 38th state (August 1); Alabama and North Carolina ratify new constitutions.

House votes to impeach War Secretary William W. Belknap for accepting bribes for sale of trading posts in Indian Territory; Belknap resigns; Senate votes to acquit him because majority feel that his resignation removes him from their jurisdiction.

Col. George Custer and 266 men are surrounded

The Centennial Exposition opens in Philadelphia, May 10, 1876. THE GRANGER COLLECTION, NEW YORK

1876

Alexander Graham Bell demonstrates his telephone at Salem, Massachusetts. THE GRANGER COLLECTION, NEW YORK

and killed at the Battle of the Little Bighorn in Montana (June 25); force of 6,000 Sioux and Cheyenne Indians are defeated at the Rosebud River in Montana.

American centennial is marked by first major U.S. industrial exhibition (in Fairmount Park, Philadelphia); 37 nations participate; more than 8 million people attend.

House passes bill that calls for free, unlimited coinage of silver; Senate takes no action.

U.S. Coast Guard Academy is founded at New London, Conn.

DEATH Former First Lady Eliza M. Johnson (1865–1869).

BUSINESS/INDUSTRY/INVENTIONS

Benjamin F. Goodrich founds tire, rubber com-

pany; Kroger grocery chain begins; first Fred Harvey restaurant opens in Santa Fe Railroad terminal in Topeka, Kans.

Alexander Graham Bell receives patent for telephone (March 7); three days later, he makes historic call: "Watson, come here; I want you."

Thomas A. Edison opens new laboratory in Menlo Park, N.J.

William A. Anthony and his Cornell University students build what is probably first American dynamo; Melville R. Bissell invents practical carpet sweeper: Halcyon Skinner, an employee of Alexander Smith Carpet Co., invents a carpet power loom to weave Axminster rugs.

Patents are issued to Albert H. Hook for cigarette-rolling machine, John C. Zachos for a stenotype device, and Daniel C. Stillson for a wrench.

Rich silver and lead ore deposits are discovered at Leadville, Colo.

SCIENCE/MEDICINE

American Chemical Society organizes in New York City.

Ira Remsen begins first American graduate research in chemistry at Johns Hopkins University.

DEATHS Solyman Brown, founder of U.S. dentistry as a profession; Walter Channing, first professor of obstetrics, medical jurisprudence (Harvard 1819–1847).

EDUCATION

American Library Assn. is organized; Melvil Dewey outlines decimal system that libraries throughout English-speaking world adopt; *Library Journal* is founded.

Johns Hopkins University, Colorado University, and Texas A. & M. are founded.

Free kindergarten opens in Florence, Mass.

RELIGION

DEATHS Rev. Edmund H. Sears, hymn writer ("It Came Upon a Midnight Clear"); Rev. Horace Bushnell, considered father of American religious liberalism.

ART/MUSIC

Thomas Eakins completes the painting *The Chess Players*; William M. Chase, *The Turkish Page*.

Electric organ, built by Hilborne L. Roosevelt, is installed in Chickering Hall, New York City; John McTammany demonstrates mechanical player piano that he develops.

SONGS (popular): "My Grandfather's Clock," "The Hat Father Wore," "I'll Take You Home Again, Kathleen," "The Rose of Killarney."

LITERATURE/JOURNALISM

American Magazine begins publication.

Philadelphia Times uses high-speed newspaper printing-and-folding machine; James E. and Edward W. Scripps acquire *St. Louis Evening Chronicle*.

BOOKS *The Adventures of Tom Sawyer* by Mark Twain, *Helen's Babies* by John Habberton, *Roderick Hudson* by Henry James.

ENTERTAINMENT

Goodspeed Opera House in East Haddam, Conn., opens.

SPORTS

National League of Professional Baseball Clubs is founded; Morgan G. Bulkeley is first president (February 2); first National League game is played in Philadelphia with Boston beating home team, 5–4, Jim O'Rourke gets first hit (April 22); Ross Barnes of Chicago hits first home run (May 2); Hartford beats Boston in first extra-inning game (April 29).

Hollis Hunnewell introduces court tennis in Boston; first court is built.

Westchester Polo Club is organized; first U.S. polo match is played in Dickel's Riding Academy, New York City.

Albert G. and James Spalding found sporting goods firm.

WINNERS *Boxing*—Joe Goss, heavyweight; *Chess*—James Mason, unofficial American championship; *Horse racing*—Vagrant, Kentucky Derby; Shirley, Preakness; Algerine, Belmont; *Track*—Princeton, first intercollegiate title; *Yachting*—U.S. yacht *Madeline*, America's Cup.

MISCELLANEOUS

First Philadelphia Mummers Parade is held.

Robert's Rules of Order is written by Henry M. Robert, military engineer.

Wild Bill Hickok is killed in a Deadwood, S. Dak., saloon while playing poker.

Felix Adler founds Society for Ethical Culture, dedicated to realizing highest human moral potential.

Railroad bridge at Ashtabula, Ohio, collapses in snowstorm, 92 die.

1877

NATIONAL

Congress creates an Electoral Commission to settle disputed Hayes–Tilden election (January 29), is composed of five members each from the House, Senate, and Supreme Court; Commission votes along straight party lines (8 Republicans, 7 Democrats), awards 20 electoral votes in four disputed states to Rutherford B. Hayes, giving him the election by 1 vote (February 28); Southern Democrats vote with Republicans (March 2) to certify Hayes the winner in return for withdrawal of federal troops stationed in the South since the Civil War and for appropriations for improvements; Hayes is inaugurated March 5.

House again passes bill authorizing silver coinage.

Thomas Alva Edison poses with his phonograph for the photographer Mathew Brady. THE GRANGER COLLECTION, NEW YORK

Congress approves Bedloe's (later Liberty) Island as site for Statue of Liberty.

Surrender of Chief Joseph ends war between Idaho nation and U.S. government.

First observance of Flag Day (June 14) is held to mark 100th anniversary of flag's adoption. Survey of the Coast office is renamed Coast and Geodetic Survey.

From Ohio, William McKinley begins to serve first of three terms in the House.

DEATH Levi Coffin, "president" of underground railway that helped escaping slaves.

BUSINESS/INDUSTRY/INVENTIONS

Bell Telephone Co. forms, succeeding Bell Patent Assn.; Charles J. Glidden establishes world's first telephone exchange in Worcester, Mass.

Pope Manufacturing Co., bicycle maker, is founded in Hartford, Conn.

Swift & Co. of Chicago ships dressed beef by refrigerated railway cars.

Massachusetts becomes first state to establish factory safeguards.

Nathanael G. Herreshoff patents a catamaran; Thomas A. Edison files for patent on phonograph.

Emile Berliner invents the microphone.

Chase National Bank in New York City is founded.

Gold is discovered on Salmon River in western Idaho.

DEATH Robert P. Parrott, inventor of first U.S. rifled cannon.

TRANSPORTATION

Strike on Baltimore & Ohio Railroad protests wage cuts (July 17); spreads to other lines, eventually involving 100,000 workers; rioting occurs in Baltimore, Pittsburgh, Chicago, St. Louis, federal troops go to Martinsburg, W. Va., after nine are killed in striker-militia battle, and to Pittsburgh, where Pennsylvania Railroad yards are destroyed, pitched battle occurs (July 21), and 26 are killed.

Cantilever railroad bridge over Kentucky River at Harrodsburg, Ky., opens.

DEATH Cornelius Vanderbilt, founder of railroad, shipping family.

SCIENCE/MEDICINE

Astronomer Asaph Hall discovers two satellites of Mars.

Edward C. Pickering begins 42 years as director of Harvard Observatory.

EDUCATION

Henry O. Flippen becomes first black graduate of U.S. Military Academy at West Point.

RELIGION

Trinity (Episcopal) Church in Boston is dedicated; replaces church lost in 1872 fire.

Question of predestination splits Lutheran Church in the U.S.

Catholic Bishop James Gibbons becomes archbishop of Baltimore.

DEATH Brigham Young, head of Mormon Church (1847–1877).

ART/MUSIC

Society of American Artists is organized.

Philadelphia Conservatory of Music is founded.

Winslow Homer completes the painting *The Carnival*; Frank Duveneck, *The Cobbler's Apprentice*.

SONGS (popular): "Abdul, the Bulbul Ameer," "Chopsticks," "In the Gloaming."

LITERATURE/JOURNALISM

Isaac Funk founds publishing company that becomes Funk & Wagnall's.

Puck, the comic magazine, is founded.

BOOKS *The American* by Henry James, *Deephaven* by Sarah Orne Jewett, "Song of the Chattahoochee" (poetry) by Sidney Lanier, *Birds and Poets* by John Burroughs.

ENTERTAINMENT

Mark Twain and Bret Harte collaborate on play *Ah, Sin*; other plays include *Our Boarding House* by L. Grover and *Zip*, starring Charlotte Crabtree.

SPORTS

William H. Hulbert becomes president of National (baseball) League; four members of Louisville (Ky.) baseball club are expelled from baseball for "crooked play."

Westminster Kennel Club stages first major dog show at Gilmore's Gardens, New York City, with 1,191 entries (May 8).

Winners of major horse races are Baden-Baden (Kentucky Derby) and Cloverbank (the Preakness Stakes and the Belmont Stakes).

American Bicycling Journal begins publication.

MISCELLANEOUS

American Humane Assn., dedicated to preventing cruelty to livestock, is founded.

First asphalt pavement is used in New York City.

Sam Bass and his gang hold up Union Pacific train at Big Springs, Neb., take $65,000 in gold and valuables.

1878

INTERNATIONAL

Treaty is signed with Samoan Islands for nonexclusive use of Pago Pago as a naval station (January 17); ratified (January 30).

Chinese Embassy in Washington, D.C., opens.

NATIONAL

Bland-Allison Act for free coinage of silver passes over President Rutherford B. Hayes's veto; calls for federal purchase of $2–4 million of silver at market price to be converted to silver dollars.

Nurses tend victims of the great yellow fever scourge in the hard-hit South, 1878. CORBIS-BETTMANN

President Hayes initiates Easter-egg roll on the White House lawn.

Senator Aaron A. Sargent (Calif.) introduces bill to give women the right to vote; fails to pass.

After Congress adjourns, President Hayes suspends Chester A. Arthur, New York City port customs collector, and Alonzo B. Cornell, port naval officer, as politically motivated appointments.

DEATHS William M. (Boss) Tweed, convicted political boss; Benjamin L. E. de Bonneville, explorer of northwestern U.S.; John S. Carlile, leader in creating West Virginia.

BUSINESS/INDUSTRY/INVENTIONS

Edison Electric Light Co. of New York is incorporated.

Louis Tiffany opens factory to make stained glass; Procter & Gamble produces soap that floats (Ivory); Robert A. Chesebrough, manufacturer of petroleum jelly, registers name *Vaseline*.

New Haven, Conn., installs telephone switchboard or exchange to serve 21 customers; issues first telephone directory (February 21).

American Bar Assn. is organized.

McKim, Mead & White form what becomes one of nation's leading architectural firms; J. Walter Thompson advertising agency is founded.

John F. Appleby patents a grain binder, knotter; Thomas A. Edison, phonograph.

Washington A. Burpee founds first successful mail-order seed business.

TRANSPORTATION

First American elevated railroad begins operations on Sixth Avenue, New York City.

Caesar Spiegler builds first American dirigible, makes maiden flight (July 3) with John Wise as pilot.

SCIENCE/MEDICINE

Yellow fever epidemic sweeps through South; 14,000 die.

Samuel P. Langley invents a bolometer with which to measure the Sun's energy output at chosen points.

American Laryngological Assn. is formed.

DEATH Joseph Henry, first secretary and director, Smithsonian Institution (1846–1878).

EDUCATION

Creighton University (Omaha, Nebr.), Duquesne University (Pittsburgh, Pa.), and Missisippi State University are founded.

RELIGION

Charles E. Cheney, who helped organize the Reformed Episcopal Church, becomes its bishop of Chicago.

Rev. Alexander Burgess becomes first Episcopal bishop of Quincy, Ill.

Catholic Bishop Charles J. Seghers becomes archbishop of Oregon City, Ore.

DEATH Charles Hodge, a leading theologian.

ART/MUSIC

Leopold Damrosch founds New York Symphony Orchestra.

John S. Sargent completes the painting *The Oyster Gatherers of Cancale*.

SONGS (popular): "In the Evening by the Moonlight," "Aloha Oe," "Skidmore Fancy Ball."

LITERATURE/JOURNALISM

Frederick E. Ives develops photoengraving process.

Adolph S. Ochs buys control of *Chattanooga Times*; Joseph Pulitzer buys bankrupt *St. Louis Dispatch*; *Yale News* begins publication.

BOOKS *The Europeans* by Henry James, *The Leavenworth Case* by Anna K. Green, "The Marshes of Glynn" (poetry) by Sidney Lanier, *Roxy* by Edward Eggleston.

DEATH William Cullen Bryant, editor (*New York Post* 1829–1878) and poet ("Thanatopsis").

ENTERTAINMENT

Clay Green's play, *M'lis*, is produced.

1879

SPORTS

Frederick W. Thayer, Harvard University catcher, patents baseball catcher's mask.

First unassisted triple play in baseball is made by Paul Hines of Providence, R.I. (May 8).

Badminton Club of New York is formed, the first in U.S.

Boston Bicycle Club is organized.

Albert G. Spalding launches annual *Official Baseball Guide*.

WINNERS *Horse racing* — Day Star, Kentucky Derby; Duke of Magenta, Preakness Stakes and Belmont Stakes; *Rowing* — Columbia, first American winner at Henley Regatta.

MISCELLANEOUS

Two anti-crime organizations are founded: New England Watch and Ward Society in Boston and the Society for the Prevention of Crime in New York City.

Sam Bass, gang leader, is fatally wounded in bank-robbery attempt in Texas.

Literary and Scientific Circle of Chautauqua Institution is founded, provides home-study course in theology.

Mrs. H. O. Ward writes *Sensible Etiquette of the Best Society*.

NATIONAL

President Rutherford B. Hayes signs act that permits women to practice law before Supreme Court (February 15); Belva A. B. Lockwood becomes first woman to do so (March 3).

California and Louisiana constitutions are ratified; Louisiana capital moves from New Orleans to Baton Rouge.

Frances E. C. Willard becomes president of Women's Christian Temperance Union.

U.S. Geological Survey is authorized; Clarence King is first director.

President Hayes vetoes bill to restrict Chinese immigration.

Specie payments resume as authorized in 1875.

BUSINESS/INDUSTRY/INVENTIONS

Developments in electricity: Thomas A. Edison invents incandescent electric lamp (October 21); demonstrates an incandescent lighting system (December 31); Wanamaker's in Philadelphia becomes first store lighted by electricity; electric arc lights are used to light Cleveland's (Ohio) Public Square; California Electric Light Co. is organized; water from Niagara Falls is used to drive waterwheel to generate power for small sawmill.

Frank W. Woolworth opens his first 5-and-10-cent store in Utica, N.Y.; it fails; is moved to Lancaster, Pa.; Anheuser-Busch Brewing Co. is founded.

Morgan G. Bulkeley becomes first president of Aetna Life Insurance Co., Hartford, Conn.

James and John Ritty patent a cash register.

Illinois prohibits employment of women in coal mines.

Terence V. Powderly heads Knights of Labor.

DEATH Charles Goodyear, founder of rubber company.

TRANSPORTATION

Glasgow (Mo.) Bridge over Missouri River opens.

SCIENCE/MEDICINE

Ira Remsen of Johns Hopkins University announces discovery of saccharin (February 27) and founds *American Chemical Journal*.

Iowa State College establishes first state veterinary school in U.S.

William H. Welch develops first American pathology laboratory at Bellevue Hospital Medical College, New York City.

Archaeological Institute of America is founded in Boston.

EDUCATION

Capt. R. H. Pratt establishes Carlisle (Pa.) Indian School.

Dwight Moody founds Northfield (Mass.) Seminary for Girls.

RELIGION

Mary Baker Eddy charters Christian Science Church in Boston (August 23).

St. Patrick's Cathedral in New York City is dedicated.

Charles Taze Russell publishes the *Watch Tower*.

ART/MUSIC

George W. Nichols, the founder, becomes first president of Cincinnati (Ohio) College of Music.

Art Institute of Chicago and Walker Art Center, Minneapolis, Minn., open.

Chicago Central Music Hall is completed.

PAINTINGS *The Pipe Dance* by Ralph A. Blakelock, *Cup of Tea* by Mary Cassatt, *The Girl in a Black Hood* by Frank Duveneck, *Luxembourg Gardens at Twilight* by John S. Sargent.

Boston Ideal Opera Co. is founded.

SONGS (popular): "Oh, Dem Golden Slippers," "Alouette," "A Tisket, A Tasket."

DEATH William M. Hunt, portrait painter.

LITERATURE/JOURNALISM

Joel Chandler Harris writes first of Uncle Remus stories, "The Wonderful Tar-Baby Story."

Walter Wellman founds *Cincinnati Post*.

BOOKS *Progress and Poverty* by Henry George (proposes "single tax" reform; sells over 2 million copies), *Old Creole Days* by George W. Cable, *Daisy Miller* by Henry James, *Rudder Grange* by Frank Stockton, *The Lady of Aroostook* by William Dean Howells.

DEATH William Lloyd Garrison, abolitionist leader and editor (*The Liberator*).

ENTERTAINMENT

William K. Vanderbilt buys Gilmore Gardens in New York City, renames it Madison Square Garden; Madison Square Theater is built, including double elevator stage to permit quick scene changes.

Ada Rehan debuts in New York City in *L'Assomoir*.

David Belasco and James A. Herne write play *Hearts of Oak*; other plays are *The Brook-Comedy* by Nate Salsbury and *The Galley Slave* by Bartley Campbell.

SPORTS

First U.S. six-day bicycle race is held in Chicago.

National Archery Assn. is founded, stages first tournament.

U.S. Amateur Lacrosse Assn. is established.

New York Athletic Club holds first interclub amateur athletic meet.

Ice-skating rink is built in Madison Square Garden.

WINNERS *Horse racing*—Lord Murphy, Kentucky Derby; Harold, Preakness Stakes; Spendthrift, Belmont Stakes; *Rowing*—University of Pennsylvania, first Child's Cup race.

MISCELLANEOUS

Rembrandt House on West 57th Street, New York City, becomes first cooperative apartment building.

1880

INTERNATIONAL

Treaty is signed with China to "regulate, limit, or suspend," but not prohibit, Chinese immigration.

NATIONAL

James A. Garfield, Republican, is elected president over Democratic Winfield S. Hancock; popular vote is close (4,449,053 to 4,442,030) but electoral vote is 214 to 155; Chester A. Arthur is elected vice president.

Tenth census reports national population at 50,155,783.

Annual immigration in U.S. reaches 457,257—a figure that will be reached almost every year until 1905.

Supreme Court holds unconstitutional a West Virginia law that excludes blacks from jury duty.

National debt is reported at $2 billion.

DEATH Ellen L. Arthur, wife of the incoming vice president.

BUSINESS/INDUSTRY/INVENTIONS

Thomas A. Edison demonstrates first experimental overhead line for incandescent lights by having main street of Menlo Park, N.J., lighted on New Year's Eve; also first direct current underground power transmission system; Edison Lamp Works opens in Menlo Park.

Small hydroelectric power installation is established at Niagara Falls, N.Y.

Grand Rapids (Mich.) Electric Light & Power Co. begins operations; New York Steam Corp. is formed; Elmer A. Sperry founds Sperry Electric Co.

Pay station telephone service begins in New Haven, Conn.

John Stevens patents flour-rolling mill that increases production 70%.

John B. Hammond invents a new-style typewriter.

Milton George, editor of *Western Rural*, a farm journal, founds National Farmers Alliance.

American Society of Mechanical Engineers is founded in New York City.

Detroit opens central market, features meat and vegetables.

TRANSPORTATION

DEATHS Thomas S. Hall, inventor of electric automatic signals for railroads, highways; Donald McKay, builder of clipper ships.

SCIENCE/MEDICINE

Astronomer Henry Draper introduces photography of nebulae.

DEATH Benjamin Peirce, mathematician and astronomer.

EDUCATION

University of California founded.

RELIGION

John Taylor is elected president of the Mormon church.

Frances Xavier (Mother) Cabrini founds Missionary Sisters of the Sacred Heart.

Phillips Brooks, Episcopal rector, is first U.S. clergyman to conduct services for British royal family in England.

Catholic Bishop Patrick A. Feehan becomes first archbishop of Chicago.

ART/MUSIC

John Philip Sousa directs U.S. Marine Band, forms own band in 1892.

Cincinnati (Ohio) Art Museum, and Rhode Island School of Design/Museum of Art open.

Sculptor Augustus Saint-Gaudens completes statue of Admiral Farragut.

The Hatfield family, infamous for its feud with the McCoys beginning in 1880. CORBIS-BETTMANN

Henry E. Krehbiel begins 43 years as music critic for *New York Tribune*.

SONGS (popular): "Blow the Man Down," "Hear Dem Bells," "Funiculi, Funicula."

DEATH Constantino Brumidi, painter of Capitol frescoes.

LITERATURE/JOURNALISM

Joseph Pulitzer combines *St. Louis Post* and *Dispatch*; James E. and Edward W. Scripps acquire *Cincinnati Post*, creating first U.S. newspaper chain.

The Dial, a journal of opinion, is founded; *Il Progresso*, Italian newspaper, begins publication in New York City.

BOOKS *Uncle Remus* by Joel Chandler Harris, *Five Little Peppers* by Harriet Lothrop, *Ben-Hur* by Lew Wallace, *The Peterkin Papers* by Lucretia P. Hale, *A Tramp Abroad* by Mark Twain, *The Stillwater Tragedy* by Thomas B. Aldrich.

DEATH Frank Leslie, newspaper and magazine publisher.

ENTERTAINMENT

Sarah Bernhardt makes U.S. debut at Booth Theater, New York City.

PLAYS *Hazel Kirke* by Steele MacKaye, *Edgewood Folks* by J. E. Brown, *Needles and Pins* with Ada Rehan and John Drew, *Widow Bedott* with Neil Burgess.

SPORTS

League of American Wheelmen is formed by 28 bicycle clubs; American Canoe Assn. is formed.

George Ligowsky patents clay-pigeon trapshooting target.

National Croquet League is organized by 18 clubs.

WINNERS *Boxing* — Paddy Ryan, U.S. heavyweight title; *Chess* — George McKenzie, unofficial U.S. champion; *Horse racing* — Fonso, Kentucky

Derby; Grenada, Preakness Stakes and Belmont Stakes; *Wrestling* — William Muldoon, world title.

MISCELLANEOUS

Salvation Army in U.S. begins with arrival in New York City of Commissioner George S. Railton and seven women workers.

Egyptian obelisk Cleopatra's Needle is erected in Central Park, New York City.

Hatfield-McCoy feud around Williamson, W. Va., begins when a Hatfield is accused of stealing a McCoy hog; continues for 10 years with numerous fatalities.

1881

NATIONAL

President James A. Garfield is shot and fatally wounded in Washington, D.C., railroad station by a disappointed office seeker, Charles J. Guiteau (July 2); President dies September 19; Vice President Chester A. Arthur sworn in as president at 2 A.M., September 20; Guiteau is convicted November 25.

Clara Barton organizes American Red Cross in Washington, D.C.

Supreme Court in *Springer v. United States* upholds constitutionality of 1862 federal income tax.

Kansas adopts state prohibition law.

National Civil Service Reform League is organized.

Grover Cleveland is elected mayor of Buffalo, N.Y.; Benjamin Harrison begins term as a senator from Indiana.

Sitting Bull and his Sioux tribe surrender to the army.

DEATH Union Gen. Ambrose E. Burnside.

BUSINESS/INDUSTRY/INVENTIONS

Wharton School of Commerce & Finance is established at University of Pennsylvania with $100,000 gift by James Wharton.

Western Union Telegraph Co., Postal Telegraph Co., and Warner & Swasey, machine tools manufacturer, are founded.

Louise B. Bethune, first U.S. woman architect, opens office in Buffalo, N.Y.; becomes first woman member of American Institute of Architects.

Frederick W. Taylor conducts first time-and-motion studies to improve efficiency.

Federation of Organized Trades and Labor Unions, forerunner of AFL, is founded in Pittsburgh.

David H. Houston patents camera roll film; Leonidas G. Woolley, a locomotive electric headlight; William Morrison designs an automobile storage battery.

Anaconda Silver Mining Co. (later Anaconda Copper) is established.

Brotherhood of Telegraphers is organized.

DEATH Lorenzo Delmonico, New York restaurateur.

TRANSPORTATION

Southern Pacific Railroad is completed from New Orleans to the Pacific.

Michigan cedes the Soo Canals to the federal government.

SCIENCE/MEDICINE

Dr. William S. Halsted performs first successful blood transfusion.

DEATH Lewis H. Morgan, pioneer U.S. ethnologist.

EDUCATION

Tuskegee (Ala.) Institute opens with 30 students; Booker T. Washington is principal.

William R. Ware founds, heads Columbia University Architectural School.

Booker T. Washington (front row, center) poses with the Tuskegee faculty council. THE GRANGER COLLECTION, NEW YORK

Moses C. Tyler is first U.S. college history professor (Cornell University).

Forerunner of University of Connecticut at Storrs and Drake University founded.

RELIGION

New Church Theological School in Waltham, Mass., incorporates; Western Theological Seminary is founded.

Rev. Francis E. Clark organizes First Christian Endeavor Society in Williston Congregational Church, Portland, Maine.

Rev. Benjamin T. Tanner becomes bishop of Philadelphia of the African Methodist Episcopal (AME) Church.

DEATHS Leonard Bacon, leading Congregational clergyman; Josiah Henson, Methodist clergyman, reputedly prototype of Uncle Tom in Harriet Beecher Stowe's book.

ART/MUSIC

Henry L. Higginson founds Boston Symphony Orchestra.

New York City music festival attracts 10,000 people.

1882

John McTammany Jr. patents a mechanical player piano.

SONGS (popular): "Dar's One More Ribber to Cross," "Loch Lomond," "My Bonnie Lies Over the Ocean," "Peek-a-Boo," "The Spanish Cavalier."

LITERATURE/JOURNALISM

Scribner's Monthly becomes *Century Illustrated Magazine*; the comic weekly *Judge* is founded.

New York Arbeiter Zeitung, a Yiddish newspaper, begins publication.

BOOKS *The Portrait of a Lady* and *Washington Square* by Henry James, *The Common Law* by Oliver Wendell Holmes Jr., *Century of Dishonor* (critique of U.S. policy toward American Indian) by Helen H. Jackson.

DEATH Sidney Lanier, leading Southern poet.

ENTERTAINMENT

P. T. Barnum and James A. Bailey combine their circuses to form the Barnum & Bailey circus.

Tony Pastor opens a theater on 14th Street, New York City; provides vaudeville entertainment suitable for families; offers door prizes.

Lillian Russell stars in comic opera *The Great Mogul*; other plays are *Esmeralda* with William Gillette, *The Passing Regiment* with Ada Rehan and John Drew.

SPORTS

U.S. Lawn Tennis Assn. is organized by 33 clubs in New York City.

American Association is organized with six charter baseball clubs; Roger Connor, Troy (N.Y.) first baseman, hits first grand-slam home run.

American Angler, first U.S. fishing magazine, begins publication.

WINNERS *Horse racing* — Hindoo, Kentucky Derby; Saunterer, Preakness Stakes and Belmont Stakes; Iroquois becomes first American horse to win English Derby; *Tennis* — Richard Sears, U.S. Lawn Tennis singles; Clarence M. Clark and Frederick W. Taylor, doubles; *Yachting* — U.S. boat *Mischief* defeats *Atalanta* to retain America's Cup.

MISCELLANEOUS

Big shootout at O.K. Corral occurs when Earp brothers and Doc Holliday fight the Clanton gang October 26; Sheriff Pat Garrett kills Billy the Kid, outlaw, July 15.

Loganberry, cross between wild blackberry and red raspberry, is introduced.

Many women wear their hair in ringlets.

1882

INTERNATIONAL

Chinese Exclusion Act is passed, restricts immigration for 10 years.

Korean–U.S. treaty recognizing Korean independence is signed.

NATIONAL

Floods along Mississippi River leave 85,000 families homeless; President Chester A. Arthur asks Congress for a levee system to control future flooding.

Supreme Court rules that the Fourteenth Amendment prevents states from infringing on civil rights but does not apply to infringement by individual persons.

Charles J. Guiteau, convicted murderer of President Garfield, is executed (see 1881).

Congress passes law that makes polygamy illegal.

Annual pensions of $5,000 are provided for presidential widows.

Tariff Commission recommends substantial reductions in tariffs.

Grover Cleveland is elected governor of New York.

DEATH Former First Lady Mary Todd Lincoln (1861–1865).

BUSINESS/INDUSTRY/INVENTIONS

Edison Electric Light Co. of New York City opens its central station to provide light and power; first hydroelectric plant opens in Appleton, Wis.

Charles H. Dow and Edward D. Jones found Dow Jones & Co.

First J. J. McCrory 5-and-10-cent store opens in Scotsdale, Pa.

Standard Oil Company of Ohio, under John D. Rockefeller's leadership, forms first modern "trust".

George Westinghouse produces an integrated automatic railway-signal system.

Peter J. McGuire, founder of Carpenter's Union, recommends creation of a "Labor Day"; Central Labor Union in New York City sponsors first Labor Day parade.

Oil fields are discovered in Ohio and Indiana.

Severe strikes hit iron and steel industry.

Henry W. Seely patents an electric flatiron.

DEATHS Cadwallader C. Washburn, flour-milling company founder; James Vick, developer of mail-order seed business.

TRANSPORTATION

Nickel Plate (New York, Chicago & St. Louis Railroad) operates between Buffalo, N.Y., and Chicago, Ill.

SCIENCE/MEDICINE

Physicist Albert A. Michelson determines speed of light to be 186,320 miles per second (in 1933, it is corrected to 186,271 miles per second).

Silk sutures replace catgut thread in surgical operations.

EDUCATION

University of North Dakota and Harvard Annex (which becomes Radcliffe College) are founded.

American Association of University Women is founded as Association of Collegiate Alumnae.

"Welcome to All!" trumpets this 1880 cartoon favoring unrestricted immigration. In 1882 the Immigration Act is passed, restricting immigration. Cartoon by Joseph Keppler. THE GRANGER COLLECTION, NEW YORK

1883

ART/MUSIC

John S. Sargent completes the paintings *The Daughter of Edward Darly Boit* and *El Juleo*.

SONGS (popular): "Goodbye, My Lover, Goodbye," "The Skaters Waltz," "Sweet Violets," "When the Clock in the Tower Strikes Twelve."

LITERATURE/JOURNALISM

Argosy Magazine begins publication in New York City as *The Golden Argosy*.

Harrison G. Otis acquires interest in *Los Angeles Times*; gains control in 1886.

BOOKS *The Prince and the Pauper* by Mark Twain, *A Modern Instance* by William Dean Howells; Frank Stockton writes popular short story "The Lady and the Tiger."

DEATHS Henry Wadsworth Longfellow, poet; Ralph Waldo Emerson, essayist; Richard Henry Dana, author.

ENTERTAINMENT

Richard Mansfield stars in *A Parisian Romance*.

Bijou Theater in Boston becomes first to be lighted by electricity.

Henrik Ibsen's play *A Doll's House* is performed in English for first time.

P. T. Barnum introduces the elephant Jumbo in circus.

Yiddish Theater and Casino Theater in New York City open.

Actors Fund of America (for needy actors) created.

SPORTS

Worcester (Mass.) and Providence (R.I.) play first major-league baseball doubleheader; Chicago Cubs (N) and Cincinnati Reds (AA) split two games in championship series; Richard Higham is first (and only) umpire expelled from baseball for dishonesty.

Brookline (Mass.) Country Club is established.

Tennis rackets are introduced in St. Paul's School, a prep school in Concord, N.H.

WINNERS *Boxing* — John L. Sullivan, heavyweight title; *Horse racing* — Apollo, Kentucky Derby; Vanguard, Preakness Stakes; Forrester, Belmont Stakes.

DEATH William A. Hulbert, National League president (1877–1882).

MISCELLANEOUS

Knights of Columbus is chartered in New Haven, Conn.

First pier in Atlantic City, N.J., is completed; storm destroys it three months later.

Members of his gang kill Jesse James, outlaw.

INTERNATIONAL

Senate ratifies 1882 treaty recognizing Korea's independence.

NATIONAL

Pendleton Act reestablishes Civil Service Commission, headed by Dorman B. Eaton.

Supreme Court holds 1866 Civil Rights Act unconstitutional because it protects social rather than political rights.

The railroads establish four standard time zones.

Congress authorizes the building of three steel cruisers, first steps toward a modern navy.

Cost of first class mail is reduced to two cents for a half-ounce.

Tariff Act lowers duties by 5%.

DEATHS Alexander H. Stephens, Confederate vice president; Montgomery Blair, Postmaster

Brooklyn Bridge (depicted here in 1915) opens on May 24, 1883. LIBRARY OF CONGRESS

General (1861–1864), who started free city delivery, postal money orders, railway post office.

BUSINESS/INDUSTRY/INVENTIONS

Lewis E. Waterman perfects first practical fountain pen.

PATENTS Oscar Hammerstein I, cigar-rolling machine; Augustus Schultz, chrome process to tan hides and skins; Jan E. Matzeliger, shoe lasting machine.

New York City Plate Glass Co. begins large-scale production of glass; Pittsburgh (Pa.) Plate Glass Co. is founded.

Yale & Towne Manufacturing Co. begins crane manufacturing; Industrial Brownhoist Corp. of Bay City Mich., erects railway wrecking crane.

John W. Mackay founds Commercial Cable Co.

Brotherhood of Railway Trainmen is organized.

National Association of Retail Druggists is founded.

William Horlick produces malted milk.

DEATH Peter Cooper, builder of first U.S. locomotive, early leader in iron and steel industry.

TRANSPORTATION

Brooklyn Bridge and cantilever bridge across Niagara River open.

Charles J. Van Depoele demonstrates electric trolley cars, which soon are used in various cities.

Northern Pacific Railroad is completed.

SCIENCE/MEDICINE

Sisters of St. Francis build hospital in Rochester, Minn., following a disastrous tornado.

American Anti-Vivisection Society is organized.

1883

Science begins publication; becomes official organ of American Association for the Advancement of Science.

DEATH Lydia Pinkham, patent medicine maker.

EDUCATION

Frederick A. F. Barnard organizes Barnard College for women at Columbia University; University of Texas opens.

Cornell University Engineering College offers its first electrical engineering course.

RELIGION

First class of rabbis ordained in U.S. after graduating from Hebrew Union College in Cincinnati.

Missionary Training College (later Institute) opens in New York City.

Catholic Bishop William H. Elder is named archbishop of Cincinnati, Ohio.

DEATH Elling Eielsen, founder of Evangelical Lutheran Church of America.

ART/MUSIC

Metropolitan Opera House opens with Gounod's *Faust*.

Lillian Nordica, opera singer who starred in Europe, makes U.S. debut in New York City.

Statue of Washington on steps of New York Sub-Treasury Building is unveiled.

Institute of Fine Arts in Minneapolis, Minn., opens.

SONGS (popular): "The Farmer in the Dell," "My Nellie's Blue Eyes," "Polly Wolly Doodle," "There Is a Tavern in the Town."

DEATH Clark Mills, sculptor of first U.S. equestrian statue (Andrew Jackson facing the White House).

LITERATURE/JOURNALISM

Cyrus H. K. Curtis founds *Ladies Home Journal*, monthly magazine.

Christian Science Monitor is founded as *Christian Science Journal*.

Joseph Pulitzer buys the *New York World* from Jay Gould.

Life, humorous magazine, and Opie Read's humorous *Arkansas Journal*, begin publication.

BOOKS *The Old Swimmin' Hole* (poetry) by James Whitcomb Riley, *Life on the Mississippi* by Mark Twain, *The Story of a Country Town* by Edgar W. Howe, *The Led-Horse Claim* by Mary H. Foote.

DEATH Isaac Adams, inventor of power printing press.

ENTERTAINMENT

B. F. Keith opens his first theater, eventually owns 400.

Buffalo Bill's Wild West Show opens in Omaha, Nebr.

New plays include *The Rajah* by William Young and *Siberia* by Bartley Campbell.

SPORTS

A. G. Mills becomes president of National (baseball) League; Union Association, baseball league of 10 teams, is formed, folds after one season; first baseball game under lights is played in Ft. Wayne, Ind., when Methodist College beats Quincy 19–11; first Ladies Day game is played by New York Giants.

National horse show opens in Madison Square Garden with 187 exhibitors, 623 entries.

First intercollegiate tennis matches are held at Trinity College, Hartford, Conn.

Hugh Baxter is first to exceed 11 feet in pole vault (11 ft., 1/4 in.).

WINNERS *Archery*—Mrs. M. C. Howell, national title (repeated 11 times between 1885 and 1907); *Bicycling*—G. M. Hendrie, first recorded championship; *Billiards*—Jacob Schaefer, balkline title; *Horse racing*—Leonatus, Kentucky Derby; Jacobus, Preakness Stakes; George Kinney, Belmont Stakes; *Tennis*—Harvard, intercollegiate title.

MISCELLANEOUS

First mail chute for high-rise buildings is installed in Elwood Building, Rochester, N.Y.

First federally purchased historic house is Custis-Lee Mansion in Arlington, Va.

Worst floods of Ohio River cause extensive damage.

1884

INTERNATIONAL

International Prime Meridian Conference is held in Washington; recommends Greenwich meridian for counting longitude and mean time.

U.S. is granted exclusive right to establish coaling and repair station at Pearl Harbor, Hawaii.

NATIONAL

Grover Cleveland, Democrat, is elected president over Republican James G. Blaine by 4,911,017 popular (219 electoral) votes to 4,848,334 popular (182 electoral) votes.

Supreme Court upholds congressional right to punish as a violation of federal law interference with a citizen's right to vote in a federal election.

AFL convention resolves that the first Monday in September be observed as Labor Day; Bureau of Labor is established in Interior Department, with Carroll D. Wright as commissioner.

Naval War College is established in Newport, R.I., with Commander Stephen B. Luce president.

Iowa adopts statewide prohibition; Montana ratifies its constitution; Alaska District is established.

Statue of Liberty is completed in France; is presented to U.S. (July 4), cornerstone is laid for pedestal (August 5).

Washington Monument is completed in Washington, D.C.

Bureau of Animal Industry is created to conduct federal meat inspection.

BUSINESS/INDUSTRY/INVENTIONS

Charles Dow publishes his first industrial average (July 3).

L. E. Waterman produces fountain pens that he invented; George A. Ball develops glass canning jar; John H. Patterson organizes National Cash Register Co.

Dorr E. Felt produces first accurate comptometer (adding machine).

More than 800,000 head of cattle are shipped East from Dodge City and Abilene (Kans.).

PATENTS John B. Meyenberg, process to make evaporated milk; John M. Browning, a repeating rifle; Hiram S. Maxim, first automatic machine gun; George Eastman, photographic film.

Home Insurance Building in Chicago is erected; first tall building to use steel as building material.

American Institute of Electrical Engineers is founded.

National Cattle & Horse Growers Assn. organizes; stockyards in Omaha, Nebr., are completed.

The eleven-story Home Insurance Building in Chicago, Illinois, designed by William Le Baron Jenney, is completed in 1884. The building is first "skyscraper" to use steel beams. CORBIS-BETTMANN

1884

DEATH Cyrus H. McCormick, agricultural machine manufacturer.

TRANSPORTATION

Sprague Electric Railway & Motor Co. is formed; introduces first large-scale electric streetcar system (Richmond, Va., 1887).

Central Pacific and Southern Pacific railroads merge.

SCIENCE/MEDICINE

Edward L. Trudeau founds tuberculosis sanitorium at Saranac Lake, N.Y.

University of Pennsylvania establishes veterinary school.

Dr. Carl Koller is first to use local anesthetic in an operation.

EDUCATION

Russell H. Conwell establishes night school that grows into Temple University; Mississippi University for Women chartered as Mississippi Industrial Institute.

Martha C. Thomas becomes first U.S. woman college dean (dean of women, Bryn Mawr).

RELIGION

Watch Tower Bible & Tract Society is founded.

Schaff-Herzog *Encyclopedia of Religious Knowledge* is published.

Catholic Bishop Patrick J. Ryan becomes archbishop of Philadelphia; Patrick W. Riordan, archbishop of San Francisco.

ART/MUSIC

Winslow Homer completes the painting, *The Life Line*; Daniel C. French, the statue of John Harvard; John S. Sargent, the painting *Madame X*.

Brooklyn (N.Y.) Museum opens.

SONGS (popular): "A Boy's Best Friend Is His Mother," "Clementine," "Love's Old Sweet Song," "Rock-a-Bye-Baby," "While Strolling Through the Park One Day."

DEATH Valentine W. L. Knabe, piano manufacturer.

LITERATURE/JOURNALISM

Ottmar Mergenthaler patents linotype machine.

McClure Syndicate supplies stories to newspapers.

The Journalist, first professional magazine for newspaper reporters, and *Cosmopolitan Magazine* are founded.

Philadelphia Tribune begins publication.

BOOKS *The Adventures of Huckleberry Finn* by Mark Twain, *Ramona* by Helen H. Jackson, *A Country Doctor* by Sarah Orne Jewett, *Poems* by Sidney Lanier, *Mingo* by Joel Chandler Harris.

ENTERTAINMENT

Charles Ringling and his four brothers present their circus.

Lyceum School of Acting opens in New York; later becomes American Academy of Dramatic Arts.

David Belasco produces the play *May Blossom*, and Charles Pidgin, *Peck's Bad Boy*.

SPORTS

Providence Nationals (N) win first baseball championship over New York Metropolitans (AA); Ned Williamson of Chicago Cubs (N) becomes first major leaguer to hit three home runs in a game; Charles Sweeney of Providence, R.I., sets National League record of 19 strikeouts in a game.

American (Soccer) Football Assn. is formed.

WINNERS *Archery*—Will H. Thompson, national title; *Fencing*—Harvard, first intercollegiate title; *Horse racing*—Buchanan, Kentucky Derby; Knight of Ellerslie, Preakness Stakes; Panique, Belmont Stakes.

MISCELLANEOUS

First U.S. bullfight is held in Dodge City, Kans.

American Historical Assn. is organized.

John J. Montgomery at Otay, Calif., makes first glider flight.

Chicago Police Department sets up identification bureau.

Sixty tornadoes, mostly in the South, kill 800.

Mrs. John Sherwood publishes *Manners and Social Usage*.

1885

NATIONAL

Washington Monument is dedicated; the Statue of Liberty, a gift of France, arrives in crates in New York City.

Post Office inaugurates special-delivery service; maximum weight of first-class mail climbs to 1 ounce for 2 cents.

William McKinley begins six years in House as a representative from Ohio.

DEATHS Vice President Thomas A. Hendricks, after eight months in office; former President Ulysses S. Grant (1869–1877); former Vice President Schuyler Colfax (1869–1873).

BUSINESS/INDUSTRY/INVENTIONS

Morton Salt Co. is founded; Swift & Co. is incorporated.

George Eastman introduces paper-backed photographic film in rolls; E. H. and A. H. Cowles introduce commercially useful electric furnace; first completely automatic can-making machine begins to function in Baltimore.

Sylvanus F. Bowser invents gasoline pump; William Stanley, an electric transformer.

Theodore N. Vail becomes first president of American Telephone & Telegraph Co. (ATT).

American Economic Assn. is founded.

Marshall Field opens bargain basement in his Chicago store.

Struggling eight-year-old Knights of Labor given boost in membership by railroad strike as workers realize their need for union.

DEATH Richard King, owner of world's largest ranch, located in Texas.

TRANSPORTATION

"Piggy-back" railroad operation begins when Long Island (N.Y.) Railroad carries farmers and their wagons and produce to market.

Ransom E. Olds produces a "horseless carriage," a three-wheeled steam-powered vehicle.

Henry M. Flagler acquires narrow-gauge railroad at St. Augustine, Fla., extends it to Miami (1896) and the Florida Keys (1912); line is abandoned after 1935 hurricane.

SCIENCE/MEDICINE

Dr. William W. Grant in Davenport, Ia., performs first appendectomy.

Dr. William S. Halsted develops local anesthesia.

Annals of Surgery and *American Journal of Archaeology* begin publication.

EDUCATION

New universities/colleges include University of Arizona, Bryn Mawr (Pa.) College, Georgia Institute of Technology, Goucher College (Towson, Md.).

RELIGION

DEATH Archbishop John McCloskey, first American cardinal.

ART/MUSIC

Augustus Saint-Gaudens completes the statue *The Puritan*; William M. Harnett, the painting *After the Hunt*; Mary Cassatt, *The Lady at the Tea Table*; John S. Sargent, a portrait of Robert Louis Stevenson.

E. C. Crocker Art Gallery in Sacramento, Calif., opens.

SONGS (popular): "The Big Rock Candy Mountain," "Remember Boy, You're Irish," "American Patrol."

DEATHS Leopold Damrosch, composer and conductor; Emmons Hamlin, piano and organ manufacturer (Mason-Hamlin).

1886

LITERATURE/JOURNALISM

Gilbert M. Hitchcock founds *Omaha World Herald*.

BOOKS *Personal Memoirs* by Ulysses S. Grant, *The Rise of Silas Lapham* by William Dean Howells, *The Money Makers* by H. F. Keenan, *My Lady Pokahontas* by J. E. Cooke, *Moral Antipathy* by Oliver Wendell Holmes Jr., *Our Country* by Josiah Strong.

DEATH Henry W. Shaw, humorist who used pseudonym Josh Billings.

ENTERTAINMENT

Producer Daniel Frohmann opens Lyceum Theater in New York City, first to be fully electrified.

E. H. Sothern stars in *One of Our Girls*.

SPORTS

Nicholas E. Young becomes president of National (baseball) League; Chicago Cubs and St. Louis Americans each win a game in championship playoff; one game is tied.

National Gun Assn. stages its first national clay-target shooting contest.

WINNERS *Horse racing*—Joe Cotton, Kentucky Derby; Tecumseh, Preakness Stakes; Tyrant, Belmont Stakes; *Yachting*—America's *Puritan* defeats England's *Genesta* to retain America's Cup.

MISCELLANEOUS

George B. Grinnell organizes forerunner of National Audubon Society.

New York State Forest preserve is created in Adirondack Mountains.

New Year's Day dinner at Palmer House, Chicago, features such entrees as ham, beef, turkey, duck, venison, and partridge for 50 cents.

NATIONAL

Presidential Succession Act passes (January 19), provides that if both the president and vice president are removed, die, resign, or are unable to serve, heads of cabinet departments will succeed them in order in which the offices were created.

President Grover Cleveland marries Frances Folsom in the White House.

President Cleveland unveils and dedicates Statue of Liberty in New York City Harbor.

Congress authorizes further shipbuilding to create modern navy; Alfred T. Mahan is named president of Naval War College.

Apache Indians of Southwest, led by Geronimo, surrender.

U.S. Forest Service is created as Division of Forestry.

Florida ratifies new state constitution.

DEATHS Former President Chester A. Arthur (1881–1885); Samuel J. Tilden, who lost presidency in 1876 by 1 electoral vote.

BUSINESS/INDUSTRY/INVENTIONS

Railroad strikers at McCormick Harvester plant in Chicago fight with strikebreakers, six die (May 3); Haymarket Massacre occurs next day when police break up a labor meeting; a bomb explodes among the police, who then open fire; seven police are killed, 70 are wounded; eight labor men are convicted (August 20), seven are sentenced to death.

American Federation of Labor (AFL) is organized in Columbus, Ohio, by 25 labor groups who represent about 150,000 workers; Samuel Gompers is named president (December 8).

Richard W. Sears starts mail-order watch business with Alvah C. Roebuck; sells out in 1889, starts Sears, Roebuck 1893; Westinghouse Electric Co. is organized to produce dynamos, transformers, and motors for alternating-current power systems.

The dedication of the Statue of Liberty in 1886 is a grand celebration. THE GRANGER COLLECTION, NEW YORK

Charles M. Hall discovers process for producing pure aluminum by electrolysis; founds what becomes Aluminum Co. of America.

Niagara Falls Power Co. is incorporated as Niagara River Hydraulic Tunnel Power & Sewer Co.; alternating current power plants begin to operate in Great Barrington, Mass., and Buffalo, N. Y.

Massachusetts requires factories to report accidents.

Elihu Thompson patents electric welding machine.

Stockyards in St. Paul, Mo., and Denver, Colo., are completed.

DEATHS Thaddeus Fairbanks, platform scale inventor; John Deere, agricultural machinery manufacturer; George H. Hammond, meatpacker; Oliver F. Winchester, firearms maker; Henry H. Richardson, architect.

TRANSPORTATION

Durant-Dort Carriage Co. is founded; becomes world's largest buggy manufacturer.

SCIENCE/MEDICINE

Johnson & Johnson Co. is organized in New Brunswick, N.J.

Arthur D. Little, one of first independent research laboratories, is founded in Boston.

Astronomer James E. Keeler discovers composition of Saturn's rings.

The Nightingale, a nurses' monthly magazine, begins publication.

DEATH Austin Flint, pioneer in heart research, founder of medical colleges (Buffalo, N.Y., Bellevue Hospital, New York City).

EDUCATION

University of Wyoming and John Carroll University are founded.

Rev. Timothy Dwight becomes president of Yale University.

RELIGION

Catholic Archbishop James Gibbons of Baltimore becomes second American cardinal; Bishop Michael A. Corrigan becomes archbishop of New York.

Henry C. Potter becomes Episcopal bishop of New York.

Dwight Moody organizes first biblical students summer conference in Northfield, Mass.; students from 250 colleges attend; Moody Bible Institute is founded in Chicago.

ART/MUSIC

Cincinnati Art Museum is founded.

SONGS (popular): "Johnny Get Your Gun," "Hot Time in the Old Town Tonight," "What the Dickie-Birds Say."

DEATH Asher B. Durand, member of Hudson River School of landscape painting.

LITERATURE/JOURNALISM

American Newspaper Publishers Assn. is organized.

New York Tribune is first paper in world to use Mergenthaler linotype machine.

BOOKS *Little Lord Fauntleroy* by Frances H. Burnett, *The Last of the Peterkins* by Lucretia P. Hale, *The Bostonians* by Henry James, *Indian Summer* by William Dean Howells.

DEATHS Emily Dickinson, poet; Edward Z. C. Judson, pioneered the "dime novel" as Ned Buntline; Richard M. Hoe, inventor of printing presses.

ENTERTAINMENT

Richard Mansfield stars in *Prince Karl* and William Gillette in *Held by the Enemy*.

SPORTS

First U.S. soccer game is played in Central Park, New York City.

The Sporting News is founded.

Aurora Ski Club forms at Red Wing, Minn.

WINNERS *Baseball* — St. Louis Americans beat Chicago Cubs for championship; *Boating* — John H. McManus, first angler's boat race; *Horse racing* — Ben Ali, Kentucky Derby; The Bard, Preakness Stakes; Inspector B., Belmont Stakes; *Polo* — England, first international series; *Yachting* — U.S.'s *Mayflower* retains America's Cup.

MISCELLANEOUS

First Tournament of Roses parade is held in Pasadena, Calif.

Boston's Children's Mission opens first playground for children.

Stanton Coit and Charles B. Stover establish first U.S. settlement house, now University Settlement, New York City.

Earthquake, felt over 1,000-mile area of Southeast, causes most damage at Charleston, S.C., 57 are killed; two-day storm along Gulf Coast causes flooding in Texas, takes 247 lives; blizzard in Kansas causes 100 deaths.

1887

INTERNATIONAL

Senate ratifies Hawaiian Reciprocity Treaty (January 20), gives U.S. right to build fortified naval base at Pearl Harbor.

NATIONAL

Congress passes Electoral Count Act whereby each state becomes absolute controller of appointment of electors and validity of election returns; is designed to prevent recurrence of disputed 1876 election.

Tenure of Office Act (1867) is repealed after President Grover Cleveland insists president has sole constitutional power to suspend or remove persons from office.

Free mail delivery begins in cities of 10,000 or more.

President Cleveland vetoes pension bill that would have granted pensions without regard for service-connected disability; first service pensions are granted for Mexican War.

Hatch Act passes, provides federal subsidies for creating state agricultural experiment stations.

President vetoes a bill requiring literacy tests for immigrants.

Susanna M. Salter becomes first woman elected mayor (Argonia, Kans.).

Oregon passes first law recognizing Labor Day as a holiday.

DEATH Former Vice President William A. Wheeler (1877–1881).

BUSINESS/INDUSTRY/INVENTIONS

Illinois Supreme Court upholds conviction of Haymarket defendants (1886); two death sentences are commuted to life imprisonment; four defendants are executed (November 11).

Thomas A. Edison demonstrates his new invention, the phonograph.

Asa G. Candler organizes Coca-Cola Co.

American Mutual Liability Insurance Co. of Boston is incorporated.

Benjamin F. Merritt patents an automatic time recorder.

American Refinery Co. begins as Sugar Refineries Co.

Fred M. Kirby opens first of a chain of five-and-ten cent stores.

Albert B. Dick invents the mimeograph.

Chemist Herman Frasch patents process to remove sulphur from petroleum.

DEATHS James B. Eads, inventor of diving bell, bridge builder; John Roach, builder of iron steamships.

TRANSPORTATION

Supreme Court rules in *Wabash, St. Louis and Pacific Company v. Illinois* that states do not have the right to regulate interstate traffic.

Interstate Commerce Commission is created to investigate, regulate railroads; is the first U.S. regulatory commission.

Frank J. Sprague installs first major U.S. electric trolley system (Richmond, Va.).

SCIENCE/MEDICINE

New York City Babies Hospital is chartered; New York Cancer Hospital (later Memorial Hospital) opens.

National Institutes of Health originates as Labora-

tory of Hygiene in Marine Hospital, New York City.

American Journal of Psychology begins publication.

DEATH Dorothea L. Dix, social worker who helped improve care of the insane.

EDUCATION

Melvil Dewey founds first U.S. library school at Columbia University; moves it to Albany, N.Y. (1889), where it becomes New York State Library School.

Newberry Library in Chicago opens.

Catholic University (Washington D.C.), North Carolina State, Clark University (Worcester, Mass.) are founded.

Perkins Institution opens kindergarten for blind in Roxbury, Mass.

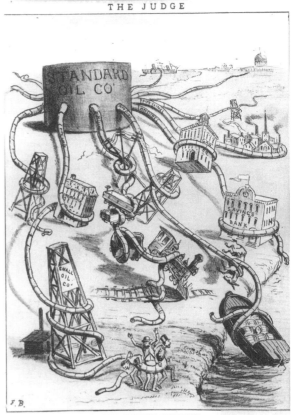

A cartoon opposing Standard Oil shows the company as a predatory octopus. The company's power continues to grow since the formation of the Standard Oil Trust (see 1882). THE GRANGER COLLECTION, NEW YORK

1888

DEATH Mark Hopkins, president of Williams College (1836–1872).

RELIGION

Alexander Kohut and Sabato Morais found Jewish Theological Seminary in New York City.

DEATHS Henry Ward Beecher, noted Congregational clergyman; Horatio Potter, Episcopal bishop of New York (1854–1887); Carl F. W. Walther, Lutheran leader; John Taylor, president of Mormon Church (1880–1887).

ART/MUSIC

Augustus Saint-Gaudens completes standing statue of Abraham Lincoln for Lincoln Park, Chicago; John Q. A. Ward completes statue of President Garfield.

SONGS (popular): "Away in a Manger," "Comrades," "The Swan."

LITERATURE/JOURNALISM

Paris edition of *New York Herald* begins publication.

William Randolph Hearst takes over *San Francisco Examiner*.

Scribner's Magazine is founded.

DEATH Emma Lazarus, poet best remembered for poem on Statue of Liberty's tablet.

ENTERTAINMENT

Actress Ada Rehan plays her most famous role, Katherine in *The Taming of the Shrew*.

PLAYS

PLAYS John Drew and Otis Skinner star in *Railroad of Love*, Bronson Howard writes *The Henrietta* and *Shenandoah*, Steele Mackaye writes *Paul Kau Var*, David Belasco and Henry DeMille write *The Wife*.

SPORTS

Oldest active American ski club, Norden (later Ishpeming) Ski Club, is founded in Ishpeming, Mich.; Skating Club of United States is organized.

American Trotting Assn. is organized; New York State legalizes racetrack betting.

New England Association Football League is created.

First indoor softball game is played at Farragut Boat Club; George W. Hancock invents game that features a broomstick for a bat, boxing glove for a ball.

Everett Horton patents fishing rod with telescoping steel tubes.

The Tribune Book of Open Air Sports is published.

WINNERS *Baseball* — Detroit Nationals defeat St. Louis Americans for title; *Horse racing* — Montrose, Kentucky Derby; Dunboyne, Preakness Stakes; Hanover, Belmont Stakes; *Yachting* — America's *Volunteer* retains America's Cup.

MISCELLANEOUS

Rev. Olympia Brown begins 30 years as president of Wisconsin Woman Suffrage Assn.

Burning bridge in Chatsworth, Ill., collapses under weight of crossing train; 100 are killed.

NATIONAL

President Grover Cleveland, Democrat, runs for a second term, wins popular vote (5,540,050 to 5,444,337), but Republican Benjamin Harrison wins electoral-vote count 233 to 168 and the presidency.

Supreme Court Chief Justice Morrison R. Waite dies at 72 after serving 14 years; Melville W. Fuller succeeds him.

Department of Labor is established, is headed by a commissioner (June 30).

Washington Monument opens to the public.

DEATH Henry Bergh, founder of American Society for Prevention of Cruelty to Animals.

George Eastman takes one of his own Kodak cameras on a trip to England in 1890. UPI/CORBIS-BETTMANN

TRANSPORTATION

Locomotive enginemen of Burlington Railroad strike for higher wages; year-long strike ends with union's return to work.

Double-decker ferryboat *Bergen* is launched at Newburgh, N.Y.

First electric automobile is demonstrated in Boston.

SCIENCE/MEDICINE

Lick Observatory of University of California opens; Woods Hole (Mass.) Marine Biological Laboratory is established.

Yellow fever epidemic strikes the South; there are 4,500 cases, more than 400 deaths.

Providence, R.I., establishes municipal health laboratory.

Agriculture Department establishes Office of Experiment Stations.

Samuel P. Langley writes *The New Astronomy*, which stimulates interest in the subject.

George E. Hale invents a spectroheliograph, a device for sun measurement.

EDUCATION

Granville Stanley Hall becomes first president of Clark University; College of William & Mary, closed since Civil War, reopens; University of Minnesota Agricultural School is established; New Mexico State University is founded.

RELIGION

Catholic Bishop John Ireland becomes first archbishop of St. Paul, Minn.

Philip Schaff founds American Society of Church History.

DEATHS Father Damien, Catholic missionary to Hawaiian leper colony; José S. Alemany, first Catholic archbishop of San Francisco (1853–1884); Isaac Errett, editor of *The Christian Standard*.

BUSINESS/INDUSTRY/INVENTIONS

George Eastman unveils fixed-focus box camera (the Kodak) that uses roll film.

William S. Burroughs develops first successful recording adding machine.

Pittsburgh Reduction Co. (later Alcoa) produces pure aluminum.

Isidor and Nathan Straus become partners in Macy's department store; gain control 1896.

American Cereal Co. combines seven largest oatmeal mills.

Oscar Mayer & Co., meatpackers; Childs restaurant chain; and Parker Bros., games manufacturer, are organized.

PATENTS Oliver B. Shallenberger for an electric meter, John J. Loud for ballpoint pen, Marvin C. Stone for drinking straw, Willard L. Bundy for employees' time clock.

DEATH Hiram Sibley, a founder of Western Union.

1889

ART/MUSIC

Charles G. Conn produces saxophones.

John Philip Sousa writes the march "Semper Fidelis."

William M. Chase completes the painting *Lady in Black*.

SONGS (popular): "Where Did You Get That Hat?" "With All Her Faults, I Love Her Still."

DEATHS Nathaniel Currier of Currier & Ives; William W. Corcoran, founder of a Washington art gallery.

LITERATURE/JOURNALISM

Colliers, a weekly magazine, is founded.

American Folk-Lore Society is created.

Acres of Diamonds, which Russell H. Conwell delivered as a lecture thousands of times, is published.

BOOKS *Looking Backward 2000–1887* by Edward Bellamy, *Lew Gansett* by Opie Read, *Pipes 'o' Pan at Zekesbury* (poetry) by James Whitcomb Riley.

DEATHS Arunah S. Abell, founder and publisher, *Baltimore Sun*; David R. Locke, writer under name of Petroleum V. Nasby; Louisa May Alcott, author.

ENTERTAINMENT

Players Club in New York City is founded.

PLAYS Eddie Foy stars in *The Crystal Slipper*, William Gillette in *A Legal Wreck*, John Drew in *The Lottery of Love*.

SPORTS

St. Andrews Golf Club opens in Yonkers, N.Y.

Ernest L. Thayer publishes "Casey at the Bat," his classic baseball poem, in *San Francisco Examiner*.

WINNERS *Archery* — Will H. Thompson, national title; *Baseball* — New York Nationals beat St. Louis Americans for title; *Horse racing* — Macbeth II, Kentucky Derby; Refund, Preakness Stakes; Sir Dixon, Belmont Stakes.

MISCELLANEOUS

Blizzard hits New York and New England with 4 feet of snow and 60 mile-per-hour winds (March 14); blizzard hits Midwest (March 12), 400 die.

Gardiner G. Hubbard founds National Geographic Society.

American Mathematical Society is founded as New York Mathematical Society.

Loyal Order of Moose is established.

Young Women's Hebrew Assn. begins in New York City.

INTERNATIONAL

Hurricane destroys U.S. and German warships in Apia Harbor, Samoa (March 15); agreement is reached in Berlin (June 4) to give autonomy to Samoan Islands with tripartite protectorate (German, British, U.S.).

International American Conference is held in Washington, D.C. (October 2), with 17 Latin American nations represented; creates International Bureau of American Republics (later Pan American Union).

NATIONAL

South Dakota adopts its constitution (May 14) and North Dakota adopts one that includes prohibition (October 1).

Four states are admitted to the Union: North Dakota is the 39th state, South Dakota the 40th (both November 2), Montana the 41st (November 8), and Washington the 42nd (November 11).

Department of Agriculture is raised to cabinet status with Norman J. Colman as commissioner; he is elevated to Secretary (February 11).

Nellie Bly (Elizabeth Cochrane) of *New York World* begins round-the-world trip to beat the then 80-day record (November 14).

Indian Territory (Oklahoma) opens to settlement; more than 50,000 settlers file homestead claims.

Theodore Roosevelt is named to Civil Service Commission.

DEATHS Former First Lady Julia G. Tyler (1844–1845); Jefferson Davis, Confederate president; Union Gen. Philip H. Sheridan.

BUSINESS/INDUSTRY/INVENTIONS

Andrew Carnegie organizes Carnegie Steel Co.; H. W. Dow begins large-scale production of bromine in Midland, Mich.

Otis Brothers installs first electric elevator (Demarest Building, New York City); Singer Sewing Machine Co. develops an electric machine.

PATENTS Charles M. Hall, process to produce pure aluminum; Herman Hollerith, a tabulating machine; William Gray, a coin telephone.

Willamette Falls (Ore.) Electric Co. supplies electricity to Portland, 13 miles away; Edison General Electric Co. is founded.

Kansas passes first antitrust law, followed closely by Maine, Michigan, and Tennessee.

DEATHS Melville R. Bissell, carpet-sweeper inventor; John Ericsson, engineer who developed screw propellor for ships.

The scene in Johnstown, Pennsylvania, following the great flood of 1889. UPI/CORBIS-BETTMANN

1889

SCIENCE/MEDICINE

Johns Hopkins Hospital opens in Baltimore, Md.; Sisters of St. Francis open St. Mary's Hospital in Rochester, Minn., with three Mayos—William W. and his sons, William J. and Charles H.—as the staff; eventually becomes the Mayo Clinic (see 1833).

DEATH Maria Mitchell, first U.S. woman astronomer.

EDUCATION

Department of Education becomes an office in Interior Department.

Archbishop James Gibbons, a founder, becomes first chancellor of Catholic University.

University of Idaho, University of New Mexico, and Clemson (S.C.) University are founded.

Rev. Daniel Dorchester is named superintendent of American Indian schools.

First county high school opens in Chapman, Kans., with 137 students.

DEATH Theodore D. Woolsey, Yale University president (1846–1871).

RELIGION

Walter Rauschenbusch and two colleagues found Society of Jesus, later named the Brotherhood of the Kingdom.

William Woodruff becomes president of the Mormon church.

Rev. Albert E. Dunning edits *The Congregationalist*.

First congress of Catholic laity is held in Baltimore.

William A. Leonard becomes Episcopal bishop of Ohio.

ART/MUSIC

John Philip Sousa writes "The Washington Post March" and "The Thunderer."

Frederic C. Beach founds *American Photography* magazine.

Thomas Eakins completes the painting *The Agnew Clinic*; Frederick W. MacMonnies, the statue of Nathan Hale.

SONGS (popular): "Slide, Kelly, Slide," "Playmates," "Down Went McGinty."

LITERATURE/JOURNALISM

Wall St. Journal begins publication; *Munsey's Magazine* starts as a weekly.

Edward W. Bok begins 30 years as editor of the *Ladies Home Journal*.

Mark Twain writes his *Connecticut Yankee in King Arthur's Court*.

ENTERTAINMENT

Lillian Russell stars in *The Brigands*; other plays are *Shenandoah* with Henry Miller, *The Christy Ball* by David Belasco and Henry DeMille, *McKenna's Flirtation* by Edgar Selden.

SPORTS

Players' (baseball) League organizes with eight teams; lasts through 1890 season.

Walter C. Camp begins annual selection of All-American football teams.

WINNERS *Baseball*—New York Nationals beat Brooklyn Americans for championship; *Boxing*—John L. Sullivan, heavyweight in last bare-knuckle fight; *Chess*—S. Lipschutz, unofficial U.S. championship; *Horse racing*—Spokane, Kentucky Derby; Buddhist, Preakness Stakes; Eric, Belmont Stakes; *Tennis*—George Kerr, international singles title.

MISCELLANEOUS

Dam breaks near Johnstown, Pa., destroys 7 towns in 15 minutes, causes 2,200 deaths (May 31).

Casa Grande, an excavated Native American pueblo in Arizona, is first federal park tract protected for historic value.

Two settlement houses are established: Hull House, Chicago, and College Settlement, New York City.

Fire destroys most of Seattle's business district.

Americans smoke 2.1 billion cigarettes a year.

1890

INTERNATIONAL

First Pan-American Conference is held in Washington, D.C.; 10 nations sign arbitration treaty.

U.S. signs international agreement for suppression of African slave trade.

NATIONAL

Sherman Anti-Trust Act passes to control industrial combinations; is not enforced vigorously.

Eleventh census reports national population at 62,979,766; census uses punched-card tabulating system invented by Herman Hollerith.

Idaho is admitted as 43rd state (July 3), Wyoming is the 44th (July 10); Oklahoma Territory is established (May 2).

General Federation of Women's Clubs is organized; National Woman Suffrage Assn. and American Woman Suffrage Assn. merge into National American Woman Suffrage Assn. with Elizabeth Cady Stanton as president.

Democrats win landslide victory in congressional elections, gain control of House.

McKinley Tariff raises average level to $49\frac{1}{2}\%$, provides for reciprocal raises to meet foreign discrimination against goods imported from the U.S.

Sequoia and Yosemite national parks are established in California.

Nellie Bly, a reporter for *New York World*, completes round-the-world trip in 72 days, 6 hours, 11 minutes (January 25), beating the 80-day record set by Phineas Fogg in Jules Verne's *Around the World in 80 Days*.

Federal law is passed that forbids use of mails in a lottery.

"The bosses of the Senate" are America's big businesses in this anti-trust cartoon by Joseph Keppler from 1889. Anti-trust legislation was passed in 1890. THE GRANGER COLLECTION

1890

Elizabeth Cochrane, the American journalist known as Nellie Bly, waves to admirers. Cochrane completes her round-the-world trip in 1890. THE GRANGER COLLECTION, NEW YORK

National debt is $1.1 billion.

New Orleans police chief is slain while investigating the Mafia.

Federal meat inspection law is approved.

Mississippi imposes $2 poll tax to vote, plus a requirement to be able to read and interpret the state constitution.

Sioux Indians are defeated at Wounded Knee, S.Dak. in the last major battle of the Indian wars.

William Howard Taft becomes Solicitor General.

BUSINESS/INDUSTRY/INVENTIONS

First long-distance transmission of electricity occurs (November 15) when streetlights in Buffalo, N.Y., switch on by power from Niagara Falls, 20 miles away.

Michael Cudahy forms meatpacking company; Charles T. Bainbridge's Sons begin to produce crepe paper; Norton Co. becomes first maker of cans for packing food.

Two historic buildings are completed: Auditorium Theater, Chicago, and Wainwright in St. Louis (Mo.), generally considered the first true skyscraper.

United Mine Workers is organized.

Frederick W. Taylor develops largest U.S. steel hammer; John M. Browning patents a machine gun powered by expansion of powder gases.

Benjamin N. and James B. Duke found what becomes American Tobacco Co.; Remington Rand Co. is established.

Cleveland opens large arcade with 112 stores, the forerunner of today's shopping malls.

DEATHS Samuel L. Mather, developer of Lake Superior iron-ore deposits; Christopher L. Sholes, inventor of typewriter.

TRANSPORTATION

Bridge across Hudson River to connect New York and New Jersey is authorized.

Packard Motor Co. is organized.

SCIENCE/MEDICINE

Johns Hopkins University creates first school of surgery.

Cold Spring Harbor (N.Y.) Biological Laboratory is founded.

Dr. William S. Halsted becomes first to wear rubber gloves in surgery.

William James prepares *The Principles of Psychology*, which remains a standard text for years.

EDUCATION

New York Library Assn. is organized, with Melvil Dewey as president.

State College of Washington and University of Oklahoma are founded.

John F. Goucher becomes president of Baltimore Women's College, later named in his honor.

Liberty H. Bailey founds New York State College of Agriculture at Cornell University; University of Wisconsin Agricultural College offers a dairy course.

RELIGION

Mormon church ends polygamy.

Philip Schaff completes seven-volume *History of the Christian Church*.

ART/MUSIC

Ralph A. Blakelock completes the painting *Brook by Moonlight*; Childe Hassam, *Washington Arch Spring*; Mary Cassatt, *The Coiffure* and *Women Bathing*; Arthur B. Davies, *Along the Erie Canal*.

SONGS (popular): "Little Annie Roonie," "Oh, Promise Me," "Passing By," "Throw Him Down, McCloskey."

LITERATURE/JOURNALISM

Literary Digest, a weekly magazine, and *Smart Set*, a monthly, begin publication.

BOOKS *Abraham Lincoln* by John Hay and J. G. Nicolay, *How the Other Half Lives* by Jacob A. Riis, *Poems* by Emily Dickinson, *Youma* by Lafcadio Hearn.

ENTERTAINMENT

Richard Mansfield stars in *Beau Brummel*, Lillian Russell in *The Grand Duchess*, Ada Rehan and John Drew in *The Last Word*, Maude Adams in *Men and Women*.

Elitch's Garden Theater in Denver, Colo., opens, the oldest U.S. summer theater.

Theatrical producer Charles Frohmann organizes a stock company.

A new showboat on the rivers, the *Theaterium*, is completed.

DEATH Dion Boucicault, playwright and actor.

SPORTS

John Owen becomes first person to run 100 yards in less than 10 seconds ($9\frac{4}{5}$ seconds).

U.S. Polo Assn. organizes.

New Madison Square Garden (New York City) is completed.

WINNERS *Baseball*—Brooklyn Nationals and Louisville Americans each win three games, the seventh is a tie, for national championship; *Chess*—Max Judd, unofficial U.S. title; *Football*—Navy 24–0 in first Army–Navy game; *Horse racing*—Riley, Kentucky Derby; Montague, Preakness Stakes; Burlington, Belmont Stakes.

MISCELLANEOUS

First electrocution is of convicted murderer William Kemmler in Auburn (N.Y.) Prison.

Daughters of American Revolution (DAR) organize.

INTERNATIONAL

Chilean mob in Valparaiso attacks U.S. military personnel on leave, kills two; Chile later (1892) apologizes, pays $75,000 in indemnity.

First international copyright agreement is adopted.

NATIONAL

Yellowstone Park Timberland Reserve is created; Forest Reserve Act empowers president to set aside lands on federal property.

Immigration and Naturalization Service is established.

Territory of Arizona adopts constitution; new Mississippi state constitution goes into effect.

New Orleans mob breaks into jail, lynches 11 Italian immigrants under indictment for murdering police chief (see 1890).

Federal prison is constructed at Leavenworth, Kans.

1891

William McKinley is elected governor of Ohio.

DEATHS Former Vice President Hannibal Hamlin (1861–1865); former First Lady Sarah C. Polk (1845–1849); Confederate Gen. Joseph E. Johnston; Union Gen. William T. Sherman.

BUSINESS/INDUSTRY/INVENTIONS

Marcellus F. Berry of American Express Co. devises traveler's checks; Thomas A. Sperry originates trading stamps, later forms Sperry & Hutchinson, which issues "green stamps."

Edward G. Acheson develops carborundum, an abrasive; William S. Burroughs improves his working calculator.

American Sugar Refining Co. is established.

Schaefer Brewing Co. introduces bottled beer; William Wrigley Jr. produces chewing gum.

Filene's department store opens in Boston.

John T. Smith patents corkboard.

John H. Galey and James McGuffey open the McDonald oil field in western Pennsylvania.

Associated Bill Posters and Distributors (later Outdoor Advertising Assn.) is founded.

TRANSPORTATION

St. Clair Railway Tunnel opens between Port Huron, Mich., and Sarnia, Canada.

Empire State Express of New York Central Railroad makes first run between New York and Buffalo in 8 hours, 27 seconds.

SCIENCE/MEDICINE

Dr. Daniel H. Williams founds interracial Provident Hospital in Chicago, including a nurses' training school for black women.

George E. Hale takes first picture of the sun with his spectroheliograph.

DEATH Joseph Leidy, anatomist.

EDUCATION

New colleges/universities include Stanford University (Stanford, Calif.) with David Starr Jordan as president; the new University of Chicago with William Rainey Harper as president; Oklahoma A. & M. (Stillwater), California Institute of Technology (Pasadena), and Hardin Simmons (Abilene, Tex.).

Thomas J. Foster opens International Correspondence Schools.

RELIGION

Midwestern Presbyterian churches found Omaha Theological Seminary; Evangelical Lutheran Theological Seminary opens in Chicago.

Katharine Drexel, wealthy Philadelphian who took vow of poverty and became a nun, founds Sisters of the Blessed Sacrament for Indians and Colored People.

Catholic Bishop Frederic X. Katzer becomes archbishop of Milwaukee.

Rev. Phillips Brooks becomes Episcopal bishop of Massachusetts.

ART/MUSIC

Carnegie Hall in New York City opens; Chicago Symphony Orchestra is founded.

Charles Ives composes *Variations on America*.

Robin Hood, comic opera by Reginald DeKoven, is produced; incorporates his earlier song, "Oh, Promise Me."

Thomas W. Dewing completes the painting *The Recitation*; John Q. A. Ward completes statue of Henry Ward Beecher.

SONGS (popular): "Hey, Rube!" "Little Boy Blue," "Narcissus," "Ta-ra-ra-boom-de-ay."

LITERATURE/JOURNALISM

Curtis Publishing Co. is founded.

BOOKS *Criticism and Fiction* by William Dean Howells, *In the Midst of Life*, by Ambrose Bierce, *Main-Traveled Roads* by Hamlin Garland.

DEATHS Herman Melville, author; James Russell Lowell, author and poet; George Jones, a founder of the *New York Times*.

ENTERTAINMENT

William Morris stars in play *The Lost Paradise*; W. J. Scanlan in *Mavourneen*, Henrietta Crosman in *Mr. Wilkinson's Widows*, DeWolf Hopper in *Wang*.

DEATH P. T. Barnum, showman.

SPORTS

American Whist League and Amateur Fencers League of America are founded.

Walter Camp writes *American Football.*

Luther Carry becomes first to run 100 meters in fewer than 11 seconds ($10\frac{3}{4}$ seconds).

First international six-day bicycle race is held; riders work alone, riding high wheelers; winner is "Plugger Bill" Martin.

WINNERS *Boxing* — Bob Fitzsimmons, middleweight; *Chess* — Jackson Showalter, first official U.S. champion; *Horse racing* — Kingman, Kentucky Derby; Foxford, Belmont Stakes; no Preakness Stakes run.

1892

NATIONAL

An Anglo-American treaty refers dispute over taking of seals in Bering Sea to arbitration.

Senate ratifies U.S. participation in ban on African slave trade.

NATIONAL

Grover Cleveland, Democratic president (1885–1889), is elected president again, defeats President Benjamin Harrison, Republican, and People's Party candidate James B. Weaver; Cleveland receives 5,554,414 popular votes, Harrison receives 5,190,802 votes, and Weaver receives 1,027,329 votes; electoral vote is 277–145–22.

"Pledge of Allegiance" first appears in *The Youth's Companion.*

Ellis Island opens as an immigration receiving station (January 1).

Congress bans sale of alcohol on Native American lands.

New York State authorizes use of voting machines; are first used (April 12) in Lockport, N.Y.

National debt is $585 million.

Louisiana abolishes state lottery.

Gifford Pinchot begins one of earliest programs of systematic forestry.

Presbyterian clergyman, Charles H. Parkhurst, preaches against political corruption and orga-

nized vice in New York City; sparks an investigation and reform government.

William McKinley begins four-year term as Ohio governor.

DEATH Union Gen. James W. Denver, public official; Denver, Colo., named for him.

BUSINESS/INDUSTRY/INVENTIONS

Ohio Supreme Court orders dissolution of Standard Oil Co. of Ohio.

Merger of Edison General Electric and Thomas Houston Electric forms General Electric Co.; Eastman Kodak Co. is organized; George A. Hormel & Co. is founded, produces first canned hams; Charles and Robert Ingersoll found company that makes $1 watches.

L. Bamberger & Co., department store, is founded.

Joseph S. Duncan invents addressograph.

Strike begins at Carnegie Steel in Homestead, Pa.; mills close (June 30); mills reopen with replacement workers; strike turns violent (July 6) when National Guard is called out; 7 guards and 11 strikers and spectators are killed; martial law is declared at strikebound lead and silver mines in northern Idaho.

Willson Aluminum Co. produces acetylene or carbide gas for first time; Taylor Iron & Steel Co. produces manganese steel; J. I. Case Co. introduces first true gasoline traction engine.

1892

PATENTS Frank Schuman for wire glass, George C. Blickensdorfer for portable typewriter, John McTammany for a voting machine, Joshua Pussey for book matches.

First three-phase hydroelectric plant is built at Mill Creek in California.

First automatic telephone exchange opens in LaPorte, Ind.

The sale of cigarettes in new push-up cardboard packages begins.

DEATH Jay Gould, financier.

TRANSPORTATION

Charles and Frank Duryea demonstrate gasoline-

Walt Whitman (1819–1892), author of *Leaves of Grass*, photographed in 1880. The Granger Collection, New York

driven automobile in Springfield, Mass.; Charles also invents a spray carburetor.

First elevated railroad in Chicago begins operation.

Printed transfers for buses, streetcars are used in Rochester, N.Y.

Jesse W. Reno invents moving stairway.

SCIENCE/MEDICINE

American School of Osteopathy is chartered in Kirksville, Mo.

William Osler prepares *The Principles and Practice of Medicine*; becomes dominant text in field for 30 years; George M. Sternberg writes *A Manual of Bacteriology*, first comprehensive work on subject.

Edwin E. Barnard of Lick Observatory (on Mt. Hamilton, near San Jose, Calif.) discovers fifth Saturn satellite (first four were discovered by Galileo).

University of Wisconsin launches bachelor's degree program for pharmacists.

American Psychological Assn. is organized in Worcester, Mass., with Granville Stanley Hall as president.

DEATH Lewis M. Rutherford, astrophysicist who designed first telescopes for celestial photography.

EDUCATION

Jacob G. Schurman begins 28 years as president of Cornell University.

RELIGION

Mary Baker Eddy and 12 followers organize Christian Science church (September 23).

Cornerstone is laid for Cathedral of St. John the Divine in New York City; designed to be largest U.S. church (still incomplete).

Baptist Theological Union becomes Divinity School of new University of Chicago.

Rev. Alfred M. Randolph becomes Episcopal bishop of southern Virginia.

DEATH Phillips Brooks, Episcopal bishop who wrote "O Little Town of Bethlehem."

ART/MUSIC

William Macbeth opens art gallery in New York City that deals exclusively in American art.

Thomas Eakins completes the painting *The Concert Singer*; William A. Harnett, *Old Models*; Childe Hassam, *Summer Sunlight*; and Augustus Saint-Gaudens completes the sculpture *Diana*.

Edward A. MacDowell composes *Indian Suite*.

SONGS (popular): "After the Ball," "A Bicycle Built for Two," "The Bowery," "The Man That Broke the Bank at Monte Carlo," "My Sweetheart's the Man in the Moon."

LITERATURE/JOURNALISM

Jacob Riis continues his exposés of urban poverty with *Children of the Poor*.

Baltimore Afro-American begins publication.

Jimmy Swinnerton draws cartoons of bears and tigers in *San Francisco Examiner*, forerunner of comic strips.

DEATHS Henry O. Houghton, publisher; Walt Whitman, poet; John Greenleaf Whittier, a founder and editor of *Atlantic Monthly*.

ENTERTAINMENT

George W. G. Ferris invents the Ferris wheel, demonstrates it first at 1893 Chicago Fair.

Maude Adams stars in *The Masked Ball*; James A. Herne writes play *Shore Acres*.

SPORTS

James Naismith invents game of basketball at International YMCA Training School, Springfield, Mass.; first game is played there (January 20).

John Doyle, reserve catcher for Cleveland, becomes first pinch hitter in baseball; hits a single.

New racing rules call for jockeys to use only a whip or spurs on a horse.

First night football game is played in Mansfield, Pa., between Teachers College and Wyoming (Pa.) Seminary; Pudge Heffelfinger, college football great, probably becomes first professional football player, receives $500 to play for Allegheny Athletic Assn.

Amos Alonzo Stagg begins 41-year football coaching career at University of Chicago.

Amateur Fencers League holds first national fencing championships.

WINNERS *Baseball*—Cincinnati beats St. Louis 5–1 in first Sunday game; Boston Nationals win national championship; *Boxing*—Jim Corbett, heavyweight, in first fight under Marquis of Queensbury rules, using padded gloves; *Chess*—S. Lipschutz, U.S. title; *Horse racing*—Azra, Kentucky Derby; Patron, Belmont Stakes; no Preakness Stakes.

MISCELLANEOUS

Dalton Brothers gang breaks up when Robert and Grattan are killed and Emmett is wounded in failed Coffeyville, Kans., bank robbery.

American Jewish Historical Society is founded.

INTERNATIONAL

U.S. Marines land on Hawaii, presumably to protect Americans; help revolutionary committee of safety to occupy government buildings; U.S. Minister John L. Stevens recognizes revolutionary regime (January 17), raises U.S. flag (February 1), declares Hawaii a U.S. protectorate with Sanford B. Dole as president; treaty on annexation submitted to Senate, which fails to act (February 15); President Grover Cleveland withdraws treaty.

International arbitration tribunal denies U.S. exclusive right to Bering Sea, prohibits ocean seal

1893

The Oklahoma Land Rush, 1893. Pioneers, hoping to stake out cheap land, race into Oklahoma's Cherokee Strip. THE GRANGER COLLECTION, NEW YORK

catching in a 60-mile zone around Pribiloff Island for part of each year (August 15).

Thomas F. Bayard is named first ambassador to Great Britain.

NATIONAL

President Cleveland is secretly operated on for cancer of the upper jaw; remains secret until 1917 when doctor who performed operation reveals story (July 1).

Columbian Exposition in Chicago opens; Ferris wheel and moving sidewalk are shown for first time. Exposition marks 400th anniversary of Columbus' arrival and features many cultural events; after close of exposition in 1894, the buildings will be nearly all destroyed by fire.

Free postal delivery is extended to rural communities; first commemorative stamp series is issued, honors Christopher Columbus.

Cherokee Strip, 6 million acres between Kansas and Oklahoma, opens to settlers; about 90,000 take part in settlements.

Katherine Lee Bates, a Wellesley professor, writes poem "America the Beautiful" after climbing Pikes Peak; poem is later set to Samuel A. Ward's music.

Colorado grants full suffrage to women.

President Benjamin Harrison proclaims amnesty for past offenses after new antipolygamy law is enacted.

Rev. H. H. Russell forms Anti-Saloon League.

Special session of Congress repeals the Sherman Silver Purchase Act, which requires government silver coinage.

DEATH Former President Rutherford B. Hayes (1877–1881).

BUSINESS/INDUSTRY/INVENTIONS

Panic of 1893 begins in part because of a drop in U.S. gold reserves below $100 million (April 21); stocks drop, before year's end 491 banks and 15,000 commercial institutions fail, beginning a severe depression until 1897.

Milton S. Hershey founds chocolate company in Lancaster, Pa.; Richard W. Sears and Alvah C. Roebuck found Sears Roebuck Co.; Procter & Gamble spends $125,000 to promote Ivory Soap; Henry Perky founds Shredded Wheat Co.

Hudson Maxim perfects a practical dynamite, establishes Maxim Powder Co. in New Jersey.

Westinghouse Electric Co. builds generating equipment for Niagara Falls power project.

American Railway Union is organized; Western Federation of Miners is founded (later becomes Mine, Mill & Smelters Union).

DEATHS Joseph Francis, inventor of lifeboats; Eben N. Hosford, developer of process to make condensed milk, baking powder; Egbert P. Judson, inventor of explosive used in railroad building.

TRANSPORTATION

Charles E. and J. Frank Duryea complete first U.S. gasoline-powered automobile; first foreign-made car, Mercedes Benz, is shown at Columbian Exposition.

Bridge across Mississippi River at Memphis (Tenn.) is completed.

SCIENCE/MEDICINE

Dr. Daniel H. Williams performs first successful heart operation in Chicago; repairs an artery damaged by a knife wound.

Johns Hopkins University Medical School is founded.

Edward L. Nichols of Cornell University founds *Physical Review*, first journal devoted to physics; Thomas C. Chamberlin issues *Journal of Geology*.

EDUCATION

New Hampshire requires townships to create libraries.

University of Chicago offers extension courses for college credits.

University of Montana, Montana State University, and American University (Washington, D.C.) open.

DEATHS Edward F. Sorin, founder and first president, Notre Dame University (1846–1865); Leland Stanford, founder of Stanford University; Anthony J. Drexel, founder, Drexel Institute of Technology.

RELIGION

World Parliament of Religions opens in Chicago as part of Columbian Exposition.

Msgr. Francesco Satolli, first permanent Catholic apostolic delegate, arrives in Washington, D.C.

Suspension of Charles A. Briggs, a theologian, by Presbyterian General Assembly causes Union Theological Seminary to break with the church, becomes nondenominational.

Mormon Tabernacle in Salt Lake City, Utah, under construction 40 years, is completed.

John R. Mott organizes Foreign Missions Conference of North America.

Catholic Bishop John Hennessy of Dubuque (Iowa) is elevated to archbishop.

ART/MUSIC

John Philip Sousa tours with his own band; writes the march "Liberty Bell."

PAINTINGS William M. Chase, *Lady in a White Shawl*; Winslow Homer, *The Fox Hunt*; George Inness, *The Home of the Heron*; Abbott H. Thayer, *The Virgin*.

SONGS (popular): "Git Along Little Dogie," "See Saw, Margery Daw," "Two Little Girls in Blue," "When the Roll Is Called Up Yonder."

DEATHS Gustav Schirmer, music publisher; John S. Dwight, editor and publisher, *Journal of Music* (1852–1881).

LITERATURE/JOURNALISM

McClure's Magazine is founded.

Finley Peter Dunne writes his humorous "Mr. Dooley" sketches in *Chicago Journal*.

Melville E. Stone becomes general manager of Associated Press.

Henry B. Fuller writes *The Cliff Dwellers*.

ENTERTAINMENT

Motion picture exhibition, using Thomas Edison's kinetoscope, is presented at Brooklyn Institute (N.Y.); Edison patents kinetoscope and kinetoscope camera.

Edward H. R. Lyman gives Northampton, Mass., Academy of Music, which it converts to municipal theater.

Empire Theater in New York City opens.

1894

Nat Goodwin stars in *In Mizzoura*; David Belasco and Franklin Fyles produce *The Girl I Left Behind*.

DEATH Edwin T. Booth, actor.

SPORTS

Senda Berenson Abbott introduces basketball at Smith College, Northampton, Mass.

Ice hockey is first played in U.S. at Johns Hopkins and Yale University.

Western (baseball) League revives; Ban Johnson is named president.

Longest boxing match (110 rounds: 7 hours, 19 minutes) occurs in New Orleans; is called "no contest" when fighters refuse to continue.

Chicago Fly-Casting Club is organized; stages first national tournament.

WINNERS *Horse racing* — Lookout wins Kentucky Derby; Comanche, Belmont Stakes; no Preakness Stakes; *Yachting* — America's *Vigilant* retains America's Cup.

DEATH Abner Doubleday, credited with inventing baseball.

MISCELLANEOUS

Three floors of Ford's Theater in Washington, D.C., collapse during reconstruction; 22 are killed.

Field Museum of Natural History is chartered as Columbian Museum.

Fire in Minneapolis destroys $2 million of property, leaves 1,500 homeless.

Tropical storm makes eight-day trip up East Coast; Savannah and Charleston (S.C.) are damaged, 1,000 are killed; later storm along Gulf Coast kills hundreds.

1894

INTERNATIONAL

Republic of Hawaii is established with Sanford B. Dole as president (July 4).

NATIONAL

Jacob S. Coxey of Massillon, Ohio, calls on unemployed (March 25) to march on Washington to deliver their demands; 400 arrive (April 30), advocate a $500 million public-works relief program; disband (May 1) when leaders are arrested.

Income tax of 2% is imposed on all personal and corporate annual income of more than $4,000.

Labor Day becomes legal national holiday.

Wilson-Gorman tariff puts wool, copper, and lumber on free list; lowers duties to 39.9%.

Postage-stamp printing is taken from private contractors; is assigned to Bureau of Engraving & Printing.

DEATH Amelia Jenks Bloomer, feminist who proposed new women's costume (full-cut trousers under a short skirt, "bloomers").

BUSINESS/INDUSTRY/ INVENTIONS

American Railway Union strikes Pullman plant in Chicago, declares boycott of trains carrying Pullman cars, ties up all Midwest roads; federal government swears in 3,400 special deputies to keep roads running; violence results (July 6), troops are sent in to keep mails and interstate commerce moving; federal injunction breaks strike in landmark defeat for organized labor.

Niagara Falls (N.Y.) plant produces hydroelectric power.

Charles W. Post develops coffee substitute, Postum; launches line of breakfast foods; Michael I. Pupin invents a system of multiplex telegraph.

Patents are granted to Charles B. King for pneumatic hammer and Daniel M. Cooper for a time-card recorder.

John H. Galey and James M. Guffey strike oil in Corsicana, Tex.

Tailors in New York City strike over "sweatshop" conditions.

TRANSPORTATION

Elwood Haynes and Elmer Apperson in Kokomo, Ind., test one of first automobiles, a one-cylinder car.

Brotherhood of Railway Switchmen is founded.

Southern Railway is organized.

SCIENCE/MEDICINE

Dr. Hermann M. Biggs introduces diphtheria antitoxin in U.S.

Saranac Laboratory is established, first U.S. laboratory devoted to study of tuberculosis.

Louisiana Leper Home at Carville is founded.

Percival Lowell founds astronomical observatory near Flagstaff, Ariz.

Dr. Samuel H. Durgin of Boston Board of Health inaugurates regular medical examination of schoolchildren.

Dr. Luther E. Holt writes *The Care and Feeding of Children.*

EDUCATION

New York City creates teachers' pension fund.

Radcliffe College is established; Ohio State University opens ceramics school.

Coxey's army of unemployed workers marches into Alleghany on their way to Washington. BROWN BROTHERS

1894

John C. Dana organizes first children's department of a public library (Denver, Colo.).

DEATH James McCosh, Princeton president (1868–1888).

RELIGION

First services are held in Christian Science Mother Church in Boston (December 30).

ART/MUSIC

Walter Damrosch organizes an opera company that tours U.S.

Winslow Homer completes the painting *High Cliff, Coast of Maine*; George G. Bernard completes the sculpture *Two Natures*.

SONGS (popular): "We Gather Together," "The Sidewalks of New York," "She Is More to Be Pitied Than Censured," "Kathleen," "I've Been Working on the Railroad," "Rambling Wreck from Georgia Tech."

DEATH George Inness, landscape painter.

LITERATURE/JOURNALISM

Richard Outcault draws first color comic strip, "Origin of New Species," appears in *New York World* (November 18); soon thereafter, Outcault begins "Hogan Alley" strip.

Atlantis, Greek newspaper, begins publication in New York.

BOOKS *Pudd'n Head Wilson* by Mark Twain, *Bayou Folk* by Kate Chopin, *A Traveler from Altruria* by William Dean Howells, *A Kentucky Cardinal* by James L. Allen.

DEATHS Oliver Wendell Holmes, author and poet; Erastus F. Beadle, originator of "dime novel," forerunner of popular paperbacks.

ENTERTAINMENT

First motion picture (*Record of a Sneeze*) on Edison Kinetoscope is copyrighted.

Billboard magazine is founded.

William Gillette stars in his play *Too Much Johnson*.

DEATH Steele MacKaye, playwright and founder of first U.S. drama school.

SPORTS

U.S. Golf Assn. is formed in New York City; *Golfing*, a weekly magazine, begins publication.

Jockey Club, governing body of thoroughbred breeding and racing, is chartered.

Bobby Lowe of Boston Braves becomes first major leaguer to hit four home runs in a game; Yale baseball players are first to use squeeze play.

Aqueduct Race Track opens.

Connie Mack, catcher, manages Pittsburgh Pirates.

Bowler's Journal begins publication.

WINNERS *Baseball*—New York beats Baltimore for league title; *Boxing*—Jim Corbett, heavyweight; *Chess*—Albert Hodges, U.S. championship; *Fencing*—Harvard, first intercollegiate title; *Horse racing*—Chant, Kentucky Derby; Assignee, Preakness Stakes; Henry of Navarre, Belmont Stakes.

MISCELLANEOUS

National Council of Jewish Women is formed.

National Municipal League is established.

National (originally United) Daughters of the Confederacy is chartered.

Midwinter International Exposition is held in San Francisco.

Fire at site of 1893 Columbian Exposition in Chicago destroys most buildings; forest fire near Hinckley, Minn., burns more than 160,000 acres, kills 418.

1895

INTERNATIONAL

President Grover Cleveland urges U.S. citizens not to give aid to Cubans rebelling against Spain during civil war in Cuba.

NATIONAL

Supreme Court in *Pollock v. Farmers Loan & Trust Co.* holds 1894 income tax invalid; ruling eventually leads to Sixteenth Amendment; also rules in *United States v. E. C. Knight Co.* that Sherman Anti-Trust Act does not apply to intrastate manufacturing combinations.

U.S. gold reserves fall to $41 million; President Cleveland arranges a $62 million loan from banking syndicate headed by J. P. Morgan and August Belmont.

Daughters of American Revolution (DAR) is chartered by Congress.

Former Vice President Levi P. Morton begins two-year term as New York governor.

DEATHS Frederick Douglass, human rights leader; Peter H. Burnett, first California governor (1849–1851).

BUSINESS/INDUSTRY/INVENTIONS

National Association of Manufacturers (NAM) is organized.

Sheffield Farms Co. markets pasteurized milk from its Bloomville, N.Y., plant.

First cafeteria in U.S. opens in Chicago on Adams St.

Underwood Typewriter Co. incorporates; Savage Arms Co. is founded; Virginia-Carolina Chemical Co., fertilizer manufacturer, is established.

Clarence W. Barron founds *Philadelphia Financial News*; Henry D. Lloyd publishes a study of Standard Oil, *Wealth Against Commonwealth.*

PATENTS Michael J. Owens of Toledo for glass-blowing machine; King Gillette, the safety razor;

Charles F. Jenkins, a motion picture projector.

International Boot & Shoe Workers Union is formed.

Reliance Building in Chicago is completed, is the forerunner of steel-frame, glass skyscraper.

DEATHS Ephraim Bull, developer of Concord grape; Rudolf Eickemeyer, inventor of hat-making machine; James Renwick, architect (Smithsonian, St. Patrick's Cathedral); Lorenzo L. Langstroth, inventor of beehive that revolutionizes honey-bee industry.

TRANSPORTATION

AUTOMOBILE DEVELOPMENTS George B. Selden patents internal combustion engine, is granted rights to royalty fees by automakers; Duryea Motor Wagon Co. becomes first automobile company; Ransom E. Olds builds cars; first organized auto race is held in Chicago, only two of six cars finish race in snowstorm; winner averages 6.6 miles per hour; first automobile club, American Motor League, organizes in Chicago; *The Horseless Age*, first automotive magazine, is published.

New York Central's Empire State Express sets record of 6 hours, 54 minutes for Buffalo–New York City run.

Van Buren St. Bridge over Chicago River opens in Chicago.

SCIENCE/MEDICINE

Dr. Joseph B. DeLee founds Chicago Lying-in Hospital.

Edward H. Angle founds first school of orthodontia in St. Louis, Mo.

Dr. Daniel H. Williams founds National Medical Assn., an organization for black physicians.

George E. Hale founds *Astrophysical Journal.*

DEATH James D. Dana, geologist and zoologist.

1895

EDUCATION

First American Catholic college for women (Notre Dame of Maryland) opens.

New York Public Library is founded by consolidating Astor and Lenox libraries and the Tilden Trust.

RELIGION

John R. Mott organizes World's Student Christian Federation.

Black Baptist groups form National Baptist Convention of the U.S.A.

ART/MUSIC

San Francisco and Cincinnati symphony orchestras are founded.

SONGS (popular): "America the Beautiful," "The Band Played On," "The Hand That Rocks the Cradle," "Just Tell Them That You Saw Me," "The Sunshine of Paradise Alley."

DEATH James M. Ives of Currier & Ives.

LITERATURE/JOURNALISM

Frederick G. Bonfils and Harry H. Tannen publish *Denver Post*; William Randolph Hearst buys *New York Morning Journal*; Scripps-McRae League of Newspapers is founded, eventually becomes United Press; William Allen White purchases *Emporia* (Kans.) *Gazette*, serves 49 years as editor.

Elbert Hubbard founds Roycroft Press in East Aurora, N.Y.

Gelett Burgess edits *Lark* Magazine, which carries his famed "purple cow" jingle.

BOOKS *The Red Badge of Courage* by Stephen Crane, *The Jacklins* by Opie Read, *Majors and Minors* (poetry) by Paul L. Dunbar, *With the Procession* by Henry B. Fuller.

DEATH Eugene Field, columnist and poet ("Little Boy Blue").

ENTERTAINMENT

Richard Mansfield stars in G. B. Shaw's *Arms and the Man*, Maurice Barrymore in *The Heart of Maryland*, E. H. Sothern in *The Prisoner of Zenda*, Virginia Harned in *Trilby*.

DuMont's Minstrels, a blackface troupe, begin in Philadelphia.

SPORTS

First professional football game is played in Latrobe, Pa.; Latrobe YMCA, which wins, pays quarterback, John Brallier, $10 (August 31).

American Bowling Congress is organized.

Robert J. Roberts invents medicine ball; William G. Morgan develops game of volleyball.

WINNERS *Auto racing*—Frank Duryea, first gasoline-powered race (54 miles at 7.5 miles per hour); *Baseball*—Cleveland, league championship; *Chess*—Jackson Showalter, U.S. championship; Harry N. Pillsbury, Hastings (England) international tournament; *Golf*—Charles B. MacDonald, first official amateur tournament; Mrs. Charles B. Brown, first U.S. women's amateur title; *Horse racing*—Halma, Kentucky Derby; Belmar, Preakness Stakes and Belmont Stakes; *Rowing*—Columbia, first intercollegiate regatta; *Yachting*—U.S.'s *Defender* retains America's cup.

MISCELLANEOUS

Cotton States and International Exposition is held in Atlanta; Booker T. Washington delivers so-called Atlanta Compromise address.

1896

INTERNATIONAL

Gold is discovered on Klondike River in northern Canada; a gold rush follows.

Boundary commission is created to resolve quarrel with British over Venezuela.

NATIONAL

William McKinley, Republican, wins the presidency over Democrat William Jennings Bryan, who also runs as People's Party candidate; McKinley receives 7,035,638 popular votes (a margin of 568,00 votes) and 271 electoral votes to Bryan's 176.

Supreme Court in *Plessy v. Ferguson* upholds Louisiana law that requires "separate but equal" accommodations on public transportation, effectively validating racial segregation.

Utah is admitted as the 45th state (January 4); along with Idaho, it provides women's suffrage; new South Carolina constitution goes into effect.

Rural free mail delivery is authorized.

Government borrows $100 million through public subscription when gold reserves fall to $79 million.

DEATH Mathew Brady, Civil War photographer.

BUSINESS/INDUSTRY/INVENTIONS

American Match Co. produces book matches; H. J. Heinz Co. uses "57 Varieties" slogan; Herman Hollerith establishes Tabulating Machine Co., forerunner of IBM; S. H. Kress & Co., five-and-ten-cent store chain, starts with store in Memphis, Tenn.; U.S. Voting Machine Co., is founded in Jamestown, N.Y.

William S. Hadaway Jr. patents an electric shaver, and Whitcomb Judson, a hookless shoe-fastener.

TRANSPORTATION

AUTOMOBILE DEVELOPMENTS Henry Ford assembles his first automobile in a Detroit workshed (June 4); Ransom E. Olds organizes Olds Motor Vehicle Co., turns out six cars the first year; Charles Brady King drives his "horseless carriage" in Detroit, marks first public appearance of an automobile; first auto accident occurs (May 30) when Henry Wells driving a Duryea, strikes Evelyn Thomas on a bicycle, breaking her leg.

SCIENCE/MEDICINE

Samuel P. Langley demonstrates his "aerodrome," a miniature steam engine with wings; flies a mile several times over Potomac River in 90 seconds.

Michael I. Pupin develops a machine with which he produces the first U.S. X-ray picture; Dr. Emil H. Grube begins X-ray treatment of breast cancer.

Wilbur O. Atwater, director of U.S. Office of Experiment Stations, publishes tables of caloric potential of many foods; tables are still in use.

Dr. Luther E. Holt writes *The Diseases of Infancy and Childhood.*

EDUCATION

John Dewey establishes Laboratory School at University of Chicago to test his education theories.

John S. Billings becomes first director of New York Public Library.

James B. Scott organizes Los Angeles Law School, which becomes part of University of Southern California.

RELIGION

John A. Dowie forms Christian Catholic Apostolic Church in Chicago; later sets up Zion City, near Chicago.

Charles M. Sheldon prepares *In His Steps*, a best-selling book calling for Christian living.

Billy Sunday, former professional baseball player, becomes successful evangelist.

ART/MUSIC

American Guild of Organists is founded.

1896

Fannie Farmer (left) with one of her pupils, Martha Hayes Ludden, at Miss Farmer's Boston cooking school, where recipes are kitchen-tested and formulated. The recipes reach the general public in 1896 through publication of the *Boston Cooking School Cookbook*. CORBIS-BETTMANN

Walter Damrosch's opera *The Scarlet Letter* is performed in Boston.

Edward A. MacDowell composes *Wonderful Sketches*; John Philip Sousa, the opera *El Capitan*; Amy M. Beach composes first important U.S. symphony, *Gaelic Symphony*.

Los Angeles Symphony Orchestra is founded.

Sculptor James E. Foster completes statue *The End of the Trail*.

Maud Nugent writes popular "Sweet Rosie O'Grady," first woman to write a one-million-copy selling song.

SONGS (popular): "Hot Time in the Old Town Tonight," "Kentucky Babe," "My Gal Is a High Born Lady" (probably first ragtime song), "Red River Valley," "When the Saints Go Marching In."

LITERATURE/JOURNALISM

Adolph S. Ochs buys control of the *New York Times*; first issue of the *Times Book Review* section is published.

Gilbert Patten, writing as Burt L. Standish, begins to turn out books (eventually 209 of them) about the Merriwell brothers, Frank and Dick.

New York Journal prints Sunday comics (October 18).

BOOKS *Country of the Pointed Firs* by Sarah Orne Jewett, *The Damnation of Theron Ware* by Harold Frederick, *Lyrics of a Lowly Life* (poetry) by Paul L. Dunbar, *A Houseboat on the Styx* by John K. Bangs, *Maggie, a Girl of the Streets* by Stephen Crane.

DEATHS Harriet Beecher Stowe, author; George Munro, publisher, *Fireside Companion*.

ENTERTAINMENT

Edison Vitascope projects motion pictures on a large screen for first time.

Theater Syndicate is founded, controls many American theaters in early 1900s; Actors' National Protective Union is chartered (becomes part of Associated Actors and Artists).

Inventor Charles W. Parker manufactures carousels with "jumping" horses.

New plays include *Secret Service* with William Gillette and *Under the Red Robe* with William Faversham.

Cakewalk, a syncopated dance, becomes popular.

DEATH George W. Ferris, builder of Ferris wheel.

SPORTS

First modern Olympic Games are held in Athens, Greece; U.S. wins 9 of 12 events; James B. Connolly, U.S. triple jump winner, is first Olympic champion in 1,500 years.

First woman's six-day bicycle race is held in New York City; New York Athletic Club stages first U.S. marathon.

Big Ten athletic conference holds its first meeting.

U.S. Hockey League is organized.

About 4 million Americans ride bicycles, which sell for about $60.

WINNERS *Auto racing*—A. H. Whiting, first race on a track (Rhode Island State Fair); *Baseball*—Baltimore, National League title; *Basketball*—Wesleyan University beats Yale in first intercollegiate game; *Bicycling*—Columbia, first intercollegiate race; *Football*—University of Chicago, first indoor game; *Hockey*—St. Nicholas club, first U.S. League game; *Horse racing*—Ben Brush, Kentucky Derby; Margrave, Preakness Stakes; Hastings, Belmont Stakes.

MISCELLANEOUS

Fannie Farmer prepares *Boston Cooking School Cookbook.*

Tornado in St. Louis kills 306 persons.

Chinese ambassador's chef prepares chop suey, a dish unknown in China, to please American and Asian tastes.

Ballington Booth, former head of U.S. Salvation Army, founds Volunteers of America.

NATIONAL

Supreme Court rules that railroads are subject to antitrust laws.

Library of Congress moves from Capitol to its own building.

Grant's Tomb in New York City is dedicated.

Dingley Tariff raises duties to average 57%, with high rates on raw and manufactured wools.

New Delaware state constitution goes into effect.

Theodore Roosevelt is named Assistant Secretary of the Navy.

DEATH Thomas F. Bayard, first ambassador to Great Britain (1893–1897).

BUSINESS/INDUSTRY/INVENTIONS

S. S. Kresge inaugurates five-and-ten-cent-store chain.

Crystal Chemical Works in Alexandria, Ind., manufactures rock wool insulation; Dow Chemical Co. is founded; Charles W. Post founds Postum Cereal Co.

Thomas A. Edison patents a movie camera.

Hydroelectric power sites develop at Niagara Falls.

Thaddeus S. C. Lowe develops an improved coke oven.

DEATHS Henry George, economist; Charles C.

1897

Fleischmann, founder of yeast manufacturing firm.

TRANSPORTATION

Alexander Winton creates Winton Motor Carriage Co., which becomes first builder of big cars; twin brothers Francis E. and Freelan Stanley build one of first successful steam-powered cars, the Stanley Steamer.

Double-deck steel bridge is constructed over Niagara Gorge, at Niagara Falls, N.Y.

South Side Elevated Railway in Chicago becomes first electrified system in U.S.; first section of Boston's Tremont St. subway opens.

SCIENCE/MEDICINE

Yerkes Observatory of University of Chicago at Williams Bay, Wis., opens, contains largest U.S. refracting telescope (40 in.).

American Dental Assn. is founded as the National Dental Assn.

Minnesota establishes first state crippled-children's hospital in U.S., Gillette State Hospital, St. Paul, Minn.

EDUCATION

National Congress of Mothers, first parent-teacher group, is formed; eventually becomes National Congress of Parents & Teachers.

Bradley University (Peoria, Ill.) is founded.

1897

DEATH John Evans, educator, a founder of Northwestern and Denver Universities.

RELIGION

Rev. Francis Hodur, who becomes prime bishop, organizes Polish National Catholic Church of America in Scranton, Pa. (March 14).

Josiah Royce's *The Conception of God* is published.

DEATH Rev. George H. Houghton, founder, rector, Little Church Around the Corner, New York City (1849–1897).

ART/MUSIC

Wilcox & White Co. manufactures completely automatic player piano.

John Philip Sousa writes the march "The Stars and Stripes Forever" and the opera *The Bride-Elect*.

DeYoung Memorial Museum in San Francisco opens.

SONGS (popular): "Asleep in the Deep," "Beautiful Isle of Somewhere," "Danny Deever," "Take Back Your Gold."

LITERATURE/JOURNALISM

Rudolph Dirks draws an early popular comic strip, "Katzenjammer Kids" in *New York Journal.*

Curtis Publishing Co. acquires *Saturday Evening Post.*

Doubleday & McClure, publishers, is founded, eventually becomes Doubleday & Co.

Jewish Daily Forward newspaper begins publication in New York City.

BOOKS *The Descendant* by Ellen Glasgow, *A Night in Acadie* by Kate Chopin, *Soldiers of Fortune* by

Women ride in a subway car reserved especially for them. The first section of Boston's subway opens in 1897. The picture actually shows New York's subway, which will open in 1899. CULVER PICTURES INC.

Richard Harding Davis, *The Choir Invisible* by James L. Allen, *The Children of the Night* (poetry) by Edwin Arlington Robinson.

ENTERTAINMENT

Maude Adams stars in *The Little Minister* by James M. Barrie; Richard Mansfield in G. B. Shaw's *The Devil's Disciple*, Chauncey Olcott in *Sweet Iniscarra*.

SPORTS

John Flanagan is first to surpass 150 feet (150 ft. 8½ in.) in hammer throw.

Yale and Pennsylvania play first five-man intercollegiate basketball game.

Willie Keeler's baseball hitting streak stops at record 44 consecutive games; Cap Anson of Chicago Cubs, at 45 years of age, becomes first to make 3,000 career hits.

First Frontier Days rodeo is held in Cheyenne, Wyo.

Chicago Fly-Casting Club sponsors national tournament.

WINNERS *Baseball*—Baltimore, National League title; *Billiards*—George F. Slosson, first tournament winner; *Boxing*—Bob Fitzsimmons, heavyweight; *Chess*—Harry Pillsbury, U.S. championship; *Golf*—Yale, intercollegiate title; *Gymnastics*—Earl Linderman, all-round AAU championship; *Handball*—Michael Egan, first national amateur title; *Horse racing*—Typhoon II, Kentucky Derby; Paul Kauvar, Preakness Stakes; Scottish Chieftain, Belmont Stakes; *Marathon*—John J. McDermott, first Boston Marathon.

MISCELLANEOUS

Tennessee Centennial Exposition is held in Nashville.

United American Zionists form in New York City.

Fire destroys Pennsylvania State Capitol in Harrisburg.

INTERNATIONAL

Spanish-American War

After a Havana riot (January 12), USS *Maine* sails to Cuba, ostensibly to protect U.S. lives; while at anchor in Havana harbor, explosion destroys battleship (February 15) killing 260. Naval inquiry blames explosion on submarine mine but cannot decide blame on people.

President William McKinley calls for 125,000 volunteers to serve two years (February 23); Theodore Roosevelt resigns as Assistant Secretary of Navy to organize volunteer cavalry regiment, the "Rough Riders."

President McKinley calls for "forcible intervention" to bring about Cuban peace (April 11); Congress passes a war resolution (April 20), Spain declares war on U.S. (April 24); U.S. declares war (April 25); Congress authorizes volunteer force of 200,000 men, increases regular army to 60,000 (April 26).

U.S. fleet bombards Matanzas, Cuba (April 27); U.S. naval force bottles up Spanish fleet of seven in Santiago de Cuba harbor (May 29).

Marines make first Cuban landing at Guantanamo Bay; U.S. expeditionary force of 17,000 sails for Cuba (June 14); first land battle in Cuba erupts at Las Guisimas (June 24).

U.S. captures heights overlooking Santiago (July 1); Spanish fleet tries to run blockade in harbor, is destroyed in the attempt (July 3); Santiago surrenders (July 16), virtually ending the fighting in Cuba; U.S. occupies Puerto Rico (July 25).

Spanish ask for peace terms (July 26), which they quickly accept (August 9).

In the Pacific phase of the war, U.S. naval force commanded by Adm. George Dewey destroys 10 Spanish vessels in Manila harbor after brief battle (May 1).

Emilio Aguinaldo, Filipino leader, establishes pro-

1898

The famous Rough Riders (the First U.S. Volunteer Cavalry Regiment) pose at the top of San Juan Hill in Cuba, 1898. Teddy Roosevelt is in the center. THE GRANGER COLLECTION, NEW YORK

visional government, declares Philippine independence from Spain (June 12); U.S. forces occupy Guam (June 20), capture Wake Island (July 4). Congress formally annexes Hawaiian Islands (August 12). With help of Filipino troops, Manila is occupied (August 13).

Peace conference opens in Paris (October 1), concludes (December 10); Spain cedes Puerto Rico, Guam, and the Philippines, surrenders all claims to Cuba.

NATIONAL

Louisiana adopts constitution that bars blacks from voting by use of property and literacy tests and a "grandfather" clause.

Congress authorizes Interstate Commerce Commission chairman and Bureau of Labor commissioner to mediate railroad dispute.

Supreme Court upholds Utah law that limits maximum working hours in mining industry.

Theodore Roosevelt is elected governor of New York.

DEATHS Former First Lady Lucy W. Hayes (1877–1881); Frances E. C. Willard, temperance crusader; Edward Bellamy, author and founder of movement to nationalize industry.

BUSINESS/INDUSTRY/INVENTIONS

Goodyear Tire & Rubber Co., International Paper Co., and National Biscuit Co. are formed.

Rev. Hannibal W. Goodwin patents celluloid photographic film and John A. Sheridan, machine to fold and seal envelopes.

Taylor-White heat-treating process is developed, increases cutting capacity of tool steels by as much as 300%.

St. Louis Iron & Marine Works build first diesel engine for commercial use; Henry C. Timken invents a roller bearing, founds company for its manufacture.

Simon Lake successfully demonstrates gasoline-engine-powered submarine in the open sea; Holland Torpedo Boat Co. launches its submarine *Holland No. 9.*

DEATH William S. Burroughs, inventor of first practical adding machine.

TRANSPORTATION

Travelers Co. issues first automobile insurance policy.

Tremont St. subway in Boston is completed.

SCIENCE/MEDICINE

New York State opens first cancer laboratory at University of Buffalo with Dr. Roswell Park as director.

Astronomer William H. Pickering discovers ninth satellite of Saturn.

American Pediatric Society is founded.

Dr. Walter Reed heads investigation of yellow-fever outbreak in army camps.

Daniel D. Palmer founds chiropractic school in Davenport, Iowa.

American Journal of Physiology begins publication.

EDUCATION

School of Comparative Jurisprudence and Diplomacy opens at George Washington University in Washington, D.C.; first forestry college opens at Cornell University.

DePaul University (Chicago) and Northeastern University (Boston) are founded.

RELIGION

Lorenzo Snow is elected president of Mormon Church, succeeds William Woodruff.

ART/MUSIC

Edward A. MacDowell composes "Sea Pieces;" Ernestine Schumann-Heink makes American debut in *Lohengrin* at the Metropolitan Opera.

National Federation of Music Clubs is founded.

SONGS (popular): "The Rosary," "She Was Bred in Old Kentucky," "Just One Girl," "Gypsy Love Song," "Ciribiribin," "Boola Boola," "It's Always Fair Weather When Good Fellows Get Together."

LITERATURE/JOURNALISM

Bernarr Macfadden publishes *Physical Culture* magazine.

BOOKS *David Harum* by Edward N. Westcott, *The Turn of the Screw* by Henry James, "The Open Boat" by Stephen Crane, *The Landlord at Lion's Head* by William Dean Howells.

ENTERTAINMENT

Richard Mansfield stars in *Cyrano de Bergerac,* William Faversham in *The Conqueror.*

Victor Herbert writes the musical *The Fortune Teller.*

SPORTS

First standardbred horse to run mile in under 2 minutes (1 min, 59¼ sec.) is the pacer Star Pointer.

National Basketball League is founded with teams in Philadelphia, New York, Brooklyn, and southern New Jersey.

Intercollegiate Shooting Assn. is formed.

WINNERS *Bicycling*—George Banker, professional sprint riding; *Horse racing*—Plaudit, Kentucky Derby; Sly Fox, Preakness Stakes; Bowling Brook, Belmont Stakes.

MISCELLANEOUS

Trans-Mississippi Exposition is held in Omaha, Nebr.

Lou Henry, later the wife of President Herbert Hoover, is first woman graduate in geology, earns degree at Stanford University (Calif.).

Stephen S. Wise founds Zionist Organization of America as the Federation of American Zionists.

Steel pier is built at Atlantic City, N.J.

Steamer *Portland* is wrecked off Cape Cod, Mass., with loss of 157 lives.

Charles W. Post introduces Grape Nuts cereal.

1899

INTERNATIONAL

Filipino nationalists, led by Emilio Aguinaldo, revolt against U.S.; revolt near end in year.

First Hague Conference (May 18) is held, 26 nations discuss disarmament, limit to warfare methods, and creation of machinery to arbitrate disputes; conference fails to agree on disarmament or warfare methods but does create Permanent Court of International Arbitration (July 29).

Senate ratifies Paris peace treaty that ends Spanish-American War (February 6).

U.S., Great Britain, and Germany agree to divide Samoan Islands; U.S. gets Tutuila.

NATIONAL

Supreme Court orders six cast-iron pipe manufacturers to discontinue an agreement that eliminates competition among them.

Use of voting machines in federal elections is authorized.

City of Greater New York comes into being with the absorption of Brooklyn, becoming the second largest in the world at the time with 3.4 million people.

World's first juvenile court opens in Denver, Colo.; Judge Ben Lindsey presides.

Mt. Rainier (Wash.) National Park is created.

Herbert Putnam begins 40 years as Librarian of Congress, develops a great national library.

DEATH Vice President Garrett A. Hobart (1897–1899).

BUSINESS/INDUSTRY/INVENTIONS

Standard Oil Co. of New Jersey organizes to replace Ohio company that dissolved in 1892; other new companies are United Shoe Machinery Co., American Agricultural Chemical Co., General Chemical Co. (later Allied Chemical), and Carnation Co., maker of evaporated milk.

Patents are issued to Humphrey O'Sullivan for rubber heel and John S. Thurman for motor-driven vacuum cleaner.

Two economics books published are *The Distribution of Wealth* by John B. Clark and *The Theory of the Leisure Class* by Thorstein B. Veblen.

DEATHS Henry B. Hyde, founder and president, Equitable Life Assurance Co.; William H. Webb, shipbuilder.

TRANSPORTATION

AUTOMOBILE DEVELOPMENTS James W. and William D. Packard produce cars; Olds Motor Works produces Oldsmobiles; New York City cab driver is first person arrested for speeding, drives at 12 miles per hour; Back Bay Cycle & Motor Co. in Boston opens public garage; first auto traffic fatality occurs in New York City when car runs over a passenger who is getting off a streetcar; Clyde J. Coleman invents an electric auto self-starter.

Congress approves construction of Galveston-Houston Ship Canal.

Holley Motor Co. produces first practical motorcycle.

First units of New York City subway system are built.

Oil is discovered in Illinois.

SCIENCE/MEDICINE

First Alaska hospital is built in Nome; first free, nonsectarian hospital for tuberculosis, National Jewish Hospital, opens in Denver, Colo.

American Physical Society is formed.

EDUCATION

Chicago becomes first city to provide special schools for the physically challenged.

University of Chicago School of Education opens as the Chicago Institute.

Fashionable young women of the 1890s are dubbed "Gibson girls" after the popular illustrator who drew this picture, Charles Dana Gibson. CORBIS-BETTMANN

John Dewey writes *School and Society*.

Clemson (S.C.) College establishes a textile school; University of San Francisco opens.

RELIGION

Gideons International is organized to distribute Bibles in hotels, motels, hospitals, and jails.

DEATHS Cyrus Hamlin, missionary and founder of Roberts College in Turkey; John Williams, presiding Episcopal bishop (1887–1899); Dwight L. Moody, evangelist.

ART/MUSIC

Scott Joplin composes "Original Rag," first ragtime song on sheet music.

University of Pennsylvania (art) Museum opens.

Winslow Homer completes the painting *The Gulf Stream*; Maurice Prendergast, *Umbrellas in the Rain*;

Thomas C. Eakins, *Between the Rounds*; Cyrus E. Dallin completes the sculpture *Medicine Man*.

SONGS (popular): "Hearts and Flowers," "Hello My Baby," "Maple Leaf Rag," "My Wild Irish Rose," "O Sole Mio," "She'll Be Comin' Round the Mountain," "Where the Sweet Magnolias Grow," "On the Banks of the Wabash Far Away."

LITERATURE/JOURNALISM

Gilbert H. Grosvenor begins 55 years as editor of *National Geographic Magazine*; *American Boy* magazine is founded.

Elbert Hubbard prints his best-known story, "A Message to Garcia," in his magazine, *The Philistine*; Edwin Markham's poem, "The Man with the Hoe," appears in the *San Francisco Examiner*.

BOOKS *When Knighthood Was in Flower* by Charles Major, *Richard Carvel* by Winston Churchill, *Janice Meredith* by Paul L. Ford, *Fables in Slang* by George

1899

Ade, *The Gentlemen from Indiana* by Booth Tarkington, *The Conjure Woman* by Charles W. Chesnutt, *The Awkward Age* by Henry James.

DEATHS Horatio Alger, author of boys' stories; Joseph Medill, owner, *Chicago Tribune* (1874–1899); Ottmar Mergenthaler, inventor of linotype.

ENTERTAINMENT

Julia Marlowe stars in *Barbara Frietchie*, Minnie Maddern Fiske in *Becky Sharp*, William Gillette in *Sherlock Holmes*, Edward Morgan and William S. Hart in *Ben-Hur*.

DEATH Augustin Daly, playwright and producer.

SPORTS

George F. Grant patents a golf tee.

Charles Murphy becomes first bicycle racer to attain speed of a mile a minute.

Intercollegiate Rowing Assn. is founded.

First two-man six-day bicycle race is held in Madison Square Garden, New York City.

WINNERS *Bicycling*—Major Taylor, world professional sprint riding; *Boxing*—Jim Jeffries, heavyweight; Frank Erne, lightweight; *Golf*—Herbert M. Harriman, U.S. Amateur; *Horse racing*—Manuel, Kentucky Derby; Half Time, Preakness Stakes; Jean Bereaud, Belmont Stakes; *Rowing*—Edward H. Ten Eyck, single sculls; *Yachting*—U.S.'s *Columbia* retains America's Cup.

MISCELLANEOUS

Bird-Lore Magazine (later *Audubon Magazine*) begins publication.

Blizzard ranging from Canada to Gulf Coast drops temperatures to as low as −61 degrees in north and zero at the Gulf.

1900

INTERNATIONAL

Siege of foreign legations in Peking is raised, Boxer Rebellion ends; 231 foreigners, many Chinese Christians are killed during two-month rebellion; U.S. announces open-door policy in China, which provides equal commercial opportunity for all nations.

First Hay-Pauncefote Treaty is signed; calls for U.S. and Great Britain jointly to protect any canal across Panama Isthmus; gives U.S. right to construct, operate such a canal; is ratified (December 20).

William Howard Taft heads commission to establish Philippines civil government; Cuban constitutional convention is held.

U.S. formally occupies Wake Island.

Negotiations are completed with Denmark for purchase of Virgin Islands.

NATIONAL

President William McKinley, Republican, is reelected with 7,219,530 popular and 292 electoral votes to Democrat William Jennings Bryan's 6,358,071 and 155.

American troops march in Beijing, China, during the Boxer Rebellion of 1900. Culver Pictures Inc.

1900

Congress grants territorial status to Hawaii (June 14); civil government is established in Puerto Rico; it becomes an unorganized U.S. territory (May 1).

Gold Standard Act establishes gold dollar as standard unit of value; all U.S.-issued money on par with gold.

National debt is $1.2 billion.

Supreme Court in *Knowlton v. Moore* finds inheritance tax to be constitutional.

Books of postage stamps are issued.

About 3.6 million immigrants arrive in U.S.

Twelfth census reports population at 76,212,168; about 4% (3.1 million) are older than 65; life expectancy is 47.3 years.

House of Representatives refuses (268–50) to seat Brigham A. Roberts of Utah because of his plural marriages (polygamy).

American Hall of Fame is established at New York University.

Chicago Drainage Canal, 40 miles long, 22 feet deep, opens.

Navy purchases its first submarine, built by John P. Holland.

First direct primary is held in Hennepin County, Minn.

DEATHS John Sherman, former Secretary of State (1897); William L. Wilson, Postmaster General (1895–1897), who started rural free delivery.

BUSINESS/INDUSTRY/INVENTIONS

Firestone Tire & Rubber Co. and Sanitas Food Co. (later W. K. Kellogg Co.) are founded.

Otis Elevator Co. manufactures first escalator; General Electric opens first industrial research laboratory in Schenectady, N.Y., Eastman Kodak opens new plant in Rochester, N.Y.

Joshua L. Cowan invents toy electric train; Hudson Maxim perfects a powerful explosive (Maximite); Allen DeVilbiss Jr. invents an automatic computing pendulum-type scale.

Coal miners strike for higher wages, win demands after a month; International Ladies Garment Workers Union is founded.

Average American worker earns 22 cents an hour; nearly 11 million work on farms, 6 million in factories; more than 100,000 women work as secretaries (there were only seven in 1870).

DEATHS Robert G. Dun, head of firm that became Dun & Bradstreet; Marcus Daly, developer of Anaconda Copper Co.

TRANSPORTATION

George B. Selden's patent for automobile engine is upheld; automakers are required to pay him royalties.

First auto show is held in New York City's Madison Square Garden.

Charles S. Palmer invents process for cracking oil to produce gasoline.

First autostage, an electric bus, operates on New York City's Fifth Avenue, carries 12 persons; fare is 5 cents.

Joseph S. Mack and his brothers build first successful bus, truck.

Automobile registrations total 8,000.

DEATHS Andrew S. Hallidie, inventor of cable railway; Collis P. Huntington and Henry Villard, railroad builders, operators.

SCIENCE/MEDICINE

Dr. Walter Reed heads army commission to study the cause of yellow fever, traces it to a certain type of mosquito.

Vladimir N. Ipatieff, Russian-born chemist, discovers high-temperature catalytic reactions in hydrocarbons; Karl Landsteiner, Austrian-born physician, discovers human blood groups that make transfusions safe.

American Society (later Association) of Orthodontists is founded.

American Journal of Nursing begins publication.

DEATHS Lewis A. Sayre, first U.S. orthopedic surgeon; Edward R. Squibb, pharmaceutical manufacturer.

EDUCATION

Carnegie Institute of Technology (now Carnegie-Mellon University) is founded.

International Federation of University Women is organized.

Alba Settlement House in Cleveland, Ohio, opens kindergarten for physically challenged children.

George H. Mead begins 30 years teaching course in social psychology at University of Chicago.

DEATH Henry Barnard, first U.S. education commissioner; Moses Coit Tyler, first U.S. college history professor.

RELIGION

Catholic Bishop John J. Keene is named archbishop of Dubuque, Iowa.

DEATH Isaac Mayer Wise, founder of American Reform Judaism.

ART/MUSIC

Boston Symphony Hall opens, first acoustically designed building in U.S.; Philadelphia Orchestra, directed by Fritz Scheel, gives first concert.

Thomas Eakins completes the painting *The Thinker*.

Edwin S. Votey patents a pneumatic player piano.

SONGS (popular): "Good Bye, Dolly Gray," "Tell Me, Pretty Maiden," "A Bird in a Gilded Cage," "Down South," "I Can't Tell Why I Love You But I Do."

DEATH Frederick E. Church, painter.

LITERATURE/JOURNALISM

William Dean Howells begins 20 years of writing "Easy Chair" column in *Harper's*; George H. Lorimer begins 37 years as editor of *Saturday Evening Post*.

Henry A. W. Wood invents automatic stereotype plate-casting machine that speeds up newspaper printing.

BOOKS *The Wonderful Wizard of Oz* by L. Frank Baum, *Sister Carrie* by Theodore Dreiser, *Monsieur Beaucaire* by Booth Tarkington, *Eben Holden* by Irving Bacheller, *To Have and to Hold* by Mary Johnston, *The Son of the Wolf* by Jack London, *Home Folks* (poetry) by James Whitcomb Riley.

DEATH Stephen Crane, author.

ENTERTAINMENT

Plays of the year include *Arizona* by Augustus Thomas, *Madame Butterfly* by David Belasco, *Mistress Nell* with Henrietta Crosman, *Richard Carvel* with John Drew, *Sag Harbor* with Lionel Barrymore, *The Duke's Jester* with Douglas Fairbanks in his debut.

First "little theater" is constructed for the Hull House Players in Chicago.

DEATH Dan Rice, greatest clown of his day.

SPORTS

Western (baseball) League reorganizes as the American League; demands (and is refused) equality with National League.

Olympic Games are held in Paris; U.S. wins 20 gold medals.

First Intercollegiate Rowing Assn. eight-oared shell race is held on Hudson River at Poughkeepsie, N.Y.

First horseshoe pitching club on Pacific Coast is formed in Long Beach, Calif.

Game of duckpins is introduced in Baltimore.

American Trapshooting Assn. is founded.

WINNERS *Auto racing*—A. L. Riker, Long Island race (50 miles in 2 hours, 3 minutes); *Baseball*—Brooklyn, National League title; *Boxing*—Jim Jeffries, heavyweight; *Golf*—Harry Vardon, U.S. Open; *Horse racing*—Lt. Gibson, Kentucky Derby; Hindus, Preakness Stakes; Ildrim, Belmont Stakes; *Marathon*—James J. Coffey, Boston Marathon; *Tennis*—U.S. first Davis Cup; *Trapshooting*—Rollo O. Heikes, first Grand American tournament.

DEATH William Steinitz, world chess champion (1866–1894).

MISCELLANEOUS

Dismal Swamp Canal opens; originally surveyed by George Washington.

Flood, tidal wave hit Galveston, Tex.; about 6,000 die in 14 days of 100+ mph winds; hurricane hits Puerto Rico, kills about 2,000.

1901

Men use straight-edge razors for shaving, pomade for their hair and mustache; many men chew plug tobacco, many smoke pipes, cigars.

Women's clothing expenditures are more than $1 billion per year ($18 million on corsets); hats are most important item, featuring lace, ribbons, flowers, and feathers.

Pier fire in Hoboken, N.J., kills more than 300, property damage of $4.6 million; explosion of blasting powder in Scofield, Utah, mine kills 200.

INTERNATIONAL

Second Hay-Pauncefote Treaty is signed (November 18), gives U.S. right to build, operate an isthmian (Panama) canal open to all shipping; is ratified (December 16).

American troops capture Filipino revolt leader, Emilio Aguinaldo (March 23); military government in Philippines ends, civil government is established (July 4) with William Howard Taft governor general.

Cuba sets up provisional independent government (June 12).

NATIONAL

President William McKinley is shot at Pan-American Exposition in Buffalo, N.Y., by an anarchist, Leon Czolgosz (September 6), dies eight days later; Vice President Theodore Roosevelt becomes president; Czolgosz is tried, convicted (September 23), electrocuted (October 29).

President Roosevelt, in first annual message, calls on Congress to consider safeguards against industrial combinations.

Bureau of Standards, Weights, and Measures is created as a separate office (July 1), becomes National Bureau of Standards (1913); permanent Census Bureau is created.

Army War College is established with Tasker H. Bliss president (November 27); first class held (1903).

Louisiana and Alabama adopt new constitutions.

American Hall of Fame at New York University dedicated (May 30).

Carry Nation, temperance crusader, makes first hatchet attack on a saloon (Wichita, Kans., January 21); she continues as do other temperance workers elsewhere.

Galveston, Tex., adopts commission form of government.

DEATHS Former President Benjamin Harrison (1889–1893); Hiram R. Revels, first black elected to Senate (Mississippi, 1870); Union Gen. Daniel Butterfield, composer of bugle call "Taps."

BUSINESS/INDUSTRY/INVENTIONS

Texas oil boom begins with Spindletop well near Beaumont; first important commercial oil well is drilled in Oklahoma.

U.S. Steel Corp., first billion dollar company, incorporates with Charles M. Schwab as president.

New companies formed include Gillette Safety Razor Co., Monsanto Chemical Co., Victor Talking Machine Co.; Guggenheim Exploration Co. takes over American Smelting & Refining Co., Quaker Oats Co. replaces American Cereal Co.

Peter Cooper Hewitt patents mercury vapor lamp, Reginald Fessenden an improved wireless transmitter.

Ellsworth Statler builds his first hotel, a temporary building of 2,100 rooms for the Pan-American Exposition in Buffalo, N.Y.

TRANSPORTATION

New York State requires license plates on automobiles.

Hendee Manufacturing Co. markets the "Indian" motorcycle with built-in gas engine; Sinclair Oil Co. is founded.

Railroad engineer Casey Jones crashes his Cannonball Express into a stopped freight train near Vaughn, Miss.

DEATHS Aaron French, inventor of coil elliptical springs that revolutionized railroad industry; Clement Studebaker, wagon and auto manufacturer.

SCIENCE/MEDICINE

Army Nurses Corps is established (February 2); Army Dental Corps is authorized.

Rockefeller Institute of Medical Research (now Rockefeller University) is founded.

Scripps Institution for Biological Research (later Oceanography) is established.

Miller R. Hutchinson produces the Acousticon, an electrical hearing aid.

Chemist Jokichi Takamine isolates adrenaline.

EDUCATION

Francis W. Parker founds University of Chicago School of Education.

Chemist Ira Remsen becomes president of Johns Hopkins University.

Andrew Carnegie gives New York City $5.2 million for 65 branch libraries.

Grambling State (La.) University and Idaho State University are founded.

Union catalog, combining alphabetically books in many catalogs and libraries, begins at Library of Congress.

RELIGION

Mother Alphonsa (Rose Hawthorne) founds Servants of Relief for Incurable Cancer, which she heads for 27 years.

Joseph Fielding Smith becomes president of Mormon church, succeeding Lorenzo Snow.

ART/MUSIC

George W. Chadwick writes lyric drama *Judith*.

King C. Gillette, who invented the safety razor in 1895, sells the first one in 1901. The new razor catches on quickly among men who are tired of cutting themselves with the old straight razors and having to "strop" or sharpen them. CORBIS-BETTMANN

Museum of Art in Toledo is founded.

Alfred H. Maurer completes the painting *An Arrangement*; Thomas Moran, *Grand Canyon of the Yellowstone*.

SONGS (popular): "Just a-Wearyin' for You," "I Love You Truly," "Mighty Lak a Rose," "Hiawatha."

DEATH Ethelbert W. Nevin, composer ("The Rosary," "Mighty Lak a Rose").

LITERATURE/JOURNALISM

Munsey newspaper chain is founded when Frank A. Munsey buys *Washington Times* and the *New York News*.

Clarence W. Barron buys Dow Jones & Co., becomes publisher of the *Wall Street Journal*.

1902

Edgar Guest writes poems that are syndicated by *Detroit Free Press*.

BOOKS *Graustark* by George B. McCutcheon, *Mrs. Wiggs of the Cabbage Patch* by Alice Hegan Rice, *The Crisis* by Winston Churchill, *The Octopus* by Frank Norris, *The Making of an American* by Jacob A. Riis.

ENTERTAINMENT

Manhattan Theater in New York City opens.

PLAYS David Warfield stars in *The Auctioneer*, Richard Mansfield in *Beaucaire*, Ethel Barrymore in *Capt. Jinks of the Horse Marines*, Mrs. Leslie Carter in *DuBarry*, E. H. Sothern in *If I Were King*, William Collier in *On the Quiet*, Julia Marlowe in *When Knighthood Was in Flower*, Lillian Russell in *Hoity Toity*, Anna Held in *The Little Duchess*.

SPORTS

First American League baseball game is played in Chicago (April 24), first doubleheader (July 15) split by Washington and Baltimore; Cy Young of Boston Red Sox wins his 300th game; Connie Mack becomes manager and part-owner of Philadelphia Athletics; National Association of Professional Baseball Leagues is organized in Chicago (September 5).

First American Bowling Congress sponsors tournament in Chicago; 41 teams from 17 cities compete for $1,592 in prize money.

WINNERS *Automobile racing* — David W. Bishop, 500-mile Buffalo–New York race; *Boxing* — Jim Jeffries, heavyweight; Joe Gans, lightweight; *Horse racing* — His Eminence, Kentucky Derby; The Parader, Preakness Stakes; Commando, Belmont Stakes; *Yachting* — U.S. boat *Columbia* retains America's Cup.

MISCELLANEOUS

Anna Edson Taylor goes over Niagara Falls in a barrel.

President Roosevelt causes uproar in South when he invites Booker T. Washington to White House (October 16).

Fire in Jacksonville, Fla., destroys 1,700 buildings, causes $11 million damage, leaves 10,000 homeless.

INTERNATIONAL

Isthmian Act provides $40 million to purchase property and rights of the new Panama Canal Co., calls on Colombia to grant U.S. perpetual control of the canal right-of-way (June 28).

Territorial government forms in Philippines (July 1).

U.S. withdraws from Cuba (May 20).

NATIONAL

President Theodore Roosevelt asks attorney general to bring first antitrust suit to dissolve Northern Securities Co., a railroad holding company (March 10).

National Reclamation Act sets aside proceeds from public-land sales in 16 states to finance, maintain irrigation projects; U.S. Reclamation Service begins (January 7).

Carnegie Institution in Washington, D.C., is founded (January 28).

U.S. Army uniform changes from blue to olive drab.

Juliette G. Low founds first troop of Girl Guides (later Girl Scouts) in Savannah, Ga.

Woman Suffrage Alliance is founded.

Crater Lake (Ore.) National Park is established.

DEATHS Former First Lady Julia D. Grant (1869–1877); cartoonist Thomas Nast, who created political party symbols; Elizabeth Cady Stanton, women's rights leader.

BUSINESS/INDUSTRY/INVENTIONS

Maryland adopts first state workmen's compensation law, later found unconstitutional.

United Mine Workers call strike against anthracite coal mines; federal mediation ends strike.

Horn & Hardart opens first automatic food-vending restaurant in U.S. at 818 Chestnut St., Philadelphia, Pa.

Merger of McCormick and Deering companies forms International Harvester Co.

PATENTS for rayon to Arthur D. Little, William H. Walker, and Harry S. York; to David D. Kenney for a vacuum cleaner.

Newt Graham founds National Farmers Union.

DuPont Co. establishes explosives laboratory at Gibbstown, N.J.

Chemist Herman Frasch begins American sulphur industry when he develops method for extracting sulphur from deep deposits in Louisiana.

DEATHS Levi Strauss, developer of pants ("levis") made of canvas; Potter Palmer, founder of store that became Marshall Field's.

TRANSPORTATION

American Automobile Assn. is founded (March 4).

Glenn H. Curtiss, motorcycle racer, develops an engine and establishes motorcycle plant.

Packard Motor Co. is founded.

Vermont passes ordinance that requires that a mature individual carrying a red flag precede every moving automobile.

SCIENCE/MEDICINE

New York City is first in U.S. to appoint a school nurse.

An early movie theater. ARCHIVE PHOTOS

Dr. Charles W. Stiles discovers the hookworm, a widespread Southern parasite.

DEATH Walter Reed, military surgeon who headed study of yellow fever.

EDUCATION

John D. Rockefeller endows General Education Board.

Simmons College in Boston opens.

University of Michigan Department of Forestry is established.

Nicholas Murray Butler becomes president of Columbia University; Woodrow Wilson, president of Princeton University.

DEATH Francis W. Parker, a founder of progressive elementary education.

RELIGION

Catholic Bishop John M. Farley becomes archbishop of New York City.

William James completes book *The Varieties of Religious Experience.*

DEATH Patrick A. Feehan, first Catholic archbishop of Chicago (1880–1902).

1903

ART/MUSIC

Alfred Stieglitz founds Photo-Secession, an organization to promote photography as an art form.

Edward A. MacDowell composes his *New England Idylls*.

Robert Henri completes the painting *Young Woman in Black*; Arthur B. Davies, *Dancing Children*; Everett Shinn, *The Hippodrome*.

SONGS (popular): "In the Good Old Summertime," "Bill Bailey, Won't You Please Come Home?" "In the Sweet Bye and Bye," "On a Sunday Afternoon," "Under the Bamboo Tree," "Because."

DEATH Albert Bierstadt, painter of Western scenes.

LITERATURE/JOURNALISM

Edward W. Scripps founds Newspaper Enterprise Assn. (NEA), a feature syndicate.

Richard Outcault draws "Buster Brown" comic strip in *New York Herald*.

BOOKS *The Virginian* by Owen Wister, *Ranson's Folly* by Richard Harding Davis, *Captain Craig* (poetry) by Edwin Arlington Robinson; *The Valley of Decision* by Edith Wharton, *The Wings of the Dove* by Henry James.

ENTERTAINMENT

Thomas L. Tally establishes first movie theater in U.S., Electric Theater, in Los Angeles.

PLAYS May Robson stars in *The Billionaire*, Marie Dressler in *The Hall of Fame*, Lillian Russell in *Twirly Whirly*; other plays are *The Sultan of Sulu* by George Ade, *The Girl with the Green Eyes* by Clyde Fitch, *The Darling of the Gods* by David Belasco.

SPORTS

John J. McGraw, manager of the Baltimore baseball club, becomes manager of New York Giants.

WINNERS *Boxing* — Jim Jeffries, heavyweight; *Football* — Michigan in first Rose Bowl 49–0 over Stanford; *Horse racing* — Alan-a-Dale, Kentucky Derby; Old England, Preakness Stakes; Masterman, Belmont Stakes; *Tennis* — U.S., Davis Cup.

MISCELLANEOUS

Fire in a Birmingham church causes 115 deaths.

Two mine disasters occur: Coal Creek, Tenn., 184 die, and Johnstown, Pa., 112 die.

INTERNATIONAL

Hay-Herran Treaty with Colombia provides for 100-year lease of 10-mile-wide strip across Isthmus of Panama for $10 million and annual payments of $250,000 (January 22); Hay-Buneau-Varilla Treaty (November 18) with Panama reaffirms earlier treaty.

U.S. and Great Britain agree to arbitrate Alaska–Canada boundary; final line excludes Canada from ocean inlets of southern Alaska.

Marine Corps formally occupies Guantanamo Bay, Cuba.

NATIONAL

Department of Commerce and Labor is established (February 14) with George B. Cortelyou secretary.

Supreme Court in *Champion v. Ames* upholds federal law that prohibits sending lottery tickets through the mails, establishes federal-law police power; Congress passes law giving antitrust suits precedence on court dockets.

Wisconsin adopts direct primary elections.

Elkins Act strengthens Interstate Commerce Commission, eliminates rebates, defines unfair discrimination.

Army General Staff Corps is established.

First national bird reservation is established on Pelican Island near Sebastian, Fla.

BUSINESS/INDUSTRY/INVENTIONS

Cable across Pacific Ocean (San Francisco to Honolulu) available for public use (January 1); cable from Honolulu to Manila is completed (July 3).

Miners strike Colorado Fuel & Iron Co.; some return in few weeks, rest come back six months later; coal mine mediation commission awards miners who struck in 1902 a 10% increase.

Oregon passes 10-hour workday for women in industry.

DEATHS Frederick Law Olmsted, pioneer landscape architect; Gordon McKay, inventor of shoemaking machinery; Ebenezer Butterick, inventor of paper patterns for shirts, suits, dresses; Luther C. Crowell, inventor of square-bottom paper bag; Gustavus F. Swift, founder of meatpacking firm.

TRANSPORTATION

Wilbur and Orville Wright demonstrate first motor-driven airplane at Kitty Hawk, N.C. (December 17); Wilbur flies 120 feet in 12 seconds, then Orville flies 852 feet in 59 seconds; nine days earlier, the *New York Times* criticizes Samuel P. Langley for "wasting" money trying to build a plane, states man would not fly for a thousand years.

First cross-country auto trip begins in San Francisco (May 23), ends in New York City (August 31); Boston YMCA opens an automobile school; New York Police Department issues "Rules for Driving" to help regulate traffic; Barney Oldfield becomes first to drive a car at a mile a minute (June 15).

Henry Ford founds Ford Motor Co.; Firestone Tire & Rubber Co. produces tires.

Clyde J. Coleman patents automobile electric self-starter.

Williamsburg Bridge over East River, New York City, is completed.

SCIENCE/MEDICINE

Vermont passes law that requires annual eye examinations of schoolchildren.

DEATH Josiah Willard Gibbs, considered U.S.'s greatest theoretical scientist.

EDUCATION

General Education Board incorporates to promote education.

Andrew Carnegie gives Cleveland $250,000 to build branch libraries.

DEATH Charles A. Cutter, father of library dictionary catalog.

RELIGION

Catholic Bishop John J. Glennon becomes archbishop of St. Louis, Mo.

Bishop Daniel S. Tuttle becomes presiding Episcopal bishop.

ART/MUSIC

Victor Herbert produces his operetta, *Babes in Toyland.*

Dallas (Tex.) Museum of Fine Arts and Berkshire Museum, Pittsfield, Mass., are founded.

SONGS (popular): "Toyland," "Sweet Adeline," "Kashmiri Love Song," "Ida, Sweet as Apple Cider," "Good-bye, Eliza Jane," "Bedelia," "The Eyes of Texas."

LITERATURE/JOURNALISM

Joseph Pulitzer gives $1 million to found Columbia University School of Journalism.

Ida M. Tarbell writes exposé of Standard Oil Co. in *McClure's.*

John T. McCutcheon begins 42 years as cartoonist for *Chicago Tribune.*

BOOKS *The Little Shepherd of Kingdom Come* by John Fox Jr., *Rebecca of Sunnybrook Farm* by Kate Douglas Wiggin, *The Call of the Wild* by Jack London, *The Pit* by Frank Norris, *The Ambassadors* by Henry James, *Children of the Tenements* by Jacob Riis.

DEATH Charles B. Smith, humorist writing as Bill Arp.

ENTERTAINMENT

John Barrymore makes stage debut in *Magda* in Chicago.

New Amsterdam Theater in New York City opens;

1903

Orville Wright in the first motor-propelled flight, December 17, 1903. His brother Wilbur Wright watches from the ground. CORBIS-BETTMANN

Majestic Theater, also in New York, hires women ushers.

Warner Brothers opens first movie theater in U.S. (New Castle, Pa.) that is called a "nickelodeon" because admission is 5 cents.

Edwin S. Porter produces movie, "The Great Train Robbery."

Dreamland amusement park costs $2 million, opens at Coney Island in Brooklyn, N.Y.

Maxine Elliott stars in *Her Own Way*, Bert Williams in *In Dahomey*, Lionel Barrymore in *The Other Girl*, Henrietta Crosman in *Sweet Kitty Bellaire*, Lillian Russell in *Whoop-dee-do*, Eddie Foy in *Mr. Bluebeard*.

SPORTS

National (baseball) League recognizes American League as an equal; Harry C. Pulliam becomes National League president; Frank Ferrell and Bill Devery purchase Baltimore baseball franchise for $18,000, move it to New York.

Jamaica Racetrack on Long Island (N.Y.) opens.

Lou Dillon, driven by Millard Sanders, is first trotter to run mile in less than 2 minutes (1 min, $58\frac{1}{2}$ sec.).

American Power Boat Assn. is formed.

WINNERS *Baseball* — Boston Red Sox beat Pittsburgh Pirates in first World Series; *Bicycling* — Iver Lawson, world professional sprint riding; *Boxing* — Jim Jeffries, heavyweight; Bob Fitzsimmons, light heavyweight; Frankie Neal, bantamweight; *Football* — Dartmouth (opening of Harvard Stadium); *Golf* — Willie Anderson, U.S. Open; *Horse racing* — Judge Himes, Kentucky Derby; Flocarline, Preakness Stakes; Africander, Belmont Stakes; *Motor cycling* — Glenn H. Curtiss, Riverdale hill climb; *Tennis* — Great Britain, Davis Cup; *Wrestling* — Tom Jenkins, heavyweight; *Yachting* — U.S.'s *Reliance* retains America's Cup.

DEATH Ed Delehanty, baseball player, falls through ties of railroad bridge into Niagara River.

MISCELLANEOUS

Fire in Iroquois Theater, Chicago, kills 602 persons; mine disaster at Hanna, Wyo., kills 169.

Martha Washington Hotel, exclusively for women, opens in New York City.

Forerunner of Big Brother movement is established in Cincinnati, Ohio.

Richard Stieff designs "teddy" bear, named for President Theodore Roosevelt.

Flooding Kansas, Missouri, and Des Moines rivers drown 200, leave 8,000 homeless, cause about $4 million in damage.

DEATHS "Judge" Roy Bean, the "law west of the Pecos;" Calamity Jane (Martha Jane Burke), frontierswoman companion of Wild Bill Hickok.

1904

INTERNATIONAL

President Theodore Roosevelt issues a corollary to Monroe Doctrine, defends U.S. intervention in Latin America to stop European aggression (December 2).

U.S. formally acquires Panama Canal Zone (February 26).

NATIONAL

President Theodore Roosevelt, Republican, is elected to full term over Judge Alton B. Parker, Democrat, by popular vote of 7,628,834 and 336 electoral votes to 5,084,401 and 140.

Supreme Court in *Northern Securities v. United States* rules that a holding company created solely to eliminate competition is an illegal combination in restraint of trade, a violation of antitrust laws.

William Howard Taft becomes Secretary of War.

Oregon adopts direct primaries for party nominations.

Louisiana Purchase Exposition is held in St. Louis, Mo., also called the World's Fair.

BUSINESS/INDUSTRY/ INVENTIONS

A. P. Giannini founds Bank of America as the Bank of Italy.

Lane Bryant stores are established.

Oil field is brought in near Bartlesville, Okla.

Roger Babson establishes Babson Business Statistical Organization to provide summaries, analysis of business conditions for investors.

Long, bitter strike of 25,000 textile workers occurs in Fall River, Mass.

The Interior Decorator magazine begins publication.

Thorstein B. Veblen writes *The Theory of Business Enterprise.*

TRANSPORTATION

First section of New York City subway operates from City Hall to 145th Street; first municipally owned transit line opens in Seattle, with a fare of $2\frac{1}{2}$ cents.

East River Tunnel in New York City is built.

New York Travelers Aid Society is organized.

New York State is first in U.S. to adopt automobile speed limits: 10 miles per hour in cities, 15 in small towns, 20 in the country.

Political cartoon from 1904 showing President Theodore Roosevelt wielding the "big stick" of American power in the Caribbean region. THE GRANGER COLLECTION, NEW YORK

1904

Harry D. Weed patents an automobile tire chain.

DEATH William R. Grace, shipping company founder.

SCIENCE/MEDICINE

National Tuberculosis Assn. is organized in Atlantic City, N.J.

EDUCATION

Mary M. Bethune opens Daytona (Fla.) Normal & Industrial Institute for Negro Girls; vocational high school for girls opens as summer experiment in Boston.

Western University of Pennsylvania moves to Pittsburgh, becomes part of University of Pittsburgh.

DEATH Francis Wayland, dean, Yale Law School (1873–1903).

RELIGION

Buddhist Temple is established in Los Angeles.

Catholic Bishop Henry Moeller becomes archbishop of Cincinnati, Ohio.

ART/MUSIC

Chicago's Orchestra Hall opens.

Robert Henri completes the painting *Willie Gee*; William J. Glackens, *Luxembourg Gardens*.

St. Louis City Art Museum and Hispanic Museum in New York City open.

SONGS (popular): "Fascination," "Give My Regards to Broadway," "Goodbye, My Lady Love," "Meet Me in St. Louis, Louis," "Teasing."

LITERATURE/JOURNALISM

Color comic books first appear in New York City, reprinting cartoons from newspapers.

Amerikai Magyar Nepszava, Hungarian daily paper, begins publication in New York City.

Bibliographical Society of America is organized.

BOOKS *The Shame of the Cities* by Lincoln Steffens, *The Sea Wolf* by Jack London, *Freckles* by Gene Stratton Porter, *Cabbages and Kings* by O. Henry (William S. Porter), *The Tar Baby* by Joel Chandler Harris, *The Crossing* by Winston Churchill, *The Golden Bowl* by Henry James.

DEATHS Prentiss Ingraham, author of about 700 "dime" novels; Mary E. M. Dodge, author (*Hans Brinker*) editor (*St. Nicholas Magazine*); Lafcadio Hearn, author.

ENTERTAINMENT

George P. Baker teaches "47 Workshop" class for playwrights at Harvard University.

Emile Berliner develops flat phonograph record.

Mrs. Minnie Maddern Fiske stars in George Ade's *The College Widow*, George M. Cohan in *Little Johnny Jones*, David Warfield in *The Music Master*, Dustin Farnum in *The Virginian*.

SPORTS

Baseball leagues cannot agree on arrangements for World Series, which is not held.

First Olympic Games in U.S. are held in St. Louis, Mo.; U.S. wins 21 track and field events, 10 in gymnastics.

Norman Dole first to surpass 12 feet (12 ft. $1\frac{1}{4}$ in.) in pole vault.

Coach Amos Alonzo Stagg of University of Chicago organizes first lettermen's club.

First Vanderbilt Cup auto race is run on 10-lap course at Hicksville, N.Y.

National Ski Assn. is organized.

Tennis & Racquet Club is built in Boston.

WINNERS *Bicycling*—Robert Waltheur, world professional motor-paced riding; *Boxing*—Jim Jeffries, heavyweight; Tommy Sullivan, featherweight; Joe Bowker, bantamweight; *Golf*—Willie Anderson, U.S. Open; *Horse racing*—Elwood, Kentucky Derby; Bryn Mawr, Preakness Stakes; Delhi, Belmont Stakes; *Motorboating*—Standard, piloted by C. C. Riotte, first race under organized rules; *Wrestling*—Frank Gotch, heavyweight.

MISCELLANEOUS

Fire destroys most of Baltimore's business district.

Steamer *General Slocum* burns in New York City's East River, 1,021 die; train wreck at Eden, Colo., kills 96.

American Academy of Arts & Letters is founded.

Carnegie Hero Fund Commission is established.

St. Louis Police Department fingerprints persons arrested on serious charges.

Evangeline Booth, daughter of founder, heads Salvation Army in U.S.; serves to 1934 when she becomes world leader.

INTERNATIONAL

President Theodore Roosevelt invites warring Japan and Russia to a peace conference in U.S. (June 8); representatives meet in Portsmouth (N.H.) Navy Yard (August 9); sign peace treaty a month later (September 5).

Panama Canal Engineering Commission recommends construction of a $250 million sea-level canal.

U.S. signs extradition treaty with Norway and Sweden.

NATIONAL

Forest Service is established.

Annual immigration to U.S. reaches 1,026,499.

Paul P. Harris founds Rotary International in Chicago.

Oris P. and Mantis Van Sweringen develop Shaker Heights, a Cleveland suburb; build streetcar line connecting it to Cleveland.

Lewis & Clark Exposition is held in Portland, Ore.

BUSINESS/INDUSTRY/INVENTIONS

Burroughs Adding Machine Co. is established; Statler Hotels chain is founded.

First air-conditioned factory is built, for Gray Manufacturing Co. in Gastonia, N.C.

Pyrene Manufacturing Co. introduces fire extinguisher with vaporized chemical; Portland (Ore.) Manufacturing Co. produces Douglas-fir plywood.

Supreme Court orders meat packers to stop making agreements on bidding, price fixing, black-lists; upholds lower court order to break up "beef trust."

Merger of Western Federation of Miners and American Labor Union forms Industrial Workers of the World.

National Boot & Shoe Manufacturers Assn. is founded.

U.S. sues Standard Oil (N.J.) under antitrust law.

DEATHS Meyer Guggenheim, founder of worldwide copper company; Charles T. Yerkes, Chicago street railway owner; Jay Cooke, financier.

TRANSPORTATION

Ferryboat service between Staten Island and Manhattan (N.Y.) begins.

William C. Durant founds Buick Motor Co.

Chicago & Northwestern Railroad are first to install electric lamps in trains.

Aerial ferry operates between Duluth and Minnesota Point.

Number of registered automobiles rises to 77,988.

SCIENCE/MEDICINE

Yellow fever epidemic begins in New Orleans, La. (July 23); ends in October with about 3,000 cases, 400 deaths.

Supreme Court rules that states have power to enact compulsory vaccination laws.

Samuel Hopkins Adams writes *The Great American Fraud*, an exposé of patent medicines that leads to passage of Pure Food & Drug Act.

Dr. Albert Einhorn produces "procaine" (Novocain).

1905

Sarah Breedlove Walker, who calls herself "Madame C. J. Walker," at the wheel of her car in the 1910s. Her business takes off in 1905 and will soon make her one of the first U.S. women millionaires. SCHOMBURG CENTER FOR RESEARCH IN BLACK CULTURE

EDUCATION

Carnegie Foundation for the Advancement of Teaching is established.

RELIGION

Russian Orthodox church moves episcopal see (area headquarters) from San Francisco to New York City.

DEATH Placide L. Chappelle, Catholic archbishop (1894–1905), Santa Fe, N.Mex., New Orleans.

ART/MUSIC

Edward J. Steichen and other photographers open famed 291 Gallery in New York City to win recognition of photography as art form.

Juilliard School of Music in New York City is founded.

Houston's Museum of Fine Arts opens.

Childe Hassam completes the painting *Southwest Wind*; William J. Glackens, *Chez Mouquin*; Jerome Myers, *The Tambourine*; Paul W. Bartlett completes the frieze figures in New York Public Library.

Henry F. B. Gilbert composes *Comedy Overture on Negro Themes*.

Victor Herbert's operetta, *The Red Mill*, opens; featured song is "Kiss Me Again."

SONGS (popular): "In My Merry Oldsmobile," "In the Shade of the Old Apple Tree," "My Gal Sal," "Wait Till the Sun Shines, Nellie," "I Don't Care," "Mary's a Grand Old Name."

LITERATURE/ JOURNALISM

Chicago Defender, African American newspaper, begins publication.

BOOKS *The House of Mirth* by Edith Wharton, *The Clansman* by Thomas Dixon, *Isidro* by Mary Austin, *The Life of Reason* by George Santayana.

DEATHS Union Gen. Lew Wallace, author (*Ben-Hur*); John Bartlett, compiler of *Familiar Quotations*.

ENTERTAINMENT

Sime Silverman founds *Variety*, entertainment journal.

Hippodrome Theater in New York City opens.

Mrs. Leslie Carter stars in *Adrea*, Blanche Bates in David Belasco's *The Girl of the Golden West*, George M. Cohan in *Forty-Five Minutes from Broadway*, Maude Adams in *Peter Pan*, William Faversham in *The Squaw Man*, Margaret Anglin in *Zira*, Julia Sanderson and Douglas Fairbanks in *Fantana*.

Harry Davis opens a nickelodeon theater in Pittsburgh, Pa.

DEATHS Two noted actors, Joseph Jefferson and Maurice Barrymore.

SPORTS

Intercollegiate Athletic Association of U.S. is founded by 62 institutions; later becomes National Collegiate Athletic Assn. (NCAA); five colleges form Intercollegiate Association Football League.

J. Scott Leary becomes first American to swim 100 yards in 60 seconds.

Touring English team introduces soccer to American public.

WINNERS *Baseball* — New York Giants, World Series; *Boxing* — Marvin Hart, heavyweight; Jack O'Brien, light heavyweight; *Golf* — Willie Anderson, U.S. Open; *Horse racing* — Agile, Kentucky Derby (in which only three horses run); Cairngorm, Preakness Stakes; Tanya, Belmont Stakes; *Tennis* — Great Britain, Davis Cup; *Wrestling* — Tom Jenkins, heavyweight; Yale, first intercollegiate title.

MISCELLANEOUS

Sarah B. Walker devises treatment to straighten tightly curled hair; becomes one of first U.S. women millionaires.

Mine disaster at Virginia City, Ala., kills 112.

American Sociological Society is organized.

1906

NATIONAL

President Theodore Roosevelt wins Nobel Peace Prize for leadership in settling Russian–Japanese war; leaves for Panama inspection trip, first president to leave country while in office.

Alice Lee Roosevelt, president's daughter, and Rep. Nicholas Longworth (later Speaker) marry in the White House.

Alaska is authorized to have delegate in Congress; Wisconsin holds first statewide primary election.

Mesa Verde (Colo.) National Park is established; President Roosevelt dedicates first national monument, Devils Tower, Wyo.

National Recreation Assn. is founded as Playground Association of America.

Congress authorizes plans for a lock canal in Panama.

DEATH Susan B. Anthony, women's rights leader.

BUSINESS/INDUSTRY/INVENTIONS

Pure Food and Drug, and Meat Inspection acts pass (June 30), the latter due in part to Upton Sinclair's book on meatpacking (*The Jungle*).

Lee De Forest invents triode electron tube, which leads to rapid growth in communications, electronics; Ernst F. W. Alexanderson develops alternator that is able to produce continuous radio waves.

President Roosevelt extends eight-hour day to all government workers; California enacts first law in U.S. to set minimum wage, $2 per day for almost all public employees.

W. K. Kellogg Co. (Battle Creek, Mich.), cereal maker, is established; Commonwealth Edison Co. in Chicago is organized; Alfred C. Fuller founds Capitol (later Fuller) Brush Co.

Hart-Parr Co. introduces first commercially successful machine, the "tractor."

Oil fields are discovered in Kansas and Oklahoma.

DEATH Joseph F. Glidden, barbed-wire inventor.

TRANSPORTATION

First double-decker bus, imported from France, is put into service on Fifth Avenue, New York City.

Hepburn Act strengthens Interstate Commerce Commission, gives it authority to fix maximum railroad rates, to prescribe uniform accounting methods; jurisdiction extends to express and sleeping car companies, oil pipelines, terminals, and ferries.

SCIENCE/MEDICINE

Mt. Wilson (Calif.) Observatory opens.

Dr. Howard T. Ricketts determines that Rocky Mountain spotted fever is spread by cattle ticks.

DEATH Samuel P. Langley, astronomer and aeronautical pioneer.

1906

EDUCATION

Rand School of Social Science in New York City is founded.

Phillips University in Enid, Okla., is chartered as Oklahoma Christian University.

DEATH Christopher C. Langdell, Harvard Law School dean (1870–1895), introduced case method of teaching.

RELIGION

Christian Science Cathedral in Boston is dedicated.

ART/MUSIC

Louis M. Eilshemius completes the painting *Figures in Landscape*; Childe Hassam, *Church at Old Lyme*.

John Herron Art Institute in Indianapolis, Ind., is founded.

Soprano Geraldine Farrar begins 16 years with Metropolitan Opera.

SONGS (popular): "At Dawning," "I Love You Truly," "You're a Grand Old Flag," "Because You're You," "Anchors Aweigh," " I Love a Lassie," "Love Me and the World Is Mine," "Waltz Me Around Again, Willie."

DEATH Eastman Johnson, painter.

LITERATURE/JOURNALISM

Fontaine Fox draws "Toonerville Trolley" cartoon.

BOOKS *The Spirit of the Border* by Zane Grey; *The Devil's Dictionary* by Ambrose Bierce, *The Four Million* by O. Henry; *Uncle Remus and Br'er Rabbit* by Joel Chandler Harris, *The Spoilers* by Rex Beach.

ENTERTAINMENT

Reginald Fessenden makes first radio broadcast of voice and music from Brant Rock, Mass. (December 24).

Bill (Bojangles) Robinson, dancer, and Sophie Tucker, singer, begin careers.

A family made homeless by the 1906 San Francisco earthquake eats dinner outdoors. CORBIS-BETTMANN

Vitagraph Studios releases the first animated movie cartoon, James S. Blackton's "Humorous Phases of Funny Faces."

Belasco Theater in New York City is built.

Margaret Anglin stars in *The Great Divide*, Minnie Maddern Fiske in *The New York Idea*, William Collier in *Caught in the Rain*, Grace George in *Clothes*, Anna Held in *A Parisian Model*.

SPORTS

Charles M. Daniels sets swimming record of 56 seconds for 100 yards.

Willie Hoppe, 18, wins his first (of many) billiards championship.

Consecutive game pitching streak of Jack Taylor, Chicago Cubs, St. Louis Cardinals, ends at 188; pitches 1,727 innings without relief.

National Coursing Assn. (now National Greyhound Assn.) is formed to govern greyhound racing.

Football forward pass is legalized; flying wedge is outlawed.

National Association of Scientific Angling Clubs is organized.

WINNERS *Baseball*—Chicago White Sox, World Series; *Boxing*—Tommy Burns, heavyweight; *Golf*—Alex Smith, U.S. Open; *Horse racing*—Sir Huon, Kentucky Derby; Whimsical, Preakness Stakes; Burgomaster, Belmont Stakes; *Tennis*—Great Britain, Davis Cup; *Wrestling*—Frank Gotch, heavyweight; *Yachting*—*Tamerlane*, first Bermuda race; *Lurline*, first transpacific race.

MISCELLANEOUS

Stanford White, prominent architect, is shot to death by Harry K. Thaw, jealous of White's earlier friendship with Mrs. Thaw.

Young Women's Christian Assn. (YWCA) is organized.

1907

INTERNATIONAL

Fleet of U.S. warships leaves Hampton Roads, Va. (December 16), on a round-the-world goodwill trip; return in 1909.

American representatives attend second Hague Conference, which again fails to agree on disarmament.

First elections are held in Philippine Islands; first legislature convenes.

U.S. Marines land in Honduras to protect U.S. lives and property.

NATIONAL

Gen. George W. Goethals is named chief engineer for construction of Panama Canal.

Corrupt Election Practices Law is enacted, prohibits corporations from contributing funds in national elections.

Oklahoma's constitution is adopted, ratified; Oklahoma is admitted as 46th state (November 16).

Army War College in Washington opens; Army organizes aeronautical unit in Signal Corps.

New York City holds first U.S. night court.

Food and Drug Administration begins operation.

Effort to unseat Senator Reed Smoot of Utah because of his Mormon church membership fails; his election is confirmed (42–28).

Tercentenary Exposition is held in Jamestown, Va.

More than a million immigrants arrive at Ellis Island, N.Y., in year.

DEATH Former First Lady Ida S. McKinley (1897–1901).

1907

The dining hall at Ellis Island in the early 1900s. THE GRANGER COLLECTION, NEW YORK

BUSINESS/INDUSTRY/INVENTIONS

Drop in stock market, followed by business failures, touches off Panic of 1907 (March 13); Knickerbocker Trust Co., New York City, fails (October 22).

Federal government files antitrust suit against American Tobacco Co.

U.S. Steel Co. acquires Tennessee Coal & Iron Co.; Bell & Howell Co. and United Parcel Service (UPS) are founded.

George F. Baker founds First Security Corp. in New York City.

Hurley Machine Co. markets a complete self-contained electric washing machine (the Thor); Maytag Co. produces its first washing machines; Hoover Co. introduces rolling vacuum cleaner with handle and dust bag.

J. C. Penney buys store in Kemperer, Wyo., starts his chain of stores.

DEATH William L. Jenney, pioneer architect.

TRANSPORTATION

First Hudson River tunnel connects New York and New Jersey (February 25).

Bendix Co., pioneer auto parts company, is formed; John N. Willys, bicycle maker, buys Overland Automobile Co., renames it Willys-Overland.

First taxicabs in U.S. appear in New York City when a fleet of "taximeter cabs" arrives from Paris.

Philadelphia's first subway operates.

SCIENCE/MEDICINE

Albert A. Michelson becomes first American to win a Nobel Prize in physics; award is given for optical measuring instruments and work in meteorology and spectroscopy.

Columbia University names Mary A. Nutting first full-time U.S. professor of nursing.

American Telephone & Telegraph Co. opens research laboratory in New York City (later moves to Murray Hill, N.J.).

William H. Taggart develops casting process that makes gold inlay fillings possible in dentistry.

DEATH Wilbur O. Atwater, founder of agricultural extension stations.

EDUCATION

Alain L. Locke, a Harvard graduate, is first black awarded a Rhodes scholarship.

RELIGION

Cornerstone is laid for St. Paul (Minn.) Cathedral (Catholic).

William H. O'Connell becomes Catholic archbishop of Boston.

Cleland K. Nelson becomes first Episcopal bishop of Atlanta, Ga.

Stephen S. Wise founds Free Synagogue in New York City.

DEATH John A. Dowie, founder of Christian Catholic Apostolic church.

ART/MUSIC

Mary Garden makes Metropolitan Opera debut in Massenet's *Thaïs*.

Irving Berlin's first song, "Marie of Sunny Italy," is published.

George W. Bellows completes the painting *Stag at Sharkey's*; John F. Sloan, *Wake of Ferry*; George B. Luks, *The Little Madonna*.

SONGS (popular): "Glow-Worm," "Merry Widow Waltz," "On the Road to Mandalay," "Harrigan," "School Days," "I Wish I Had a Girl."

LITERATURE/JOURNALISM

United Press, a wire service, begins.

H. C. (Bud) Fisher draws first daily comic strip, "Mutt and Jeff," in *San Francisco Chronicle*.

BOOKS *Sister Carrie* by Theodore Dreiser, *The Shepherd of the Hills* by Harold Bell Wright, *Sonnets to Duse* (poetry) by Sara Teasdale, *The Education of Henry Adams* by Henry Adams (privately printed).

DEATH William T. Adams, who wrote more than 125 books, 1,000 stories under name of Oliver Optic among others.

ENTERTAINMENT

Lee De Forest transmits Rossini's *William Tell Overture* from Telharmonic Hall in New York City to Brooklyn in first musical program radio broadcast (March 5).

Ringling Bros. buy Barnum & Bailey's to become nation's leading circus.

Florenz Ziegfeld stages *Follies of 1907*, the first American "revue."

George M. Cohan writes and produces *The Talk of New York*, David Warfield stars in *Grand Army Man*, Augustus Thomas writes *The Witching Hour*.

The two-step becomes a popular dance.

DEATH Richard Mansfield, actor.

SPORTS

Committee is named to study origin of baseball; Chairman A. G. Mills, former National League president, reports (personally) (December 30) that game began with New York Knickerbocker Base Ball Club (1845).

WINNERS *Baseball*—Chicago Cubs, World Series; *Boxing*—Tommy Burns, heavyweight; *Cross-country*—Asario Autio, first national race; *Golf*—Alex Ross, U.S. Open; *Horse racing*—Pink Star, Kentucky Derby; Don Enrique, Preakness Stakes; Peter Pan, Belmont Stakes.

MISCELLANEOUS

Emily P. Bissell designs first Christmas seals; initial drive to aid tubercular children is held.

Russell Sage Foundation to improve social and living conditions is created with $10 million endowment.

Frank Lloyd Wright completes Robie House in Chicago.

Coal-mine explosion in Monongah, W. Va., results in 361 deaths; another at Jacob's Creek, Pa., kills 239.

1908

INTERNATIONAL

Root–Takahira agreement provides for Japanese confirmation of the Open Door policy in China (November 30).

NATIONAL

William Howard Taft, Republican, is elected president over William Jennings Bryan, Democrat; Taft receives 7,679,006 popular and 321 electoral votes to Bryan's 6,409,106 and 162.

Supreme Court in *Adair v. United States* strikes down a provision of the 1898 Erdman Act that requires railroad workers to sign promise not to join the union, terming it an unreasonable violation of freedom of contract and property rights; in *Loew v. Lawler* (the Danbury [Conn.] hatters' case), the Court rules that a secondary boycott is a violation of the antitrust act; *Muller v. Oregon* upholds the state law that sets maximum working hours for women.

Federal Bureau of Investigation (FBI) begins as Bureau of Investigation (July 26).

President Theodore Roosevelt calls a meeting on conservation, results in creation of National Conservation Commission with Gifford Pinchot chairman (June 8).

The motto "In God We Trust," first used briefly in 1860s, is restored on U.S. coins.

Aldrich–Vreeland Act establishes National Monetary Commission to study existing monetary and banking systems, eventually leads to creation of Federal Reserve System.

Charles E. Ashburner becomes first-named city manager; post is in Staunton, Va.

An American family proudly poses in their new Model T, introduced by Henry Ford in 1908.
CORBIS-BETTMANN

North Carolina and Mississippi establish statewide prohibition.

The 47-story Singer Building in New York City is completed.

U.S. Army buys first aircraft, a dirigible; only its inventor, T. S. Baldwin, can fly the craft.

DEATHS Former President Grover Cleveland (1885–1889, 1893–1897); Ainsworth R. Spofford, Librarian of Congress (1864–1897).

BUSINESS/INDUSTRY/INVENTIONS

U.S. Circuit Court of Appeals finds American Tobacco Co. guilty of restraining trade and violating antitrust law.

Federal workmen's compensation law goes into effect (August 1).

Racine (Wis.) Confectioner's Machinery Corp. develops machine to make lollipops; John H. Breck Co., maker of hair-care products, is founded.

General Electric patents electric iron and electric toaster.

William D. Coolidge develops method of making fine tungsten wire for light bulbs, radio tubes.

TRANSPORTATION

East River Tunnel from Battery to Brooklyn (N.Y.) and the first railroad tunnel under the Hudson River are completed.

Henry Ford introduces the Model T, price $850; with higher production, price continuously drops ($310 by 1926).

Fisher Body Co. is founded; General Motors incorporates.

SCIENCE/MEDICINE

First child-hygiene bureau is established in New York City; International Children's Welfare Congress meets in Washington.

Louisville (Ky.) extends its health services into surrounding Jefferson County.

University of Minnesota establishes School of Nursing.

A 60-inch reflecting telescope goes into service at Mt. Wilson (Calif.) Observatory.

Richard Tolman and Gilbert N. Lewis deliver first U.S. paper on theory of relativity.

Henry Fairfield Osborn, vertebrate paleontology curator, becomes president of American Museum of Natural History.

Clifford W. Beers launches Connecticut Society for Mental Hygiene, first such organization in world.

EDUCATION

New York City provides school lunches, establishes first Division of School Hygiene.

DEATH Daniel C. Gilman, first president, Johns Hopkins University (1875–1901).

RELIGION

Federal Council of Churches of Christ is organized.

Andover Theological Seminary moves to Cambridge, Mass., affiliates with Harvard University.

Merger of several small religious groups forms Church of the Nazarene.

Methodist Conference of New England lifts ban on dancing, card playing, theatergoing.

Gideons place their first Bible in a hotel room (Superior, Mont.).

ART/MUSIC

Young American artists who revolted against conservatism of National Academy hold first "Ashcan School" art exhibit.

Arturo Toscanini arrives from Milan to conduct Metropolitan Opera orchestra.

PAINTINGS George W. Bellows, *Up the Hudson*; Frederic Remington, *The Scout, Friends or Enemies*; Joseph Stella, *Pittsburgh Winter*.

SONGS (popular): "Cuddle Up a Little Closer," "Take Me Out to the Ball Game," "Smarty," "Sweet Violets," "Shine On, Harvest Moon."

DEATH Edward A. MacDowell, composer (*Indian Suite, Woodland Sketches*).

LITERATURE/JOURNALISM

First issue of *Christian Science Monitor* is published; replaces *Christian Science Sentinel*.

1908

School of Journalism is created at University of Missouri.

Julia Ward Howe, author of "Battle Hymn of the Republic," is first woman elected to American Academy of Arts & Letters.

BOOKS *The Trail of the Lonesome Pine* by John Fox Jr., *The Circular Staircase* by Mary Roberts Rinehart, *The Vermilion Pencil* by Homer Lea, *The Last of the Plainsmen* by Zane Grey, *Get-Rich-Quick Wallingford* by George R. Chester.

ENTERTAINMENT

Henry J. Miller stars in *The Servant in the House*, Mrs. Minnie Maddern Fiske in *Salvation Nell*, Douglas Fairbanks in *The Gentleman from Mississippi*, Anna Held in *Miss Innocence*.

Modern Electrics, first radio magazine, begins publication.

DEATH Tony Pastor, theater operator.

SPORTS

Automobile race from New York to Paris by way of Seattle and Yokohama begins in New York City (February 12); race takes 170 days; car built by Thomas Motor Co., Buffalo, N.Y., wins.

Olympic Games are held in London; U.S. wins 15 of 28 events; Ray Ewry wins standing high jump for fourth time; John J. Hayes, the marathon.

Football game between University of Pittsburgh and Washington & Jefferson College is first where numbers are sewn on the back of jerseys.

Forbes Field baseball stadium in Pittsburgh opens (June 30).

First steel ski jump in U.S. is built at Chippewa Falls, Wis.

WINNERS *Archery* — Will H. Thompson, national title; *Baseball* — Chicago White Sox, World Series; *Boxing* — Tommy Burns (until December 26), then Jack Johnson, heavyweight; Stanley Ketchel, middleweight; Abe Attell, featherweight; *Cross country* — Cornell, first intercollegiate race; *Golf* — Fred McLeod, U.S. Open; *Harness racing* — Allen Winter, first U.S. Trotting Derby; *Horse racing* — Stone Street, Kentucky Derby; Royal Tourist, Preakness Stakes; Colin, Belmont Stakes; *Tennis* — Australia, Davis Cup; *Wrestling* — Frank Gotch, heavyweight.

MISCELLANEOUS

Glenn H. Curtiss wins his first aeronautical trophy flying his "June Bug" at 40 miles per hour at Hammondsport, N.Y.; first aviation casualty in world occurs at Ft. Myer, Va., when plane goes out of control, killing the pilot, Lt. Thomas Selfridge; Orville Wright is seriously injured.

Four disasters occur: fire in Rhoads Theater, Boyertown, Pa., kills 170; fire in Collinwood, Ohio, school claims 176 lives; mine accident at Marianna, Pa., kills 154; fire destroys Chelsea, Mass., leaves 10,000 homeless.

New York City makes smoking in public by women illegal.

American Home Economics Assn. is founded.

Alpha Kappa Alpha, first black sorority, is founded at Howard University, Washington, D.C.

Permanent wave for hair is introduced to U.S. from England.

Very narrow skirts without petticoats are in style for women; also huge hats and dotted veils, boned collars and "fishnet" stockings.

1909

INTERNATIONAL

U.S. and Great Britain agree to submit continuing controversy over North Atlantic fisheries to arbitration (January 27).

U.S. and Canada create an international joint commission to settle disputes, set limits on water diversion at Niagara Falls (January 11).

Fleet of 16 U.S. battleships complete 15-month around-the-world cruise.

NATIONAL

Robert E. Peary and his assistant, Matthew Henson, accompanied by four Inuit, reach the North Pole (April 6).

Congress passes the Sixteenth Amendment to permit a federal income tax (June 12); submits to states for ratification.

Payne-Aldrich Tariff reduces duties to about 38%.

Salary of President increases from $50,000 to $75,000, Vice President to $12,000.

Lincoln penny is first issued (August 2).

First White House Conference on Children recommends creation of a federal children's bureau.

National Conference on the Negro is held, leads to creation of National Association for the Advancement of Colored People (NAACP).

Tennessee enacts statewide prohibition.

Robert Edwin Peary, the American Arctic explorer. THE GRANGER COLLECTION, NEW YORK

Matthew Henson, American Arctic explorer and Peary's assistant. The two reach the North Pole on April 6, 1909. THE GRANGER COLLECTION, NEW YORK

1909

First report of National Conservation Commission provides an inventory of U.S. natural resources.

Hudson–Fulton Celebration in New York commemorates 300th anniversary of Henry Hudson's arrival and 100th of Robert Fulton's steamboat.

Alaska–Yukon–Pacific Exposition is held in Seattle.

DEATHS Geronimo, Apache chief; Carroll D. Wright, first labor commissioner (1885–1905); William M. Stewart, Nevada senator, author of Fifteenth Amendment.

BUSINESS/INDUSTRY/INVENTIONS

U.S. Circuit Court holds that Standard Oil Co. is an illegal monopoly, orders its dissolution.

Henry E. Warren invents an electric clock.

Kansas enacts law that gives state insurance commissioner power over rates charged by fire insurance companies.

DeVilbiss Co. produces a paint sprayer; Murphy Door Bed Co. manufactures "in-a-door" beds; Kraft Foods begins as S. L. Kraft Co.

Patents are granted to Leo H. Baekeland for thermosetting plastic (Bakelite) and Adon J. Hoffman for steam-operated pressing machine.

Caddo oil pool in Louisiana is discovered.

DEATHS Edwin Reynolds, developer of Corliss-Reynolds engine; Joseph Wharton, benefactor of Wharton School of Finance.

TRANSPORTATION

Annual production of automobiles reaches 123,900; Roy D. Chapin and Howard E. Coffin found Hudson Motor Car Co.

Queensborough and Manhattan suspension bridges over East River in New York City open.

Chicago, Milwaukee & St. Paul Railroad is completed to Pacific coast.

DEATH Albert A. Pope, founder of U.S. bicycle industry.

SCIENCE/MEDICINE

Walter Reed Hospital in Washington, D.C., opens.

Robert A. Millikan of University of Chicago demonstrates that all electrons are identically charged particles.

Navy Nurses Corps is created.

Clifford W. Beers founds National Commission for Mental Hygiene.

EDUCATION

A. Lawrence Lowell begins 24 years as president of Harvard University; Harvard offers course in city planning.

Berkeley (Calif.) opens first U.S. junior high school.

Arkansas State University founded.

DEATHS Arthur Gilman, developer of Radcliffe College; Sheldon Jackson, supervisor of public instruction in Alaska.

RELIGION

Cyrus I. Scofield publishes Scofield Reference Bible.

ART/MUSIC

Leopold Stokowski becomes principal conductor of Cincinnati Symphony.

Henry K. Hadley composes opera *Safie*.

Rockwell Kent completes the painting *Road Roller*.

SONGS (popular): "By the Light of the Silvery Moon," "From the Land of the Sky Blue Water," "Put On Your Old Grey Bonnet," " I Wonder Who's Kissing Her Now," "I've Got Rings on My Fingers" "My Pony Boy."

DEATH Frederic Remington, painter and sculptor.

LITERATURE/JOURNALISM

Harvard Classics, "five-foot shelf" of books, begin to appear.

BOOKS *A Girl of the Limberlost* by Gene Stratton Porter, *The Calling of Dan Matthews* by Harold Bell Wright, *The Valor of Ignorance* by Homer Lea, *The Man in Lower Ten* by Mary Roberts Rinehart, *Martin Eden* by Jack London.

DEATHS Martha F. Finley, author (Elsie Dinsmore books); Sarah Orne Jewett, author.

ENTERTAINMENT

First color motion pictures are exhibited at Madison Square Garden, New York City.

National Board of Censorship (later Review) of Motion Pictures is established.

John Barrymore stars in *The Fortune Hunter*, Florence Reed in *Seven Days*, Grace George in *A Woman's Way*, Walter Hampden in *The City*.

SPORTS

Benjamn F. Shibe invents cork-center baseball.

Ole Evinrude develops first commercially successful outboard motor.

Eastern Canada Hockey League and Federal League merge to form National Hockey Assn., predecessor of National Hockey League.

Present Indianapolis (Ind.) Speedway opens as dirt track for auto testing.

Shortstop Neal Ball of Cleveland Indians completes baseball's first unassisted triple play.

John A. Heydler is named president of National (baseball) League, serves only five months; is renamed in 1918 for 16 years.

Ralph Rose is first to throw shot more than 50 feet.

WINNERS *Auto racing* — Bert W. Scott and C. James Smith, first transcontinental race; *Baseball* — Pittsburgh Pirates, World Series; *Bicycling* — Georges Parent, world professional motor-paced riding; *Boxing* — Jack Johnson, heavyweight; *Chess* — Frank Marshall, U.S. champion; *Golf* — George Sargent, U.S. Open; *Horse racing* — Wintergreen, Kentucky Derby; Effendi, Preakness Stakes; Joe Madden, Belmont Stakes; *Tennis* — Australia, Davis Cup.

MISCELLANEOUS

Carlisle (Pa.) Trust Co. begins first Christmas Club account.

Mine disaster at Cherry, Ill., kills 259 miners.

1910

INTERNATIONAL

International Court of Arbitration settles long-running dispute between U.S. and Great Britain over Newfoundland fishing rights.

NATIONAL

Postal savings bank system is established (June 25).

Thirteenth census reports population of 92,228,496.

Supreme Court Chief Justice Melville W. Fuller dies; Justice Edward D. White succeeds him.

Washington amends its state constitution to provide women's suffrage; women march down Fifth Avenue, New York City, demanding right to vote; New Mexico holds its constitutional convention.

First domestic relations court is established in Buffalo, N.Y.

Forest Service Chief Gifford Pinchot accuses In-

terior Secretary Richard A. Ballinger of hurting conservation by aiding corporations; President William Howard Taft dismisses Pinchot for making the dispute public.

Speaker Joseph G. Cannon's power to appoint powerful House Rules Committee is taken from him; Committee, in which the Speaker could not serve, is to be named by House vote.

Congress requires statements of financial contributions in House elections.

U.S. Bureau of Mines is established.

Rockefeller Foundation is founded.

Glacier (Mont.) National Park is created.

Benjamin D. Foulois establishes Air Force.

Franklin D. Roosevelt is elected to New York Senate; Woodrow Wilson is elected governor of New Jersey.

State governors hold first national meeting.

Victor L. Berger of Wisconsin is elected to House

Women march in New York City, demanding the right to vote. CORBIS-BETTMANN

of Representatives, first Socialist to serve in Congress.

National debt stands at $1.1 billion; Gross National Product is $30.4 billion.

About 8.7 million immigrants have arrived in U.S. since 1900.

BUSINESS/INDUSTRY/INVENTIONS

Eastman Kodak produces a copying machine (photostat), American Viscose Co. makes rayon; George Hughes builds first electric range.

Charles R. Walgreen founds drug-store chain (Walgreen Co.); Joyce C. Hall establishes forerunner of Hallmark Cards Inc.; Elizabeth Arden begins cosmetics career as partner in a beauty salon.

Mann-Elkins Act gives Interstate Commerce Commission power over telephone, telegraph, cable, and wireless companies; creates Court of Commerce to hear appeals from rate decisions.

Julius Rosenwald begins 15-year career as president of Sears Roebuck; then becomes chairman.

Newly formed Sperry Gyroscope Co. installs first gyrocompass on battleship *Delaware*.

DEATH Octave Chanute, pioneer aviator, designer of biplane glider.

TRANSPORTATION

First auto show is held in Madison Square Garden, New York City, with 31 exhibitors of cars, 20 of accessories; more than 460,000 cars are sold in last decade.

Charles Kettering and Edward A. Deeds found Dayton Engineering Co., which becomes Delco; Henry L. Doherty establishes Cities Service Co.

Installment buying of automobiles begins.

Trackless trolley system is installed between Laurel Canyon and Los Angeles (Calif.).

SCIENCE/MEDICINE

Abraham Flexner does major study that results in modern medical education.

Moses Gomberg discovers trivalent carbon.

Columbia University offers courses in optics and optometry.

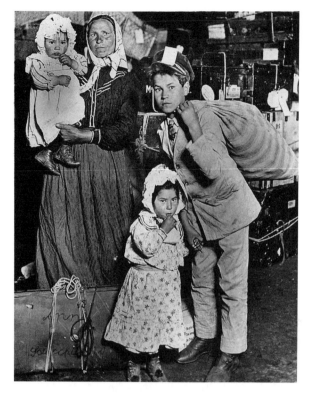

An Italian immigrant family at Ellis Island, photographed by Lewis Hine. CORBIS-BETTMANN

New York School of Chiropody is organized.

Halley's Comet passes the Sun without incident.

Dr. Peyton Rous is first to isolate a cancer-causing virus.

EDUCATION

Women's College of Baltimore becomes Goucher College.

Harvard University names first climatology professor, Robert D. Ward.

RELIGION

St. Patrick's Cathedral in New York City is dedicated.

DEATH Mary Baker Eddy, founder of Christian Science Church.

ART/MUSIC

Metropolitan Opera House presents first Ameri-

1910

can opera, *The Pipe of Desire* by Frederick S. Converse; Giacomo Puccini's *The Girl of the Golden West* premieres there, too, conducted by Toscanini (see 1905) and starring Enrico Caruso.

Victor Herbert presents his operetta *Naughty Marietta*; features song, "Ah, Sweet Mystery of Life."

Ballerina Anna Pavlova makes New York debut.

Arthur B. Davies completes the painting *Crescendo*; Childe Hassam, *Against the Light*; Maurice Prendergast, *Seashore*.

SONGS (popular): "Come, Josephine, in My Flying Machine," "Down by the Old Mill Stream," "Let Me Call You Sweetheart," "Mother Machree," "A Perfect Day," "Some of These Days," "Put Your Arms Around Me, Honey."

DEATHS Winslow Homer, painter of seascapes; John Q. A. Ward, first U.S.-trained sculptor; John La Farge, painter.

LITERATURE/JOURNALISM

Yale University Press is founded.

Loeb Classical Library of Greek and Latin literature is founded.

Pittsburgh Courier begins publication.

"Krazy Kat" cartoon by George Herriman first appears.

Doubleday Co., publishers, is founded.

BOOKS *Twenty Years at Hull House* by Jane Addams; *The Town Down the River* (poetry) by Edwin Arlington Robinson.

ENTERTAINMENT

Fanny Brice debuts on Broadway in Ziegfeld Follies.

George M. Cohan's *Get-Rich-Quick-Wallingford* is produced.

Pathe News shows first screen newsreels in world, and the first animated movie cartoon, "Little Nemo," is shown.

H. B. Warner stars in *Alias Jimmy Valentine*; Lina Abarbanell in *Madame Sherry*, Blanche Bates in *Nobody's Widow*, Julia Sanderson in *The Arcadians*.

SPORTS

First aviation meet is held in Los Angeles; first international air races in U.S. are held at Belmont Park, Calif.

President Taft begins tradition of chief executive throwing out first ball to start the baseball season.

Thomas J. Lynch becomes president of National (baseball) League.

League Park, home of Cleveland Indians, and White Sox (later Comiskey) Park in Chicago open.

Barney Oldfield sets automobile land speed record of 131.7 miles per hour.

Patent is issued to Arthur F. Knight for golf club with steel shaft.

Cy Young of Cleveland Indians pitches 500th victory.

John Flanagan sets hammer-throw record of 184 feet, 4 inches.

First Pendleton (Ore.) Round-Up is held.

Stanley Ketchel, middleweight boxing champion, is shot and killed in Springfield, Ohio.

WINNERS *Baseball*—Philadelphia Athletics, World Series; *Boxing*—Jack Johnson, heavyweight; Ad Wolgast, lightweight; *Golf*—Alex Smith, U.S. Open; *Horse racing*—Donan, Kentucky Derby; Layminster, Preakness Stakes; Sweep, Belmont Stakes; *Tennis*—William Larned, U.S. Open.

MISCELLANEOUS

Boy Scouts of America incorporate; Luther H. and Charlotte V. Gulick found Camp Fire Girls.

Explosion in *Los Angeles Times* building kills 41 persons.

Eugene B. Ely becomes first pilot to land on a ship, the cruiser *Philadelphia* (January 18); is first to take off from a ship (cruiser *Birmingham*, November 10).

Spokane (Wash.) Ministerial Assn. and YMCA launch observance of Father's Day.

Carnegie Endowment for International Peace is founded.

Rose C. O'Neill produces Kewpie dolls.

1911

INTERNATIONAL

U.S. and Canada sign agreement to reduce or eliminate duties on Canadian farm goods and U.S. manufactured products (January 26).

U.S., Great Britain, and Japan sign treaty to abolish seal hunting in North Pacific waters for 15 years.

NATIONAL

California adopts women's suffrage; Illinois passes law that provides assistance to women with dependent children.

Postal savings service begins at 48 second-class post offices (January 3).

Arizona adopts state constitution; President William Howard Taft vetoes joint resolution to admit Arizona to statehood because its constitution permits recall of judges.

National Urban League is founded as National League on Urban Conditions.

Insurgent Republicans, led by Wisconsin Sen. Robert M. La Follette, is organized as National Progressive Republican League.

Roosevelt Dam in Arizona is dedicated.

DEATHS Norman J. Colman, first Agricultural Secretary (1885–1889); Carry A. Nation, axe-wielding temperance crusader.

BUSINESS/INDUSTRY/INVENTIONS

Supreme Court orders dissolution of Standard Oil Co. as a monopoly (May 1); similar order is issued on the "tobacco trust" (American Tobacco Co.) (May 29) and DuPont Co. (June 21); each Standard Oil Co. subsidiary assumes control of its own operations, becomes independent (November 30).

Triangle Shirtwaist Co. factory in New York City burns, killing 146 workers (March 25); leads to stringent building codes, revision of state labor laws.

First workmen's compensation law goes into effect in New Jersey (July 4); 10 other states quickly follow; Equitable Life Insurance Co. issues first group insurance policy for employees of a company.

Merger of three companies forms Computing-Tabulating Recording Co.; Jay R. Monroe founds Monroe Calculating Machine Co.

James McCurdy demonstrates feasibility of two-way radio contact between air and ground.

Broome County (N.Y.) Farm Bureau, first of its kind, is established.

Willis S. Farnsworth patents a coin-operated locker; John M. Browning invents automatic pistol.

Procter & Gamble introduces a shortening, Crisco.

Herman Hollerith and others form the C-T-R Company, later to be known as International Business Machines.

DEATHS Franklin H. King, inventor of cylindrical silo; Tom L. Johnson, inventor of coin farebox; John D. Archbold, Standard Oil executive; Milton Bradley, founder of games company; John M. Carrere, architect; Seaman A. Knapp, developer of Louisiana rice growing.

TRANSPORTATION

Galbraith M. Rogers makes first transcontinental flight, takes 68 hops in 49 days with flying time of 82 hours.

Glenn Curtiss, inventor, flies first successful hydroplane.

Charles F. Kettering perfects automobile electric self-starter.

First Chevrolet motor car is produced.

SCIENCE/MEDICINE

Arnold L. Gesell founds Yale Clinic of Child Development.

1911

The fire in the Triangle Shirtwaist factory in New York, March 25, 1911. Underwood & Underwood/Corbis-Bettmann

Greensboro, N.C., turns its health department into a county unit; typhoid epidemic in Yakima, Wash., leads to appointment of full-time county health worker.

EDUCATION

Philander P. Claxton becomes U.S. Education Commissioner.

Carnegie Corporation of New York is created to support educational projects.

Southern Methodist University, Dallas, is founded.

RELIGION

Completed portion of the Cathedral of St. John the Divine in New York City is dedicated.

Catholic Bishop James J. Keane becomes archbishop of Dubuque (Iowa).

Rev John G. Murray is named Episcopal bishop of Maryland; Rev. James DeW. Perry becomes Episcopal bishop of Rhode Island.

ART/MUSIC

Los Angeles County Museum and Isaac Delgado Museum of Art in New Orleans, La., are founded.

Victor Herbert presents his opera *Natoma*, in Philadelphia; Scott Joplin's ragtime opera, *Treemonisha*, is produced.

Leon Kroll completes the painting *The Bridge*.

SONGS (popular): "Goodnight, Ladies," "Oh, You Beautiful Doll," "I Want a Girl Just Like the Girl," "The Whiffenpoof Song," "Alexander's Ragtime Band," "Memphis Blues."

DEATH Thomas Bell, sculptor

(equestrian Washington in Boston Public Gardens); James A. Bland, minstrel musician and composer.

LITERATURE/JOURNALISM

BOOKS *Mother* by Kathleen Norris, *The Harvester* by Gene Stratton Porter, *The Winning of Barbara Worth* by Harold Bell Wright, *Ethan Frome* by Edith Wharton, *Jennie Gerhardt* by Theodore Dreiser, *Mother Carey's Chickens* by Kate Douglas Wiggin.

DEATHS Joseph Pulitzer, publisher (*St. Louis Post-Dispatch, New York World*); Howard Pyle, author and illustrator of children's books.

ENTERTAINMENT

Sophie Tucker first sings "Some of These Days," which becomes her trademark.

Winter Garden Theater in New York City opens.

David Warfield stars in *The Return of Peter Grimm*, Mrs. Minnie Maddern Fiske in *Mrs. Bumpstead-Leigh*, Ina Claire in *The Quaker Girl*, George M. Cohan in *The Little Millionaire*, Otis Skinner in *Kismet*.

SPORTS

WINNERS *Auto racing* — Ray Harroun, first Indianapolis 500 race; *Baseball* — Philadelphia Athletics, World Series; *Golf* — John J. McDermott, first U.S.-born winner of U.S. Open; *Horse racing* — Meridian, Kentucky Derby; Watervale, Preakness Stakes; Belmont Stakes not run; *Squash* — Dr. Alfred Stillman 2d, first national tournament; *Tennis* — Australia, Davis Cup; William Larned, U.S. Open.

MISCELLANEOUS

Harriet Quimby is licensed as first American woman pilot; Earl L. Ovington is sworn in as first airmail pilot.

First uniformed Boy Scout troop is organized in Troy, N.Y.; *Boys' Life* magazine, official Boy Scout magazine, begins publication.

Mine disaster at Littleton, Ala., kills 128.

Dartmouth College stages first collegiate ice festival.

1912

INTERNATIONAL

U.S. Marines land in Nicaragua to protect U.S. interest (August 14); a small contingent remains until 1925.

American Institute of International Law is founded.

NATIONAL

Woodrow Wilson, Democrat, is elected president, defeating former President Theodore Roosevelt, who runs on the Progressive ticket, and Republican President William Howard Taft; Wilson receives 6,286,214 popular and 435 electoral votes to 4,126,020 and 88 for Roosevelt and 3,483,922 and 8 for Taft.

Elihu Root, Secretary of State (1905–1909), is awarded Nobel Peace Prize for work on various treaties.

New Mexico is admitted as 47th state (January 6); Arizona is admitted as 48th state (February 14) after removing a judicial-recall provision in its constitution (see 1911); Territory of Alaska is established (August 24).

Ohio voters ratify new constitution; an amendment to permit women's suffrage is turned down; Arizona, Kansas, and Oregon approve women's suffrage.

Parcel post service is authorized.

United States Chamber of Commerce is founded in Washington, D.C.

National Monetary Commission proposes various legislative steps on banking and financial matters

1912

Boy Scouts raising money to help survivors of the Titanic, which sank in the North Atlantic in the early hours of April 15, 1912. CORBIS-BETTMANN

that lead to creation of Federal Reserve System.

Panama Canal Act exempts U.S. coastwise traffic from tolls; this is rescinded after British protest.

Juliette G. Low establishes Girl Scouts (see 1902).

First Japanese cherry trees are planted at Tidal Basin in Washington, D.C.

Children's Bureau is created in Labor Department.

First National Safety Congress meets in Milwaukee, Wis.

Mt. Katmai in Alaska erupts, forms Valley of the Ten Thousand Smokes.

Former President Theodore Roosevelt, while campaigning for president, is shot and slightly wounded.

Plant quarantine legislation goes into effect.

DEATH Vice President James S. Sherman (1909–1912).

BUSINESS/INDUSTRY/INVENTIONS

Montgomery Ward & Co. signs contract with Equitable Life Insurance Society for health insurance for its 3,000 employees, the first important group policy.

Massachusetts enacts minimum-wage law for women and minors; eight-hour day is authorized for all workers under federal contracts.

Alfred C. Gilbert produces Erector Set, a new type of toy.

Textile workers strike in Lawrence, Mass.

Bradley A. Fiske patents an airplane torpedo.

Fred M. Kirby chain of five-and-ten-cent stores merge with Woolworth chain.

DEATH Daniel H. Burnham, architect, supervised construction of 1893 World's Fair.

TRANSPORTATION

Steamer *Titanic* sinks on maiden voyage in Atlantic Ocean with 1,513 of its 2,340 passengers, including many Americans, lost.

First U.S. dirigible, *Akron*, explodes in midair over Atlantic City, N.J.

Supreme Court dissolves merger of Union Pacific and Southern Pacific railroads, calls it a combination in restraint of trade.

Staten Island to Brooklyn to Manhattan (N.Y.) ferry begins to operate.

Vincent Bendix develops automobile starter drive.

William Burton introduces thermal process for refining petroleum.

SCIENCE/MEDICINE

Navy Dental Corps is authorized.

Dr. Alexis Carrel of Rockefeller Institute is awarded Nobel Prize in physiology/medicine for research on vascular suture, transplants of blood vessels, organs.

Casimir Funk announces isolation of thiamine in brown rice, which is used to cure beriberi.

University of California establishes Scripps Institution for Biological Research.

American College of Surgeons is incorporated.

National Organization for Public Health Nursing is founded.

U.S. Public Health Service is established.

EDUCATION

William M. Rice endows Rice University in Houston; Memphis State University and Loyola University of New Orleans are established.

RELIGION

Richard Wolfe organizes Liberal Church of America, which has no creed, dogma, or theology.

ART/MUSIC

Gaston Lachaise completes massive bronze statue, *Standing Woman*.

PAINTINGS Lyonel Feininger, *Bicycle Riders*; John Sloan, *McSorley's Bar* and *Sunday, Women Drying Their Hair*; Paul Burlin, *Figure of a Woman*.

Leopold Stokowski begins 24 years as conductor of the Philadelphia Orchestra.

Rudolf Friml writes the operetta *The Firefly*.

SONGS (popular): "In the Evening by the Moonlight," "It's a Long Way to Tipperary," "My Melancholy Baby," "Sweetheart of Sigma Chi," "Ragtime Cowboy Joe," "Row, Row, Row Your Boat," "When Irish Eyes Are Smiling," "You Can't Stop Me from Loving You."

LITERATURE/JOURNALISM

Columbia School (now Graduate School) of Journalism opens, is endowed by Joseph Pulitzer.

Harriet Monroe founds *Poetry* magazine.

Authors League of America is created.

BOOKS *Riders of the Purple Sage* by Zane Grey, *The Financier* by Theodore Dreiser, *A Dome of Many-Colored Glass* (poetry) by Amy Lowell, *Lee, the American* by Gamaliel Bradford.

DEATH Whitelaw Reid, editor, *New York Tribune* (1877–1905).

ENTERTAINMENT

Jerome Kern writes the musical *The Red Petticoat*.

Lewis Stone stars in *The Bird of Paradise*, Laurette Taylor in *Peg o' My Heart*, Jane Cowl in *Within the Law*, Elsie Janis in *The Lady of the Slipper*.

Carl Laemmle founds Universal Pictures Corp.; Mack Sennett founds the Keystone Co.; Actors Equity Assn. is founded.

Ragtime music brings out such dances as the fox trot, turkey trot, and bunny hug.

SPORTS

Fenway Park in Boston, Mass., and Tiger Stadium in Detroit, Mich., open.

Olympic Games are held in Stockholm; U.S. wins 23 events, including Jim Thorpe's victories in the decathlon and pentathlon.

George Horine, using the "western roll," high-jumps 6 feet, 7 inches; James Duncan becomes first to surpass 150 feet (156 ft., $1\frac{1}{4}$ in.) in discus throw; Robert Gardner becomes first to pole vault higher than 13 feet (13 ft., $\frac{3}{4}$ in.).

1913

Duke Kahanamoku sets 100-meter freestyle swimming record of 61.6 seconds.

Football double-wing formation is first used in Carlisle Indian School's 27–6 win over Army.

WINNERS *Auto racing* — Joe Dawson, Indianapolis 500; *Baseball* — Boston Red Sox, World Series; *Bicycling* — George Wiley, world motor-paced riding; Frank Kramer, sprint riding; *Boxing* — Willie Ritchie, lightweight; Johnny Kilbane, featherweight; *Golf* — John McDermott, U.S. Open; *Horse racing* — Worth, Kentucky Derby; Colonel Holloway, Preakness Stakes; Belmont Stakes not run; *Tennis* — Maurice McLaughlin, U.S. Open.

MISCELLANEOUS

George E. Haynes becomes first African American to receive Ph.D. degree at Columbia University.

Glenn L. Martin makes first overwater plane flight, flies one of his own planes from Los Angeles to Catalina Island; Capt. Albert Lewis makes first U.S. parachute jump.

1913

INTERNATIONAL

New Chinese Republic is recognized.

U.S. blockades Mexico in support of revolutionaries.

NATIONAL

States ratify Sixteenth Amendment, authorizing a federal income tax (February 25), also ratify Seventeenth Amendment, calling for popular election of senators (May 31).

Department of Commerce and Labor divide into two departments, Commerce headed by William C. Redfield, Labor headed by William B. Wilson (March 4).

President Woodrow Wilson appears before Congress (April 8), first president to do so since John Adams (1800); calls for tariff revision; the Underwood Tariff Act lowers duties to about 30%, with iron, steel, and raw wool on free list (October 3).

Congress, over President William Howard Taft's veto, prohibits shipment of liquor into states that forbid its sale.

Cleveland Municipal Court establishes small claims court, Kansas authorizes small debtor's court; Los Angeles County creates public defender's office.

Newlands Act creates Board of Mediation and Conciliation.

Parcel Post Service begins (January 1).

First regular White House news conference is held.

Alice Paul and others found Congressional Union for Woman Suffrage; Illinois allows women to vote in local elections.

Keokuk Dam across the Mississippi River is completed.

National Safety Council is organized.

Franklin D. Roosevelt is named Assistant Secretary of the Navy.

Growing number of immigrants in U.S. is reflected in fact that there are 538 newspapers printed in 29 foreign languages.

DEATH Harriet Tubman, organizer of Underground Railroad to help fleeing slaves.

BUSINESS/INDUSTRY/INVENTIONS

Armstrong Cork Co. introduces insulating brick; Hood Rubber Co. manufactures synthetic rubber.

Sheaffer Pen Co. is established.

Textile workers in Paterson, N.J., strike; miners strike Colorado Fuel & Iron Co. for second time; 150,000 garment workers win shorter hours, wage increase after short strike.

Mellon Institute of Industrial Research is founded.

Sale of "hump" hairpins, bobbie-pin predecessor, begins.

Gideon Sundback patents zipper.

Federal Reserve System is established with 12 district banks and a Federal Reserve Board to set rediscount rates (December 23).

Sixty-story Woolworth Building and 50-story Metropolitan Tower in New York City are completed.

TRANSPORTATION

Gulf Oil in Pittsburgh, Pa., opens first drive-in gasoline station.

Grand Central Terminal in New York City opens.

Interstate Commerce Commission is empowered to establish railroad costs and physical valuations as basis for rate making.

Ford Motor Co. introduces conveyor-belt assembly-line production of cars.

Stutz Car Co., maker of Stutz Bearcat, is founded; Hudson Motors produces first auto sedan.

Lincoln Highway Assn. forms to promote transcontinental highway; work begins in 1914.

Igor I. Sikorsky flies first multimotor airplane.

Passenger car registrations reach 1,258,062.

SCIENCE/MEDICINE

Dr. Bela Schick devises a skin test for diphtheria.

American Association of Immunologists is organized.

Biochemist Elmer McCollum isolates vitamins A and B.

John B. Watson founds behaviorist school of psychology.

DEATH Daniel D. Palmer, pioneer chiropractor.

EDUCATION

Massachusetts Institute of Tech-

nology offers first aeronautical engineering course.

RELIGION

Solomon Schechter founds United Synagogue of America.

ART/MUSIC

Armory Show in New York City introduces European and new American works.

Metropolitan Opera presents Walter Damrosch's opera *Cyrano de Bergerac*; Victor Herbert's operetta, *Sweethearts*, and Rudolf Friml's *High Jinks* open.

Sculptor Alexander Archipenko completes *Geometric Statue*; Arthur B. Davies completes the painting *Dances*; George W. Bellows, *Cliff Dwellers*; Robert

"STEP UP TO THE CAPTAIN'S OFFICE AND SETTLE!"

UNCLE SAM. — I'm sorry for you, my unfortunate friends; — I know the Income Tax is "inquisitorial and oppressive;" but I've *got* to meet the one hundred and sixty million dollars of pension appropriation, somehow!

Uncle Sam collects income taxes from famous millionaires, who weep bitter tears over having to write checks to the government for the first time. The Sixteenth Amendment is ratified on February 25, 1913. CORBIS-BETTMANN

Henri, *Himself and Herself*; Lyonel Feininger, *Sidewheeler*.

SONGS (popular): "Danny Boy," "Peg o' My Heart," "You Made Me Love You," "Sweethearts," "Brighten the Corner Where You Are," "There's a Long, Long Trail."

LITERATURE/JOURNALISM

Franklin P. Adams (FPA) writes column, "The Conning Tower," and Don(ald) Marquis writes daily humorous column, "The Sun Dial," in which characters Archy and Mehitabel appear.

Vachel Lindsay's poem, "General William Booth Enters Into Heaven," is published in *Poetry*.

New York Times Index begins.

Ogden Mills Reid edits and publishes *New York Tribune* succeeding his father, Whitelaw Reid.

Masses, a magazine of art, literature, and socialism, begins publication.

BOOKS *Pollyanna* by Eleanor H. Porter, *Laddie* by Gene Stratton Porter, *O Pioneers!* by Willa Cather, *A Preface to Politics* by Walter Lippmann, *Seven Keys to Baldpate* by Earl Derr Biggers, *Merchants from Cathay* (poetry) by William Rose Benet.

ENTERTAINMENT

Cecil B. DeMille, Jesse Lasky, and Samuel Goldwyn form movie company; *The Squaw Man* is the first full-length movie; the movie *The Perils of Pauline* is also produced.

Vernon and Irene Castle make their dancing debut in *The Sunshine Girl*, in which Julia Sanderson stars; other plays: Emily Stevens stars in *Today*, Al Jolson in *The Honeymoon Express*, and Montagu Glass writes *Potash and Perlmutter*.

New York's Palace Theater begins 20 years' reign as outstanding U.S. vaudeville house.

The dance, "ballin-the-jack" becomes popular.

SPORTS

John K. Tener is named National (baseball) League president.

International Olympic Committee strips Jim Thorpe of his 1912 victories and medals because he played professional baseball before the Olympics (action reversed in 1982).

New York State Athletic Commission bans fights between black and Caucasian boxers.

Present-day game of shuffleboard begins in Daytona Beach, Fla.

Ebbetts (baseball) Field in Brooklyn, N.Y., opens.

Merger of American Football Assn. and American Amateur Football Assn. forms U.S. Soccer Football Assn.

Patrick Ryan sets hammer-throw record of 189 feet, 6½ inches.

WINNERS *Auto racing* — Jules Goux, Indianapolis 500; *Baseball* — Philadelphia Athletics, World Series; *Golf* — Francis Ouimet, U.S. Open; *Horse racing* — Donerail (91–1 longshot), Kentucky Derby; Buskin, Preakness Stakes; Prince Eugene, Belmont Stakes; *Tennis* — U.S., Davis Cup; Maurice McLaughlin, U.S. Open.

MISCELLANEOUS

Four major disasters occur: a dynamite explosion in Baltimore Harbor kills 55, a mine accident at Finleyville, Pa., kills 96, a similar accident at Dawson, N.Mex., takes 263 lives, and three days of flooding in March in Ohio and Indiana cause 732 deaths.

Veterans of Foreign Wars (VFW) is founded.

Monument by Mahouri Young to honor sea gulls is unveiled in Salt Lake City; gulls had consumed an army of grasshoppers that were destroying the 1848 wheat crop.

Arthur Wynne prepares first crossword puzzle; is published in *New York World*.

1914

INTERNATIONAL

President Woodrow Wilson issues neutrality proclamation when war breaks out in Europe.

U.S. sailors buying supplies in Tampico, Mexico, are arrested, released a short time later (April 9); Congress grants President Wilson right to use force if needed to uphold U.S. rights.

U.S. Marines land in Veracruz, Mexico (April 22), to prevent landing of German munitions; Mexico breaks off relations with U.S.; the ABC powers (Argentina, Brazil, Chile) meet in Niagara Falls, N.Y. (July 2), resolve the U.S.–Mexico dispute.

Convention signed with Panama defines boundaries of the Panama Canal Zone (September 2); George W. Goethals becomes first governor of the zone.

Bryan-Chamorro Treaty gives U.S. exclusive right to build an interoceanic canal across Nicaragua.

NATIONAL

Clayton Anti-Trust Act passes to strengthen Sherman Act; Food and Fuel Control Act passes.

Margaret Sanger founds National Birth Control League, which later becomes Planned Parenthood Foundation.

Dayton, Ohio, becomes first large U.S. city to adopt commission–city manager form of government (January 1).

Air Service of U.S. Army is established in Signal Corps.

Women march on the Capitol, demand the right to vote.

Prohibition goes into effect in Tennessee and West Virginia; Nevada and Montana approve women's suffrage.

Congress establishes second Sunday in May as Mother's Day.

DEATHS First Lady Ellen Wilson; former Vice President Adlai E. Stevenson (1893–1897); Samuel W. Allerton, a builder of modern Chicago.

BUSINESS/INDUSTRY/INVENTIONS

Federal Trade Commission is established (September 26), replaces Bureau of Corporations; is designed to guard against unfair competition in interstate commerce.

Port of Houston is opened to international commerce.

Merrill, Lynch brokerage firm is founded.

Thomas J. Watson becomes president of Computing-Tabulating Recording Co., which becomes IBM in 1924.

Sidney Hillman begins 32 years as first president of Amalgamated Clothing Workers union.

Robert H. Goddard patents a liquid fuel rocket.

Grossinger's resort in the Catskills (N.Y.) opens.

DEATHS John P. Holland, submarine developer; Charles W. Post, cereal maker; Frederick Weyerhaeuser, lumber "king;" Joseph Fels, founder of Fels-Naphtha (soaps); Herman Frasch, developer of smelting process that led to sulphur industry; Richard W. Sears, a founder of Sears Roebuck.

TRANSPORTATION

A self-propelled crane boat makes first passage of Panama Canal (January 7); commercial traffic begins (August 15).

Ford Motor Co. assembly line production cuts time for assembling a car from $12\frac{1}{2}$ hours to 93 minutes; company raises basic wage from $2.40 for nine-hour day to $5 for eight hours.

First electric traffic signals in U.S. are installed (Euclid Avenue and 105th Street, Cleveland, Ohio).

First eight-cylinder automobile motor is developed; Charles Lawrence develops first successful air-cooled airplane engine.

1914

Seasonal commercial air passenger service begins between Tampa and St. Augustine, Fla.

SCIENCE/MEDICINE

Theodore W. Richards is awarded Nobel Prize in chemistry for determination of atomic weight of chemical elements.

Dr. Simon Flexner announces successful isolation of infantile paralysis virus.

Astronomer Seth B. Nicholson discovers ninth moon of Jupiter, discovers three more by 1952; Walter S. Adams develops method of calculating distances of faraway stars.

Museum of Science and Industry in New York City is established as Museum of Peaceful Arts.

RELIGION

Assemblies of God church is organized (April 2).

DEATH Joseph Smith, son of Mormon Church founder and head of Reorganized Latter Day Saints church (1860–1914).

ART/MUSIC

ASCAP (American Society of Composers, Authors, and Publishers) forms in New York City.

Metropolitan Opera presents Victor Herbert's opera, *Madeline*.

John Sloan completes the painting *Backyards, Greenwich Village*; Lyonel Feininger, *Allée*; William J. Glackens, *Washington Square*.

Margaret Anderson founds *Little Review*, a magazine of the arts.

Original Dixieland Jazz Band forms in Chicago.

SONGS (popular): "St. Louis Blues," "That's A-Plenty," "They Didn't Believe Me," "When You Wore a Tulip," "By the Beautiful Sea," "Love's Old Sweet Song," "Missouri Waltz," "Twelfth Street Rag."

DEATH Rudolph Wurlitzer, musical instrument maker.

LITERATURE/JOURNALISM

Carl Sandburg's poems, "Fog" and "I Am the People," and Joyce Kilmer's poem, "Trees," appear in *Poetry* magazine.

Association of American Advertisers organizes Audit Bureau of Circulation.

First newspaper rotogravure sections appear in seven papers.

Herbert D. Croly founds *New Republic* magazine.

H. L. Mencken edits *The Smart Set* magazine.

BOOKS *Tarzan of the Apes* by Edgar Rice Burroughs, *Penrod* by Booth Tarkington, *The Eyes of the World* by Harold Bell Wright, *The Titan* by Theodore Dreiser, *The Congo and Other Poems* by Vachel Lindsay, *North of Boston* (poetry) by Robert Frost.

ENTERTAINMENT

Louella Parsons writes movie column for *Chicago Record-Herald*; Alexander Woollcott begins eight years as the *New York Times* drama critic.

Tillie's Punctured Romance with Charlie Chaplin and Marie Dressler is produced, the first American feature-length movie comedy; Theda Bara stars in *A Fool There Was*.

Al Jolson stars in *Dancing Around*, Vernon and Irene Castle in *Watch Your Step*, Ruth Chatterton in *Daddy Long-Legs*, John Barrymore in *Kick In*, Douglas Fairbanks in *The Show Shop*, Frank Craven in *Too Many Crooks*.

The waltz and two-step are the fashionable society dance steps; other popular dances are the grizzly bear, bunny hug, turkey trot, and fox-trot.

DEATHS Benjamin F. Keith, vaudeville circuit founder; George C. Tilyou, amusement rides inventor and developer of Coney Island (Brooklyn, N.Y.).

SPORTS

U.S. Power Squadrons are formed.

Southwest Intercollegiate Athletic Conference is established.

Honus Wagner of Pittsburgh Pirates and Nap Lajoie of Cleveland Indians each get their 3,000th base hits.

Grand League of American Horseshoe Players is organized.

WINNERS *Auto racing*—Rene Thomas, Indianapolis 500; *Baseball*—Boston Braves, World

Series; *Boxing*—Jack Johnson, heavyweight; Kid Williams, bantamweight; *Figure skating*—Theresa Weld, women's international title; Norman Scott, men's; *Golf*—Walter Hagen, U.S. Open; *Horse racing*—Old Rosebud, Kentucky Derby; Holiday, Preakness Stakes; Luke McLuke, Belmont Stakes; *Motorcycling*—Glenn R. Boyd, first race (300 miles); *Rowing*—Harvard, first U.S. winner of Henley Grand Challenge Cup; *Tennis*—Australia, Davis Cup; Richard Williams, U.S. Open.

MISCELLANEOUS

Mine disaster at Eccles, W. Va., kills 181.

Women give up tight corsets, but fashionable skirts are so tight that they impede walking; skirts are shorter, and women wear high-buttoned shoes.

1915

INTERNATIONAL

World War I

German submarine sinks wheat-laden U.S. vessel *William Frye* (January 28). Germany announces area around British Isles is a war zone, enemy merchant ships will be destroyed beginning February 18; German mines sink U.S. steamers *Evelyn* (February 19) and *Carib* (February 23); German torpedoes sink tanker *Gulflight*. Germany warns that U.S. vessels entering war zone do so at their own peril.

British steamer *Lusitania* sunk (May 7) off Ireland, taking 1,198 lives, including 128 Americans (author Elbert Hubbard, producer Charles Frohmann, Alfred G. Vanderbilt). U.S. steamer *Nebraskan* (May 25) and *Leelanaw* (July 25) are sunk.

War-related activities at home include opening of military training camp at Plattsburgh, N.Y. (August 10); an explosion in DuPont plant (Wilmington, Del.), believed due to sabotage, kills 31; Henry Ford and a peace delegation travel to Europe (December 4) to end war; Ford leaves the group (December 22), returns to U.S.; President Woodrow Wilson outlines comprehensive national defense program (December 7).

—∿—

U.S. Marines land at Santo Domingo, Dominican Republic, to begin occupation (May 5); Marines land in Haiti (July 29), following a revolution; new government signs treaty making Haiti a virtual U.S. protectorate for 10 years.

NATIONAL

Secretary of State William Jennings Bryan resigns in disagreement with presidential policy on *Lusitania* sinking.

Bomb is placed by Eric Muenter, German instructor, explodes in Senate reception room (July 2); no one is injured; the next day, Muenter slightly wounds J. P. Morgan, war contract agent for British; Muenter commits suicide three days later.

Combining Life Saving and Revenue Cutter services creates Coast Guard (January 28).

William J. Simmons of Atlanta revives Ku Klux Klan (November 25).

Young Men's Progressive Civic Assn. (later Junior Chamber of Commerce) is organized.

Prohibition goes into effect in Alabama, Arizona, Idaho; and South Carolina, Oregon, and Colorado pass prohibition laws.

National Committee for Aeronautics is created, forerunner of National Aeronautics and Space Administration (NASA) (March 3).

Widowed President Wilson marries a widow, Mrs. Edith B. Galt.

Warren G. Harding begins term as senator from Ohio; Herbert Hoover is named chairman of Commission for Relief in Belgium.

Alexander Graham Bell in New York and his

1915

Charlie Chaplin dressed in his classic tramp costume, with hat and cane. CORBIS-BETTMANN

assistant, Thomas A. Watson, in San Francisco hold first transcontinental telephone conversation; costs $20.70 for first three minutes (January 25).

San Diego hosts Panama-California Exposition.

Rocky Mountain (Colo.) National Park is established.

DEATHS Anthony Comstock, reformer; John A. Holmes, first director, Bureau of Mines (1910–1915), who popularized phrase, "Safety first."

BUSINESS/INDUSTRY/INVENTIONS

John T. Thompson invents submachine gun; David Sarnoff, a radio set.

La Follette Seamen's Act regulates employment conditions of maritime workers.

Willis H. Carrier founds Carrier Corp.

Oil is discovered at El Dorado, Kans.

American Association of Engineers is founded.

DEATHS Frank W. Taylor, industrial engineer, father of scientific management; W. Atlee Burpee, plant-seed merchant; John McTammany, inventor.

TRANSPORTATION

One-millionth Ford comes off assembly line; Chevrolet Motor Co. is founded.

First automobile finance company is Bankers Commercial Corp., New York City; Guarantee Securities Co. is organized to buy consumers' installment notes from Willys-Overland dealers.

DEATHS Lorenzo S. Coffin, led successful campaign for railroad automatic coupling.

SCIENCE/MEDICINE

Mayo Clinic in Rochester, Minn., opens.

Dinosaur National Monument in Utah and Colorado is established to preserve paleontological finds.

Zoological Society of America is founded.

DEATHS Greene V. Black, pioneer dentist; Francis Delafield, founder, Association of American Physicians.

EDUCATION

Xavier University in New Orleans, La., opens.

American Association of University Professors is founded.

DEATH Booker T. Washington, founder, head of Tuskegee (Ala.) Institute.

RELIGION

Catholic Bishop George W. Mundelein becomes archbishop of Chicago; Bishop Edward J. Hanna archbishop of San Francisco.

DEATH Frances J. Crosby, blind Protestant hymn writer ("Blessed Assurance," "Sweet Hour of Prayer").

ART/MUSIC

Ruth St. Denis and Ted Shawn establish Denishawn School of Dance.

Arthur G. Dove completes the painting *Plant Forms*; John F. Kensett, *Lake George*; Max Weber, *Chinese Restaurant*.

SONGS (popular): "Auf Wiedersehen," "The Magic Melody," "The Old Gray Mare," "Pack Up Your Troubles in Your Old Kit Bag," "Fascination," "Jelly Roll Blues," "Keep the Home Fires Burning," "Memories," "Song of the Islands."

DEATH John W. Alexander, muralist (*Evolution of the Book* in Library of Congress).

LITERATURE/JOURNALISM

Alfred A. Knopf establishes publishing company.

BOOKS *The Harbor* by Ernest Poole, *Spoon River Anthology* by Edgar Lee Masters, *The Bent Twig* by Dorothy Canfield Fisher, *Ruggles of Red Gap* by Harry L. Wilson, *Rivers to the Sea* (poetry) by Sara Teasdale, *Old Judge Priest* by Irvin S. Cobb, *The Song of the Lark* by Willa Cather.

ENTERTAINMENT

Movies of the year include Charles Chaplin in *The Tramp*, and D. W. Griffith's *The Birth of a Nation*.

W. C. Fields begins six-year run in the Ziegfeld Follies.

Ralph Morgan stars in *Fair and Warmer*, Alice Brady in *Sinners*; two musicals are produced: *Alone at Last* with music by Franz Lehar and *Princess Pat* with music by Victor Herbert.

Neighborhood Playhouse and Washington Square Players begin in New York City; Provincetown (Mass.) Players organized; moves to New York in 1916.

SPORTS

Jacob Ruppert and T. L. Huston buy New York Yankees for $460,000.

Babe Ruth, then a Boston Red Sox pitcher, hits his first home run.

Federal League ends legal battle with National and American leagues, folds as its players sign with other teams.

American Lawn Bowling Assn. is formed.

Pacific Coast Intercollegiate Athletic Conference is founded.

WINNERS *Auto racing*—Ralph DePalma, Indianapolis 500; *Baseball*—Boston Red Sox, World Series; *Boxing*—Jess Willard, heavyweight; Ted Lewis, welterweight; *Golf*—Jerome Travers, U.S. Open; *Horse racing*—Regret, first filly to win Kentucky Derby; Rhine Maiden, Preakness Stakes; The Finn, Belmont Stakes; *Tennis*—William Johnston, U.S. Open.

MISCELLANEOUS

Submarine F-4 sinks outside Honolulu Harbor with loss of 21 men.

Lewisohn Stadium in New York City is dedicated.

Kiwanis International is founded in Detroit.

Four major disasters occur: Excursion steamer *Eastland* capsizes in Chicago River, kills 812; floods in Galveston, Tex., cause 275 deaths; gasoline tank car explodes in Ardmore, Okla., kills 47; mine accident at Layland, W. Va., kills 46.

Dancer Irene Castle popularizes bobbed hair.

DEATH Fannie Farmer, cooking expert.

1916

INTERNATIONAL

World War I

President Woodrow Wilson tours nationally to urge preparedness (January 27); Congress votes to increase army to 175,000 men, then to 223,000 at end of five years (June 3); authorizes 450,000-man National Guard, establishes Officers Reserve Training Corps.

Fire and explosion in munitions plant at Black Tom Island, N.J., causes $22 million damage (July 30), is attributed to sabotage.

National Research Council organizes to promote wartime research (September 20); Council of National Defense is organized (October 11) with six cabinet members, headed by War Secretary Newton D. Baker, and an Advisory Commission.

Germany announces (February 10) that enemy-armed merchant ships will be treated as war vessels; U.S. steamer *Lanso* (October 28) and steamer *Columbian* (November 7) are sunk by German submarines; Germany announces its willingness to discuss peace (December 12); Allies turn it down because no peace terms are disclosed; President Wilson calls on both sides to disclose peace terms (December 18).

Pancho Villa leads 1,500 Mexicans in setting Columbus, N.Mex., on fire, killing 19 Americans (March 9); President Wilson orders U.S. troops into Mexico to capture Villa (March 10); 4,000 troops led by Gen. John J. Pershing conduct nine-month fruitless chase.

U.S. and Great Britain (for Canada) sign migratory bird treaty.

U.S. and Haiti sign treaty for U.S. control of the island (May 3).

U.S. buys Virgin Islands (Danish West Indies) from Denmark for $25 million (August 4); is ratified by Senate (September 7).

NATIONAL

President Wilson, Democrat, is reelected over Supreme Court Justice Charles Evans Hughes, Republican; receives 9,129,606 popular and 277 electoral votes to Hughes's 8,538,221 and 254.

Supreme Court upholds constitutionality of federal income tax; Louis D. Brandeis is confirmed as first Jewish Supreme Court justice.

U.S. Shipping Board is created to acquire vessels through an Emergency Fleet Corp. (September 7).

Bomb explodes during Preparedness Day parade in San Francisco, kills nine (July 22); two men later are found guilty.

National Park Service is established; Lassen (Calif.) National Park is created.

Margaret Sanger and others open birth-control clinic at 46 Amboy Street, Brooklyn, N.Y.

Farm Loan Act gives farmers long-term credit facilities similar to those for industry and commerce; creates Federal Farm Loan Board and 12 district banks.

Statewide prohibition begins in Arkansas, Iowa, Virginia; is enacted in Utah.

Jeanette Rankin of Montana is first woman elected to House of Representatives.

Tariff Commission is established.

Calvin Coolidge becomes lieutenant governor of Massachusetts.

BUSINESS/INDUSTRY/INVENTIONS

Adamson Act passes, reduces railroad workers' day from 10 to 8 hours without reducing pay.

William G. Mennen founds toiletries company; A. C. Gilbert Co., toymaker, is established; Hall Brothers produces Hallmark greeting cards; Clarence Saunders opens Piggly Wiggly grocery chain, features self-service.

Nearly 2,100 strikes and lockouts occur in first six months of year.

General John Pershing (fourth from the left) and members of his staff at Durban, on Mexican Expedition. CORBIS-BETTMANN

DEATHS Hetty (Henrietta H.) Green, financier, reputedly richest woman of era; William Stanley, inventor of electrical transformer, generator; James J. Hill, financier and railroad president; Hiram S. Maxim, machine-gun inventor.

TRANSPORTATION

Nash Motor Co. and Fruehauf Trailer Co. are founded.

More than 1 million (1,525,578) automobiles are manufactured.

Boeing Airplane Co., Sinclair Oil & Refining Co., and Getty Oil Co. are founded.

Aviation and Aeronautical Engineering magazine begins publication, later becomes *Aviation* magazine.

SCIENCE/MEDICINE

Gilbert N. Lewis sets forth new theory on structure of atom.

Severe polio epidemic strikes country.

Lewis M. Terman, psychologist, coins term *IQ* (*intelligence quotient*) in widely used test for measuring intelligence.

EDUCATION

John Dewey's *Democracy and Education* is published.

RELIGION

Mordecai Kaplan founds Jewish Center in New York City.

DEATHS Charles Taze Russell, founder of Jehovah's Witnesses; Samuel D. Ferguson, first black Episcopal bishop.

ART/MUSIC

Saturday Evening Post accepts Norman Rockwell's first cover painting.

Baltimore Symphony Orchestra gives its first concert.

Cleveland (Ohio) Museum of Art opens.

Rudolf Friml's operetta *Katinka* is published.

Louis M. Eilshemius completes the painting *The Funeral*; Naum Gabo completes the sculpture *Head of a Woman*.

Player-piano music rolls are introduced.

SONGS (popular): "Bugle Call Rag," "If You Were

the Only Girl in the World," "Nola," "Poor Butter-fly," "Roses of Picardy," "Beale Street Blues," "I Ain't Got Nobody," "Pretty Baby."

LITERATURE/JOURNALISM

McGraw-Hill Publishing Co. is founded.

Journal of Negro History begins publication.

BOOKS *A Heap o' Livin'* (poetry) by Edgar A. Guest; *When a Man's a Man* by Harold Bell Wright, *Mountain Interval* (poetry) by Robert Frost, *Sea Garden* (poetry) by Hilda Doolittle, *You Know Me, Al* by Ring Lardner, *Chicago Poems* by Carl Sandburg, *Seventeen* by Booth Tarkington, *Tish* by Mary Roberts Rinehart.

ENTERTAINMENT

Ernst F. W. Alexanderson invents modern radio-tuning device.

Theater Arts Magazine begins publication as a quarterly.

The musical *Have a Heart*, by Jerome Kern and P. G. Wodehouse, is produced.

Marjorie Rambeau stars in *Cheating Cheaters*, Walter Hampden in *Good Gracious, Annabelle*, William Collier in *Nothing But the Truth*, Elsie Janis in *The Century Girl*.

In movies, Mary Pickford stars in *Daddy Long Legs*, William S. Hart in *The Aryan*, Enid Markey in *Civilization*, Lillian Gish in *Intolerance*.

SPORTS

Ed "Strangler" Lewis and Joe Stecher wrestle $5\frac{1}{2}$ hours to a draw.

Professional Golfers Assn. (PGA) is organized.

Women's National Bowling Assn. (now Women's International Bowling Congress) is organized; AAU holds its first national women's swimming competition; Grand American Handicap awards prizes for first time to women trapshooters.

Weeghman Park (later Wrigley Field), home of baseball's Chicago Cubs, opens.

Dan Patch, all-time great harness race horse, dies.

WINNERS *Auto racing*—Dario Resta, Indianapolis 500; *Baseball*—Boston Red Sox, World Series; *Golf*—Chick Evans, U.S. Open; Jim Barnes, first PGA tournament; *Football*—Washington State, first annual Rose Bowl; Georgia Tech, in most one-sided game (220–0 over Cumberland, of Lebanon, Tenn.); *Horse racing*—George Smith, Kentucky Derby; Damrosch, Preakness Stakes; Friar Rock, Belmont Stakes; *Tennis*—Richard Johnson, U.S. Open.

MISCELLANEOUS

Fire in Paris, Tex., burns 1,400 buildings, does $11 million damage.

First Mother's Day is observed in Philadelphia and in Grafton, W. Va.

Henrietta Szold founds Hadassah, American women's Zionist organization.

INTERNATIONAL

World War I

President Woodrow Wilson issues a program for peace settlement, calls for an international organization to keep the peace (January 22); Germany notifies U.S. that unrestricted submarine warfare will be resumed February 1;

President Wilson announces breaking relations with Germany (February 3); U.S. arms merchant vessels (March 12); the president calls a special session of Congress, asks for a war declaration against Germany; Congress approves (April 6).

U.S. steamer *Magnolia* fires first U.S. shots of war beating off a submarine attack; first U.S. destroyers arrive in Ireland (May 3); President Wilson sends one army division to France (May 18), arrives June 26; Gen. John J. Pershing, head of American Expeditionary Force, arrives (June 14).

First regular U.S. convoy of merchant ships sails for Europe (July 2). German subs that earlier sank the *Heraldton* killing 20 (March 21) and the *Aztec* step up their attacks: oil steamer *Montano* (July 31), sinks transport *Minehaha* with loss of 48 (September 7), destroyer *Cassin* (October 15), sinks transport *Antilles* with 70 lost (October 17), and sinks destroyer *Jacob Jones* (December 6).

Rainbow Division arrives in France (November 30).

Congress declares war on Austria-Hungary.

—⁓—

At home, war-related activities include: President Wilson calls up National Guard from Eastern states (March 25), extends the call nationwide (July 3); Selective Service Act is signed (May 18), calls for registration of 21–30-year-old men; is amended to include men 18 to 45 (August 31); more than 9 million register for the draft (June 5); executive order calls 678,000 men into service (July 13); drawing is held (July 20) to determine order of entry into service; National Guard is absorbed into army (August 5).

First government aviation training field opens at Rantoul, Ill. (July 4); Army Balloon School is established (April 6).

General Munitions Board is created (March 31) to coordinate procurement of war materials (becomes War Industries Board) (July 28); Committee on Public Information is created (April 14); President is given power (August 10) to regulate production and distribution of food and fuel, names Herbert Hoover food administrator, Harry Garfield, fuel administrator.

Law passes that forbids trading with enemy (Octo-

U.S. soldiers on the way to fight in World War I in Europe wave farewell. CORBIS-BETTMANN

ber 6), creates Alien Property Custodian to handle U.S. property owned by enemy aliens; President issues proclamation (November 16) requiring registration of enemy aliens.

To help finance the war, first Liberty Loan drive begins (May 2); 4 million subscribe more than $2 billion in first drive; another drive in November results in $3.8 billion. War Revenue Act (October 3) sets up graduated income and excess profits taxes, increases excise taxes.

President Wilson issues proclamation placing all railroads under federal control (December 26); railroads return to private owners in 1920.

Two explosions, thought to be caused by sabotage, occur at Kingsland (N.J.) car and foundry plant (January 11) and Eddystone (Pa.) munitions plant, where 133 die (April 10).

— m —

U.S. takes possession of Virgin Islands (March 31), which were purchased from Denmark (see 1916); Puerto Rico becomes U.S. territory, its residents U.S. citizens (March 2).

NATIONAL

Congress submits Eighteenth (Prohibition) Amendment to states for ratification (December 18).

Supreme Court in *Wilson v. New* upholds constitutionality of act that sets eight-hour day on interstate railways.

Congressional Union for Woman Suffrage pickets White House; a number of states enact women's suffrage statutes: North Dakota, Ohio, Indiana, Texas, Rhode Island, Michigan, Nebraska.

More than 100 blacks are killed or wounded in two-day riot in East St. Louis, Ill. (July 2).

Immigration Act is passed, which requires literacy tests; bill passes over president's veto. Similar bill was vetoed 20 years earlier.

Julius Rosenwald Foundation is created with $40 million endowment to be used for the "welfare of mankind."

First class postage increases a penny to 3 cents an ounce.

National Travelers Aid Society is formed.

American Friends Service Committee is created.

Mt. McKinley (now Denali) National Park is established in Alaska.

DEATH Stephen B. Luce, founder of Naval War College.

BUSINESS/INDUSTRY/INVENTIONS

Mary Lathrop is first woman lawyer admitted to American Bar Assn.

Otto Y. Schnering founds what is now Curtiss Candy Co.

DEATHS Irving W. Colburn, invented process for making continuous sheets of flat glass; James B. (Diamond Jim) Brady, financier; George H. Hartford, developer of Atlantic–Pacific food chain.

TRANSPORTATION

Robert Manley develops an automobile-wrecking crane.

Chance M. Vought founds company to design and build military aircraft.

Hell Gate Bridge in New York City opens.

Phillips Petroleum and Humble Oil companies are founded.

Registered cars in U.S. reach 4.8 million.

SCIENCE/MEDICINE

Harlow Shapley measures distances in the Milky Way.

Hundred-inch telescope at Mt. Wilson (Calif.) Observatory is completed.

DEATH Andrew T. Still, founder of osteopathy.

EDUCATION

Alaska territorial legislature appropriates $60,000 to start University of Alaska at Fairbanks.

ART/MUSIC

Violinist Jascha Heifetz makes American debut at Carnegie Hall.

Society for Independent Artists is organized.

Sigmund Romberg's operetta, *Maytime*, opens;

Reginald De Koven composes the opera *The Canterbury Pilgrims*.

University of Kansas Museum of Art opens.

PAINTINGS Charles Burchfield, *Church Bells Ringing* and *Rainy Winter Nights*; George Grosz, *Memories of New York*; Marsden Hartley, *Movement No. 10*.

SONGS (popular): "The Bells of St. Mary's," "Darktown Strutters Ball," "For Me and My Gal," "Back Home Again in Indiana," "McNamara's Band," "Over There," "Oh, Johnny, Oh, Johnny, Oh!"

DEATHS Scott Joplin, composer; Albert P. Ryder, painter.

LITERATURE/JOURNALISM

Boni & Liveright, publishers, is founded.

Columbia University confers first Pulitzer Prize awards: Herbert B. Swope for reporting, *New York Tribune* for editorial writing, J. J. Jusserand for U.S. history, Laura E. Richards and Maude H. Elliot for biography.

Arthur Brisbane writes editorial column "Today"; is syndicated to more than 1,000 daily and weekly newspapers.

BOOKS *His Family* by Ernest Poole, *Three Black Pennies* by Joseph Hergesheimer, *Love Songs* (poetry) by Sara Teasdale, *A Son of the Middle Border* by Hamlin Garland, *The Amazing Interlude* by Mary Roberts Rinehart, *King Coal* by Upton Sinclair, *Just Folks* (poetry) by Edgar A. Guest, *Renascence and Other Poems* by Edna St. Vincent Millay.

DEATHS Robert T. S. Lowell, poet and translator; Edward Cary, editor, the *New York Times* (1871–1917); Harrison G. Otis, publisher, *Los Angeles Times* (1886–1917).

ENTERTAINMENT

Fred and Adele Astaire make Broadway debut in *Over the Top*.

Ina Claire stars in *Polly with a Past*, Lenore Ulric in *Tiger Rose*, Marjorie Rambeau in *Eyes of Youth*, Leo Carrillo in *Lombardi Ltd.*, Nat Wills in *Cheer Up*, Frank Craven in *Going Up*, Lionel Barrymore in *Peter Ibbetson*, Helen Hayes in *Pollyanna*.

In movies, Charles Chaplin stars in both *The Adventurer* and *The Immigrant*.

DEATHS Vernon Castle, dancer, in plane crash; Buffalo Bill (William Cody), hunter and showman.

SPORTS

Jim Vaughn of Chicago Cubs and Fred Toney of Cincinnati Reds pitch nine-inning no-hit games against each other; Cincinnati wins 1–0 in tenth on a hit and two errors (May 2); Toney also pitches both games in a doubleheader (July 20), allowing only three hits in each game.

National Hockey League (NHL) is organized (November 22); first game is played in Toronto (December 19).

First baseball game in New York City's Polo Grounds results in arrest of Managers John McGraw and Christy Mathewson for playing on Sunday (August 19).

WINNERS *Baseball*—Chicago White Sox, World Series; *Boxing*—Benny Leonard, lightweight; Pete Herman, bantamweight; *Football*—Oregon, Rose Bowl; *Horse racing*—Omar Khayyam, Kentucky Derby; Kalitan, Preakness Stakes; Hourless, Belmont Stakes; *Tennis*—Richard Murray, U.S. Open.

MISCELLANEOUS

Lions Clubs form Lions International.

Father Edward J. Flanagan founds Boys Town, near Omaha, as Home for Boys.

American Girl magazine, official Girl Scout publication, is founded.

Three mine disasters occur: Hastings, Colo., 121 die; Butte, Mont., 163; and Clay, Ky., 62.

Fire destroys about 2,000 buildings in Atlanta.

1918

INTERNATIONAL

World War I

President Woodrow Wilson outlines his 14 points for a peace program, including creation of an international peace-keeping organization (January 8).

U.S. Army air squadron sees its first action in France when it is attacked while on reconnaissance flight (April 12); U.S. planes make first air raid, bomb railroad station near Metz (June 11); Capt. Eddie Rickenbacker is credited with shooting down 22 enemy planes and four balloons between April and October.

U.S. troops capture Cantigny (May 28), take Vaux, Bouresches, and Belleau Wood, play large role in Battle of the Marne. First U.S. troops land in Italy (May 30). U.S. and French troops turn back German attack on Champagne (July 15); second Battle of Marne begins (July 18); German offensive ends (August 6).

First independent U.S. army is formed, fights with Allies in Oise-Aisne and Ypres-Lys offensives; plays major role in St. Mihiel fighting in the Meuse-Argonne offensive.

Germans, followed the next day by Austria, ask President Wilson for an armistice (October 6).

Allies are reluctant to accept Wilson's 14-point formula and armistice; Kaiser Wilhelm abdicates (November 9) and German Republic is formed;

Children of families stricken with the terrible influenza virus are fed by volunteers equipped with gauze masks, Cincinnati, Ohio. CORBIS-BETTMANN

armistice is signed at 5 A.M., November 11; firing stops at 11 A.M.

Activity at sea is minimal, though submarine sinks British ship *Tuscania* carrying 2,000 U.S. troops off Irish coast; 210 men are lost.

First issue of *Stars and Stripes*, official Army weekly, is published.

First American troops return from Europe (December 1).

—⁓—

War-related activities at home include third Liberty Loan drive in May, which raises $4.2 billion, another in October for $6 billion; War Finance Corp. is created (April 5) to finance war industries.

Government takes over operation of nation's railroads (January 1), telephone and telegraph systems (August 1).

Supreme Court in *Arver v. United States* upholds constitutionality of Selective Service Act; executive order exempts conscientious objectors from military service.

Americans are asked to observe "wheatless" Mondays and Wednesdays, "meatless" Tuesdays, "porkless" Thursdays and Saturdays, and are urged to eat Victory bread (January 10); sugar rationing goes into effect (July 1); Herbert Hoover is named to represent U.S. on European food-relief organization.

Bernard M. Baruch heads War Industries Board; War Labor Board is created with Frank P. Walsh and former President Taft cochairmen; U.S. shipyards launch 98 vessels in one day (July 4).

Sedition Act enlarges 1917 Espionage Act to include acts of antiwar and pacifist proponents.

Government orders baseball to end its season September 1; allows playing of World Series.

Chemical Warfare Service is created in the Army.

NATIONAL

Daylight saving time begins March 30; is repealed in August 1919.

U.S. Employment Service is created in Labor Department.

First experimental airmail route is flown from Washington, D.C., to New York via Philadelphia (May 15); regular service is established August 12; first airmail stamp (24 cents) is issued.

Mississippi becomes first state to ratify Eighteenth Amendment (January 8); several states enact statewide prohibition: Indiana, Texas, Colorado, Nevada, Montana.

Annette A. Adams becomes first woman U.S. district attorney (North California District).

Laura Spelman Rockefeller Memorial Foundation is endowed.

Calvin Coolidge is elected governor of Massachusetts.

DEATHS Former First Lady Lucretia P. Garfield (1881); former Vice President Charles W. Fairbanks (1905–1909); Margaret Olivia Sage, founder of foundation to improve U.S. social and living conditions; Luther H. Gulick, cofounder of Camp Fire Girls.

BUSINESS/INDUSTRY/INVENTIONS

Construction of Muscle Shoals Dam on Tennessee River is ordered.

American Express Co. absorbs Adams Express Co. and several others.

Elmer A. Sperry invents arc searchlight; Henry E. Warren invents electric clock that only has to be plugged into an electric circuit, needs no timekeeping elements.

Brinks, Inc., in Chicago puts first armored car into use.

TRANSPORTATION

Glenn L. Martin Co. builds first successful twin-engine plane; William W. Stout builds U.S.'s first commercial monoplane.

Charles R. Wittemann builds first automatic pilot system.

SCIENCE/MEDICINE

Army School of Nursing is authorized.

President Wilson signs order that perpetuates wartime National Research Council.

Influenza epidemic spreads from Europe to U.S.;

1918

American soldiers fighting in France in 1918. Painting by Mal Thompson. THE GRANGER COLLECTION

sweeps through nation, kills about 500,000 by 1919.

Edwin H. Armstrong invents superheterodyne circuit, basis for most modern radio, television, and radar reception.

EDUCATION

Smith-Hughes Act provides federal grants to be matched by states for agricultural and vocational instruction.

RELIGION

Merging three branches of denomination forms United Lutheran Church; Native American church, composed of many members, incorporates in Oklahoma.

Heber J. Grant becomes president of Mormon church.

Catholic Bishop Dennis J. Dougherty becomes archbishop of Philadelphia.

Aimee Semple McPherson, evangelist, founds International Church of the Four-Square Gospel in Los Angeles.

DEATHS Washington Gladden, Congregational minister considered founder of American Social Gospel movement; Walter Rauschenbusch, Baptist theologian who founded Brotherhood of the Kingdom; John Ireland, Catholic archbishop of St. Paul (1888–1918).

ART/MUSIC

Cleveland Symphony Orchestra is formed; Summer concerts begin in Lewisohn Stadium, New York.

George Gershwin writes "Swanee," Irving Berlin writes show *Yip, Yip, Yaphank*, which includes song "Oh, How I Hate to Get Up in the Morning."

Phillips Collection (art) opens in Washington.

SONGS (popular): "I'm Always Chasing Rainbows," "A Good Man Is Hard to Find," "Somebody Stole My Gal," "After You've Gone," "Hinky Dinky Parley Voo," "K-K-K-Katy," "Till We Meet Again."

LITERATURE/JOURNALISM

Little Review serializes James Joyce's *Ulysses*; issues

are seized by postal authorities during three-year serialization; court upholds obscenity charges.

Robert L. Ripley, cartoonist, develops "Believe It or Not" syndicated feature.

BOOKS *Dere Mabel* by Edward Streeter, *The U.P. Trail* by Zane Grey, *My Antonia* by Willa Cather, *The Magnificent Ambersons* by Booth Tarkington, *Corn Huskers* (poetry) by Carl Sandburg.

DEATHS Henry Adams, author; James Gordon Bennett, editor *New York Herald*; Joyce Kilmer, poet ("Trees").

ENTERTAINMENT

Louis B. Mayer founds motion picture company.

Helen Hayes stars in *Penrod*, Lionel Barrymore in *The Copperhead*, Helen Menken in *Three Wise Fools*, Richard Bennett in *The Unknown Purple*, Conrad Nagel in *Forever After*, DeWolf Hopper in *Everything*, Al Jolson in *Sinbad*, Ed Wynn and Mae West in *Sometime*.

Charles Chaplin stars in movie *A Dog's Life*.

SPORTS

John A. Heydler becomes president of American (baseball) League.

Casey Stengel's return to Brooklyn's Ebbets Field is memorable: he steps to the plate and takes off his cap, and a bird flies out.

WINNERS *Baseball*—Boston Red Sox, World Series; *Horse racing*—Exterminator, Kentucky Derby; War Cloud and Jack Hare Jr. (dead heat), Preakness Stakes; Johnson, Belmont Stakes; *Horseshoe pitching*—Fred Burst, first world championship; *Tennis*—Richard Murray, U.S. Open.

DEATH John L. Sullivan, world heavyweight boxing champion (1882–1892).

MISCELLANEOUS

Numerous disasters occur: forest fire in Cloquet, Minn., area (October 12) kills 400; 600 others perish in fires in adjoining Minnesota, Wisconsin areas; excursion steamer *Columbia* sinks in Illinois River with loss of 200 lives; earthquake destroys San Jacinto and Hemet, Calif.; explosions destroy chemical plant in Oakdale, Pa. (193 die), and a shell-loading plant in Morgan, N.J. (90 die); three railroad accidents take 266 lives (Nashville, Tenn., Brooklyn, N.Y., and Ivanhoe, Ind.).

INTERNATIONAL

Peace negotiations begin in Versailles, France (January 18); Allies agree to include League of Nations creation in peace settlement (January 25); President Woodrow Wilson returns to U.S. to find Republican-controlled Congress opposed to League until after peace; President goes back to France with proposed changes.

Germany signs peace treaty (June 28); it calls for Germany to admit guilt, give up Alsace-Lorraine, Saar basin, Posen, parts of Schleswig and Silesia; reparations are sought (set at $56 billion later); League of Nations covenant is attached.

Herbert Hoover is named head of international relief efforts.

1919

International Labor Organization (ILO) holds first meeting (October 29).

NATIONAL

President Wilson presents peace treaty to Senate (July 10); committee adds 45 amendments, four reservations; President tries to get public support, makes 9,500-mile western tour with 37 speeches in 29 cities.

President collapses in Pueblo, Colo. (September 25), is rushed back to Washington, suffers stroke (October 2), virtually incapacitating him for remainder of his term.

Nebraska becomes 36th state to ratify Eighteenth Amendment (January 16); to become effective January 16, 1920.

1919

Congress passes joint resolution approving the Nineteenth Amendment, granting women's suffrage (June 5); is sent to states for ratification; League of Women Voters is organized.

President Wilson is awarded Nobel Peace Prize for founding the League of Nations.

Supreme Court in *Schenck v. United States* upholds 1917 Espionage Act, finds that free speech can be restrained in wartime; also upholds 1918 Sedition Act.

Telephone and telegraph lines return to private owners after year of government operation.

National debt increases because of World War I to $25.2 billion; Victory Loan bond sale raises $4.5 billion.

Boston police strike; riots and disorders follow; Gov. Calvin Coolidge orders state militia to restore order; strike ends.

Grand Canyon (Ariz.) and Zion (Utah) national parks are established.

First daily airmail service begins between New York City and Chicago (July 1); price of first-class postage stamp is reduced to 2 cents from 3.

Communist Party of America and Communist Labor Party organize; U.S. transport *Buford* with 249 deported "agitators" sails for Russia.

DEATH Former President Theodore Roosevelt (1901–1909).

BUSINESS/INDUSTRY/INVENTIONS

Reynolds Aluminum Co. is founded as U.S. Foil Co.

Owen D. Young organizes Radio Corporation of America (RCA), with David Sarnoff as president.

First American general strike occurs in Seattle to protest elimination of western cost-of-living differential by U.S. Shipping Board; lasts six days.

Bruce Barton and two partners found advertising agency, which later becomes a giant in the industry (Batton, Barton, Durstine & Osborne).

First U.S.-built fighter plane, the Thomas-Morse

Volunteers collect books on the steps of the New York Public Library to send to the troops overseas. UPI/Corbis-Bettmann

MB-1 Scout, is unveiled; Glenn L. Martin develops a bomber.

DEATHS Josiah C. Cady, architect (original Metropolitan Opera); William C. W. Sabine, founder of architectural acoustics.

TRANSPORTATION

Oregon becomes first state to pass gasoline tax (1 cent per gallon); two other states (Colorado, New Mexico) follow.

Henry Ford turns over presidency of Ford Motor Co. to his son, Edsel.

First municipally owned airport opens in Tucson, Ariz.

SCIENCE/MEDICINE

American Association for the Hard of Hearing is founded.

DEATHS Jane Delano, organizer of World War I Red Cross nursing service; Dr. Abraham Jacobi, founder of American pediatrics; Edward C. Pickering, director, Harvard Observatory (1876–1919).

EDUCATION

New School of Social Research is founded in New York City.

Roger Babson founds Babson Park near Boston and Babson Institute, a two-year business school.

James H. Breasted founds Oriental Institute at University of Chicago with grant from John D. Rockefeller Jr.

RELIGION

Two U.S. Catholic bishops are elevated to archbishop: Patrick J. Hayes of New York and Albert A. Daeger of Santa Fe, N. Mex.

Archbishop Edward J. Hannon becomes first chair of National Catholic Welfare Council.

ART/MUSIC

Fritz Kreisler's operetta *Apple Blossoms* is produced.

Eastman School of Music is founded in Rochester, N.Y.

Paul Whiteman organizes his band.

Stuart Davis completes the painting, *Yellow Hills*; George B. Luks, *Otis Skinner as Colonel Bridan*; Joseph Stella, *Orange Bars*; Rockwell Kent, *North Wind*; Georgia O'Keeffe, *Lake George, Coat and Red*.

SONGS (popular): "Alice Blue Gown," "Baby, Won't You Please Come Home," "Dardanella," "I'm Forever Blowing Bubbles," "Irene," "A Pretty Girl Is Like a Melody," "The World Is Waiting for the Sunrise," "How Ya Gonna Keep Them Down on the Farm."

DEATHS Augustus D. Juilliard, benefactor of music school; Oscar Hammerstein I, founder of what later became Metropolitan Opera.

LITERATURE/JOURNALISM

Illustrated Daily News begins publication in New York City.

True Story magazine is founded.

BOOKS *Jurgen* by James Branch Cabell, *Java Head* by Joseph Hergesheimer, *Winesburg, Ohio* by Sherwood Anderson, *Prejudices* (first of six volumes) and *The American Language* by H. L. Mencken, *Ten Days That Shook the World* by John Reed, *Lad, A Dog* by Albert Payson Terhune, *Humoresque* by Fannie Hurst, *Banners* (poetry) by Babette Deutsch.

Harcourt, Brace, publishers, is founded.

Arthur ("Bugs") Baer syndicates his column in *New York American*.

Emanuel Haldeman-Julius publishes Little Blue Books, which sell for 10 cents.

Frank King syndicates his comic strip, "Gasoline Alley" (Uncle Walt and Skeezix); Elzie C. Segar draws cartoon, "Thimble Theater," featuring Olive Oyl and (later) Popeye.

DEATHS Ella Wheeler Wilcox, popular syndicated poet; Henry M. Alden, editor, *Harper's Magazine* (1863–1919); L. Frank Baum, author (*The Wonderful Wizard of Oz*).

ENTERTAINMENT

United Artists motion picture company is founded.

John Murray Anderson stages first *Greenwich Village Follies*.

Alfred Lunt stars in *Clarence*, Ethel Barrymore in *Déclassée*, Ina Claire in *The Gold Diggers*, Edith Day in *Irene*, Peggy Wood in *Buddies*.

Theatre Guild stages its first production, Jacinto Benavente's *The Bonds of Interest*.

Lillian Gish stars in movie *Broken Blossoms*.

SPORTS

Branch W. Rickey, president of St. Louis Cardinals baseball team, inaugurates farm system for developing players.

Baseball outlaws the spitball and shineball and the use of foreign substances on a ball.

National League of Horseshoe and Quoit Pitchers is formed.

WINNERS *Auto racing* — Howdy Wilcox, Indianapolis 500; *Baseball* — Cincinnati Reds, World Series; *Boxing* — Jack Dempsey, heavyweight; Jack Britton, welterweight; *Golf* — Walter Hagen, U.S. Open; *Horse racing* — Sir Barton becomes first Triple Crown winner, takes Kentucky Derby, Preakness Stakes, and Belmont Stakes; *Tennis* — William Johnston, U.S. Open.

MISCELLANEOUS

Lena M. Phillips founds National Federation of Business & Professional Women's Clubs.

American Legion is organized in Paris, is incorporated by Congress.

Order of DeMolay, related to Masonic Order, is founded for young men.

Women's International League for Peace & Freedom is organized.

Balloon crashes into downtown Chicago building; 12 die.

1920

INTERNATIONAL

Supreme Court in *Missouri v. Holland* upholds constitutionality of 1918 Migratory Bird Treaty.

NATIONAL

Warren G. Harding, Republican, is elected president over Democrat James M. Cox with a popular vote of 16,152,200 and 404 electoral votes to Cox's 9,147,353 popular and 127 electoral votes; election returns are broadcast on radio (Station KDKA, Pittsburgh) for the first time.

Nineteenth Amendment gives women the right to vote (August 26); Eighteenth Amendment (Prohibition) goes into effect (January 16).

Senate fails to get required two-thirds (49–35) to ratify League of Nations Covenant and Versailles Peace Treaty (March 19).

Fourteenth census reports national population of 106,021,537.

End of World War I brings increase in immigration to U.S. (430,001).

Post Office approves use of postage meters; transcontinental airmail service is established between New York City and San Francisco.

Helen H. Gardener is sworn in as first woman member of Civil Service Commission; Women's Bureau is created in Labor Department.

American Civil Liberties Union is founded; Rev. Harry F. Ward is president.

Nation's railroads return to private ownership after two years of government operation.

Junior Chamber of Commerce holds first national convention.

First pension for Civil War service is granted.

National debt is reported at $24.2 billion; Gross National Product is $71.6 billion.

DEATH Former Vice President Levi Morton (1889–1893).

BUSINESS/INDUSTRY/INVENTIONS

Federal Power Commission is established (June 10); Railroad Labor Board is created (February 28).

Strike for union recognition at Gary (Ind.) U.S. Steel plant fails.

John L. Lewis begins 40-year presidency of United Mine Workers Union.

Navy Department constructs helium plant at Ft. Worth, Tex.

American Farm Bureau Federation is established.

National Bureau of Economic Research is founded.

Sosthenes Behn founds International Telephone & Telegraph Co. (ITT).

DEATHS John W. Hyatt, discovered fundamental principles for making celluloid; Theodore N. Vail, first president, ATT (1885–1897, 1907–1919).

TRANSPORTATION

Douglas Aircraft Co. is founded.

Americans buy 10 million automobiles in the decade.

SCIENCE/MEDICINE

Langley Research Center at Hampton, Va., opens as the Langley Memorial Aeronautical Laboratory.

Karl A. Menninger founds Menninger Clinic for psychiatric research and therapy.

Andrew E. Douglass develops dendrochronology, dating wood from tree rings.

Edward W. Scripps founds Science Service, a newspaper feature syndicate.

DEATH William C. Gorgas, Surgeon General who led effort to eliminate yellow fever in Cuba, Panama.

Scott, Zelda, and Scottie Fitzgerald (b. 1921) dance in front of their Christmas tree. CORBIS-BETTMANN

EDUCATION

Scholastic Magazine is founded.

RELIGION

Arthur W. Moulton becomes Episcopal bishop of Utah.

DEATH John H. Vincent, Methodist bishop and cofounder, Chautauqua Movement.

ART/MUSIC

Guy Lombardo organizes nine-man band; Joseph ("King") Oliver forms jazz band.

Chicago Opera Assn. presents Reginald De Koven's opera *Rip Van Winkle*; Henry K. Hadley composes opera, *Cleopatra's Night*.

Sculptor Lorado Taft completes *Fountain of Time* in Chicago; Alexander Archipenko the statue *Standing Figure*.

Charles Burchfield completes the painting *February Thaw*; George Grosz, *Cafe Neptune*; Rockwell Kent, *Wilderness*; Lyonel Feininger, *Viaduct*.

Freer Art Gallery in Washington, D.C., opens.

SONGS (popular): "Avalon," "Margie," "Whispering," "Hold Me," "I Never Knew I Could Love Anybody," "When My Baby Smiles at Me."

LITERATURE/ JOURNALISM

Station WMJ, Detroit, makes first radio news broadcasts (August 31).

BOOKS *The Americanization of Edward Bok* by Edward Bok, *Main Street* by Sinclair Lewis, *The Age of Innocence* by Edith Wharton, *This Side of Paradise* by F. Scott Fitzgerald, *The Domesday Book* (poetry) by Edgar Lee Masters, *Smoke and Steel* (poetry) by Carl Sandburg, *Flame and Shadow* (poetry) by Sara Teasdale, *The Story of Dr. Dolittle* by Hugh Lofting, *Poor White* by Sherwood Anderson.

DEATH John Reed, radical journalist, only American buried in the Kremlin in Moscow.

ENTERTAINMENT

Public radio begins to broadcast at Station KDKA, Pittsburgh, Pa. (November 2).

Douglas Fairbanks marries movie star Mary Pickford, makes movie *The Mark of Zorro*; Lillian Gish stars in *Way Down East*.

Milton Berle makes stage debut in *Floradora*; Ed Wynn presents his *Carnival*.

Marilyn Miller stars in musical *Sally*, Fred Stone in *Tip Top*, Eva Le Gallienne in *Not So Long Ago*, Richard Bennett in Eugene O'Neill's *Beyond the Horizon*, Arnold Daly in *The Tavern*.

SPORTS

Chicago grand jury indicts eight Chicago White Sox players accused of "throwing" the 1919 World Series; the "Black Sox" scandal results in election of Judge Kenesaw M. Landis as the first baseball commissioner (November 2).

American Professional Football Assn., forerunner of National Football League, forms (September 17) with 11 clubs; Jim Thorpe is elected president.

Ray Chapman of Cleveland Indians dies (August 17) from being struck in the head by a pitch from Carl Mays of New York Yankees the previous day.

Radio broadcasts of sports begin: first college football game (November 25) (Texas vs. Texas A&M); first prizefight (September 6) (Jack Dempsey vs. Billy Miske).

Olympic Games are held in Antwerp; U.S. wins 39 gold medals; Olympic flag with five interlocking rings flies for first time.

John B. Kelly of Philadelphia's Vespers Boat Club is barred from the Henley Regatta in England; Kelly and club are barred because of alleged amateur violations.

Walter Johnson of Washington Senators pitches 300th winning game.

First dog racetrack is built in Emeryville, Calif.

WINNERS *Auto racing*—Gaston Chevrolet, Indianapolis 500; *Baseball*—Cleveland Indians, World Series; *Boxing*—Jack Dempsey, heavyweight; Georges Carpentier, light heavyweight; Joe Lynch, bantamweight; *Football*—Harvard, Rose Bowl; *Golf*—Edward Ray, U.S. Open; *Handball*—William Ranft, first AAU senior title; *Horse racing*—Paul Jones, Kentucky Derby; Man o' War, Preakness Stakes and Belmont Stakes; *Tennis*—U.S. Davis Cup; Bill Tilden, U.S. Open; *Yachting*—U.S. boat *Resolute* retains America's Cup.

MISCELLANEOUS

Anarchists Nicola Sacco and Bartolomeo Vanzetti are arrested for alleged murder of two men in a payroll holdup at a shoe factory in South Braintree, Mass.

Floods of Arkansas River nearly destroy Pueblo, Colo.

Bomb explodes on Wall Street, New York City; kills 35, injures 100.

1921

INTERNATIONAL

Congress by joint resolution terminates war with Germany and Austria-Hungary (July 21); ratifies separate treaties with them (October 18).

Treaty with Colombia is ratified; Colombia receives $25 million for loss of Panama and is provided free access to canal.

Conference on Limitation of Armaments is held in Washington, D.C.; nine nations are represented.

NATIONAL

Johnson Act is passed by Congress, limiting the number of aliens admitted annually to 3% of the number of that foreign-born nationality already in the U.S.; total is about 358,000 (May 10).

Monument to the Unknown Soldier in Arlington (Va.) National Cemetery is unveiled on first observance of Armistice Day (November 11).

U.S. Budget Bureau is created (June 10) with Charles G. Dawes as first director; Comptroller

1921

General's office is established (June 21); U.S. Veterans Bureau is founded (August 9).

Andrew Mellon begins 11 years as Secretary of the Treasury; Herbert Hoover becomes Secretary of Commerce.

Former President Taft is named Chief Justice of the Supreme Court.

Nevada is first state to authorize capital punishment by lethal gas.

West Virginia levies first state sales tax (July 1); Iowa enacts first state tax on cigarettes (April 11).

Rep. Alice Robertson of Oklahoma presides over House for 30 minutes, first woman to do so (June 20).

Infantile paralysis strikes Franklin D. Roosevelt.

Hot Springs (Ark.) National Park is established.

Emergency tariff act raises rates on agricultural products.

National unemployment rate is 5.7%.

DEATH Philander C. Knox, Secretary of State (1909–1913) who started "dollar diplomacy."

BUSINESS/INDUSTRY/INVENTIONS

Congress passes the Packers and Stockyards Act and Grain Futures Act to prevent unfair and discriminatory practices or price manipulation.

Crosley Radio Corp. and Seiberling Rubber Co. are founded.

John A. Larson invents polygraph (lie detector).

John Robert Powers agency (modeling) opens.

DEATHS Francis B. Parker, instrumental in setting U.S. electrical standards; William Robinson, inventor of automatic electric signaling system; Samuel S. Laws, inventor of stock ticker.

TRANSPORTATION

Port Authority of New York and New Jersey is established.

A traveling style show of the National Association of Cotton Manufacturers, demonstrating the adaptability of new cotton and cotton-rayon fabrics, 1927. Outfit on the left is a bathing suit, and outfit in the middle is sleepwear ("Lido Beach pajamas") with bathrobe. UPI/CORBIS-BETTMANN

SCIENCE/MEDICINE

Dr. George W. Crile and others found Cleveland Clinic Hospital.

Ernest O. Lawrence, University of California physicist, founds what will become the Lawrence Radiation Laboratory.

Harlow Shapley begins 31 years as director of the Harvard Observatory.

University of Rochester (N.Y.) School of Medicine and Dentistry is founded.

EDUCATION

John J. Tigert IV becomes U.S. Education Commissioner.

Lafayette College in Easton, Pa., establishes civil rights chair; Graduate School of Geography opens at Clark University, Worcester, Mass.

RELIGION

First religious service broadcast on radio is that of Calvary Episcopal Church in Pittsburgh, Pa. (January 2).

International Missionary Council forms with John R. Mott chairman.

First general synod of African Orthodox Church meets in New York City with George McGuire as first bishop.

Dennis J. Dougherty, Catholic archbishop of Philadelphia, is elevated to cardinal.

William T. Manning becomes Episcopal bishop of New York.

DEATH Antoinette L. B. Blackwell, first woman ordained as a minister (Congregational).

ART/MUSIC

Sigmund Romberg's operetta *Blossom Time* is produced.

Stuart Davis completes the paintings *Lucky Strike* and *Cigarette Papers*; Samuel Halpert, *Her First Book of Lessons*.

SONGS (popular): "Ain't We Got Fun," "April Showers," "Look for the Silver Lining," "My Man," "Sally," "Second-Hand Rose," "Wabash Blues," "Ma, He's Making Eyes at Me," "There'll

Be Some Changes Made," "Kitten on the Keys."

DEATH Enrico Caruso, opera tenor.

LITERATURE/JOURNALISM

Barron's Weekly begins publication; Newhouse newspaper chain is founded.

Little Review, arts magazine that serialized James Joyce's *Ulysses* and was found guilty of obscenity, moves from New York to Paris.

Heywood Broun writes column, "It Seems to Me," in *New York World*.

United Press becomes a major news service.

BOOKS *A Daughter of the Middle Border* by Hamlin Garland, *The Brimming Cup* by Dorothy Canfield Fisher, *Alice Adams* by Booth Tarkington, *Erik Dorn* by Ben Hecht, *Three Soldiers* by John Dos Passos, *Scaramouche* by Rafael Sabatini, first edition of Emily Post's *Etiquette*, *Poems* by Marianne Moore.

ENTERTAINMENT

Eva Le Gallienne stars in *Liliom*, Ed Wynn in *The Perfect Fool*, Otis Skinner in *Blood and Sand*, Lynn Fontanne in *Dulcy*, Pauline Lord in *Anna Christie*, Al Jolson in *Bombo*, Katharine Cornell debuts in *Nice People*.

In the movies, John Barrymore stars in *Dr. Jekyll and Mr. Hyde*, Lillian Gish in *Orphans of the Storm*, Charles Chaplin in *The Kid*, Douglas Fairbanks in *The Three Musketeers*, Rudolph Valentino in *The Sheik*.

SPORTS

Eight Chicago White Sox baseball players who were accused of "throwing" the 1919 World Series are acquitted on a technicality (August 3); Baseball Commissioner Kenesaw M. Landis bars the players from baseball for life.

Radio broadcasts of baseball games air (August 25); first radio coverage of World Series begins with play-by-play bulletins.

Joe E. Carr is named president of the National Football League.

American Soccer League forms; National Horseshoe Pitching Assn. incorporates.

Babe Ruth becomes all-time home run leader

when he hits 120th; Ty Cobb of Detroit Tigers gets his 3,000th hit.

Edwin Gourdin becomes first to surpass 25 feet (25 ft., 3 in.) in the long jump.

Southern Intercollegiate Conference is formed; becomes Southeastern Conference.

WINNERS *Auto racing* — Tommy Milton, Indianapolis 500; *Baseball* — New York Giants, World Series; *Boxing* — Jack Dempsey, heavyweight; Johnny Wilson, middleweight; Johnny Buff, bantamweight; *Fencing* — U.S., first international competition; *Football* — California, Rose Bowl; *Golf* — Jim Barnes, U.S. Open; *Horse racing* — Behave Yourself, Kentucky Derby; Broomspun, Preakness Stakes, Grey Lag, Belmont Stakes; *Tennis* — U.S., Davis Cup; Bill Tilden, U.S. Open; *Track* — Illinois, first NCAA championship; *Wrestling* — Ed "Strangler" Lewis, heavyweight.

MISCELLANEOUS

Nicola Sacco and Bartolomeo Vanzetti are found guilty of murdering two men in a South Braintree, Mass., payroll robbery.

Floods in San Antonio cause 250 deaths.

St. Louis Zoo opens.

Christian K. Nelson invents the Eskimo Pie.

Race riots in Tulsa, Okla., result in death of 25 white and 60 black persons.

Women's fashion feature cloche hats, silk stockings, knee-length skirts, and fake jewelry; men wear their hair slicked down and parted in the middle, wear snappy hats and saddle shoes. Smoking increases and doubles sales of tobacco products during the decade.

1922

INTERNATIONAL

Washington Armament Conference of nine nations ends (February 6) with the signing of both treaties that set naval strength and restrict use of submarines, and an agreement on Pacific operations.

Second Central American conference meets in Washington.

NATIONAL

Supreme Court upholds constitutionality of Nineteenth Amendment, which gives women the vote.

Interior Secretary Albert B. Fall secretly leases naval oil reserve lands to oil operator Harry F. Sinclair; Edward L. Doheny leases California lands.

Seven states sign Colorado River Compact to regulate river's water.

First U.S. aircraft carrier, *Langley*, is converted from the collier *Jupiter*.

Florence E. Allen is first woman justice of a state

(Ohio) Supreme Court, later (1934) becomes first woman justice of Circuit Court of Appeals; Rebecca Felton of Georgia is first woman U.S. senator, serving from October 3 to November 22.

President Warren G. Harding dedicates Francis Scott Key Memorial in Baltimore, Md., in first presidential radio broadcast.

Fordney-McCumber Tariff raises rates generally.

BUSINESS/INDUSTRY/INVENTIONS

Herrin (Ill.) massacre occurs during coal-mine strike when union miners and nonunion men clash; 20 nonunion men die.

American Rolling Mill Co. builds continuous-sheet steel mill at Ashland, Ky.

Raytheon Manufacturing Co. begins as American Appliance Corp.

Bradley A. Fiske patents microfilm reading device; a sonic depth finder is introduced.

First mechanical telephone switchboard is installed in New York City.

DEATH Alexander Graham Bell, inventor of telephone.

TRANSPORTATION

Ford Motor Co. acquires Lincoln Motor Co.

U.S. dirigible *Roma* explodes over Hampton, Va.; 34 are killed.

Glenn L. Martin Co. builds first U.S. metal monoplane; Henry A. Berliner demonstrates a helicopter for government officials.

DEATH George B. Selden, inventor of gasoline motor.

SCIENCE/MEDICINE

DEATH George W. Gould, inventor of bifocal lens glasses.

EDUCATION

Cornell University opens School of Hotel Administration.

Texas Tech University, Lubbock, opens.

DEATH John F. Goucher, benefactor and president of what became Goucher College.

RELIGION

Harry Emerson Fosdick resigns from Presbyterian church over differences between liberal and traditional doctrine.

American Episcopal church deletes word *obey* from marriage service.

Alfred Haatanen begins 28 years as president of American Finnish Lutheran Evangelical church.

Stephen S. Wise founds Jewish Institute of Religion.

ART/MUSIC

Edwin Franko Goldman band begins 33 years of open-air concerts in New York City's Central Park.

Seated statue of Abraham Lincoln by Daniel C. French in Lincoln Memorial is dedicated.

The Teapot Dome Scandal. Albert B. Fall and Edward Doheny on their way to court. CORBIS-BETTMANN

Childe Hassam completes the painting *Montauk*.

Museum of the American Indian in New York City opens.

SONGS (popular): "Goin' Home," "My Buddy," "Toot, Toot Tootsie," "Way Down Yonder in New Orleans," "Carolina in the Morning," "Chicago," "Limehouse Blues," "Hot Lips."

LITERATURE/JOURNALISM

DeWitt Wallace and his wife, Lila Bell, launch *Reader's Digest*.

Scripps-Howard newspaper chain is established.

Will Rogers writes weekly column in the *New York Times*.

BOOKS *Babbitt* by Sinclair Lewis, *One of Ours* by Willa Cather, *Ballad of the Harp Weavers* (poetry) by Edna St. Vincent Millay, *The Breaking Point* by Mary Roberts Rinehart, *Under the Tree* (poetry) by Elizabeth M. Roberts, *Merton of the Movies* by Harry L. Wilson, *The Covered Wagon* by Emerson Hough.

1923

ENTERTAINMENT

Will R. Hays begins 23 years as "movie czar" (president, Motion Picture Producers & Distributors).

Herbert T. Kalmus develops Technicolor process.

Ed Wynn produces first radio broadcast of a Broadway show (*The Perfect Fool*) (June 12), is also the first broadcast with a studio audience.

Robert Benchley delivers classic monologue, "The Treasurer's Report," is later one of first movie "shorts."

The play, *Abie's Irish Rose*, begins its record 2,327 performances.

Helen Hayes stars in *To the Ladies*, Florence Eldridge in *The Cat and the Canary*, Jeanne Eagels in *Rain*, Helen Menken in *Seventh Heaven*, Eddie Dowling in *Sally, Irene and Mary*.

MOVIES *Blood and Sand* with Rudolph Valentino, *Robin Hood* with Douglas Fairbanks, *Cops* with Buster Keaton.

DEATHS Lillian Russell, actress and feminine ideal of her time; Marcus Loew, movie industy pioneer.

SPORTS

Jacob Ruppert is sole owner of New York Yankees baseball team.

Johnny Weissmuller breaks four swimming records: 300 and 400 meters, 440 and 500 yards.

Eddie Collins of Philadelphia Athletics steals six bases in a game, setting American League and major leagues baseball record; duplicates feat 11 days later.

U.S. Field Hockey Assn. and International Star Class Yacht Racing Assn. are established.

WINNERS *Auto racing*—Jimmy Murphy, Indianapolis 500; *Baseball*—New York Giants, World Series; *Boxing*—Gene Tunney, light heavyweight; Mickey Walker, welterweight; Joe Lynch, bantamweight; *Football*—Washington–Jefferson and California (tie), Rose Bowl; *Golf*—U.S., first Walker Cup matches with England; Gene Sarazen, U.S. Open and PGA; *Horse racing*—Morvich, Kentucky Derby; Pillory, Preakness Stakes and Belmont Stakes; *Polo*—Princeton, first indoor intercollegiate title; *Tennis*—U.S., Davis Cup; Bill Tilden, U.S. Open; *Track*—Cornell, first indoor IC4A meet; *Volleyball*—Pittsburgh YMCA, first national tournament; *Wrestling*—Ed "Strangler" Lewis, heavyweight.

MISCELLANEOUS

Two-day snowstorm in Washington, D.C., results in collapse of Knickerbocker Theater roof, killing 100.

Ten days of hurricanes in Florida and Alabama kill 243.

Ancient Chinese game of mah-jongg is introduced in U.S., becomes a craze.

INTERNATIONAL

Treaty signed by U.S., Great Britain, France, and Japan covers handling of Pacific possessions (December 13).

Central American conference ends with a neutrality treaty, limitation of armaments, and a Central American court of justice (February 7).

U.S. and Turkey sign treaty of friendship and commerce.

1923

NATIONAL

President Warren G. Harding dies in San Francisco during his return trip from Alaska (August 2); Vice President Calvin Coolidge is sworn in as president (August 3).

First equal rights amendent is introduced in Congress, does not pass.

Montana and Nevada are first states to enact an old-age pension.

Congress passes over president's veto a veteran's bonus of $1.25 per day for overseas duty, $1 a day for U.S. service; bonus given in form of 20-year endowment policy.

The *Baltimore Sun* and *New York Times* print exposés of Ku Klux Klan activities; articles lead to decline in membership.

President Coolidge gives first presidential message specifically for radio (December 6).

DEATH Henry Cabot Lodge, senator who led successful fight against League of Nations.

BUSINESS/INDUSTRY/INVENTIONS

U.S. Steel Co. adopts an eight-hour day, reducing it from 12 hours.

Zenith Radio Corp. and Burlington Industries are founded.

Young & Rubicam advertising agency is founded.

Intermediate Credit Act makes it easier to get crop financing loans.

DEATHS Francis W. Ayer, pioneer advertising executive; Charles P. Steinmetz, electrical inventor who helped make alternating current commercially feasible; John Davey, tree-care specialist; William Holabird, architect who established skeleton method of skyscraper building.

TRANSPORTATION

First ethyl gasoline is marketed in Dayton, Ohio (February 2).

Firestone Tire & Rubber Co. produces balloon tires.

First transcontinental nonstop plane flight (New York City to San Diego) is completed in 26 hours, 50 minutes.

Registered automobiles total about 13.3 million.

DEATH Alexander McDougall, designer of Great Lakes "whaleback" freighter.

SCIENCE/MEDICINE

Robert A. Millikan is awarded Nobel Prize in

Dancers and musicians pause during a Charleston-dancing marathon to show off for a news photographer. UPI/CORBIS-BETTMANN

physics for work on the elementary charge of electricity and on the photoelectric effect.

Physicist Arthur H. Compton discovers the photon, a particle unit of light.

Naval Research Laboratory opens in Washington, D.C.

New York Cancer Institute on Welfare Island is dedicated.

George and Gladys Dick isolate the scarlet fever toxin, develop an effective antitoxin.

EDUCATION

Merger of Daytona Normal and Cookman Institute forms Bethune-Cookman College; Mary M. Bethune is first president.

John D. Rockefeller Jr. endows International Education Board.

RELIGION

Edgar J. Goodspeed prepares *New Testament: An American Translation*.

DEATH Daniel S. Tuttle, presiding American Episcopal bishop (1903–1923).

ART/MUSIC

Bessie Smith, blues singer, records "Down Hearted Blues," the first phonograph record to sell more than 2 million copies.

Martha Graham makes solo debut as a ballerina in the *Greenwich Village Follies*.

George W. Bellows completes the painting *Emma and Her Children*; Charles Sheeler, *Bucks County Barn*; George Grosz, *Ecce Homo*; Naum Gabo completes the sculpture *Column*.

Denver (Colo.) Art Museum is founded.

Roger Sessions composes orchestral suite *The Black Maskers*.

SONGS (popular): "Barney Google," "It Ain't Gonna Rain No Mo'," "Linger Awhile," "That Old Gang of Mine," "Who's Sorry Now?," "Yes, We Have No Bananas," "Bugle Call Rag," "Mexicali Rose," "Charleston."

DEATH Edward C. Potter, sculptor of animals (lions at entrance to New York Public Library).

LITERATURE/JOURNALISM

Henry R. Luce and Briton Hadden launch *Time* magazine (March 3).

College Humor magazine and *Kiplinger Washington Newsletter* begin publication.

BOOKS *New Hampshire* (poetry) by Robert Frost, *Cane* by Jean Toomer, *Black Oxen* by Gertrude Atherton, *A Lost Lady* by Willa Cather, *Tulips and Chimneys* (poetry) by E. E. Cummings.

ENTERTAINMENT

Warner Bros. Pictures Inc. is established.

Lee De Forest shows first sound-on-film motion picture, *Phonofilm*.

Eddie Cantor stars in *Kid Boots*, Walter Hampden in *Cyrano de Bergerac*, W. C. Fields in *Poppy*, George M. Cohan in *The Song and Dance Man*, Edna May Oliver in *Icebound*, H. B. Warner in *You and I*.

MOVIES *Safety Last* with Harold Lloyd, *The Hunchback of Notre Dame* with Lon Chaney, *The Pilgrim* with Charlie Chaplin, *The Ten Commandments* with Theodore Roberts, *The Covered Wagon* with Ernest Torrence.

Dance marathons become popular and new dance, the Charleston, sweeps country.

SPORTS

Henry F. Sullivan of Lowell, Mass., becomes first American to swim English Channel, does it in 27 hours, 23 minutes.

Yankee Stadium in New York City opens (April 18); before 72,400 spectators, Babe Ruth hits three home runs.

WINNERS *Auto racing*—Tommy Milton, Indianapolis 500; *Baseball*—New York Yankees, World Series; *Boxing*—Jack Dempsey, heavyweight; Mike McTigue, light heavyweight; Harry Greb, middleweight; Johnny Dundee, featherweight; *Fencing*—Army, three-weapon intercollegiate title; *Football*—Southern California, Rose Bowl; *Golf*—U.S., Walker Cup; Bobby Jones, U.S. Open; Gene Sarazen, PGA; *Horse racing*—Zev, Kentucky Derby and Belmont Stakes; Vigil, Preakness Stakes; *Tennis*—U.S., Davis Cup; Bill Tilden, U.S. Open (men); Helen Wills, USLTA (women); *Track*—Prudential, AAU women's meet.

MISCELLANEOUS

Mine disaster at Dawson, N. Mex., kills 120.

1924

INTERNATIONAL

Dawes Plan on German reparations calls for stabilizing German currency, setting up a five-year schedule of payments (April 9); plan is adopted.

U.S. Marines withdraw from Nicaragua, only to return nine months later.

NATIONAL

President Calvin Coolidge, Republican, is elected to first full term, defeats Democrat John W. Davis; Coolidge receives 15,725,016 popular and 382 electoral votes to Davis's 8,385,586 popular and 136 electoral votes; Progressive Party candidate Robert M. La Follette receives 4,822,856 popular and 13 electoral votes.

Charles G. Dawes shares Nobel Peace Prize with Sir J. Austen Chamberlain of England for developing German reparations plan.

Former Interior Secretary Albert B. Fall is indicted in Teapot Dome scandal, later is convicted and sentenced to one year, $100,000 fine; Oilmen Harry F. Sinclair and Edward L. Doheny are also indicted but later are acquitted.

Annual admissions quota for immigrants is reduced to 2% of the number of that foreign-born nationality in U.S.; new law also requires that immigrants obtain visas, which is a complicated and lengthy process.

Foreign Service Act is reorganized, consolidates U.S. diplomatic and consular service.

Indian Citizenship Act makes all U.S.-born Native Americans U.S. citizens.

Nellie Tayloe Ross becomes first woman state governor (Wyoming) when elected to complete unexpired term of her husband.

Two U.S. Army planes complete 26,103 mile flight around the world from Seattle in 35 days, 1 hour, 11 minutes.

First wilderness area is set aside in the Gila (N. Mex.) National Forest.

J. Edgar Hoover becomes acting head of Federal Bureau of Investigation (May 10), begins 48 years' service as director December 10.

DEATHS Former President Woodrow Wilson (1913–1923); former First Lady Florence Harding (1921–1923).

BUSINESS/INDUSTRY/INVENTIONS

William Green assumes AFL presidency on the death of Samuel Gompers.

Howard Johnson enters food business in Wollaston, Mass. (see 1929).

DuPont plant in Buffalo, N.Y., first produces cellophane.

Ernst F. W. Alexanderson transmits first transatlantic facsimile message.

J. C. Penney opens 500th store in Hamilton, Mo., where he first worked as a clerk in 1904 for $2.27 a month.

Jacob Schick introduces first successful electric shaver.

DEATHS Samuel Gompers, president of AFL (1886–1924); Louis H. Sullivan, father of modernist architecture; Henry Bacon, architect who designed Lincoln Memorial.

TRANSPORTATION

Chrysler Motors is founded, introduces first six-cylinder car.

National Association of Finance Companies adopts minimum standards of one-third down payment for a new car, two-thirds for a used car.

Midland Transit Co. of West Virginia, which later becomes Atlantic Greyhound Co., is founded.

Regular transcontinental air service begins.

Big Lake oil field in western Texas is discovered.

Diesel electric locomotive is put into service.

1924

George Gershwin, composer, at the piano. Gershwin's *Rhapsody in Blue* premieres in 1924. UPI/CORBIS-BETTMANN

Bear Mountain Bridge across Hudson River opens.

DEATH Clifford M. Holland, New York tunnel builder.

SCIENCE/MEDICINE

Morris Fishbein begins 25 years editorship of *AMA Journal* (American Medical Assn.).

Western Electric Co. demonstrates new electrical portable stethoscope.

Dr. George R. Minot develops liver treatment for pernicious anemia.

DEATH T. Mitchell Prudden, pathologist, first American to make diphtheria antitoxin.

EDUCATION

National Congress of Parents and Teachers is established.

Trinity College (Durham, N.C.) is renamed Duke University in honor of school's benefactors.

RELIGION

Methodist General Conference lifts traditional ban on dancing and theatergoing.

Rev. Harry Emerson Fosdick is cleared of heresy charges by New York Presbytery.

Two Catholic archbishops, Patrick J. Hayes of New York and George W. Mundelein of Chicago, elevated to cardinal.

Edward L. Parsons becomes Episcopal bishop of California.

ART/MUSIC

Howard H. Hanson begins 40 years as director of Eastman School of Music.

The operettas *Rose Marie* by Rudolf Friml and *The Student Prince* by Sigmund Romberg are presented.

Serge Koussevitsky arrives from Russia to begin 25 years as conductor of the Boston Symphony Orchestra.

Paul Whiteman and his orchestra give first formal jazz concert at Aeolian Hall, New York City; features George Gershwin at the piano playing his *Rhapsody in Blue* (February 12).

Charles Burchfield completes the painting *House of Mystery*; Preston Dickinson, *Factory*.

Pierpont Morgan Library (art) in New York City opens.

SONGS (popular): "All Alone," "Fascinating Rhythm," "I Wonder What's Become of Sally," "I'll See You in My Dreams," "Tea for Two," "Indian Love Call," "Shine," "Amapola," "It Had to Be You," "Rose-Marie," "California, Here I Come."

DEATH Victor Herbert, composer.

LITERATURE/JOURNALISM

Saturday Review of Literature begins publication; George Jean Nathan and H. L. Mencken found *The American Mercury*.

New York City tabloid, *Daily Mirror*, begins publication; Ogden Mills Reid purchases *New York Herald* and combines it with *New York Tribune*.

Walter Winchell begins 49 years of writing show-business gossip column in *New York Graphic* (later in the *Mirror*).

Simon & Schuster, publishers, is founded.

Harold L. Gray draws the cartoon strip "Little Orphan Annie" in *Chicago Tribune*.

BOOKS *So Big* by Edna Ferber, *The Old Maid* by Edith Wharton, *Arrowsmith* by Sinclair Lewis, *Tamar and Other Poems* by Robinson Jeffers, *Israfel* by Hervey Allen, *Sunrise Trumpets* (poetry) by Joseph Auslander.

DEATH Frances H. Burnett, author (*Little Lord Fauntleroy*).

ENTERTAINMENT

First coast-to-coast radio hookup is used successfully.

Combining the Metro, Mayer, and Goldwyn companies creates Metro-Goldwyn-Mayer; Harry Cohn founds Columbia Pictures.

American own 2.5 million radios compared to 5,000 in 1920.

PLAYS Alfred Lunt and Lynn Fontanne star in *The Guardsman*, Paul Robeson in *The Emperor Jones*, Helen Hayes in *Dancing Mothers*, Walter Huston in *Desire Under the Elms*, Fred and Adele Astaire in *Lady Be Good* (music by George Gershwin), Roland Young in *Beggar on Horseback*.

MOVIES *Beau Brummel* with John Barrymore, *Forbidden Paradise* with Pola Negri, *Janice Meredith* with Marion Davies, *The Thief of Bagdad* with Douglas Fairbanks.

DEATH Lew Dockstader, minstrel and entertainer.

SPORTS

First Winter Olympics are held in Chamonix, France; U.S. wins one gold medal; Summer Olympics are held in Paris; U.S. wins 48 golds, with William Hubbard winning the long jump, the first African American to win a gold medal.

Frank Caruna of Buffalo becomes first bowler to roll two consecutive 300 games; rolls 274 in third game.

Jim Bottomley of St. Louis Cardinals sets National League record, driving in 12 runs in a game.

Newly formed American Motorcyclist Assn. holds three-day rally.

WINNERS *Auto racing*—L. L. Corum and Joe Boyer, Indianapolis 500; *Baseball*—Washington Senators, World Series; *Boxing*—Joe Goldstein, bantamweight; *Football*—Navy–Washington (tie), Rose Bowl; *Golf*—U.S., Walker Cup; Cyril Walker, U.S. Open; Walter Hagen, PGA; *Horse racing*—Black Gold, Kentucky Derby; Nellie Morse, Preakness Stakes; Mad Play, Belmont Stakes; *Tennis*—U.S., Davis Cup; Bill Tilden, U.S. Open (men).

MISCELLANEOUS

Two mine disasters occur; Castle Gate, Utah (171 are killed), and Benwood, W. Va. (119 deaths).

First crossword puzzle book is published.

First national cornhusking championship is held near Alleman, Iowa.

Tornadoes destroy 35 towns in Midwest, killing 800.

Shipwreck Kelly begins career of flagpole sitting.

1925

INTERNATIONAL

U.S. and Canada agree to improve St. Lawrence River between Montreal and Lake Ontario.

NATIONAL

Supreme Court in *Gitlow v. New York* rules that the First Amendment prohibition against governmental abridgment of free speech applies to both federal and state governments.

Court-martial finds Col. Billy Mitchell, outspoken critic of U.S. air power, guilty of conduct prejudicial to good order and military discipline; he later resigns from army.

National Aircraft Board is named to investigate government's role in aviation; Dwight W. Morrow is chairman.

Guggenheim Foundation is established.

U.S. Chamber of Commerce headquarters in Washington, D.C., is dedicated.

DEATHS Former Vice President Thomas R. Marshall (1913–1921), remembered for quote: "What this country needs is a really good five-cent cigar"; William Jennings Bryan, former Secretary of State (1912–1915), three-time Democratic presidential candidate; Robert M. La Follette, Wisconsin governor and senator.

BUSINESS/INDUSTRY/INVENTIONS

Bell Telephone Laboratories organize as non-profit corporation.

Wilson Dam on Tennessee River in Alabama is completed.

Dry ice is first produced commercially; A. A. Walter Co. erects plant in Albany to produce potato chips.

Armstrong Cork & Insulation Co. introduces embossed inlaid linoleum.

A. Philip Randolph organizes Brotherhood of Sleeping Car Porters, becomes strong civil rights leader.

DEATHS Frank S. Baldwin, inventor of what became Monroe calculator; Charles F. Chandler, inventor of flushing toilet water closet, who refused to patent it in the public interest; James B. Duke, American Tobacco Co. president.

TRANSPORTATION

Ford Motor Co. introduces eight-hour day, five-day workweek.

National Air Transport Inc., which later becomes United Air Lines, is founded.

Merger of GM Laboratories and Delco forms General Motors Research Corp.; Charles Kettering is first president.

DEATH Elwood Haynes, pioneer automobile manufacturer, patented stainless steel process.

SCIENCE/MEDICINE

John T. Scopes, high school teacher, is arrested in Dayton, Tenn., for violating state law that makes it illegal to teach any theory that denies the story of "the Divine creation of man" in any public school; Clarence Darrow is defense lawyer, William Jennings Bryan is part of prosecution team; Scopes is found guilty, is fined $100.

Robert A. Millikan announces discovery of a cosmic ray.

Annie Jump Cannon, astronomer, becomes first woman to receive honorary doctorate (Oxford).

Battelle Memorial Institute in Columbus, Ohio, incorporates to conduct research.

EDUCATION

Yale University Aeronautics School receives $500,000 endowment from Daniel Guggenheim.

RELIGION

Rev. Harry Emerson Fosdick leaves Presbyterian church, refuses to accept General Assembly requirements for his continued stay (see 1924).

Clarence S. Darrow (left), prominent American lawyer (1857–1938) defends John Scopes in 1925 when he is charged with violating state law forbidding the teaching of evolution in the public school system. Darrow is seated with William Jennings Bryan, prosecuting attorney. CORBIS-BETTMANN

Episcopal Bishop William M. Brown of Arkansas is deposed for heresy; author of *Communion and Christianity*.

Catholic Bishop John T. McNichols becomes Archbishop of Cincinnati.

ART/MUSIC

The operetta *The Vagabond King* by Rudolf Friml is presented.

Edward Hopper completes the paintings *House by the Railroad* and *Model Reading*; Robert Laurent, *Wave*; Arthur G. Dove, *Portrait of A.S.*; Jacques Lipchitz completes the sculpture *Bather*.

Herbert Elwell composes the ballet *The Happy Hypocrite*.

SONGS (popular): "Always," "Dinah," "Drifting and Dreaming," "Sleepy Time Gal," "Sweet Georgia Brown," "Who?," "Yes, Sir, That's My Baby," "Clap Hands, Here Comes Charlie," "Jalousie," "Show Me the Way to Go Home," "I'm Sittin' on Top of the World."

DEATHS John Singer Sargent, portrait painter; Willard L. Metcalf, artist of New England scenes.

LITERATURE/ JOURNALISM

Harold W. Ross founds *The New Yorker*, features Helen Hokinson's cartoons of middle-aged matrons and Peter Arno's work.

Viking Press is founded.

Robert R. McCormick becomes editor, publisher of *Chicago Tribune*; Westbrook Pegler writes his column in the *Tribune*.

BOOKS *Gentlemen Prefer Blondes* by Anita Loos, *The Man Nobody Knew* by Bruce Barton, *The Great Gatsby* by F. Scott Fitzgerald, *An American Tragedy* by Theodore Dreiser, *Porgy* by DuBose Hayward, *Roan Stallion* (poetry) by Robinson Jeffers, *Barren Ground* by Ellen Glasgow, *Collected Poems* by Hilda Doolittle.

DEATHS Amy Lowell, poet; Frank Munsey, magazine and newspaper publisher.

ENTERTAINMENT

PLAYS Marilyn Miller stars in *Sunny*, Charles Winninger in *No, No, Nanette*, George Jessel in *The Jazz Singer*, Fay Bainter and Walter Abel in *The Enemy*.

MOVIES *The Freshman* with Harold Lloyd, *The Phantom of the Opera* with Lon Chaney, *The Gold Rush* with Charlie Chaplin, *The Merry Widow* with Marion Davies, *The Big Parade* with John Gilbert.

The "Grand Ole Opry" broadcasts locally on radio.

Brooks Atkinson begins 35 years as the *New York Times* drama critic.

SPORTS

Lou Gehrig enters baseball as a pinch hitter and first baseman for New York Yankees (June 1), starts a 2,130-consecutive-game streak; Everett Scott, New York Yankees shortstop, ends his consecutive-game streak at 1,307 (May 6).

Tris Speaker of Cleveland Indians and Eddie

Collins of Chicago White Sox each get their 3,000th base hits.

American (basketball) League is organized.

First contract-bridge game is played aboard a steamer waiting to enter Panama Canal (November 1); players are Harold S. Vanderbilt, game's inventor, and friends.

St. Petersburg (Fla.) Kennel Club opens greyhound racing track.

First East-West Shrine football game is played.

New Madison Square Garden opens.

Tim Mara buys New York Giants football franchise for $500.

WINNERS *Auto racing* — Peter DePaolo, Indianapolis 500; *Baseball* — Pittsburgh Pirates, World Series; *Boxing* — Paul Berlenbach, light heavyweight; Rocky Kansas, lightweight; Fidel La Barba, flyweight; *Football* — Notre Dame, Rose Bowl; *Golf* — Willie MacFarlane, U.S. Open; Walter Hagen, PGA; *Gymnastics* — Alfred Jochim, AAU all-around title; *Horse racing* — Flying Ebony, Kentucky Derby; Coventry, Preakness Stakes; American Flag, Belmont Stakes; *Tennis* — U.S., Davis Cup; Bill Tilden, U.S. Open (men); *Wrestling* — Ed "Strangler" Lewis, heavyweight.

DEATH Christy Mathewson, Hall of Fame baseball pitcher.

MISCELLANEOUS

Tornadoes in Missouri, Illinois, and Indiana claim 689 lives (March 18).

Earthquake destroys downtown Santa Barbara, Calif.

Louisville Courier-Journal inaugurates national spelling bee.

The flapper dress, featuring a drop waist, is introduced.

1926

INTERNATIONAL

Senate ratifies World War I debt-funding agreements with European countries.

U.S. fails to join Permanent Court of International Justice and Arbitration.

NATIONAL

Philadelphia Sesquicentennial Exposition is held.

Army Air Corps is created (July 2).

Personal income and inheritance taxes are reduced; some excise taxes are abolished.

DEATHS Sanford B. Dole, first governor, Territory of Hawaii; Eugene V. Debs, radical labor leader and Social Democratic Party presidential candidate.

BUSINESS/INDUSTRY/INVENTIONS

American Arbitration Assn. is founded.

Railroad Labor Board replaces an independent Board of Mediation.

Dr. Colin G. Fink patents chromium-plating process.

McGraw Electric Co. markets electric toaster (Toastmaster); Electrolux unveils gas household refrigerator.

Neiman Marcus inaugurates department-store fashion shows.

George F. Doriot begins 40 years of teaching manufacturing at Harvard University; is credited with creating American professional managers.

DEATHS John M. Browning, machine gun and automatic gun inventor; Leonidas Merritt, discoverer of Mesabi iron-ore deposits; Luther Burbank, plant breeder; Washington A. Roebling, builder of Brooklyn Bridge.

TRANSPORTATION

Air Commerce Act places civil aviation under the Commerce Department.

The *Governor Moore*, a ferryboat built exclusively to carry cars, is placed in service between New York City and New Jersey.

Richard E. Byrd and Floyd Bennett fly over North Pole (May 9).

Carl E. Wickman founds what later becomes Greyhound Corp.

Benjamin Franklin Bridge over Delaware River in Philadelphia opens.

SCIENCE/MEDICINE

Robert H. Goddard successfully demonstrates a liquid fuel rocket in flight of 184 feet in 22 seconds at Auburn, Mass.

Paul de Kruif writes *Microbe Hunters*, and Thomas H. Morgan *The Theory of the Gene*.

EDUCATION

University of California, Los Angeles (UCLA), is dedicated.

DEATH Charles W. Eliot, Harvard University president (1869–1909).

RELIGION

International Eucharistic Congress holds first U.S. meeting in Chicago suburb.

Henry Sloane Coffin becomes president of Union Theological Seminary.

Rev. Andrew J. Brennan becomes Catholic bishop of Richmond, Va.

Charles M. (Daddy) Grace, evangelist, founds House of Prayer for All People.

ART/MUSIC

National Broadcasting Co. broadcasts its first major orchestra, carries a Boston Symphony concert.

John A. Carpenter composes two ballets, *The Birthday of the Infanta* and *Skyscrapers*; Sigmund Romberg's operetta, *The Desert Song* is presented.

Georgia O'Keeffe completes the painting *Black Iris*; Lyonel Feininger, *Church of the Minorities*; William J. Glackens, *Promenade*; Kenneth H. Davis, *Day Dream*; Preston Dickinson, *Plums on a*

Mrs. Calvin Coolidge poses with a group of Girl Scouts and the magazine *The American Girl*. Mrs. Coolidge is First Lady 1923–1929. UPI/Corbis-Bettmann

Plate; Alexander Calder completes wire sculpture *Josephine Baker*.

Louis Armstrong (Satchmo) forms band.

SONGS (popular): "Baby Face," "Birth of the Blues," "Bye, Bye, Blackbird," "In a Little Spanish Town," "When Day Is Done," "Charmaine," "Tip Toe Through the Tulips," "One Alone," "Someone to Watch Over Me."

DEATHS Rida Young, librettist (*Naughty Marietta*); Carl E. Akeley, sculptor who made large habitat animal groups; Mary Cassatt, Impressionist painter.

LITERATURE/JOURNALISM

Book of the Month Club issues its first selection, *Lolly Willowes* by Sylvia Townsend Warner; Harold K. Guinzburg founds Literary Guild.

BOOKS *Elmer Gantry* by Sinclair Lewis, *The Story of Philosophy* by Will Durant, *The Sun Also Rises* by Ernest Hemingway, *Show Boat* by Edna Ferber, *Enough Rope* (poetry) by Dorothy Parker, *Dark of the Moon* by Sara Teasdale, *Soldier's Pay* by William Faulkner.

DEATH Edward W. Scripps, newspaper publisher.

ENTERTAINMENT

First talking moving picture, a series of short features, is shown at Warner Theater, New York City (August 5); Warner Bros.' *Don Juan* is first movie with sound accompaniment (August 26).

National Broadcasting Co. (NBC) goes on air with 24 radio stations (November 25), first major radio network.

Edgar Bergen begins act with a dummy, Charlie McCarthy, in vaudeville.

Civic Repertory Theatre, led by Eva Le Gallienne, stages its first production.

Cities Service radio concerts start 20-year run on the air.

PLAYS Gertrude Lawrence stars in *Oh, Kay*, with music by George Gershwin; Eddie Dowling in

Honeymoon Lane, Charles Ruggles in *Queen High*, Helen Morgan in *Americana*, Lee Tracy in *Broadway*, Mae West in *Sex*, the Marx Brothers in *Coconuts*.

MOVIES *Ben-Hur* with Ramon Novarro, *The Black Pirate* with Douglas Fairbanks, *Beau Geste* with Ronald Colman, *Don Juan* with John Barrymore, *The Scarlet Letter* with Lillian Gish, *The General* with Buster Keaton.

DEATH Harry Houdini, escape artist; Rudolph Valentino, silent screen idol.

SPORTS

Gertrude Ederle becomes first woman to swim English Channel (August 6), takes 14 hours, 34 minutes.

Eddie Rickenbacker, World War I ace, buys controlling interest in Indianapolis Speedway.

Charles C. Pyle promotes national tennis tour for Suzanne Lenglen and Vinnie Richards.

International Greyhound Racing Assn. is established.

Lillian Copeland becomes first woman to throw javelin farther than 110 feet (112 ft., $5\frac{1}{2}$ in.).

WINNERS *Auto racing* — Frank Lockhart, Indianapolis 500; *Baseball* — St. Louis Cardinals, World Series; *Boxing* — Gene Tunney, heavyweight; Pete Latzo, welterweight; Mickey Walker, middleweight; Sammy Mandell, lightweight; *Football* — Alabama, Rose Bowl; *Golf* — U.S., Walker Cup; Bobby Jones, U.S. Open; Walter Hagen, PGA; *Harness racing* — Guy McKinney, first Hambletonian; *Horse racing* — Bubbling Over, Kentucky Derby; Display, Preakness Stakes; Crusader, Belmont Stakes; *Tennis* — U.S., Davis Cup; Rene Lacoste, U.S. Open (men); Molla Mallory, U.S. Open (women).

MISCELLANEOUS

Hurricane near Miami causes 370 deaths, thousands of injuries.

DEATH Annie Oakley, frontierswoman.

1927

INTERNATIONAL

Naval conference is held in Geneva with no concrete results.

About 1,000 marines land in China to protect property in civil war.

NATIONAL

President Calvin Coolidge announces he will not run for president in 1928 (August 2).

Supreme Court invalidates Elks Hill lease of oil lands involved in Teapot Dome scandal.

Merger of three organizations establishes Brookings Institution in Washington, D.C.

Food & Drug Administration is created as the Food, Drug and Insecticide Administration; Congress creates Bureau of Customs and a Bureau of Prohibition in Treasury Department.

Drive-up mailboxes for motorists are first installed in Houston, Tex.

BUSINESS/INDUSTRY/INVENTIONS

Commercial transatlantic telephone service is established between New York and London.

John D. and Mack D. Rust invent mechanical cotton picker.

Buckminster Fuller builds first luxury house using Dymaxion principle, is designed to achieve maximum output with a minimum of material and energy.

TRANSPORTATION

Spectacular airplane flights: Charles A. Lindbergh flies solo across the Atlantic, lands in Paris 33 hours, 29 minutes, 30 seconds after leaving Long Island, N.Y. (May 20); Richard E. Byrd lands off French coast in transatlantic plane flight; Clarence D. Chamberlin flies nonstop from New York City to Germany; two Army Air Corps pilots (Lester J. Maitland and Albert F. Hegenberger) make first successful San Francisco–Honolulu flight (June 28).

Massachusetts becomes first state to impose compulsory auto insurance; requires $5,000/$10,000 liability coverage.

Lockheed Aircraft Corp. is founded; Clyde V. Cessna builds first cantilever plane; Juan Trippe founds Pan American Airways.

Production of Model T Ford discontinues after 15 millionth car.

Holland Tunnel under Hudson River at New York City opens.

International Peace Bridge across Niagara River at Buffalo opens.

American Express and airlines establish air express.

SCIENCE/MEDICINE

Albert A. Compton shares Nobel Prize in physics with Charles T. R. Wilson of England for discovery of the Compton effects, the scattering of X rays by matter.

Philip Drinker and Louis A. Shaw invent the iron lung (respirator).

EDUCATION

Second Maimonides College opens in New York City.

DEATH Elizabeth Harrison, a leader in kindergarten movement.

RELIGION

Henry S. Tucker becomes Episcopal bishop of Virginia.

ART/MUSIC

Metropolitan Opera presents *The King's Henchmen* by Deems Taylor and Edna St. Vincent Millay.

Lindbergh poses in front of his monoplane *Spirit of St. Louis,* in which he is the first to fly alone across the Atlantic (1927). CORBIS

Victor Talking Machine Co. introduces phonograph with automatic record changer.

Lawrence Welk and Duke Ellington form bands.

First regular series of opera broadcasts begins from Chicago Civic Opera; regular concert broadcasts from Boston and New York symphonies follow.

Paul Whiteman hires Bing Crosby, Al Rinker, and Harry Barris to form successful Rhythm Boys.

Gaston Lachaise completes the sculpture *Standing Woman*; Preston Dickinson completes the painting *Old Quarter, Quebec*; Glenn O. Coleman, *The Mirror*.

Detroit Institute of Arts, Philadelphia Museum of Art, and Fogg Art Museum in Cambridge, Mass., open.

George Antheil composes *Ballet Mecanique*.

SONGS (popular): "Ain't She Sweet," "Among My Souvenirs," "The Best Things in Life Are Free," "Chloe," "I'm Looking Over a Four-Leaf Clover,"

"My Blue Heaven" (Gene Austin's record sells 1 million copies), "The Song Is Ended," "Varsity Drag," "Ol' Man River," "Let a Smile Be Your Umbrella."

DEATH Isadora Duncan, a founder of modern expressive dancing.

LITERATURE/JOURNALISM

Random House and Doubleday Doran & Co., publishers, are founded.

Roy W. Howard purchases *New York Telegram*.

BOOKS *Death Comes for the Archbishop* by Willa Cather, *The Bridge of San Luis Rey* by Thornton Wilder, *Black April* by Julia Peterkin, *Tristram* (poetry) by Edwin Arlington Robinson, *Oil* by Upton Sinclair, *Copper Sun* (poetry) by Countee Cullen.

ENTERTAINMENT

Television is demonstrated for first time (April 7).

Federal Radio Commission is created.

Columbia Broadcasting System (CBS) is organized with William S. Paley president.

Academy of Motion Picture Arts and Sciences is founded; awards first Oscars: best actor, Emil Jannings (*The Way of All Flesh*); best actress, Janet Gaynor (*Seventh Heaven*); best picture, *Wings*.

Ziegfeld Theater in New York City opens.

PLAYS Fred and Adele Astaire star in Gershwin's *Funny Face*, Charles Winninger in *Show Boat*, Ethel Waters in *Africana*, Helen Hayes in *Coquette*, Marx Brothers in *Animal Crackers*, Barbara Stanwyck in *Burlesque*, Ruth Gordon in *Saturday's Children*, Ann Harding in *The Trial of Mary Dugan*.

MOVIES *The King of Kings* with H. B. Warner, *Seventh Heaven* with Janet Gaynor, *The Jazz Singer* with Al Jolson, *Wings* with Gary Cooper, *Dracula* with Bela Lugosi, *The Divine Woman* with Greta Garbo, *It* with Clara Bow, *My Best Girl* with Mary Pickford.

SPORTS

Babe Ruth of New York Yankees hits 60th home run to set new season major-league record; Ty Cobb of Detroit Tigers gets 4,000th base hit.

Ben Johnson, president of American (baseball) League for 26 years, resigns because of poor health; Ernest S. Barnard succeeds him.

Harlem Globetrotters play their first basketball game.

Sabin Carr becomes first to pole vault 14 feet.

Major H. O. Seagrave drives his car at 203.79 miles per hour at Daytona Beach, Fla.

First Golden Gloves boxing matches are held.

WINNERS *Auto racing*—George Souders, Indianapolis 500; *Baseball*—New York Yankees, World Series; *Boxing*—Gene Tunney, heavyweight; Tommy Loughran, light heavyweight; Joe Dundee, welterweight; *Football*—Alabama–Stanford (tie), Rose Bowl; *Golf*—U.S., Ryder Cup; Tommy Armour, U.S. Open; Walter Hagen, PGA; *Hockey*—Ottawa, Stanley Cup; *Horse racing*—Whiskery, Kentucky Derby; Bostonian, Preakness Stakes; Chance Shot, Belmont Stakes; *Rowing*—Yale, first Blackwell Cup race; *Tennis*—France, Davis Cup; Rene Lacoste, U.S. Open (men); Helen Wills, U.S. Open (women).

MISCELLANEOUS

Tornadoes in Arkansas and Poplar Bluffs, Mo., kill 92; in St. Louis 90; floods in lower Mississippi Valley bring death to 313, $300 million in damage.

Nicola Sacco and Bartolomeo Vanzetti are executed for payroll holdup slaying of two (1920).

Submarine S-4 sinks after colliding with Coast Guard destroyer off Provincetown, Mass., 40 men are lost.

INTERNATIONAL

Fourteen nations sign Kellogg-Briand Treaty to outlaw war (August 27); eventually 62 nations sign; the Senate later ratifies the pact.

NATIONAL

Herbert Hoover, Republican, is elected president, receives 21,392,190 popular and 444 electoral votes to 15,016,443 popular and 87 electoral votes for Democrat Alfred E. Smith.

Flood Control Act is signed (May 15), provides

$325 million for a 10-year flood control program in the Mississippi Valley.

Harry F. Sinclair is acquitted of charges involving his role in Teapot Dome scandal.

Airmail postage rate is set at 5 cents per ounce.

The "Motogram" flashes election returns on the New York Times building for the first time (November 6).

Franklin D. Roosevelt is elected governor of New York.

1928

Airmail flight from San Francisco to New York. Airmail postage rate is 5 cents per ounce in 1928. CORBIS-BETTMANN

Bryce Canyon (Utah) National Park is established.

DEATH George W. Goethals, directed construction of Panama Canal.

BUSINESS/INDUSTRY/INVENTIONS

Transamerica Corp. is founded.

DuPont Co. in Wilmington, Del., establishes new research laboratory.

Milan Building in San Antonio, Tex., first air-conditioned building in U.S. opens.

Vannevar Bush develops differential analyzer, an early analog computer.

Commercial Cable Co. and Postal Telegraph merge into International Telephone & Telegraph Co.

First training school for fashion models, L'Ecole des Mannequins, opens in Chicago.

Marriott hotel and restaurant chain is founded.

Sears Roebuck opens its first retail store.

DEATH Sara A. M. Conroy, first woman named to national labor post (Secretary-Treasurer, United Textile Workers).

TRANSPORTATION

Merchant Marine Act provides $250 million loan program for ship rebuilding, construction.

Three bridges open: Arthur Kill Cantilever Bridge connects Staten Island and New Jersey; James River Bridge in Virginia, world's longest highway bridge; and Goethals Bridge connects Staten Island and Elizabeth, N.J.

Yellow Bus Line begins transcontinental bus service; trip takes 5 days, 14 hours.

Chrysler Corp. acquires Dodge Brothers firm.

First autogiro (helicopter) flies at Pitcairn Field, Willow Grove, Pa.

Graf Zeppelin flies from Germany to U.S. with 20 passengers.

Amelia Earhart, a passenger, becomes first woman to fly over Atlantic Ocean.

Newark Airport is completed.

SCIENCE/MEDICINE

Dr. George N. Papanicolau develops pap smear test for early detection of cervical cancer.

Dr. Willis R. Whitney constructs diathermy machine for medical use.

Iron lung is used for treatment of polio.

Dr. William H. Park of New York City Health Department develops tuberculosis vaccine.

Mead, Johnson & Co. markets vitamin D.

Clifford W. Beers founds American Foundation for Mental Hygiene.

DEATH Dr. Robert Abbe, first American to use radium in cancer treatment.

EDUCATION

Yeshiva College in New York City is chartered.

RELIGION

Samuel F. Cadman, president, Federal Council of Churches of Christ, becomes first U.S. radio minister.

ART/MUSIC

Arturo Toscanini conducts New York Philharmonic Symphony Orchestra; merger of the Symphony Society and Philharmonic forms this ensemble.

Boston Symphony performs Walter Piston's Symphonic Piece for first time in U.S.

Doris Humphrey and Charles Weidman form ballet company.

Sigmund Romberg's operetta *The New Moon* and Rudolf Friml's *The Three Musketeers* open.

Rudy Vallee forms band.

Thomas Hart Benton completes the painting *Baptism in Kansas.*

SONGS (popular): "Coquette," "I Can't Give You Anything But Love," "I'll Get By," "Lover Come Back to Me," "Marie," "Sonny Boy," "Sweet Sue,"

"Button Up Your Overcoat," "Sweethearts on Parade," "There's a Rainbow 'Round My Shoulder," "Jeanine, I Dream of Lilac Time."

DEATHS Nora Bayes, singer and actress who was co-author of "Shine On, Harvest Moon;" Henry Gilbert, first composer to rely primarily on American folk music.

LITERATURE/JOURNALISM

President Coolidge dedicates National Press Club in Washington.

BOOKS *Scarlet Sister Mary* by Julia Peterkin, *John Brown's Body* (poetry) by Stephen Vincent Benét, *Coming of Age in Samoa* by Margaret Mead, *Cawdor* (poetry) by Robinson Jeffers, *A Lantern in Her Hand* by Bess Streeter Aldrich, *Good Morning, America* (poetry) by Carl Sandburg.

DEATHS Clarence W. Barron, owner of Dow Jones, founder of *Barron's Weekly*; Edwin T. Meredith, founder and publisher, *Better Homes and Gardens.*

Amelia Earhart, the first woman pilot to cross the Atlantic. In 1928 she is a passenger, and in 1932 she will set her own transatlantic record. SCHLESINGER LIBRARY, RADCLIFFE COLLEGE

1929

ENTERTAINMENT

Walt Disney releases first cartoon, "Plane Crazy."

First radio broadcast of *Amos 'n Andy* show is aired, is broadcast nationwide in 1929.

March of Time and *Voice of Firestone* radio progams begin.

PLAYS Lynn Fontanne stars in *Strange Interlude*, Lee Tracy in *The Front Page*, Ethel Barrymore in *Kingdom of God*, Eddie Cantor in *Whoopee*, Paul Robeson in *Porgy*, Bert Lahr in *Hold Everything*, Alfred Lunt in *Marco Millions*, Marilyn Miller in *Rosalie*, Will Rogers in *Three Cheers*.

MOVIES *The Actress* with Norma Shearer, *My Man* with Fanny Brice, *Our Dancing Daughters* with Joan Crawford, *The Singing Fool* with Al Jolson.

DEATH Eddy Foy, musical entertainer.

SPORTS

Winter Olympics are held in St. Moritz, Switzerland; U.S. wins two gold medals; Summer Games are held in Amsterdam; U.S. wins 22 gold medals, Peter Desjardins scores two perfect 10s in springboard diving; women's track events are included for first time.

First organized men's field hockey match is played at Germantown (Pa.) Cricket Club.

U.S. Volleyball Assn. is formed.

WINNERS *Auto racing*—Louis Meyer, Indianapolis 500; *Baseball*—New York Yankees, World Series; *Boxing*—Gene Tunney, heavyweight; Andre Routis, featherweight; *Football*—Stanford, Rose Bowl; *Golf*—U.S., Walker Cup; John Farrell, U.S. Open; Leo Diegel, PGA; *Hockey*—New York Rangers, Stanley Cup; *Horse racing*—Reigh Count, Kentucky Derby; Victorian, Preakness Stakes; Vito, Belmont Stakes; *Lawn bowling*—David White, first U.S. singles; *Skeet shooting*—Yale, first college tournament; *Tennis*—France, Davis Cup; Henri Cochet, U.S. Open (men), Helen Wills, U.S. Open (women); *Wrestling*—Ed "Strangler" Lewis, heavyweight.

MISCELLANEOUS

St. Francis Dam at Saugus, Calif., bursts, floods cause 950 deaths; hurricane moves from Caribbean islands to Florida, causes 4,000 deaths, 1,800 in Florida.

Two-day frog-jumping contest is held for first time in Calaveras County, Calif.

Jean Lassier goes over Niagara Falls in a rubber ball.

Detroit Zoological Park opens.

INTERNATIONAL

German reparations are reduced to $8.04 billion, payable over $58\frac{1}{2}$ years at $5\frac{1}{2}$% interest; Bank for International Settlements is created.

Canada and U.S. sign convention (agreement) to preserve Niagara Falls (January 2).

NATIONAL

Frank B. Kellogg, Secretary of State (1925–1929), awarded 1929 Nobel Peace Prize for working out the Kellogg-Briand Peace Pact.

Supreme Court upholds presidential pocket veto.

Fire in White House destroys a portion of the executive offices; official papers are saved.

Albert B. Fall, former Interior Secretary, is found guilty of accepting a bribe to grant valuable oil leases in Teapot Dome scandal; is sentenced to a year in prison.

New smaller dollar bills are issued.

Grand Teton (Wyo.) National Park is established.

DEATHS Wyatt Earp, frontier lawman; Francis E. Warren, Wyoming senator known as the father of reclamation.

"$100 will buy this car. Must have cash. Lost all on the stock market." Following the stock-market crash of 1929, a dapper young man contemplates his sudden change in circumstances. UPI/Corbis-Bettmann

BUSINESS/INDUSTRY/INVENTIONS

Stock market begins crash (October 29) when 13 million shares are traded, continues for several days; stocks lose $30 million in market value by mid-November; touches off worst depression in U.S. history.

Federal Farm Board is created to promote marketing of farm commodities through cooperatives and stabilization boards (June 15).

Since 1920, installment buying quintuples to $6 billion a year, accounts for 90% of all piano, sewing and washing machine sales; 80% of vacuum, radio, and refrigerator sales; 70% of furniture sales, 60% of auto sales.

Republic Steel Co., R. G. LeTourneau Inc. (heavy

equipment maker), and Levitt & Sons, Inc. (home builder) are founded.

Benton & Bowles advertising agency is created.

Business Week magazine begins publication.

First Howard Johnson restaurant opens in Massachusetts.

Indiana enacts tax on chain stores.

Frances Perkins is named New York State Industrial Commissioner.

Violence occurs when police raid a union strike meeting in Gastonia, N.C.; the Gastonia police chief and seven strikers are killed.

Ford Motor Co. raises daily pay from $6 to $7.

DEATHS Herman Hollerith, inventor of punch-card tabulating system; Minor C. Keith, founder of United Fruit Co.

TRANSPORTATION

Grumman Aircraft Engineering Corp. and Bendix Aviation Corp. are founded.

Several bridges are completed: Brockport Bridge in Paducah (Ky.); Lake Champlain Bridge, connecting Vermont and New York; Ambassador Bridge at Detroit; Mt. Hope Bridge in Rhode Island.

Richard E. Byrd and Bernt Balchen become first to fly over the South Pole (October 28).

SCIENCE/MEDICINE

Baylor University Hospital inaugurates group hospitalization insurance plan.

Journal of Allergy is published.

Edwin G. Boring writes *History of Experimental Psychology*, major contribution to the field.

DEATHS Joseph Goldberger, physician whose work on pellagra led to its virtual elimination; Robert Ridgway, U.S. National Museum bird curator (1880–1929).

EDUCATION

Morehouse and Spelman colleges merge with Atlanta University to form Atlanta University System.

Robert M. Hutchins becomes president of University of Chicago, the youngest (30) major university president.

DEATHS Charles H. Cooley, founder of U.S. sociology; Willam F. Warren, cofounder and first president, Boston University (1873–1903).

RELIGION

DEATH Charles H. Brent, chief of World War I chaplains in Europe.

ART/MUSIC

New York Philharmonic inaugurates regular Sunday broadcasts.

Edgard Varèse founds the Symphony Orchestra in New York City.

Grant Wood completes the painting *Woman with Plants*; Charles Sheeler, *Upper Deck*; Arthur G. Dove, *Fog Horns*.

Baltimore Museum of Art opens.

SONGS (popular): "Ain't Misbehavin'," "Am I Blue?," "Honeysuckle Rose," "Mean to Me," "Pagan Love Song," "Singin' in the Rain," "With a Song in My Heart," "Love, Your Magic Spell Is Everywhere," "More Than You Know," "Basin Street Blues," "Stardust."

DEATH Robert Henri, artist and teacher who influenced American art.

LITERATURE/JOURNALISM

H. V. Kaltenborn becomes chief news commentator for Columbia Broadcasting System.

Ellery Queen, a pseudonym of Frederic Dannay and Manfred B. Lee, begins to write with *The Roman Hat Mystery*.

The Embassy, a newsreel theater, opens in New York City.

BOOKS *Magnificent Obsession* by Lloyd C. Douglas, *A Farewell to Arms* by Ernest Hemingway, *Laughing Boy* by Oliver La Farge, *Selected Poems* by Conrad Aiken, *Dodsworth* by Sinclair Lewis, *Look Homeward, Angel* by Thomas Wolfe, *The Sound and the Fury* by William Faulkner, *Blue Juniata* by Malcolm Cowley, *Rome Haul* by Walter D. Edmonds.

ENTERTAINMENT

Bell Telephone Laboratories demonstrate color television.

Alexander Woollcott hosts his weekly *Town Crier* radio show; *The Goldbergs* radio show airs.

Gypsy Rose Lee begins her burlesque career.

PLAYS Leslie Howard stars in *Berkeley Square*, Jack Haley in *Follow Through*, Humphrey Bogart in *It's a Wise Child*, Helen Morgan in *Sweet Adeline*, Marc Connelly's *The Green Pastures* is produced.

MOVIES *Disraeli* with George Arliss, *Sunny Side Up* with Janet Gaynor, *The Virginian* with Gary Cooper, *The Vagabond Lover* with Rudy Vallee, *The Iron Mask* with Douglas Fairbanks.

SPORTS

Babe Ruth hits 500th home run.

Ernie Nevers of Chicago Cardinals rushes for record six touchdowns, adds four extra points.

Ely Culbertson publishes magazine, *Bridge World.*

Dr. William E. Code invents codeball, combination of golf and soccer.

WINNERS *Auto racing* — Ray Keech, Indianapolis 500; *Baseball* — Philadelphia Athletics, World Series; *Boxing* — Chris (Battling) Battalino, featherweight; *Football* — Georgia Tech, Rose Bowl; Green Bay, first NFL title; *Golf* — Great Britain, Ryder Cup; Bobby Jones, U.S. Open; Leo Diegel, PGA; *Hockey* — Boston, Stanley Cup; *Horse racing* — Clyde Van Dusen, Kentucky Derby; Dr. Freeland, Preakness Stakes; Blue Larkspur, Belmont Stakes; *Tennis* — France, Davis Cup; Bill Tilden, U.S. Open (men); Helen Wills, U.S. Open (women); *Wrestling* — Gus Sonnenberg, heavyweight.

DEATH Tex Rickard, boxing promoter.

MISCELLANEOUS

St. Valentine's Day massacre occurs in Chicago when a rival gang executes seven gangsters in a garage.

Poisonous fumes from burning X-ray film kill 125 in Crile Hospital, Cleveland, Ohio.

Chrysler Building in New York City, then world's tallest, is completed.

The Seeing Eye, for training guide dogs, is incorporated.

Mine disaster at Mather, Pa., kills 195.

1930

INTERNATIONAL

London Naval Conference results in agreement among U.S., Great Britain, and Japan on cruiser limitations, ratios for all vessels (April 22); Senate ratifies (July 21).

NATIONAL

President Herbert Hoover asks for, receives $116 million for emergency construction projects to aid the unemployed, $45 million for drought relief; unemployment reaches 4.5 million.

Former President Taft resigns as Supreme Court Chief Justice (February 3) because of poor health; Charles Evans Hughes succeeds him; Taft dies March 8.

Fifteenth census reports population at 123,202,624.

Annual immigration to U.S. totals 241,700; it drops to under 100,000 until after World War II.

National debt is reduced to $16.1 billion.

Veterans Administration is created (July 3); Bureau of Prisons is established.

Construction of Boulder (later Hoover) Dam begins.

USS *Constitution* ("Old Ironsides"), reconditioned by public subscription, is relaunched.

Carlsbad (N. Mex.) National Park is established.

Streamlined submarine *Nautilus* is commissioned.

DEATHS Irving Hale, founder of Veterans of

Unemployed people try to sell apples for 5 cents during the Great Depression. CORBIS-BETTMANN

Foreign Wars (VFW); Tasker H. Bliss, World War I Army chief of staff; Stephen T. Maher, first National Park Service director.

BUSINESS/INDUSTRY/INVENTIONS

Thomas Midgley of General Motors announces development of refrigerant Freon.

Butler Consolidated Coal Co., Wildwood (Pa.) plant, opens with 100% mechanical operation.

Use of reflector seismograph results in discovery of Edwards (Okla.) oil field; East Texas oil field is tapped for first time.

Bank of the United States (New York City) closes; about 1,300 banks close between late 1929 and summer of 1930; 827 more close in September and October.

David Sarnoff begins 17 years as president of RCA.

DEATHS Dorr E. Felt, inventor of first wholly key-operated calculator; Henry E. House, inventor of button-holing machine; Henry C. Folger, oil company executive, endower of Shakespeare library; Daniel Guggenheim, industrialist who created philanthropic and aeronautics foundations; Elmer A. Sperry, inventor of gyrocompass.

TRANSPORTATION

Maritime Administration is established.

Braniff Airlines and Greyhound Corp. are established.

Thomas Edison runs first electric passenger train experimentally from Hoboken to Montclair, N.J.

Motor Car Transport Co. is founded; later becomes Commercial Carriers Inc.

Jimmy Doolittle, military aviator, makes first successful test of a blind, instrument-controlled landing.

Passenger-car registrations total 26,545,281.

First airline stewardess, Ellen Church, flies on United Airlines from San Francisco to Cheyenne, Wyo.

Detroit-Windsor Tunnel under the Detroit River opens.

Mid-Hudson Bridge at Poughkeepsie, N.Y., and Longview (Wash.) Bridge over Columbia River open.

SCIENCE/MEDICINE

Karl Landsteiner is awarded Nobel Prize for physiology/medicine for work on blood groups.

DuPont Co. produces sulfanilamide.

Clyde W. Tombaugh of Lowell Observatory (Flagstaff, Ariz.) discovers the planet Pluto (February 18); astronomers make first photograph of the planet.

Woods Hole (Mass.) Oceanographical Institute is established.

Ernest O. Lawrence constructs first cyclotron.

Adler Planetarium in Chicago opens.

Radar is first used to detect airplanes.

Drs. Fred Allison and Edgar J. Murphy discover element 87, francium.

Mental Hygiene International Congress meets in Washington, D.C., 3,000 from 53 countries attending.

DEATH Samuel Theobald, ophthalmologist who introduced use of boric acid for eye diseases.

EDUCATION

Abraham Flexner, organizer of Institute for Advanced Study at Princeton University, is named its first director.

Robert G. Sproul becomes president of University of California; Karl T. Compton of MIT.

DEATH Arthur T. Hadley, president of Yale University (1899–1921).

RELIGION

Merger of Buffalo Lutheran and Iowa and Ohio Evangelical Lutheran synods forms American Lutheran church; *International Lutheran Hour* broadcasts on 36-station radio network, Dr. Walter A. Maier is speaker.

Sarah E. Dickson of Milwaukee becomes first woman Presbyterian elder.

Jesse E. Bader begins 33 years as president and general secretary of World Convention of Churches of Christ (Disciples).

1930

An American family tunes in to a radio program during the 1930s. BROWN BROTHERS

Rev. Fulton Sheen preaches regularly on NBC radio's *Catholic Hour*.

Rev. Henry K. Sherrill becomes Episcopal bishop of Massachusetts.

ART/MUSIC

Sculptor Gutzon Borglum unveils the first of four 60-foot-high heads of presidents (Washington) carved out of rock in Mt. Rushmore in Black Hills (S. Dak.).

Arthur Fiedler founds Boston Pops Orchestra.

Walter Piston composes Suite for Orchestra; Aaron Copland, Piano Variations.

Grant Wood completes his most famous painting, *American Gothic*; George B. Luks, *Mrs. Gamely*; Sculptor George G. Bernard finishes the marble *Refugee*.

SONGS (popular): "Beyond the Blue Horizon," "Body and Soul," "Little White Lies," "Three Little Words," "I've Got Rhythm," "Old Rockin'

Chair," "Ten Cents a Dance," "Georgia on My Mind," "Bidin' My Time," "On the Sunny Side of the Street."

Ringling Museum of Art in Sarasota, Fla., opens.

DEATH Preston Dickinson, modern art pioneer.

LITERATURE/JOURNALISM

Sinclair Lewis becomes first U.S. writer to win Nobel Prize for literature for his novels.

Henry B. Luce founds *Fortune*, monthly magazine.

Lowell Thomas newscasts for CBS, serves more than 40 years.

Chic Young draws comic strip "Blondie."

BOOKS *Cimarron* by Edna Ferber, *Years of Grace* by Margaret Ayer Barnes, *Collected Poems* by Robert Frost, *The Deepening Stream* by Dorothy Canfield Fisher, *Arundel* by Kenneth Roberts, *The Maltese Falcon* by Dashiell Hammett, *N by E* by Rockwell Kent, *New Found Land* (poetry) by Archibald MacLeish, *The Woman of Andros* by Thornton Wilder, *Flowering Judas* by Katherine Anne Porter.

DEATHS Clare A. Briggs, cartoonist ("When a Feller Needs a Friend"); Edward Stratemeyer, author (*Rover Boys*, *Tom Swift*, *Bobbsey Twins*) under various pseudonyms; George P. Putnam, founder and head of family publishing firm (1872–1930).

ENTERTAINMENT

Americans own 13 million radio sets.

Arthur Godfrey announces on radio in Washington; Walter Winchell begins his radio gossip program.

PLAYS Alfred Lunt and Lynn Fontanne star in *Elizabeth the Queen*, Ethel Merman in *Girl Crazy* by the Gershwins, Ethel Waters in *Blackbirds*, Bert Lahr in *Flying High*, Spencer Tracy in *The Last Mile*.

MOVIES *Abraham Lincoln* with Walter Huston, *The Green Goddess* with George Arliss, *Min and Bill* with Marie Dressler and Wallace Beery, *Whoopee* with Eddie Cantor, *Morocco* with Marlene Dietrich and Gary Cooper, *Hell's Angels*, with Jean Harlow, *Little Caesar* with Edward G. Robinson, *Cimarron* with Richard Dix, *All Quiet on the Western Front* with Lew Ayres. Donald Duck makes his screen debut.

New radio programs include *Rin Tin Tin*, *Ripley's Believe It or Not*, *Death Valley Days*, and Kate Smith's show.

DEATH Lon Chaney, screen actor ("the man of a thousand faces").

SPORTS

Bobby Jones wins U.S. amateur golf tournament, becomes first (and only) golfer to win U.S. and British Opens, U.S. and British amateur titles in same year; is awarded first Sullivan Medal as year's outstanding amateur athlete.

Stella Walsh becomes first woman to run 100 yards in less than 11 seconds (10.8 sec.)

WINNERS *Auto racing* — Billy Arnold, Indianapolis 500; *Baseball* — Philadelphia Athletics, World Series; *Boxing* — Max Schmeling, heavyweight; Maxie Rosenbloom, light heavyweight; Tony Canzoneri, lightweight; Baby Arizmendi, featherweight; *Football* — Southern California, Rose Bowl; Green Bay, NFL title; *Golf* — U.S., Walker Cup; Bobby Jones, U.S. Open; Tommy Armour, PGA; *Harness racing* — Hanover's Bertha, Hambletonian; *Hockey* — Montreal, Stanley Cup; *Horse racing* — Gallant Fox wins Kentucky Derby, Preakness Stakes, and Belmont Stakes to become second Triple Crown winner; *Marathon* — Clarence De Mar, Boston Marathon for seventh time; *Tennis* — France, Davis Cup; John Doeg, U.S. Open (men); Betty Nuttall, U.S. Open (women); *Yachting* — U.S. boat *Enterprise* retains America's Cup.

MISCELLANEOUS

Fire in Ohio Penitentiary in Columbus kills 320.

Judge Joseph F. Crater of New York State Supreme Court vanishes mysteriously; no trace of him is ever found.

Empire State Building, then the world's tallest, is completed.

In & Outdoor Games Co. of Chicago manufactures pinball game machine.

1931

INTERNATIONAL

President Herbert Hoover calls for a one-year moratorium on interallied debts and reparations because of universal economic crisis (June 20); is generally accepted.

NATIONAL

Congress designates "Star-Spangled Banner" as the national anthem (March 3).

President Hoover sends Congress the Wickersham Report on prohibition; calls for revisions of law but opposes repeal of Eighteenth Amendment; Supreme Court upholds constitutionality of the amendment.

Overriding a presidential veto, Congress authorizes improvement of veterans' bonus benefits.

Smoot-Hawley Tariff raises rates on agricultural raw materials from 38% to 49%, other commodities from 31% to 34%, gives special protection to sugar and textiles.

Jane Addams of Chicago's Hull House and Dr. Nicholas Murray Butler, president of Columbia University, share Nobel Peace Prize for their work toward international peace.

Civil government is established in the Virgin Islands.

Gangster Al Capone is found guilty of tax evasion, is sentenced to 11 years.

Representative Maria Norton of New Jersey becomes first woman chair of a congressional committee.

The keel is laid for first aircraft carrier, the *Ranger.*

BUSINESS/INDUSTRY/INVENTIONS

Vladimir K. Zworykin, RCA research head, invents the iconoscope, which makes all-electronic television possible.

DuPont Co. manufactures synthetic rubber (neoprene); fiberglass is introduced.

Wilcox's Pier Restaurant, West Haven, Conn., installs a "magic eye" (photoelectric cell) to operate a door.

Robert Van de Graaff builds first electrostatic generator.

Caterpillar Tractor Co. produces first diesel-powered tractor.

Schick, Inc. produces electric dry shavers.

Sears, Roebuck founds All-State Insurance Co.

ATT begins commercial teletype service.

Henry J. Kaiser organizes group of contractors, the Six Companies, to build Boulder (Hoover) Dam; it is completed in 1936, two years ahead of schedule.

Unemployment is estimated between 4 and 5 million.

DEATHS Thomas A. Edison, inventor; Edward G. Acheson, discoverer of silicon carbide (carborundum); Isaac Gimbel, department store cofounder; George Eastman, camera and film developer.

TRANSPORTATION

Wiley Post and Harold Getty complete round-the-world flight in 8 days, 16 hours; Clyde Pangborn and Hugh Herndon Jr. complete first nonstop flight across Pacific Ocean.

First transcontinental helicopter flight begins May 14 in Philadelphia; is completed May 28 in San Diego.

Piper Cub airplane is introduced.

Four bridges are completed: George Washington over Hudson River at New York City; St. John's at Portland, Ore.; Maysville (Ky.) over the Ohio River; and Bayonne, N.J., over the Kill van Kull.

SCIENCE/MEDICINE

Harold C. Urey announces discovery of heavy

hydrogen, a hydrogen atom of double weight (deuterium) (December 29).

Langley (Va.) Research Center of National Advisory Committee for Aeronautics places full-scale wind tunnel in operation.

Elk City, Okla., dedicates first community hospital (August 13).

DEATHS George A. Dorsey, anthropologist and author (*Why We Behave Like Human Beings*); Albert A. Michelson, first American to win Nobel Prize in physics.

EDUCATION

Municipal College for Negroes opens as part of University of Louisville (Ky.).

Pitrim A. Sorokin begins 25 years as first chair of Harvard University sociology department.

DEATHS Melvil Dewey, librarian who originated decimal classification system; John W. Burgess, father of U.S. political science.

RELIGION

Merger of Christian and Congregational denominations forms General Council of Congregational and Christian Churches.

Park Ave. Baptist Church (New York City) becomes the interdenominational Riverside Church; Harry Emerson Fosdick is pastor.

Jehovah's Witnesses becomes new name of Adventist sect known as Russellites or International Bible Students.

As the Depression continues, people gather outside a bank where their money has been lost. CORBIS-BETTMANN

1931

The Marx Brothers—Chico, Zeppo, Groucho, and Harpo—take the country by storm during the early 1930s with their hilarious films. PHOTOFEST

First Baha'i house of worship opens in Wilmette, Ill.

ART/MUSIC

Metropolitan Opera presents Deems Taylor's opera, *Peter Ibbetson*; broadcasts full performance of *Hansel and Gretel* for the first time.

Ferde Grofé completes the *Grand Canyon* Suite; Robert Russell Bennett the symphony *Abraham Lincoln*.

Ruth St. Denis founds the Society of Spiritual Arts, which attempts to demonstrate the potential of dance as a form of worship.

Lily Pons joins Metropolitan Opera Co.

Walt Kuhn completes the painting *Blue Clown*; Georgia O'Keeffe, *Cow's Skull: Red, White and Blue*; Alexander Calder completes the mobile *Dancing Torpedo Shape*.

Whitney Museum of American Art (New York City) and Joslyn Art Museum (Omaha, Nebr.) open.

SONGS (popular): "All of Me," "Dancing in the Dark," "Goodnight, Sweetheart," "I Surrender, Dear," "Lazy River," "Love Letters in the Sand," "Minnie the Moocher," "Mood Indigo," "Wrap Your Troubles in Dreams," "Got a Date with an Angel."

DEATHS Leon ("Bix") Beiderbecke, jazz cornetist; Buddy Bolden, legendary creator of New Orleans jazz; Daniel C. French, sculptor (seated Lincoln in Memorial); Henry O. Tanner, painter of biblical scenes.

LITERATURE/ JOURNALISM

Roy Howard buys *New York World*, merges it with *Telegram* to form *World-Telegram*.

Walter Lippmann writes syndicated newspaper column, "Today and Tomorrow"; Emily Post writes her column on etiquette.

Chester Gould draws comic strip "Dick Tracy" in *Chicago Tribune*.

Story, a monthly magazine, begins publication.

BOOKS *The Good Earth* by Pearl Buck, *Shadows on the Rock* by Willa Cather, *Sanctuary* by William Faulkner, *John Henry* by Roark Bradford, *Back Street* by Fannie Hurst, *Guys and Dolls* by Damon Runyon, *Grand Hotel* by Vicki Baum.

DEATHS William L. McLean, publisher, *Philadelphia Bulletin* (1895–1931); Edward Channing, historian; Vachel Lindsay, poet.

ENTERTAINMENT

PLAYS Fred and Adele Astaire star in *The Band Wagon*, Katharine Cornell in *The Barretts of Wimpole Street*, Paul Muni in *Counsellor-at-Law*, Paul Robeson in *The Hairy Ape*, Alfred Lunt and Lynn Fontanne in *Reunion in Vienna*, Ethel Waters in *Rhapsody in Black*.

Easy Aces radio program debuts; Emmett Kelly begins his career as the clown Weary Willie.

MOVIES *City Lights* with Charles Chaplin, *The Champ* with Wallace Beery, *The Sin of Madelon Claudet* with Helen Hayes, *Dr. Jekyll and Mr. Hyde* with Fredric March, *Mata Hari* with Greta Garbo, *Street Scene* with Sylvia Sidney, *Dracula* with Bela Lugosi, *Monkey Business* with the Marx Brothers.

DEATH David Belasco, playwright and producer.

SPORTS

Will Harridge, American (baseball) League secretary-treasurer since 1911, is named president.

Ely Culbertson and partner win bridge battle of century, defeat Sidney Lenz and partner, 77 rubbers to 73.

WINNERS *Auto racing* — Louis Schneider, Indianapolis 500; *Baseball* — St. Louis Cardinals, World Series; *Boxing* — Max Schmeling, heavyweight; Lou Brouillard, welterweight; *Football* — Alabama, Rose Bowl; Green Bay, NFL title; *Golf* — U.S., Ryder Cup; William Burke, U.S. Open; Tom Creavy, PGA; *Gymnastics* — Roberta C. Rauck, first national woman's all-round title; *Hockey* — Montreal, Stanley Cup; *Horse racing* — Twenty Grand, Kentucky Derby and Belmont Stakes; Mate, Preakness Stakes; *Table tennis* — Marcus Schussheim, first national title; *Tennis* — Ellsworth Vines, U.S. Open (men); Helen Wills (Moody), U.S. Open (women).

DEATHS Knute Rockne, Notre Dame football coach, in plane crash; Charles A. Comiskey, baseball player and owner, Chicago White Sox (1900–1931); first two presidents of baseball's American League, Byron (Ban) Johnson and Ernest S. Barnard.

MISCELLANEOUS

Original mosque of Temple of Islam (Black Muslims) opens in Detroit; Elijah Muhammad becomes movement's leader.

1932

INTERNATIONAL

Scheduled Lausanne Conference to discuss remaining German reparations is cancelled.

NATIONAL

Depression reaches new low with monthly wages 60% below 1929 average; more than 5,000 banks close; business losses are reported at $6 billion; average monthly unemployment is 12 million.

Reconstruction Finance Corp. (RFC) is created (January 22) to provide emergency financing for various businesses; Charles G. Dawes is director; RFC is liberalized (July 21) to include agriculture; Federal Home Loan Bank Board is established (July 22).

Franklin D. Roosevelt, Democrat, is elected president by 22,809,638 popular and 472 electoral votes to President Herbert Hoover's 15,758,901 popular and 59 electoral votes; Roosevelt breaks tradition by appearing in person to accept Democratic nomination; the term *New Deal* is first used in that speech. He said, "I pledge you, I pledge myself, to a New Deal for the American people."

Twentieth Amendment is submitted to states for ratification; provides for Congress to convene January 3, presidential inauguration January 20; both traditionally in March.

About 1,000 veterans arrive in Washington (May 29) to urge cash payment of their bonus; "bonus army" grows to 17,000; a bonus bill fails to pass, but money is provided to pay vets for trip home; 2,000 elect to stay until forced out by police and army (July 28).

Wisconsin enacts first unemployment insurance act.

Tomb of the Unknown Soldier in Arlington National Cemetery (Va.) is dedicated.

Cost of first-class postage rises to 3 cents an ounce.

Mrs. Hattie W. Caraway of Arkansas becomes first woman elected to U.S. Senate.

Cornerstone is laid for new Supreme Court building.

DEATHS Robert S. Brookings, a founder and benefactor, Brookings Institution; Enoch H. Crowder, World War I Selective Service director; Charles E. Ashburner, first U.S. city manager.

BUSINESS/INDUSTRY/INVENTIONS

Norris–LaGuardia Act prohibits use of injunctions in labor disputes.

1932

David Dubinsky begins 34 years as president of International Ladies Garment Workers Union.

Revlon Inc., cosmetics and fragrance firm, is founded.

William N. Goodwin Jr. patents camera exposure meter.

DEATHS King C. Gillette, safety razor inventor; John J. Carty, engineer who helped develop telephone switchboard; Paul M. Warburg, banker who helped plan Federal Reserve; Julius Rosenwald, Sears executive and philanthropist; Reginald A. Fessenden, inventor of high-frequency alternator; William Wrigley Jr., chewing-gum manufacturer.

TRANSPORTATION

Amelia Earhart becomes first woman to fly solo across Atlantic Ocean (May 20).

Federal gasoline tax of 1 cent per gallon is enacted.

Beech Aircraft Co. is founded; Robert E. Gross purchases Lockheed Aircraft Co. for $40,000.

Auguste Piccard reaches an altitude of more than 55,000 feet in a pressurized balloon.

DEATHS Henry M. Leland, developer of first eight-cylinder engine; Robert Dollar, shipping-line founder.

SCIENCE/MEDICINE

Irving Langmuir is awarded Nobel Prize in chemistry for discoveries in surface chemistry.

Karl G. Jansky determines source of radio waves from outside solar system, begins radio astronomy.

Charles G. King isolates vitamin C.

Reporters gather in Hopewell, New Jersey, to cover the Lindbergh kidnapping, 1932. CORBIS-BETTMANN

Yellow-fever vaccine for humans is announced.

Sonic locator, measuring water depth with sound waves, is developed.

DEATH William W. Keen, first U.S. brain surgeon.

EDUCATION

Folger Shakespeare Memorial Library in Washington, D.C., opens.

RELIGION

Norman Vincent Peale becomes pastor of Marble Collegiate Church in New York City.

DEATH Rev. Francis P. (Father) Duffy, chaplain of 165th Infantry in Mexico and Europe.

ART/MUSIC

War Memorial Opera House in San Francisco opens with *Tosca*.

PAINTINGS John Steuart Curry, *Flying Codonàs*; Edward Hopper, *Room in Brooklyn*; Robert Laurent, *Goose Girl*; Thomas Hart Benton, *Cotton Pickers*; Georgia O'Keeffe, *Stables*.

SONGS (popular): "April in Paris," "Brother, Can You Spare a Dime?," "I'm Gettin' Sentimental over You," "Night and Day," "Have You Ever Been Lonely?," "I Surrender, Dear," "I've Got the World on a String," "Lullaby of the Leaves," "One Hour with You," "Try a Little Tenderness," "You're an Old Smoothie."

LITERATURE/JOURNALISM

Teletype Corp. produces its first machine.

Drew Pearson and Robert Allen write "Washington Merry-Go-Round" column.

BOOKS *Tobacco Road* by Erskine Caldwell, *Conquistador* (poetry) by Archibald MacLeish, *Death in the Afternoon* by Ernest Hemingway, *Life Begins at Forty* by Walter B. Pitkin, *Mutiny on the Bounty* by James Hall and Charles B. Nordhoff.

DEATHS Charles W. Chesnutt, first African American novelist (*Conjure Woman*).

ENTERTAINMENT

PLAYS Leslie Howard stars in *Animal Kingdom*,

Ethel Merman in *Take a Chance*, Fred Astaire in Cole Porter's *The Gay Divorce*, Ina Claire in *Biography*.

MOVIES *Grand Hotel* with John Barrymore and Greta Garbo, *A Farewell to Arms* with Helen Hayes and Gary Cooper, *Back Street* with Irene Dunne, *Rebecca of Sunnybrook Farm* with Mary Pickford, *Smilin' Through* with Norma Shearer, *Scarface* with Paul Muni.

New radio shows and personalities include Bing Crosby, Fred Allen, Fred Waring, George Burns and Gracie Allen, Jack Benny, and *One Man's Family*.

Radio City Music Hall in New York City opens; Palace Theater closes as a vaudeville house, becomes movie theater.

DEATHS Minnie Maddern Fiske, actress; Chauncey Olcott, singer, actor, and composer ("My Wild Irish Rose"); Florenz Ziegfeld, theatrical producer; Leonard T. Troland, invented multicolor process for movies.

SPORTS

Winter Olympic Games are held in Lake Placid, N.Y.; U.S. wins 10 gold medals; Summer Games are held in Los Angeles, U.S. wins 16 golds, 9 in swimming.

John McGraw resigns as manager of New York Giants baseball team after 31 years.

Lou Gehrig of New York Yankees becomes first American Leaguer to hit four consecutive home runs.

Hialeah racetrack in Miami, Fla., uses first totalisator (tote board) to record track bets and odds.

WINNERS *Auto racing* — Fred Frame, Indianapolis 500; *Baseball* — New York Yankees, World Series; *Boxing* — Jack Sharkey, heavyweight; Jackie Fields, welterweight; *Football* — Southern California, Rose Bowl; Chicago Bears, NFL; *Golf* — U.S., Walker Cup; Gene Sarazen, U.S. Open; Olin Dutra, PGA; *Hockey* — Toronto, Stanley Cup; *Horse racing* — Burgoo King, Kentucky Derby and Preakness Stakes; Faireno, Belmont Stakes; *Tennis* — France, Davis Cup; Ellsworth Vines, U.S. Open (men); Helen Jacobs, U.S. Open (women).

1933

DEATH Nat(haniel W.) Niles, pioneer U.S. figure skater.

MISCELLANEOUS

Two-year-old son of Charles and Anne Lindbergh is kidnapped from their New Jersey home; is later found murdered; a carpenter, Bruno Hauptmann, is convicted, executed for crime.

Series of tornadoes in Alabama kill 268.

New York City Mayor Jimmy Walker, charged with corruption, resigns.

INTERNATIONAL

U.S. recognizes U.S.S.R; William C. Bullitt is named ambassador (November 16).

Congress passes law providing independence for Philippine Islands after 12 years (January 13); reserved right to military bases is later modified.

U.S. Marines withdraw from Nicaragua (January 2) after nearly eight years' stay.

American nations sign treaty of nonaggression and conciliation; is ratified by Senate.

Ruth Bryan Owen (Rohde), daughter of William Jennings Bryan, becomes first U.S. woman diplomatic representative (minister to Denmark) (April 12).

NATIONAL

An assassin shoots at President-Elect Franklin D. Roosevelt in Florida, hits Chicago Mayor Anton J. Cermak (February 15); Cermak dies March 6; Joseph Zangara, convicted assassin, is electrocuted (March 20).

President Roosevelt at his inauguration (March 4) states: "The only thing we have to fear is fear itself"; pledges a "good neighbor" policy in world affairs.

For the 100 days between March 9 and June 16, a great many steps are taken by president and Congress to help nation's economy (see also Business and Transportation categories).

President Roosevelt uses the "fireside chat" on radio, tries to keep nation advised of federal actions.

Economy Act (March 20) cuts federal salaries 15%, reduces veterans' pensions, reorganizes government agencies; Volstead Act (Prohibition) is modified (March 22) to permit 3.2% wine and beer; Civilian Conservation Corps (CCC) is created (March 31) to provide 250,000 jobs for unemployed 18–25-year-old men; first camp opens near Luray, Va. (April 17).

Federal Emergency Relief Administration is created (May 12) to help states with $500 million for relief; Public Works Administration is established (June 16); Federal Surplus Relief Corp. is founded (October 4); Civil Works Administration is created as an unemployment relief program (November 9).

Twenty-first Amendment repealing the Eighteenth (Prohibition) Amendment, goes into effect (December 5).

National debt stands at $22.2 billion.

Francis E. Townsend devises plan for national sales tax with which to pay all retirees $200 per month in scrip, all to be spent within the month.

Francis Perkins, new Secretary of Labor, becomes first woman cabinet member; Eleanor Roosevelt conducts first press conference by a First Lady; Mrs. Nellie Tayloe Ross, first woman governor (Wyoming), becomes first woman to serve as director of U.S. Mint.

Twentieth ("Lame Duck") Amendment is ratified (February 6); called for presidential inauguration January 20 (rather than March); Congress to begin term January 3.

First aircraft carrier (*Ranger*) is launched (February 25).

Admiral William D. Leahy becomes first White

House chief of staff, serves until 1949.

DEATH Former President Calvin Coolidge (1923–1929).

BUSINESS/INDUSTRY/INVENTIONS

President Roosevelt proclaims four-day bank holiday (March 6) (most banks already closed by state actions), permits use of scrip, embargoes export of gold, silver, and currency; three-fourths of the banks open March 12.

Farm Credit Administration (March 27) authorizes refinancing farm mortgages at low interest (effective June 16); U.S. officially abandons gold standard (April 19), Congress ratifies action (June 5).

Agricultural Adjustment Act is approved to restore purchasing power of farmers (May 12); Tennessee Valley Authority (TVA) is created to build dams and power plants to improve economy of the area (May 18).

Federal Securities Act (May 27) requires full disclosure of information on new securities.

Federal Savings and Loan Association is authorized (June 13), with first S&L created in Miami (August 8).

Home Owners Loan Corp. is authorized to refinance nonfarm home mortgages (June 13); Federal Deposit Insurance Corp. is created (June 16) to guarantee bank deposits under $5,000.

Congress passes National Industrial Recovery Act, gives federal government control of industry through codes (June 16); the Blue Eagle becomes the NIRA symbol.

National Labor Board is created (August 5); Commodity Credit Corp. is founded (October 16) to help handle agricultural and other commodities; Wages and Hours Act goes into effect, sets minimum wages and maximum weekly hours; seven states pass minimum wage laws.

First "sit-down" strike occurs at Hormel & Co. plant in Austin, Minn. (November 13).

DEATHS Louis C. Tiffany, developer of Tiffany glass; Edward N. Hurley, founder of pneumatic tool industry.

The defeated Herbert Hoover (left) and Franklin Delano Roosevelt ride together to the 1933 presidential inauguration, in this illustration by artist Peter Arno. THE GRANGER COLLECTION, NEW YORK

TRANSPORTATION

Emergency Railroad Transportation Act provides for reorganization of the industry (June 16).

Wiley Post flies solo around the world in 7 days, 18 hours.

Great Lakes–Gulf Waterway between Chicago and New Orleans is completed (June 21).

Construction begins on Golden Gate Bridge; University Bridge in Seattle opens.

SCIENCE/MEDICINE

Thomas H. Morgan is awarded Nobel Prize for physiology/medicine for discoveries on role of chromosomes in heredity.

First large-scale cyclotron ("atom smasher") is developed under direction of its inventor, Ernest O.

1933

Lawrence at University of California.

Physicist Carl D. Anderson artificially produces a subatomic particle, the positron, by gamma-ray bombardment.

Dr. Evarts Graham in St. Louis performs first lung removal.

Scientist Albert Einstein arrives from Germany to make his home in Princeton, N.J.

EDUCATION

James Bryant Conant begins 20 years as president of Harvard University.

Leonard Bloomfield writes *Language*, an important contribution to linguistics.

Five thousand Chicago schoolteachers, paid in scrip, storm banks for 10 months' back pay.

DEATH John G. Hibben, president of Princeton University (1912–1932).

ART/MUSIC

Diego Rivera and Ben Shahn complete series of murals, *Man at the Crossroads*, in Rockefeller Center; John Flanagan completes the sculpture *Dragon Motif.*

Seattle Art Museum opens.

Aaron Copland composes Short Symphony.

Jazz singer Billie Holiday ("Lady Day") makes first recordings.

Jimmy and Tommy Dorsey form band.

SONGS (popular): "Easter Parade," "It's Only a Paper Moon," "The Last Roundup," "Lazy Bones," "Shuffle Off to Buffalo," "Smoke Gets in Your Eyes," "Sophisticated Lady," "Stormy Weather," "Who's Afraid of the Big Bad Wolf?," "I Like Mountain Music," "Let's Fall in Love," "Maria Elena," "Did You Ever See a Dream Walking?"

LITERATURE/JOURNALISM

Long legal battle ends when Bennett Cerf succeeds in having ban lifted on U.S. publication of James Joyce's *Ulysses.*

American Newspaper Guild organizes with Heywood Broun president.

Newsweek, Esquire, and *U.S. News and World Report* are founded.

Erle Stanley Gardner publishes his first Perry Mason book, *The Case of the Velvet Claws.*

BOOKS *Anthony Adverse* by Hervey Allen, *The Autobiography of Alice B. Toklas* by Gertrude Stein, *Collected Verse* by Robert Hillyer, *God's Little Acre* by Erskine Caldwell, *Miss Lonelyhearts* by Nathanael West, *My Life and Hard Times* by James Thurber.

DEATHS Sara Teasdale, author and poet; Earl Derr Biggers, author (Charlie Chan stories); Richard R. Bowker, founder, American Library Assn. and *Library Journal*; Horace B. Liveright, publisher; Sime Silverman, editor, *Variety* (1905–1933); Ring Lardner, sportswriter and author.

ENTERTAINMENT

Edwin H. Armstrong demonstrates FM (frequency modulation) radio transmission eliminating static.

First drive-in movie theater in U.S. opens in Camden, N.J. (June 6).

PLAYS Henry Hull stars in *Tobacco Road*, Katharine Cornell in *Alien Corn*, Noel Coward, Alfred Lunt, and Lynn Fontanne in *Design for Living*, Ethel Waters in *As Thousands Cheer* with music by Irving Berlin.

MOVIES *King Kong* with Fay Wray, *State Fair* with Will Rogers, *Flying Down to Rio* with Fred Astaire and Ginger Rogers, *Tugboat Annie* with Marie Dressler, *Dinner at Eight* with Jean Harlow, *Lady for a Day* with May Robson, *Henry the Eighth* with Charles Laughton.

Don McNeill's *Breakfast Club* begins 35-year run on radio; other new shows are *The Lone Ranger, National Barn Dance, Kraft Music Hall, Information Please.*

DEATH Edward H. Sothern, Shakespearian actor.

SPORTS

First major-league baseball All-Star Game is played (July 6); American League wins 4–2, Babe Ruth hits game's first home run.

Boxer Primo Carnera knocks out Ernie Schaaf; Schaaf dies a few days later.

Football goal posts are returned to goal line; forward pass is allowed anywhere behind the line of scrimmage.

WINNERS *Auto racing*—Louis Meyer, Indianapolis 500; *Baseball*—New York Giants, World Series; *Boxing*—Primo Carnera, heavyweight; Jimmy McLarnin, welterweight; Barney Ross, lightweight; *Football*—Southern California, Rose Bowl; Chicago Bears, NFL; *Golf*—Great Britain, Ryder Cup; John Goodman, U.S. Open; Gene Sarazen, PGA; *Hockey*—New York Rangers, Stanley Cup; Boston Olympics, world amateur title; *Horse racing*—Broker's Tip, Kentucky Derby; Head Play, Preakness Stakes; Hurryoff, Belmont Stakes; *Horseshoe pitching*—Ted Allen, national singles; *Tennis*—Fred Perry, U.S. Open (men); Helen Jacobs, U.S. Open (women).

DEATHS William Muldoon, champion wrestler; James J. Corbett, heavyweight boxing champion (1892–1897).

MISCELLANEOUS

Century of Progress Exposition opens in Chicago.

Earthquake at Long Beach, Calif., claims 115 lives.

Western Union introduces singing telegram.

1934

INTERNATIONAL

All nations who are indebted to the U.S., except Finland, default.

U.S. troops in Haiti are withdrawn.

Trade Agreements Act authorizes President Franklin Roosevelt to negotiate tariffs on a most-favored-nation principle; U.S. and Cuba sign reciprocal trade agreement; duty on sugar is reduced from 2.5 cents to 0.9 cents per pound.

NATIONAL

Congress overrides presidential veto of a bill to restore cuts in federal salaries and pensions.

Federal Communications Commission is created (June 19).

Civil Works Emergency Act provides $950 million for civil works and public relief.

National Archives are founded (June 19).

Naval Parity Act authorizes construction of 100 warships and more than 5,000 planes over a five-year period; National Guard becomes part of U.S. Army during war or emergency.

Anti-New Deal groups emerge: Liberty League and Rev. Charles Coughlin's National Union for Social Justice.

Dust storms occur in Midwest due to overplowing; thousands of tons of topsoil blow away.

Nebraska adopts a unicameral legislature.

Ohio Supreme Court Justice Florence E. Allen is sworn in as the first woman justice of U.S. Circuit Court of Appeals.

Great Smoky Mountains (N.C.) National Park is established.

DEATH William B. Wilson, first Secretary of Labor (1913–1921).

BUSINESS/INDUSTRY/INVENTIONS

Export-Import Bank organizes to encourage overseas commerce (February 2); Securities & Exchange Commission is created.

Federal Housing Administration is founded (June 28) to insure housing loans; Federal Farm Mortgage Corp. is established (January 31) to refinance farm debts.

Federal Credit Union Act passes (June 26); first credit union is created in Texarkana, Tex. (October 1).

U.S. Board of Mediation is organized (July 21); National Labor Relations Board is created (June 19) to replace 1933 National Labor Board.

Federal Trade Commission is reestablished (June 19).

Gold content of dollar is reduced to 13.71 grains.

1934

Two strangers share a hotel room in a scene from *It Happened One Night*, starring Claudette Colbert and Clark Gable (1934). PHOTOFEST

John C. Garand patents semi-automatic rifle (MI); rifle is adopted by Army in 1936.

Ninety state liquor stores open in Pennsylvania.

Chemist Wallace Carothers of DuPont produces nylon.

National Society of Professional Engineers is founded.

DEATHS Albert B. Dick, founder and head of mimeograph machine company; Ivy L. Lee, developed public relations as a profession; William C. Procter, soap manufacturer (Procter & Gamble); Cass Gilbert, architect (Woolworth Building).

TRANSPORTATION

Railway Labor Act gives workers right to organize and bargain; sets up National Railroad Adjustment Board (June 27).

Streamlined all-steel diesel train, the "Zephyr" of Burlington Railroad, makes first trip (November 11), a round trip from Lincoln, Nebr., to Kansas City, Mo.

Jean F. Piccard and wife reach height of 57,500 feet in balloon.

William A. Patterson is named president of United Air Lines; William P. Lear founds Lear Avia Corp.

DEATH Frank J. Sprague, father of electric traction.

SCIENCE/MEDICINE

Harold C. Urey is awarded Nobel Prize in chemistry for discovery of heavy hydrogen; George R. Minot, William P. Murphy, and G. H. Whipple share physiology/medicine prize for work on liver therapy in anemia.

Charles William Beebe descends a then-record 3,028 feet into ocean in a bathysphere that he invented.

Joseph B. Rhine writes book *Extra-Sensory Perception*.

DEATH William H. Welch, pathologist who helped found Johns Hopkins Hospital/Medical School.

EDUCATION

John W. Studebaker becomes U.S. Commissioner of Education.

RELIGION

Merger (June 24) of Reformed Church, founded in 1725, and Evangelical Synod of North America, founded in 1840, creates Evangelical & Reformed church.

Catholic Archbishop of Chicago George W. Mundelein is elevated to cardinal.

ART/MUSIC

Arnold Schoenberg, composer, debuts as conductor with Boston Symphony Orchestra.

Annual Summer Berkshire Symphonic Festival is founded in Tanglewood, Mass.

Metropolitan Opera presents Howard Hanson's opera, *Merrymount*; *Four Saints in Three Acts*, an opera by Virgil Thomson and Gertrude Stein, is produced in Hartford, Conn.

Lincoln Kirstein and George Balanchine found School of American Ballet.

Laurens Hammond patents pipeless organ.

Ella Fitzgerald begins singing career with Chick Webb's band; Benny Goodman organizes band.

Walter Piston composes Concerto for Orchestra; William Levi, *Negro Folk* Symphony.

SONGS (popular): "Anything Goes," "I Get a Kick Out of You," "I Only Have Eyes for You," "Moonglow," "Stay as Sweet as You Are," "Wagon Wheels," "Cocktails for Two," "Deep Purple," "June in January," "P.S. I Love You," "Santa

Claus Is Coming to Town," "You're the Top," "Solitude," "Be Still, My Heart."

DEATH Otto H. Kahn, banker and one of U.S.'s greatest art patrons.

LITERATURE/JOURNALISM

Milton Caniff draws comic strip "Terry and the Pirates"; Al Capp, the "L'il Abner" strip.

BOOKS *Tender Is the Night* by F. Scott Fitzgerald, *Wine from These Grapes* (poetry) by Edna St. Vincent Millay, *Appointment in Samarra* by John O'Hara, *Heaven's My Destination* by Thornton Wil-

Vaudeville and movie theaters in New York City in the 1930s. ARCHIVE PHOTOS

der, *While Rome Burns* by Alexander Woollcott, *Lust for Life* by Irving Stone, *The Thin Man* by Dashiell Hammett, *Stars Fell on Alabama* by Carl Carmer.

ENTERTAINMENT

Catholic Legion of Decency censors and grades movies.

"March of Time" documentary film series begins.

Decca Records Inc. is established.

PLAYS Walter Huston stars in *Dodsworth*, Ethel Merman in *Anything Goes*, Grace George in *Personal Appearance*.

MOVIES *The Thin Man* with William Powell and Myrna Loy, *It Happened One Night* with Claudette Colbert and Clark Gable, *Of Human Bondage* with Bette Davis and Leslie Howard, *The Gay Divorcee* with Fred Astaire and Ginger Rogers, *The Scarlet Pimpernel* with Leslie Howard.

DEATH Marie Dressler, screen actress.

SPORTS

Ford Frick is named National (baseball) League president.

In baseball All-Star Game, Carl Hubbell strikes out Babe Ruth, Lou Gehrig, Jimmie Foxx, Al Simmons, and Joe Cronin in succession.

Babe Ruth of New York Yankees hits his 700th home run.

First National Hockey League All-Star Game is played.

Golfer Bobby Jones founds annual Masters Tournament.

First ski tow (rope) operates at Woodstock, Vt.

WINNERS *Auto racing*—Bill Cummings, Indianapolis 500; *Baseball*—St. Louis Cardinals, World Series; *Boxing*—Max Baer, heavyweight; Jimmy McLarnin, welterweight; *Football*—Columbia, Rose Bowl; New York Giants, NFL; *Golf*—U.S., Walker Cup; Olin Dutra, U.S. Open; Paul Runyon, PGA; Horton Smith, first Masters tourney; *Hockey*—Chicago, Stanley Cup; *Horse racing*—Cavalcade, Kentucky Derby; High Quest, Preakness Stakes; Peace Chance, Belmont Stakes; *Tennis*—Great Britain, Davis Cup; Fred Perry, U.S. Open (men); Helen Jacobs, U.S. Open (women); *Wrestling*—Jim Londos, heavyweight; *Yachting*—U.S. boat *Rainbow* retains America's Cup.

DEATH John McGraw, baseball player and manager (New York Giants 1902–1932).

MISCELLANEOUS

Steamer *Morro Castle* burns off Asbury Park, N.J.; 134 die.

Clyde Barrow and Bonnie Parker, bank robbers, shot to death by Texas Rangers; John Dillinger, Public Enemy No. 1, shot and killed by lawmen outside a Chicago theater.

Florida Keys are hit by hurricane that causes 400 deaths.

Brookfield Zoo in Chicago opens.

American Youth Hostels incorporate.

Clark Gable takes off his shirt in *It Happened One Night*, revealing that he is not wearing an undershirt; undershirt sales immediately plummet.

1935

INTERNATIONAL

President Franklin D. Roosevelt approves Philippine Islands constitution (February 8); Senate ratifies (May 14); Manuel Quezon is elected first president (September 17) and Commonwealth of the Philippines is inaugurated (November 15).

After years of consideration, Senate rejects U.S. membership in World Court (January 16).

NATIONAL

Supreme Court in *Schechter v. United States* rules that National Industrial Recovery Act of 1933 is unconstitutional (May 27).

Social Security Act is approved (August 24).

Senator Huey P. Long of Louisiana is shot and killed in Baton Rouge by Dr. Carl A. Weiss, who is killed by Long's bodyguards.

George H. Gallup founds Institute of Public Opinion, which holds Gallup polls.

First U.S. Savings Bonds ($25 to $100) are issued.

Boulder (later Hoover) Dam is dedicated; produces power (1936) to serve Los Angeles area.

National Youth Administration is formed to aid 16–23 year olds (June 26).

Federal Register is authorized.

Trenton, N.J., hosts two-day national conference on crime; 41 states are represented.

Pan American Airways makes first airmail flight across Pacific Ocean.

FBI opens police training school.

Shenandoah (Va.) National Park is established.

Harry S. Truman begins 10-year service as a senator from Missouri.

DEATHS Oliver Wendell Holmes Jr., Supreme Court justice (1902–1932), known as the Great Dissenter; Jane Addams, social worker (Hull House); Frank H. Hitchcock, Postmaster General

(1909–1913) who began parcel post, airmail, and postal savings.

BUSINESS/INDUSTRY/INVENTIONS

United Auto Workers holds first convention; Committee of Industrial Organization, predecessor of CIO, is established.

New National Labor Relations Board is established (July 5).

Congress passes law that provides three-year moratorium on farm foreclosures; Resettlement Administration is created to provide relief to low-income farm families.

Soil Conservation Service is created to stop erosion.

Shirley Temple, the most popular child star in Hollywood history. THE GRANGER COLLECTION, NEW YORK

1935

Works Progress Administration (WPA) is created; Harry L. Hopkins administrates.

Public Utility Holding Company Act gives Federal Power Commission more authority over electric transmission and gas, gives Securities & Exchange Commission authority over holding companies practices.

Rural Electrification Administration (REA) is created to provide electricity to rural areas.

Sylvia Porter writes syndicated financial column in *New York Post*.

DEATH David White, developer of carbon ratio theory that leads to development of petroleum industry.

TRANSPORTATION

Supreme Court declares Railroad Retirement Act of 1934 unconstitutional.

Oklahoma City installs first automatic parking meter.

Motor Carrier Act places interstate buses and trucks under Interstate Commerce Commission.

Bell Aircraft Corp. is founded.

Amelia Earhart is first to fly solo across Pacific (Honolulu to Oakland) (January 11).

DEATH John N. Willys, automaker.

SCIENCE/MEDICINE

Arthur Dempster discovers U-235, an isotope of uranium used in nuclear weapons and plants.

DEATHS Franklin H. Martin, founder of American College of Surgeons; Henry Fairfield Osborn, head of American Museum of Natural History (1908–1933).

EDUCATION

Isaiah Bowman begins 14 years as president of Johns Hopkins University.

St. Joseph's College in Philadelphia offers course in combating communism.

RELIGION

Two new Catholic archbishops named: John J. Mitty to San Francisco and Joseph F. Rummel to New Orleans.

Oral Roberts begins evangelistic career.

DEATH Billy Sunday, evangelist and revivalist.

ART/MUSIC

American Ballet, forerunner of New York City Ballet, is founded with George Balanchine director; Littlefield (later Philadelphia) Ballet is formed.

WPA Federal Art Project Gallery opens in New York City; San Francisco Museum of Art opens.

Marian Anderson, one of world's great contraltos, debuts in New York City.

Antonia Brico founds New York Women's Symphony.

Aaron Copland composes *Statements*.

Robert Laurent completes the painting *Spanning the Continent*.

Count Basie forms a band.

SONGS (popular): "I'm in the Mood for Love," "Cheek to Cheek," "Footloose and Fancy Free," "Lullaby of Broadway," "Moon over Miami," "Red Sails in the Sunset," "Summertime," "The Music Goes Round and Round," "Just One of Those Things," "Begin the Beguine."

DEATHS Childe Hassam, leading U.S. impressionist painter; Charles Demuth, painter who helped introduce cubist technique to U.S.

LITERATURE/JOURNALISM

Charles S. Addams draws his macabre cartoons for *New Yorker* magazine; Edward R. Murrow joins Columbia Broadcasting System.

Gardner Cowles acquires the *Minneapolis Star*.

BOOKS *Tortilla Flat* by John Steinbeck, *Life with Father* by Clarence S. Day Jr., *It Can't Happen Here* by Sinclair Lewis, *Butterfield 8* by John O'Hara, *Of Time and the River* by Thomas Wolfe, *Vein of Iron* by Ellen Glasgow, *R. E. Lee* by Douglas Southall Freeman.

DEATHS Sidney Smith, cartoonist ("The Gumps"); Adolph S. Ochs; publisher, the *New York Times* (1896–1935); Lucius W. Nieman, endower of journalism fellowships at Harvard; Edwin Arlington Robinson, poet.

ENTERTAINMENT

Federal Theater Project is founded.

Spyros Skouras founds Twentieth Century-Fox movie company.

PLAYS Leslie Howard and Humphrey Bogart star in *The Petrified Forest*, Burgess Meredith in *Winterset*, Helen Hayes in *Victoria Regina*, Judith Anderson in *The Old Maid*; George Gershwin's opera *Porgy and Bess* opens on Broadway.

MOVIES *The Informer* with Victor McLaglen, *Mutiny on the Bounty* with Charles Laughton, *Anna Karenina* with Greta Garbo, *Top Hat* and *Roberta* with Fred Astaire and Ginger Rogers, *The Little Colonel* with Shirley Temple, *Magnificent Obsession* with Irene Dunne, *Les Miserables* with Frederic March, *The 39 Steps* with Robert Donat.

New radio shows include *Cavalcade of America*, *Fibber McGee and Molly*, *Lights Out*, *Major Bowes' Original Amateur Hour*, *Your Hit Parade*.

DEATH DeWolf Hopper, actor.

SPORTS

Roller derby for 50 skaters is held in Chicago.

Sir Malcolm Campbell drives Bluebird Special at 304.33 miles per hour at Bonneville (Utah) Salt Flats.

First night game in major-league baseball is played in Crosley Field, Cincinnati; Reds beat Philadelphia.

Babe Ruth hits his 714th, and last, home run.

Mary Hirsch becomes first woman licensed to train race horses.

New York Downtown Athletic Club presents first Heisman Memorial Trophy; recipient is Jay Berwanger, University of Chicago halfback.

WINNERS *Auto racing*—Kelly Petillo, Indianapolis 500; *Baseball*—Detroit Tigers, World Series; *Boxing*—Jim Braddock, heavyweight; Barney Ross, welterweight; Tony Canzoneri, light-

With the passage of the Social Security Act, some Americans feel that they have been reduced to mere numbers, as this political cartoon illustrates. THE GRANGER COLLECTION

weight; *Football* (bowls)—Alabama, Rose; Bucknell, Orange; Tulane, Sugar; Detroit Lions, NFL; *Golf*—U.S., Ryder Cup; Sam Parks Jr., U.S. Open; Johnny Revolta, PGA; Gene Sarazen, Masters; *Hockey*—Montreal Maroons, Stanley Cup; *Horse racing*—Omaha, third Triple Crown winner (Kentucky Derby, Preakness Stakes, Belmont Stakes); *Skeet shooting*—Lovell S. Pratt, men's national; Esther A. Ingalls, women's; *Tennis*—Great Britain, Davis Cup; Wilmer Allison, U.S. Open (men); Helen Jacobs, U.S. Open (women).

MISCELLANEOUS

Wiley Post and his passenger, Will Rogers, die in an Alaska plane crash.

William G. Wilson and Dr. Robert Smith found Alcoholics Anonymous.

1936

INTERNATIONAL

Inter-American Conference is held in Buenos Aires.

NATIONAL

President Franklin D. Roosevelt, Democrat, is reelected, carries every state but Maine and Vermont; receives 27,751,612 popular and 523 electoral votes to Republican Alfred M. Landon's 16,681,913 popular and 8 electoral votes.

Supreme Court in *United States v. Butler* declares unconstitutional the Agricultural Adjustment Act (January 24); Congress then passes law to replace the act (February 29), restricts agricultural output through benefit payments to growers practicing soil conservation; Court also deems unconstitutional the Bituminous Coal Conservation Act; upholds the constitutionality of dam building by TVA.

Congress passes bill (January 24) over president's veto to give World War I veterans cash bonuses; distributes more than $1.5 million to about 3 million veterans.

Three dams are completed: Hoover (originally Boulder) Dam on Colorado River, Norris Dam on Clinch River in Tennessee, and Wheeler Dam on Tennessee River in Alabama.

Ford Foundation, philanthropic organization, is established.

DEATHS Former Vice President Charles Curtis (1929–1933); Admiral William S. Sims, commanded World War I naval operations.

BUSINESS/INDUSTRY/INVENTIONS

Drs. Vladimir Zworykin and George Morton describe their invention, the electron tube.

United Auto Workers stage sit-down strikes in several General Motors plants in Flint, Mich.; last 44 days; are copied by other workers.

Philip Murray heads Steel Workers Organizing Committee (later United Steelworkers).

Owens-Illinois Glass Co. completes all-glass windowless packaging laboratory in Toledo, Ohio.

Great American Oil Co. and Hunt Oil Co. are founded.

Government Contracts Act calls for 40-hour week for companies with government contracts, plus time-and-a-half for overtime.

Anti-price discrimination law makes illegal unreasonably low prices by interstate chain stores.

DEATHS William Horlick, originator of malted milk; Edward Weston, inventor of cadmium cell; Hiram P. Maxim, inventor of firearm silencer.

TRANSPORTATION

Triborough Bridge in New York City and San Francisco–Oakland Bridge open.

Socony-Vacuum Oil Co. produces aviation gasoline.

U.S. Maritime Commission replaces Shipping Board, is designed to develop merchant marine.

German dirigible *Hindenburg* arrives at Lakehurst, N.J., completing first scheduled transatlantic flight.

SCIENCE/MEDICINE

Carl D. Anderson shares Nobel Prize in physics with Viktor F. Hess of Austria for discovery of the positron; Otto Loewi shares the prize for physiology/medicine with Sir Henry H. Dale of England for chemical transmission of nerve impulses.

New York State enacts law requiring annual testing of pupils' hearing.

William A. White Foundation founds Washington School of Psychiatry.

EDUCATION

Spring Hill (Ala.) College is chartered; first Catholic college in the deep South.

Jesse Owens, winner of four gold medals at the 1936 Summer Olympics in Berlin. UPI/CORBIS-BETTMANN

DEATH Thomas J. Foster, founder of International Correspondence School.

RELIGION

John G. Machen founds Presbyterian Church of America (later becomes Orthodox Presbyterian church).

Evangelical Bishop John S. Stamm becomes president of Board of Bishops.

ART/MUSIC

Sculptor Gutzon Borglum unveils the second 60-foot-high presidential head (Jefferson) at Mt. Rushmore in the Black Hills, S. Dak.

Samuel Barber's Symphony in One Movement is first American work played at Salzburg (Austria) music festival; Walter Piston composes Prelude and Fugue for Orchestra.

William G. Still becomes first African American to conduct major symphony orchestra (Los Angeles Philharmonic).

Edwin H. Marshfield completes mural *Progress of Civilization* on Library of Congress dome; Paul Burlin completes the painting *The Ghost City*;

Louis Guglielmi, *Wedding in South Street*; Charles Sheeler, *City Interior*.

SONGS (popular): "I'm an Old Cowhand," "I've Got You Under My Skin," "Let Yourself Go," "Pennies from Heaven," "Stompin' at the Savoy," "Goody, Goody," "There's a Small Hotel," "These Foolish Things."

DEATHS Ernestine Schumann-Heink, one of greatest contraltos; Lorado Z. Taft, sculptor (Chicago's *Fountain of Time*).

LITERATURE/ JOURNALISM

Margaret Bourke-White begins her 33-year career as a *Life* photographer.

BOOKS *How to Win Friends and Influence People* by Dale Carnegie, *Gone with the Wind* by Margaret Mitchell, *A Further Range* (poetry) by Robert Frost, *The People, Yes* (poetry) by Carl Sandburg, *Absalom, Absalom!* by William Faulkner, *Inside Europe* by John Gunther, *Drums Along the Mohawk* by Walter D. Edmonds, *U.S.A.*, a trilogy by John Dos Passos.

DEATHS Arthur Brisbane, newspaper columnist; Lincoln Steffens, reform journalist (*Shame of the Cities*).

ENTERTAINMENT

Eugene O'Neill wins Nobel Prize in literature for his plays.

Washington State Theater in Seattle opens.

PLAYS Katharine Cornell stars in *St. Joan*, Ilka Chase in *The Women*, Alfred Lunt and Lynn Fontanne in *Idiot's Delight*, Ray Bolger in *On Your Toes*.

MOVIES *Mr. Deeds Goes to Town* with Gary Cooper and Jean Arthur, *Modern Times* with Charlie Chaplin, *Camille* with Greta Garbo, *My Man Godfrey* with Carole Lombard, *Poppy* with W. C. Fields, *Follow the Fleet* with Fred Astaire and Ginger Rogers.

RADIO Fanny Brice as "Baby Snooks," *Gangbusters*, *The Green Hornet*, Edgar Bergen and Charlie McCarthy.

DEATHS Irving Thalberg, movie producer; Samuel L. (Roxy) Rothafel, founder of Radio City Music Hall; John Gilbert, silent-screen actor; H. B. Walthall, pioneer screen actor (*Birth of a Nation*).

SPORTS

U.S. two-man bobsled team wins Winter Olympics gold medal at Garmisch-Partenkirchen, Germany; Jesse Owens wins four golds at Summer Olympics in Berlin, Germany.

Professional football teams draft college players for first time.

Tony Lazzeri of New York Yankees sets American League record by driving in 11 runs in one game with three home runs, two of them grand slams.

Sally Stearns is first woman coxswain of a men's collegiate varsity crew (Rollins College).

WINNERS *Auto racing* — Louis Meyer, Indianapolis 500; *Baseball* — New York Yankees, World Series; *Boxing* — Lou Ambers, lightweight; *Chess* — Samuel Reshevsky, U.S. champion; *Football* (bowls) — Stanford, Rose; Catholic University, Orange; Texas Christian, Sugar; Green Bay, NFL; *Golf* — U.S., Walker Cup; Tony Manero, U.S. Open; Denny Shute, PGA; Horton Smith, Masters; *Hockey* — Detroit, Stanley Cup; *Horse racing* — Bold Venture, Kentucky Derby and Preakness Stakes; Granville, Belmont Stakes; *Table Tennis* — Ruth Aaron, first U.S. woman world champion; *Tennis* — Fred Perry, U.S. Open (men); Alice Marble, U.S. Open (women).

MISCELLANEOUS

Congress charters Veterans of Foreign Wars (VFW).

Tornadoes in Mississippi and Georgia kill 455.

Two expositions are held: Ft. Worth Frontier Centennial and Great Lakes Exposition–Cleveland Centennial.

1937

INTERNATIONAL

Japanese planes, while bombing China, sink U.S. gunboat *Panay* and three supply ships (December 12); Japan accepts blame, apologizes, pays indemnities.

President Franklin D. Roosevelt urges international quarantine of aggressors as only way to peace.

Congress forbids shipment of arms to either side in Spanish Civil War.

NATIONAL

President Roosevelt submits plan to increase Supreme Court from 9 to 15 if judges decline to retire at 70; calls for increasing number of federal court judges to as many as 50 (February 5); Chief Justice Charles Evans Hughes says court does not need more justices (March 11); Senate by 70-20 vote recommits plan to Judiciary Committee (July 22), where it dies.

Supreme Court upholds series of New Deal measures: Washington minimum-wage law, National Labor Relations Act (*NLRB v. Jones & Laughlin Steel*), and Social Security laws.

William H. Hastie is first African American federal judge.

President Roosevelt, starting his second term, is first to be inaugurated in January rather than March under the Twentieth Amendment.

Bonneville Dam on Columbia River is dedicated.

Lyndon B. Johnson begins 12 years as a representative from Texas.

DEATHS Andrew W. Mellon, Treasury Secretary (1921–1933); Joseph Lee, a leader in playground development; Henry T. Mayo, commander-in-chief, Atlantic Fleet (1916–1919); Frank B. Kellog, Secretary of State (1925–1929).

This temporary pontoon bridge connects the flooded section of Louisville, Kentucky, and the city highlands, 1937. UPI/CORBIS-BETTMANN

BUSINESS/INDUSTRY/INVENTIONS

Congress of Industrial Organizations (CIO) is created with John L. Lewis president (November 14).

U.S. Steel Corp. recognizes Steelworkers union (March 2); Steelworkers demonstrate in front of South Chicago Republic Steel plant, are fired on by police; 4 are killed, 84 are injured.

Rockefeller Center in New York City is completed.

Edwin H. Land founds Polaroid Corp.

General Motors and Chrysler recognize United Auto Workers as bargaining agent for their employees.

DEATHS John R. Pope, architect (National Gallery of Art); Dr. Wallace H. Carothers, research chemist (neoprene, nylon); John D. Rockefeller, Standard Oil founder; Charles E. Hires, root-beer developer; Edward A. Filene, Boston department-store founder; Jacob Schick, razor manufacturer.

TRANSPORTATION

German zeppelin, *Hindenburg*, burns at its mooring in Lakehurst, N.J.; 36 die.

Golden Gate Bridge opens; first Lincoln Tunnel tube under Hudson River is completed.

Amelia Earhart and pilot Fred Noonan disappear in Pacific Ocean while on round-the-world flight.

SCIENCE/MEDICINE

Clinton J. Davisson shares Nobel Prize in physics

with George P. Thomson of England for discovery of the diffraction of electrons by crystals; Albert Szent-Györgyi is awarded prize for physiology/medicine for work on biological combustion processes.

Cook County Hospital, Chicago, establishes first blood bank (March 15).

Physicist I. I. Rabi develops atomic and molecular beam method for observing spectra in radio frequency range; Grote Reber builds first radio telescope; James Hiller develops first practical electron microscope.

National Foundation for Infantile Paralysis and National Cancer Institute are founded.

Dr. Max Theiler develops a vaccine for yellow fever.

DEATH Charles Hayden, a founder of New York City planetarium named for him.

RELIGION

Rev. Norman Vincent Peale and others found American Foundation for Religion and Psychiatry.

Catholic Archbishop Edward F. Mooney of Rochester, N.Y., becomes first archbishop of Detroit, Mich.

ART/MUSIC

Andrew Mellon turns over large art collection to federal government and sufficient funds to build and endow National Gallery of Art; Tanglewood in Berkshires is given to Boston Symphony Orchestra as permanent summer-festival home.

Gutzon Borglum unveils the head of President Lincoln, the third head carved on Mt. Rushmore in the Black Hills, S. Dak.

Arturo Toscanini conducts NBC Symphony, especially created for him.

Gian Carlo Menotti composes opera, *Amelia Goes to the Ball*.

Glenn Miller forms band.

Museum of Costume Arts incorporates in New York City.

George Biddle completes the painting *William Gropper*; Peter Blume, *The Eternal City*; Lyonel Feininger, *Towers at Halle*; Joseph Hirsch, *Two Men*; Jack Levine, *The Feast of Pure Reason*; John Flanagan completes the sculpture *Triumph of the Egg*.

SONGS (popular): "Bei Mir Bist Du Schön," "Blue Hawaii," "Boo Hoo," "The Lady Is a Tramp," "My Funny Valentine," "Rosalie," "September in the Rain," "Sweet Leilani," "That Old Feeling," "Where or When," "Whistle While You Work."

DEATHS George Gershwin, composer; Bessie Smith, one of the greatest blues singers.

LITERATURE/JOURNALISM

Dr. Seuss (Theodore S. Geisel) completes his first book, *To Think That I Saw It on Mulberry Street*.

Look magazine begins publication.

Eleanor M. Patterson leases (later buys) *Washington Herald* and *Washington Times*, combines them.

Edward R. Murrow in London heads CBS European bureau.

BOOKS *Of Mice and Men* by John Steinbeck, *The Late George Apley* by John P. Marquand, *Strictly from Hunger* by S. J. Perelman, *Northwest Passage* by Kenneth Roberts, *The Chute* by Albert Halper, *Patterns of Culture* by Ruth Benedict.

DEATHS Edith Wharton, author; Paul E. More, cofounder of modern humanism.

ENTERTAINMENT

Mobile television units are produced for NBC.

Term *disc jockey* is coined in *Variety*.

PLAYS Luther Adler stars in *Golden Boy*, Gertrude Lawrence in *Susan and God*, Burgess Meredith in *High Tor*, George M. Cohan in *I'd Rather Be Right*, Broderick Crawford in *Of Mice and Men*.

MOVIES *Snow White and the Seven Dwarfs*, *Lost Horizon* with Ronald Colman, *Heidi* with Shirley Temple, *The Good Earth* with Paul Muni, *Captains Courageous* with Spencer Tracy, *The Awful Truth* with Cary Grant and Irene Dunne, *In Old Chicago* with Alice Faye and Tyrone Power, *A Star Is Born* with Janet Gaynor.

New radio programs include *American Forum of the Air*, *Big Town*, *Meet Corliss Archer*, and *Mary Margaret McBride*.

The dance, Big Apple, sweeps the country.

DEATHS Jean Harlow, screen actress; Mrs. Leslie Carter, actress sometimes called America's Sarah Bernhardt.

SPORTS

WINNERS *Auto racing*—Wilbur Shaw, Indianapolis 500; *Baseball*—New York Yankees, World Series; *Bicycling*—Doris Kopsky, first U.S. women's title; *Boxing*—Joe Louis, heavyweight; Benny Lynch, flyweight; *Football* (bowls)—Pittsburgh, Rose; Duquesne, Orange; Santa Clara, Sugar; Texas Christian, Cotton; Washington, NFL; *Golf*—U.S., Ryder Cup; Ralph Guldahl, U.S. Open; Denny Shute, PGA; Byron Nelson, Masters; *Hockey*—Detroit, Stanley Cup; *Horse racing*—War Admiral wins Kentucky Derby, Preakness Stakes, and Belmont Stakes to become fourth Triple Crown winner; *Tennis*—U.S., Davis Cup; Don Budge, U.S. Open (men); Anita Lizana, U.S.

Open (women); *Yachting*—U.S. boat *Ranger* retains America's Cup.

DEATHS Ray C. Ewry, track gold medalist in 1904, 1908 Olympics; Howie Morenz, hockey great.

MISCELLANEOUS

Explosion at New London (Tex.) school kills 413 pupils and teachers.

Charles W. Howard conducts one-week "Santa Claus" school in Albion, N.Y.

First animated cartoon electric sign lights up on Broadway in New York City.

Ohio River floods (especially at Cincinnati and Louisville) result in 137 deaths, $500 million damage.

1938

INTERNATIONAL

Mexico nationalizes British and U.S. oil companies; property valued at $415 million.

President Franklin D. Roosevelt asks Hitler and Mussolini for peaceful solution of growing European problem.

NATIONAL

Congress authorizes $1-billion expansion of two-ocean navy in next 10 years.

House Committee on Un-American Activities is created to investigate subversive activities.

Dr. Francis E. Townsend, old-age pension-plan advocate, is pardoned from 30-day prison term for contempt of Congress.

New York State law requires marriage-license applicants to have medical tests.

Olympic (Wash.) National Park is established.

Pickwick Landing Dam on Tennessee River is completed.

DEATHS Helen M. Shepard, endower of American Hall of Fame at New York University; Clarence S. Darrow, defense attorney.

BUSINESS/INDUSTRY/INVENTIONS

Congress reduces taxes on business; the Food, Drug, and Cosmetic Act passes, prohibits misbranding or false advertising of products; Fair Labor Standards Act establishes 40-cents-per-hour minimum wage and 40-hour workweek and sets 16 as minimum age for workers.

Federal Crop Insurance Corp. is authorized; Federal National Mortgage Assn. is created; Agricultural Administration Act is signed.

William McC. Martin becomes first salaried president of New York Stock Exchange.

DuPont Co. announces development of nylon, first usable synthetic fiber.

DEATHS Charles R. Walgreen, founder of drugstore chain; Harvey S. Firestone, rubber company founder.

1938

TRANSPORTATION

Howard Hughes flies around the world in record 3 days, 19 hours, 14 minutes, 28 seconds (July 14); Douglas ("Wrong Way") Corrigan flies from New York to Dublin in 28 hours, 13 minutes, says he thought he was flying to Los Angeles (July 18).

Civil Aeronautics Authority is created to supervise nonmilitary aviation (June 23).

John K. Northrop creates Northrop Aviation Corp.

Honeymoon Bridge at Niagara Falls collapses under pressure of a huge ice jam (January 27); Thousand Islands Bridge over St. Lawrence River opens; bridge connecting Port Huron, Mich., and Port Edward, Canada, is dedicated.

Airlines carry 1,365,706 revenue passengers.

DEATH Joseph B. Strauss, bridge designer (Golden Gate).

SCIENCE/MEDICINE

Enrico Fermi is awarded Nobel Prize in physics for work on nuclear reactions.

National Society for Legalization of Euthanasia is founded.

DEATHS William H. Pickering, astronomer; John J. Abel, who isolated adrenaline and insulin in crystalline form.

EDUCATION

Harvard University observes its tercentenary.

Institute of General Semantics is founded in Chicago.

RELIGION

Mother Francis Xavier Cabrini becomes first American citizen beatified in Catholic church.

Supreme Court upholds right of Jehovah's Witnesses to distribute religious literature without a license.

DEATH Patrick J. Hayes, Catholic archbishop of New York (1919–1938).

ART/MUSIC

Aaron Copland presents ballet *Billy the Kid*; Walter Piston composes First Symphony and *The Incredible Flutist*.

Walter Gropius chairs Harvard Graduate School of Design.

Our Town, written by Thornton Wilder in 1938, is destined to become one of America's best-loved plays. Pictured here is the original Broadway production of that same year. © MUSEUM OF THE CITY OF NEW YORK THEATRE COLLECTION

Charles Sheeler completes the painting *Upstairs*; Lyonel Feininger, *Dawn*; Robert Laurent, *Kneeling Woman*.

Benny Goodman's orchestra presents first jazz concert in Carnegie Hall; Lawrence Welk describes his style as "champagne music."

SONGS (popular): "A-Tisket, A-Tasket," "My Heart Belongs to Daddy," "I'll Be Seeing You," "Jeepers Creepers," "Music, Maestro, Please," "One O'Clock Jump," "You Must Have Been a Beautiful Baby," "San Antonio Rose," "Thanks for the Memories."

DEATHS William J. Glackens, artist and illustrator; Alma Gluck, lyric soprano; King (Joseph) Oliver, pioneer jazz cornetist.

LITERATURE/JOURNALISM

Pearl Buck is awarded Nobel Prize in literature for books on China and biographies.

H. V. Kaltenborn, chief CBS news commentator, makes almost nonstop radio broadcasts during Munich crisis; on air 102 times in 18 days.

BOOKS *The Yearling* by Marjorie Kinnan Rawlings, *Benjamin Franklin* by Carl Van Doren, *The Long Valley* by John Steinbeck, *I'm a Stranger Here Myself* (poetry) by Ogden Nash, *Dynasty of Death* by Taylor Caldwell, *The Unvanquished* by William Faulkner.

DEATHS Thomas Wolfe, author; Elzie C. Segar, cartoonist ("Popeye"); O. O. McIntyre, syndicated newspaper columnist.

ENTERTAINMENT

Radio dramatization of H. G. Wells's *War of the Worlds* by Orson Welles and Mercury Theater is so realistic that it creates a brief nationwide scare.

Marineland, south of St. Augustine, Fla., opens.

Massachusetts Television Institute is established.

Vladimir K. Zworykin develops first practical television camera.

Hedda Hopper syndicates a Hollywood newspaper gossip column.

American Guild of Variety Artists is formed.

PLAYS Raymond Massey stars in *Abe Lincoln in Illinois*, Walter Huston in *Knickerbocker Holiday*,

Ethel Waters in *Mamba's Daughters*, Ole Olson and Chic Johnson in *Hellzapoppin*; Thornton Wilder completes *Our Town*.

MOVIES *Room Service* and *A Day at the Circus* with the Marx Brothers, *Boys Town* with Spencer Tracy, *You Can't Take It With You* with Jean Arthur, *Robin Hood* with Errol Flynn, *Algiers* with Charles Boyer, *Jezebel* with Bette Davis.

Bob Hope begins his radio show; Clifton Fadiman moderates *Information Please*; Kay Kyser's *Kollege of Musical Knowledge* debuts.

The British dance, Lambeth Walk, is introduced in U.S.

DEATH Pearl White, silent screen actress (*The Perils of Pauline*).

SPORTS

Johnny Vander Meer of Cincinnati Reds pitches no-hit game against Boston (June 11); repeats no-hitter four days later against Brooklyn Dodgers.

Jockey Eddie Arcaro rides 4,000th winner.

Eastern College Athletic Conference is organized.

WINNERS *Auto racing*—Floyd Roberts, Indianapolis 500; *Baseball*—New York Yankees, World Series; *Basketball*—Temple, first National Invitation Tourney (NIT); *Boxing*—Joe Louis, heavyweight; Henry Armstrong, welterweight and lightweight titles; Joey Archibald, featherweight; *Football* (bowls)—California, Rose; Auburn, Orange; Santa Clara, Sugar; Rice, Cotton; New York Giants, NFL; *Golf*—Great Britain, Walker Cup; Ralph Guldahl, U. S. Open; Paul Runyan, PGA; Henry Picard, Masters; *Hockey*—Chicago, Stanley Cup; *Horse racing*—Laurin, Kentucky Derby; Dauber, Preakness Stakes; Pasteurized, Belmont Stakes; *Tennis*—U.S., Davis Cup; Don Budge, U.S. Open (men); Alice Marble, U.S. Open (women).

DEATH Nathanael G. Herreshoff, designer of America's Cup yachts.

MISCELLANEOUS

Hurricane along Atlantic Coast from Long Island, N.Y., to Cape Cod, Mass., leaves nearly 700 dead; Southern California floods, landslides kill 144, destroy thousands of homes.

Fairchild Tropical Gardens in Florida is created.

1939

INTERNATIONAL

U.S. declares its neutrality in World War II, which begins in Europe (September 5); Inter-American Conference warns belligerent nations to keep naval actions out of Western Hemisphere.

American arms embargo is repealed, adopts policy of "cash-and-carry" arms exports (November 4).

U.S. agrees to provide financial help to Brazil for economic development.

NATIONAL

President Franklin D. Roosevelt's budget request includes $1.3 billion for national defense (January 5); requests additional $525 million later; president orders purchase of 571 military aircraft, asks for immediate construction of new naval bases.

Federal Security Agency is established to combine activities promoting social and economic security; Federal Works Agency sets up to do the same with public works; Office of Emergency Management is created in Executive Office.

Scientists, including Albert Einstein, notify president of possibilities of an atomic bomb (October 11).

King George VI and Queen Elizabeth arrive in U.S. from Canada for a week's visit, the first by a British monarch.

Social Security amendments are adopted to improve system.

Food-stamp plan that uses agricultural surpluses for those on relief is instituted in Rochester, N.Y.

Hatch Act passes, prevents federal workers from taking part in political campaigns.

Gunterville Dam on Tennessee River in Alabama is completed.

Transatlantic mail service from New York begins.

Judge Ben Lindsey creates new conciliation court in Los Angeles.

DEATHS Joel Spingarn, a founder and head of NAACP; Robert Fechner, director, Civilian Conservation Corps (1933–1939).

BUSINESS/INDUSTRY/INVENTIONS

Supreme Court upholds right of peaceful assemblage in *Hague v. CIO*; Court outlaws sit-down strikes but upholds right to collective bargaining in railroad industry.

Nylon stockings are sold for first time when DuPont puts 4,000 pairs on sale.

DEATH Arthur E. Kennelly, established electrical units and standards, adopted worldwide.

TRANSPORTATION

Pan American Airways begins regular transatlantic passenger air service.

Packard manufactures first air-conditioned automobile.

Igor I. Sikorsky develops first successful helicopter.

McDonnell Aircraft Co. is founded.

Bronx-Whitestone Bridge over East River in New York City and Deer Isle Bridge in Maine open.

SCIENCE/MEDICINE

Ernest O. Lawrence is awarded Nobel Prize in physics for invention of the cyclotron.

Dr. George B. Pegran of Columbia University helps carry out first successful U.S. demonstration of nuclear fission.

DEATHS Dr. Harvey W. Cushing, brain surgeon; Dr. Charles H. Mayo, cofounder of Mayo Clinic.

EDUCATION

Archibald MacLeish begins five years as Librarian of Congress.

Frank Aydelotte is named director of Institute of Advanced Study at Princeton University.

DEATH Henry S. Pritchett, president, Carnegie Foundation for Promotion of Teaching (1906–1930).

RELIGION

Merger of Methodist Episcopal church, Methodist Church South, and Methodist Protestant church results in 8-million member Methodist church.

Kateri Tekakwitha, "the lily of the Mohawks," is beatified in Rome, first Native American so honored.

Catholic Bishop Francis J. Spellman becomes archbishop of New York; Archbishop Samuel A. Stritch of Milwaukee is transferred to Chicago.

DEATH Catholic Archbishop George W. Mundelein of Chicago (1915–1939).

ART/MUSIC

Mt. Rushmore (S. Dak.) presidential sculptures are complete with unveiling of head of Theodore Roosevelt.

Daughters of American Revolution refuse to rent Constitution Hall for a concert by Marian Anderson; First Lady Eleanor Roosevelt resigns from DAR; concert is held Easter Sunday on the Lincoln Memorial steps with 75,000 in attendance.

Museum of Modern Art, New York City, is dedicated.

Arnold Branch completes the painting *Carolina Low Country*; Aaron Bohrod, *Chicago Street*; Ben Shahn, *Seurati's Lunch* and *Handball*; Julian E. Levi, *Fisherman's Family*; Joseph Stella, *The Bridge*.

Frank Sinatra is hired as vocalist with Harry James's orchestra; later moves to Tommy Dorsey's orchestra.

Institute of Design is established in Chicago.

The opera, *The Devil and Daniel Webster* by Douglas Moore, is presented.

SONGS (popular): "God Bless America," "All the

Dorothy wipes the Cowardly Lion's tears away!

A scene from the *Wizard of Oz*, released in 1939. PHOTOFEST

Things You Are," "Beer Barrel Polka," "In the Mood," "Little Sir Echo," "Moonlight Serenade," "Over the Rainbow," "Brazil," "I'll Never Smile Again."

DEATH Artur Bodanzky, conductor, Metropolitan Opera Co. (1915–1939).

LITERATURE/JOURNALISM

Pocket Books, inexpensive reprints, are introduced.

Elmer Davis joins CBS News; James B. Reston joins the *New York Times*.

John Crowe Ransom founds *Kenyon Review*.

BOOKS *The Grapes of Wrath* by John Steinbeck, *Wickford Point* by John P. Marquand, *Huntsman, What Quarry?* (poetry) by Edna St. Vincent Millay, *Here Lies* by Dorothy Parker, *The Web and the Rock* by Thomas Wolfe, *The Nazarene* by Sholem Asch, *Children of God* by Vardis Fisher, *Abraham Lincoln* (4 volumes) by Carl Sandburg.

DEATHS Heywood Broun, columnist; Zane Grey, author of Western novels.

ENTERTAINMENT

Grand Ole Opry goes on national television.

1939

PLAYS Tallulah Bankhead stars in *The Little Foxes*, Monty Woolley in *The Man Who Came to Dinner*, Ethel Merman in Cole Porter's *DuBarry Was a Lady*, Bill Robinson in *The Hot Mikado*, Howard Lindsay in *Life with Father*, Gertrude Lawrence in *Skylark*.

MOVIES *Stagecoach* with John Wayne, *Gone with the Wind* with Vivien Leigh and Clark Gable, *The Wizard of Oz* with Judy Garland, *Mr. Smith Goes to Washington* with James Stewart, *Goodbye, Mr. Chips* with Robert Donat, *Wuthering Heights* with Merle Oberon and Laurence Olivier.

Among the new radio shows are *Ellery Queen*, *The Aldrich Family*, *Dr. I.Q.*

A new dance, the Samba, arrives from Brazil.

DEATHS Douglas Fairbanks, silent-screen actor; Sidney Howard, playwright; Alice Brady, stage and screen actress.

SPORTS

Baseball Hall of Fame in Cooperstown, N.Y., is dedicated.

Television comes into sports: first college baseball game (May 17), first major league game (Brooklyn–Cincinnati, August 26), first college football game (Fordham–Waynesburg, September 30), pro football game (Brooklyn–Philadelphia, October 22), first prizefight (June 1).

Lou Gehrig takes himself out of lineup as New York Yankees first baseman (May 2), ends consecutive-game streak at 2,130 (dies less than two years later at 38).

Underwater photography is used for first time to determine finish in swimming races.

WINNERS *Auto racing*—Wilbur Shaw, Indianapolis 500; *Baseball*—New York Yankees, World Series; *Basketball*—Long Island, NIT; Oregon, first NCAA tournament; *Boxing*—Joe Louis, heavyweight; Billy Conn, light heavyweight; Lou Ambers, lightweight; *Football* (bowls)—Southern California, Rose; Tennessee, Orange; Texas Christian, Sugar; St. Mary's, Cotton; Green Bay, NFL; *Golf*—Byron Nelson, U.S. Open; Henry Picard, PGA; Ralph Guldahl, Masters; *Hockey*—Boston, Stanley Cup; *Horse racing*—Johnstown, Kentucky Derby and Belmont Stakes; Challedon, Preakness Stakes; *Tennis*—Australia, Davis Cup; Bobby Riggs, U.S. Open (men); Alice Marble, U.S. Open (women); *Waterskiing*—Bruce Parker, first national title (men); Esther Yates (women).

DEATHS Joe E. Carr, NFL president (1921–1939); Floyd Roberts, winner of 1938 Indianapolis 500 is killed in 1939 race; Jacob Ruppert, brewer and owner, New York Yankees baseball team; James Naismith, developer of basketball.

MISCELLANEOUS

New York World's Fair and Golden Gate Exposition in San Francisco are held.

U.S. submarine *Squalus* sinks at Portsmouth, N.H.; 33 of 59 crewmen are saved by using a diving bell.

1940

INTERNATIONAL

World War II (prelude)

President Franklin D. Roosevelt requests $1.8 billion for national defense, $1.2 billion for producing 50,000 planes a year; then asks for $1.3 billion more.

U.S. Air Defense Command is created (February 26); War Department releases outdated stocks (June 3) and transfers 50 overage destroyers to Great Britain in return for bases in Newfoundland and the Caribbean (September 3); U.S. announces embargo on scrap iron and steel to all countries outside the Western Hemisphere except Great Britain (October 16).

Alien Registration Act passes (June 28); 5 million aliens register between August 27 and December 26; Congress approves first peacetime draft for military service of men 21–35 and training of 1.2 million troops and 800,000 reserves in a year (September 16); 16.4 million register by October 16; numbers for the order of service are drawn October 29: first number is 158.

National Defense Research Committee is established, directed by Dr. Vannevar Bush; later becomes Office of Scientific Research and Development.

Pan-American Union approves steps to prevent transfer of European colonies in Western Hemisphere (June 30); all 21 American republics approve Act of Havana (July 30); permits takeover of any colony endangered by aggression.

President Roosevelt and Canadian Prime Minister W. L. McKenzie King agree to set up a Permanent Joint Board on Defense (October 18).

NATIONAL

President Roosevelt is elected to unprecedented third term, receives 27,243,466 popular and 449 electoral votes compared to Republican Wendell L. Willkie's 22,304,755 popular and 82 electoral votes; Republican national convention (June 4) is first to be televised.

Sixteenth census reports national population at 132,164,569.

Chickamauga Dam on Tennessee River and Ft. Peck Dam on Missouri River in Montana are completed.

Benjamin O. Davis becomes first African American army general.

John F. Kennedy becomes secretary to his father, ambassador to Great Britain.

Franklin D. Roosevelt Library at Hyde Park, N.Y., is dedicated.

National debt is $43 billion.

DEATH Marcus Garvey, founder of first important African American organization, Universal Negro Improvement Assn.

In 1940, in Bridgeport, Connecticut, Ivor Sikorsky makes the first successful fully controlled helicopter flight. The device goes straight up for 30 feet, flies 200 feet around the field, and comes straight down. UPI/CORBIS-BETTMANN

1940

BUSINESS/INDUSTRY/INVENTIONS

Chester E. Carlson patents the xerography process.

Charles Eames and Eero Saarinen design revolutionary contour-molded plywood chair that leads to machine-produced furniture.

National unemployment rate reaches 14.6%.

Forty-hour workweek goes into effect (October 24).

Philip Murray begins 12 years as president of CIO; George Meany becomes secretary-treasurer of AFL.

Supreme Court upholds the right of peaceful picketing.

DEATHS John T. Thompson, co-inventor of submachine gun; Walter P. Chrysler, founder, Chrysler Corp.; Claude W. Kress, cofounder, dime-store chain; Charles S. Tainter, inventor of Dictaphone.

TRANSPORTATION

National Airport in Washington, D.C., is dedicated.

Lake Washington Floating Bridge in Seattle opens; suspension bridge over the Narrows in Tacoma, Wash., collapses.

Igor I. Sikorsky flies helicopter for 15 minutes at Stamford, Conn.

Automobile registrations for year reach 27,465,826.

SCIENCE/MEDICINE

National Institute of Health in Bethesda, Md., is dedicated.

Vladimir K. Zworykin demonstrates his electron microscope.

Edwin M. McMillan and Philip H. Abelson discover neptunium (element 93); McMillan and Glenn T. Seaborg discover plutonium (element 94).

DEATHS Raymond Pearl, a founder of biometry; S. Adolphus Knopf, founder of New York City and national tuberculosis associations.

RELIGION

Aurelia H. Reinhardt, president of Mills College, becomes first woman moderator of Unitarian church.

Supreme Court in *Cantwell v. Connecticut* upholds right of Jehovah's Witnesses to solicit funds for religious purposes.

Israel Rosenberg becomes president of Union of Orthodox Rabbis.

DEATH Cyrus Adler, a leader of Conservative Judaism.

ART/MUSIC

American Ballet Theater gives its first performance.

Licia Albanese debuts at Metropolitan Opera.

John Steuart Curry completes the painting *Wisconsin Landscape*; Lyonel Feininger, *The River*; Marsden Hartley, *Mount Katahdin, Autumn No. 1*; Joseph Stella, *Full Moon* (*Barbados*); John Flanagan completes the sculpture *Not Yet*.

A musical quartet written by Benjamin Franklin is found in Paris Conservatory.

Bernard Herrmann composes dramatic cantata *Moby Dick*.

SONGS (popular): "Blueberry Hill," "Fools Rush In," "Frenesi," "How High the Moon," "I'll Never Smile Again," "Pennsylvania 6-5000," "You Are My Sunshine," "All the Things You Are," "Polka Dots and Moonbeams."

DEATHS Hal Kemp, bandleader of 1930s; Jonas Lie, artist (*Brooklyn Bridge*).

LITERATURE/JOURNALISM

Norman Cousins begins 31 years as executive editor of *Saturday Review of Literature*.

BOOKS *For Whom the Bell Tolls* by Ernest Hemingway, *The Heart Is a Lonely Hunter* by Carson McCullers, *Pal Joey* by John O'Hara, *My Name Is Aram* by William Saroyan, *You Can't Go Home Again* by Thomas Wolfe, *Native Son* by Richard Wright, *Homeward to America* (poetry) by John Ciardi, *The Ox-Bow Incident* by Walter V. Clark.

C. C. Beck draws comic strip "Captain Marvel."

DEATHS Edwin Markham, poet ("Man with a Hoe"); F. Scott Fitzgerald, author; Lewis W. Hine, photographer who originated photo story; Robert S. Abbott, publisher, *Chicago Defender* (1905–1940).

ENTERTAINMENT

FM (frequency-modulation) radio introduced (January 5); Peter C. Goldmark develops color television.

American Theater Wing, which operates Stage Door Canteens, originates.

PLAYS Alfred Lunt and Lynn Fontanne star in *There Shall Be No Night*, Ethel Waters in *Cabin in the Sky*, Ethel Merman in *Panama Hattie*, Gene Kelly in *Pal Joey*.

MOVIES *The Great Dictator* with Charlie Chaplin, *The Road to Singapore* with Bing Crosby and Bob Hope, two Disney films *Fantasia* and *Pinocchio*, *The Grapes of Wrath* with Henry Fonda, *The Philadelphia Story* with Katharine Hepburn, *Rebecca* with Laurence Olivier.

RADIO *The Shadow, Superman, Bell Telephone Hour, Double or Nothing, The Quiz Kids, Truth or Consequences,* and *Abbott and Costello*.

DEATHS Ben Turpin, silent-screen comedian; Tom Mix, silent-screen cowboy.

SPORTS

Cornelius Warmerdam is first to clear 15 feet in pole vault.

Jimmie Foxx of Philadelphia Athletics hits 500th home run.

Belle Martell of Van Nuys, Calif., becomes first woman licensed as a prizefight referee.

WINNERS *Auto racing*—Wilbur Shaw, Indianapolis 500; *Baseball*—Cincinnati Reds, World Series; *Basketball*—Colorado, NIT; Indiana, NCAA; *Boxing*—Joe Louis, heavyweight; Fritzie Zivic, welterweight; Tony Zale, middleweight; Lew Jenkins, lightweight; *Football* (bowls)—Southern California, Rose; Georgia Tech, Orange; Texas A&M, Sugar; Clemson, Cotton; Chicago Bears, NFL; *Golf*—Lawson Little, U.S. Open; Byron Nelson, PGA; Jimmy Demaret, Masters; *Gymnastics*—Illinois, first intercollegiate title; *Hockey*—New York Rangers, Stanley Cup; *Horse racing*—Gallahadion, Kentucky Derby; Bimelech, Preakness Stakes and Belmont Stakes; *Tennis*—Don McNeill, U.S. Open (men), Alice Marble, U.S. Open (women).

MISCELLANEOUS

Fire in a Natchez, Miss., dance hall kills 198.

INTERNATIONAL

World War II

After almost a year of preparing and helping allies under attack, U.S. enters World War II with shocking speed.

Japanese planes in surprise dawn attack December 7 on Pearl Harbor destroy or damage 19 U.S. warships and 150 planes; 2,400 are killed. Japanese also attack Philippines, Guam, Midway, Hong Kong, and the Malay Peninsula.

Congress on December 8 takes 33 minutes to declare war on Japan with Montana Rep. Jeannette Rankin casting the only dissenting vote (she

1941

voted the same way in 1917). Germany and Italy declare war on U.S. (December 11); U.S. declares war on them.

Japanese troops land on Luzon in the Philippines (December 10), capture Guam (December 11).

Admiral Chester Nimitz commands Pacific fleet, Admiral Ernest King heads U.S. naval forces.

Before these December events, U.S. had created Lend-Lease Program (March 11), allowing nations deemed vital to U.S. to get arms and equipment by sale, transfer, or lease; $7 billion was appropriated. U.S. promises to help Russia after it is

1941

New York Yankee Joe DiMaggio bats during a game in Washington, D.C., on June 29, 1941. His consecutive-game hitting streak ends in 1941 at 56 games. UPI/CORBIS-BETTMANN

invaded by Germany, granting $1 billion in credit; signs agreement for lend-lease with China.

U.S. pledges defense of Denmark's Greenland after getting right to build installations there (April 9); U.S. lands troops on Denmark's Iceland after agreement on bases (July 7).

U.S. involved in war even before formal entry: merchant ship *Robin Moor* is sunk in the Atlantic by German submarine (May 21); U.S. destroyer *Kearney* is torpedoed (October 17), destroyer *Reuben James* is sunk (October 30). The 1939 Neutrality Act is amended (November 17) to permit arming merchant ships; all German and Italian (and later Japanese) assets in U.S. are frozen.

After a secret meeting at sea, President Franklin D. Roosevelt and British Prime Minister Winston Churchill issue Atlantic Charter (August 14), assures the right of people to choose and retain own governments, renounces territorial ambitions, and calls for disarmament of aggressor nations.

Preparations at home include creation of various agencies: Office of Production Management (January 7), War Shipping Administration (February 7), Office of Price Administration (April 15), Office of Civilian Defense (May 20), Office of Defense Transportation (December 18), Office of Censorship (December 19). United Service Organizations (USO) is formed (April 7).

President proclaims national emergency (May 27), orders closing of German and Italian consulates; a dimout 15 miles wide along the Atlantic Coast is put into effect (April 28) to combat submarine attacks; President orders step-up of production of heavy bombers from 9 a month to 50.

Selective Service is extended for 18 months (August 18), ages change from 21–35 to 20–45; rationing begins with automobile tires (December 27).

U.S. Civil Air patrol is created (December 1) as part of civil-defense operation.

Navy takes over French liner *Normandie* in New York Harbor.

NATIONAL

President enunciates "four freedoms" in a speech to Congress: freedom of speech and religion, freedom from want and fear.

Supreme Court Chief Justice Charles Evans Hughes resigns; Associate Justice Harlan F. Stone succeeds him.

Supreme Court in *Edwards v. California* rules "Okie" law designed to exclude indigent immigrants unconstitutional; upholds 1938 Fair Labor Standards Act in *United States v. Darby.*

Grand Coulee Dam, world's largest hydroelectric facility, generates power in Washington; Los Angeles and other Southern California cities receive water from Colorado River Aqueduct.

Mammoth Cave (Ky.) National Park is established.

Adam Clayton Powell, pastor of a Harlem Baptist church, becomes first African American member of New York City Council.

Lanham Act authorizes $150 million for defense housing.

BUSINESS/INDUSTRY/INVENTIONS

National Defense Mediation Board is given power to deal with labor disputes in defense industries; Government takes over North American Aviation plant in Inglewood, Calif., to end strike impairing defense production.

Fair Employment Practice Committee is set up to curb discrimination in war production and government employment.

Dacron is introduced.

Simmons Co. manufactures electric blankets.

TRANSPORTATION

Ford Motor Co. recognizes United Auto Workers as bargaining agent for its employees.

Rainbow Bridge over Niagara River at Niagara Falls opens.

DEATH Frederic J. Fisher of Fisher Body Co.

SCIENCE/MEDICINE

Glenn T. Seaborg and Emilio Segre produce plu-

tonium, first manufactured fissionable material.

First atomic reactor is built.

EDUCATION

Supreme Court rules that religious training in public schools is unconstitutional.

RELIGION

Rev. Karl M. Block becomes Episcopal bishop of California.

ART/MUSIC

National Gallery of Art opens in Washington, D.C.

Ted Shawn founds Jacob's Pillow Dance Festival in Massachusetts.

Grandma (Anna M.) Moses completes the painting *Black Horses*; Louis Guglielmi, *Terror in Brooklyn*; Joseph Hirsch, *The Senator.*

SONGS (popular) "The Anniversary Waltz," "Bewitched, Bothered, and Bewildered," "Chattanooga Choo Choo," "Deep in the Heart of Texas," "The Last Time I Saw Paris," "I Don't Want to Walk Without You," "Jersey Bounce," "Take the A Train," "There I've Said It Again."

DEATHS Gutzon Borglum, sculptor of Mt. Rushmore president heads; Jelly Roll Morton, jazz musician and composer.

LITERATURE/JOURNALISM

Chicago Sun is founded.

BOOKS *The Last Tycoon* by F. Scott Fitzgerald, *Keys of the Kingdom* by A. J. Cronin, *Saratoga Trunk* by Edna Ferber, *H. M. Pulham, Esquire* by John P. Marquand, *Berlin Diary* by William L. Shirer.

DEATH Edward J. H. O'Brien, editor of annual best short-stories collections (1915–1940).

ENTERTAINMENT

WNBT, New York City, shows first audience participation telecast; first commercial television license is issued to NBC (July 1); Nielsen gauges radio ratings.

PLAYS Josephine Hull starts in *Arsenic and Old Lace*, Gertrude Lawrence in *Lady in the Dark*, Mady Christians in *Watch on the Rhine.*

1942

MOVIES *Citizen Kane* with Orson Welles, *The Maltese Falcon* with Humphrey Bogart, *Sergeant York* with Gary Cooper, *Suspicion* with Cary Grant, *How Green Was My Valley* with Walter Pidgeon, *Sun Valley Serenade* with Sonja Henie.

Milton Berle and Red Skelton begin radio shows; other new programs are *Duffy's Tavern* and *Mr. and Mrs. North*.

DEATH Screen actress Carole Lombard, in plane crash.

SPORTS

American Bowling Congress Hall of Fame is founded.

New York Yankee Joe DiMaggio's consecutive-game hitting streak ends at 56 games.

Lefty Grove of Boston Red Sox wins 300th baseball game.

WINNERS *Auto racing*—Floyd Davis, Mauri Rose, Indianapolis 500; *Baseball*—New York Yankees, World Series; *Basketball*—Long Island, NIT; Wisconsin, NCAA; *Bowling*—John Crimmins, first all-star tournament; *Boxing*—Joe Louis, heavyweight; Gus Lesnevich, light heavyweight; Freddie Cochrane, welterweight; Tony Zale, middlweight; Sammy Angott, lightweight; Chalky Wright, featherweight; *Football* (bowls)—Stanford, Rose; Mississippi State, Orange; Boston College, Sugar; Texas A&M, Cotton; Chicago Bears, NFL; *Golf*—Craig Wood, U.S. Open and Masters; Victor Ghezzi, PGA; *Hockey*—Boston, Stanley Cup; *Horse racing*—Whirlaway wins Kentucky Derby, Preakness Stakes, and Belmont Stakes to become fifth Triple Crown winner; *Tennis*—Bobby Riggs, U.S. Open (men); Sarah Palfrey Cooke, U.S. Open (women).

DEATH Lou Gehrig, baseball player who set consecutive-game record at 2,130 games

MISCELLANEOUS

Blizzard strikes upper Midwest, claims 70 lives.

INTERNATIONAL

World War II

1942

PACIFIC THEATER Manila and Cavite fall to Japanese (January 2); U.S. and Filipino troops abandon Bataan Peninsula (April 9), 37,000 men are taken prisoner, led on "death march" with about 5,200 dying en route; last stronghold, island fort of Corregidor falls (May 6).

Pacific fleet attacks Marshall and Gilbert islands (February 1); Allies lose four cruisers, four destroyers in two-day battle of Java Sea and Sunda Strait, a delaying action (February 27); U.S. troops land on New Caledonia (March 12); in Battle of Coral Sea (May 7), Allies halt Japanese drive on Australia; one Japanese carrier is lost, two are damaged; U.S. carrier *Lexington* is lost.

Three-day Battle of Midway (June 3–6) is first defeat of Japanese forces, who lose four aircraft carriers, 275 planes; U.S. loses carrier *Yorktown*; U.S. forces land on Guadalcanal (August 7); Allied naval forces lose four cruisers in Battle of Savo Island; Guadalcanal is gained (November 15).

First battle for Solomon Islands (October 11) costs Japan an aircraft carrier, four destroyers; the second battle, two weeks later, inflicts heavy losses on Japanese fleet; U.S. carrier *Hornet* is sunk.

U.S. B-25s led by Maj. Gen. James H. Doolittle, bomb Tokyo (April 18); Japanese bomb Alaskan bases (June 3), occupy Attu and Kiska in Aleutian Islands.

EUROPEAN THEATER U.S. troops arrive in North Ireland (January 26); U.S. destroyer *Truxton* and cargo ship are sunk off Newfoundland (February 18), 204 perish; agreement is reached with Denmark on military bases in Greenland (April 10); first U.S. air operation in Europe occurs when air force crews take part in British raid on Netherlands (July 4); first U.S. attack by 8th Air Force on railroad yards is at Rouen, France (August 17).

A flying wedge of dive bombers during the Battle of Midway, June 1942. The bombers will sink four Japanese carriers. THE GRANGER COLLECTION, NEW YORK

Allied forces land in North Africa (November 8), take Oran, Casablanca, and Algiers; enter Tunisia (November 15).

Allied nations sign declaration (January 1), affirm Atlantic Charter principles, a joint effort to defeat the Axis powers, and pledge not to make separate peace.

U.S. and Mexico establish joint defense commission (January 12); two-week Rio de Janeiro Conference of 21 American republics ends (January 29) with diplomatic break with Axis, sets up defense for Panama Canal; Act of Chapultepec (March 3) provides that an attack on one American state will be regarded as attack on all, resulting in use of force.

U.S., Great Britain, Russia, and China hold nine-day strategy session; first Moscow Conference meets (August 12), informs Russia that a second European front not possible in 1942.

NATIONAL

American military leadership is created, names Gen. Douglas MacArthur Allied commander in the Pacific (March 17), Gen. Dwight D. Eisenhower commander in Europe (June 11); later Eisenhower becomes Allied commander of North African invasion.

Women's service corps are created: Women Ap-pointed for Voluntary Emergency Service (WAVES), the women's navy branch (July 30), with Wellesley President Mildred McAfee director; Women's Army Auxiliary Corps (WAAC, later WAC) (May 14) with Oveta Culp Hobby director; Women's Auxiliary Ferrying Squadron (WAFS) created by Air Transport Command (September 10); Coast Guard Women's Reserve (SPARS) (November 23), Dorothy C. Stratton, commander.

Various agencies handle war effort: National War Labor Board, which replaces Defense Mediation Board; War Production Board, Office of Civil Defense; Office of Price Administration issues ration books for sugar, coffee, and gasoline; War Shipping Administration, National Housing Agency, War Manpower Commission; Office of War Information, which is headed by Elmer Davis; Office of Strategic Services, which is headed by William Donovan; Office of Economic Stabilization.

Efforts are concentrated on producing war materials: $4-billion program is created to increase synthetic rubber production (January 7); President Franklin D. Roosevelt appeals on radio for scrap rubber; more than 300,000 tons are collected in two weeks.

Manhattan Project is organized (June 18) for production of an atomic bomb; other facilities are at Oak Ridge, Tenn., and Los Alamos, N.Mex.;

plutonium production plant is built at Hanford, Wash.; Enrico Fermi, Arthur Compton, Leo Szilard, and other scientists at University of Chicago achieve first self-sustaining nuclear chain reaction (December 2), marks beginning of atomic age.

Draft age is lowered from 20 to 18 years.

About 10,000 Japanese Americans on West Coast and in Arizona are relocated to camps in interior area.

V-mail is started.

FBI announces capture of eight Nazi saboteurs who landed by submarine on Long Island and Florida.

First war bond drive opens November 30; nearly $13 billion in bonds are sold by December 23.

Social Justice, publication of Rev. Charles E. Coughlin's radical group, is barred from the mails, ceases publication; his Catholic superiors impose silence on him.

Nationwide daylight saving time goes into effect.

French liner *Normandie*, in conversion to transport duty, capsizes and burns at New York City dock.

BUSINESS/INDUSTRY/INVENTIONS

Kaiser Shipyards, north of Richmond, Calif., sets record of constructing a ship in $4\frac{1}{2}$ days, builds 1,460 ships during World War II; Henry J. Kaiser, finding it difficult to find enough steel for his shipyards, builds first steel plant on Pacific Coast.

General Electric in Bridgeport produces bazooka rocket gun.

DEATH Ralph Cram, architect, helped design West Point.

TRANSPORTATION

First U.S. jet flight is made in a Bell XP-59A at Edwards Air Force Base, Cal. (October 1).

Pan American Airways completes first round-the-world commercial flight.

Alcan Highway, 1,523 miles from British Columbia to Alaska, is completed (December 1).

In *Casablanca* (1942), Humphrey Bogart (right) plays Rick, who defends his true love, played by Ingrid Bergman, and her husband, a French Resistance fighter, from the Nazis. PHOTOFEST

Two-place army helicopter makes cross-country helicopter flight from Stratford, Conn., to Wright Field, Ohio.

SCIENCE/MEDICINE

Bethesda (Md.) Naval Medical Center is dedicated.

Permanente (now Kaiser) Foundation, a pioneer nonprofit health maintenance organization, is established.

DEATH Franz Boas, established modern structure of anthropology.

EDUCATION

DEATH Martha M. Berry, founder of schools for underprivileged Georgia children.

RELIGION

Nathan H. Knorr becomes president of Watch Tower Bible and Tract Society.

DEATH Joseph F. Rutherford, head of Jehovah's Witnesses (1916–1942).

ART/MUSIC

William Schuman composes Secular Cantata no. 2; Leonard Bernstein presents first work, "Sonata for Clarinet and Piano;" Aaron Copland produces *Lincoln Portrait*, for orchestra and speaker, and the ballet *Rodeo*; Gian Carlo Menotti composes opera, *The Island God*.

Edward Hopper completes the painting *Nighthawks*; Albert E. Gallatin, *Composition*.

SONGS (popular): "Don't Get Around Much Anymore," "For Me and My Gal," "Manhattan Serenade," "One Dozen Roses," "Praise the Lord and Pass the Ammunition," "Tangerine," "That Old Black Magic," "Don't Sit Under the Apple Tree," "White Christmas."

DEATHS Grant Wood, artist; Tony Sarg, marionette maker; Bunny Berrigan, swing trumpeter.

LITERATURE/JOURNALISM

George Baker draws "Sad Sack" cartoons in *Yank Magazine*.

Negro Digest, a monthly magazine, is founded.

Earl Wilson writes syndicated column, "It Happened Last Night."

BOOKS *The Robe* by Lloyd C. Douglas, *Paul Revere* by Esther Forbes, *Admiral of the Ocean Sea* by Samuel Eliot Morison, *A Witness Tree* (poetry) by Robert Frost, *Generation of Vipers* by Philip Wylie, *Dragon Seed* by Pearl Buck, *They Were Expendable* by William L. White, *The Moon Is Down* by John Steinbeck.

DEATH Condé Nast, publisher (*Vanity Fair, Vogue*).

ENTERTAINMENT

PLAYS Fredric March stars in *The Skin of Our Teeth*, Ethel Barrymore in *The Corn Is Green*, Ray Bolger in *By Jupiter*, Arlene Francis in *The Doughgirls*.

MOVIES *Casablanca* with Humphrey Bogart, *Yankee Doodle Dandy* with Jimmy Cagney, *Mrs. Miniver* with Greer Garson, *Holiday Inn* with Bing Crosby, *My Sister Eileen* with Rosalind Russell, *For Me and My Gal* with Judy Garland.

CBS signs columnist Ed Sullivan to weekly radio show; other new shows are *Can You Top This?*, *People Are Funny*, *Suspense*.

The jitterbug becomes an extremely popular dance.

DEATHS John Barrymore, stage and screen actor; Otis Skinner, actor; George M. Cohan, actor, playwright, and composer; Graham McNamee, radio announcer; Joseph M. Weber of Weber & Fields comedy team.

SPORTS

Paul Waner of Pittsburgh Pirates gets his 3,000th hit.

Cornelius Warmerdam sets outdoor pole vault record of 15 feet $7\frac{3}{4}$ inches.

National Boxing Assn. freezes titles of boxers in service.

Torger Tokle breaks own ski jump record, reaches 289 feet.

WINNERS *Baseball*—St. Louis Cardinals, World Series; *Basketball*—West Virginia, NIT; Stanford, NCAA; *Boxing*—Joe Louis, heavyweight; Beau Jack, lightweight; Willy Pep, featherweight; *Football* (bowls)—Oregon State, Rose; Georgia, Or-

1943

ange; Fordham, Sugar; Alabama, Cotton; Washington, NFL; *Golf*—Sam Snead, PGA; Byron Nelson, Masters; *Hockey*—Toronto, Stanley Cup; *Horse racing*—Shut Out, Kentucky Derby and Belmont Stakes; Alsab, Preakness Stakes; *Tennis*—Ted Schroeder, U.S. Open (men); Pauline Betz, U. S. Open (women).

MISCELLANEOUS

Fire in Boston nightclub (Cocoanut Grove) kills 491 people.

James Farmer leads in founding CORE (Congress of Racial Equality).

Eddie Rickenbacker, on government mission with seven others, is forced down in Pacific; survives 23 days with only fish and rainwater to sustain them.

Zoot suits become a popular male garb, featuring a long, one-button jacket with padded shoulders and high-waisted trousers that grip the ankles.

INTERNATIONAL

World War II

PACIFIC THEATER In Battle of Bismarck Sea (March 2), Japanese suffer heavy losses (12 troop convoy ships, 10 warships), leads to recapture of much of New Guinea; U.S. begins offensive in South Pacific, retakes most of Solomon Islands (June 30); Allied troops capture Lae, New Guinea (September 16). In Alaska, U.S. forces secure Attu Island after 19 days of fighting (May 30); U.S. and Canadian troops regain Aleutians.

NORTH AFRICA U.S. troops are thrown back at Kasserine Pass (February 14); U.S. troops join British on Mareth Line in Tunisia (March 19), encircle Germans (April 7); British take Tunis; Americans, Bizerte (May 7); section of North African theater collapses when 250,000 Axis troops surrender (May 13).

EUROPEAN THEATER Allied planes hammer Axis positions: Wilhelmshaven (January 27), U.S. planes bomb major oil refineries at Ploesti, Rumania (August 1); ball-bearing plants in Regensburg and Schweinfurt (August 17). U.S. and British forces launch air and sea invasion of Sicily (July 10); Palermo falls (July 14), followed by Catania (August 5) and Messina (August 17), completing island takeover. Allies launch invasion of Italy from Sicily (September 3), Italy surrenders (September 8), Germans move into Rome (Sep-

1943

tember 10), Italian fleet surrenders (September 11), Allies take Salerno (September 18); Allied control commission for Italy is established (November 10).

Throughout year, Allied leaders confer: Ten-day Casablanca meeting declares war will go on until "unconditional surrender" is secured (January 24); two-week conference in Washington plans second European front (May 26); President Franklin Roosevelt and British Prime Minister Winston Churchill meet for a week in August; first Cairo Conference finds U.S., British, and Chinese leaders agreeing to fight against Japan until unconditional surrender (November 22); Teheran Conference (November 28) discusses second front in Europe; second Cairo Conference includes Turkish President Ismet İnönü (December 4).

There are also meetings of what become United Nations organizations: Food & Agricultural Organization (May 18), Relief & Rehabilitation Administration (November 9).

DEATH Army Gen. Frank M. Andrews, in plane crash.

NATIONAL

War-related events include: Minimum workweek is lengthened from 40 to 48 hours (with overtime pay for the additional hours) (February 9); War Manpower Commission issues regulations that freeze workers into war jobs; War Production Board halts nonessential housing and highway construction.

Point rationing begins (March 1) for meats, fats and oils, butter, cheese, and processed food; shoes are added later; president orders freeze on prices, wages, and salaries, effective May 12; government takes over Eastern coal mines for a day and later the railroads to prevent a strike.

Office of War Mobilization is created; pay-as-you-go income tax goes into effect (July 1).

Two Depression-era programs end: Civilian Conservation Corps (CCC), which gave young men jobs, and Works Project Administration (WPA), which in eight years employed 8.5 million people on 1.4 million projects that cost $11 billion.

President finds time to dedicate new Merchant Marine Academy, Kings Point, N.Y., and the Jefferson Memorial in Washington, D.C.

New Defense Department home, the Pentagon, is completed.

White anger over hiring blacks in war plants in Detroit (June 20) sparks race riots, 34 deaths result.

Two Tennessee dams completed: Douglas on French Broad River and Ft. Loudon on Tennessee River.

DEATH Former First Lady Helen H. Taft (1909–1913).

BUSINESS/INDUSTRY/INVENTIONS

World's longest oil pipeline (1,254 miles), between Longview, Tex., and Phoenixville, Pa., operates.

DEATHS Michael J. Owens, a founder of Libbey-Owens Glass; Nikola Tesla, inventor of many electrical devices and systems; J. P. Morgan, banker.

TRANSPORTATION

Chicago's first subway is dedicated (October 16).

DEATH Edsel B. Ford, auto company president (1919–1943).

SCIENCE/MEDICINE

Polio epidemic kills 1,151 persons, cripples thousands.

Otto Stern is awarded Nobel Prize in physics for discovery of magnetic momentum of the proton and contribution to molecular ray method; Edward A. Doisy shares physiology/medicine prize with Henrik C. P. Dam of Denmark for discovery of chemical nature of vitamin A.

Selman A. Waksman, microbiologist, and his coworkers discover antibiotic, streptomycin.

DEATHS Aleš Hrdlička, helped establish U.S. physical anthropology; Clifford W. Beers, public health pioneer; Winford L. Lewis, developer of lewisite (poison gas); George Washington Carver, agronomist, developed hundreds of by-products of peanuts.

EDUCATION

Milton S. Eisenhower becomes president of Kansas State University.

United Negro College Fund is organized.

RELIGION

Supreme Court rules that schoolchildren cannot be compelled to salute the flag if it conflicts with their religion.

ART/MUSIC

WRGB, Schenectady (N.Y.), televises first complete opera (*Hansel and Gretel*) (February 23).

Howard Hanson composes Symphony no. 4, op. 34; Marc Blitzstein, *Freedom Morning*; William H. Schuman, "A Free Song."

PAINTINGS Robert Motherwell, *Pancho Villa, Dead and Alive*; Thomas Hart Benton, *July Hay*; Julio DeDiego, *The Portentous City*; Arshile Gorky, *Waterfall*; Jackson Pollock, *The She-Wolf*.

SONGS (popular): "Besame Mucho," "Holiday for Strings," "I'll Be Home for Christmas," "You'd Be So Nice To Come Home To," "I've Heard That Song Before," "Mairzy Doats," "Pistol Packing Mama."

DEATHS Sergei Rachmaninoff, pianist and composer; Fats Waller, pianist and composer ("Honeysuckle Rose").

LITERATURE/JOURNALISM

Bill Mauldin's cartoons appear in *Stars & Stripes*, the army newspaper.

1944

BOOKS *A Tree Grows in Brooklyn* by Betty Smith, *Western Star* (poetry) by Stephen Vincent Benét, *At Heaven's Gate* by Robert Penn Warren, *The Fountainhead* by Ayn Rand, *The Apostle* by Sholem Asch.

DEATH Albert W. Marquis, founder of *Who's Who*.

ENTERTAINMENT

PLAYS Alfred Drake stars in *Oklahoma!*, Mary Martin in *One Touch of Venus*, Margaret Sullavan in *The Voice of the Turtle*, Moss Hart writes *Winged Victory*.

MOVIES *For Whom the Bell Tolls* with Gary Cooper, *Girl Crazy* with Judy Garland, *Jane Eyre* with Joan Fontaine, *Lassie Come Home* with Roddy McDowall, *Stormy Weather* with Lena Horne, *The Song of Bernadette* with Jennifer Jones.

New radio programs include *Life of Riley*, *Perry Mason*, and Jimmy Durante.

DEATH Leslie Howard, screen actor.

SPORTS

William D. Cox, part-owner of Philadelphia Phillies baseball team, is banned for life by Commissioner Kenesaw M. Landis for betting on own team.

Women's International Bowling Congress (WIBC) Hall of Fame is founded.

WINNERS *Baseball* — New York Yankees, World Series; *Basketball* — St. Johns, NIT; Wyoming, NCAA; *Bowling* — Ned Day, bowler of year; *Boxing* — Beau Jack, lightweight; *Football* (bowls) — Georgia, Rose; Alabama, Orange; Tennessee, Sugar; Texas, Cotton; Chicago Bears, NFL; *Hockey* — Detroit, Stanley Cup; *Horse racing* — Count Fleet becomes sixth Triple Crown winner taking the Kentucky Derby, Preakness Stakes, and Belmont Stakes; *Tennis* — Joseph Hunt, U.S. Open (men); Pauline Betz, U.S. Open (women).

MISCELLANEOUS

Four chaplains aboard the *Dorchester* give up their life jackets to others and go down with the ship.

Two railroad accidents occur: Frankfort Junction in Philadelphia (79 lives are lost), and between Rennert and Buie, N.C. (72 lives).

INTERNATIONAL

World War II

EUROPEAN THEATER More than 150,000 Allied troops make amphibious landings (June 6) on northern French coast, 4,000 invasion craft and 11,000 planes support; Germans counter with pilotless aircraft (V2s) attacks on London. U.S. troops land on western shore of Cherbourg Peninsula (June 18), take the city (June 27); British capture Caen (July 9), U.S. takes St.-Lô (July 25) and Brest (August 7) and overrun Brittany Peninsula by August 10. Allied troops move rapidly, liberating Paris (August 25), Brussels and Antwerp (September 4), Luxembourg (September 11). U.S. troops enter Germany (September 12), capture Aachen (October 21), Metz (November 22), and Strasbourg (November 23).

1944

Germans launch counteroffensive (Battle of the Bulge) (December 16), hoping to split Allied armies; stubborn resistance at Bastogne gives time for Allied reinforcements to arrive (December 26) and end the threat.

Allies are also busy in Italy with amphibious landings at Anzio (January 22), but stiff German resistance stalls drive for months; Rome falls (June 4), U.S. takes Leghorn, the British Florence (July 9). Other Allied forces land in Southern France (August 15), drive up the Rhône Valley.

PACIFIC THEATER U.S. forces advance in southern and central Pacific with invasion of Marshall Islands (January 31); recapture Kwajalein (February 6), Eniwetok (February 22), Admiralty Islands (March 25), Hollandia (April 22); U.S. forces land on Mariana Islands (June 15), take Saipan

(July 9), Guam (August 10), Tinian (August 11).

Battle of the Philippine Sea (June 19) costs Japanese 3 aircraft carriers, 200 planes; Gen. Douglas MacArthur returns to Philippines, leads invasion of Leyte (October 20); three-day Battle of Leyte Gulf destroys most remaining Japanese naval strength.

Some activities for postwar living: Forty-four nations attend three-week U.N. Monetary and Financial Conference at Bretton Woods, N.H., create International Monetary Fund and International Bank for Reconstruction and Development. Dumbarton Oaks Conference in Washington follows, lays groundwork for United Nations. An agreement (November 19) is signed at White House to create U.N. Relief and Rehabilitation Administration (UNRRA).

A German plot to assassinate Hitler (July 20) and take over Germany fails.

U.S., Great Britain, and Russia recognize French Provisional Government in Exile; President Franklin Roosevelt and British Prime Minister Winston Churchill meet in Quebec to discuss postwar problems.

NATIONAL

Congress passes GI Bill of Rights, provides benefits to World War II veterans; War Production Board permits limited conversion of industry to civilian production; Office of War Mobilization and Reconversion is created.

President Roosevelt is elected to a fourth term, receives 25,602,505 popular and 432 electoral votes to 22,006,278 popular and 99 electoral votes for Republican Thomas E. Dewey.

Supreme Court upholds wartime exclusion of Japanese Americans from the West Coast.

Agreement is reached with Mexico on the shared use of water from Rio Grande, Colorado, and Tijuana rivers.

Big Bend (Tex.) National Park is established.

DEATHS Former First Lady Lou Hoover (1929–1933); Wendell Willkie, Republican presidential candidate (1940); Alfred E. Smith, New York governor and 1928 Democratic presidential candidate; Manuel L. Quezon, first Philippines president (1935–1941).

BUSINESS/INDUSTRY/INVENTIONS

Howard H. Aiken of IBM completes Mark I, first large-scale digital computer; it is given to Harvard University.

Marvin Camras patents wire recorder.

DEATHS James H. Rand, devised visible file divider system; Leo H. Baekeland, inventor of Bakelite, a plastic.

TRANSPORTATION

Nation's railroads return to private ownership.

SCIENCE/MEDICINE

Isidor I. Rabi is awarded Nobel Prize in physics for method of recording properties of atomic nuclei; Joseph Erlanger and Herbert S. Gasser share physiology/medicine prize for discoveries of differentiated functions of single nerve fibers.

Dr. Alfred Blalock develops operation to save "blue babies" by increasing oxygen in blood.

New York Hospital establishes first eye bank.

University of California scientists discover three new elements, 95 (americium), 96 (curium), and 97 (berkelium).

DEATHS Thomas Midgley, chemist who discovered antiknock properties of tetraethyl lead in fuel; Joseph M. Flint, surgeon and founder of first mobile hospital for troops.

RELIGION

Methodist Bishop G. Bromley Oxnam becomes president of Federal Council of Churches.

Angus Dun becomes Episcopal bishop of Washington, D.C.

DEATHS Catholic Archbishop Edward J. Hanna of San Francisco; Aimee Semple McPherson, evangelist.

ART/MUSIC

Leopold Stokowski founds, conducts second New York Symphony Orchestra (1944–1945).

Walter Piston composes Second Symphony; Leonard Bernstein composes ballet, *Fancy Free*, and symphony, *Jeremiah*; Aaron Copland composes *Appalachian Spring*.

Dizzy Gillespie forms band to play "bop" jazz.

American women take over as factory workers at home while the men who usually do such work are away fighting the war. UPI/CORBIS-BETTMANN

Jackson Pollock completes the painting *Mural*.

SONGS (popular): "Don't Fence Me In," "Spring Will Be a Little Late This Year," "I'll Get By," "Shoo-Shoo Baby," "Swinging on a Star," "I Couldn't Sleep a Wink Last Night."

LITERATURE/JOURNALISM

BOOKS *Brave Men* by Ernie Pyle, *Forever Amber* by Kathleen Winsor, *Strange Fruit* by Lillian Smith, *A Bell for Adano* by John Hersey, *V-Letter and Other Poems* by Karl Shapiro, *The Lost Weekend* by Charles Jackson, *Yankee from Olympus* by Catherine Drinker Bowen.

DEATHS George Ade, humorist (*Fables in Slang*);

William Allen White and Harry Chandler, newspaper editors and publishers; two early cartoonists, Billy DeBeck ("Barney Google") and George Herriman ("Krazy Kat"); Ida Tarbell, author of Standard Oil history that led to federal investigation.

ENTERTAINMENT

PLAYS Frank Fay stars in *Harvey*, Eddie Dowling in Tennessee Williams's *The Glass Menagerie*, Celeste Holm in *Bloomer Girl*; Leonard Bernstein writes *On the Town*.

MOVIES *Going My Way* with Bing Crosby, *Meet Me in St. Louis* with Judy Garland, *Up in Arms* with Danny Kaye, *Cover Girl* with Rita Hayworth, *Gas-*

light with Charles Boyer, *Pin-Up Girl* with Betty Grable.

Popular new radio shows are *Ozzie and Harriet*, Alan Young, Roy Rogers, and Perry Como.

SPORTS

NCAA adopts two new basketball rules; ban on goal-tending, and increased maximum number of personal fouls from 4 to 5.

WINNERS *Baseball*—St. Louis Cardinals, World Series; *Basketball*—St. Johns, NIT; Utah, NCAA; *Chess*—Arnold Danker, U.S. champion; *Football* (bowls)—Southern California, Rose; Louisiana State, Orange; Georgia Tech, Sugar; Randolph Field, Cotton; Green Bay, NFL; *Golf*—Bob Hamilton, PGA; *Hockey*—Montreal, Stanley Cup; *Horse racing*—Pensive, Kentucky Derby and Preakness Stakes; Bounding Home, Belmont Stakes; *Tennis*—Frank Parker, U.S. Open (men); Pauline Betz, U.S. Open (women).

DEATHS Tommy Hitchcock, world-great polo player, in plane crash; Kenesaw M. Landis, baseball commissioner (1921–1944); John L. Griffith, first Big Ten football commissioner.

MISCELLANEOUS

Year is filled with disasters: tornadoes in Ohio, Pennsylvania, West Virginia, and Maryland kill 150; hurricanes along Atlantic Coast from Long Island to Cape Cod kill 400; a fire followed by a stampede at a Hartford (Conn.) circus kills 168; explosion on Port Chicago, Calif., pier claims 322 lives, and liquid gas tank explosion followed by widespread fires in Cleveland (Ohio) cause 135 deaths.

INTERNATIONAL

World War II

1945

War on both fronts grinds to a halt, but before it does, the sudden death of President Franklin D. Roosevelt (April 12) shocks world.

PACIFIC THEATER War against Japan ends with dramatic suddenness by use of the first atomic bombs. Two bombs are dropped in early August on Hiroshima and Nagasaki, killing thousands, causing unparalleled devastation; Japanese quickly surrender.

U.S. troops land on Luzon in Philippines (January 9), take Manila (February 23); Marines land on Iwo Jima (February 19), capture island (March 7) at cost of 4,189 killed, 15,308 wounded; Army forces invade Okinawa (March 19), take island (July 21) after more than 11,000 deaths.

First atomic bomb is exploded successfully at Alamagordo (N. Mex.) base (July 16); U.S. plane *Enola Gay*, piloted by Col. Paul W. Tibbetts Jr., drops bomb on Hiroshima (August 6), destroys 4 square miles of city, kills or injures 160,000.

A second bomb is dropped on Nagasaki (August 9), kills 40,000. The next day, Japanese offer to surrender, accept terms (August 14). U.S. forces begin occupation (August 27); formal surrender is signed aboard the USS *Missouri* in Tokyo Bay (September 2).

EUROPEAN THEATER U.S. troops drive into Ruhr Valley (February 23), reach the Rhine (March 2), which they cross (March 7) after capturing bridge at Remagen. Cologne and Düsseldorf are taken (March 7), also Mannheim and Frankfurt (March 27), Nuremberg (April 21); U.S. joins Russian troops at Elbe River (April 25).

Mussolini is captured and killed by Italian partisans at Lake Como as he tries to escape to Switzerland (April 28). Provisional German government announces that Hitler committed suicide in Berlin (May 1).

Berlin falls to Allies, and German forces in Italy surrender (May 2); German units in the Netherlands, Denmark, and northwest Germany surrender (May 4). Germany agrees to unconditional surrender at "the little red schoolhouse" in Reims,

France (May 7); VE Day is proclaimed May 8. Germany is placed under an Allied Control Council (June 5), German occupation zones are established.

United Nations forms as representatives of 50 nations meet in San Francisco (April 25), work out draft charter; President Harry Truman addresses delegates by phone (April 28); Senate approves draft charter (July 28), which is signed by president (August 8); charter goes into effect October 24.

World leaders meet in Yalta February 4–11 to discuss war problems and postwar plans, give Russia important concessions for its declaring war on Japan; meet again (July 7) in Potsdam with emphasis on Japan and war criminals. Allies sign agreement (August 8) to set up International War Crimes Tribunal; trials begin in Nuremberg (November 20), with Supreme Court Justice Robert H. Jackson chief American prosecutor (12 are convicted, 10 hanged in 1946, Hermann Göring commits suicide, Martin Bormann is convicted in absentia).

Lend-Lease program terminates; supplied $50.6 billion in aid to foreign nations.

Point system is announced for the discharge of enlisted men (May 10).

DEATHS Gen. Simon B. Buckner Jr., killed in Okinawa action, Gen. George S. Patton, Third Army commander, in automobile accident in Germany.

NATIONAL

Sudden death of President Roosevelt occurs while he vacations in Warm Springs, Ga.; Vice President Truman is sworn in as president (April 12).

The devastation in Hiroshima, Japan, in 1945 after the United States dropped the atomic bomb. UPI/CORBIS-BETTMANN

Former Secretary of State Cordell Hull is awarded Nobel Peace Prize for work in founding U.N.

War Production Board (October 4) and Office of Civil Defense (June 30) terminate; gasoline and fuel oil rationing ends; food rationing (except sugar) stops (November 23); daylight saving time ends in September, its use restored to local option.

Eleanor Roosevelt, the president's widow, is named a delegate to United Nations.

Japanese Americans who were evacuated from West Coast in 1943 are free to return home.

New York State Commission Against Discrimination is established; New Jersey adopts new constitution, replacing the 1844 document.

House Un-American Activities Committee is given permanent status; recommends dismissal of 3,800 government employees; Justice Department finds only 36 warranted dismissal.

Atomic Energy Commission is created (August 1).

BUSINESS/INDUSTRY/INVENTIONS

Wage Stabilization Board is created to replace National War Labor Board.

J. Presper Eckhert and John W. Mauchly of the Moore School at the University of Pennsylvania produce ENIAC, the first all-electronic digital computer.

TRANSPORTATION

United Auto Workers stage 113-day strike against General Motors.

Burlington Railroad initiates the "Vista Dome," a car with an observation dome.

Flying Tigers Line is founded.

Second tube of Lincoln Tunnel under Hudson River is completed.

DEATH Vincent Bendix, inventor of automobile starter.

SCIENCE/MEDICINE

Wolfgang Pauli is awarded Nobel Prize in physics for discovery of the exclusion principle.

Grand Rapids, Mich., becomes first city to fluoridate municipal water.

Weather radar is developed.

DEATH Robert H. Goddard, physicist who pioneered modern rocketry.

EDUCATION

School for Industrial and Labor Relations opens at Cornell University.

Harold Taylor becomes first male president of Sarah Lawrence College, Bronxville, N.Y.

RELIGION

George A. Smith is elected president of Mormon church.

ART/MUSIC

Leo Sowerby composes *Canticle of the Sun*.

Charles Sheeler completes the painting *Water*; Mark Rothko, *Baptismal Scene*; Isamu Noguchi completes the sculpture *Kouros*.

SONGS (popular): "Have I Told You Lately That I Love You?," "It Might as Well Be Spring," "June Is Bustin' Out All Over," "Laura," "There I've Said It Again," "Rum and Coca-Cola."

DEATHS Jerome Kern, musical-comedy composer; Béla Bartók, composer; Newell C. Wyeth, mural painter and book illustrator.

LITERATURE/JOURNALISM

Ebony magazine begins publication.

BOOKS *The Black Rose* by Thomas B. Costain, *The Egg and I* by Betty McDonald, *The Age of Jackson* by Arthur M. Schlesinger Jr., *Captain from Castile* by Samuel Shellabarger, *Cass Timberlane* by Sinclair Lewis, *Cannery Row* by John Steinbeck, *Stuart Little* by E. B. White.

DEATHS Theodore Dreiser, author; Robert C. Benchley, author and screen actor; Gilbert Patten, author as Burt Standish (Frank and Dick Merriwell series); Ernie Pyle, war correspondent, killed by sniper.

ENTERTAINMENT

PLAYS John Raitt stars in *Carousel*, Ralph Bellamy in *State of the Union*; Sigmund Romberg writes music for *Up in Central Park*.

1945

The scene on Wall Street in New York City as Americans celebrate the end of World War II in Europe ("V-E Day"). CORBIS-BETTMANN

MOVIES *National Velvet* with Elizabeth Taylor, *The Bells of St. Mary's* with Bing Crosby, *Spellbound* with Ingrid Bergman, *The Lost Weekend* with Ray Miland, *The Clock* with Judy Garland.

New radio shows include *Break the Bank, Meet the Press, Green Hornet, Inner Sanctum, Queen for a Day.*

DEATHS Gus Edwards, entertainer and composer ("School Days"); H. B. Warner, screen actor.

SPORTS

Happy (Albert B.) Chandler is named baseball commissioner.

Red (Walter W.) Smith writes syndicated sports column.

WINNERS *Baseball* — Detroit Tigers, World Series; *Basketball* — DePaul, NIT; Oklahoma A&M, NCAA; *Bowling* — Buddy Bomar, bowler of year; *Football* (bowls) — Southern California, Rose; Tulsa, Orange; Duke, Sugar; Oklahoma A&M, Cotton; Cleveland, NFL; *Golf* — Byron Nelson, PGA; *Hockey* — Toronto, Stanley Cup; *Horse racing* — Hoop Jr., Kentucky Derby; Polynesian, Preakness Stakes; Pavot, Belmont Stakes; *Tennis* — Frank Parker, U.S. Open (men); Sarah Palfrey Cooke, U.S. Open (women).

DEATHS Ski champion Torger Tokle killed in action with army; Dwight F. Davis, donor of tennis cup.

MISCELLANEOUS

An army B-25 crashes into Empire State Building in New York City, kills 14 (July 28).

Tornadoes in Oklahoma and Arkansas kill 102.

1946

INTERNATIONAL

Peace conference to end European phase of World War II formally is held in Paris; Japanese war-crimes trial sentences seven to death (hanged in 1948), 14 to life imprisonment.

U.S. gives Philippine Islands independence (July 4).

U.N. General Assembly holds first session in Flushing Meadows on Long Island (October 23); John D. Rockefeller Jr. gives $8.5 million toward purchase of New York City property for permanent U.N. headquarters; Mrs. Eleanor Roosevelt, U.S. delegate to U.N., named head of U.N. Commisssion on Human Rights.

World Bank organizes with Eugene I. Meyer as president.

British Prime Minister Winston Churchill makes "iron curtain" speech at Westminster College, Fulton, Mo.

NATIONAL

Atomic explosion tests are held on Bikini Atoll in the Pacific in July.

Emily G. Balch and John R. Mott share Nobel Peace Prize for their work.

Frederick M. Vinson is named Supreme Court Chief Justice.

President Harry S. Truman proposes merging

Harry Truman takes the podium as the new United Nations assembly convenes in Flushing, New York, in 1946. UPI/CORBIS-BETTMANN

1946

Army and Navy departments into Defense Department.

President Truman asks for Commerce Secretary Henry A. Wallace's resignation because of his public criticism of U.S. policy on Russia.

Judge William H. Hastie becomes first African American governor of the Virgin Islands.

New agencies created are the Central Intelligence Agency, Council of Economic Advisors, and Bureau of Land Management in Interior Department.

Republicans gain control of both houses of Congress for first time in 14 years.

DEATHS Gen. Joseph M. ("Vinegar Joe") Stilwell, Burma-China Theater commander; Jimmy Walker, New York City mayor (1926–1932); Gifford Pinchot, first U.S. professional forester; Harry L. Hopkins, federal relief administrator (1933–1938).

BUSINESS/INDUSTRY/INVENTIONS

End of war brings much labor unrest because unions tried to freeze wage increases during the war: 7,700 Western Electric telephone mechanics strike in 44 states, United Electrical Workers in 16 states; United Steelworkers shut down industry briefly, United Mine Workers strike bituminous mines.

Most price and wage controls end.

Hilton Hotels Corp. is organized.

Exchange National Bank, Chicago, provides first bank drive-in service.

Southwestern Bell Telephone Co. initiates mobile telephone service.

DEATHS George W. Hill, American Tobacco Co. president (1925–1946); Sidney Hillman, president, Amalgamated Clothing Workers (1914–1940); Louis K. Liggett, founder and head, United Drug Co.

TRANSPORTATION

Government seizes railroads (May 17) to avert general strike; threat ends a week later.

Four-passenger commercial helicopter (S-51), built by Sikorsky Aircraft, is flown for first time.

SCIENCE/MEDICINE

Percy W. Bridgman is awarded Nobel Prize in physics for discoveries in field of high-pressure physics; James B. Sumner, John H. Northrop, and Wendell M. Stanley share chemistry prize for their work on enzymes and viruses; Hermann J. Muller is awarded physiology/medicine prize for production of mutations by X-ray irradiation.

New York Orthopedic Hospital and Hospital for Special Surgery establish bone banks.

Chemist Irving Langmuir develops method to produce rain artificially by seeding clouds with dry ice and silver iodide.

Best-selling book by Dr. Benjamin Spock, *Baby and Child Care*, is published.

EDUCATION

Fulbright Act sets up educational exchange program with foreign countries.

Sarah G. Blanding becomes first woman president of Vassar College.

Oliver C. Carmichael becomes president of Carnegie Foundation for Advancement of Teaching.

Champlain College, primarily for war veterans, opens in Plattsburgh, N.Y.

RELIGION

United Brethren and Evangelical churches merge to form Evangelical United Brethren church (November 16).

International Council of Religious Education publishes Revised Standard Version of the New Testament.

Mother Cabrini (Francis Xavier Cabrini) becomes first U.S. citizen to be canonized.

Three U.S. Catholic archbishops are elevated to cardinal: John J. Glennon of St. Louis, Mo., Francis J. Spellman of New York, Samuel A. Stritch of Chicago. Archbishop Joseph E. Ritter of Indianapolis, Ind., transfers to St. Louis.

Maurice N. Eisendrath becomes president of Union of American Hebrew Congregations.

DEATH Archbishop John J. Glennon of St. Louis (1903–1946).

The first general-purpose electronic calculator, dedicated at the Moore School of Electrical Engineering at the University of Pennsylvania in February 1946. Built to perform ballistic calculations for the U.S. Army, it is called the ENIAC ("Electronic Numerical Integrator and Computer"). UPI/CORBIS-BETTMANN

ART/MUSIC

Grandma Moses completes the painting *From My Window*; Adolph Gottlieb, *The Voyagers' Return*; George Grosz, *The Pit*; Ben Shahn, *Father and Child*.

Gian Carlo Menotti composes the opera *The Medium*.

SONGS (popular): "All I Want for Christmas," "Five Minutes More," "The Girl That I Marry," "Let It Snow," "Shoo Fly Pie," "Zip-a-Dee-Doo-Dah," "On the Atchison, Topeka, and the Santa Fe," "You Always Hurt the One You Love."

DEATHS Alfred Stieglitz, pioneer of modern photography; Arthur G. Dove, first U.S. abstract painter; Carrie Jacobs Bond, composer ("I Love You Truly"); Vincent Youmans, composer ("Tea for Two"); John Steuart Curry, painter; Charles W. Cadman, composer.

LITERATURE/JOURNALISM

Herblock (Herbert Block), editorial cartoonist, joins *Washington Post* staff.

BOOKS *Peace of Mind* by Joshua L. Liebman, *The Foxes of Harrow* by Frank Yerby, *This Side of Innocence* by Taylor Caldwell, *Lord Weary's Castle* (poetry) by Robert Lowell, *A Member of the Wedding* by Carson McCullers, *Hiroshima* by John Hersey,

1947

Delta Wedding by Eudora Welty, *All the King's Men* by Robert Penn Warren.

DEATHS Booth Tarkington and Gertrude Stein, authors; Damon Runyon, journalist and author; Joseph M. Patterson, founder and publisher, *New York Daily News*.

ENTERTAINMENT

American Repertory Theatre in New York City opens with Shakespeare's *Henry VIII*.

Arthur Godfrey begins *Talent Scouts* program on radio (later on television).

PLAYS Ethel Merman stars in *Annie Get Your Gun*, Judy Holliday in *Born Yesterday*, Helen Hayes in *Happy Birthday*; Eugene O'Neill writes *The Iceman Cometh*.

DEATHS William S. Hart, silent-screen cowboy; W. C. Fields, actor; "Major" Edward Bowes, amateur-hour originator; George Arliss, actor.

SPORTS

Basketball Association of America, forerunner of National Basketball Assn., is founded.

Bert Bell is named National Football League commissioner; All-American Football Conference begins with eight teams.

Players receive permanent representation on a new baseball governing body; collective-bargaining election is ordered for Pittsburgh Pirates players (vote is 15–3 against American Baseball Guild, most players abstain).

WINNERS *Auto racing* — Gene Robson, Indianapolis 500; *Baseball* — St. Louis Cardinals, World Series; *Basketball* — Kentucky, NIT; Oklahoma A&M, NCAA; *Bowling* — Joseph Wilman, bowler of year; *Boxing* — Joe Louis, heavyweight; Sugar Ray Robinson, welterweight; Tony Zale, middleweight; *Chess* — Samuel Reshevsky, U.S. title; *Football* (bowls) — Alabama, Rose; Miami (Fla.), Orange; Oklahoma A&M, Sugar; Texas, Cotton; Chicago Bears, NFL; Cleveland, AAFC; *Golf* — Lloyd Mangrum, U.S. Open; Ben Hogan, PGA; Sam Snead, Masters; Patty Berg, first U.S. Women's Open; *Hockey* — Montreal, Stanley Cup; *Horse racing* — Assault becomes seventh Triple Crown winner; *Tennis* — U.S., Davis Cup; Jack Kramer, U.S. Open (men); Pauline Betz, U.S. Open (women).

DEATHS Former Heavyweight Champion Jack Johnson, in auto accident; Barney Oldfield, first to drive car at more than 60 miles per hour; Walter Johnson, Hall of Fame baseball pitcher.

MISCELLANEOUS

Forest fire destroys most of Bar Harbor, Maine; damages Acadia National Park; fire in Winecoff Hotel, Atlanta, Ga., kills 119.

D. S. Harder, Ford vice president, coins word *automation*.

"Ranch-type" houses — low slung, single story — become popular.

INTERNATIONAL

1947

Secretary of State George C. Marshall launches (June 15) European aid plan to promote conditions in which free institutions can exist; 16 nations set up Committee for European Economic Cooperation (July 12); President Harry S. Truman asks approval of $17 billion for Marshall Plan.

President Truman pledges aid to Greece and Turkey; Congress approves the Truman Doctrine, provides $400 million for aid.

Peace treaties with Italy, Hungary, Rumania, and Bulgaria are signed (June 14).

North Atlantic Council agrees on integrated European defense under a supreme commander, Dwight D. Eisenhower.

Jackie Robinson, the first African American baseball player to play in a major-league club, prepares with his Brooklyn Dodgers teammates to open the 1947 season with a game against the Boston Braves. UPI/CORBIS-BETTMANN

Nineteen American nations sign Treaty of Rio de Janeiro (September 2), a defense pact.

NATIONAL

National Security Act combines Army, Navy, and Air Force departments into Defense Department (July 26), under a Defense Secretary (James E. Forrestal); creates Joint Chiefs of Staff, National Security Council; W. Stuart Symington is sworn in as first Secretary of Air Force (September 18).

Presidential Succession Act revises 1886 law, makes house speaker first in line to succeed president and vice president, followed by president pro tem of Senate, secretary of state, and other cabinet members according to rank.

Selective Service Act for military draft expires.

Sugar rationing ends (June 11).

Former President Hoover leads study of European food and economic conditions, calls for $475 million aid program.

Housing & Home Finance Agency is created, predecessor of Department of Housing & Urban Development.

Puerto Rico is given right to elect own governor; Luis Munoz-Marin, first native appointed governor, is first to be elected.

Supreme Court in *Friedman v. Schwellenbach* upholds 1947 loyalty order authorizing dismissal of disloyal federal employees.

Domestic airmail rate drops to 5 cents per ounce.

Everglades (Fla.) National Park is established.

Americans for Democratic Action is founded.

Richard M. Nixon begins three years in House from California; John F. Kennedy begins six years in House from Massachusetts; Ronald Reagan begins 13 years as president of Screen Actors Guild.

Freedom Train, a historic exhibit, is dedicated in Philadelphia (September 17) before starting 33,000-mile tour.

1947

DEATHS Former First Lady Frances F. Cleveland (1886–1890, 1894–1898); Carrie Chapman Catt, woman's rights leader; Fiorello La Guardia, New York City mayor (1933–1945); Al Capone, gangster.

BUSINESS/INDUSTRY/INVENTIONS

Its inventor, Edwin H. Land, demonstrates Polaroid camera (February 21).

Congress passes Taft-Hartley Act over President Truman's veto; bans closed shop, requires 30 days cooling-off before strike, requires union financial statements, forbids political contributions, and institutes other strict requirements.

DEATH Henry Ford, automaker.

TRANSPORTATION

B. F. Goodrich Co. produces tubeless tires.

Radar for commercial and private planes is demonstrated.

Howard Hughes flies world's largest plane, the 220-ton plywood flying boat, which he designed and built.

Chesapeake & Ohio Railroad absorbs Pere Marquette Railroad.

SCIENCE/MEDICINE

Drs. Carl F. Cori and his wife, Gerty, share Nobel Prize in physiology/medicine for discoveries relating to glycogen.

Mt. Palomar Observatory in California installs a 200-inch telescope lens.

Bell X-1 rocket plane flown by Major Charles E. Yeager breaks sound barrier.

Willard F. Libby develops carbon-14 dating technique.

EDUCATION

Brandeis University in Waltham, Mass., is founded.

Gen Dwight D. Eisenhower is installed as president of Columbia University.

DEATH Nicholas Murray Butler, president, Columbia University (1902–1945).

RELIGION

Conservative Baptist Association of America is founded.

Catholic Bishop Francis P. Keough becomes archbishop of Baltimore, Md.

ART/MUSIC

Leopold Stokowski becomes conductor of New York Philharmonic Orchestra.

Walter Piston composes Symphony no. 3; Roger H. Sessions the opera *The Trial of Lucullus*; Gian Carlo Menotti, *The Telephone*.

Jackson Pollock completes the painting *Full Fathom Five*; Arshile Gorky, *The Betrothal II*.

SONGS (popular): "Almost Like Being in Love," "How Are Things in Glocca Morra?," "I Believe," "Old Devil Moon," "Sixteen Tons," "Tenderly," "Cool Water," "Open the Door, Richard."

DEATHS Jimmie Lunceford, orchestra leader; Walter Donaldson, composer ("My Blue Heaven").

LITERATURE/JOURNALISM

BOOKS *Gentleman's Agreement* by Laura Z. Hobson, *Tales of the South Pacific* by James A. Michener, *Across the Wide Missouri* by Bernard De Voto, *Rocket Ship Galileo* by Robert A. Heinlein, *The Vixen* by Frank Yerby, *The Big Sky* by A. B. Guthrie.

DEATHS Authors Willa Cather, Hugh Lofting, and Charles B. Nordhoff; Ogden M. Reid, publisher, *New York Tribune, Herald*; Francis W. Crowninshield, editor (*Vanity Fair* 1914–1935); Frederick W. Goudy, type designer.

ENTERTAINMENT

Robert J. Keeshan begins television career as clown Clarabelle on *Howdy Doody* show; other new shows are *Meet the Press* and *Kraft Television Theater*.

PLAYS Marlon Brando stars in *A Streetcar Named Desire*, Ella Logan in *Finian's Rainbow*, Judith Anderson and John Gielgud in *Medea*; Arthur Miller writes *All My Sons*.

MOVIES *Life with Father* with William Powell, *The Secret Life of Walter Mitty* with Danny Kaye, *Gentleman's Agreement* with Gregory Peck, *Miracle on 34th*

Street with Edmund Gwenn, *The Road to Rio* with Bing Crosby and Bob Hope.

DEATHS Grace Moore, opera soprano, in plane crash; Eva Tanguay, entertainer.

SPORTS

Baseball major-league annuity plan goes into effect; National Hockey League adopts players' pension fund.

National Hockey League plays first all-star game; World Hockey Assn. organizes with franchises in seven U.S. cities.

National Association for Stock Car Auto Racing (NASCAR) is formed.

Jackie Robinson of Brooklyn Dodgers, first African American baseball player in majors, plays his first major league game (April 11); Larry Doby becomes first African American ballplayer in American League (Cleveland) (July 5).

Babe Didrikson Zaharias becomes first U.S.-born woman golfer to win British amateur title.

Babe Ruth Day is observed by 58,339 in Yankee Stadium, N.Y.

WINNERS *Auto racing*—Mauri Rose, Indianapolis 500; *Baseball*—New York Yankees, World Series; *Basketball*—Utah, NIT; Holy Cross, NCAA; Philadelphia, first BAA title; *Bowling*—Buddy Bomar, bowler of year; *Boxing*—Joe Louis, heavyweight; Sugar Ray Robinson, welterweight; Rocky Graziano, middleweight; *Football* (bowls)—Illinois, Rose; Rice, Orange; Georgia, Sugar; Arkansas, Cotton; Chicago Cardinals, NFL; Cleveland, AAFC; *Golf*—U.S., Ryder and Walker cups; Lew Worsham, U.S. Open; Jim Ferrier, PGA; Fred Daly, Masters; *Hockey*—Toronto, Stanley Cup; *Horse racing*—Jet Pilot, Kentucky Derby; Faultless, Preakness Stakes; Phalanx, Belmont Stakes; *Rowing*—Jack Kelly, Henley diamond challenge sculls; *Tennis*—U.S., Davis Cup; Jack Kramer, U.S. Open (men); Louise Brough, U.S. Open (women).

DEATH Charles W. Bidwill, owner of Chicago Cardinals football team.

MISCELLANEOUS

Amvets is chartered by Congress.

Most of Texas City, Tex., is destroyed when a French freighter explodes in harbor (April 16), kills 516.

Big Brothers of America is founded.

Tornadoes in Texas, Oklahoma, and Kansas kill 169; mine disaster in Centralia, Ill., kills 111; New York City receives heaviest snowfall on record (25.8 inches), paralyzing city, causing 80 deaths.

1948

INTERNATIONAL

Soviet Russia blockades Allied sectors of Berlin (April 1); British and U.S. planes airlift food and coal into city (June 26); when blockade ends in 1949, 276,926 flights had carried 2.3 million tons of supplies.

Economic Cooperation Administration is created to assist foreign countries; $6.1 billion is set aside for program.

Twenty-one Western Hemisphere republics form Organization of American States (OAS) (April 30).

U.N. General Assembly adopts Universal Declaration of Human Rights.

Israel is declared an independent state (May 14); Arabs unsuccessful in military attempt to overthrow action.

NATIONAL

President Harry S. Truman, Democrat, is elected to full term, defeating Republican Thomas E. Dewey with 24,105,802 popular and 303 electoral votes against Dewey's 21,970,065 and 189; Dixiecrat candidate J. Strom Thurmond receives 1,169,063 and 39 votes.

Babe Ruth (1895–1948) at bat during the first game at the new Yankee Stadium, Bronx, New York, April 19, 1923. UPI/CORBIS-BETTMANN

Whittaker Chambers, an admitted Communist, accuses Alger Hiss, State Department official, of being a communist; Hiss sues for libel, is indicted for perjury.

New Selective Service Act calls for registration of men 18–25; induction is restricted to 21 months' service in the military for those 19 to 25.

President Truman issues an executive order outlawing racial segregation in the armed forces.

Three atomic bombs are tested at Eniwetok in the Pacific.

Air Force bombers complete nonstop round-the-world flight, refuel in air four times.

Lyndon B. Johnson begins 12 years of service in Senate from Texas.

DEATHS Former First Lady Mary S. L. Harrison (1889–1893) and Edith K. C. Roosevelt (1901–1909); Gen. John J. Pershing, head of American World War I forces; Orville Wright, aviation pioneer; Charles Evans Hughes, Supreme Court Chief Justice (1930–1941); John A. Lomax, folklorist.

BUSINESS/INDUSTRY/INVENTIONS

Haloid Corp. and Battelle Institute give first public demonstration of xerography; John Bardeen and Walter H. Brattain demonstrate their invention, the transistor.

Federal Communications Commission authorizes use of telephone recording devices.

More than 350,000 soft-coal miners strike for $100-a-month pensions; agreement is reached a month later.

DEATH John R. Gregg, shorthand-system developer.

TRANSPORTATION

Idlewild (later Kennedy) International Airport opens.

DEATHS William S. Knudsen, General Motors official; Charles W. Nash, pioneer automaker.

SCIENCE/MEDICINE

Blue Cross is instituted when group of school-teachers enter an agreement with Baylor Hospital in Dallas.

Dr. Benjamin M. Duggar discovers aureomycin chlortetracycline, an antibiotic.

Dr. George G. Wright of Army Chemical Laboratory develops anthrax vaccine for humans.

University of Indiana Institute for Sex Research releases report by Dr. Alfred Kinsey on sexual behavior of men.

Dr. Norbert Wiener completes his book, *Cybernetics*.

National Institute of Dental Health is established.

Vitamin B-12 is isolated from liver extract.

DEATHS Abraham A. Brill, pioneer U.S. psychoanalyst; Emily P. Bissell, Christmas Seal founder.

RELIGION

Supreme Court rules religious training in public schools is unconstitutional.

World Council of Churches is founded; Methodist Bishop G. Bromley Oxnam is president.

Helen Kenyon becomes first woman moderator of Congregational-Christian churches.

Christmas Eve midnight mass at St. Patrick's Cathedral in New York City is televised for first time.

Two new Catholic archbishops named: James F. McIntyre of Los Angeles and Patrick A. O'Boyle of Washington, D.C.

ART/MUSIC

New York City Ballet is organized, directed by George Balanchine.

Columbia Records introduces long-playing records, developed by Peter Goldmark; Wire Recording Corp. develops a magnetic tape recorder.

Miles Davis, who started "cool jazz," forms band.

Robert Shaw Chorale is founded.

Mark Rothko completes the painting *No. 2, 1948*; Saul Baizerman completes the sculpture *Slumber*.

Des Moines (Iowa) Art Center is founded.

SONGS (popular): "Hooray for Love," "If I Had a Hammer," "Nature Boy," "On a Slow Boat to China," "Red Roses for a Blue Lady," "Buttons and Bows," "Tennessee Waltz," "Baby, It's Cold Outside."

DEATH Oley Speaks, composer ("On the Road to Mandalay").

LITERATURE/JOURNALISM

Walter C. Kelly draws comic strip "Pogo" for New York papers.

After his victory over Dewey in the 1948 presidential election, Harry Truman stops in Chicago on his way back to Washington D.C. He holds up early edition of the November 4, 1948, *Chicago Tribune*; the erroneous headline was based on early election returns. UPI/CORBIS-BETTMANN

1948

BOOKS *High Towers* by Thomas B. Costain, *The Naked and the Dead* by Norman Mailer, *Guard of Honor* by James G. Cozzens, *Other Voices, Other Rooms* by Truman Capote, *Crusade in Europe* by Dwight D. Eisenhower, *The Seven-Storey Mountain* by Thomas Merton, *The Young Lions* by Irwin Shaw, *The Age of Anxiety* (poetry) by W. H. Auden.

DEATHS Gertrude Atherton, author (*Black Oxen*); James H. McGraw, publisher; Charles A. Beard, historian; Carl T. Anderson, cartoonist ("Henry").

ENTERTAINMENT

Ed Sullivan debuts Sunday night television variety show that lasts 23 years; Milton Berle emcees Texaco Star Theater; Kukla, Fran, and Ollie, part-puppet show, airs; other new shows include *Candid Camera* with Allen Funt, Arthur Godfrey's *Talent Scouts*, and Perry Como.

PLAYS Paul Muni stars in *Key Largo*, Rex Harrison in *Anne of the Thousand Days*, Ray Bolger in *Where's Charley?*, Henry Fonda in *Mr. Roberts*, Alfred Drake in *Kiss Me, Kate*.

MOVIES *The Treasure of Sierra Madre* with Humphrey Bogart, *Fort Apache* with John Wayne, *Johnny Belinda* with Jane Wyman, *Easter Parade* with Fred Astaire and Judy Garland.

Eve Arden stars in radio's *Our Miss Brooks*.

DEATH D. W. Griffith, pioneer filmmaker (*Birth of a Nation*).

SPORTS

Olympic Games are held in London; U.S. wins 33 gold medals, including Bob Mathias's in decathlon.

National Boxing Assn. announces new safety program for professional boxers: more-thorough examinations, 8-ounce gloves, mandatory eight count after a knockdown.

Dick Button becomes first American to win men's world figure-skating championship.

Mel Patton sets record of 9.3 seconds for 100-yard dash.

Satchel Paige, legendary Negro League pitcher, makes first major-league start.

WINNERS *Auto racing* — Mauri Rose, Indianapolis 500; *Baseball* — Cleveland Indians, World Series; *Basketball* — St. Louis, NIT; Kentucky, NCAA; Baltimore, BAA; *Bowling* — Andy Varipapa and Val Mikiel, bowlers of year; *Boxing* — Joe Louis, heavyweight; Freddie Mills, light heavyweight; Tony Zale, middleweight; *Chess* — Herman Steiner, U.S. champion; *Football* (bowls) — Michigan, Rose; Georgia Tech, Orange; Texas, Sugar; Southern Methodist, Cotton; Philadelphia, NFL; Cleveland, AAFC; *Golf* — Ben Hogan, U.S. Open and PGA; Henry Cotton, Masters; Babe Didrikson Zaharias, U.S. Women's Open; *Hockey* — Toronto, Stanley Cup; Michigan, NCAA; *Horse racing* — Citation becomes eighth Triple Crown winner taking Kentucky Derby, Preakness Stakes, and Belmont Stakes; *Tennis* — U.S., Davis Cup; Pancho Gonzales, U.S. Open (men); Margaret Osborne du Pont, U.S. Open (women).

DEATHS Babe Ruth, home run king; Jock Sutherland, college football coach.

MISCELLANEOUS

American Association of Registration Executives begins uniform system of birth registration numbering.

Long-playing records ("LPs") begin to replace "78s."

1949

INTERNATIONAL

U.S., Great Britain, Canada, France, Belgium, Italy, Netherlands, Luxembourg, Denmark, Norway, Iceland, Portugal sign North Atlantic Treaty (April 4); create NATO.

President Harry S. Truman calls for Point Four program of assistance to underprivileged areas.

U.S. recognizes Israel after Israel creates a permanent government (January 31).

Berlin airlift ends (September 30) when Russian blockade is lifted; airlift delivered 2.3 million tons of food and coal to Allied portions of Berlin.

U.S., Great Britain, and France agree to establish West German Republic (April 8); President Truman creates office of U.S. High Commissioner for Germany (June 6); John J. McCloy is first commissioner.

Cornerstone is laid for U.N. headquarters in New York City.

Eugenie Anderson becomes first U.S. woman with ambassador rank (to Denmark).

NATIONAL

Supreme Court in *Terminiello v. Chicago* upholds free speech even when it causes unrest or disturbances.

Eleven top U.S. Communists are found guilty of conspiring to overthrow the government, are sentenced to five years in prison.

Hoover Commission issues report on government operations; leads to Reorganization Act of 1949.

Salary of president is raised to $100,000 annually; vice president and house speaker to $30,000.

Flag Day, June 14, is established.

General Services Administration (GSA) is established to manage government property.

Gen. Henry H. (Hap) Arnold becomes first general of Air Force; Gen. Omar N. Bradley becomes first permanent chairman of Joint Chiefs of Staff.

William H. Hastie becomes first African American judge on U.S. Circuit Court of Appeals.

American Museum of Atomic Energy opens at Oak Ridge, Tenn.

Gerald R. Ford begins 24 years of service in House from Michigan.

National Trust for Historic Preservation is created.

DEATHS James V. Forrestal, first defense secretary; Edward R. Stettinius Jr., first U.S. delegate to the U.N.

BUSINESS/INDUSTRY/INVENTIONS

Supreme Court rules that states have right to ban the closed shop.

Minimum wage is raised from 40 cents an hour to 75 cents, effective 1950.

Federal government seizes North American Aviation plant in Inglewood, Calif., to end strike.

Goodyear Tire & Rubber Co. manufactures belt conveyor for Weirton mine of National Mines to convey coal 10,000 feet from mine to Monongahela River in West Virginia.

DEATH Atwater Kent, pioneer radio manufacturer.

TRANSPORTATION

More than 5 million (5,119,466) cars are manufactured in year.

SCIENCE/MEDICINE

William F. Giauque is awarded Nobel Prize for chemistry for work on chemical thermodynamics.

Morehead Planetarium at University of North Carolina opens.

EDUCATION

Earl J. McGrath is named U.S. Education Commissioner.

1949

The Berlin Airlift, 1948–1949. Children in blockaded city of West Berlin eagerly await American planes bringing supplies. CORBIS-BETTMANN

DEATHS Ray Lyman Wilbur, president and chancellor, Stanford University (1916–1949); James R. Angell, Yale University president (1921–1937), a founder of functional psychology.

RELIGION

Billy Graham begins nationwide evangelistic program with eight weeks of meetings in Los Angeles.

Cornerstone is laid for Islamic Center in Washington, D.C.

DEATH Rabbi Stephen S. Wise, founder of American Zionist movement.

ART/MUSIC

Roy E. Harris composes *Kentucky Spring*.

Peter Blume completes the painting *The Rock*.

SONGS (popular): "Dear Hearts and Gentle People," "Mule Train," "Rudolph, the Red-Nosed Reindeer," "Some Enchanted Evening," "I'm Gonna Wash That Man Right Out of My Hair."

LITERATURE/JOURNALISM

William Faulkner is awarded Nobel Prize for Literature for contributions to the U.S. novel.

BOOKS *The Big Fisherman* by Lloyd C. Douglas, *Annie Allen* (poetry) by Gwendolyn Brooks, *A Rage to Live* by John O'Hara, *The Man with the Golden Arm* by Nelson Algren, *The Apostle* by Sholem Asch, *The Lottery* by Shirley Jackson, *The Dream Merchants* by Harold Robbins, *The Golden Apples* by Eudora Welty.

The Reporter and *American Heritage* magazines begin publication.

DEATHS Margaret Mitchell and Hervey Allen, authors; Helen Hokinson, cartoonist; John T. McCutcheon, editorial cartoonist (*Chicago Tribune* 1903–1945).

ENTERTAINMENT

PLAYS Mary Martin and Ezio Pinza star in *South Pacific*, Carol Channing in *Gentlemen Prefer Blondes*, Lee J. Cobb in *Death of a Salesman*, Ralph Bellamy in *Detective Story*.

MOVIES *All the King's Men* with Broderick Crawford, *Adam's Rib* with Katharine Hepburn and Spencer Tracy.

New television shows are *Stop the Music* with Bert Parks, *Quiz Kids*, *One Man's Family*, *Mama* with Peggy Wood, *Life of Riley* with William Bendix, *Hopalong Cassidy* with William Boyd, *Aldrich Family*, *Lights Out*, the Fred Waring and Dave Garroway shows.

DEATHS Maxwell Anderson, playwright; Burns Mantle, editor of annual play collection (1919–1947); Wallace Beery, screen actor; Bill ("Bojangles") Robinson, dancer.

SPORTS

Merger of National Basketball League and Basketball Association of America forms National Basketball Assn.; National Football League and All-American Conference merge.

WINNERS *Auto racing*—Bill Holland, Indianapolis 500; Red Byron, NASCAR Winston Cup Champion; *Baseball*—New York Yankees, World Series; *Basketball*—San Francisco, NIT; Kentucky, NCAA; Minneapolis, NBA; *Bowling*—Connie Schwegler and Val Mikiel, bowlers of year; *Boxing*—Ezzard Charles, heavyweight; Jake LaMotta, middleweight; Willie Pep, featherweight; *Football* (bowls)—Northwestern, Rose; Texas, Orange; Oklahoma, Sugar; Southern Methodist, Cotton; Philadelphia, NFL; *Golf*—U.S., Ryder and Walker cups; Cary Middlecoff, U.S. Open; Sam Snead, PGA; Bobby Locke, Masters; Louise Suggs, U.S. Women's Open; *Hockey*—Toronto, Stanley Cup; *Horse racing*—Ponder, Kentucky Derby; Capot, Preakness Stakes and Belmont Stakes; *Tennis*—U.S., Davis Cup; Pancho Gonzales, U.S. Open (men); Margaret Osborne du Pont, U.S. Open (women).

MISCELLANEOUS

Two planes collide over Washington, D.C., kill 55.

Fire in Effingham (Ill.) hospital kills 77 persons.

Bikinis are introduced as swimwear.

1950

INTERNATIONAL

Korean War

One hundred thousand North Koreans invade South Korea (June 25); President Harry Truman orders U.S. air, sea forces to support Korean Republican Army (June 27), adds ground forces (June 30); Gen. Douglas MacArthur is named commander of U.N. troops (July 8). U.S. Marines take Womi Island, Inchon (September 15), U.S. troops recapture Seoul (September 26); 18 Communist China divisions launch surprise attack (September 30), force U.N. retreat to 38th parallel.

North Atlantic Council agrees on integrated European defense force; Gen. Dwight D. Eisenhower becomes NATO commander.

U.S. recalls consular officials from China after U.S. consul general was seized; shipments to Communist China are banned.

U.N. official Ralph Bunche is awarded Nobel Peace Prize for work in Middle East war; U.N. headquarters in New York City is completed.

U.S. sends arms, supplies, and instructors to South Vietnam; military assistance pact is signed with France, Cambodia, Laos, and Vietnam.

U.S. and Canada sign 50-year treaty (February 27), to regulate Niagara Falls power output, preserve falls' beauty.

NATIONAL

Two Puerto Rican nationalists attempt to assassiate President Truman (November 1); one nationalist and a White House guard are killed.

President Truman announces that U.S. will develop hydrogen bomb; Wernher von Braun, German rocket engineer, is named director of missile research facility at Huntsville, Ala.

U.S. citizenship and limited self-government granted to people of Guam; Puerto Rico Commonwealth Act is signed.

Sixteenth census reports population at 151,325,798.

Annual immigration to U.S. totals 249,187.

Alger Hiss, former State Department official, is found guilty of perjury, is sentenced to five-year prison term.

McCarran Act passes over president's veto, calls for registration of Communists and their internment during national emergencies.

Senate Judiciary Committee televises hearings on organized crime.

Senator Joseph McCarthy of Wisconsin announces in Wheeling, W. Va., that he has a list of many Communists in the State Department, leading to several years of congressional hearings.

Residential mail deliveries are cut to once a day.

Selective Service for military draft is extended for another year.

National deficit is $3.1 million; public debt climbs to $256.1 billion.

DEATHS Henry L. Stimson, War Secretary (1911–1913, 1940–1945), Secretary of State (1929–1933); Clarence A. Dykstra, Selective Service head (1940–1941); Henry H. (Hap) Arnold, Air Force general.

BUSINESS/INDUSTRY/INVENTIONS

Supreme Court in *American Communications Workers v. Douds* upholds Taft-Hartley Act provision that requires non-Communist affidavits from union officers.

Maritime Administration is established.

Grand Coulee Dam in Washington State is dedicated.

Bic Pen Co. is founded; Hazel Bishop forms cosmetics company; J. Paul Getty negotiates oil concessions in Saudi Arabia, Kuwait.

CIO expels International Longshoremen's and Warehousemen's Union.

Minimum wage becomes 75 cents an hour.

DEATHS Walter H. Beech, founder and head, Beech Aircraft; Charles L. Lawrence, designer of first air-cooled aeronautical engine; Eliel Saarinen, architect.

TRANSPORTATION

President Truman orders seizure of the railroads to prevent general strike (August 27).

New York Port Authority bus terminal opens.

Brooklyn–Battery Tunnel, longest in U.S., opens; Tacoma (Wash.) Narrow Bridge is completed.

DEATH Ransom E. Olds, pioneer automaker.

Desi Arnaz and Lucille Ball in *I Love Lucy*, one of the new television shows in 1950. PHOTOFEST

SCIENCE/MEDICINE

Philip S. Hench and Edward C. Kendall share Nobel Prize for physiology/medicine for discoveries about hormones of the adrenal cortex.

President Truman signs act creating National Science Foundation.

Richard H. Lawler performs first kidney transplant from one human to another in Chicago.

Charles Pfizer & Co. announces the antibiotic tetramycin.

Fluoro-record reflector X-ray camera is developed.

Dr. Helen Taussig becomes first woman member of Association of American Physicians.

Element 98 (californium) is discovered at University of California.

DEATHS Charles R. Drew, developer of blood banks; Arthur J. Dempster, builder of first mass spectrometer; George R. Minot, discoverer of liver therapy for anemia.

EDUCATION

Yale University founds Department of Design,

headed by Josef Albers; University of North Carolina offers nuclear engineering course.

DEATH Isaiah Bowman, Johns Hopkins University president (1935–1948).

RELIGION

National Council of Churches is formed by 29 major American Protestant, seven Eastern Orthodox churches.

Rose Philippine Duchesne, founder of first American Sacred Heart convent, is beatified.

American Synod of Russian Orthodox church elects New York Archbishop Leonty as Metropolitan for the United States and Canada.

DEATHS William T. Manning, Episcopal bishop of New York (1921–1946); Edwin H. Hughes, senior Methodist bishop (1932–1950).

ART/MUSIC

Age of Anxiety, ballet by Jerome Robbins and Leonard Bernstein, is presented; Gian Carlo Menotti composes opera *The Consul*.

PAINTINGS Jackson Pollock's first "action" work, *Lavender Mist*; Andrew Wyeth's temperas, *Young*

1950

SONGS (popular): "Mona Lisa," "C'est Si Bon," "A Bushel and a Peck," "From This Moment On," "Good Night, Irene," "May the Good Lord Bless and Keep You."

DEATHS George G. (Buddy) De Sylva, lyricist ("April Showers"); Kurt Weill, composer (*Three-penny Opera*); Walter Damrosch, conductor.

LITERATURE/ JOURNALISM

Gwendolyn Brooks, poet, becomes first African American woman to win Pulitzer Prize (for *Annie Allen*).

Charles M. Schulz creates cartoon, "Peanuts."

Walter Cronkite begins CBS television news career.

Tan magazine is founded.

BOOKS *The Wall* by John Hersey, *I, Robert* by Isaac Asimov; *The Disenchanted* by Budd Schulberg, *Kon-Tiki* by Thor Heyerdahl, *The 13 Clocks* by James Thurber, *Complete Poems* by Carl Sandburg, *The Cardinal* by Henry M. Robinson, *The Family Moskat* by Isaac Bashevis Singer, *Giant* by Edna Ferber.

DEATHS Poets Edna St. Vincent Millay and William Rose Benét; authors Edgar Lee Masters, Carl Van Doren, and Edgar Rice Burroughs.

ENTERTAINMENT

CBS television broadcasts in color.

Comedy and musical personalities star on television shows: Jimmy Durante, Steve Allen, Jack Benny, Sid Caesar and Imogene Coca, George Burns and Grace Allen, and Frank Sinatra; other new shows

The Korean War. In South Korea, 1950, women and children flee Communist invaders as U.S. soldiers march ahead to fight those invaders. UPI/CORBIS-BETTMANN

America and *Northern Point*; Ben Shahn, *Epoch*; Hans Hofmann, *The Window*; Stuart Davis, *Little Giant Still-Life*.

include *I Love Lucy*, *Your Hit Parade*, *What's My Line?*, *Truth or Consequences*, *Beat the Clock*.

PLAYS Robert Alda stars in *Guys & Dolls*, Ethel Waters and Julie Harris in *The Member of the Wedding*, Ethel Merman in *Call Me Madam*, Shirley Booth in *Come Back, Little Sheba*, Uta Hagen in *The Country Girl*.

MOVIES *Born Yesterday* with Judy Holliday, *Cyrano de Bergerac* with Jose Ferrer, *The Great Caruso* with Mario Lanza, *Harvey* with James Stewart, *The Asphalt Jungle* with Sterling Hayden, *All About Eve* with Bette Davis.

DEATHS Actresses Julia Marlowe and Jane Cowl; actors Walter Huston and Al Jolson; producers William A. Brady and Brock Pemberton.

SPORTS

Connie Mack retires after managing Philadelphia Athletics baseball team for 50 years.

Florence Chadwick swims English Channel both ways.

Sportswriters and broadcasters name Jack Dempsey greatest prizefighter of 1900–1950 era; George Mikan, best basketball player; Man o' War, greatest racehorse.

U.S. soccer team upsets England in World Cup play; three days later, Chile eliminates U.S.

WINNERS *Auto racing*—Johnny Parsons, Indianapolis 500; Bill Rexford, NASCAR; *Baseball*—New York Yankees, World Series; *Basketball*—City College of New York, NIT and NCAA; Minneapolis, NBA; *Bobsledding*—U.S. four-man team, world title; *Bowling*—Junie McMahon, Marion Ladewig, bowlers of year; *Boxing*—Ezzard Charles, heavyweight; Joey Maxim, light heavyweight; Sugar Ray Robinson, middleweight; Sandy Saddler, featherweight; *Chess*—Arthur B. Bisguier, U.S. Open; *Figure skating*—Dick Button, men's world singles; Peter and Karol Kennedy, first from U.S. to win world pairs; *Football* (bowls)—Ohio State, Rose; Santa Clara, Orange; Oklahoma, Sugar; Rice, Cotton; Cleveland, NFL; *Golf*—Ben Hogan, U.S. Open; Chandler Harper, PGA; Jimmy Demaret, Masters; Babe Didrikson Zaharias, U.S. Women's Open; *Hockey*—Detroit, Stanley Cup; *Horse racing*—Middleground, Kentucky Derby and Belmont Stakes; Hill Prince, Preakness Stakes; *Tennis*—Australia, Davis Cup; Arthur Larsen, U.S. Open (men); Margaret Osborne du Pont, U.S. Open (women).

DEATHS Carl L. Storck, NFL secretary-treasurer (1921–1939)/president (1939–1941); Frank Buck, wild-game hunter.

MISCELLANEOUS

Brinks Express office in Boston is robbed of $2.8 million.

New York City's Aircall, Inc. begins radio paging service.

Standing commuter train in Richmond Hill, N.Y., is hit by oncoming train, kills 79.

INTERNATIONAL

Korean War

Retreating U.N. forces abandon Seoul (January 4) to North Koreans and Chinese; President Harry S. Truman relieves Gen. Douglas MacArthur of his post as U.N. commander and American Far East commander for constant public criticism of U.S. policy (April 11); armistice negotiations in Korea begin (July 10).

Japanese peace treaty is signed in San Francisco by 49 nations (September 8).

U.S., Australia, and New Zealand sign mutual security pact (September 1).

U.S. and Iceland sign agreement calling for U.S. defense of the island in return for right to build major U.S. air base.

NATIONAL

Twenty-second Amendment sets a maximum of

1951

two terms for the presidency, is ratified (February 26).

Supreme Court in *Dennis v. United States* upholds 1946 Smith Act that makes it a criminal offense to advocate forceful overthrow of the government; also upholds 1949 conviction of 11 American Communist Party leaders.

Gen. Douglas McArthur, relieved of his Far East posts, addresses a joint session of Congress.

Julius Rosenberg and his wife, Ethel, are convicted of atomic espionage, are sentenced to death.

DEATHS Former Vice President Charles G. Dawes (1925–1929); Lincoln Ellsworth, explorer.

BUSINESS/INDUSTRY/INVENTIONS

Franklin National Bank of New York introduces the credit card.

Electric power is obtained for first time from nuclear energy at Atomic Energy Commission station at Idaho Falls, Idaho.

Pittsburgh Coal Consolidation Co. (Cadiz, Ohio) demonstrates coal pipeline.

Remington Rand builds UNIVAC I, first electronic computer.

Plant in Henderson, Nev., opens to produce titanium metal from ore.

Dial telephone service coast-to-coast without operators is instituted.

DEATH Will K. Kellogg, cereal company founder.

TRANSPORTATION

First section of New Jersey Turnpike (Bordentown–Deepwater) opens.

Delaware Memorial Bridge at Wilmington opens.

Park-o-Mat Garage (Washington, D.C.), completely automatic push-botton 16-story garage, opens.

Passenger car registrations total 42,700,000.

SCIENCE/MEDICINE

Edwin M. McMillan and Glenn T. Seaborg share Nobel Prize for chemistry for discoveries in chemistry of transuranium elements; Max Theiler is awarded Nobel Prize for physiology/medicine for discoveries concerning yellow fever.

Walter H. Zinn develops first breeder reactor.

EDUCATION

Clarence A. Faust becomes president of Fund for the Advancement of Education.

RELIGION

David O. McKay becomes president of Mormon church on death of George A. Smith.

Catholic Bishop John F. O'Hara becomes archbishop of Philadelphia.

DEATHS Henry A. Ironside, evangelist known as the archbishop of fundamentalists; Catholic Archbishop Dennis J. Dougherty of Philadelphia (1918–1951).

ART/MUSIC

Gian Carlo Menotti writes *Amahl and the Night Visitors*, first opera for television; becomes annual Christmas Eve show.

Gail Kubik composes *Symphony Concertante*; Douglas S. Moore, the opera *Giants in the Earth*.

Dave Brubeck forms his quartet.

Adolph Gottlieb completes the painting *The Frozen Sounds*; David Hare completes the sculpture *Figure Waiting in the Cold*.

SONGS (popular): "Cold, Cold Heart," "I Whistle a Happy Tune," "Kisses Sweeter Than Wine," "Too Young," "In the Cool, Cool, Cool of the Evening," "Getting to Know You."

LITERATURE/JOURNALISM

The Village Voice, New York City newspaper, is founded.

Jet magazine is founded.

BOOKS *The Sea Around Us* by Rachel Carson, *The Caine Mutiny* by Herman Wouk, *From Here to Eternity* by James Jones, *Collected Poems* by Marianne Moore, *Catcher in the Rye* by J. D. Salinger, *Requiem for a Nun* by William Faulkner, *Piano Player* by Kurt Vonnegut, *A Man Called Peter* by Catharine Marshall.

DEATHS Authors Sinclair Lewis and Lloyd C. Douglas; publishers William Randolph Hearst and

Emanuel Haldeman-Julius; Dorothy Dix (Elizabeth M. Gilmer), advice to lovelorn columnist.

ENTERTAINMENT

Transcontinental television is inaugurated with President Truman's speech at Japanese peace conference in San Francisco (September 4); Zenith Radio Corp. demonstrates first pay television system.

Philadelphia opens city-owned and -operated playhouse in Fairmount Park.

PLAYS Yul Brynner stars in *The King and I*, Julie Harris in *I Am a Camera*, Barbara Bel Geddes in *The Moon Is Blue*, Shirley Booth in *A Tree Grows in Brooklyn*.

MOVIES *The African Queen* with Katharine Hepburn and Humphrey Bogart, *An American in Paris* with Gene Kelly, *The Lavender Hill Mob* with Alec Guinness, *A Streetcar Named Desire* with Vivien Leigh and Marlon Brando.

New television shows include *Strike It Rich*, *Mark Saber*, *Wild Bill Hickok*, and Red Skelton.

SPORTS

Happy Chandler resigns as baseball commissioner, is succeeded by Ford Frick; Warren C. Giles succeeds Frick as National League president.

Bobby Thomson hits three-run home run in the bottom of the ninth against Brooklyn to give New York Giants the playoff and National League pennant.

Norm Van Brocklin of Los Angeles Rams completes 27 passes for record 554 yards, 5 touchdowns.

First Pan-American Games are held.

First NBA all-star basketball game and first Pro Bowl (football) game are played.

Eddie Gaedel, 3-foot-7-inch baseball player, pinchhits for St. Louis Browns, walks; use of little people in baseball is outlawed by commissioner the next day.

WINNERS *Auto racing*—Lee Wallard, Indianapolis 500; Herb Thomas, NASCAR; *Baseball*—New York Yankees, World Series; *Basketball*—Brigham Young, NIT; Kentucky, NCAA; Rochester, NBA; *Bowling*—Lee Jouglard, Marion Ladewig, bowlers of year; *Boxing*—Jersey Joe Walcott, heavyweight; Sugar Ray Robinson, middleweight; Kid Gavilan, welterweight; *Chess*—Larry Evans, U.S. men; Mary Bain, U.S. women; *Figure skating*—Dick Button, world men's title; *Football* (bowls)—Michigan, Rose; Clemson, Orange; Kentucky, Sugar; Tennessee, Cotton; Los Angeles Rams, NFL; *Golf*—U.S., Walker and Ryder cups; Ben Hogan, U.S. Open and Masters; Sam Snead, PGA; Betsy Rawls, U.S. Women's Open; *Hockey*—Toronto, Stanley Cup; *Horse racing*—Count Turf, Kentucky Derby; Bold, Preakness Stakes; Counterpoint, Belmont Stakes; *Tennis*—Australia, Davis Cup; Frank Sedgman, U.S. Open (men); Maureen Connolly, U.S. Open (women).

MISCELLANEOUS

Hart, Schaffner & Marx introduces men's suits made of Dacron.

Mine disaster at West Frankfort, Ill., kills 119; commuter train plunges through temporary overpass in Woodbridge, N.J., kills, 85, injures 500; plane plunges into river on takeoff from Elizabeth (N.J.) Airport taking 56 lives; Kansas and Missouri floods leave 200,000 homeless, 41 dead.

1952

INTERNATIONAL

Korean War continues.

Gen. Matthew B. Ridgway succeeds Gen. Dwight D. Eisenhower as NATO supreme commander.

U.S., Great Britain, France, and West Germany sign peace compact (May 26).

United Nations headquarters in New York City is completed.

NATIONAL

President Harry S. Truman announces that he will not seek reelection; Gen. Eisenhower is picked by Republicans and Adlai E. Stevenson by the Democrats. Eisenhower is elected with 33,900,000 popular and 442 electoral votes to Stevenson's 27,300,000 and 89.

First hydrogen device explodes at Eniwetok in the Pacific (November 1).

Supreme Court clears the Italian film *The Miracle*, declares movies are "a significant medium" for communicating ideas and are fully shielded by First Amendment.

President and Mrs. Truman move back to renovated White House after four-year project.

Puerto Rico becomes first overseas U.S. commonwealth.

Immigration and Naturalization Act removes last racial and ethnic barriers to citizenship.

John F. Kennedy is elected to Senate from Massachusetts.

DEATH Harold L. Ickes, Interior Secretary (1933–1946), headed Public Works Administration.

BUSINESS/INDUSTRY/INVENTIONS

President Truman orders seizure of steel mills to avert strike; Supreme Court rules seizure unconstitutional.

George Meany, AFL secretary-treasurer, succeeds to presidency on death of William Green; Walter P. Reuther, president of United Auto Workers, becomes CIO president after Philip Murray's death.

Lever House in New York City is completed; sets style for office-building design for a decade.

More than 2,500 new television stations are started.

First Holiday Inn (Memphis) opens.

DEATHS Albert D. Lasker, advertising executive; Charles H. Kraft, cofounder of cheese firm.

TRANSPORTATION

Chesapeake Bay Bridge at Annapolis, Md., opens.

Two Army helicopters complete transatlantic flight from Westover (Mass.) to Germany.

SCIENCE/MEDICINE

Felix Bloch and Edward N. Purcell share Nobel Prize in physics for new methods of nuclear precision measurements; Selman A. Waksman is awarded prize in physiology/medicine for discovery of streptomycin.

More than 21,000 cases of polio are reported in U.S.

University of California scientists identify element 99 (einsteinium).

DEATH Forest R. Moulton, co-author of spiral nebulae theory.

EDUCATION

Rev. Theodore M. Hesburgh becomes president of Notre Dame University; Henry T. Heald, chancellor of New York University.

DEATH John Dewey, pioneer in progressive education.

"We like Ike." Republican women show their support for presidential candidate General Dwight D. Eisenhower. UPI/CORBIS-BETTMANN

RELIGION

Rev. Fulton Sheen appears weekly on television program *Life Is Worth Living*.

ART/MUSIC

Leonard Bernstein composes opera *Trouble in Tahiti*; the Brecht-Weill *Threepenny Opera* is adapted by Marc Blitzstein.

Helen Frankenthaler completes the painting *Mountains and Sea*, Jackson Pollock, *Blue Poles*; Naum Gabo completes the sculpture *Construction Suspended in Space*.

SONGS (popular): "Don't Let the Stars Get in Your Eyes," "I Saw Mommy Kissing Santa Claus," "I'm Yours," "Takes Two to Tango," "You Belong to Me," "High Noon."

LITERATURE/JOURNALISM

BOOKS *The Silver Chalice* by Thomas B. Costain, *East of Eden* by John Steinbeck, *Glory Road* by Bruce Catton, *The Natural* by Bernard Malamud, *Charlotte's Web* by E. B. White, *Invisible Man* by Ralph Ellison, *The Old Man and the Sea* by Ernest Hemingway, *Collected Poems* by Archibald MacLeish, *The Power of Positive Thinking* by Norman Vincent Peale.

DEATH H. T. Webster, cartoonist ("The Timid Soul").

ENTERTAINMENT

Cinerama, a three-film strip process, is demonstrated.

PLAYS Alfred Lunt and Lynn Fontanne star in *Quadrille*, Tom Ewell in *The Seven Year Itch*, Jose Ferrer in *The Shrike*.

MOVIES *Hans Christian Andersen* with Danny Kaye, *Singin' in the Rain* with Gene Kelly, *The Quiet Man* with John Wayne, *Viva Zapata!* with Marlon Brando, *Limelight* with Charlie Chaplin.

1953

New television shows include *This Is Your Life* with Ralph Edwards, *See It Now* with Edward R. Murrow, *I've Got a Secret* with Garry Moore, *Dragnet*, and Ernie Kovacs.

DEATH Gertrude Lawrence, actress.

SPORTS

Winter Olympics are held in Oslo, with U.S. winning four gold medals; Summer Olympics are held in Helsinki, with U.S. winning 40 golds, including Bob Mathias's second decathlon.

Avery Brundage, former head of AAU and U.S. Olympic Assn., begins 20 years as president of International Olympic Committee.

American Bowling Congress approves use of automatic pinspotters.

Professional Golfers Assn. approves participation of African Americans in golf tournaments.

First U.S. woman bullfighter, Patricia McCormick, debuts in Mexico, kills three bulls.

WINNERS *Auto racing*—Tony Ruttman, Indianapolis 500; Tim Flock, NASCAR; *Baseball*—New York Yankees, World Series; *Basketball*—LaSalle, NIT; Kansas, NCAA; Minneapolis, NBA; *Bowling*—Steve Nagy, Marion Ladewig, bowlers of year; *Boxing*—Rocky Marciano, heavyweight; Archie Moore, light heavyweight; *Figure skating*—Dick Button, U.S. and world men's singles; Tenley Albright, world women's singles; *Football* (bowls)—Illinois, Rose; Georgia Tech, Orange; Maryland, Sugar; Kentucky, Cotton; Detroit, NFL; *Golf*—Julius Boros, U.S. Open; Jim Turnesa, PGA; Sam Snead, Masters; Louise Suggs, U.S. Women's Open; *Hockey*—Detroit, Stanley Cup; *Horse racing*—Hill Gail, Kentucky Derby; Blue Man, Preakness Stakes; One Count, Belmont Stakes; *Tennis*—Australia, Davis Cup; Frank Sedgman, U.S. Open (men); Maureen Connolly, U.S. Open (women).

MISCELLANEOUS

Series of tornadoes in Arkansas, Missouri, and Tennessee claim 208 lives.

DEATH Shipwreck (Alvin) Kelly, flagpole sitter who spent 20,613 hours aloft.

INTERNATIONAL

Armistice in Korea is signed (June 26) after two years of intermittent negotiations; U.S. approves $200 million for Korean relief, rehabilitation (August 3).

President Dwight D. Eisenhower proposes international "atoms for peace" program.

Spain authorizes U.S. to establish military bases there.

U.S. gives $60 million to France to help war in Indochina.

NATIONAL

Former Secretary of State George C. Marshall is awarded Nobel Peace Prize for his plan to assist other nations.

1953

Earl Warren is confirmed as Supreme Court chief justice.

Julius and Ethel Rosenberg are electrocuted in Sing Sing Prison; first civilians executed for wartime espionage, first ever executed for that crime in peacetime.

Former President Hoover is named head of second commission to study reorganization of Executive Department.

Department of Health, Education, and Welfare is created with Oveta Culp Hobby as secretary.

Submerged Land Act gives federal government right to offshore lands of seaboard states.

Refugee Relief Act admits escapees from Communist aggression into U.S.

Two dams completed: Hungry Horse on Flathead

River in Montana and McNary on Columbia River in Washington.

DEATHS Robert F. Wagner, New York senator responsible for much social legislation; Jonathan Wainwright, general who defended Bataan, Corregidor; Robert A. Taft, Ohio senator known as Mr. Republican; Supreme Court Chief Justice Frederick M. Vinson (1946–1953).

BUSINESS/INDUSTRY/INVENTIONS

Alcoa Building, 30-story aluminum-faced building in Pittsburgh, is completed.

DEATH William L. Hutcheson, president, Carpenters Union (1915–1952).

TRANSPORTATION

Helicopter service between New York City airports begins.

Work begins on Eugene Talmadge Memorial Bridge in Savannah.

DEATH William M. Jeffers, president, Union Pacific Railroad (1937–1946).

SCIENCE/MEDICINE

Fritz A. Lipmann shares Nobel Prize for physiology/medicine with Hans A. Krebs of Great Britain for discovery of coenzyme A.

Dr. Jonas Salk announces successful experimental use of a polio vaccine.

Dr. James D. Watson and Francis C. H. Crick successfully create a three-dimensional molecular model of deoxyribonucleic acid (DNA), a discovery comparable in importance to Newton's laws of motion, Darwin's theory of evolution, and Einstein's relativity theory.

First privately operated atomic reactor put into operation by North Carolina and North Carolina State universities at Raleigh.

Julius and Ethel Rosenberg, executed in 1953, are shown here in the U.S. Marshal's van, divided by wire screening, as they left federal court after their conviction in 1951 on charges of espionage and conspiracy in transmitting atomic secrets to Soviet Russia. UPI/CORBIS-BETTMANN

1953

University of California scientists identify element 100 (fermium).

Argonne Cancer Research Hospital in Chicago opens.

Companion study to original 1948 study by Institute of Sex Research, *Sexual Behavior in the Human Female*, is published.

DEATH Robert A. Millikan, physicist who was first to isolate the electron.

EDUCATION

Detlev N. Bronk becomes president of Rockefeller Institute; Nathan M. Pusey of Harvard University.

RELIGION

Catholic archbishop James F. McIntyre of Los Angeles is elevated to cardinal; Albert G. Meyer becomes archbishop of Milwaukee, Wis.

ART/MUSIC

New York City Opera presents Aaron Copland's *Tender Land*; Quincy Porter composes Concerto for Two Pianos and Orchestra.

Leonard Bernstein becomes first U.S. composer to conduct at Milan's (Italy) La Scala opera house.

Robert Joffrey founds and directs American Ballet Center.

Andrew D. White Museum of Art at Cornell University opens.

Jackson Pollock completes the painting *Portrait and a Dream*; Helen Frankenthaler, *Open Wall*; Franz Kline, *New York*.

SONGS (popular): "How Much Is That Doggie in the Window?," "From This Moment On," "I Believe," "I Love Paris," "O, Mein Papa," "That's Amore," "Your Cheatin' Heart," "Secret Love."

LITERATURE/JOURNALISM

Hugh Hefner founds *Playboy* magazine.

BOOKS *Poems 1942–53* by Karl Shapiro, *A Stillness at Appomattox* by Bruce Catton, *Go Tell It on the Mountain* by James Baldwin, *The Adventures of Augie March* by Saul Bellow; *The Bridges at Toko-Ri* by James A. Michener, *Fahrenheit 451* by Ray Bradbury.

DEATHS Authors Douglas Southall Freeman and Walter B. Pitkin.

ENTERTAINMENT

The movie *The Robe* introduces Cinemascope.

First U.S. educational television station, KUHT in Houston, broadcasts.

PLAYS Henry Fonda stars in *The Caine Mutiny Court-Martial*, Deborah Kerr in *Tea and Sympathy*, Margaret Sullavan in *Sabrina Fair*; Leonard Bernstein writes music for *Wonderful Town*; Arthur Miller writes *The Crucible*; Paddy Chayefsky, *Marty*; Cole Porter, *Can-Can*; and William Inge, *Picnic*.

MOVIES *From Here to Eternity* with Burt Lancaster and Deborah Kerr, *Shane* with Alan Ladd, *The Desert Song* with Gordon MacRae, *The Bandwagon* with Fred Astaire.

Danny Thomas and Loretta Young premiere television shows, Edward R. Murrow interviews on *Person to Person*; other new shows are *Name That Tune* and *General Electric Theater*.

DEATHS Eugene O'Neill, playwright; Maude Adams, actress who played Peter Pan about 1,500 times.

SPORTS

Supreme Court rules that baseball is a sport, not a business, and therefore not subject to antitrust laws.

National League owners approve transfer of Boston baseball franchise to Milwaukee, Wis.; American League, move of St. Louis to Baltimore.

Maureen ("Little Mo") Connolly wins tennis grand slam by winning the Australian, French, British, and U.S. championships in one year.

WINNERS *Auto racing*—Bill Vukovich, Indianapolis 500; Herb Thomas, NASCAR; *Baseball*—New York Yankees, World Series; *Basketball*—Seton Hall, NIT; Indiana, NCAA; Minneapolis, NBA; *Bobsledding*, U.S. four-man team, world title; *Bowling*—Don Carter, Marion Ladewig, bowlers of year; *Boxing*—Rocky Marciano, heavyweight; Carl Olson, middleweight; *Figure skating*—Hayes Jenkins, men's world singles; Tenley Albright, women's world singles; *Football* (bowls)—Southern California, Rose; Alabama, Orange; Georgia

Tech, Sugar; Texas, Cotton; Detroit, NFL; *Golf*— U.S., Walker and Ryder cups; Ben Hogan, U.S. Open and Masters; Walter Bukermo, PGA; Betsy Rawls, U.S. Women's Open; *Hockey*—Montreal, Stanley Cup; *Horse racing*—Dark Star, Kentucky Derby; Native Dancer, Preakness Stakes and Belmont Stakes; *Tennis*—Australia, Davis Cup; Tony Trabert, U.S. Open (men); Maureen Connolly, U.S. Open (women); *Wrestling*—Bill Kerslake, first AAU Greco-Roman heavyweight.

DEATHS Two former athletes, Jim Thorpe, one of greatest all-around athletes, and Bill Tilden, a tennis great.

MISCELLANEOUS

Tornadoes in Texas kill 114 and in Michigan and Ohio, 142.

U.S. Air Force C-124 crashes and burns near Tokyo, 129 die.

Bermuda shorts become popular among men.

1954

INTERNATIONAL

Senate approves construction of St. Lawrence Seaway; corporation is established to develop, operate, and maintain seaway.

U.S., Australia, Great Britain, France, New Zealand, Pakistan, Philippines, and Thailand create Southeast Asia Treaty Organization (SEATO) (September 8).

U.S., Great Britain, France, Canada, Australia, and South Africa join to explore peacetime uses of atomic energy.

U.S. and Canada agree to create third line of radar stations across northern Canada, the Distant Early Warning (DEW) line.

U.S. signs mutual defense treaties with Japan (March 8) and Nationalist China (December 2).

Libya gives U.S. long-term (to 1970) rights to air base near Tripoli.

NATIONAL

Five members of House of Representatives are slightly wounded by four Puerto Rican nationalists who fire from spectators' gallery (March 1).

Senator Joseph R. McCarthy of Wisconsin attacks alleged Communists in government and Democratic Party; he conducts televised hearings; Senate censures him (December 2) for failing to explain a financial transaction and for abusing fellow senators.

Atomic Energy Commission holds secret hearings on J. Robert Oppenheimer, consultant, for alleged Communist ties; he is cleared as "loyal" but it is recommended that he not be rehired.

Air Force Academy is authorized; opens in temporary quarters at Lowry AFB, then in permanent home at Colorado Springs, Colo.

Housing Act authorizes construction of 35,000 houses a year for those displaced by federal programs.

Congress outlaws Communist Party.

Benjamin O. Davis Jr. becomes first African American Air Force general; his father was first African American Army general.

Nautilus, first atomic-powered submarine, is launched; USS *Forrestal*, largest aircraft carrier, is launched; explosion aboard carrier *Bennington* kills 103.

Second H-bomb experimental explosion occurs at Bikini Atoll in Pacific.

DEATHS Air Force Gen. Hoyt S. Vandenberg; Ruth Bryan (Rohde), first U.S. woman diplomat; Arthur Garfield Hays, director, American Civil Liberties Union (1912–1954).

BUSINESS/INDUSTRY/INVENTIONS

Atomic Energy Act authorizes private power companies to own and use reactors for electric power; ground is broken in Pittsburgh for first atomic power plant.

1954

Senator McCarthy shows the other senators at the hearings his view of the growth of Communism in the United States (June 9, 1954). On the left with a dejected expression is Army counsel Joseph N. Welch, who has just denounced McCarthy as a "cruelly reckless character assassin." UPI/CORBIS-BETTMANN

Buckminster Fuller founds Geodesics Inc. to produce geodesic domes.

Hilton Hotel Corp. acquires controlling interest of Statler Hotels.

TRANSPORTATION

General Motors announces $1 billion expansion program.

First automatic toll-collection station opens at Union Toll Plaza on the Garden State Parkway in New Jersey.

SCIENCE/MEDICINE

Linus Pauling is awarded Nobel Prize for chemistry for research into the nature of chemical bond; John F. Enders, Frederic C. Robbins, and Thomas H. Weller share prize for physiology/medicine for

discovery that polio viruses grow in various types of tissue.

First mass inoculation with Salk vaccine begins in Pittsburgh; field trials involving 400,000 children prove vaccine safe and 70% effective in preventing polio.

Rutgers University dedicates Institute of Microbiology.

Plastic contact lenses are introduced.

DEATH Enrico Fermi, nuclear scientist.

EDUCATION

Supreme Court in *Brown v. Board of Education* (May 17) holds that racial segregation in public schools violates Fourteenth Amendment guarantee of equal protection of the laws; in a series of decisions (May 24), Court outlaws segregation in tax-supported educational institutions, public housing, and public park, recreational, and entertainment facilities.

University of Alaska at Anchorage is founded.

DEATHS Alain L. Locke, first African American Rhodes scholar; Liberty H. Bailey, founder of agricultural college at Cornell University.

ART/MUSIC

Annual American jazz festivals begin at Newport, R.I.

Gian Carlo Menotti composes *The Saint of Bleeker Street*.

Elvis Presley makes his first recordings, "That's All Right, Mama" and "Blue Moon of Kentucky."

PAINTINGS *Double Portrait of Birdie* by Larry Rivers; *Light, Earth, and Blue* by Mark Rothko; *Construction with a Piano* by Jasper Johns; *Midi* by Stuart Davis; *The Garden* by John Ferrer.

SONGS (popular): "Fly Me to the Moon," "Hey There," "Home for the Holidays," "Mister Sandman," "Shake, Rattle and Roll," "Sh-Boom," "Smile," "This Ole House."

DEATH Charles Edward Ives, composer of polytonal harmonies, unusual rhythms.

LITERATURE/JOURNALISM

Ernest Hemingway is awarded Nobel Prize in literature.

BOOKS *Poems 1923–54* by E. E. Cummings, *A Fable* by William Faulkner, *The Ponder Heart* by Eudora Welty, *Blackboard Jungle* by Evan Hunter, *The Tunnel of Love* by Peter DeVries, *The View from Pompey's Head* by Hamilton Basso, *George Washington* by Douglas Southall Freeman.

DEATHS Maxwell Bodenheim, poet ("Bard of Greenwich Village"); two pioneer cartoonists, George McManus ("Bringing Up Father") and Bud Fisher ("Mutt and Jeff"); Bertie C. Forbes, founder and editor *Forbes Magazine*.

ENTERTAINMENT

PLAYS Pearl Bailey stars in *House of Flowers*, John Raitt in *The Pajama Game*, Ezio Pinza in *Fanny*; Thornton Wilder writes *The Matchmaker* (which becomes *Hello, Dolly!*).

MOVIES *Rear Window* with James Stewart, *The Country Girl* with Grace Kelly, *A Star Is Born* with Judy Garland, *On the Waterfront* with Marlon Brando, *20,000 Leagues Under the Sea* with James Mason, *The Barefoot Contessa* with Ava Gardner.

New shows on television include *Tonight Show* with Steve Allen, *People Are Funny* with Art Linkletter, *Sid Caesar's Hour*, *Father Knows Best*, *The Lineup*, and *Lassie*.

A new dance, the Mambo, becomes popular.

DEATHS Lionel Barrymore, actor; Claude E. Hooper, radio market analyst; Edwin H. Armstrong, developer of FM radio transmission.

SPORTS

NBA adopts rule requiring a shot on basket within 24 seconds after getting the ball.

Parry O'Brien becomes first to throw shot more than 60 feet (60 ft., $5\frac{1}{4}$ in.).

Jonas E. Salk looks at the vaccine that bears his name and is reducing drastically the incidence of paralytic polio in the U.S. UPI/CORBIS-BETTMANN

1955

Maureen Connolly, tennis star, suffers career-ending horseback-riding injury.

American League approves transfer of baseball franchise from Philadelphia to Kansas City, Mo.

National Ski Hall of Fame is founded.

Sports Illustrated magazine begins publication.

WINNERS *Auto racing*—Bill Vukovich, Indianapolis 500; Lee Petty, NASCAR; *Baseball*—New York Giants, World Series; *Basketball*—Holy Cross, NIT; LaSalle, NCAA; Minneapolis, NBA; *Bowling*—Don Carter, Marion Ladewig, bowlers of year; *Boxing*—Rocky Marciano, heavyweight; Johnny Saxton, welterweight; Jimmy Carter, lightweight; *Chess*—Arthur Bisguier, U.S. title; *Figure skating*—Hayes Jenkins, U.S. and world men's singles; *Football* (bowls)—Michigan State, Rose; Oklahoma, Orange; Georgia Tech, Sugar; Rice, Cotton; Cleveland, NFL; *Golf*—Ed Furgol, U.S.

Open; Melvin Harbert, PGA; Sam Snead, Masters; Babe Didrikson Zaharias, U.S. Women's Open; *Hockey*—Detroit, Stanley Cup; *Horse racing*—Determine, Kentucky Derby; Hasty Road, Preakness Stakes; High Gun, Belmont Stakes; *Tennis*—U.S., Davis Cup; Vic Seixas, U.S. Open (men); Doris Hart, U.S. Open (women); Yale, first intercollegiate title.

DEATHS Grantland Rice, sportswriter; Glenn S. (Pop) Warner, college-football coach; Wilbur Shaw, auto racer, in plane crash.

MISCELLANEOUS

Hurricane Hazel rakes Haiti and eastern U.S. for 13 days, kills 347 persons; Hurricane Carol sweeps East Coast, kills 68, causes $500 million damage.

Killing tornadoes hit Waco, Tex. (114 die), Flint, Mich. (116), Worcester, Mass. (90).

INTERNATIONAL

American occupation of Germany ends (April 21).

U.S. agrees to help train South Vietnamese army.

U.S. and Guatemala sign military assistance pact (June 18); U.S. and Panama sign treaty of cooperation on Panama Canal (January 25).

President Dwight D. Eisenhower and Soviet Premier Nikita Khruschev discuss disarmament.

NATIONAL

President Eisenhower, on Colorado vacation, suffers heart attack (September 24); resumes limited activities a short time later.

Salaries are raised for vice president by $5,000 to $35,000; members of Congress by $7,500 to $22,500; Supreme Court chief justice by $9,550 to $35,000; associate justices by $10,000 to $30,000.

Rosa Parks refuses to give her seat to a white man

1955

on a Montgomery, Ala., bus (December 1); her arrest leads to major boycott of buses, eventually to Supreme Court decision that outlaws segregation on public transportation.

National Association of Social Workers is established.

DEATHS Cordell Hull, Secretary of State (1933–1944); John R. Mott, YMCA leader; Walter F. White, executive secretary, NAACP (1931–1955); Matthew Henson, who accompanied Peary to North Pole; Maud Park, first president, League of Women Voters.

BUSINESS/INDUSTRY/INVENTIONS

AFL and CIO merge to form 15-million-member union headed by AFL President George Meany.

McDonald's fast-food chain is founded by Ray A. Kroc in Des Plaines, Ill.

C. G. Glasscock Drilling Co. puts first seagoing oil drill in service.

Rosa Parks rides a Montgomery, Ala., bus after the successful boycott against the city's bus lines. Mrs. Parks is arrested on December 1, 1955, when she sits in the "white" section of the bus and refuses to give up her seat to a white man. UPI/CORBIS-BETTMANN

Tappan Stove Co. introduces electronic range for domestic use.

General Electric researchers form synthetic diamonds.

DEATHS Samuel H. Kress, cofounder of five-and-ten-cent-store chain; Daniel J. Tobin, Teamsters Union president (1907–1952); Glenn L. Martin, aircraft manufacturer.

TRANSPORTATION

President Eisenhower asks Congress for $101 billion over 10 years for interstate highways.

More than 7 million cars (7,920,186) are manufactured in year.

Tappan Zee Bridge over Hudson River at Nyack, N.Y., opens.

Illinois law requires attachments to which seat belts can be fastened.

SCIENCE/MEDICINE

Polykarp Kusch and Willis E. Lamb share Nobel Prize for physics for precision determination of electron's magnetic moment; Vincent du Vigneaud is awarded chemistry prize for work on sulphur compounds.

Emilio Segre and University of California associates discover new atomic particle, the antiproton; other university scientists discover Element #101 (mendelevium).

1955

National Hurricane Center is established.

DEATHS Albert Einstein, physicist; George H. Parker, early U.S. experimental zoologist.

EDUCATION

Supreme Court orders "all deliberate speed" in integrating public schools.

White House Conference on Education calls on government to increase financial help for public education.

DEATHS George H. Denny, University of Alabama president (1912–1955); Herbert Putnam, Librarian of Congress (1899–1939).

RELIGION

Betty Robbins of Massapequa, N.Y., first Jewish woman cantor, sings her first service at Temple Avodah, Oceanside, N.Y.

DEATH Mary Josephine Rogers, founder of Maryknoll Sisters.

ART/MUSIC

Marian Anderson debuts at Metropolitan Opera, the first African American to perform at the Met; Arthur Mitchell becomes first African American to dance with major company (New York City Ballet).

Jackson Pollock completes the painting *Autumn Rhythm*; Willem de Kooning, *Woman: Ochre*; Morris Graves, *Flight of Power*; Herbert Ferber completes the sculpture *Mercury*; sculptor David Hare, *Sunrise*.

SONGS (popular): "Ain't That a Shame," "Cry Me a River," "Hearts of Stone," "Love Is a Many-Splendored Thing," "Rock Around the Clock," "Cherry Pink and Apple Blossom White," "Maybellene," "Mack the Knife."

DEATH Charlie Parker, jazz musician and composer who helped develop "bop" or "bebop."

LITERATURE/JOURNALISM

Ann Landers' (Esther P. Friedman Lederer) first advice-to-lovelorn column appears in *Chicago Sun-Times*; *San Francisco Chronicle* hires her twin sister (Paula E. Friedman Philips) to do similar column ("Dear Abby").

William F. Buckley Jr. founds *National Review*.

BOOKS *Marjorie Morningstar* by Herman Wouk, *Andersonville* by MacKinlay Kantor, *Lolita* by Vladimir Nabokov, *10 North Frederick* by John O'Hara, *The Man in the Grey Flannel Suit* by Sloan Wilson, *The Edge of the Sea* by Rachel Carson, *Candy* by Terry Southern.

DEATHS Ham(mond E.) Fisher, cartoonist ("Joe Palooka"); authors Dale Carnegie and James Agee; publishers Joseph A. Pulitzer and Robert R. McCormick.

ENTERTAINMENT

Disneyland in Anaheim, Calif., opens.

PLAYS Susan Strasberg stars in *The Diary of Anne Frank*, Burl Ives in *Cat on a Hot Tin Roof*, Paul Muni in *Inherit the Wind*; Cole Porter writes *Silk Stockings*.

MOVIES *The Seven Year Itch* with Marilyn Monroe, *Mister Roberts* with Henry Fonda and Jimmy Cagney; *Marty* with Ernest Borgnine, *Rebel Without a Cause* with James Dean, *The Blackboard Jungle* with Glenn Ford, *The Rose Tattoo* with Anna Magnani.

Jackie Gleason stars in *The Honeymooners* with Art Carney and Audrey Meadows; Jim Henson creates first of the Muppets, Kermit the Frog; other new television shows are: *Gunsmoke* with Jim Arness, *The $64,000 Question* with Hal March, *Wyatt Earp* with Hugh O'Brien, Soupy Sales, Phil Silvers, Alfred Hitchcock.

DEATHS James Dean, screen actor; Walter Hampden, actor; Theda Bara, silent-screen "vamp"; Robert E. Sherwood, playwright.

SPORTS

Ted Allen sets horseshoe pitching record of 72 consecutive ringers.

U.S. Auto Club, which sanctions major auto races, is established.

WINNERS *Auto racing* — Bob Sweikert, Indianapolis 500; Tim Flock, NASCAR; *Baseball* — Brooklyn Dodgers, World Series; *Basketball* — Duquesne, NIT; San Francisco, NCAA; Syracuse, NBA; *Bowling* — Steve Nagy, Sylvia Martin, bowlers of year; *Boxing* — Rocky Marciano, heavyweight; Carmen Basilio, welterweight; Sugar Ray Robinson, middleweight; *Figure skating* — Hayes

Jenkins, world men's singles; Tenley Albright, U.S. and world women's singles; *Football (bowls)*—Ohio State, Rose; Duke, Orange; Navy, Sugar; Georgia Tech, Cotton; Cleveland, NFL; *Golf*—U.S., Walker and Ryder cups; Jack Fleck, U.S. Open; Doug Ford, PGA; Cary Middlecoff, Masters; Fay Crocker, U.S. Women's Open; Beverly Hanson, LPGA; *Hockey*—Detroit, Stanley Cup; *Horse racing*—Swaps, Kentucky Derby; Nashua, Preakness Stakes and Belmont Stakes; *Tennis*—Australia, Davis Cup; Tony Trabert, U.S. Open (men); Doris Hart, U.S. Open (women).

DEATHS Bill Vukovich, auto racer, while seeking third Indianapolis 500 win; Ely Culbertson, bridge expert; baseball greats Honus Wagner and Cy Young, pitcher who won 511 career games.

MISCELLANEOUS

Hurricane Diane sweeps Eastern U.S. for two weeks, 400 die; tornadoes in Midwest claim 115 lives; heavy rains in Pacific Northwest cause much damage, claim 74 lives.

INTERNATIONAL

Egypt closes Suez Canal after U.S. and Great Britain stop financing Aswan Dam; Britain and France send troops to retake canal; United Nations intervenes, clears situation; canal reopens 1956.

U.S. and Iceland renew agreement to continue operating U.S. air base.

U.S. signs treaty with Panama to increase canal annuity to $1.93 million.

Eighteen American republics meet in Panama City to discuss economic problems.

NATIONAL

President Dwight D. Eisenhower, Republican, is reelected, receives 35,590,472 popular and 457 electoral votes to 26,022,752 popular and 74 electoral votes for his Democratic challenger, Adlai E. Stevenson; Democrats regain control of Congress.

President Eisenhower suffers an ileitis attack, undergoes successful surgery.

Responding to Supreme Court decision, nonsegregated bus service begins in Montgomery, Ala.; 101 Southern members of Congress call for massive resistance against Court ruling.

The national motto, "In God We Trust," is authorized.

Alaska voters approve territorial constitution.

Virgin Islands National Park is established.

Ft. Randall Dam on Missouri River in South Dakota is completed.

DEATHS Jesse H. Jones, commerce secretary (1940–1945); Former Vice President Alben W. Barkley (1949–1953); Hiram Bingham, explorer who discovered Inca ruins; Admiral Ernest J. King, head of World War II naval operations.

BUSINESS/INDUSTRY/INVENTIONS

Commercial telephone service over transoceanic cable begins; $12 for each three-minute call.

Minimum wage is raised to $1 an hour (March 1).

Smith-Corona Inc. announces portable electric typewriter.

Getty Oil Co. is founded.

Louis Harris & Associates, opinion polling organization, is formed.

DEATHS Clarence Birdseye, inventor of food-freezing process; Harry F. Sinclair, founder and president, Sinclair Oil (1916–1949); Hattie Carnegie, fashion designer.

TRANSPORTATION

Highway Act provides $32.5 billion over 13 years to build 41,000-mile interstate highway system (June 29).

Elvis Presley performs in Dallas, Texas, to a crowd of 26,000 people on October 15, 1956. Two of his songs that are especially popular are "Blue Suede Shoes" and "Love Me Tender." UPI/CORBIS-BETTMANN

First nonstop transcontinental helicopter flight is completed in 31 hours, 40 minutes.

SCIENCE/MEDICINE

John Bardeen, Walter H. Brattain, and William Shockley share Nobel Prize for physics for discovery of transistor effect; Andre F. Cournand and Dickinson W. Richards Jr. share prize for physiology/medicine for discoveries concerning heart catheterization.

Drs. James W. Watts and Walter Freeman perform first prefrontal lobotomy in Washington, D.C.

DEATH Alfred C. Kinsey, zoologist who headed landmark studies of sexual behavior.

RELIGION

Ninth World Methodist conference meets at Lake Junaluska, N.C., representatives from 40 nations are present; Methodist General Conference grants full clergy rights to women in the U.S., orders abolition of racial segregation in Methodist churches.

Congregational Christian and Evangelical and Reformed churches pass vote on proposed merger in 1957.

Margaret Ellen Tanner becomes first woman ordained as Presbyterian minister (October 24).

Universal chapel for eight faiths is dedicated in Universalist Church of the Divine Paternity in New York City.

ART/MUSIC

Robert Joffrey organizes ballet company.

Norman Dello Joio composes *Meditations on Ecclesiastes*; Douglas S. Moore, the opera *The Ballad of Baby Doe*.

Philip Guston completes the painting *Dial*; Grace Hartigan, *City Life*; Georgia O'Keeffe, *Patio with Cloud*.

SONGS (popular): "Blue Suede Shoes," "Don't Be Cruel," "I Could Have Danced All Night," "Memories Are Made of This," "On the Street Where You Live," "Que Será, Será," "I Walk the Line," "Love Me Tender."

DEATHS Jackson Pollock, pop art founder; Albert Von Tilzer, composer ("Take Me Out to the Ball Game"); composer Victor Young ("Love Letters"); bandleader Tommy Dorsey; Art Tatum, jazz pianist.

LITERATURE/JOURNALISM

BOOKS *The Last Hurrah* by Edwin O'Connor, *Peyton Place* by Grace Metalious, *Homage to Mistress Bradstreet* by John Berryman, *Things of This World* (poetry) by Richard Wilbur.

Huntley-Brinkley news report appears on NBC.

DEATHS Clarence E. Mulford, author of Westerns; H. L. Mencken, journalist and author; Alex Raymond, cartoonist ("Flash Gordon").

ENTERTAINMENT

Ampex Corp. demonstrates magnetic tape recorder of sound and picture.

Grace Kelly, screen actress, marries Prince Rainier of Monaco.

Ringling Brothers Barnum & Bailey Circus closes because of rising costs.

PLAYS Sammy Davis Jr. stars in *Mr. Wonderful*, Rex Harrison and Julie Andrews in *My Fair Lady*,

Rosalind Russell in *Auntie Mame*; Leonard Bernstein writes music for *Candide*, Frank Loesser writes *The Most Happy Fella*.

MOVIES *Around the World in 80 Days* with David Niven, *High Society* with Grace Kelly, *Bus Stop* with Marilyn Monroe, *Giant* with Rock Hudson, *The King and I* with Yul Brynner, *Picnic* with William Holden.

Ernie Kovacs hosts *The Tonight Show*; new shows include *To Tell the Truth* with Bud Collyer, and Tennessee Ernie Ford.

DEATHS Elsie Janis, entertained troops in World War I; Fred Allen, radio humorist; Bela Lugosi, screen actor.

SPORTS

Don Larsen of New York Yankees pitches first (and only) perfect game in World Series, allows no hits, no walks, no runs against Brooklyn Dodgers (October 8).

Charles Dumas, Compton College freshman, becomes first to clear 7 feet in high jump.

Summer Olympic Games are held in Melbourne, Australia; U.S. wins 33 gold medals.

WINNERS *Auto racing* — Pat Flaherty, Indianapolis 500; Buck Baker, NASCAR; *Baseball* — New York Yankees, World Series; *Basketball* — Louisville, NIT; San Francisco, NCAA; Philadelphia, NBA; *Bobsledding* — U.S. four-man team, world title; *Bowling* — Bill Lillard, Anita Canteline, bowlers of year; *Boxing* — Floyd Patterson, heavyweight; Carmen Basilio, welterweight; Joe Brown, lightweight; *Chess* — Arthur B. Bisguier, U.S. title; *Figure Skating* — Hayes Jenkins, men's world singles; Tenley Albright, women's world singles; *Football* (bowls) — Michigan State, Rose; Oklahoma, Orange; Georgia Tech, Sugar; Mississippi, Cotton; New York Giants, NFL; *Golf* — Cary Middlecoff, U.S. Open; Jack Burke, PGA and Masters; Kathy Cornelius, U.S. Women's Open; Marlene Hagge, LPGA; *Hockey* — Montreal, Stanley Cup; *Horse racing* — Needles, Kentucky Derby and Belmont Stakes; Fabius, Preakness Stakes; *Tennis* — Australia, Davis Cup; Ken Rosewall, U.S. Open (men); Shirley Fry, U.S. Open (women).

DEATHS Connie Mack, Philadelphia baseball manager for 50 years; Babe Didrikson Zaharias, one of greatest women athletes.

MISCELLANEOUS

Italian liner *Andrea Doria* and Swedish liner *Stockholm* collide off Nantucket, 51 die.

TWA Super-Constellation and United DC-7 collide over Grand Canyon, 128 die.

Suburbs grow in the post-World War II period, and single-story ranch houses are popular. Shown here is a street in Levittown, N.Y., in 1956, an influential development of low-cost houses 90% of whose residents are World War II veterans and their families (constructed 1946–1951). UPI/CORBIS-BETTMANN

1957

INTERNATIONAL

President Dwight D. Eisenhower announces U.S. will use its military and economic power to protect Middle East against Communist aggression (January 5); Congress endorses doctrine.

U.S. ratifies International Atomic Energy Agency treaty, created by 80 nations.

U.S. combat troops withdraw from Japan (August 1).

U.S. renews agreement to maintain air base in Saudi Arabia.

NATIONAL

First civil rights act since 1875 establishes Civil Rights Commission to investigate and seek correction of any violations (September 9).

Supreme Court in *Roth v. United States* defines obscenity more permissively than previously accepted; in *Sweezy v. New Hampshire*, Court rules that academic freedom is protected by Constitution's due process clause.

President Eisenhower suffers mild stroke (November 25); recovers quickly, returns to duty in two weeks.

Southern Christian Leadership Conference is founded with Rev. Martin Luther King Jr. as president.

Law providing pensions for former presidents goes into effect.

First underground nuclear explosion occurs at Nevada testing grounds; National Committee for Sane Nuclear Policy is organized.

Queen Elizabeth II and Prince Philip visit Jamestown, Va., on 350th anniversary of first English settlement in U.S.

Federal troops enforce desegregation at Central High School in Little Rock, Ark., in 1957.
UPI/CORBIS-BETTMANN

Harry S. Truman Library in Independence, Mo., is dedicated.

The Dallas Dam on Columbia River and Palisades Dam on Snake River in Idaho are completed.

DEATHS Former First Lady Grace Coolidge (1923–1929); Richard E. Byrd, aviator and polar explorer; Joseph R. McCarthy, Wisconsin senator whose investigative methods gave rise to term *McCarthyism*.

BUSINESS/INDUSTRY/INVENTIONS

Shippingport (Pa.) Atomic Power Station begins operating.

Pittsburgh Consolidation Coal Co. puts 108-mile pipeline to Eastlake (Ohio) power station into operation.

Charles F. Carlson founds Haloid Co., forerunner of Xerox Corp.

Jimmy Hoffa becomes president of Teamsters Union, which was ousted from AFL–CIO on grounds of corruption.

Hamilton Watch Co. introduces electric watch.

First solar-heated building in U.S. is completed in Albuquerque, N. Mex.

DEATHS Sosthenes Behn, founder and head, International Telephone & Telegraph; Ernest T. Weir, founder of Weirton, National Steel companies; Paul Starrett, builder of Empire State Building; Gerard Swope, president, General Electric (1922–1940, 1942–1944).

TRANSPORTATION

Third tube of Lincoln Tunnel under Hudson River is completed.

Mackinac Bridge at Straits of Mackinac, Mich., and Walt Whitman Bridge in Philadelphia are completed.

Three B-52 Air Force bombers complete round-the-world flight in 45 hours, 19 minutes.

SCIENCE/MEDICINE

Tsung-dao Lee and Chen Ning Yang share Nobel Prize in physics for work on left-right symmetry in physical processes.

World Health Organization begins to use polio vaccine developed by Dr. Albert B. Sabin.

Arthur Kornberg produces artificial DNA, the substance in a cell that carries genetic code.

Argonne National Laboratory announces discovery of Element #102 (nobelicum).

Leon N. Cooper, John Bardeen, and J. R. S. Schrieffer develop theory of superconductivity.

DEATH George W. Merck, pharmaceutical firm head.

EDUCATION

Arkansas Governor Orval Faubus uses National Guard to keep nine black students from entering all-white high school in Little Rock (September 4); after court order and arrival of federal troops (September 24), students enter.

RELIGION

Evangelical and Reformed Church and Congregational Christian Church merge to form United Church of Christ (June 25).

First worldwide Lutheran meeting in U.S. is held in Minneapolis; Rev. Franklin C. Fry, president of United Lutheran Church in U.S., is named president of world body.

ART/MUSIC

American Ballet Theater is founded; Edward Villela joins New York City Ballet.

Conductor Sarah Caldwell founds Boston Opera Co.

Leontyne Price makes operatic debut with San Francisco Opera.

Leonard Baskin completes the sculpture *Laureate Standing*; Richard Stankiewicz, the sculpture *Instruction*; Seymour Lipton, the sculpture *Sorcerer*.

Jasper Johns completes the painting *Book*; Philip Guston, *The Clock*.

Museum for Contemporary Arts in Dallas and Museum for Primitive Art in New York City are founded.

SONGS (popular): "April Love," "Bye Bye Love," "Jailhouse Rock," "Little Darlin'," "Maria," "76 Trombones," "Singin' the Blues," "Tammy,"

1957

"Wake Up, Little Susie," "Till There Was You."

LITERATURE/JOURNALISM

BOOKS *By Love Possessed* by James G. Cozzens, *Promises* (poetry) by Robert Penn Warren, *A Death in the Family* by James Agee, *How the Grinch Stole Christmas* by Dr. Seuss, *Atlas Shrugged* by Ayn Rand, *The Town* by William Faulkner, *The Wapshot Chronicle* by John Cheever, *On the Road* by Jack Kerouac.

DEATHS Angela Morgan, poet; Edna W. Chase, editor of *Vogue*; Frank E. Gannett, founder of newspaper chain; authors Sholem Asch and Kenneth Roberts.

ENTERTAINMENT

PLAYS Anthony Perkins stars in *Look Homeward, Angel*, Robert Preston in *The Music Man*, Cyril Ritchard in *A Visit to a Small Planet*; Leonard Bernstein writes music for *West Side Story*.

MOVIES *The Bridge on the River Kwai* with Alec Guinness, *St. Joan* with Jean Seberg, *The Three Faces of Eve* with Joanne Woodward, *Twelve Angry Men* with Henry Fonda, *Peyton Place* with Lana Turner.

New television shows include *Wagon Train*, *The Price Is Right* with Bill Cullen, *Perry Mason* with Raymond Burr, *Maverick* with James Garner, *Leave It to Beaver*, *Have Gun, Will Travel* with Richard Boone; Jack Paar hosts *The Tonight Show*, Dinah Shore begins program.

DEATHS Oliver Hardy of Laurel and Hardy comedy team; John Van Druten, playwright; Humphrey Bogart, actor; Louis B. Mayer, movie executive.

SPORTS

Two New York teams announce that they will move to Pacific Coast in 1958: New York Giants to move to San Francisco, Brooklyn Dodgers to Los Angeles.

National Hockey League Players Assn. is formed.

Don Bowden becomes first American to run mile in less than 4 minutes (3 min., 58.7 sec.).

Jim Spalding sets nine-game bowling record of 2088 points at ABC tournament.

WINNERS *Auto racing* — Sam Hanks, Indianapolis 500; Buck Baker, NASCAR; *Badminton* — U.S. women's team, world title; *Baseball* — Milwaukee Braves, World Series; *Basketball* — Bradley, NIT; North Carolina, NCAA; Boston, NBA; *Boxing* — Floyd Patterson, heavyweight; Carmen Basilio, middleweight; Alphonse Halimi, featherweight; *Figure skating* — Dave Jenkins, U.S. and world men's singles; Carol Heiss, U.S. and world women's singles; *Football* (bowls) — Iowa, Rose; Colorado, Orange; Baylor, Sugar; Texas Christian, Cotton; Detroit, NFL; *Golf* — Great Britain, Walker and Ryder cups; Dick Mayer, U.S. Open; Lionel Hebert, PGA; Doug Ford, Masters; Betsy Rawls, U.S. Women's Open; Louise Suggs, LPGA; *Hockey* — Montreal, Stanley Cup; *Horse racing* — Iron Liege, Kentucky Derby; Bold Ruler, Preakness Stakes; Gallant Man, Belmont Stakes; *Table tennis* — Leah Thall Neuberger, national singles; *Tennis* — Australia, Davis Cup; Malcolm Anderson, U.S. Open (men); Althea Gibson, U.S. Open (women), she also is first African American to win at Wimbledon.

DEATH Tom Jenkins, wrestling champion.

MISCELLANEOUS

Louisiana and Texas struck by Hurricane Audrey and tidal wave; 531 are dead or missing.

California company introduces the Frisbee.

Sack dresses become popular.

DEATH Elizabeth S. Kingsley, inventor of double-crostic puzzle.

1958

INTERNATIONAL

U.N. announces neutrality in Indonesia civil war.

Marines are sent to Lebanon to restore order after uprising by Arab nationalists.

Vice President Richard M. Nixon makes three-week goodwill tour of eight South American countries; Venezuelans and Peruvians greet him angrily.

NATIONAL

National Aeronautics and Space Administration (NASA) is created.

Atomic-powered submarine *Nautilus* makes first underwater crossing of North Pole; another atomic submarine, *Skate*, crosses Atlantic Ocean both ways submerged in 15 days, 16 hours.

First-class postage increases to 4 cents per ounce.

Robert H. W. Welch Jr. founds John Birch Society.

Nelson A. Rockefeller begins 15 years as New York governor.

DEATH James M. Curley, colorful Boston mayor for 16 years and Massachusetts governor.

BUSINESS/INDUSTRY/INVENTIONS

Arthur Melin and Richard Knerr create hula-hoop, a circle of plastic tubing that people twirl on their hips; within year, 25 million such hoops are sold in U.S.

Manufacture of aluminum cans begins.

DEATHS Malcolm Lockheed, airplane manufacturer; James D. Dole, founder of Hawaiian pineapple industry; Arde Bulova, watch manufacturer; Norman Bel Geddes, foremost proponent of streamlining; John Moody, financial analyst; Eugene F. McDonald, founder and head, Zenith Radio Corp.

TRANSPORTATION

First domestic jet airline service begins between New York City and Miami.

Mississippi River Bridge at New Orleans opens.

DEATH Charles F. Kettering, developer of automobile self-starter.

SCIENCE/MEDICINE

George W. Beadle, Edward L. Tatum, and Joshua Lederberg share Nobel Prize in physiology/medicine; Beadle and Tatum for discovery that heredity-transmitting genes do so by chemical reaction; Lederberg for discoveries of genetic recombination and organization of genes in bacteria.

Explorer I is first U.S. satellite placed in orbit (January 31), discovers Van Allen radiation belt; *Score* satellite is launched, transmits first voice messages from space.

Bifocal contact lens is introduced.

More than 11,000 scientists sign petition that is presented to U.N.; demands end to nuclear-weapons testing.

DEATHS Ernest O. Lawrence, developer of cyclotron; Earnest A. Hooton, laid foundation for U.S. physical anthropology.

EDUCATION

Air Force Academy begins operation in permanent home near Colorado Springs, Colo.

RELIGION

Presbyterian Church (USA) merges with U.S. Presbyterian Church of North America to form United Presbyterian Church (May 28).

Catholic Cardinal Samuel A. Stritch becomes first American named to Roman Curia; Archbishop Albert G. Meyer of Milwaukee is moved to Chicago; Archbishops John F. O'Hara and Richard J. Cushing are elevated to cardinal.

Bishop Arthur Lichtenberger becomes presiding bishop of American Episcopal Church.

National Council of Churches reports church membership at 109,557,741.

1958

George Washington University, 1958. Anne Sneeringer, the school's 97-pound cheerleader, attempts to coach Ed Rurbach, the 270-pound tackle, in the art of spinning a hula-hoop. UPI/CORBIS-BETTMANN

ART/MUSIC

Van (Harvey K.) Cliburn Jr. of Texas wins first prize at International Tchaikovsky Piano Competition in Moscow.

John LaMontaine composes *Concerto for Piano and Orchestra*; Samuel Barber completes opera *Vanessa*; Walter Piston composes *Seventh Symphony*.

Leonard Bernstein becomes permanent conductor of New York Philharmonic.

Jerome Robbins's *Ballets: USA* tours the country; Alvin Ailey forms ballet company, presents *Blues Suite*.

Stereo long-playing records are introduced.

Isabel Bishop completes the painting *Subway Scene*; Adolph Gottlieb, *Ascent*; Franz Kline, *Siegfried*; Louise Nevelson completes the sculpture *Sky Cathedral*; Alexander Calder, *Spiral*.

Guggenheim Museum in New York City is completed.

SONGS (popular): "The Chipmunk Song," "Gigi," "It's Only Make Believe," "Jingle Bell Rock," "Satin Doll," "Volare," "Summertime," "The Purple People Eater."

DEATHS Artur Rodzinski, conductor; John Held Jr., illustrator of "jazz age"; Doris Humphrey, pioneer of American modern dance; W. C. Handy, blues composer.

LITERATURE/ JOURNALISM

United Press and International News Service merge to become UPI.

BOOKS *Anatomy of a Murder* by Robert Traver, *The Travels of Jaimie McPherson* by Robert L. Taylor, *Breakfast at Tiffany's* by Truman Capote, *From the Terrace* by John O'Hara, *Exodus* by Leon Uris, *Only in America* by Harry Golden; *The Dharma Bums* by Jack Kerouac, *Paterson* (poetry) by William Carlos Williams.

DEATHS George Jean Nathan, editor and drama critic; James Branch Cabell, author.

ENTERTAINMENT

PLAYS Ralph Bellamy stars in *Sunrise at Campobello*, Helen Hayes in *A Touch of the Poet*, Cyril Ritchard in *The Pleasure of His Company*; Archibald MacLeish writes a biblical allegory, *J.B.*, Tennessee Williams, *Suddenly Last Summer*.

MOVIES *The Old Man and the Sea* with Spencer Tracy, *Cat on a Hot Tin Roof* with Elizabeth Taylor, *Gigi* with Leslie Caron, *Damn Yankees* with Gwen Verdon, *Auntie Mame* with Rosalind Rusell.

New television shows include *77 Sunset Strip* with Efrem Zimbalist Jr., *Peter Gunn* with Craig Stevens, *Seahunt* with Lloyd Bridges, and the Garry Moore and Andy Williams shows.

DEATHS Harry M. Warner, Warner Brothers president (1923–1956); Jesse Lasky, movie pioneer; Michael Todd, stage and screen producer, in plane crash; Ronald Colman, screen actor.

SPORTS

Jim Brown, Cleveland running back, rushes for record 1527 yards in season.

Stan Musial, St. Louis Cardinals, gets 3000th base hit.

Glenn Davis sets 100-meter hurdles record of 49.2 seconds.

WINNERS *Auto racing* — Jimmy Bryan, Indianapolis 500; Lee Petty, NASCAR; *Baseball* — New York Yankees, World Series; *Basketball* — Xavier (Ohio), NIT; Kentucky, NCAA; St. Louis, NBA; *Bowling* — Don Carter, Marion Ladewig, bowlers of year; *Boxing* — Don Jordon, welterweight; Sugar Ray Robinson, middleweight; *Figure skating* — David Jenkins, U.S. and world men's singles; Carol Heiss, U.S. and world women's singles; *Football* (bowls) — Ohio State, Rose; Oklahoma, Orange; Mississippi, Sugar; Navy, Cotton; Baltimore, NFL; *Golf* — Tommy Bolt, U.S. Open; Dow Finsterwald, PGA; Arnold Palmer, Masters; Mickey Wright, U.S. Women's Open and LPGA; *Hockey* — Montreal, Stanley Cup; *Horse racing* — Tim Tam, Kentucky Derby and Preakness Stakes; Cavan, Belmont Stakes; *Lawn bowling* — Leonard Schofield, first singles title; *Tennis* — U.S., Davis Cup; Great Britain, Wightman Cup; Ashley Cooper, U.S. Open (men); Althea Gibson, U.S. Open (women); *Yachting* — U.S. sloop *Columbia* retains America's Cup.

DEATHS Mel Ott, New York Giants baseball great; Clarence DeMar, seven-time winner of Boston Marathon.

MISCELLANEOUS

Our Lady of Angels parochial school in Chicago burns; 92 students, 3 teachers die.

1959

INTERNATIONAL

Cuba confiscates U.S.-owned oil refineries and business firms (June 29); U.S. places embargo on Cuban sugar imports, U.S. exports (except food and medicine).

Queen Elizabeth and President Dwight D. Eisenhower dedicate St. Lawrence Seaway (June 26); The Queen and Vice President Richard M. Nixon dedicate St. Lawrence Hydroelectric Power Project at Massena, N.Y. (June 27).

President Eisenhower makes three-week trip to 11 countries in Europe, Asia, and Africa; Soviet Premier Khruschev makes 12-day visit to U.S.

International Atomic Energy Agency is created to explore peaceful atomic-energy uses.

NATIONAL

Alaska is admitted as 49th state (January 3), Hawaii as 50th (August 21).

Secretary of State John Foster Dulles resigns (April 15) because of an incapacitating illness; dies May 4; Christian A. Herter succeeds him (April 18).

First ballistic missile submarine, *George Washington*, is launched.

DEATHS Admiral William F. Halsey, headed World War II Pacific Fleet; Gen. George C. Marshall, Army chief of staff (1939–1945), Secretary of State (1947–1950).

BUSINESS/INDUSTRY/INVENTIONS

Haloid-Xerox Co. (later Xerox Corp.) introduces first commercial xerographic copier.

Four-month steel strike ends when 80-day federal injunction is issued.

DEATHS Food critic and writer Duncan Hines; Frank Lloyd Wright, architect.

TRANSPORTATION

World's first atomic-powered merchant ship, *Savannah*, is launched in Camden, N.J.

1959

SCIENCE/MEDICINE

Albert B. Sabin develops oral polio vaccine.

Owen Chamberlain and Emilio G. Segre share Nobel Prize in physics for discovery of antiproton; Arthur Kornberg and Severo Ochoa share prize in physiology/medicine for contributions to understanding of life process.

Explorer VI satellite is launched to send back pictures of Earth; unmanned spacecraft *Luna 2* lands on moon (September 12); *Luna 3* is first to circle moon (October 4) and send back pictures of far side.

EDUCATION

Federal district court and Virginia Supreme Court both rule that closing public schools to avoid desegregation violates Fourteenth Amendment; desegregation begins in Norfolk and Arlington.

DEATH Abraham Flexner, medical educator, organizer and director (1930–1939), Institute for Advanced Study, Princeton, N.J.

RELIGION

Evangelical Lutheran and United Evangelical Lutheran churches merge to form American Lutheran Church.

Unitarian and Universalist churches vote to merge.

Two Catholic archbishops are elevated to cardinal: Aloysius J. Muench of Fargo, N. Dak., and Albert G. Meyer of Chicago.

ART/MUSIC

Elliott Carter composes *Second String Quartet.*

Thomas Hart Benton completes murals in Harry S. Truman Library; Adolph Gottlieb completes the painting *Counterpoise*; Jasper Johns, *Device Circle*; Louise Nevelson completes the sculpture *Dawn's Wedding.*

SONGS (popular): "Climb Every Mountain," "Everything's Coming Up Roses," "Put Your Head on My Shoulder," "My Favorite Things," "There Goes My Baby," "Mister Blue," "Dream Lover," "Lonely Boy."

DEATHS George Antheil, ultramodern composer; Buddy Holly, singer and major influence on rock and roll, in a plane crash; Billie Holiday, jazz singer.

LITERATURE/JOURNALISM

BOOKS *Advise and Consent* by Allen Drury, *Henderson the Rain King* by Saul Bellow, *Hawaii* by James Michener, *The Cave* by Robert Penn Warren, *Two Weeks in Another Town* by Irwin Shaw.

DEATHS Raymond T. Chandler, mystery writer; Edgar A. Guest, columnist and poet.

ENTERTAINMENT

PLAYS Anne Bancroft stars in *The Miracle Worker*, Tom Bosley in *Fiorello!*, Ethel Merman in *Gypsy*; Lorraine Hansberry writes *A Raisin in the Sun*, Lillian Hellman, *The Little Foxes*, Richard Rodgers and Oscar Hammerstein II, *The Sound of Music.*

MOVIES *Ben Hur* with Charlton Heston, *Some Like It Hot* with Jack Lemmon and Tony Curtis, *The Diary of Anne Frank* with Joseph Schildkraut, *Porgy and Bess* with Sidney Poitier, *Rio Bravo* with John Wayne.

Rod Serling writes television series *The Twilight Zone*; a radio soap opera, *One Man's Family*, written by Carlton F. Morse, completes 27-year run of 3,256 episodes; new television shows include *Hawaiian Eye* with Robert Conrad, *Bonanza* with Lorne Greene, *The Untouchables*, *Bell Telephone Hour.*

DEATHS Lou Costello of Abbott and Costello comedy team; Errol Flynn and Victor McLaglen, screen actors; Cecil B. DeMille, pioneer movie producer and director; Ethel Barrymore, actress; Maxwell Anderson, playwright.

SPORTS

William Harridge, American (baseball) League president since 1931, resigns, is succeeded by Joe Cronin; Continental League forms with Branch Rickey as president.

Supreme Court rules that Louisiana law barring boxing matches between whites and blacks is unconstitutional.

Harvey Haddix, Pittsburgh Pirates, pitches 12 perfect innings but loses in 13th on an error, sacrifice, and hit.

1959

WINNERS *Auto racing*—Roger Ward, Indianapolis 500; Lee Petty, NASCAR; *Baseball*—Los Angeles Dodgers, World Series; *Basketball*—St. Johns, NIT; California, NCAA; Boston, NBA; *Bowling*—Ed Lubanski, Marion Ladewig, bowlers of year; *Boxing*—Ingemar Johansson, heavyweight; Gene Fulmer, middleweight; *Figure skating*—Dave Jenkins, U.S. men's singles; Carol Heiss, U.S. and world women's singles; *Football* (bowls)—Iowa, Rose; Oklahoma, Orange; Louisiana State, Sugar; Texas Christian–Air Force (tie), Cotton; Baltimore, NFL; *Golf*—U.S., Walker and Ryder cups; Billy Casper, U.S. Open; Bob Rosburg, PGA; Art Wall, Masters; Mickey Wright, U.S. Women's Open; Betsy Rawls, LPGA; *Hockey*—Montreal, Stanley Cup; *Horse racing*—Tommy Lee, Kentucky Derby; Royal Orbit, Preakness Stakes; Sword Dancer, Belmont Stakes; *Tennis*—Australia, Davis Cup; Neale Fraser, U.S. Open (men); Maria Bueno, U.S. Open (women).

DEATHS Bert Bell, NFL commissioner; Molla Mallory and Vincent Richards, tennis players; Tim Mara, founder, New York Giants football team; Nap(oleon) Lajoie, all-time baseball great; Willie Hoppe, one of greatest billiards players.

1960

INTERNATIONAL

Russia announces it shot down an American U-2 reconnaissance plane (May 1); the pilot, Francis Gary Powers, alive, confesses; President Dwight D. Eisenhower says he had authorized the flight (May 11).

Act of Bogota calls for social and economic reform in Latin America with U.S. help (September 13).

Mob attacks U.S. Embassy in Panama in dispute over flying U.S., Panamanian flags.

NATIONAL

Presidential contenders Republican Vice President Richard M. Nixon and Democratic Senator John F. Kennedy hold four televised debates before election; Sen. Kennedy wins election by a margin of 118,550 popular votes out of 68.8 million cast; Kennedy receives 303 electoral votes, 219 for Nixon.

Four black students stage sit-in at a Greensboro, N.C., lunch counter; many such acts follow; Student Non-Violent Coordinating Committee (SNCC) is established.

Connecticut abolishes county governments; state assumes necessary county functions.

Annual immigration to U.S. totals 265,398.

First atomic-powered aircraft carrier, *Enterprise*, is launched.

Eighteenth census reports national population at 179,323,175.

Robert C. Weaver becomes administrator of Housing & Home Finance Agency, predecessor of Department of Housing & Urban Development.

USS *Triton*, nuclear-powered submarine, makes submerged trip around the world, covering 41,500 miles in 84 days.

Garrison Dam on Missouri River in North Dakota is completed.

DEATHS John D. Rockefeller Jr., philanthropist (Colonial Williamsburg, U.N. headquarters); Frank T. Hines, Veterans Administration head (1930–1945).

BUSINESS/INDUSTRY/INVENTIONS

Freeport Sulphur Co. mines sulphur off Louisiana coast.

DEATHS Eugene G. Grace, president, Bethlehem Steel Co. (1913–1946); Sewell Avery, Montgomery Ward president (1931–1955).

TRANSPORTATION

Robert S. McNamara becomes president of Ford Motor Co.

Delaware, Lackawanna & Western, and Erie lines merge to create Erie Lackawanna Railroad.

Auto registrations for the year reach 61,671,390.

Ogdensburg (N.Y.) Bridge over St. Lawrence River opens.

DEATH George N. Borg, helped develop disc auto and truck clutch.

SCIENCE/MEDICINE

Donald A. Glaser is awarded Nobel Prize in physics for inventing bubble chamber to study elementary particles; Willard F. Libby is awarded Chemistry Prize for method of using radioactive carbon to determine age of objects.

Pioneer V satellite is launched (March 11) to investigate space between orbits of Earth and Venus; *Tiros I*, first weather satellite, is launched (April 1); *Echo I*, a giant balloon reflector that relays voice and some TV signals, is launched (August 12); *Courier 1-B*, first successful active communications satellite, is launched (October 10).

Theodore Maiman develops first laser.

Birth-control pills are made available to public.

Senator John F. Kennedy and Vice President Richard M. Nixon contend in the second of the "Great Debates," 1960. At center, rear, is moderator Frank McGee of NBC news. UPI/CORBIS-BETTMANN

DEATH Roy Chapman Andrews, naturalist and explorer.

EDUCATION

Kenneth B. Clark, psychologist, becomes first African American tenured professor (City College of New York).

RELIGION

Inter-Church Center in New York City is completed; becomes headquarters for several church denominations, National Council of Churches.

Catholic Archbishop Joseph E. Ritter of St. Louis is elevated to cardinal.

DEATHS Cardinal John F. O'Hara of Philadelphia; Rev. John W. Keogh, founder of Newman Club.

ART/MUSIC

Aaron Copland composes *Piano Fantasy*.

Leonard Baskin completes the sculpture *Man with Owl*; completed paintings include *Second Story*

Sunlight by Edward Hopper, *The Physicist* by Ben Shahn, *The French Line* by Robert Motherwell.

SONGS (popular): "Cathy's Clown," "If Ever I Should Leave You," "Only the Lonely," "Save the Last Dance for Me," "The Twist," "Why," "I Want to Be Wanted."

DEATHS Lawrence Tibbett, opera baritone; James Montgomery Flagg, illustrator best known for World War I poster ("I Want You"); Dmitri Mitropoulos, conductor.

LITERATURE/ JOURNALISM

Many mergers occur in publishing world: Henry Holt & Co. with Rinehart & Winston, Meridian and World, Macmillan and Crowell-Collier, Appleton-Century-Crofts and Meredith, Alfred A. Knopf Inc. and Random House.

Supreme Court clears D. H. Lawrence's novel *Lady Chatterley's Lover* for general distribution.

BOOKS *Times Three* (poetry) by Phyllis McGinley, *The Rise and Fall of the Third Reich* by William L. Shirer, *Rabbit, Run* by John Updike, *Hard Times* by E. L. Doctorow, *The Child Buyer* by John Hersey, *To Kill a Mockingbird* by Harper Lee.

DEATHS Richard Wright and John P. Marquand, authors; Emily Post, etiquette writer; Franklin P. Adams, columnist and critic; Richard L. Simon, publisher.

ENTERTAINMENT

Broadway theaters close for 10 days because of Actors Equity strike.

PLAYS Richard Burton and Julie Andrews star in *Camelot*, Melvyn Douglas in *The Best Man*, Dick Van Dyke in *Bye, Bye Birdie*, Jason Robards in *Toys in the Attic*.

MOVIES *Butterfield 8* with Elizabeth Taylor, *The Alamo* with John Wayne, *Exodus* with Paul Newman, *Spartacus* with Kirk Douglas, *The Magnificent Seven* with Yul Brynner.

New television shows include *Route 66* with Martin Milner, *My Three Sons* with Fred MacMurray, *The Flintstones*, and *The Andy Griffith Show*.

DEATHS Mack Sennett, pioneer moviemaker; Clark Gable, screen actor; Oscar Hammerstein II, lyricist.

SPORTS

Pete (Alvin) Rozelle becomes National Football League commissioner; American Football League (AFL) debuts eight teams; Chicago Cardinals move to St. Louis.

Candlestick Park in San Francisco opens; demolition begins on Ebbets Field in Brooklyn.

Winter Olympics are held in Squaw Valley, Calif., U.S. ice hockey team wins gold; Summer Games are held in Rome, U.S. wins 34 gold medals.

Floyd Patterson becomes first to regain heavyweight boxing championship, knocks out Ingemar Johansson.

Continental (baseball) League disbands without playing a game; loses promised four franchises; National League awards franchises to New York and Houston.

John Thomas sets new world high-jump record of 7 feet, $3\frac{3}{4}$ inches.

Dolph Schayes becomes first NBA player to score 15,000 career points; Elgin Baylor of Los Angeles

Lakers sets NBA single-game scoring record of 71 points.

Ted Williams of Boston Red Sox hits 500th home run.

WINNERS *Auto racing*—Jim Rathman, Indianapolis 500; Rex White, NASCAR; *Baseball*—Pittsburgh Pirates, World Series; *Basketball*—Bradley, NIT; Ohio State, NCAA; Boston, NBA; *Bowling*—Don Carter, PBA national title; *Boxing*—Floyd Patterson, heavyweight; *Chess*—Robert Bryce, U.S. Open; *Figure skating*—David Jenkins, U.S. men's singles; Carol Heiss, U.S. and world women's singles; *Football* (bowls)—Washington, Rose; Georgia, Orange; Mississippi, Sugar; Syracuse, Cotton; Philadelphia, NFL; Houston, AFL; *Golf*—Arnold Palmer, U.S. Open and Masters; Jay Hebert, PGA; Betsy Rawls, U.S. Women's Open; Mickey Wright, LPGA; *Hockey*—Montreal, Stanley Cup; *Horse racing*—Venetian Way, Kentucky Derby; Bally Ache, Preakness Stakes; Celtic Ash, Belmont Stakes; *Tennis*—Neale Fraser, U.S. Open (men); Darlene Hard, U.S. Open (women).

MISCELLANEOUS

United DC-8 and TWA Super-Constellation collide in fog over New York City; 134 die.

Fire aboard aircraft carrier *Constellation* under construction in Brooklyn, N.Y., kills 50, injures 150, does $50 million damage.

Hurricane Donna sweeps across Eastern Seaboard, causes 148 deaths.

1961

INTERNATIONAL

U.S. breaks off diplomatic relations with Cuba (January 3); Bay of Pigs invasion of Cuba by 1,200 anti-Castro exiles is crushed (April 17); President John F. Kennedy says U.S. will not abandon Cuba to Communists (April 20).

President Kennedy offers Alliance for Progress program to raise Latin American living standards (March 13); U.S. and 19 Latin American countries sign the alliance (August 17).

Adlai E. Stevenson is named U.S. ambassador to U.N.

Agency for International Development is created.

U.S. and Canada sign 60-year Columbia River Treaty, agree on waterpower and storage.

NATIONAL

President Kennedy calls for project to land astronaut on the moon and return him safely to Earth by 1970 (May 25); speaking to U.N. General Assembly, he proposes eventual nuclear disarmament.

Twenty-third Amendment is ratified (March 29); allows District of Columbia residents to vote for president.

Peace Corps is created (March 1); Sargent Shriver is named director.

Edward R. Murrow heads U.S. Information Agency; Glenn T. Seaborg becomes first scientist to head Atomic Energy Commission.

Hawaii Volcanoes and Haleakala (Hawaii) national parks are established.

Ice Harbor Dam on Snake River in Washington is completed.

Supreme Court in *Mapp v. Ohio* rules that Fourth Amendment guarantee against evidence obtained by unreasonable search and seizure applies to state as well as federal trials.

DEATHS Former First Lady Edith B. Wilson (1915–1921); Sumner Welles, undersecretary of state who laid groundwork for U.S.'s "good neighbor" policy; Sam Rayburn, House Speaker (1937–1961, except for four years); Walter B. Smith, World War II general.

BUSINESS/INDUSTRY/INVENTIONS

Congress votes minimum-wage increase from $1 an hour to $1.25 in two-year period: $1.15 on September 3, $1.25 on September 3, 1963.

President Kennedy dedicates Freeport (Tex.) desalination plant.

DEATHS Alfred C. Gilbert, toymaker; James F. Bell, first president, General Mills (1928–1934); Eero Saarinen, architect; Lee De Forest, various communications inventions.

TRANSPORTATION

Throgs Neck Bridge over Long Island Sound opens.

DEATHS John D. Hertz, founder and head, car rental service; Louis Hupp, pioneer automaker.

SCIENCE/MEDICINE

Robert Hofstadter shares Nobel Prize in physics with Rudolf L. Mossbauer of Germany for discov-eries concerning atom nucleus; Melvin Calvin is awarded chemistry prize for discoveries on photosynthesis; George von Bekesy is awarded physiology/medicine prize for discoveries of mechanism of the ear.

Alan B. Shepard becomes first U.S. astronaut to make space flight (May 5).

Lawrence Radiation Laboratory at University of California produces Element #103 (lawrencium).

Experimental reactor near Idaho Falls, Idaho, fails, kills three workers.

DEATH Earle E. Dickson, inventor of adhesive bandage.

EDUCATION

Sterling M. McMurrin is named U.S. Education Commissioner.

RELIGION

National Council of Churches endorses birth control as means of family limitation.

Ernest Hemingway (1899–1961), American writer. THE GRANGER COLLECTION, NEW YORK

1961

Two Catholic archbishops are named: Lawrence J. Shehan of Baltimore and John J. Krol of Philadelphia.

DEATH Frank N. D. Buchman, founder of Moral Rearmament movement.

ART/MUSIC

Robert Ward composes the opera *The Crucible*; Douglas S. Moore, the opera *Wings of the Dove*; Milton B. Babbitt composes two revolutionary pieces, "Composition for Synthesizer" and "Vision and Prayer."

Jasper Johns completes the painting *Map*; Philip Guston, *The Tale*.

SONGS (popular): "Where Have All the Flowers Gone?," "Big Bad John," "Can't Help Falling in Love," "Hey, Look Me Over," "Moon River," "Travelin' Man," "Hit the Road, Jack," "Please, Mister Postman," "Raindrops."

DEATHS Grandma (Anna M.) Moses, "primitive" painter; Wallingford Riegger, a leader in avant garde twentieth-century music.

LITERATURE/JOURNALISM

President Kennedy holds first live presidential news conference.

BOOKS *Franny and Zooey* by J. D. Salinger; *Nobody Knows My Name* by James Baldwin, *The Agony and the Ecstasy* by Irving Stone, *Mila 18* by Leon Uris, *Catch-22* by Joseph Heller, *The Carpetbaggers* by Harold Robbins.

DEATHS Dashiell Hammett, Ernest Hemingway, and Kenneth Fearing, authors; Hilda Doolittle (HD), poet; James Thurber, author and cartoonist; Dorothy Thompson, columnist.

ENTERTAINMENT

Newton N. Minow, FCC chairman, describes television as "vast wasteland."

PLAYS Robert Morse stars in *How to Succeed in Business without Really Trying*, Kim Stanley in *A Far Country*, Fredric March in *Gideon*; Neil Simon writes *Come Blow Your Horn*, Tennessee Williams writes *The Night of the Iguana*.

MOVIES *The Hustler* with Jackie Gleason, *West Side Story* with Natalie Wood, *The Misfits* with Clark Gable and Marilyn Monroe, *Breakfast at Tiffany's* with Audrey Hepburn.

New television shows include *Sing Along with Mitch*, *Mr. Ed* with Alan Young, *Hazel* with Shirley Booth, *Dr. Kildare* with Richard Chamberlain, Dick Van Dyke and Mary Tyler Moore, Joey Bishop, and David Susskind.

DEATHS Playwrights Moss Hart and George S. Kaufman; Gary Cooper, actor.

SPORTS

Roger Maris of New York Yankees hits 61st home run, a new season's record (October 1).

Ralph Boston is first to long jump more than 27 feet (27 ft., $\frac{1}{2}$ in.).

WINNERS *Auto racing*—A. J. Foyt, Indianapolis 500; Ned Jarrett, NASCAR; *Baseball*—New York Yankees, World Series; *Basketball*—Providence, NIT; Cincinnati, NCAA; Boston, NBA; *Bowling*—Dave Soutar, PBA national; *Boxing*—Floyd Patterson, heavyweight; Benny Paret, welterweight; Eder Jofre, bantamweight; *Figure skating*—Bradley Lord, U.S. men's singles; Laurence Owen, U.S. women's singles; *Football* (bowls)—Washington, Rose; Missouri, Orange; Mississippi, Sugar; Duke, Cotton; Green Bay, NFL; Houston, AFL; *Golf*—U.S., Walker and Ryder cups; Gene Littler, U.S. Open; Jerry Barber, PGA; Gary Player, Masters; Mickey Wright, U.S. Women's Open and LPGA; *Hockey*—Chicago, Stanley Cup; *Horse racing*—Carry Back, Kentucky Derby and Preakness Stakes; Sherluck, Belmont Stakes; *Tennis*—Roy Emerson, U.S. Open (men); Darlene Hard, U.S. Open (women).

DEATHS Maribel Vinson (Owen), figure-skating champion, in plane crash; Ty Cobb, probably greatest offensive baseball player.

1962

INTERNATIONAL

President John F. Kennedy announces Soviet Russia is building offensive weapons bases in Cuba (October 22); he orders naval and air quarantine of offensive military equipment (October 24); Russia agrees to halt construction, dismantle, and remove Soviet rockets (October 28); dismantling is complete (November 2), U.S. quarantine ends (November 20).

U.S. military forces are ordered to Laos (May 12); President Kennedy says U.S. advisors in Vietnam will fire if fired on.

NATIONAL

Supreme Court upholds "one-man, one-vote" apportionment of seats in state legislatures; Felix Frankfurter and Charles E. Whittaker resign from the Court; Arthur J. Goldberg and Byron R. White succeed them.

Linus Pauling is awarded Nobel Peace Prize, becomes only person to win two unshared Nobel prizes (awarded 1954 chemistry prize).

U.S. establishes Communications Satellite Corp. (COMSAT).

First U.S. world's fair in more than 20 years, Century 21 Exposition, is held in Seattle, Wash.

Dwight D. Eisenhower Library in Abilene, Kans., and Herbert Hoover Library in West Branch, Iowa, open.

Trinity Dam on Trinity River in California is completed.

Petrified Forest (Ariz.) National Park is established.

DEATHS Former First Lady Eleanor Roosevelt (1933–1945); Vihjalmur Stefansson, Arctic explorer.

BUSINESS/INDUSTRY/INVENTIONS

Cesar Chavez organizes National Farm Workers Assn.; it later merges with United Farm Workers Organizing Committee.

DEATHS Samuel C. Prescott, bacteriologist who found method to keep canned food sanitary; Benjamin Fairless, U.S. Steel president (1938–1952); Arthur V. Davis, Alcoa president (1910–1928), chairman (1928–1957); Abraham Levitt, housing developer; E. F. Hutton, financier.

TRANSPORTATION

William P. Lear founds Lear Corp.

DEATHS Eugene J. Houdry, inventor of catalytic cracking process to make gasoline; Ralph Budd, railroad president (Burlington), introduced streamlined trains.

SCIENCE/MEDICINE

John H. Glenn Jr. becomes first U.S. astronaut to orbit the Earth (February 20).

James D. Watson shares Nobel Prize in physiology/medicine with Frances Crick and Maurice Wilkins of Great Britain for discoveries of molecular structure of deoxyribonucleic acid (DNA), the substance of heredity.

U.S. satellite reaches moon after 229,541-mile flight from Cape Canaveral, Fla. (April 26); first U.S. unmanned space flight, *Mariner 2*, passes within 22,000 miles of Venus.

DEATHS William Beebe, naturalist and inventor of bathysphere; Arthur H. Compton, physicist.

EDUCATION

U.S. Circuit Court orders University of Mississippi to admit African American student James H. Meredith, who had been refused admission (September 24); Meredith is admitted a week later.

Louisiana Archbishop Joseph F. Rummel orders end to segregation in Catholic schools; Atlanta Archbishop Paul J. Hallinan announces Catholic schools will admit students on a nonracial basis.

Supreme Court in *Engel v. Vitale* holds sanctioning

1962

Astronaut John Glenn pulls himself up into the Mercury Space Capsule that will make a three-circuit orbit of the earth. Cape Canaveral, Florida. UPI/CORBIS-BETTMANN

of religious "utterances," such as reading an official prayer, to be unconstitutional.

Francis Keppel is named U.S. Commissioner of Education.

RELIGION

Merger of United Lutheran Church in America, Augustana Evangelical Lutheran Church, and Finnish Evangelical Church creates Lutheran Church in America.

Rt. Rev. Melville Burgess is consecrated as Suffragan Bishop of Massachusetts, first black Episcopal bishop in a white diocese.

ART/MUSIC

Aaron Copland composes *Connotations for Orchestra*; Samuel Barber, *Piano Concerto #1*.

Leopold Stokowski forms American Symphony Orchestra.

Lincoln Center in New York City opens.

Robert A. Moog develops first practical electronic synthesizer.

Andy Warhol, pop-art leader, completes the painting *Green Coca-Cola Bottles*; Hans Hofmann, *Sanctum Sanctorum*; Jasper Johns, *Fool's House*.

SONGS (popular): "Days of Wine and Roses," "I Can't Stop Loving You," "Johnny Angel," "Roses Are Red, My Love," "Stranger on the Shore," "Walk on By," "You Don't Know Me."

LITERATURE/JOURNALISM

John Steinbeck, U.S. author, is awarded Nobel Prize in literature.

BOOKS *The Reivers* by William Faulkner, *The Guns of August* by Barbara W. Tuchman, *Herzog* by Saul Bellow, *Silent Spring* by Rachel Carson, *Ship of Fools* by Katherine Anne Porter, *One Flew over the Cuckoo's Nest* by Ken Kesey, *The Wish Tree* (poetry) by John Ciardi.

DEATHS Howard R. Garis, author of children's stories; William Faulkner, author; Robinson Jeffers, poet.

ENTERTAINMENT

Telstar I relays first satellite transmission of television signals between U.S. and Europe.

Johnny Carson emcees *The Tonight Show*; new shows include *The Lucy Show* with Lucille Ball, *McHale's Navy* with Ernest Borgnine, *Beverly Hillbillies* with Buddy Ebsen and Irene Ryan, *Wild Kingdom* with Marlin Perkins.

PLAYS Uta Hagen stars in *Who's Afraid of Virginia Woolf?*, Zero Mostel in *A Funny Thing Happened on the Way to the Forum*, Jason Robards in *A Thousand Clowns*.

MOVIES *Lawrence of Arabia* with Peter O'Toole, *Gigot* with Jackie Gleason, *To Kill a Mockingbird* with Gregory Peck, *The Music Man* with Robert Preston, *The Miracle Worker* with Anne Bancroft.

DEATHS Frank Borzage, screen director and producer; Charles Laughton and Dick Powell, screen actors; Marilyn Monroe, screen actress; Ted Husing, radio announcer of 1920s.

SPORTS

John Uelses is first to clear 16 feet (by a quarter-inch) in pole vault; Jim Beatty becomes first American to break 4-minute mile indoors; Al Oerter first to surpass 200 feet in discus throw (200 ft., 5 in.).

Wilt Chamberlain of Philadelphia scores 100 points in basketball game against New York (36 field goals, 28 free throws).

Dodgers Stadium in Los Angeles opens.

New York Mets receive franchise from National (baseball) League.

WINNERS *Auto racing*—Rodger Ward, Indianapolis 500; Joe Weatherly, NASCAR; *Baseball*—New York Yankees, World Series; *Basketball*—Dayton, NIT; Cincinnati, NCAA; Boston, NBA; *Bowling*—Carmen Salvino, PBA national; *Boxing*—Sonny Liston, heavyweight; Harold Johnson, light heavyweight; Emile Griffith, welterweight; Carlos Ortiz, lightweight; *Chess*—Bobby Fischer, U.S. title; *Figure skating*—Monty Hoyt, U.S. men's singles; Barbara R. Pursley, U.S. women's singles; *Football* (bowls)—Minnesota, Rose; Louisiana State, Orange; Alabama, Sugar; Texas, Cotton; Green Bay, NFL; Dallas, AFL; *Golf*—Jack Nicklaus, U.S. Open; Gary Player, PGA; Arnold Palmer, Masters; Marie Lindstrom, U.S. Women's Open; Judy Kimball, LPGA; *Hockey*—Toronto, Stanley Cup; *Horse racing*—Decidedly, Kentucky Derby; Greek Money, Preakness Stakes; Jaipur, Belmont Stakes; *Tennis*—Rod Laver, U.S. Open (men); Margaret Smith, U.S. Open (women); *Yachting*—U.S. boat *Weatherly* retains America's Cup.

DEATHS Walt Kiesling, football player and coach; Taylor Spink, editor, *Sporting News* (1914–1962).

INTERNATIONAL

U.S., Soviet Russia, and Great Britain agree to Nuclear Test Ban Treaty, ban tests in the atmosphere, outer space, and underwater (August 5); 99 nations agree.

U.S. and Soviet Russia establish a "hot line" for quick communication (August 30).

Former British Prime Minister Winston S. Churchill is granted honorary U.S. citizenship.

By year's end, 15,000 U.S. troops are in Vietnam.

NATIONAL

President John F. Kennedy is assassinated in

1963

Dallas (November 22) while traveling in a motorcade through city; Texas Gov. John B. Connally is also shot but not seriously wounded; Lee Harvey Oswald is arrested for the killing; Vice President Lyndon B. Johnson is sworn in as president aboard *Air Force One*; two days later, Oswald is shot to death in city jail by nightclub owner Jack Ruby.

President Johnson pledges to continue policies of late President Kennedy; Warren Commission is created to investigate assassination.

Medgar Evers, NAACP field secretary, is shot to death from ambush in front of his Jackson, Miss., home (June 12).

1963

About 200,000 demonstrate peacefully in Washington to support African Americans' demands for equal rights, hear Dr. Martin Luther King Jr. speech, "I have a dream..." (August 28).

Antisegregation demonstrations begin in Birmingham, Ala. (April 2); race riot follows bombing (September 15) of black church in which four girls are killed, 20 are hurt.

Supreme Court rules congressional districts should have equal populations; in *Gideon v. Wainwright*, Court holds that all defendants are entitled to an attorney.

Atomic submarine *Thrasher* sinks in North Atlantic; 29 die.

First-class postage increases to 5 cents.

Jimmy Carter begins four-year term in Georgia state senate.

DEATHS Herbert H. Lehman, New York governor, senator; Elsa Maxwell, noted hostess; Gen. Royal B. Lord, inventor of portable steel cableway.

BUSINESS/INDUSTRY/INVENTIONS

Polaroid introduces color film for its camera.

Minimum wage increases to $1.25 an hour (September 3).

TRANSPORTATION

Chesapeake & Ohio Railroad takes over financially troubled Baltimore & Ohio line.

DEATHS Alfred P. Sloan, General Motors president and chairman (1923–1956); Charles T. Fisher of Fisher Body Corp.

SCIENCE/MEDICINE

Maria Goeppert-Mayer and Eugene P. Wigner share Nobel Prize in physics: Mayer for research on atomic nucleus structure, Wigner for laws of symmetry governing nuclear particle reactions.

DEATHS Dr. Franz Alexander, pioneer in psychosomatic medicine; Otto Struve, astronomer.

EDUCATION

Supreme Court rules in *School District of Abington Township v. Schempp* that recitation of Lord's Prayer or Bible verses in public schools is unconstitutional.

Two African American students enter state university at Birmingham, Ala., under court order; President Kennedy federalizes Alabama National Guard to speed integration.

Federal government launches $1.2 billion construction program for college buildings.

One-day boycott is staged in Chicago as 225,000 students stay home to protest segregation.

DEATH Edith Hamilton, popularized classical literature in U.S.

RELIGION

National Council of Churches elects its first woman president, Cynthia C. Wedel.

Lutheran Free Church merges into American Lutheran Church.

Elizabeth Ann Seton, founder of Sisters of Charity, and former Philadelphia Bishop John Neumann are beatified.

Malcolm X becomes "national minister" of the Black Muslims.

Use of English instead of Latin for parts of Catholic mass and sacraments is approved.

DEATH Methodist Bishop G. Bromley Oxnam, a founder of National Council of Churches.

ART/MUSIC

Leonard Bernstein composes the symphony *Kaddish*; Gian Carlo Menotti, the opera *The Last Savage*.

SONGS (popular): "Call Me Irresponsible," "Can't Get Used to Losing You," "Hey Paula," "More," "Our Day Will Come," "Rhythm of the Rain," "Walk Right In," "You Don't Own Me," "Puff the Magic Dragon."

DEATHS Patsy Cline, country-music singer, in plane crash; Dinah Washington, "queen" of blues; Fritz Reiner, conductor.

LITERATURE/JOURNALISM

New York Review of Books begins publication.

BOOKS *The Feminine Mystique* by Betty Friedan,

Raise High the Roof Beams, Carpenter and *Seymour: An Introduction* by J. D. Salinger, *The Group* by Mary McCarthy, *The Other America* by Michael Harrington.

DEATHS Robert Frost, Theodore Roethke, and William Carlos Williams, poets; Jimmy Hatlo, cartoonist ("Little Iodine"); Alicia Patterson, publisher, *Newsday*; Oliver H. P. La Farge, anthropologist and author (*Laughing Boy*).

ENTERTAINMENT

Robert Redford stars in Neil Simon's play *Barefoot in the Park*.

MOVIES *Cleopatra* with Elizabeth Taylor and Richard Burton, *Hud* with Paul Newman, *Irma la Douce* with Shirley MacLaine and Jack Lemmon, *The Pink Panther* with Peter Sellers.

New television shows include *Twilight Zone*, *My Favorite Martian* with Ray Walston, *Petticoat Junction* with Bea Benadaret, *Burke's Law* with Gene Barry.

SPORTS

John Pennel clears 17 feet in the pole vault (17 ft., $\frac{3}{4}$ in.).

Willie Mays of San Francisco Giants hits 400th home run; Early Wynn, Cleveland Indians, pitches his 300th victory.

Pro Football Hall of Fame in Canton, Ohio, opens.

Liberty Bell Racetrack in Philadelphia opens.

WINNERS *Auto racing* — Parnelli Jones, Indianapolis 500; Joe Weatherly, NASCAR; *Baseball* — Los Angeles Dodgers, World Series; *Basketball* — Providence, NIT; Loyola (Ill.), NCAA; Boston, NBA; *Bowling* — Billy Hardwick, PBA National; *Boxing* — Sonny Liston, heavyweight; Willie Pastrano, light heavyweight; Emile Griffith, welterweight; *Figure skating* — Tommy Litz, U.S. men's singles; Lorraine Hanlon, U.S. women's singles; *Football* (bowls) — Southern California, Rose; Alabama, Orange; Mississippi, Sugar; Louisiana State, Cotton; Chicago, NFL; San Diego, AFL; *Golf* — U.S., Walker and Ryder cups; Julius Boros, U.S. Open; Jack Nicklaus, PGA and Masters; Mary Mills, U.S. Women's Open; Mickey Wright, LPGA; *Hockey* — Toronto, Stanley Cup; *Horse racing* — Chateaugay, Kentucky Derby and Belmont Stakes; Candy Spots, Preakness Stakes; *Tennis* — U.S., Davis Cup; Rafael Osuna, U.S. Open (men); Maria Bueno, U.S. Open (women).

DEATHS Two professional football players, Quarterback Bernie Masterson and Eugene "Big Daddy" Lipscomb.

MISCELLANEOUS

Fire in Indiana State Fair Coliseum in Indianapolis kills 73.

1964

INTERNATIONAL

President Lyndon B. Johnson announces U.S. air attacks on North Vietnam in answer to attacks on U.S. warships (August 4); Tonkin Gulf Resolution is passed (August 7), gives president authority to retaliate against North Vietnamese attacks.

Panama suspends relations with U.S. after riots; U.S. offers to renegotiate canal treaty.

NATIONAL

President Johnson, Democrat, is elected to full term in biggest landslide of century: 486 electoral votes and 43.1 million popular votes to Republican Sen. Barry M. Goldwater's 52 electoral and 27.1 million popular votes.

Warren Commission, after investigating President Kennedy's assassination, concludes that Lee Harvey Oswald was lone assassin; Jack Ruby is convicted of killing Oswald and sentenced to death; after appeal, new trial is ordered.

Twenty-fourth Amendment is ratified (January 23), bars the poll tax as a requisite in federal elections.

1964

Ed Sullivan flanked by the Beatles as they rehearse a show sequence at CBS Television studios on February 8, 1964. From left to right: Ringo Starr, George Harrison, John Lennon, and Paul McCartney. UPI/CORBIS-BETTMANN

Civil Rights Act goes into effect (July 2).

Congress approves Office of Economic Opportunity (War on Poverty).

Glen Canyon Dam on Colorado River in Arizona is completed.

Canyonland (Utah) National Park is established.

New Hampshire introduces state lottery to help pay for schools.

Vice President's salary is raised $8,000 to $43,000.

DEATHS Former President Herbert Hoover (1929–1933); Gen. Douglas MacArthur, commander of Pacific forces; Alvin C. York, most decorated U.S. soldier in World War I.

TRANSPORTATION

Three major bridges open: Vincent Thomas over Los Angeles Harbor; Verrazano-Narrows over New York Harbor; Chesapeake Bay Bridge Tunnel, 17.6-mile span connecting Eastern Shore of Virginia and Norfolk.

Norfolk and Western Railroad acquires Nickel Plate and Wabash railroads.

SCIENCE/MEDICINE

Charles H. Townes shares Nobel Prize in physics with Nikolai Basov and Aleksander Procherov for work on maser-laser principle of magnifying electromagnetic radiation; Konrad E. Bloch shares prize in physiology/medicine with Feodor Lynen of Germany for work on cholesterol and fatty-acid metabolism.

Surgeon General Luther L. Terry issues warning against cigarette smoking; cigarette manufacturers are required to put hazard notice on cigarette packages.

Mariner 4, unmanned satellite, photographs surface of Mars.

Polio vaccinations cut new cases from 35,600 in 1953 to fewer than 100 in 1964.

DEATHS Dr. Alfred Blalock, developed technique for saving "blue babies"; Norbert Wiener, mathematician, developer of cybernetics.

RELIGION

Presbyterian Church in U.S. votes to permit ordination of women as deacons, elders, and ministers.

First Catholic mass offered completely in English in U.S. is celebrated in St. Louis.

ART/MUSIC

Roger H. Sessions composes opera *Montezuma*.

Vatican exhibit at World's Fair features Michelangelo's *Pieta*.

Thieves steal $410,000 worth of jewels from Museum of Natural History, including world's largest sapphire, 565-carat "Star of India."

Jasper Johns completes the painting *Field Painting*.

SONGS (popular): "Dang Me," "Everybody Loves Somebody," "Hello, Dolly!," "I Want to Hold Your Hand," "My Guy," "Rag Doll," "Walk on By."

DEATHS Jim Reeves, country-music singer, in plane crash; Pierre Monteaux, conductor; Cole Porter, musical comedy composer; Jack Teagarden, trombonist and band leader.

LITERATURE/JOURNALISM

Supreme Court in *The New York Times v. Sullivan* upholds freedom of the press, protects the press from libel suits unless malice can be proved.

BOOKS *Flood* by Robert Penn Warren, *The Keepers of the House* by Shirley Ann Grau, *The Wapshot Scandal* by John Cheever, *Reuben, Reuben* by Peter DeVries, *The Honey Badger* by Robert C. Ruark.

DEATHS Percy L. Crosby, cartoonist ("Skippy"); J. Frank Dobie, author of Southwest histories; Rachel Carson, environmental author; Ted Patrick, editor, *Holiday* (1946–1964); Roy W. Howard, Scripps-Howard newspapers executive; Ben Hecht, author and playwright.

ENTERTAINMENT

PLAYS Sammy Davis Jr. stars in *Golden Boy*, Jason Robards in Arthur Miller's *After the Fall*, Barbra Streisand in *Funny Girl*, Carol Channing in *Hello, Dolly!*, Eli Wallach in *Luv*.

MOVIES *Mary Poppins* with Julie Andrews, *My Fair Lady* with Rex Harrison and Audrey Hepburn, *The Night of the Iguana* with Richard Burton, *Dr. Strangelove* with Peter Sellers.

The Beatles arrive for first U.S. tour; their record, *Meet the Beatles*, sells 2 million copies.

Popular rock-and-roll dances are the Watusi and the Frug.

New television shows include *The Man from U.N.C.L.E.* with Robert Vaughn, *Bewitched* with Elizabeth Montgomery, *Daniel Boone* with Fess Parker, *Peyton Place*.

DEATHS Eddie Cantor, entertainer; Joseph Schildkraut, screen actor; Gracie Allen of Burns and Allen comedy team; Alan Ladd, screen actor.

SPORTS

New York Mets open new home park, Shea Stadium.

Billy Mills becomes first American to win Olympic 10,000-meter race; Don Schollander wins four gold medals in swimming.

Astro-Turf, popular covering for baseball and football fields, is first used in Providence, R.I., private school.

WINNERS *Auto racing*—A. J. Foyt, Indianapolis 500; Richard Petty, NASCAR; *Baseball*—St. Louis, World Series; *Basketball*—Bradley, NIT; UCLA, NCAA; Boston, NBA; *Bowling*—Bob Strampee, PBA national; *Boxing*—Muhammad Ali, heavyweight; *Chess*—Pal Benkö, U.S. Open; *Figure skating*—Scott Allen, U.S. men's singles; Peggy Fleming, U.S. women's singles; *Football (bowls)*—Illinois, Rose; Nebraska, Orange; Alabama, Sugar; Texas, Cotton; Cleveland, NFL; Buffalo, AFL; *Golf*—Ken Venturi, U.S. Open; Bob Nichols, PGA; Arnold Palmer, Masters; Mickey Wright, U.S. Women's Open; Mary Mills, LPGA; *Hockey*—Toronto, Stanley Cup; *Horse racing*—Northern Dancer, Kentucky Derby and Preakness Stakes; Quadrangle, Belmont Stakes; *Tennis*—Australia, Davis Cup; Roy Emerson, U.S. Open (men); Maria Bueno, U.S. Open (women).

DEATHS Two Chicago Bears football players in auto accident: Willie Gallimore and Bo Farrington; Steve Owen, New York Giants football player and coach; Glenn Roberts, auto racer.

MISCELLANEOUS

Earthquake east of Anchorage, Alaska, kills 131, does $500–700 million damage (March 27).

1965

INTERNATIONAL

VIETNAM WAR U.S. air strikes are ordered over North Vietnam (February 8); first combat troops land in South Vietnam, two Marine battalions to defend Danang air base (March 8); additional 50,000 troops are sent, brings total to 125,000; holiday truce begins (December 24).

About 14,000 troops are sent to Dominican Republic during civil war.

NATIONAL

Dr. Martin Luther King Jr. is awarded Nobel Peace Prize.

Police and sheriff's deputies turn back civil rights marchers from Selma, Ala., as they start for Montgomery (March 7); with an Alabama National Guard escort, the 54-mile march to Montgomery is made two weeks later; Rev. James Reeb, Unitarian clergyman, dies in Selma from beating received while working for civil rights.

Six days of rioting begins (August 11) in Watts section of Los Angeles; results in 34 deaths, 1,000+ injuries, $175 million in fire damage.

Department of Housing & Urban Development is created (September 9); Robert C. Weaver is named Secretary, becomes first African American cabinet member; Economic Development Administration is established (September 1); Environmental Science Services Administration is created, takes in Coast & Geodetic Survey and Weather Bureau; Equal Employment Opportunity Commission is founded.

Supreme Court rules in *Griswold v. Connecticut* that a state cannot prohibit use of contraceptives.

National origins quota system of immigration is abolished (October 3), in effect since 1921.

Arthur J. Goldberg resigns from Supreme Court to become U.N. ambassador; Abe Fortas succeeds him.

A 13½-hour power failure blacks out northeastern U.S. and southeastern Canada (November 9); New York City is hardest hit.

DEATHS Malcolm X, black nationalist, is fatally shot in New York City; Adlai E. Stevenson, Democratic presidential candidate, U.N. ambassador; Bernard M. Baruch, financier; former Vice President Henry A. Wallace.

BUSINESS/INDUSTRY/INVENTIONS

Housing Act providing $7.5 billion for housing and rent subsidies is signed.

DEATHS Colby M. Chester, first president, General Foods (1929–1935); Oscar G. Mayer, meat packer; Allen B. Du Mont, television pioneer; Helena Rubinstein, cosmetics maker; Joshua L. Cowan, inventor of toy electric train.

TRANSPORTATION

Ralph Nader publishes *Unsafe at Any Speed*, a book that shakes automobile industry.

SCIENCE/MEDICINE

Richard P. Feynman and Julius S. Schwinger share Nobel Prize in physics for study of subatomic particles; Robert B. Woodward is awarded chemistry prize for synthesis of complex organic compounds.

James A. McDivitt and Edward H. White II fly 62 orbits in space (June 3), during which White becomes first U.S. astronaut to walk in space.

First commercial satellite, *Early Bird I*, is launched; first space rendezvous is completed (December 15) when astronauts Walter M. Schirra Jr. and Thomas P. Stafford join their spaceship with that of Frank Borman and James A. Lovell Jr.

EDUCATION

Elementary and Secondary Education Act passes, provides large-scale direct federal aid to schools.

Dr. Martin Luther King, Jr. (front row, center) leads a fifty-mile march from Selma to Montgomery, Ala., to promote civil rights. Others in photo: Mrs. King, John Davis of SNCC (2nd from left), Dr. Ralph Bunche (5th from left), and Rev. Hosea Williams (carrying little girl, right). UPI/BETTMANN

RELIGION

Pope Pius VI delivers peace message to U.N. while on visit to U.S.

Catholic Archbishop John P. Cody of New Orleans moves to Chicago; Archbishop Laurence J. Shehan is elevated to cardinal.

DEATH Father Divine (George Baker), founder of Peace Mission.

ART/MUSIC

Leslie Bassett composes *Variations for Orchestra*; Walter Piston composes the *Eighth Symphony*.

Georgia O'Keeffe completes the painting *Sky above Clouds IV*; James A. Rosenquist, the 51 panels of *F-111*; Robert Motherwell, *Africa*; Alexander Calder, the sculpture *Ticket Window*.

SONGS (popular): "Downtown," "The Game of Love," "I Got You, Babe," "King of the Road," "My Girl," "Over and Over," "The Shadow of Your Smile," "What the World Needs Now," "You've Lost That Lovin' Feelin'," "Back in My Arms Again."

DEATHS Nat "King" Cole, popular singer; Spike Jones, orchestra leader; Paul Manship, sculptor (Prometheus Fountain, Rockefeller Center); Edgard Varèse, conductor and composer.

LITERATURE/JOURNALISM

BOOKS *In Cold Blood* by Truman Capote, *Hotel* by Arthur Hailey, *An American Dream* by Norman Mailer, *A Thousand Days* by Arthur M. Schlesinger Jr.

DEATHS Wilfred J. Funk of Funk & Wagnalls, publishers; Edward R. Murrow, radio and televi-

1965

sion newsman; Marshall Field IV, editor and publisher; H. V. Kaltenborn, radio news reporter; Shirley Jackson, author; Randall Jarrell, poet.

ENTERTAINMENT

PLAYS Richard Kiley stars in *Man of La Mancha*, Henry Fonda in *Generation*, Lauren Bacall in *Cactus Flower*, Art Carney and Walter Matthau in *The Odd Couple*.

MOVIES *Who's Afraid of Virginia Woolf?* with Richard Burton and Elizabeth Taylor, *The Sound of Music* with Julie Andrews, *Cat Ballou* with Lee Marvin, *Dr. Zhivago* with Omar Sharif, *The Great Race* with Jack Lemmon.

New television shows include *I Spy* with Robert Culp and Bill Cosby, *Green Acres* with Eva Gabor and Eddie Albert, *The FBI* with Efrem Zimbalist Jr., *I Dream of Jeannie* with Barbara Eden and Larry Hagman.

DEATHS Francis X. Bushman, silent-screen actor; David O. Selznick, movie producer; Stan Laurel of Laurel and Hardy comedy team; Clara Bow, 1920s screen actress.

SPORTS

William D. Eckert is named baseball commissioner; Joe Cronin is named president of American League.

Houston Astrodome opens (April 9).

Ernie Banks of Chicago Cubs hits 400th career home run; Willie Mays, San Francisco Giants, his 500th.

Atlanta is awarded National Football League franchise; Miami in American Football League.

Randy Matson is first to throw shot more than 70 feet (70 ft., $7\frac{1}{4}$ in.).

WINNERS *Auto racing*—Jim Clark, Indianapolis 500; Ned Jarrett, NASCAR; *Baseball*—Los Angeles Dodgers, World Series; *Basketball*—St. Johns, NIT; UCLA, NCAA; Boston, NBA; *Bowling*—Dave Davis, PBA national; *Boxing*—Muhammad Ali, heavyweight; Jose Torres, light heavyweight; Dick Tiger, middleweight; Carlos Ortiz, lightweight; *Figure skating*—Gary Viscount, U.S. men's singles; Peggy Fleming, U.S. women's singles; *Football* (bowls)—Michigan, Rose; Texas, Orange; Louisiana State, Sugar; Arkansas, Cotton; Green Bay, NFL; Buffalo, AFL; *Golf*—U.S., Ryder Cup; Gary Player, U.S. Open; Dave Marr, PGA; Jack Nicklaus, Masters; Carol Mann, U.S. Women's Open; Sandra Haynie, LPGA; *Harness racing*—Egyptian Candor, Hambletonian; *Hockey*—Montreal, Stanley Cup; *Horse racing*—Lucky Debonair, Kentucky Derby; Tom Rolfe, Preakness Stakes; Hail to All, Belmont Stakes; *Tennis*—Manuel Santana, U.S. Open (men); Margaret Smith, U.S. Open (women).

DEATHS Curly (Earl) Lambeau, player, founder, and coach, Green Bay Packers; Jack Mara, New York Giants football team president; Branch Rickey, baseball executive.

MISCELLANEOUS

Hurricane Betsy hits Florida and Louisiana, kills 80 and causes $1.4 billion in damage; 37 tornadoes strike Midwest on Palm Sunday (April 11), kill 271.

Roy Wilkins becomes executive director of NAACP.

Missile silo explodes at Searcy, Ark., kills 53.

The miniskirt is introduced.

1966

INTERNATIONAL

VIETNAM WAR U.S. resumes bombing of North Vietnam after China rejects peace overtures (January 30); U.S. planes bomb Hanoi area (June 29). Seven-nation Manila Conference pledges to continue efforts in Vietnam until aggression ends (October 25).

President Lyndon Johnson, visiting in Mexico, reaffirms support of the Alliance for Progress.

NATIONAL

Supreme Court in *Miranda v. Arizona* rules that suspects in police custody must be informed of their right to remain silent and have right of counsel; also upholds Voting Rights Act of 1965.

Uniform Time Act calls for nationwide daylight saving time; lasts one year, then becomes local option.

Postal Savings Bank System ends after 55 years.

American Revolution Bicentennial Commission is created.

More than 10,000 anti–Vietnam War protestors demonstrate in front of the White House.

Betty Friedan establishes National Organization for Women (NOW).

Andrew F. Brimmer becomes first African American member of Federal Reserve Board; Edward W. Brooke is elected to U.S. Senate from Massachusetts, the first popularly elected African American senator.

National Historic Preservation Act goes into effect.

Ronald Reagan is elected governor of California.

Guadalupe Mountains (Tex.) National Park is established.

DEATHS Chester W. Nimitz, World War II admiral; Rev. Henry F. Ward, chairman, American Civil Liberties Union (1920–1940); Margaret Sanger, pioneer advocate of birth control.

BUSINESS/INDUSTRY/INVENTIONS

Truth in Packaging Law passes, requires clear, accurate statement of ingredients, amounts.

Minimum wage is raised to $1.40 an hour, to be effective February 1, 1967; to $1.60 an hour on February 1, 1968.

RCA uses integrated circuits in television sets.

DEATHS Bernard F. Gimbel, retail merchant; S. S. Kresge, head of five-and-ten-cent-store chain (1907–1966); Elizabeth Arden, founder and owner, cosmetics firm.

Many people—both men and women—find the mini-skirt a surprising fashion development in 1966. UPI/CORBIS-BETTMANN

1966

The new television series *Star Trek*, 1966, with William Shatner as Captain Kirk (left) and Leonard Nimoy as Mr. Spock (right). PHOTOFEST

TRANSPORTATION

Department of Transportation is established (October 15).

New York City undergoes first subway strike; lasts 12 days.

Interstate Commerce Commission approves merger of Pennsylvania and New York Central railroads.

National Traffic and Motor Vehicle Safety Act passes.

Columbia River Bridge at Astoria, Ore., opens.

Nation has registered 78 million passenger cars and 16 million trucks and buses.

SCIENCE/MEDICINE

Medicare program to assist elderly goes into effect (July 1).

Robert S. Mulliken is awarded Nobel Prize in chemistry for work on the chemical bond and electronic structure of molecules; Charles B. Huggins and Peyton Rous share physiology/medicine prize, Rous for discovering a cancer virus, Huggins for developing methods of treating cancer.

Surveyor I becomes first U.S. satellite to make soft landing on the moon (June 2).

EDUCATION

Harold Howe II becomes U.S. Education commissioner.

RELIGION

Merger of Methodist and Evangelical United Brethren churches is ratified (November 11), forms largest American Protestant church, the 10,750,000 member United Methodist Church.

National Conference of Catholic Bishops is established, issues rule that Catholics must abstain from eating meat only on Ash Wednesday and Fridays in Lent.

ART/MUSIC

Old Metropolitan Opera House (New York City) gives final performance (April 16); company opens new home in Lincoln Center (September 16) with Samuel Barber's opera, *Antony and Cleopatra*.

Barnett Newman completes the painting *Stations of the Cross*; Isamu Noguchi completes the sculpture *Euripides*.

SONGS (popular): "Alfie," "Born Free," "The Impossible Dream," "Lara's Theme," "My Love," "Strangers in the Night," "When a Man Loves a Woman," "Georgy Girl," "If I Were a Carpenter."

DEATHS Hans Hofmann, painter who introduced European styles to U.S.; Malvina Hoffman, sculptor; Deems Taylor, music critic and composer.

LITERATURE/JOURNALISM

BOOKS *The Fixer* by Bernard Malamud, *Giles Goat-Boy* by John S. Barth, *Valley of the Dolls* by Jacqueline Susann, *The Arrangement* by Elia Kazan,

Taipan by James D. Clavell, *Division Street America* by Studs Terkel.

ENTERTAINMENT

PLAYS Joel Grey stars in *Cabaret*, Jessica Tandy in *A Delicate Balance*, Gwen Verdon in Neil Simon's *Sweet Charity*.

MOVIES *A Man for All Seasons* with Paul Scofield, *Batman* with Adam West, *The Fortune Cookie* with Walter Matthau, *The Spy Who Came in from the Cold* with Richard Burton.

New television shows include *Mission Impossible*, *Star Trek* with William Shatner.

DEATHS Russel Crouse, playwright; Sophie Tucker, singer and last of the "red hot mamas"; Hedda Hopper, movie gossip columnist; Billy Rose, producer and composer; Gertrude Berg, radio and television actress; Buster Keaton, silent-screen comedian; Walt Disney, filmmaker and theme-park creator.

SPORTS

American and National Football leagues merge (June 8).

Bill Russell is named player-coach of Boston Celtics, is first African American coach of a major professional sports team.

Three new stadiums open: Fulton County (Atlanta), California (Anaheim), Busch (St. Louis).

New records are set in track and field: Bob Seagren, indoor pole vault (17 ft., $\frac{1}{4}$ in.); John Pennel, outdoor pole vault (17 ft., $6\frac{1}{4}$ in.); Tommie Smith, 220-yard dash (20 sec.); Jim Ryun, mile run (3 min., 51.3 sec.).

WINNERS *Auto racing* — Grahman Hill, Indianapolis 500; David Pearson, NASCAR; *Baseball* — Baltimore Orioles, World Series; *Basketball* — Brigham Young, NIT; Texas Western, NCAA; Boston, NBA; *Bowling* — Wayne Zahn, PBA national; *Boxing* — Muhammad Ali, heavyweight; Emile Griffith, middleweight; Curtis Cokes, welterweight; *Figure skating* — Peggy Fleming, U.S. and world women's title; Scott Allen, U.S. men's; *Football* (bowls) — UCLA, Rose; Alabama, Orange; Missouri, Sugar; Louisiana State, Cotton; *Golf* — Billy Casper, U.S. Open; Al Geiberger, PGA; Jack Nicklaus, Masters; Gloria Ehret, LPGA; Sandra Spuzich, U.S. Women's Open; *Harness racing* — Kerry Way, Hambletonian; *Hockey* — Montreal, Stanley Cup; *Horse racing* — Kaui King, Kentucky Derby and Preakness Stakes; Amberoid, Belmont Stakes; *Tennis* — Fred Stolle, U.S. Open (men); Maria Bueno, U.S. Open (women).

DEATH "Sunny" Jim Fitzsimmons, horse trainer who saddled 2,275 winners.

MISCELLANEOUS

Tornadoes kill 57 in Jackson, Miss., 61 others in Alabama and Mississippi.

Huey Newton and Bobby Seale organize Black Panther Party.

Charles Starkweather barricades himself in University of Texas tower, shoots and kills 13, wounds 31 before being killed by law enforcers.

The mini-skirt is introduced as the latest fashion for women.

1967

INTERNATIONAL

U.S., Great Britain, and Russia agree to limit use of outer space for military purposes.

Western Hemisphere nations vote to form Latin American common market.

President Lyndon B. Johnson makes round-the-world trip in a week; meets with Soviet Premier Aleksei Kosygin for three days at Glassboro (N.J.) State College.

NATIONAL

Twenty-fifth Amendment is ratified, sets up presidential succession (February 10).

Thurgood Marshall becomes first African American Supreme Court justice (August 30).

Freedom of Information Act goes into effect.

Five days of rioting by African Americans begins in Newark, N.J. (July 12), 26 persons are killed, 1,500 are injured; week-long rioting begins in

A view of Detroit, Michigan, on July 25, 1967, after the first two of four days of race riots. After two days, more than 23 people have been killed and some thousand injured. UPI/Corbis-Bettmann

Detroit (July 23), results in 40 deaths, 600 injuries, destruction of 5,000 homes.

Tennessee repeals law that forbids teaching of evolution in public schools, which led to 1925 Scopes trial.

U.S. Coast Guard moves from Treasury to new Transportation Department.

First two African American mayors of major cities are elected: Carl B. Stokes, Cleveland; Richard Hatcher, Gary, Ind.

National Commission of Product Safety is created.

Nickajack Dam on Tennessee River in Tennessee is completed.

Spiro T. Agnew is elected governor of Maryland.

DEATHS Former Vice President John N. Garner (1933–1941); William F. Gibbs, directed production of World War II cargo ships.

BUSINESS/INDUSTRY/INVENTIONS

Teamsters President Jimmy Hoffa begins eight-year prison term for mail fraud and mishandling union funds.

Minimum wage rises to $1.40 an hour (February 1).

DEATHS Henry J. Kaiser, builder of ships, dams, autos; Bruce Barton, advertising executive and author; Roger W. Babson, economist.

TRANSPORTATION

Alan S. Boyd is named first secretary of transportation (April 1).

Douglas and McDonnell aircraft companies merge.

Merger of Atlantic Coast Line and Seaboard Air Line railroads forms Seaboard Coast Line.

SCIENCE/MEDICINE

Hans A. Bethe is awarded Nobel Prize in physics for discovery of the energy production of stars; Haldan K. Hartline and George Wald share physiology/medicine prize for discoveries on primary visual processes of the eye.

Fire in spacecraft *Apollo* on ground at Cape Canaveral, Fla., kills three astronauts: Virgil I. Grissom, Edward H. White II, and Roger B. Chaffee (January 27).

DEATHS Elmer V. McCollum, discoverer of vitamin D, codiscoverer of vitamin A; Gregory Pincus, biologist, codeveloper of oral contraceptive pill; J. Robert Oppenheimer, physicist; Bela Schick, pediatrician, developer of diphtheria test; George F. Dick, who with wife, Gladys, isolated scarlet fever germ, developed serum.

EDUCATION

Merger of Case Institute and Western Reserve forms Case-Western Reserve University in Cleveland; Merger of Carnegie and Mellon institutes creates Carnegie-Mellon University in Pittsburgh.

RELIGION

Janie McGaughey becomes first Presbyterian woman named moderator of a presbytery (Atlanta).

United Presbyterian Church in the USA adopts new confession, first change since 1647.

Two Catholic archbishops are elevated to cardinal: Patrick A. O'Boyle of Washington (D.C.) and John P. Cody of Chicago.

ART/MUSIC

Helen Frankenthaler completes the painting *The Human Edge.*

SONGS (popular): "By the Time I Get to Phoenix," "Can't Take My Eyes off You," "Light My Fire," "A Little Help from My Friends," "Ode to Billy Joe," "Something Stupid," "Up, Up, and Away," "I Heard It Through the Grape Vine."

DEATHS Otis Redding, rhythm-and-blues artist, in plane crash; Geraldine Farrar, dramatic soprano; Paul Whiteman, orchestra leader; Woody Guthrie, folksinger and composer; Muggsy Spanier, Dixieland jazz cornetist; Edward Hopper, painter of contemporary life.

LITERATURE/JOURNALISM

BOOKS *The Confessions of Nat Turner* by William Styron, *The Armies of the Night* by Norman Mailer, *Topaz* by Leon Uris, *Rosemary's Baby* by Ira Levin, *The Chosen* by Chaim Potok.

1967

DEATHS Carl Sandburg, poet and biographer; Carson McCullers, author; Henry R. Luce, publisher; Langston Hughes, "poet laureate" of Harlem.

ENTERTAINMENT

Corporation for Public Broadcasting is established.

PLAYS *Hair* and Clark Gesner's *You're a Good Man, Charlie Brown.*

MOVIES *Guess Who's Coming to Dinner* with Spencer Tracy and Katharine Hepburn; *Bonnie and Clyde* with Warren Beatty and Faye Dunaway, *The Dirty Dozen* with Lee Marvin, *The Graduate* with Dustin Hoffman, *Thoroughly Modern Millie* with Julie Andrews.

New television shows include the Smothers Brothers, Jonathan Winters, Jerry Lewis, Carol Burnett, *The Newlywed Game* with Bob Ewbanks, *The Flying Nun* with Sally Field, *Kraft Music Hall.*

DEATHS Bert Lahr, Paul Muni, and Spencer Tracy, actors; Martin Block, disc jockey of 1930–1940s; Nelson Eddy, singer and screen actor.

SPORTS

American League approves transfer of baseball franchise from Kansas City, Mo., to Oakland, Calif., authorizes expansion to 12 clubs. National Basketball Assn. grants franchise to San Diego and Seattle; American Basketball Assn. is founded.

Muhammad Ali is sentenced to five years and $10,000 fine for refusing military service; sentence is appealed.

Mickey Mantle, New York Yankees, and Eddie Mathews, Houston Astros, each hit their 500th career home runs.

A. J. Foyt and Dan Gurney become first Americans to win 24 Hours of LeMans sports-car race.

Jim Baaken of St. Louis kicks record seven field goals in a football game.

WINNERS *Auto racing*—A. J. Foyt, Indianapolis 500; Richard Petty, NASCAR; *Baseball*—St. Louis Cardinals, World Series; *Basketball*—Southern Illinois, NIT; UCLA, NCAA; Philadelphia, NBA; *Bowling*—Dave Davis, PBA national; *Boxing*—Muhammad Ali, heavyweight; Emile Griffith, middleweight; *Figure skating*—Peggy Fleming, world and U.S. championship; Gary Visconti, U.S. title (men); *Football* (bowls)—Purdue, Rose; Florida, Orange; Alabama, Sugar; Georgia, Cotton; Green Bay, Super Bowl I; *Golf*—U.S., Walker and Ryder cups; Jack Nicklaus, U.S. Open; Don January, PGA; Gary Brewer Jr., Masters; Catherine Lacoste, U.S. Women's Open; Kathy Whitworth, LPGA; *Harness racing*—Speedy Streak, Hambletonian; *Hockey*—Toronto, Stanley Cup; *Horse racing*—Proud Clarion, Kentucky Derby; Damascus, Preakness Stakes and Belmont Stakes; *Tennis*—John Newcombe, U.S. Open (men); Billie Jean King, U.S. Open (women); *Yachting*—U.S. boat *Intrepid* retains America's Cup.

DEATHS Eleanora Sears, Tennis Hall of Famer; Francis Ouimet, popularized golf in U.S.

MISCELLANEOUS

Silver Bridge over Ohio River that connects Pt. Pleasant, W. Va., and Kanauga, Ohio, collapses; 46 are killed.

Piedmont Boeing 727 and Cessna 310 collide over Hendersonville, N.C.; 82 are killed.

Floods damage much of Fairbanks, Alaska.

Aircraft carrier *Forrestal* catches fire off North Vietnam; 134 die.

1968

INTERNATIONAL

VIETNAM WAR Communist forces launch Tet offensive (January 30); U.S. and North Vietnam agree to preliminary talks to end war (May 3); begin a week later.

North Korea seizes U.S. intelligence ship *Pueblo*; 83 men on board are held as spies.

Island of Iwo Jima is returned to Japan.

NATIONAL

Two assassinations shock nation: Rev. Martin Luther King Jr., civil rights leader, at a Memphis motel (April 4), and Senator Robert F. Kennedy in a Los Angeles hotel (June 5); Kennedy dies the next morning.

President Lyndon B. Johnson announces he will not seek reelection (March 31); Republican Richard M. Nixon is elected president with 31,785,480 popular and 301 electoral votes to Democratic Vice President Hubert H. Humphrey's 31,275,166 popular and 191 electoral votes; Independent George A. Wallace receives 9,906,473 popular and 46 electoral votes.

Supreme Court Chief Justice Earl Warren resigns (June 13).

Nuclear submarine *Scorpion* sinks near the Azores; 99 men are lost.

First-class postage rises to 6 cents.

HemisFair 68 opens in San Antonio, Tex., marking city's 200th birthday.

Oroville Dam on Feather River in California is completed.

North Cascades (Wash.) and Redwood (Calif.) national parks are established.

Rep. Shirley Chisholm becomes first African American woman elected to Congress.

DEATHS Helen Keller, blind lecturer on behalf of blind; Norman Thomas, five-time Socialist presidential candidate (1928–1948).

BUSINESS/INDUSTRY/INVENTIONS

Truth in Lending Act is signed.

Minimum wage increases to $1.60 an hour.

DEATHS Sanford L. Cluett, shirt and collar maker, invented Sanforizing process; Chester F. Carlson, inventor of xerography.

TRANSPORTATION

Supreme Court approves merger of Pennsylvania and New York Central railroads, which creates the Penn Central.

Mississippi River Bridge at Baton Rouge, La., and second span of Delaware Memorial Bridge at Wilmington open.

Lockheed unveils world's largest plane, the C-5A.

Merger of unions representing railway trainmen, locomotive firemen and engineers, switchmen, and conductors forms United Transportation Union.

DEATH Ralph H. Upson, designer of first metal-clad airplane.

SCIENCE/MEDICINE

Luis W. Alvarez is awarded Nobel Prize in physics for contributions to physics and detection of elementary particles; Lars Onsager is awarded chemistry prize for work on thermodynamics of irreversible processes; Robert W. Holley, H. Gobind Khorama, and Marshall W. Nirenberg share physiology/medicine prize for interpreting the genetic code and its role in making certain proteins.

Frank Borman, James A. Lovell Jr., and William A. Anders complete six-day first flight to the moon (December 27), send back pictures of moon's surface; earlier, unmanned *Surveyor VII* made soft landing on moon, sending back data and pictures.

Scientists synthesize an enzyme for the first time.

American troops in Vietnam, fighting in the city of Hue. UPI/CORBIS-BETTMANN

Dr. Norman Shumway performs first successful U.S. heart transplant.

EDUCATION

Supreme Court rules that "freedom of choice" desegregation is inadequate if other methods can correct Southern school segregation more rapidly; Court also rules that public-school teachers may not be discharged for good faith criticism of school officials.

Internal Revenue Service revokes tax-exempt status of private schools that continue to practice racial discrimination in admission policies.

Carnegie Commission on Higher Education urges multibillion-dollar federal aid for colleges and college students.

RELIGION

Terence J. Cooke becomes Catholic archbishop of New York.

DEATH Franklin C. Fry, president, United Lutheran, American Lutheran churches (1944–1968).

ART/MUSIC

New York Philharmonic observes 125th anniversary with Leonard Bernstein conducting Walter Piston's *Ricercare*.

Pop artist Roy Lichtenstein completes painting *Preparedness*.

SONGS (popular): "Do You Know the Way to San Jose?" "The Dock of the Bay," "Hey Jude," "Harper Valley PTA," "Honey," "Mrs. Robinson," "This Guy's in Love with You," "Wichita Lineman," "Piece of My Heart."

DEATH Ruth St. Denis, dancer.

LITERATURE/JOURNALISM

BOOKS *Iberia* by James A. Michener, *Couples* by John Updike, *Myra Breckenridge* by Gore Vidal, *Airport* by Arthur Hailey, *Lonesome Cities* (poetry) by Rod McKuen.

DEATHS Authors John Steinbeck, Vardis Fisher, Edwin G. O'Connor, Edna Ferber, and Upton B. Sinclair; Harold L. Gray, cartoonist ("Little Orphan Annie").

ENTERTAINMENT

Restored Ford's Theater in Washington, D.C., is dedicated.

Classification of movies begins: "G," "PG," "R," and "X" ratings.

PLAYS Jerry Orbach stars in *Promises, Promises*, James Earl Jones in *The Great White Hope*, Maureen Stapleton and George C. Scott in Neil Simon's *Plaza Suite*.

MOVIES *The Lion in Winter* with Katharine Hepburn, *2001:A Space Odyssey*, *Funny Girl* with Barbra Streisand, *The Green Berets* with John Wayne, *The Detective* with Frank Sinatra.

New television shows include *Laugh-In* with Dan Rowan and Dick Martin, *60 Minutes* with Mike Wallace, *Hawaii 5-0* with Jack Lord.

SPORTS

Club owners fire Baseball Commissioner William D. Eckert with five years left on his contract.

Three new sports facilities open: New York City's Madison Square Center, including a new garden; Oakland (Calif.) Coliseum, home of baseball A's; Belmont Park after $30 million renovation.

Naismith Memorial Basketball Hall of Fame opens in Springfield, Mass.

Hank Aaron of Atlanta Braves hits 500th home run.

Olympic Games are held in Mexico City; U.S. wins 45 gold medals.

National Basketball Assn. awards franchises to Milwaukee and Detroit.

National Football league Players Assn. strikes for six days.

Don Drysdale of Los Angeles Dodgers sets record for consecutive scoreless innings pitched (58⅔).

WINNERS *Auto racing*—Bobby Unser, Indianapolis 500; David Pearson, NASCAR; *Baseball*—Detroit Tigers, World Series; *Basketball*—Dayton, NIT; UCLA, NCAA; Boston, NBA; *Bowling*—Wayne Zahn, PBA national; *Boxing*—Joe Frazier, heavyweight; Bob Foster, light heavyweight; Nino Benevenuti, middleweight; *Figure skating*—Peggy Fleming, U.S. and world titles (women); Tim Wood, U.S. title (men); *Football* (bowls)—Southern California, Rose; Oklahoma, Orange;

Louisiana State, Sugar; Texas A&M, Cotton; Green Bay, Super Bowl II; *Golf*—Lee Trevino, U.S. Open; Julius Boros, PGA; Bob Goalby, Masters; Susie M. Browning, U.S. Women's Open; Sandra Post, LPGA; *Harness racing*—Nevele Pride, Hambletonian; *Hockey*—Montreal, Stanley Cup; *Horse racing*—Dancer's Image, Kentucky Derby; Forward Pass, Preakness Stakes; Stage Door Johnny, Belmont Stakes; *Horseshoe pitching*—Elmer Hohe, world title; *Tennis*—U.S., Davis Cup; Arthur Ashe, U.S. Open (men); Virginia Wade, U.S. Open (women).

DEATHS Bill Masterson, Minnesota hockey player, first death in NHL from game injury; Stanislaus Zybyszko, wrestler; Paddy Driscoll, early football great; Earl Sande, one of premier jockeys of 1920s.

MISCELLANEOUS

Explosion and fire in Mannington, W. Va., coal mine kills 78 miners.

Braniff Electra crashes in storm near Dawson, Tex.; 85 die.

Janis Joplin performs in New York. Her 1968 album *Cheap Thrills,* featuring the song "Piece of My Heart" sells 1 million copies in its first month of release. CORBIS-BETTMANN

1969

INTERNATIONAL

VIETNAM WAR Peace talks to end war in Vietnam begin (January 18); about 250,000 persons take part in anti–Vietnam War demonstration in Washington, D.C. (November 15).

NATIONAL

Warren E. Burger becomes Supreme Court chief justice (June 23); Justice Abe Fortas resigns after criticism of his acceptance of a fee.

President Richard M. Nixon signs tax reform bill, which was expected to lower taxes by 5%, remove 9 million people from income tax rolls.

Car driven by Sen. Edward M. Kennedy of Massachusetts plunges off bridge on Chappaquiddick Island (Mass.); a 28-year-old secretary with him drowns.

Sirhan Sirhan, accused murderer of Sen. Robert Kennedy, is found guilty and sentenced to death; sentence is later commuted to life imprisonment.

World's largest mint opens in Philadelphia.

Destroyer *Evans* collides with an Australian carrier in South China Sea; 74 men are lost.

Vice president's salary is raised from $43,000 to $62,500.

DEATHS Former President Dwight D. Eisenhower (1953–1961); Allen W. Dulles, head of CIA (1953–1961); Assistant Attorney General Thurman Arnold, who filed 230 antitrust suits (1938–1943); World War II Admiral Raymond A. Spruance.

BUSINESS/INDUSTRY/INVENTIONS

DEATHS John L. Lewis, president, United Mine Workers (1920–1960), CIO (1935–1940); Ludwig Mies van der Rohe, architect who developed glass-and-steel skyscraper; Robert E. Wood, merchant (Sears).

TRANSPORTATION

Penn Central completes takeover of bankrupt New York, New Haven & Hartford Railroad.

Metroliner completes first New York City–Washington run in 3 hours, 7 minutes.

Newport Bridge over Narragansett Bay (R.I.) is completed.

SCIENCE/MEDICINE

Neil A. Armstrong, Edwin E. Aldrin Jr., and Michael Collins make eight-day flight to the moon; Armstrong becomes first man to set foot on moon (July 20), saying, "That's one small step for a man, one giant leap for mankind."

Murray Gell-Mann is awarded Nobel Prize in physics for discoveries concerning elementary particles; Max Delbruck, Alfred D. Hershey, and Salvador Luria

The Apollo 11 lunar landing, July 1969. Astronaut Edwin E. Aldrin Jr. is shown standing beside the United States flag. Neil Armstrong takes the photograph with a 70-mm. Hasselblad lunar surface camera, while millions of Americans watch the action live on television. NASA

The young crowd at the Woodstock music festival in 1969. TOM MINER/THE IMAGE WORKS

share physiology/medicine prize for discoveries of viruses and viral diseases.

Dr. Denton A. Cooley implants in a human being in Houston world's first totally artificial heart (April 4); patient lives four days.

EDUCATION

Supreme Court rules that schools must end segregation "at once"; school systems must be integrated "now and hereafter"; rules that public school officials cannot interfere with students' nondisruptive public-opinion expressions during school hours; rules that states can spend more on schools in wealthy districts than in disadvantaged areas.

RELIGION

Catholic Church issues revised liturgical calendar, eliminating more than 200 saints (including Christopher, Valentine).

Cynthia C. Wedel becomes first woman president of National Council of Churches.

Norman Vincent Peale becomes president of Reformed Church in America.

Catholic Archbishop Terence J. Cooke of New York is elevated to cardinal.

DEATHS Rev. Francis Brennan, first U.S. dean of Sacred Rota, Catholic Church's highest appeal court; Rev. Harry Emerson Fosdick, leader of modern liberal Christianity.

ART/MUSIC

New Juilliard School of Music opens in Lincoln Center, New York City.

Woodstock, music festival attended by about 300,000 young people, is held near Bethel, N.Y.

SONGS (popular): "Aquarius/Let the Sunshine In," "A Boy Named Sue," "Games People Play,"

"Hair," "Leaving on a Jet Plane," "Something," "Wedding Bell Blues."

DEATHS Ben Shahn, artist of social, political causes; Thomas H. Jones, sculptor of Tomb of the Unknown Soldier in Arlington (Va.) Cemetery; Frank Loesser, composer.

LITERATURE/JOURNALISM

Jack Anderson takes over "Washington Merry-Go-Round" column on death of Drew Pearson.

BOOKS *Portnoy's Complaint* by Philip Roth, *Slaughterhouse Five* by Kurt Vonnegut, *The Godfather* by Mario Puzo, *The Poseidon Adventure* by Paul Gallico, *The French Connection* by Robin Moore, *The Inheritors* by Harold Robbins.

DEATHS Westbrook Pegler, syndicated columnist; Jack Kerouac, "beat generation" author; Harry Scherman, founder, Book of the Month Club.

ENTERTAINMENT

PLAYS James Coco stars in *Last of the Red Hot Lovers*; Kenneth Tynan contributes to *Oh, Calcutta*; Leonard Gershe writes *Butterflies Are Free*; Woody Allen, *Play It Again, Sam*.

MOVIES *True Grit* with John Wayne, *Butch Cassidy and the Sundance Kid* with Paul Newman and Robert Redford, *Midnight Cowboy* with Jon Voight, *Easy Rider* with Peter Fonda, *Cactus Flower* with Ingrid Bergman.

New on television are *Marcus Welby, M.D.* with Robert Young, *Medical Center* with Chad Everett, *Hee Haw!* with Roy Clark, *The Brady Bunch*, and Merv Griffin, John Davidson, Johnny Cash, Glen Campbell, Dick Cavett, and David Frost.

DEATHS Irene Castle, dancer; Judy Garland, entertainer and screen actress; Boris Karloff, actor.

SPORTS

Bowie Kuhn is named baseball commissioner.

Willie Mays of San Francisco Giants hits his 600th home run.

Jack Murphy (baseball) Stadium in San Diego opens.

WINNERS *Auto racing* — Mario Andretti, Indianapolis 500; David Pearson, NASCAR; *Baseball* — New York Mets, World Series; *Basketball* — Temple, NIT; UCLA, NCAA; Boston, NBA; *Bowling* — Mike McGrath, PBA national; *Boxing* — Joe Frazier, heavyweight; Jose Napoles, welterweight; Mando Ramos, lightweight; *Chess* — Samuel Reshevsky, U.S. title; *Figure skating* — Tim Wood, U.S., world men's titles; Janet Lynn, U.S. women's singles; *Football* (bowls) — Ohio State, Rose; Penn State, Orange; Arkansas, Sugar; Texas, Cotton; New York Jets, Super Bowl III; *Golf* — U.S., Walker Cup; Orville Moody, U.S. Open; Ray Floyd, PGA; George Archer, Masters; Donna Caponi, U.S. Women's Open; Betsy Rawls, LPGA; *Harness racing* — Lindy's Pride, Hambletonian; *Hockey* — Montreal, Stanley Cup; *Horse racing* — Majestic Prince, Kentucky Derby and Preakness Stakes; Arts and Letters, Belmont Stakes; *Tennis* — U.S., Davis Cup; Rod Laver, U.S. Open (men); Margaret Court, U.S. Open (women).

DEATHS Rocky Marciano, heavyweight boxing champion, in plane crash; Arnie Herber, football quarterback; Max Hirsch, dean of U.S. thoroughbred trainers; Walter Hagen, famed golfer.

MISCELLANEOUS

Hurricane Camille strikes Gulf Coast, kills 292, causes $1 billion damage.

Pants suits become acceptable for everyday wear by women.

1970

INTERNATIONAL

President Richard M. Nixon announces that U.S. troops are being sent into Cambodia (April 30).

Terrorists in Montevideo, Uruguay, kidnap U.S. diplomat Daniel A. Mitrione (July 31); body is found 10 days later.

NATIONAL

Nearly 200,000 postal workers strike (March 18) in New York City; strike spreads through nation (except South), ends six days later.

U.S. Postal Service law is signed (August 12), is effective 1971.

Newly created agencies are Council of Environmental Quality (January 1); Environmental Protection Agency (December 2); National Oceanic and Atmospheric Administration (including Weather Service, Ocean Survey, Marine Fisheries), and Office of Management and Budget (July 1).

Nineteenth census reports national population at 203,302,031.

Two deadly college demonstrations occur: four students at Kent State University are killed by Ohio National Guards during an anti–Vietnam War rally; two students at Jackson (Miss.) State College are killed when police fire on demonstrators.

Norman E. Borlaug is awarded Nobel Peace Prize for contributions to spurring food production in developing nations.

First draft lottery since World War II is held.

Guam and Virgin Islands elect their first governors.

National debt is reported at $370.1 billion.

First Earth Day is observed (April 22).

DEATHS Benjamin O. Davis, first African American Army general; Gen. Leslie R. Groves, headed Manhattan Project that developed atomic bomb.

BUSINESS/INDUSTRY/INVENTIONS

IBM has sold 18,000 mainframe computer systems in U.S. since early 1950s; Intel introduces its first memory chip, which holds one kilobyte of information.

Paul A. Samuelson is awarded Nobel Prize in economics for raising level of scientific analysis in economic theory.

Occupational Safety and Health Act is signed, authorizes setting of federal standards.

DEATHS Walter P. Reuther, United Auto Workers president (1946–1970), in plane crash; Richard J. Neutra, architect, introduced international style to U.S.; Harry A. Noyes, developer of food-freezing process.

TRANSPORTATION

General Motors redesigns cars to operate on lower octane gas.

President Nixon signs clean-air bill that sets six-year deadline for auto industry to develop pollution-free engine.

Merger of Chicago, Burlington, and Northern and Northern Pacific roads creates Burlington Northern Railroad.

Lee Iacocca becomes president of Ford Motor Co.

DEATHS William T. Piper, designer of Piper Cub planes; Arthur W. S. Herrington, developer of World War II jeep.

SCIENCE/MEDICINE

Julius Axelrod shares Nobel Prize in physiology/medicine with Sir Bernard Katz of Great Britain and Ulf Von Euler of Sweden for independent basic research on chemistry of nerve transmission.

Apollo 13 mission develops serious problems about 200,000 miles from Earth when oxygen tanks and service module explode; completes mission around moon, returns to Earth successfully (April 17).

1970

Kent State University, Ohio. National Guard skirmish line advances up a hill on campus on May 4, 1970, just before they turn and fire upon students participating in an anti-war demonstration. UPI/CORBIS-BETTMANN

EDUCATION

Supreme Court rules that election of school board members must adhere to one-man, one-vote principle.

University of Hawaii is established.

RELIGION

Joseph Fielding Smith becomes tenth head of Mormon Church, on death of David O. McKay.

Catholic Bishop Humberto S. Medeiros is named archbishop of Boston following death of Archbishop Richard J. Cushing (1947–1970).

ART/MUSIC

Mario Davidovsky composes *Synchronisms #6*.

SONGS (popular): "Bridge over Troubled Water," "Everything Is Beautiful," "I Never Promised You a Rose Garden," "Let It Be," "No Sugar Tonight,"
"Raindrops Keep Fallin' on My Head," "We've Only Just Begun."

DEATHS Mark Rothko, artist of abstract expressionism who during year completed *Black on Grey*; George Szell, conductor; Janis Joplin, rock star.

LITERATURE/JOURNALISM

BOOKS *Jonathan Livingston Seagull* by Richard D. Bach, *Hard Times* by Studs Terkel, *The Rising Sun* by John Toland, *The Trumpet of the Swan* by E. B. White, *Love Story* by Erich Segal, *Rich Man, Poor Man* by Irwin Shaw.

DEATHS Richard Hofstadter, historian; Rube Goldberg, cartoonist; Erle Stanley Gardner and John O'Hara, authors; Joseph Wood Krutch, editor, *The Nation* (1924–1952).

ENTERTAINMENT

PLAYS Dean Jones stars in *Company*, Lauren

Bacall in *Applause*; Paul Zindel writes *The Effect of Gamma Rays on Man-in-the-Moon Marigolds*.

MOVIES *Airport* with Burt Lancaster and Helen Hayes, *Patton* with George C. Scott, *Catch-22* with Alan Arkin, *Love Story* with Ali McGraw, *The Reivers* with Steve McQueen.

New television shows include *The Odd Couple* with Tony Randall and Jack Klugman, *The Partridge Family* with Shirley Jones, *The Mary Tyler Moore Show*, and *The Flip Wilson Show*.

DEATHS Gypsy Rose Lee, entertainer; Billie Burke, screen actress.

SPORTS

Two college football teams and staff are killed in air crashes: Wichita State University in Colorado, 29 die; Marshall University in West Virginia, 43 die.

Bill Shoemaker rides 6,033rd winning horse to set new record.

Three baseball parks open: Texas Rangers in Arlington, Riverfront Stadium in Cincinnati, and Three Rivers Stadium in Pittsburgh.

International Lawn Tennis Assn. approves nine-point tie-breaking scoring.

National Basketball Assn. expands to 18 teams, awards franchises to Buffalo, Cleveland, Houston, and Portland, Ore.

Charles S. Feeney becomes National (baseball) League president.

Hank Aaron of Atlanta Braves and Willie Mays of San Francisco Giants each gets his 3,000th hit.

Tom Dempsey kicks longest field goal (63 yards) in NFL history.

Gary Gabelich sets land speed record of 622.407 miles per hour.

Seattle baseball franchise moves to Milwaukee.

WINNERS *Auto racing*—Al Unser, Indianapolis 500; Bobby Isaac, NASCAR; *Baseball*—Baltimore Orioles, World Series; *Basketball*—Marquette, NIT; UCLA, NCAA; New York, NBA; *Bowling*—Mike McGrath, PBA national; *Boxing*—Joe Frazier, heavyweight; Billy Backus, welterweight; Carlos Monzon, middleweight; Ismael Laguna, lightweight; *Figure skating*—Tim Wood, U.S. and world men's titles; Janet Lynn, U.S. women's; *Football* (bowls)—Southern California, Rose; Penn State, Orange; Mississippi, Sugar; Texas, Cotton; Kansas City, Super Bowl IV; *Golf*—Tony Jacklin, U.S. Open; Dave Stockton, PGA; Billy Casper, Masters; Donna Caponi, U.S. Women's Open; Shirley Engelhorn, LPGA; *Harness racing*—Timothy T., Hambletonian; *Hockey*—Boston, Stanley Cup; *Horse racing*—Dust Commander, Kentucky Derby; Personality, Preakness Stakes; High Echelon, Belmont Stakes; *Marathon*—Gary Muhrcke, first New York City race; Sara Berman, first woman's championship; *Tennis*—U.S., Davis Cup; Ken Rosewall, U.S. Open (men); Margaret Court U.S. Open (women); *Yachting*—U.S. boat *Intrepid* retains America's Cup.

DEATHS Vincent Lombardi, football coach; Harold S. Vanderbilt, winner of America's Cup three times, developer of contract bridge.

MISCELLANEOUS

North tower of World Trade Center in New York City tops out, world's tallest (1,350 feet).

Tornado strikes Lubbock, Tex., kills 26, causes $135 million in damage.

1971

INTERNATIONAL

VIETNAM WAR U.S. bombs Vietnam for five days, beginning December 26, for alleged violations of 1968 bombing halt.

Treaty is signed, returns Okinawa to Japan; Ryukyu and Daito islands are also returned.

Trade embargo on Communist China is lifted after 21 years.

Japanese Government allows Chrysler Motors to acquire 35% interest in Mitsubishi Motors over three-year period.

NATIONAL

National voting age is lowered to 18 with ratification of Twenty-sixth Amendment (July 1).

President Richard M. Nixon announces 90-day wage-price freeze (August 15); Cost of Living Council is established.

U.S. Postal Service comes into existence, replaces Post Office Department.

Radical Weather Underground bombs a room in Capitol; no one is injured, $300,000 damage.

Kennedy Center for the Performing Arts in Washington, D.C., opens.

First-class postage rises to 8 cents an ounce (May 16).

Three-day holiday weekends (Washington's Birthday, Memorial Day, Columbus Day, Veterans Day) go into effect (January 1).

More than 1,000 New York State troopers and police storm Attica prison to end four-day uprising; 9 hostages, 28 convicts are killed.

Lyndon B. Johnson Library at University of Texas is dedicated.

ACTION is created as an independent agency to administer volunteer programs (Peace Corps, VISTA, Foster Grandparents, etc.).

Jimmy Carter is elected Georgia governor.

Cowans Ford Dam on Catawba River in North Carolina is completed.

DEATHS Thomas E. Dewey, New York governor, twice Republican presidential candidate; Arthur B. Spingarn, NAACP president (1940–1965); Dean G. Acheson, secretary of state (1949–1953); Rosey (Emmett) O'Donnell, Air Force general; Ralph Bunche, U.N. undersecretary.

BUSINESS/INDUSTRY/INVENTIONS

Simon Kuznets is awarded Nobel Prize in economics for developing economic interpretation of national growth.

Cigarette advertising is banned from television.

Interior Department recommends trans-Alaska oil pipeline to help meet critical oil need.

Texaco completes world's deepest producing oil well at Stockton, Tex.

DEATHS James C. Penney, department-store-chain founder; Gar Wood, boat racer and builder (Navy PT boat); Philo T. Farnsworth, television pioneer.

TRANSPORTATION

Amtrak announces rates and schedules, begins operations (May 1); Alan S. Boyd is named chief executive officer.

Dent Bridge in Clearwater County, Idaho, opens.

SCIENCE/MEDICINE

Earl W. Sutherland Jr. is awarded Nobel Prize in physiology/medicine for discoveries concerning hormone action.

EDUCATION

Supreme Court upholds constitutionality of busing to eliminate segregation; also overturns Mobile, Ala., desegregation plan.

Sidney P. Marland Jr. is named U.S. Education Commissioner.

Ford Foundation announces six-year, $100-million program to assist African American private colleges and minority students.

RELIGION

Supreme Court rules unconstitutional the reimbursement of religious schools for secular instruction.

DEATH Reinhold Niebuhr, theologian.

ART/MUSIC

Jacob Druckman composes the work *Windows*; Leonard Bernstein composes *Mass* for opening of Kennedy Center.

SONGS (popular): "Joy to the World," "Knock Three Times," "Me and Bobby McGee," "Mister Bojangles," "Put Your Hand in the Hand," "She's a Lady," "Take Me Home, Country Road," "You've Got a Friend," "Day by Day."

DEATHS Rockwell Kent, artist and author; Louis (Satchmo) Armstrong, jazz musician, singer, and orchestra leader; Ted Fio Rito, early orchestra leader and composer.

LITERATURE/JOURNALISM

The *New York Times* publishes classified Pentagon Papers; Supreme Court upholds right to their publication.

Look magazine ceases publication.

BOOKS *Rabbit Redux* by John Updike, *The Winds of War* by Herman Wouk, *The Betsy* by Harold Robbins, *Wheels* by Arthur Hailey, *Yazoo* by Willie Morris, *Wonderland* by Joyce Carol Oates, *Our Gang* by Philip Roth.

DEATHS Bennett Cerf, publisher; Margaret Bourke-White, *Life* photographer; Ogden Nash, poet; James F. Stevens, author of Paul Bunyan stories.

ENTERTAINMENT

PLAYS Peter Falk stars in *The Prisoner of Second Avenue*; John M. Tebelak and Stephen Schwartz write *Godspell*, Tim Rice and Andrew Lloyd Webber, *Jesus Christ Superstar*.

Chief of the presses William Frazer makes a "V" for victory as he displays the first edition of the *Washington Post* on June 30, 1971, after the Supreme Court's 6–3 decision allowing newspapers freedom to resume publication of a top secret Pentagon study of the Vietnam War. CORBIS-BETTMANN

MOVIES *A Clockwork Orange* with Malcolm McDowell, *The French Connection* with Gene Hackman, *Dirty Harry* with Clint Eastwood, *Klute* with Jane Fonda, *The Last Picture Show* with Timothy Bottoms and Jeff Bridges.

New television shows include *All in the Family* with Carroll O'Connor, *Sonny and Cher*, *Hollywood Squares*, *Columbo* with Peter Falk.

SPORTS

Supreme Court overturns conviction of Muhammad Ali as a draft evader; rules that he qualified as a conscientious objector.

New York (football) Giants announce move to Flushing Meadows in New Jersey in 1975; Washington Senators baseball club announces move to Texas in 1972.

World Hockey Assn. is founded; to begin play in 1972.

New York City begins first legal off-track horse-race betting in U.S.

Hank Aaron of Atlanta Braves hits 600th home run.

1972

WINNERS *Auto racing*—Al Unser, Indianapolis 500; Richard Petty, NASCAR; *Baseball*—Pittsburgh Pirates, World Series; *Basketball*—North Carolina, NIT; UCLA, NCAA; Milwaukee, NBA; *Bowling*—Mike Lemongello, PBA national; *Boxing*—Joe Frazier, heavyweight; Jose Napoles, welterweight, Ruben Olivares, bantamweight; *Figure skating*—John M. Petkevich, U.S. men's title; Janet Lynn, U.S. women's; *Football* (bowls)—Stanford, Rose; Nebraska, Orange; Tennessee, Sugar; Notre Dame, Cotton; Baltimore, Super Bowl V; *Golf*—Great Britain, Walker Cup; U.S., Ryder Cup; Lee Trevino, U.S. Open; Jack Nicklaus, PGA; Charlie Coody, Masters; JoAnne Carner, U.S. Women's Open; Kathy Whitworth, LPGA; *Harness racing*—Speedy Crown, Hambletonian; *Hockey*—Montreal, Stanley Cup; *Horse racing*—Canonero II, Kentucky Derby and Preakness Stakes; Pass Catcher, Belmont Stakes; *Tennis*—U.S. Davis Cup; Stan Smith, U.S. Open (men); Billie Jean King, U.S. Open (women).

DEATHS Bobby Jones, all-time great golfer; Will Harridge, American (baseball) League president (1931–1958).

MISCELLANEOUS

Hurricane Agnes kills 130, does $2 billion damage along Atlantic Coast; tornado in Mississippi Delta kills 110.

Earthquake rocks San Fernando Valley in California; 64 are killed, damage is set at $1 billion.

Alaska Airlines Boeing 727 crashes into mountain near Juneau, 111 die.

INTERNATIONAL

VIETNAM WAR North Vietnam forces launch attack across demilitarized zone (March 30); U.S. resumes bombing Hanoi and Haiphong (April 15); peace talks resume April 27; bombing resumes December 18 after peace talks stall.

U.S. and Russian representatives sign Strategic Arms Limitation Treaty I (SALT I) in Moscow (May 26); in effect until 1977.

President Nixon makes week-long visit to China; first president to visit a nation not recognized by U.S.; restriction on China travel by U.S. ships and planes is lifted.

President Nixon visits Russia in May.

NATIONAL

President Nixon, Republican, is elected to second term, receives 47,165,234 popular and 520 electoral votes to 29,170,774 popular and 17 electoral for Democratic Sen. George S. McGovern.

Alabama Gov. George A. Wallace is shot at a Laurel (Md.) political rally, is paralyzed from waist down; this ends his effort to attain Democratic presidential nomination; Arthur Bremer is sentenced to 63 years for the crime.

Five men are arrested for breaking into Democratic national headquarters in Watergate building in Washington (June 17).

Supreme Court rules the death penalty to be unconstitutional in *Furman v. Georgia*.

Consumer Product Safety Commission is created.

American Museum of Immigration opens at base of Statue of Liberty.

Eisenhower Center, including library, in Abilene, Kan., and Herbert Hoover Library in West Branch, Iowa, are dedicated.

DEATHS Former President Harry S. Truman (1945–1953); J. Edgar Hoover, FBI director (1924–1972); James F. Byrnes, Supreme Court justice, secretary of state (1945).

BUSINESS/INDUSTRY/INVENTIONS

Kenneth J. Arrow shares Nobel Prize in economics with John R. Hicks of Great Britain for contributing to general economic equilibrium theory and welfare theory.

Dow-Jones industrial average closes above 1,000 for the first time.

Near-total ban on use of DDT goes into effect.

Congress overrides president's veto of a 20% increase in railroad retirement benefits.

Major cigarette companies agree to include health warning in advertising.

DEATHS Howard H. Aiken, inventor of Mark I, forerunner of digital computer; Howard Johnson, restaurant and hotel-chain founder; Igor Sikorsky, engineer, developer of several planes, helicopter.

Robert Duvall and Marlon Brando in *The Godfather,* 1972. UPI/CORBIS-BETTMANN

TRANSPORTATION

Senate passes antihijacking bill; U.S. airlines tighten security to prevent acts of sabotage; government orders search of all carry-on luggage, boarding passengers.

First portion of San Francisco's BART transit system opens.

Merger of Gulf, Mobile and Ohio Railroad and Illinois Central Railroad forms Illinois Central Gulf Railroad.

SCIENCE/MEDICINE

John Bardeen, Leon N. Cooper, and John R. Schrieffer share Nobel Prize for physics for theory of superconductivity; Christian B. Anfinsen, Stanford Moore, and William H. Stine share chemistry prize for major contributions to enzyme chemistry; Gerald M. Edelman shares prize in physiology/medicine with Rodney R. Porter of Great Britain for research on chemical structure of antibodies.

President Nixon approves plan to develop space shuttle.

Pioneer 10 is launched, is designed to explore asteroid belt and fly by Jupiter.

Acupuncture is used for first time in U.S.

EDUCATION

Congress provides $2 billion to help public schools desegregate, establishes federal aid program for college and university students.

National Institute of Education is established to conduct, coordinate basic and applied educational research.

RELIGION

Supreme Court rules that state laws requiring school attendance violate constitutional freedom of religion, rules that Amish children cannot be required to attend beyond eighth grade.

Historic separation of white and black Methodist conferences in South Carolina ends.

Sally J. Priesand becomes first U.S. woman rabbi; Judith Herd becomes first woman Lutheran pastor.

Four Episcopal bishops defy church law, ordain 11 women priests; Rev. Harold S. Jones is consecrated Episcopal bishop of South Dakota, the first Sioux Indian bishop; Rt. Rev. Paul Moore Jr. becomes Episcopal bishop of New York.

Harold B. Lee heads the Mormon Church on the death of Joseph Fielding Smith.

ART/MUSIC

Elliott Carter composes *String Quartet #3.*

1972

SONGS (popular): "Alone Again," "Baby, Don't Get Hooked on Me," "The Candy Man," "I Can See Clearly Now," "Lean on Me," "Song Sung Blue," "Without You."

DEATHS Ferde Grofé and Rudolf Friml, composers; Howard Barlow, conductor; Mahalia Jackson, gospel singer.

LITERATURE/ JOURNALISM

Supreme Court rules that journalists have no right to withhold confidential information from grand juries.

Gloria Steinem founds *Ms* magazine.

BOOKS *The Optimist's Daughter* by Eudora Welty, *Chimera* by John Barth, *Up Country* (poetry) by Maxine Kumin, *The Ward* by Irving Wallace, *The Blue Knight* by Joseph Wambaugh.

DEATHS Four poets: John Berryman, Ezra Pound, Marianne Moore, and Mark Van Doren; reporters: Walter Winchell, Louella Parsons, and Gabriel Heatter; Edmund Wilson, *New Yorker* critic and author; Walter van Tilburg Clark, author.

ENTERTAINMENT

PLAYS Ben Vereen stars in *Pippin*; Jack Albertson and Sam Levene in *The Sunshine Boys*; Jason Miller writes *That Championship Season*; Jim Jacobs and Warren Casey, *Grease*.

MOVIES *The Godfather* with Marlon Brando, *Cabaret* with Liza Minelli, *Lady Sings the Blues* with Diana Ross, *The Poseidon Adventure* with Gene Hackman, *The Candidate* with Robert Redford.

New television shows include *Maude* with Bea Arthur, *M*A*S*H* with Alan Alda, *Sanford and Son* with Redd Foxx, *The Waltons*, and *Bob Newhart*.

President Richard Nixon walks through the Forbidden City, Peking, China, with Chinese officials. At left in foreground is Wang Hsing-ting, deputy chief of the General Staff of the People's Liberation Army; at right foreground is Yeh Chien-ying, chief of the Military Affairs Committee. UPI/Corbis-Bettmann

SPORTS

Winter Olympics are held in Sapporo, Japan; U.S. wins 3 gold medals; Summer Games are held in Munich, Germany, with U.S. winning 33 golds, including 7 by swimmer Mark Spitz.

New York State Athletic Commission approves letting women journalists into dressing rooms at boxing, wrestling matches when men are "properly attired."

Cincinnati pro basketball team moves to Kansas City, Mo.

John Wooten is first to be enshrined in Basketball Hall of Fame as a player (Purdue 1960) and coach (UCLA).

Roberto Clemente of Pittsburgh Pirates gets his 3,000th hit.

WINNERS *Auto racing*—Mark Donohue, Indianapolis 500; Richard Petty, NASCAR; *Baseball*—Oakland Athletics, World Series; *Basketball*—Maryland, NIT; UCLA, NCAA (for sixth consecutive year); Immaculata, first AIAW title; *Bowling*—Johnny Guenther, PBA title; *Boxing*—Joe Frazier, heavyweight; Roberto Duran, lightweight; Enrique Pinder, bantamweight; *Chess*—Bobby Fischer, first American to win world title; *Figure skating*—Janet Lynn, U.S. women's title; Ken Shelley, U.S. men's;

Football (bowls)—Stanford, Rose; Nebraska, Orange; Oklahoma, Sugar; Penn State, Cotton; Miami, Super Bowl VI; *Golf*—U.S., Ryder Cup; Jack Nicklaus, U.S. Open and Masters; Gary Player, PGA; Susie M. Berning, U.S. Women's Open; Kathy Ahem, LPGA; *Harness racing*—Super Bowl, Hambletonian; *Hockey*—Boston, Stanley Cup; *Horse racing*—Riva Ridge, Kentucky Derby and Belmont Stakes; Bee Bee Bee, Preakness Stakes; *Soccer*—New York Cosmos, North American League; *Tennis*—U.S., Davis Cup; Ilie Nastase, U.S. Open; Billie Jean King, U.S. Open (women).

DEATHS Gil Hodges, baseball player and manager; Roberto Clemente, baseball player, in plane crash; Jackie Robinson, first African American major-league baseball player; Nat Fleischer, founder and editor, *Ring Magazine* (1922–1972).

MISCELLANEOUS

Eastern Airlines plane crashes on approach to Miami Airport; 101 die.

Tropical Storm Agnes hits U.S. from Florida to New York in nine-day period, kills 177, causes $3 billion damage.

Flash flood in Rapid City, S. Dak., causes 237 deaths, $160 million damage; dam at Buffalo Creek, W. Va., collapses; 118 die.

1973

INTERNATIONAL

VIETNAM WAR U.S., South and North Vietnam sign cease-fire (January 27), end Vietnam War.

Arab oil producers reduce exports to U.S. and other pro-Israel nations by 5% (October 17); Saudi Arabia reduces exports 10% (October 18); Mideast nations ban all exports (October 19); Iraq nationalizes Exxon and Mobil oil properties.

U.S. and Cuba sign treaty, calls for extradition or punishment of air pirates.

Ambassador Cleo A. Noel Jr. and Chargé d'Af-

faires George C. Moore are killed by Palestinian guerrillas in Khartoum, Sudan.

U.S. and China agree to set up in each country permanent liaison offices.

NATIONAL

WATERGATE Senate establishes Select Committee headed by Sen. Sam Ervin (February 7); Archibald Cox is named special prosecutor (April 17); three top presidential aides—H. R. Haldeman, John Ehrlichmann, and John W. Dean—and Attorney General Richard Kleindienst resign

1973

Washington Post reporters Bob Woodward (left) and Carl Bernstein uncover the "Watergate" scandal. UPI/Corbis-Bettmann

(April 30); Senate committee holds nationally televised hearings (May 17); Court of Appeals orders President Richard M. Nixon to turn over Watergate tapes to Judge John Sirica (October 14); President orders Special Prosecutor Cox fired (October 20); Attorney General Elliot Richardson resigns rather than fire Cox; Deputy William Ruckelshaus is fired for refusing to fire Cox; Leon Jaworski is named special prosecutor (November 1).

Vice President Spiro T. Agnew resigns in wake of a tax scandal (October 10), is succeeded by Rep. Gerald R. Ford of Michigan.

Secretary of State Henry Kissinger shares Nobel Peace Prize with Le Duc Tho of North Vietnam.

Military draft ends.

Price control on gas, oil, and refinery products is reimposed; government lifts price controls on automobile industry.

Supreme Court in *Roe v. Wade* rules that a state may not prevent a woman from having an abortion in the first six months of pregnancy.

Confrontation between American Indian Move-

ment (AIM) protesters and white authorities over a murder case leads to AIM takeover of village of Wounded Knee, S. Dak.; two activists are killed during 71-day standoff, ends when activist leaders sign a "peace pact" with the government.

Atlanta becomes first major Southern city to elect an African American mayor, Maynard Jackson.

DEATHS Former President Lyndon B. Johnson (1963–1969); Jeannette Rankin of Montana, first woman member of Congress, voted against U.S. entry in both World Wars.

BUSINESS/INDUSTRY/INVENTIONS

Congress and the president approve construction of trans-Alaska pipeline.

Federal Trade Commission charges eight major companies with conspiring for 23 years to monopolize petroleum refining.

Wassily Leontief is awarded Nobel Prize in economics for development of input-output method.

DEATHS William Benton, advertising executive, founder, Voice of America; Alfred C. Fuller, of brush fame; Eddie Rickenbacker, World War I

436 • THE AMERICAN YEARS

flying ace, Eastern Airlines president (1938–1963).

TRANSPORTATION

Volvo announces it will build $100 million assembly plant in Chesapeake, Va.

Grand Central Station in New York City closes from 1:30 to 5:30 A.M.; new passenger terminal at remodeled Newark (N.J.) Airport opens.

Dallas–Ft. Worth Airport opens.

Largest American merchant ship is christened at Brooklyn (N.Y.) Navy Yard; first Soviet passenger ship in 25 years arrives in New York.

SCIENCE/MEDICINE

Ivar Giaever shares Nobel Prize in physics with Lee Esaki of Japan and Brian Josephson of Great Britain for work on semiconductors and superconductors.

EDUCATION

Supreme Court upholds lower court ruling that Richmond, Va., desegregation plan is unconstitutional; rules Denver's school districting unconstitutional because it represents state-imposed segregation; strikes down as unconstitutional New York State financial assistance to private and parochial schools.

Student Loan Marketing Assn. (Sallie Mae) is created to support $4.5 billion federal student-loan program.

DEATH Ada Louise Comstock, president, Radcliffe College (1923–1943).

RELIGION

Rev. Lawrence W. Bottoms is named moderator of Presbyterian Church of the U.S., first African American leader in Southern denomination in 113 years.

Members of the American Indian Movement stand guard outside the Sacred Heart Catholic Church in Wounded Knee, S. Dak., on March 3, 1973, during negotiations with federal officials. UPI/CORBIS-BETTMANN

1973

Judge M. A. Haywood of Washington, D.C., is named moderator of United Church of Christ general synod, first African American woman named to leadership position in U.S. biracial denomination.

Spencer W. Kimball is named president of Mormon Church.

Conservatives in Presbyterian Church of the U.S. form National Presbyterian Church.

Catholic Archbishop Humberto S. Medeiros of Boston is elevated to cardinal.

DEATH Maurice N. Eisendrath, president, Union of American Hebrew Congregations (1946–1973).

ART/MUSIC

Donald Martino composes *Notturno*.

SONGS (popular): "Send in the Clowns," "Big Bad Leroy Brown," "Delta Dawn," "Killing Me Softly with His Song," "Midnight Train to Georgia," "My Love," "Tie a Yellow Ribbon Round the Old Oak Tree," "Keep on Truckin'."

DEATHS Jim Croce, rock star, in plane crash; Gene Krupa, drummer and band leader; Lauritz Melchior, opera tenor; Edward Steichen, pioneer photographer; Vaughn Monroe, singer and orchestra leader.

LITERATURE/JOURNALISM

BOOKS *Burr* by Gore Vidal, *Fear of Flying* by Erica Jong, *Gravity's Rainbow* by Thomas Pynchon, *The Dolphin* (poetry) by Robert Lowell, *The Last of the Southern Girls* by Willie Morris.

DEATHS Poets W. H. Auden and Conrad Aiken; Cartoonists Chic Young ("Blondie") and Walter C. Kelly ("Pogo"); Pearl S. Buck, author.

ENTERTAINMENT

PLAYS Stephen Sondheim writes *A Little Night Music*; Lanford Wilson, *Hot-L Baltimore*.

MOVIES *The Way We Were* with Barbra Streisand, *The Exorcist* with Ellen Burstyn, *The Sting* with Paul Newman and Robert Redford, *Serpico* with Al Pacino.

New television shows are *Kojak* with Telly Savalas, *Barnaby Jones* with Buddy Ebsen.

DEATH John Ford, screen director.

SPORTS

American League approves trial of designated hitter; Ron Blumberg of New York Yankees is first designated hitter; he walks with bases loaded.

Baseball players and owners sign three-year contract, end spring training boycott; NBA and players sign first comprehensive contract, which provides $20,000 minimum annual salary, pensions.

National Hockey League Hall of Fame opens in Eveleth, Minn.

O. J. Simpson of Buffalo sets football season rushing record of 2,003 yards.

WINNERS *Auto racing*—Gordon Johncock, Indianapolis 500; Benny Parsons, NASCAR; *Baseball*—Oakland Athletics, World Series; *Basketball*—Virginia Tech, NIT; UCLA, NCAA; Immaculata, AIAW; New York, NBA; *Bowling*—Earl Anthony, PBA; *Boxing*—George Foreman, heavyweight; *Figure skating*—Janet Lynn, U.S. women; Gordon McKellen Jr., U.S. men; *Football (bowls)*—Southern California, Rose; Nebraska, Orange; Oklahoma, Sugar; Texas, Cotton; Miami, Super Bowl VII; *Golf*—Johnny Miller, U.S. Open; Jack Nicklaus, PGA; Tommy Aaron, Masters; Susie M. Berning, U.S. Women's Open; Mary Mills, LPGA; *Harness racing*—Firth, Hambletonian; *Hockey*—Montreal, Stanley Cup; *Horse racing*—Secretariat, ninth Triple Crown winner, takes the Kentucky Derby, Preakness Stakes, and Belmont Stakes; *Tennis*—Australia, Davis Cup; John Newcombe, U.S. Open; Margaret Court, U.S. Open (women).

MISCELLANEOUS

Delta jetliner crashes in fog at Boston's Logan Airport; 89 die.

Mississippi River floods cause $322 million damage, leave 35,000 homeless.

1974

INTERNATIONAL

President Gerald R. Ford becomes first incumbent president to visit Japan, confers with leaders; goes to Vladivostok where he and Russian leader Leonid Brezhnev set framework for more-comprehensive agreement on offensive nuclear arms (November 24); earlier, President Richard M. Nixon signed treaty with Russia that limited underground testing of nuclear weapons.

Ambassador to Cyprus, Rodger P. Davies, is killed by a sniper in Nicosia.

NATIONAL

WATERGATE Watergate scandal ends with resignation of President Nixon (August 9); he is succeeded by Vice President Ford; vice presidency is filled by Nelson A. Rockefeller (December 19). Before these events, former Attorney General John N. Mitchell and presidential aides John Erlichmann and H. R. Haldeman were found guilty of coverup charges (January 1); House of Representatives authorized an impeachment investigation (February 6), voted three articles of impeachment (July 27–30) and without debate approved impeachment articles (412–3) (August 20); Supreme Court ruled (July 24) that President Nixon must turn over 64 tapes to Watergate prosecutor.

President Ford grants an unconditional pardon to former President Nixon (September 8) for offenses he "committed or may have committed" while in office.

Most Arab oil producing countries lift ban on shipments to U.S. (March 18) after five-month embargo; wage and price controls end.

Supreme Court rules that women must receive equal pay for equal work.

Violent protests in Boston as white students opposed to busing for school desegregation attack African American students (September–November).

Cost of first-class postage increases to 10 cents; soon thereafter, to 13 cents.

Life expectancy in U.S. rises to 71.3 years; 10.3% of population (21.8 million) is older than 65.

Expo '74 held in Spokane, Wash.

DEATHS Charles A. Lindbergh, first to fly solo nonstop across Atlantic (1927); Earl Warren, Supreme Court chief justice (1953–1969); Gen. Carl Spaatz, first Air Force chief of staff; Gen. Creighton Abrams, commanding general in Vietnam War (1968–1972).

BUSINESS/INDUSTRY/INVENTIONS

Work begins on trans-Alaska oil pipeline.

Justice Department files civil antitrust suit against ATT.

Duke Ellington (1889–1974), American composer and arranger, in a photograph dating from circa 1910. CORBIS-BETTMANN

President Richard Nixon goes before television cameras to announce his resignation. UPI/CORBIS-BETTMANN

Franklin National Bank of New York City fails, largest U.S. bank failure.

Two-stage coal gasification process is patented; can also be used for producing synthetic oil and gasoline.

Minimum wage rises to $2 an hour (May 1).

Sears Tower in Chicago, 110 stories, is completed; world's tallest building.

DEATHS H(aroldson) H. Hunt, oil magnate; Vannevar Bush, builder of first analog computer; Edwin G. Nourse, first chairman, Council of Economic Advisers; Alexander P. De Seversky, aeronautical engineer and inventor.

TRANSPORTATION

President Nixon signs law, sets highway speed limit at 55 miles per hour.

Union Pacific and Rock Island railroads merger is approved.

Supreme Court rules that cities can levy high taxes on downtown parking to try to reduce congestion.

Commodore Barry Bridge at Chester, Pa., opens.

SCIENCE/MEDICINE

Paul J. Flory is awarded Nobel Prize in chemistry for developing analytic methods to study properties, architecture of long chain molecules; Albert Claude and George E. Palade share prize in physiology/medicine for contributions to understanding inner workings of living cells.

Spacecraft *Pioneer II* passes planet Jupiter on way to Saturn.

DEATH Selman A. Waksman, codiscoverer of streptomycin.

EDUCATION

Supreme Court rules that female teachers cannot be forced to take maternity leave before last weeks of pregnancy; also rules that states may provide funds for nonsectarian purposes to church-affiliated schools.

Federal district court rules that Boston's schools are racially segregated; orders dismantling of dual system.

RELIGION

Christian Science Church Center opens in Boston.

Bishop John M. Alin is installed as presiding bishop of Episcopal Church; Harold L. Wright becomes first African American Episcopal bishop in New York diocese.

ART/MUSIC

Hirschhorn Museum in Washington, D.C., opens.

Dominick Argento composes *From the Diary of Virginia Woolf*.

SONGS (popular): "Annie's Song," "Don't Let the Sun Go Down on Me," "Having My Baby," "My Melody of Love," "Seasons in the Sun," "The Streak," "Time in a Bottle."

DEATHS Harry Ruby, composer ("Three Little Words"); Duke Ellington, jazz pianist and composer; Johnny Mercer, composer.

LITERATURE/JOURNALISM

BOOKS *The Power Broker* by Robert A. Caro; *Jaws*

by Peter Benchley, *Centennial* by James A. Michener, *The Fan Club* by Irving Wallace, *The Rhinemann Exchange* by Robert Ludlum.

DEATHS Francis M. Flynn, publisher, *New York Daily News* (1947–1973); Abel Green, editor, *Variety*; Chet Huntley of Huntley-Brinkley television news team; Otto Soglow, cartoonist ("The Little King"); Walter Lippmann, author and columnist.

ENTERTAINMENT

PLAYS Edward Albee writes *Seascape*; Bob Randall, *The Magic Show*.

MOVIES *The Towering Inferno* with Paul Newman, *Blazing Saddles* with Gene Wilder, *The Godfather, Part II* with Al Pacino, *The Great Gatsby* with Robert Redford, *Harry and Tonto* with Art Carney.

New television shows include *The Tony Orlando and Dawn Show*, *The Rockford Files* with James Garner, *Little House on the Prairie* with Michael Landon, *Happy Days* with Henry Winkler.

DEATHS Three comedians die: Jack Benny, Bud Abbott of Abbott and Costello, and Charlie Weaver; Samuel Goldwyn, movie producer; Charles Boyer, screen actor; Ed Sullivan, variety-show master of ceremonies; Tex Ritter, singer and Western screen actor; Katharine Cornell, actress.

SPORTS

Henry Aaron of Atlanta Braves hits 715th home run (April 8), breaks 39-year-old record of 714 set by Babe Ruth.

Frank Robinson becomes first African American major-league baseball manager (Cleveland Indians).

President Ford dedicates Golf Hall of Fame in Pinehurst, N.C.

Baseball Commissioner Bowie Kuhn suspends George Steinbrenner of New York Yankees for two years because of his federal conviction for illegal political contributions.

Consecutive winning streak of UCLA basketball team ends at 88 by Notre Dame.

New Jersey Superior Court rules that girls must be permitted to play in Little League baseball games.

Al Kaline of Detroit Tigers gets his 3,000th base hit; Lou Brock of St. Louis Cardinals steals 700th base, ends season with record 118.

Tom Waldrop sets world indoor-mile record of 3 minutes, 55 seconds.

WINNERS *Auto racing*—Johnny Rutherford, Indianapolis 500; Richard Petty, NASCAR; *Baseball*—Oakland Athletics, World Series; *Basketball*—Purdue, NIT; North Carolina State, NCAA; Immaculata, AIAW; Boston, NBA; *Bowling*—Earl Anthony, PBA; *Boxing*—Muhammad Ali, heavyweight; *Figure skating*—Gordon McKeller, U.S. men's; Dorothy Hamill, U.S. women's; *Football (bowls)*—Ohio State, Rose; Penn State, Orange; Notre Dame, Sugar; Nebraska, Cotton; Miami, Super Bowl VIII; *Golf*—Hale Irwin, U.S. Open; Lee Trevino, PGA; Gary Player, Masters; Sandra Haynie, U.S. Women's Open and LPGA; *Harness racing*—Christopher T., Hambletonian; *Hockey*—Philadelphia, Stanley Cup; *Horse racing*—Cannonade, Kentucky Derby; Little Current, Preakness Stakes and Belmont Stakes; *Tennis*—Jimmy Connors, U.S. Open (men); Billie Jean King, U.S. Open (women); *Yachting*—U.S. yacht *Courageous* retains America's Cup.

MISCELLANEOUS

Thirteen states are hit by 148 tornadoes in 24 hours (April 3–4); the storms kill 315, injure 600, destroy or damage 27,000 homes.

David Kunst is first to circle the Earth on foot, returns to Waseca, Minn., after 14,500 miles in 4 years, 3 months, 16 days.

"Streaking" craze sweeps the nation.

1975

INTERNATIONAL

VIETNAM WAR Saigon is shelled; remaining U.S. military evacuated (April 27); South Vietnam announces its unconditional surrender to Vietcong (April 30).

All-out attack results in recovery of U.S. ship *Mayaguez*, which Cambodian forces captured (May 14).

U.S. vetoes admission of North and South Vietnam to U.N.

NATIONAL

President Gerald R. Ford is unharmed in two apparent assassination attempts; Secret Service agent grabs pistol aimed at the president in Sacramento (September 5), and a political activist fires at him and misses in San Francisco (September 22).

Ohio Gov. John Rhodes and 27 of the National Guard are exonerated in 1970 Kent State shooting in which four students were killed.

Supreme Court rules that federal government has exclusive rights to oil and gas resources beyond 3-mile limit in Atlantic Ocean.

Nuclear Regulatory Agency is established, takes over functions of Atomic Energy Commission.

First-class postage rises to 13 cents an ounce (December 31).

U.S. military academies open to women.

DEATH Gen. Anthony J. McAuliffe, commander at Bastogne, remembered for answer ("Nuts!") to German surrender demand.

BUSINESS/INDUSTRY/INVENTIONS

Automobile companies give rebates to stimulate sales.

Minimum wage is raised to $2.10 an hour for nonfarmworkers, $1.80 for farmworkers (January 1).

Tjalling Koopmans shares Nobel Prize in economics with Leonid Kantrovich of U.S.S.R. for contributions to theory of "optimum allocation of resources."

Jimmy Hoffa, former Teamsters Union president, mysteriously disappears.

Altair, a microcomputer kit that takes hobbyists 40 or more hours to assemble, appears on the cover of *Popular Electronics*.

TRANSPORTATION

Plan to revitalize six bankrupt northeastern and midwestern railroads is announced.

Staten Island ferry fare, which had been 5 cents since 1898, is raised to 25 cents.

SCIENCE/MEDICINE

L. James Rainwater shares Nobel Prize in physics with Ben Mottelson and Aage Bohr of Denmark for discovery of connection between collective and particle motion in atomic nucleus; David Baltimore, Renato Dulbeco, and Howard Temin share prize in physiology/medicine for discoveries of interaction between tumor viruses and genetic cell material.

Center for Disease Control is established.

U.S. and Russian spacecraft link up 140 miles above Earth, exchange visits.

DEATHS Detlev W. Bronk, founder of biophysics; John R. Dunning, first to demonstrate fission of uranium 235.

EDUCATION

Supreme Court rules that school pupils cannot be suspended without notice of charges against them and a chance to be heard; rules that school officials who discipline pupils unfairly cannot claim ignorance of pupils' rights if sued; rules that states may permit teachers to spank misbehaving students.

April 1975 in Saigon, South Vietnam. An Air America helicopter crewman helps evacuees up the ladder on top of a Saigon building. UPI/CORBIS-BETTMANN

Federal district court orders Detroit to begin school integration.

Louisville and Jefferson County, Ky., becomes first metropolitan area to achieve racial balance in public schools by cross-district busing.

DEATH Robert G. Sproul, president of University of California (1930–1958).

RELIGION

Elizabeth Ann Seton is canonized, first U.S.-born Catholic saint (September 24).

Internal Revenue Service announces that tax exemption will be denied to church-affiliated schools that refuse to accept children of all racial and ethnic groups.

ART/MUSIC

Beverly Sills debuts with Metropolitan Opera.

Ned Rorem composes "Air Music."

SONGS (popular): "Have You Never Been Mellow," "I'm Sorry," "Love Will Keep Us Together," "Mandy," "Rhinestone Cowboy," "Thank God, I'm a Country Boy," "Another Somebody Done Somebody Wrong Song."

DEATHS Thomas Hart Benton, artist of realistic portraits; Richard Tucker, opera tenor; "Cannonball" Adderly, jazz saxophonist; Vincent Lopez, pianist and orchestra leader.

LITERATURE/JOURNALISM

BOOKS *Humboldt's Gift* by Saul Bellow, *Shogun* by

James D. Clavell, *Ragtime* by E. L. Doctorow, *Looking for Mr. Goodbar* by Judith L. Rossner, *In the Beginning* by Chaim Potok.

DEATHS Authors Thornton Wilder, P. G. Wodehouse, and Rex Stout; George Baker, cartoonist.

ENTERTAINMENT

A Chorus Line is written by Michael Bennett, Marvin Hamlisch, and others; F. Murray Abraham stars in *The Ritz*; Ellen Burstyn in *Same Time, Next Year*.

MOVIES *One Flew over the Cuckoo's Nest* with Jack Nicholson, *Shampoo* with Warren Beatty, *The Sunshine Boys* with George Burns and Walter Matthau, *Jaws* with Roy Scheider and Richard Dreyfuss.

New television shows include *Welcome Back, Kotter* with John Travolta, *Wheel of Fortune*, *One Day at a Time* with Bonnie Franklin, *The Jeffersons* with Sherman Hemsley, *Barney Miller* with Hal Linden.

DEATHS Fredric March, screen actor; Rod Serling, television playwright (*Twilight Zone*).

SPORTS

Bowie Kuhn is reelected baseball commissioner; former postmaster Lawrence R. O'Brien is named NBA commissioner.

Bobby Fischer forfeits world chess championship after rule changes that he requests for a match are refused.

Three sports facilities are completed: New Orleans Superdome; Pontiac (Mich.) Metropolitan Stadium, home of Detroit Lions; Meadowlands Harness Track in the sports complex near Hackensack, N.J.

World Football League disbands after two years.

WINNERS *Auto racing* — Bobby Unser, Indianapolis 500; Richard Petty, NASCAR; *Baseball* — Cincinnati Reds, World Series; *Basketball* — Princeton, NIT; UCLA, NCAA; Golden State, NBA; *Bowling* — Earl Anthony, PBA; *Boxing* — Muhammad Ali, heavyweight; Victor Galindez, light heavyweight; Carlos Monzon, middleweight; *Figure skating* — Gordon McKellen Jr., U.S. men; Dorothy Hamill, U.S. women; *Football* (bowls) — Southern California, Rose; Notre Dame, Orange; Nebraska, Sugar; Penn State, Cotton; Pittsburgh, Super Bowl IX; *Golf* — Lou Graham, U.S. Open; Jack Nicklaus, PGA and Masters; Sandra Palmer, U.S. Women's Open; Kathy Whitworth, LPGA; *Harness racing* — Bonefish, Hambletonian; *Hockey* — Philadelphia, Stanley Cup; *Horse racing* — Foolish Pleasure, Kentucky Derby; Master Derby, Preakness Stakes; Avatar, Belmont Stakes; *Tennis* — Manuel Orantes, U.S. Open (men); Chris Evert, U.S. Open (women).

DEATHS Jockey Alvaro Pineda in accident at starting gate; Steve Prefontaine, runner, in car crash; Jim Londos, wrestler; Casey Stengel, baseball player and manager; Avery Brundage, leader in national, international amateur athletics.

MISCELLANEOUS

Air Force plane carrying Vietnamese children crashes near Saigon, 172 are killed; Eastern Boeing 727 crashes in storm at Kennedy Airport, 113 die.

INTERNATIONAL

Ambassador to Lebanon Francis E. Maloy Jr. and an aide are killed by an unidentified man.

Cuban Premier Fidel Castro cancels antihijacking pact with U.S., charges U.S. complicity in crash of a Cuban airliner.

1976

NATIONAL

Democrat Jimmy Carter is elected president, defeats President Gerald R. Ford; Carter receives 40,828,929 popular and 297 electoral votes against 39,149,940 popular and 240 electoral for Ford.

Nation celebrates 200th anniversary with a "tall

ships" parade in New York Harbor, presidential visit to Independence Hall in Philadelphia, and other events throughout the country.

Supreme Court in *Gregg v. Georgia* holds that death penalty in first-degree murder cases is not in and of itself cruel and unusual punishment.

Pesticides containing mercury are banned.

Supreme Court rules that the president has right to impose fees on imported oil.

Homestead Act of 1862 is repealed for all states except Alaska because there no longer is cultivable public land available.

DEATHS James A. Farley, former postmaster general (1933–1940); Richard J. Daley, Chicago mayor (1955–1976); Perle Mesta, Washington hostess (model for play *Call Me Madam*); Howard R. Hughes, reclusive millionaire.

BUSINESS/INDUSTRY/ INVENTIONS

Milton Friedman is awarded Nobel Prize in economics for work in consumption analysis, monetary history and theory.

Minimum wage rises to $2.30 an hour (January 1).

Stephen G. Wozniak and Steven P. Jobs introduce Apple I desktop computer.

DEATHS William Zeckendorf, real-estate developer; J. Paul Getty, oil industry leader.

TRANSPORTATION

Transportation Department postpones mandatory air bags in all cars for two years.

Approval is given for $2.4 million aid to improve commuter rail service between Washington

(D.C.), New York, and Boston.

Washington, D.C., subway service begins.

Concorde SST service from Paris and London to Washington begins.

Astronaut Frank Borman is named chairman of Eastern Air Lines.

The largest birthday cake ever made was created by Kitchens of Sara Lee as a bicentennial gift to Philadelphia. Fifty feet high and forty-two feet wide at its base, the eight-tiered cake is decorated with symbols of American history handmade with icings and confections. © MARTIN ADLER LEVICK

SCIENCE/MEDICINE

Burton Richter and Samuel C. C. Ting share Nobel Prize in physics for discoveries of new type of elementary particle (PSI or J); William N. Lipscomb is awarded prize in chemistry for studies on structure of boranes; Baruch S. Blumberg and Daniel C. Gajdusek share prize in physiology/medicine for discoveries of new mechanisms for origin and dissemination of infectious diseases.

Flu-shot program is launched (March 24), halts after 58 persons suffered paralysis from shots.

Unmanned spacecraft successfully lands on Mars (July 20).

A mysterious "Legionnaire's disease" kills 29 persons who attended convention in Philadelphia.

DEATH Morris Fishbein, editor, *AMA Journal* (1924–1949).

EDUCATION

Supreme Court rules that courts cannot require school authorities to readjust attendance zones each year to keep up with population shifts; also rules that private nonsectarian schools cannot exclude African American children because of race.

U.S. Appeals Court upholds court-ordered integration of Boston schools.

RELIGION

International Eucharistic Congress is held in Philadelphia.

Episcopal Church bishops and deputies' vote to permit ordination of women as priests and bishops is approved by general convention.

Thelma D. Adair is elected moderator of United Presbyterian Church, first African American woman to hold that post.

Catholic Archbishop William W. Baum of Washington, D.C., is elevated to cardinal.

ART/MUSIC

Richard Wernick composes *Visions of Terror and Wonder*.

Christo, the artist, designs *Running Fence*, a 24-mile curtain of fabric along Pacific Coast.

SONGS (popular): "I Write the Songs," "Tonight's the Night," "Disco Lady," "Fifty Ways to Leave Your Lover," "If You Leave Me Now."

DEATHS Lily Pons, opera soprano; Alexander Calder, sculptor; Eddie Condon, Dixieland band leader; painters Man Ray, surrealist, and Mark Tobey.

LITERATURE/JOURNALISM

Saul Bellow is awarded Nobel Prize in literature.

BOOKS *Beautiful Swimmers* by William W. Warner, *The Deep* by Peter Benchley, *Roots* by Alex Haley, *The Boys from Brazil* by Ira Levin, *Trinity* by Leon Uris, *The Zodiac* (poetry) by James Dickey, *Collected Poems* by W. H. Auden, *Slapstick* by Kurt Vonnegut.

DEATHS Samuel Eliot Morison, historian; Munro Leaf, author and illustrator (*Ferdinand*, *Wee Gillis*); Arnold Gingrich, founder and publisher, *Esquire* magazine; Mary Margaret McBride, radio commentator.

ENTERTAINMENT

PLAYS Jules Feiffer writes *Knock, Knock*; David Rabe, *Streamers*.

MOVIES *Network* with Peter Finch, *Rocky* with Sylvester Stallone, *All the President's Men* with Robert Redford, *Marathon Man* with Dustin Hoffman, *Taxi Driver* with Robert DeNiro.

TELEVISION *Wonder Woman* with Lynda Carter, *Laverne and Shirley* with Penny Marshall and Cindy Williams, *Charlie's Angels*, *The Muppets*, and Donny and Marie Osmond.

DEATHS Jo Mielziner, stage designer for 360 Broadway plays; Rosalind Russell, stage and screen actress; Busby Berkeley, stage and screen choreographer; Paul Robeson, singer and actor.

SPORTS

Winter Olympics are held in Innsbruck, Austria; Bill Koch becomes first from U.S. to win medal (silver) in Nordic events; Summer Games are held in Montreal, U.S. wins 34 golds.

NBA's 18 teams merge with four of remaining six teams of American Basketball Assn.

Baseball owners and players agree to change in reserve clause, give players free agency after five years.

New York's Yankee Stadium opens after $70 million renovation.

Dan Ripley sets pole-vault record of 18 feet, 1¼ inches.

U.S. Croquet Assn. is founded.

WINNERS *Auto racing*—Johnny Rutherford, Indianapolis 500; Cale Yarborough, NASCAR; *Baseball*—Cincinnati Reds, World Series; *Basketball*—Kentucky, NIT; Indiana, NCAA; Boston, NBA; *Bowling*—Paul Colwell, PBA; *Boxing*—Muhammad Ali, heavyweight; *Figure skating*—Dorothy Hamill, U.S. and world women's title; Terry Kubicka, U.S. men's; *Football* (bowls)—UCLA, Rose; Oklahoma, Orange; Alabama, Sugar; Arkansas, Cotton; Pittsburgh, Super Bowl X; *Golf*—Jerry Pate, U.S. Open; Dave Stockton, PGA; Ray Floyd, Masters; Jo Anne Carner, U.S. Women's Open; Betty Burfeindt, LPGA; *Harness racing*—Steve Lobell, Hambletonian; *Hockey*—Montreal, Stanley Cup; *Horse racing*—Bold Forbes, Kentucky Derby and Belmont Stakes; Elocutionist, Preakness Stakes; *Tennis*—Jimmy Connors, U.S. Open (men); Chris Evert, U.S. Open (women).

MISCELLANEOUS

Ferry and tanker collide in Mississippi River near Luling, La.; 77 die; *Argo Merchant* runs aground off Nantucket Island, causes 7.7-million-gallon oil spill.

Museum of American Jewish History opens in Philadelphia.

1977

INTERNATIONAL

President Jimmy Carter and Panamanian Gen. Omar Herrera sign treaties to transfer control of Panama Canal to Panama by year 2000.

U.S. and Soviet Russia agree to continue abiding by SALT I treaty to limit strategic arms despite its 1977 expiration date.

U.S. and Canada agree on joint construction of 2,700-mile natural-gas pipeline from Alaska to continental U.S.

U.S. and Great Britain reach new civil aviation agreement.

NATIONAL

President Carter pardons most Vietnam War draft resisters.

Department of Energy is created (August 9) with James R. Schlesinger as first secretary; functions of Federal Power Commission transfer to new department.

President Carter restores gasoline price controls.

DEATHS Alice Paul, women's rights leader; Gen. Lewis B. Hershey, head, Selective Service System (1941–1970).

BUSINESS/INDUSTRY/ INVENTIONS

Oil flows in 800-mile trans-Alaska pipeline, arrives in southern terminus, Valdez.

Five oil companies agree to build and operate Louisiana offshore oil port.

Sales of Apple computers reach $2.5 million; Paul Allen and William Henry Gates III form Microsoft, which will by early 1990s be world's largest manufacturer of personal-computer software, operating systems, and programming languages.

TRANSPORTATION

Supreme Court rules that Concorde SST may land at Kennedy Airport; issues rules limiting Concorde operations in U.S.

Pipe and cigar smoking is banned on all commercial airlines.

Federal court orders imposition of tolls on 13 East River and Harlem River bridges to reduce New York City mass-transit fares.

1977

Francis Scott Key Bridge in Baltimore opens.

First overnight-cruise paddle-wheel steamboat is built in 50 years in U.S.; the 500-passenger *Mississippi Queen* is commissioned.

SCIENCE/MEDICINE

John H. Van Vleck and Philip W. Anderson share Nobel Prize in physics for work basic to development of computer memories; Rosalyn S. Yalow, Roger C. Guillemin, and Andrew V. Schally share prize in physiology/medicine, Yalow for development of radio immunoassay, Schally and Guillemin for research in production of peptide hormones in the brain.

DEATHS Wernher von Braun, rocket scientist; Eli Lilly, pharmaceutical firm head.

EDUCATION

Supreme Court upholds right of federal courts to order citywide school desegregation plans; upholds plan for Detroit.

Health, Education, and Welfare Department issues regulations to prevent discrimination against disabled schoolchildren.

Ernest L. Boyer is named U.S. Education Commissioner.

DEATH Robert M. Hutchins, educator.

RELIGION

John N. Neumann, Catholic bishop of Philadelphia (1852–1860), becomes first U.S. man to be canonized.

Rev. Jacqueline Means becomes first woman ordained an Episcopal priest; some Episcopalians opposed to feminine ordination form Anglican Church of North America.

Supreme Court rules that states may finance counseling for parochial school children on off-school "neutral" sites.

ART/MUSIC

Michael Colgrass composes *Déjà Vu for Percussion and Orchestra.*

SONGS (popular): "Evergreen," "How Deep Is Your Love," "Slip, Slidin' Away," "Southern

The space shuttle Enterprise flies on after separating from its 747 carrier during a test flight in August 1977. NASA

Nights," "You Light Up My Life," "Baby, Come Back."

DEATHS Elvis Presley, singer; Leopold Stokowski, conductor; Bing Crosby, singer and actor; Guy Lombardo, orchestra leader; Ethel Waters, singer and actress; Maria Callas, opera soprano.

LITERATURE/JOURNALISM

BOOKS *The Dragons of Eden* by Carl Sagan, *The Thorn Birds* by Colleen McCullough, *Dreams Die First* by Harold Robbins, *Condominium* by John D. MacDonald, *Falconer* by John Cheever, *Collected Poems* by Howard Nemerov.

DEATHS MacKinlay Kantor, author; Bruce Bliven, editor, *New Republic* (1923–1955).

ENTERTAINMENT

PLAYS Andrea McArdle stars in *Annie,* Judd

Hirsch in *Chapter Two*, Jessica Tandy and Hume Cronyn in *The Gin Game*; Michael Cristofer writes *The Shadow Box*.

MOVIES *Annie Hall* with Diane Keaton; *Close Encounters of the Third Kind* with Richard Dreyfuss; *New York, New York* with Liza Minelli; *Oh, God!* with George Burns; *Smokey and the Bandit* with Burt Reynolds; *Star Wars* with Mark Hamill, Harrison Ford, and Carrie Fisher; *Saturday Night Fever* with John Travolta.

New television shows include the miniseries *Roots*, *The Love Boat* with Gavin McLeod, *Eight Is Enough* with Dick Van Patten, *Chips* with Erik Estrada.

DEATHS Zero (Sam) Mostel, actor; Joan Crawford and Charlie Chaplin, screen actors; Alfred Lunt, actor; Groucho Marx, entertainer and actor.

SPORTS

Reggie Jackson of New York Yankees hits three consecutive home runs on three consecutive pitches against Los Angeles Dodgers in World Series game.

Lou Brock of St. Louis Cardinals breaks Ty Cobb's base-stealing record of 892.

Two baseball stadiums open: King Dome in Seattle and Olympic Stadium in Montreal.

National Hockey League rejects merger with World Hockey League.

Fifteen members of Evansville (Ind.) University basketball squad die in plane crash.

Jockey Steve Cauthen sets record for purses in a year: $6,151,750.

Janet Guthrie becomes first woman to drive in Indianapolis 500 auto race; mechanical problems force her out after 27 laps.

WINNERS *Auto racing*—A. J. Foyt, Indianapolis 500; Cale Yarborough, NASCAR; *Baseball*—New York Yankees, World Series; *Basketball*—St. Bonaventure, NIT; Marquette, NCAA; Portland, NBA; *Bowling*—Tommy Hudson, PBA; *Boxing*—Muhammad Ali, heavyweight; *Figure skating*—Linda Fratianne, U.S. and world women's titles; Charles Tickner, U.S. men's; *Football* (bowls)—Southern California, Rose; Ohio State, Orange; Pittsburgh, Sugar; Houston, Cotton; Oakland, Super Bowl XI; *Golf*—Hubert Green, U.S. Open; Lanny Wadkins, PGA; Tom Watson, Masters; Hollis Stacy, U.S. Women's Open; Chako Higuchi, LPGA; *Harness racing*—Green Speed, Hambletonian; *Hockey*—Montreal, Stanley Cup; *Horse racing*—Seattle Slew becomes 10th Triple Crown winner, wins Kentucky Derby, Preakness Stakes, and Belmont Stakes; *Tennis*—Australia, Davis Cup; Guillermo Vilas, U.S. Open (men); Chris Evert, U.S. Open (women); *Yachting*—U.S. yacht *Courageous* retains America's Cup.

MISCELLANEOUS

Fire in a Southgate, Ky., nightclub kills 164.

A Boeing 747 completes round-the-world flight over both poles in 54 hours, 7 minutes, 12 seconds.

INTERNATIONAL

Senate approves two treaties to turn Panama Canal over to Panama by year 2000 (March 16, April 18); President Jimmy Carter and General Herrera of Panama sign the treaties.

Talks begin at Camp David, Md., between President Carter, Egyptian President Anwar Sadat, and Israeli Prime Minister Menachem Begin to seek Mideast peace.

Solomon Islands become independent; U.S. protectorate since World War II.

NATIONAL

Members of the People's Temple in South America shoot Rep. Leo J. Ryan of California and four other U.S. citizens to death; soon thereafter, 900 members of the Temple are murdered or commit suicide.

Supreme Court refuses to allow firm quota system in affirmative action plans; also rules that New York City can prohibit construction of 53-story office building atop landmark Grand Central Terminal.

President Carter places more than 56 million acres of Alaska federal lands into National Park system.

Cost of first-class postage increases to 15 cents.

DEATH Former Vice President Hubert H. Humphrey (1965–1969).

BUSINESS/INDUSTRY/INVENTIONS

Herbert A. Simon is awarded Nobel Prize in economics for research in decision-making process in economic organizations.

Minimum wage increases to $2.65 an hour (January 1).

Longest U.S. coal strike, nearly four months, ends (March 25).

DEATHS John D. MacArthur, Bankers Life Insurance Co. president; Edward Durrell Stone, architect (Kennedy Center); Charles Eames, furniture designer; William P. Lear, aircraft manufacturer.

TRANSPORTATION

First Volkswagen comes off New Stanton, Pa., assembly line; first U.S. mass production of foreign cars.

Ben Abruzzo, Max Anderson, and Larry Newman make first successful balloon crossing of Atlantic.

Airline industry is freed from federal regulation.

Seaboard Coast Line Industries and Chessie Systems announce merger to form largest U.S. railroad.

SCIENCE/MEDICINE

Arno Penzies and Robert Wilson share Nobel Prize in physics for discovery of cosmic microwave background radiation; Daniel Nathans and Hamilton O. Smith share prize in physiology/medicine for discovery of restriction enzymes.

DEATH Margaret Mead, anthropologist.

EDUCATION

Federal appeals court bars mandatory retirement at 65.

Supreme Court rules that a student dismissed from medical school for low grades and poor performance has little right to challenge the action; also upholds constitutionality of college admissions programs that give special advantage to minorities.

Hannah H. Gray becomes president of University of Chicago, first woman president of a major U.S. university.

Congress passes legislation, makes more than 1 million students from middle-income families eligible for college tuition help.

DEATH James Bryant Conant, Harvard University president (1933–1953).

RELIGION

Reformed Protestant Dutch Church of New York City celebrates its 350th anniversary.

Rev. M. William Howard Jr., at 32, becomes youngest president of National Council of Churches.

ART/MUSIC

Joseph Schwantner composes *Aftertones of Infinity*; Leonard Bernstein, *An American Song Book*.

SONGS (popular): "Three Times a Lady," "With a Little Luck," "You Don't Bring Me Flowers," "You Needed Me," "If I Can't Have You," "Shadow Dancing."

DEATH Norman Rockwell, painter and illustrator.

LITERATURE/JOURNALISM

Isaac Bashevis Singer is awarded Nobel Prize in literature.

Life magazine reappears as a monthly.

BOOKS *Now and Then Poems* by Robert Penn Warren, *The World According to Garp* by John Irving, *Chesapeake* by James A. Michener, *War and Remembrance* by Herman Wouk, *The Coup* by John Updike, *A Distant Mirror* by Barbara Tuchman.

DEATHS Phyllis McGinley, poet; Faith Baldwin, novelist; Bruce Catton, Civil War historian.

ENTERTAINMENT

PLAYS Jack Lemmon stars in *Tribute*, Fats (Thomas) Waller in *Ain't Misbehavin'*, Bob Fosse produces *Dancin'*, Ira Levin writes *Deathtrap*.

MOVIES *The Boys from Brazil* with Gregory Peck, *The Deer Hunter* with Robert DeNiro, *Grease* with John Travolta, *Superman* with Christopher Reeve.

New television shows include *Dallas* with Larry Hagman, *Mork and Mindy* with Robin Williams, *20/20*.

DEATHS Edgar Bergen, ventriloquist; Jack Warner, movie executive.

Norman Rockwell (1894–1978) captured the lives of working-class Americans in his engaging magazine illustrations. This photograph shows him at work in 1950. UPI/CORBIS-BETTMANN

SPORTS

Pete Rose gets his 3,000 hit; ties National League consecutive game-hitting streak (44).

College Football Hall of Fame is dedicated at King's Island, Ohio.

WINNERS *Auto racing* — Al Unser, Indianapolis 500; Cale Yarborough, NASCAR; *Baseball* — New York Yankees, World Series; *Basketball* — Texas, NIT; Kentucky, NCAA; Washington, NBA; *Bowling* — Warren Nelson, PBA; *Boxing* — Muhammad Ali, heavyweight; *Figure skating* — Charles Tickner, U.S., world men's titles; Linda Fratianne, U.S. women's title; *Football* (bowls) — Washington, Rose; Arkansas, Orange; Alabama, Sugar; Notre Dame, Cotton; Dallas, Super Bowl XII; *Golf* — Andy North, U.S. Open; John Mahaffey, PGA; Gary Player, Masters; Hollis Stacy, U.S. Women's Open; Nancy Lopez, LPGA; *Harness racing* — Speedy Somoli, Hambletonian; *Hockey* — Montreal, Stanley Cup; *Horse racing* — Affirmed becomes 11th Triple Crown winner, wins Kentucky Derby, Preakness Stakes, and Belmont Stakes; *Tennis* — U.S., Davis Cup; Jimmy Connors, U.S. Open (men); Chris Evert, U.S. Open (women).

DEATHS Theresa W. Blanchard, figure skater; Ford Frick, baseball commissioner (1961–1965).

MISCELLANEOUS

Boeing 727 and Cessna 172 collide over San Diego, 150 die.

1979

INTERNATIONAL

Iranian militants seize U.S. Embassy in Teheran (November 4), hold 63 U.S. hostages; release African Americans and women hostages (November 19); President Jimmy Carter orders immediate suspension of oil imports from Iran (November 12).

Mob attacks U.S. Embassy in Islamabad, Pakistan, four are killed (November 21).

Muslim extremists in Kabul kill Ambassador Adolph Dubs in Afghanistan.

Egyptian President Anwar Sadat and Israeli Prime Minister Menachem Begin sign peace treaty at White House after Camp David, Md., meetings to seek Middle East peace (March 26).

U.S. and Soviet Union sign SALT II treaty in Vienna to continue limitations on strategic weapons; treaty not ratified because President Carter withdraws it from Senate consideration after Soviets invade Afghanistan.

Panama assumes control of Panama Canal Zone.

China and U.S. resume full diplomatic relations; U.S. severs relations with Taiwan.

NATIONAL

President Carter announces deferral in production of neutron bomb; approves development of MX missile.

Congress approves bill to divide Department of Health, Education, and Welfare into the Department of Health and Human Services and the Department of Education; Patricia R. Harris becomes secretary of HHS; Shirley Hufstedler, of Education.

Congress approves windfall profits tax that is expected to raise $23.2 billion.

Supreme Court rules that police cannot stop motorists at random unless there is some reason to believe motorist is violating the law; upholds voluntary affirmative action programs.

John F. Kennedy Memorial Library is dedicated in Boston.

DEATHS Omar N. Bradley, World War II general; former Vice President Nelson A. Rockefeller (1974–1977); former First Lady Mamie Eisenhower (1953–1961); Jacob L. Devers, World War II general who led southern France invasion; Rexford G. Tugwell, New Deal "brain truster."

BUSINESS/INDUSTRY/INVENTIONS

Worst U.S. nuclear accident occurs at Three Mile Island reactor at Middletown, Pa.; coolant loss and partial core meltdown are symptoms; no deaths or injuries (March 28).

Theodore W. Schultz shares Nobel Prize in economics with Sir Arthur Lewis of Great Britain for work on economic problems of developing nations.

President Carter decontrols price of heavy crude oil.

Minimum wage increases to $2.90 an hour (January).

DEATHS A. Philip Randolph, labor and civil-rights leader; Conrad Hilton, hotel-chain founder; Cyrus S. Eaton, financier, industrialist.

TRANSPORTATION

Lee Iacocca becomes chief executive officer of Chrysler Motors; Congress approves $1.5 billion federal loan to save Chrysler.

Southern Railway Co. is fined $1.9 billion for providing shippers free use of three company-owned resorts.

SCIENCE/MEDICINE

Steven Weinberg and Sheldon L. Glashow share Nobel Prize in physics for theory of unity of electromagnetic and weak atomic forces; Herbert C. Brown shares prize in chemistry with George

Wittig of Germany for development of temporary chemical links for complex molecules; Alan M. Cormack shares prize in physiology/medicine with Godfrey N. Hounsfield of Great Britain for developing the CAT scan.

EDUCATION

House defeats a bill to ban busing as a means of desegregating schools.

RELIGION

Reformed Church of America votes to allow ordination of women as ministers.

Supreme Court rules unconstitutional Tennessee law that bans priests and ministers from running for public office; last such state law.

Pope John Paul II becomes first pope to be received in the White House.

DEATHS Catholic Archbishop James F. McIntyre of Los Angeles; Catholic Bishop Fulton Sheen, popular radio and television personality.

ART/MUSIC

David Del Tredici composes *In Memory of a Summer Day.*

Opera star Beverly Sills becomes music director of New York City Opera Co.

The Icebergs, a painting by Frederick E. Church, is auctioned for $2.5 million, highest price for an American painting.

SONGS (popular): "Sad Eyes," "Please Don't Go," "Rise," "Le Freak," "Reunited," "Too Much Heaven," "No More Tears," "I Will Survive."

DEATHS Stan Kenton, band leader; Dimitri Tiomkin, composer of film scores; Richard Rodgers, composer of musicals; Leonide Massine, ballet dancer and choreographer; Arthur Fiedler, founder and conductor, Boston Pops (1930–1979).

LITERATURE/JOURNALISM

BOOKS *The Executioner's Song* by Norman Mailer, *The Island* by Peter Benchley, *Sophie's Choice* by William Styron, *Broca's Brain* by Carl Sagan, *The Strength of Fields* (poetry) by James Dickey, *Great Days* by Donald Barthelme.

DEATHS Malcolm Muir, founder of *Business Week* and editor-in-chief, *Newsweek* (1937–1961); Al Capp, cartoonist ("Lil Abner"); Allen Tate, poet and critic.

After the 1979 accident, the observation center at the Three-Mile Island nuclear reactor closes. FRANKEN; OWEN/CORBIS

1979

ENTERTAINMENT

PLAYS Neil Simon writes *They're Playing Our Song*; Patti LuPone stars in *Evita*, Angela Lansbury in *Sweeney Todd* with music by Stephen Sondheim; Michael Weller writes *Loose Ends*.

MOVIES *Kramer versus Kramer* with Dustin Hoffman and Meryl Streep, *Apocalypse Now* with Martin Sheen, *The China Syndrome* with Jane Fonda, *Rocky II* with Sylvester Stallone, *Star Trek* with William Shatner.

New television shows include *Knot's Landing*, *Hart to Hart* with Robert Wagner, *The Dukes of Hazard*.

DEATHS Merle Oberon, screen actress; Mary Pickford, early screen star called America's Sweetheart; John Wayne, screen actor; Darryl F. Zanuck, screen producer.

SPORTS

First all-sports cable network, ESPN (Entertainment, Sports Network), debuts on the air (September 9).

Four World Hockey League franchises (New England, Quebec, Winnipeg, Edmonton) merge into National Hockey League.

Stan Barrett sets land speed record of 739.66 miles per hour in a rocket-powered car at Edwards Air Force Base, Calif., is first to break sound barrier on the ground.

Carl Yastrzemski of Boston at 40 and Lou Brock of St. Louis each gets his 3,000th base hit.

Pro Rodeo Hall of Champions and Museum of the American Cowboy opens in Colorado Springs, Colo.

WINNERS *Auto racing* — Rick Mears, Indianapolis 500; Richard Petty, NASCAR; *Baseball* — Pittsburgh Pirates, World Series; *Basketball* — Indiana, NIT; Michigan State, NCAA; Seattle, NBA; *Bowling* — Mike Aulby, PBA; *Boxing* — Larry Holmes, heavyweight; Matthew Franklin, light heavyweight; Vito Antuofermo, middleweight; *Figure skating* — Linda Fratianne, U.S. and world women's titles; Charles Tickner, U.S. men's title; Tai Babilonia and Randy Gardner, world pairs title; *Football* (bowls) — Southern California, Rose; Oklahoma, Orange; Alabama, Sugar; Notre Dame, Cotton; Pittsburgh, Super Bowl XIII; *Golf* — Hale Irwin, U.S. Open; David Graham, PGA; Fuzzy Zoeller, Masters; Jerilyn Britz, U.S. Women's Open; Donna Caponi, LPGA; *Harness racing* — Legend Hanover, Hambletonian; *Hockey* — Montreal, Stanley Cup; *Horse racing* — Spectacular Bid, Kentucky Derby and Preakness Stakes; Coastal, Belmont Stakes; *Tennis* — U.S., Davis Cup; John McEnroe, U.S. Open (men); Tracy Austin, U.S. Open (women).

DEATHS Thurman Munson, New York Yankees catcher, in plane crash; Warren Giles, National (baseball) League president.

MISCELLANEOUS

Hurricane David rakes Caribbean and eastern U.S. for a week; 1,100 die.

American Airlines jet crashes on takeoff at Chicago's O'Hare Airport killing all 272 aboard in worst U.S. air disaster.

1980

INTERNATIONAL

U.S. severs diplomatic relations with Iran as a result of 1979 takeover of U.S. Embassy; military mission to rescue U.S. hostages in Teheran aborts after plane and helicopter collide; Secretary of State Cyrus Vance resigns over the mission.

U.S. and Great Britain announce increase in reciprocal air service; U.S. and China sign first airline service pact since 1949.

NATIONAL

Ronald Reagan, Republican, is elected president, receives 43,889,248 popular and 489 electoral votes to President Jimmy Carter's 35,481,435 popular and 49 electoral votes.

Twentieth census reports national population at 226,542,203.

President Carter orders evacuation of 710 families

Steam and ash rise some 60,000 feet in the air as Mt. St. Helens erupts, July 22, 1980. Mt. Hood is visible in the background. UPI/Corbis-Bettmann

1980

from Love Canal area in Niagara Falls, a former toxic-waste dump.

Nineteen- and twenty-year-old men are required to register for the military draft.

Three Alaska national parks are created: Katmai, Kenai Fjords, and Lake Clark; Mt. McKinley National Park is renamed Denali National Park.

DEATH William O. Douglas, Supreme Court justice (1939–1976).

BUSINESS/INDUSTRY/INVENTIONS

Lawrence R. Klein is awarded Nobel Prize in economics for development, analysis of empirical models of business fluctuations.

Standard Oil Co. (Indiana) agrees to settle price-violations charges by reimbursing $300 million and spending $400 million on new refining and production facilities, and exploration.

Minimum wage increases to $3.10 an hour (January 1).

DEATHS George Meany, AFL–CIO president (1955–1979); John W. Mauchly, co-inventor of electronic computer.

TRANSPORTATION

Honda Motor Co. announces that it will build assembly plant in Ohio; Nissan Motor Co. to build plant near Smyrna, Tenn.

Interstate trucking industry is deregulated.

Two railroad mergers complete: Seaboard Coast Line and Chessie form CSX Inc. and Southern and Norfolk Western.

Interstate Commerce Commission denies railroads the power to set freight rates collectively; Civil Aeronautics Board agrees to give airlines more freedom to change domestic rates without government approval.

Maxie Anderson and son, Kim, complete first nonstop transcontinental balloon flight.

DEATH Jacqueline Cochran, aviator.

SCIENCE/MEDICINE

James W. Cronin and Val L. Fitch share Nobel Prize in physics for research on subatomic particles that reveal that natural laws of symmetry can be violated; Paul Berg and Walter Gilbert share prize in chemistry for development of methods for detailed mapping of DNA structure and function; Barruj Benacerraf and George Snell share prize in physiology/medicine for research in immunology.

Unmanned spacecraft *Voyager I* passes within 77,000 miles of Saturn, sends back data.

Supreme Court rules that biological organisms can be patented.

EDUCATION

Supreme Court rules that unionizing faculty members of private universities are not protected by federal law because they are "managerial" employees.

Federal court rules unconstitutional a Texas law that bars children of illegal aliens from attending public schools.

St. Louis public schools integrate after eight-year program of desegregation.

RELIGION

Rev. Marjorie S. Mathews of Traverse City, Mich., is elected Methodist bishop, is first woman named to ruling hierarchy of a U.S. church.

Mormons travel from around the world to Salt Lake City to observe church's 150th anniversary; convention rejects ordination of women.

Jesuit order forbids Rev. Robert Drinan, only priest in Congress, to run for reelection.

U.S. Appeals Court bars students from holding prayer meetings in public schools.

National Council of Churches calls for major effort to introduce "nonsexist" language in worship.

DEATHS Henry K. Sherrill, Episcopal presiding bishop; Dorothy Day, publisher, *Catholic Worker*.

ART/MUSIC

Former Beatle John Lennon is murdered outside his New York City apartment.

Eugene Ormandy ends 44 years as musical director of Philadelphia Symphony; Mikhail Baryshnikov becomes director of American Ballet Theater.

John Williams, composer and conductor, conducts Boston Pops Orchestra.

SONGS (popular): "Call Me," "Funkytown," "Magic," "Starting Over," "Upside Down," "All the Gold in California," "Coward of the County," "On the Road Again," "Stand by Me."

DEATH André Kostelanetz, conductor.

LITERATURE/JOURNALISM

BOOKS *Loon Lake* by E. L. Doctorow, *The Transit of Venus* by Shirley Hazzard, *Floater* by Calvin Trillin, *The Ring* by Danielle Steel, *China Men* by Maxine H. Kingston.

DEATH Rube Goldberg, cartoonist.

ENTERTAINMENT

PLAYS Mark Meddoff writes *Children of a Lesser God*; *42nd Street* is produced.

MOVIES *Coal Miner's Daughter* with Sissy Spacek; *The Empire Strikes Back* with Harrison Ford, Carrie Fisher, and Mark Hamill; *Raging Bull* with Robert DeNiro; *The Hunter* with Steve McQueen; *Nine to Five* with Dolly Parton; *Urban Cowboy* with John Travolta.

New on television are Barbara Mandrell, Tim Conway, and *Magnum P.I.* with Tom Selleck.

DEATHS Jimmy Durante, entertainer; Steve McQueen, screen actor; Gower Champion, dancer and director; Alfred Hitchcock, director; Mae West, screen and stage actress; Marc Connelly, playwright.

SPORTS

President Carter announces U.S. will not participate in Summer Olympics in Moscow because of Soviet invasion of Afghanistan; Winter Games held in Lake Placid, N.Y.; U.S. wins six gold medals, five of them by speed skater Eric Heiden.

Baseball owners and players sign four-year contract.

Plane crash at Warsaw Airport takes the lives of 22 U.S. amateur-boxing team members.

WINNERS *Auto racing*—Johnny Rutherford, Indianapolis 500; Dale Earnhardt, NASCAR; *Baseball*—Philadelphia Phillies, World Series; *Basketball*—Virginia, NIT; Louisville, NCAA; Los Angeles, NBA; *Bowling*—Johnny Petraglia, PBA; *Boxing*—Larry Holmes, heavyweight; Marvin Hagler, middleweight; Sugar Ray Leonard, welterweight; *Football* (bowls)—Southern California, Rose; Oklahoma, Orange; Alabama, Sugar; Houston, Cotton; Pittsburgh, Super Bowl XIV; *Golf*—Jack Nicklaus, U.S. Open and PGA; Severiano Ballesteros, Masters; Amy Alcott, U.S. Women's Open; Sally Little, LPGA; *Harness racing*—Burgomeister, Hambletonian; *Hockey*—New York Islanders, Stanley Cup; *Horse racing*—Genuine Risk, Kentucky Derby; Codex, Preakness Stakes; Temperance Hill, Belmont Stakes; *Tennis*—John McEnroe, U.S. Open (men); Chris Evert, U.S. Open (women); *Yachting*—U.S. boat *Freedom* retains America's Cup.

DEATH Stella Walsh, Olympic runner.

MISCELLANEOUS

Mt. St. Helens, Washington volcano, erupts for first time in 123 years, kills 26; 46 missing.

Week-long Hurricane Allen hits Caribbean and Texas, 272 die.

Freighter rams Sunshine Skyway Bridge over Tampa (Fla.) Bay, collapses one span; 35 die.

Fire in MGM Grand Hotel in Las Vegas kills 84; fire in Stouffer Inn, Harrison, N.Y., kills 26.

Two days of rioting in New Mexico State Prison results in 33 deaths.

Searchers find wreckage of *Titanic* 12,000 feet deep in Atlantic Ocean, 400 miles southeast of Newfoundland; liner sank on its maiden voyage (April 14, 1912).

1981

INTERNATIONAL

Iran releases 52 U.S. hostages whom they held more than a year in Teheran.

President Ronald Reagan imposes sanctions on Polish military government for its role in cracking down on Polish independent labor unions.

U.S. and Japan reach agreement to reduce Japanese car exports to U.S. for three years.

NATIONAL

President Reagan is shot and seriously wounded in downtown Washington by John W. Hinckley; Press Secretary James Brady, Secret Service Agent Timothy J. McCarthy, and Thomas Delahanty, a Washington police officer, are also wounded (March 30).

Sandra Day O'Connor becomes first woman Supreme Court justice (September 25).

Cost of first-class postage increases to 18 cents (March 22), then to 20 cents (November 1).

Federal Trade Commission drops eight-year-old antitrust suit against eight major oil firms.

Price controls on domestic oil and gasoline are lifted.

Henry G. Cisneros is first Mexican American elected mayor of a U.S. city (San Antonio, Tex.).

Gerald R. Ford Library at Ann Arbor, Mich., is dedicated.

DEATHS Roy Wilkins, NAACP leader; Robert Moses, New York state and city park commissioner, headed 1964–1965 World's Fair.

BUSINESS/INDUSTRY/INVENTIONS

James Tobin is awarded Nobel Prize in economics for analysis of financial markets and their effect on how people spend and save money.

Louisiana Offshore Oil Port opens, costs $100 million.

United Auto Workers rejoins AFL–CIO after 13-year separation.

Minimum wage increases to $3.35 an hour (January 1).

Two mergers of the year are Du Pont with Conoco Oil and Marathon Oil Co. with U.S. Steel.

IBM introduces a personal computer.

DEATH Wallace K. Harrison, architect (U.N. building, Rockefeller Center).

TRANSPORTATION

Ben Abruzzo, Larry Newman, Rocky Aoki, and Ron Clark complete first nonstop balloon crossing of Pacific Ocean (November 12).

Professional Air Traffic Controllers Assn. strikes nationwide (August 3); most of the 12,000 controllers are fired and replaced.

Ford Motor Co. turns down proposal to merge with Chrysler Motors.

Pan American Airways begins New York to Peiping (now Beijing) air service.

SCIENCE/MEDICINE

First manned space shuttle, *Columbia*, orbits earth 36 times (April 12–14); crew is John W. Young and Robert L. Crippen.

Nicolass Bloembergen and Arthur Schaalow share Nobel Prize in physics for work in developing technologies with lasers and other devices to study matter; Roald Hoffmann shares prize in chemistry with Kenichi Fukui of Japan for work in applying theories of quantum mechanics to predict course of chemical reactions; Roger W. Sperry, David H. Hubel, and Tosten N. Wiesel share prize in physiology/medicine for studies of the brain.

DEATH Harold C. Urey, chemist who discovered heavy hydrogen.

EDUCATION

Terrell H. Bell becomes secretary of education.

Former Indiana congressman, John Brademas, is named president of New York University.

RELIGION

Supreme Court upholds constitutionality of religious services by college student organizations in campus buildings.

Representatives from 56 nations attend Christian Science Church convention in Boston.

Christ Episcopal Church in Stevensville, Md., observes its 350th anniversary.

ART/MUSIC

Roger Sessions composes *Concerto for Orchestra*.

SONGS (popular): "Endless Love," "I Love a Rainy Night," "Jessie's Girl," "Rapture," "Elvira," "Games People Play," "Nine to Five."

LITERATURE/JOURNALISM

BOOKS *Rabbit Is Rich* by John Updike, *Zuckerman Unbound* by Philip Roth, *Gorky Park* by Martin C. Smith, *Remembrance* by Danielle Steel.

DEATHS Three publishers die: DeWitt Wallace, cofounder, *Reader's Digest*; John S. Knight, founder of newspaper chain, and Robert F. DeGraff, founder, Pocket Books; authors Anita Loos, William Saroyan, and Will Durant, coauthor of 11-volume *Story of Civilization*; Lowell Thomas, radio news reporter and author.

ENTERTAINMENT

PLAYS Charles Fuller writes *A Soldier's Play*; Beth Henley, *Crimes of the Heart*; Charles Egan and Henry Krieger, *Dreamgirls*; Lanford Wilson, *The Fifth of July*.

MOVIES *Chariots of Fire* with Ben Cross, *On Golden Pond* with Katharine Hepburn and Henry Fonda, *Raiders of the Lost Ark* with Harrison Ford, *Mommie Dearest* with Faye Dunaway.

New television shows include *Dynasty* with John Forsythe and Linda Evans, *Harper Valley PTA* with Barbara Eden, *Hill St. Blues*.

DEATHS Playwrights Mary C. Chase (*Harvey*) and Paul E. Green (*Lost Colony*, *In Abraham's Bosom*); Melvyn Douglas, stage and screen actor.

U.S. hostages, free at last, arrive in Germany from Iran. UPI/CORBIS-BETTMANN

SPORTS

Baseball players strike for seven weeks over free-agent compensation.

Jockey Bill Shoemaker rides his 8,000th winner.

Coach Paul (Bear) Bryant of Alabama sets record (315) for college football wins.

Phil Mahre becomes first American to win World Cup Alpine skiing title.

WINNERS *Auto racing*—Bobby Unser, Indianapolis 500; Darrell Waltrip, NASCAR; *Baseball*—Los Angeles Dodgers, World Series; *Basketball*—Tulsa, NIT; Indiana, NCAA; Boston, NBA; *Bowling*—Earl Anthony, PBA; *Boxing*—Larry Holmes, heavyweight; Sugar Ray Leonard, middleweight; *Figure skating*—Scott Hamilton, U.S. and world men's titles; Elaine Zayak, U.S. women's; *Football (bowls)*—Michigan, Rose; Oklahoma, Orange;

Georgia, Sugar; Alabama, Cotton; Oakland, Super Bowl XV; *Golf*—David Graham, U.S. Open; Larry Nelson, PGA; Tom Watson, Masters; Pat Bradley, U.S. Women's Open; Donna Caponi, LPGA; *Harness racing*—Shiaway St. Pat, Hambletonian; *Horse racing*—Pleasant Colony, Kentucky Derby and Preakness Stakes; Summing, Belmont Stakes; *Tennis*—U.S., Davis Cup; John McEnroe, U.S. Open (men); Tracy Austin, U.S. Open (women).

DEATHS Joe Louis, heavyweight boxing champion (1937–1949); Jim Morgan, bobsled driver, killed in world-title race.

MISCELLANEOUS

Two "skywalks" in Hyatt Regency Hotel in Kansas City, Mo., collapse; 113 are killed.

INTERNATIONAL

U.S. imposes an embargo on Libyan oil imports, curtails export of high technology to Libya because of its support of terrorism.

U.S. and Soviet Union hold arms-control talks in Geneva.

NATIONAL

Equal rights amendment to Constitution fails when three state legislatures do not approve it before the midnight deadline on June 30.

Cyanide-laced Tylenol capsules cause seven deaths in Chicago area; killer is not found; federal regulations are issued (November 4), require tamper-proof packaging for nearly all nonprescription drugs.

Supreme Court rules that individuals may sue state and local officials and agencies directly in federal court; also rules that federal and state officials are entitled to "qualified immunity" from civil damage suits for their official acts and that the president cannot be sued for damages for any official act.

Federal jury finds John W. Hinckley Jr. not guilty in shooting of President Reagan and three others by virtue of insanity.

Secretary of State Alexander M. Haig resigns; George P. Shultz succeeds him.

Supreme Court rules that members of Old Order Amish Church who operate businesses must pay Social Security and unemployment taxes despite their religious belief that paying taxes is a sin.

World's Fair is held in Knoxville, Tenn.

Death penalty is reinstated in New Jersey.

DEATHS Former First Lady Bess Truman (1945–1953); Leon Jaworski, Watergate special prosecutor.

BUSINESS/INDUSTRY/INVENTIONS

George J. Sigler is awarded Nobel Prize in economics for research on industry and role of government regulation in economics.

Justice Department drops antitrust suit against ATT.

Supreme Court rules that seniority systems that outlaw race or sex discrimination are legal.

Cities Service and Occidental Petroleum merge.

Johns Manville Co. files for bankruptcy.

Sales of Apple computers reach $1 billion.

DEATH David Dubinsky, president, International Ladies Garment Workers Union (1932–1966).

TRANSPORTATION

U.S. Appeals Court rules that new cars sold after September 1983 must be equipped with air bags or automatic seat belts; House of Representatives rejects Federal Trade Commission rules that require used-car dealers to disclose major defects in cars to buyers.

A scene from *E.T. The Extra-Terrestrial*, 1982. PHOTOFEST

Ford Motor Co. workers accept contract that trades wages and benefits for increased job security.

U.S. Appeals Court upholds government decision to decertify striking Professional Air Traffic Controllers Organization.

Intercity bus industry is freed from many government regulations.

Braniff Airways suspends all operations (May 12), files for bankruptcy; is first airline to do so.

Congress approves 5-cents-per-gallon tax increase and higher taxes for heavy trucks.

Missouri Pacific, Western Pacific, and Union Pacific railroads merge.

SCIENCE/MEDICINE

Kenneth G. Wilson is awarded Nobel Prize in physics for his method of analyzing basic changes in matter under influence of pressure and temperature.

First "permanent" artificial heart is implanted in a human being, 61-year-old Barney Clark, at University of Utah Medical Center; he lives about three months.

Centers for Disease Control terms AIDS, disease that has spread to 24 states, an epidemic; initially disease spreads predominantly among young homosexual men.

Space shuttle completes nine-day mission, makes numerous scientific studies; June flight includes first U.S. woman astronaut, Sally K. Ride.

Supreme Court upholds order that permits doctors to advertise nontraditional arrangements for medical practice.

EDUCATION

Supreme Court rules that law that bars sex discrimination in federally aided education programs applies to employees as well as students; upholds lower-court ruling that children of illegal aliens must have access to free public education; rules that handicapped children are entitled to

1982

public education from which they derive "some educational benefit."

New Jersey Senate passes bill over governor's veto that requires public schools to start each day with a minute of "silent contemplation and introspection."

Arkansas federal judge strikes down Arkansas law that requires teaching of creation based on the Bible in schools where theory of evolution is taught, rules that this violates separation of church and state.

Supreme Court rules that First Amendment limits discretion of public school officials to remove books they deem offensive from school libraries.

RELIGION

Agreement is announced to merge American Lutheran Church, Association of Evangelical Lutheran Churches, and Lutheran Church in America.

Presbyterian Church in the U.S. and the United Presbyterian Church in the U.S. vote to merge, end 122-year-old schism caused by slavery question.

Seven largest African American denominations with 65,000 churches and 20 million members create Congress of National Black Churches.

National Cathedral in Washington, D.C., celebrates its 75th anniversary by unveiling new west front; two more towers remain to be built.

Dr. Norman Vincent Peale celebrates 50th anniversary with Marble Collegiate Church in New York City.

Catholic Archbishop Joseph L. Bernardin of Cincinnati is moved to Chicago.

President Reagan proposes constitutional amendment to permit organized prayer in schools.

ART/MUSIC

Ellen T. Zwilich composes *Three Movements for Orchestra*; William Bolcom, *Songs of Innocence* and *Songs of Experience*; John Conigliano, *Three Hallucinations for Orchestra* and *Pied Piper Fantasy*.

Edward Kienholz completes the painting *Bout, Round Eleven.*

SONGS (popular): "Ebony and Ivory," "Eye of the Tiger," "I Love Rock and Roll," "Up Where We Belong," "Chariots of Fire," "Heartbreak Express," "Mountain Music," "What's Forever For."

DEATHS Arthur Rubinstein, pianist; Calvin Simmons, first African American conductor of a major orchestra (Oakland Symphony); Earl ("Fatha") Hines, jazz pianist and orchestra leader.

LITERATURE/JOURNALISM

BOOKS *The Color Purple* by Alice Walker, *The Dean's December* by Saul Bellow, *Crossings* by Danielle Steel, *Prizzi's Honor* by Richard Condon.

DEATHS Erwin D. Canham, editor, *Christian Science Monitor* (1941–1974); Archibald MacLeish, poet; John Cheever, author; cartoonists Hal Foster ("Prince Valiant") and Ernie Bushmiller ("Nancy").

ENTERTAINMENT

PLAYS Andrew Lloyd Webber writes *Cats*, which becomes U.S.'s longest-running play; Arthur Kopit and Maury Yeston, *Nine*; Lanford Wilson, *Angels Fall.*

MOVIES *Gandhi* with Ben Kingsley, *Tootsie* with Dustin Hoffman, *Blade Runner* with Harrison Ford, *Cannery Row* with Nick Nolte, *Pennies from Heaven* with Steve Martin, *Sophie's Choice* with Meryl Streep, *Victor/Victoria* with Julie Andrews, *E.T., The Extra-Terrestrial* directed by Steven Spielberg.

DEATHS Henry Fonda, actor; Ingrid Bergman, actress.

SPORTS

National Football League players strike for nine weeks; U.S. Football League is founded, set to play in Spring 1983; federal jury finds NFL guilty of antitrust action in trying to block Oakland Raiders' move to Los Angeles; NFL owners accept five-year $2 billion television contract.

Club owners refuse to renew Bowie Kuhn's contract as baseball commissioner.

Wayne Gretzky of Edmonton, Canada, becomes first National Hockey League player to surpass 200 points in a season, first to be selected unanimously as NHL most-valuable player.

International Olympic Committee restores amateur status and approves posthumously the two gold medals won by Jim Thorpe in 1912 Olympics; they were taken from him for amateur-rule violation.

WINNERS *Auto racing*—Gordon Johncock, Indianapolis 500; Darrell Waltrip, NASCAR; *Baseball*—St. Louis Cardinals, World Series; *Basketball*—Bradley, NIT; North Carolina, NCAA; Louisiana Tech, first NCAA (women); Los Angeles, NBA; *Bowling*—Earl Anthony, PBA; *Boxing*—Larry Holmes, heavyweight; Sugar Ray Leonard, welterweight; *Figure skating*—Scott Hamilton, U.S. and world men's titles; Elaine Zayak, world women's; Rosalynn Sumners, U.S. women's; *Football* (bowls)—Washington, Rose; Clemson, Orange; Pittsburgh, Sugar; Texas, Cotton; San Francisco, Super Bowl XVI; *Golf*—Tom Watson, U.S. Open; Ray Floyd, PGA; Craig Stadler, Masters; Janet Alex, U.S. Women's Open; Jan Stephenson, LPGA; *Harness racing*—Speed Bowl, Hambletonian; *Hockey*—New York Islanders, Stanley Cup; *Horse racing*—Gato del Sol, Kentucky Derby; Aloma's Ruler, Preakness Stakes; Conquistador, Belmont Stakes; *Swimming*—Florida, first NCAA women's title; *Tennis*—U.S., Davis Cup; Jimmy Connors, U.S. Open (men); Chris Evert, U.S. Open (women).

DEATHS Gordon Smiley, auto racer; Salvador Sanchez, featherweight boxing champion, in auto accident; Red (Walter W.) Smith, syndicated sports columnist.

MISCELLANEOUS

Air Florida 737 crashes into Potomac River after takeoff at Washington's (D.C.) National Airport, 78 die; Pan Am 727 crashes after takeoff in Kenner, La., 153 die.

Women become full-fledged firefighters in New York City with graduation of 11 from Fire Academy.

INTERNATIONAL

U.S. Embassy in Beirut is bombed (April 18), 17 U.S. citizens die; a bomb-filled truck smashes through barriers at U.S. Marine compound in Beirut, kills 241 Americans (October 23).

U.S. troops land on Grenada in West Indies to halt Cuban buildup and protect U.S. students (October 25); island is secured within few days.

Russians shoot down Korean Airlines plane that had drifted over Soviet territory (September 1); all 269 aboard, including 52 Americans, die.

NATIONAL

Social Security is amended to include federal employees after April 1, 1984; raises age of eligibility from 65 to 66 by year 2009, to 67 by 2027.

Third Monday in January becomes national holiday in honor of Dr. Martin Luther King Jr.

Chicago elects its first African American mayor, Harold Washington.

Supreme Court upholds constitutionality of windfall profits tax on decontrolled crude oil.

BUSINESS/INDUSTRY/INVENTIONS

Apple introduces "mouse," hand-held computer pointing device, and screens with pictures ("icons") to represent programs.

Supreme Court approves an agreement that settles antitrust suit against ATT (August 5); ATT gives up its 22 Bell System companies; in return it is permitted to enter previously prohibited areas (data processing, equipment sales, etc.).

General Motors agrees to pay $42.5 million to settle charges of employment discrimination against blacks, Hispanics, and women.

Gerard Debreu is awarded Nobel Prize in economics for work on the way prices operate to balance supply and demand.

Job Training Partnership Act establishes job training and employment services for underprivileged persons.

Compact disks ("CDs") begin to appear in record stores, replacing LP records.

DEATHS R. Buckminster Fuller, developer of geodesic dome; Earl S. Tupper, developer of Tupperware.

TRANSPORTATION

Federal Trade Commission approves plan by General Motors and Toyota for joint production of a subcompact car.

Federal gasoline tax increases 5 cents per gallon to pay for highway, bridges, and mass-transit improvements.

Connecticut Turnpike bridge over Mianus River at Greenwich collapses; three are killed.

American Airlines simplifies fare structure to four basic fees tied to miles traveled.

Houston voters reject $2.35-billion bond issue for urban rail system.

Mississippi River Bridge at Luling, La., opens.

SCIENCE/MEDICINE

Subrahmanyan Chandrasekhar and William A. Fowler share Nobel Prize in physics for work on what happens when stars age; Barbara McClintock is awarded prize in physiology/medicine for discovery that genes can move on chromosomes of plants and effect of the moves on future plants.

Eighth successful shuttle flight is completed; first flight for an African American astronaut, Guion S. Buford III.

Rescue workers survey the damage after the bombing of the U.S. Marine base in Beirut, Lebanon, October 1983. AP WIDE WORLD PHOTOS

EDUCATION

Federal District Court rules that New Jersey law that mandates a minute of silence or meditation for public school students is unconstitutional (see 1982).

National Commission on Excellence in Education reports that U.S. elementary and secondary education is "mediocre."

Supreme Court rules that IRS can deny tax exemptions to private schools that practice racial discrimination.

RELIGION

National Conference of Catholic Bishops condemns nuclear arms race, calls for end of nuclear arms production and deployment.

National Council of Churches completes translation of Bible readings to eliminate references to God as solely male.

Presbyterian Church (USA) comes into being as the United Presbyterian Church and the Presbyterian Church in the U.S. formally merge; Rev. John R. Taylor of Charlotte, N.C., is named first moderator of merged church.

Catholic Archbishop Joseph L. Bernardin of Chicago is elevated to cardinal.

ART/MUSIC

Bernard Rands composes *Canti del Sole*.

SONGS (popular): "All Night Long," "Beat It," "Down Under," "Every Breath You Take," "Islands in the Stream," "Say Say Say," "Total Eclipse of the Heart," "Somebody's Baby," "Sweet Dreams."

DEATHS George Balanchine, choreographer; Eubie Blake, pianist and composer; Harry James, trumpeter and bandleader; Marty Robbins, country-music singer and composer; Ira Gershwin, lyricist for brother, George.

LITERATURE/JOURNALISM

BOOKS *Ironweed* by William Kennedy, *American Primitive* by Mary Oliver, *Winter's Tale* by Mark Helprin, *Voice of the Heart* by Barbara T. Bradford, *Thurston House* by Danielle Steel.

ENTERTAINMENT

PLAYS David Mamet writes *Glengarry Glen Ross*; Neil Simon, *Brighton Beach Memoirs*; Marsha Norman, *'Night, Mother*; Stockard Channing stars in *The Lady and the Clarinet*.

MOVIES *Terms of Endearment* with Shirley MacLaine; *Return of the Jedi* with Harrison Ford, Carrie Fisher, and Mark Hamill; *The Big Chill* with Glenn Close; *Breathless* with Richard Gere; *Sudden Impact* with Clint Eastwood; *Silkwood* with Meryl Streep.

DEATHS Tennessee Williams, playwright; screen personalities Norma Shearer, Gloria Swanson, Raymond Massey, and Pat O'Brien; television hosts Dave Garroway and Arthur Godfrey; Lynn Fontanne, actress.

SPORTS

Peter F. Ueberroth becomes baseball commissioner.

American Medical Assn. urges ban on boxing because of brain damage resulting from bouts.

ABC and NBC agree to pay $1.1 billion for six years of regular-season baseball broadcasts.

U.S. District Court awards $11.5 million in antitrust damages to Los Angeles Raiders, $4.86 million to Los Angeles Coliseum in suit against NFL.

Nolan Ryan records 3,509th strikeout, breaking Walter Johnson's long-standing record; Brian Downing, California Angels outfielder, sets record of 244 consecutive errorless games; Steve Garvey of San Diego Padres sets National League playing record, 1,207 consecutive games.

WINNERS *Auto racing* — Tom Sneva, Indianapolis 500; Bobby Allison, NASCAR; *Baseball* — Baltimore Orioles, World Series; *Basketball* — Fresno State, NIT; North Carolina State, NCAA; Southern California, NCAA (women); Philadelphia, NBA; *Bowling* — Earl Anthony, PBA; *Boxing* — Larry Holmes, heavyweight; Sugar Ray Leonard, welterweight; Vito Antuofermo, middleweight; *Figure skating* — Scott Hamilton, U.S. and world men's title; Rosalynn Sumners, U.S. and world women's title; *Football* (bowls) — UCLA, Rose; Nebraska, Orange; Penn State, Sugar; Southern Methodist, Cotton; Washington, Super Bowl XVII; Michigan, first USFL title; *Golf* — Larry Nelson, U.S. Open;

Hal Sutton, PGA; Severiano Ballesteros, Masters; Jan Stephenson, U.S. Women's Open; Patty Sheehan, LPGA; *Harness racing* — Duenna, Hambletonian; *Hockey* — New York Islanders, Stanley Cup; *Horse racing* — Sunny's Halo, Kentucky Derby; Deputed Testamony, Preakness Stakes; Caveat, Belmont Stakes; *Skiing* — Phil Mahre, world Alpine Cup; Tamara McKinney, first American to win world women's title; *Tennis* — Jimmy Connors, U.S. Open (men); Martina Navratilova, U.S. Open (women); *Yachting* — Australian boat

Australia II wins America's Cup, first U.S. loss since race began in 1851.

DEATHS Jack Dempsey, heavyweight boxing champion (1919–1926); George Halas, pro-football pioneer; Paul (Bear) Bryant, Alabama football coach.

MISCELLANEOUS

Worst snowstorm in 36 years blankets 600-mile stretch of the East Coast.

1984

INTERNATIONAL

Explosives-filled truck strikes U.S. Embassy annex in Beirut; 23 are killed.

U.S. Marines are withdrawn from Beirut (February 26); three Americans are kidnapped in that city: TV reporter Jeremy Levin, who escapes later; CIA Station Chief William Buckley, who is killed (March 7); and Presbyterian Minister Benjamin Weir (May 8).

U.S. and Vatican resume full diplomatic relations after 117 years (January 10); William A. Wilson is named ambassador to the Vatican.

U.S. withdraws from UNESCO (U.N. Educational, Scientific, and Cultural Organization) because of agency's mismanagement and politicization.

Kuwaiti plane en route to Pakistan is hijacked; 161 in plane are held hostage at Teheran; Iranian security men capture plane; two Americans are killed before rescue.

President Ronald Reagan makes six-day visit to China.

NATIONAL

President Reagan, Republican, is reelected, receives 54,281,858 popular and 525 electoral votes to 37,457,215 popular and 13 electoral votes for former vice president Walter Mondale; Rep. Geraldine Ferraro is Mondale's vice presidential candidate, the first woman nominated by a major party.

Supreme Court rules that the Federal Aviation Administration (and by inference, other agencies) cannot be sued for damages for mistakes that contribute to disasters.

Vietnam Memorial in Washington, D.C., is dedicated.

DEATHS Mark W. Clark, World War II and Korea general; William A. Egan, first Alaska governor; George H. Gallup, pollster.

BUSINESS/INDUSTRY/INVENTIONS

ATT divests itself of 22 wholly owned local Bell telephone companies (January 1) as a result of 1982 consent decree with Justice Department.

E. F. Hutton brokerage firm pleads guilty to 2,000 federal charges of checking-account manipulations.

Stock market sets record when 236 million shares change hands in one day; 696 million shares are traded in week.

Environmental Protection Agency proposes 90% reduction of lead in gasoline by 1986, complete elimination by 1995.

Major U.S. oil companies agree to allow service-station operators to sell any gasoline they choose.

Mergers during the year include Gulf Oil and Chevron, Texaco and Getty Oil, Superior Oil and Mobil, Carnation and Nestle, Electronic Data Systems and General Motors.

TRANSPORTATION

Joe Kittinger completes first successful transatlantic balloon flight (September 17).

New York State becomes first to require driver and front-seat passenger seat belts.

SCIENCE/MEDICINE

Bruce Merrifield is awarded Nobel Prize in chemistry for research that revolutionized study of proteins.

Astronaut Bruce McCandless becomes first person to walk in space with no ties to the mother ship; Astronaut Kathryn D. Sullivan becomes first American woman to walk in space.

Astronauts successfully repair in space damaged satellite that had been inoperative for four years.

DEATH Dr. John Rock, codeveloper of oral contraceptive pill.

EDUCATION

Supreme Court rules that prohibition of sex discrimination by federally aided schools and colleges applies only to department or program that receives the aid, not entire school; also upholds law that makes college men who fail to register for the draft ineligible for federal scholarships.

New York State Board of Regents issues strict new high-school graduation requirements.

RELIGION

Supreme Court reaffirms its ruling that organized prayer in public schools is unconstitutional; also rules that public financing of a Nativity scene does not of itself violate doctrine of separation of church and state.

Senate rejects proposed constitutional amendment to permit silent or spoken prayers in public schools.

Congress approves measure that permits public high-school students to hold religious meetings in

Mary Lou Retton scores a perfect 10 on the vault to win the Olympic gold medal for the U.S. in women's gymnastics, August 3, 1984. UPI/CORBIS-BETTMANN

the schools during off-hours.

Basis is reached for merging nine Protestant denominations by Consultation on Church Union after 22 years of effort.

Two Catholic archbishops are named: John J. O'Connor of New York and Bernard F. Law of Boston.

ART/MUSIC

Stephen Albert composes *Symphony, River Run*.

John Baldessori completes the painting *Kiss/Panic*.

SONGS (popular): "Against All Odds," "Footloose," "Ghostbusters," "I Just Called to Say I Love You," "Jump," "What's Love Got to Do with It?," "When Doves Cry," "Another Woman in Love."

DEATHS Ansel Adams, photographer; Mabel Mercer, jazz singer; Meredith Willson, composer (*The Music Man*); Jan Peerce, opera tenor; two orchestra leaders, Fred Waring and Count Basie.

LITERATURE/JOURNALISM

BOOKS *The American Blues* by Ward Just, *Duplicate Keys* by Jane Smiley, *Full Circle* by Danielle Steel,

1984

The Good War by Studs Terkel, *Yin* by Caroline Kizer.

DEATHS Authors Irwin Shaw and Truman Capote.

ENTERTAINMENT

PLAYS Stephen Sondheim and James Lapine write *Sunday in the Park with George*; Jerry Herman, *La Cage aux Folles*.

MOVIES *Indiana Jones and the Temple of Doom* with Harrison Ford, *Beverly Hills Cop* with Eddie Murphy, *Falling in Love* with Robert DeNiro, *The Terminator* with Arnold Schwarzenegger, *Harry and Son* with Paul Newman, *The Natural* with Robert Redford, *Romancing the Stone* with Michael Douglas.

DEATHS Lillian Hellman, playwright; William Powell, screen actor; Brooks Atkinson, *New York Times* drama critic.

SPORTS

Supreme Court rules that NCAA's exclusive control of college-football television coverage violates antitrust laws; five universities form National Independent Football Network.

Supreme Court rules that NFL cannot prevent teams from moving to other cities.

U.S. Football League abandons spring playing schedule, to play in fall.

Winter Olympics are held in Yugoslavia; Bill Johnson first from U.S. to win gold medal in skiing; Debbi Armstrong, a gold in women's giant slalom; Russia announces that it will not participate in Summer Games in Los Angeles; Karen Stives becomes first U.S. woman to win an equestrian event; Mary Lou Retton, first to win all-around women's gymnastics; Joan Benoit, the first women's marathon.

Reggie Jackson hits 500th home run; Elvin Hayes of Houston ends basketball career with record 1,303 games; Kareem Abdul Jabbar becomes pro-basketball's leading scorer with 31,421 points; Walter Payton of Chicago Bears breaks career rushing record with 12,400 yards; Eric Dickerson of Los Angeles Rams sets single-season rushing record with 2,105 yards.

WINNERS *Auto racing*—Rick Mears, Indianapolis 500; Tery Labonte, NASCAR; *Baseball*—Detroit Tigers, World Series; *Basketball*—Michigan, NIT; Georgetown, NCAA; Southern California, NCAA (women); Boston, NBA; *Bowling*—Bob Chamberlain, PBA; *Boxing*—Thomas Hearns, superwelterweight; Marvin Hagler, middleweight; Livingston Bramble, lightweight; *Figure skating*—Scott Hamilton, U.S. and world men's titles; Rosalynn Sumners, U.S. women's title; *Football* (bowls)—UCLA, Rose; Miama (Fla.), Orange; Auburn, Sugar; Georgia, Cotton; Los Angeles Raiders, Super Bowl XVIII; *Golf*—Fuzzy Zoeller, U.S. Open; Lee Trevino, PGA; Ben Crenshaw, Masters; Hollis Stacy, U.S. Women's Open; Pat Sheehan, LPGA; *Harness racing*—Historic Freight, Hambletonian; *Hockey*—Edmonton, Stanley Cup; *Horse racing*—Swale, Kentucky Derby and Belmont Stakes; Gate Dancer, Preakness Stakes; *Tennis*—Sweden, Davis Cup; John McEnroe, U.S. Open (men); Martina Navratilova, U.S. Open (women).

DEATHS Johnny Weissmuller, swimmer and screen actor (Tarzan); Walter Alston, baseball manager (Dodgers 1954–1976); Anne Townsend, leading U.S. field-hockey player.

1985

INTERNATIONAL

Cruise ship *Achille Lauro* is hijacked in Mediterranean; one U.S. citizen is killed before rescue.

Barber B. Conable, former New York congressman, is named president of World Bank.

Four U.S. citizens are kidnapped in Beirut: Catholic priest Lawrence Jenco; Terry Anderson, Associated Press correspondent; Thomas Sutherland, American University dean; and David Jacobsen, director, American University hospital; Rev. Benjamin Weir, kidnapped in 1984, is released.

U.S. and Soviet Union disarmament talks begin in Geneva.

President Ronald Reagan and Canadian Prime Minister Brian Mulroney sign several agreements, create joint committee to study acid rain.

NATIONAL

President Reagan undergoes successful abdominal surgery (July 13).

First-class postage rises to 22 cents an ounce (February 17).

Philadelphia police bomb house to get radical group out, results in fire that causes 11 deaths, destruction of 61 houses (May 13).

Labor Secretary Raymond Donovan resigns after being indicted for business practices before becoming secretary.

U.S. District Court finds Yonkers, N.Y., guilty of "illegally and intentionally" segregating public schools and housing.

DEATHS Henry Cabot Lodge, legislator, ambassador to South Vietnam; Sam Ervin, North Carolina senator who headed Watergate committee.

BUSINESS/INDUSTRY/INVENTIONS

General Electric buys RCA for $6.28 billion; other corporate combinations of year are General Motors and Hughes Aircraft, Nabisco and R. J. Reynolds.

Largest U.S. civil judgment ($10.53 billion) assessed against Texaco Inc. in favor of Penzoil Co.

President Reagan vetoes bill that would limit imports of textiles.

Bank failures nearly double in year to 120.

Franco Modigoliani is awarded Nobel Prize in economics for analyzing behavior of household savers and functioning of financial markets.

DEATH Robert W. Woodruff, Coca-Cola president and chairman (1923–1955).

TRANSPORTATION

Chrysler Corp. and Mitsubishi Motors Corp. announce joint venture to build subcompact cars in U.S.

Groundbreaking is held in Michigan for new Mazda auto plant; Honda Motors says it will build engines for a subcompact at an Ohio plant.

Lock of Welland Canal that connects Lakes Erie and Ontario collapses, halts shipping (October 15).

Norfolk Southern Corp. is chosen to take over government-controlled Conrail system.

Court of Appeals finds Exxon Corp. guilty of overcharging customers; fines it $1.9 billion.

Texas Air Corp. announces it will acquire TWA (Trans World Airlines).

New security measures against airline and airport terrorism are issued.

Ford Motor Co. announces it will cut its white-collar force by 20% over next five years.

SCIENCE/MEDICINE

Herbert A. Hauptman and Jerome Karle share Nobel prize in chemistry for developing tech-

Michael Jackson and Lionel Ritchie win the Grammy Award for their song "We Are The World." UPI/CORBIS-BETTMANN

niques used to determine structures of molecules vital to life; Michael S. Brown and Joseph L. Goldstein share prize in physiology/medicine for research on cholesterol.

DEATHS John F. Enders, developer of tissue culture of polio virus that led to Salk vaccine; Charles F. Richter, developer of scale for measuring earthquakes.

EDUCATION

Supreme Court rules that public-school systems may not send teachers into parochial schools for remedial or enriched instruction; also rules that public-school teachers and officials may search students if there are "reasonable grounds" to believe search will give evidence of law or school-rule violation.

William J. Bennett becomes Secretary of Education.

RELIGION

Supreme Court strikes down Alabama law that permits one minute of prayer or meditation in public schools.

Ezra Taft Benson is named president of Mormon Church.

Amy Eilberg is ordained as first woman Conservative rabbi.

Episcopal Bishop Edmund L. Browning of Hawaii is elected presiding bishop.

Two Catholic archbishops are elevated to cardinal: John J. O'Connor of New York and Bernard F. Law of Boston.

DEATHS Eugene Carson Blake, general secretary, World Council of Churches (1966–1972); Catholic Cardinal Terence J. Cooke of New York.

ART/MUSIC

George Perle composes *Wind Quintet IV*; John Conigliaro composes *Fantasia on an Obstinato*.

SONGS (popular): "Can't Fight This Feeling," "Careless Whisper," "Everybody Wants to Rule the World," "I Want to Know What Love Is," "Money for Nothing," "The Power of Love," "Say You, Say Me," "We Are the World."

DEATHS Rick Nelson, rock 'n roll star, in plane crash; Wayne King, orchestra leader; Johnny Marks, composer ("Rudolph, the Red-Nosed Reindeer"); Eugene Ormandy, concert violinist and conductor; Roger Sessions, opera composer.

LITERARY/JOURNALISM

BOOKS *Lonesome Dove* by Larry McMurtry, *Caracole* by Edmund White, *Family Album* by Danielle Steel, *The Mammoth Hunters* by Jean M. Auel, *Galapagos* by Kurt Vonnegut Jr.

DEATHS E. B. White and Taylor Caldwell, authors; Chester Gould, cartoonist ("Dick Tracy").

ENTERTAINMENT

Capital Cities Communications Inc. purchases ABC (American Broadcasting Co.).

MOVIES *Back to the Future* with Michael Fox, *Out*

of Africa with Meryl Streep, *Rambo, First Blood* with Sylvester Stallone, *The Color Purple* with Whoopi Goldberg, *Pale Rider* with Clint Eastwood, *Into the Night* with Michelle Pfeiffer.

DEATHS Phil Silvers, entertainer; Yul Brynner, actor; Burr Tillstrom, puppeteer (*Kukla, Fran, and Ollie*); Rock Hudson, screen actor, of AIDS, encouraging open national discussion of the disease.

SPORTS

Basketball Hall of Fame in Springfield, Mass., is dedicated.

Eddie Robinson, Grambling University football coach, becomes winningest coach with 324th win; later rises to 371.

U.S. Olympic Committee to test U.S. athletes for drugs up to 1988 games; major league baseball personnel, except unionized players, to submit to drug tests.

Nolan Ryan of Houston Astros becomes first pitcher to achieve 4,000 career strikeouts; Tom Seaver, Chicago White Sox, and Phil Niekro, New York Yankees, each wins his 300th game; Pete Rose of Cincinnati Reds breaks Ty Cobb's 1928 record with 4,192 career base hits; Rod Carew of California Angels scores his 3,000th base hit.

WINNERS *Auto racing*—Danny Sullivan, Indianapolis 500; Darrell Waltrip, NASCAR; *Baseball*—

Kansas City Royals, World Series; *Basketball*—UCLA, NIT; Villanova, NCAA; Old Dominion, NCAA (women); Los Angeles Lakers, NBA; *Bowling*—Mike Aulby, PBA; *Boxing*—Michael Spinks, heavyweight; Marvin Hagler, middleweight; Donald Curry, welterweight; *Figure skating*—Brian Boitano, U.S. men's title; Tiffany Chin, U.S. women's title; *Football* (bowls)—Southern California, Rose; Washington, Orange; Nebraska, Sugar; Boston College, Cotton; San Francisco, Super Bowl XIX; *Golf*—Andy North, U.S. Open; Hubert Green, PGA; Bernhard Langer, Masters; Kathy Baker, U.S. Women's Open; Nancy Lopez, LPGA; *Harness racing*—Prakas, Hambletonian; *Hockey*—Edmonton, Stanley Cup; *Horse racing*—Spend a Buck, Kentucky Derby; Tank's Prospect, Preakness Stakes; Creme Fraiche, Belmont Stakes; *Rowing*—Princeton, Men's Intercollegiate; Washington, Women's; *Tennis*—Ivan Lendl, U.S. Open (men); Hana Mandlikova, U.S. Open (women).

DEATHS Peter Desjardins, Olympic diving champion; Pelle Lindbergh, Philadelphia goaltender, in car crash; Roger Maris, current holder of season home-run record (61).

MISCELLANEOUS

Charter DC-8 bringing troops home for Christmas crashes at Gander, Newfoundland; 256 are killed.

INTERNATIONAL

President Ronald Reagan signs secret order, authorizes arms shipments to Iran (January 17); National Security Advisor John M. Poindexter resigns (November 25); his aide, Lt. Col. Oliver North is dismissed after it is learned that some Iran arms sales proceeds went to finance military aid for Nicaraguan Contras.

U.S. planes bomb "terrorist" targets in Libya (April 15).

Two U.S. hostages in Beirut are released, three

others kidnapped; released are Rev. Lawrence Jenco and David Jacobsen; kidnapped are Frank Reed, educator; Edward Tracy, writer; and Joseph Cicippio.

Congress overrides presidential veto to impose economic sanctions against South Africa.

Canada and U.S. agree on plan to reduce acid rain.

NATIONAL

President Reagan announces that Supreme Court

1986

Chief Justice Warren Burger will retire, nominates Associate Justice William Rehnquist for post; he is confirmed September 17.

Congress virtually eliminates mandatory retirement at 70.

Congress passes major tax-reform law.

More than 5 million Americans join hands trying to form a human chain across the nation in Hands Across America, designed to raise money for the hungry.

Titan 34-D rocket carrying secret military payload explodes shortly after liftoff.

Supreme Court denies Yonkers, N.Y., a stay in effecting court-ordered desegregation plan for schools and housing; also rules that police cannot question defendant at arraignment if his requested lawyer is not present; also rules that military personnel cannot sue superiors for damages even if their constitutional rights are violated.

Senate ratifies U.N. treaty outlawing genocide.

Elie Wiesel is awarded Nobel Peace Prize.

President Carter Memorial Library in Atlanta is dedicated.

DEATH Admiral Hyman Rickover, father of atomic-powered Navy.

BUSINESS/INDUSTRY/INVENTIONS

James M. Buchanan is awarded Nobel Prize in economics for pioneering new methods of analyzing economic and political decision-making.

Dow Jones industrial average drops 86.61 points when a record 237.6 million shares change hands (September 11); drops another 34.17 points the following day.

Year's bank failures climb to 145.

LTV Corp. becomes largest U.S. corporation to file for bankruptcy.

Among the year's mergers are Beatrice Foods and KKR (Kohlberg Kravis Roberts), General Foods and Philip Morris, Sperry and Burroughs, Allied Stores and Campeau.

DEATHS Abram N. Pritzer, founder of Hyatt Hotels; J. Willard Marriott, founder of hotel/restaurant chain; Minoru Yamasaki, architect (New York's World Trade Center).

TRANSPORTATION

Supreme Court upholds ruling that Exxon Corp. pay $2.1 billion in refunds for overcharges.

Some airline mergers and purchases occur: Northwest buys Republic, United acquires Frontier, Texas Air buys People's Express, Delta and Western plan merger, Texas Air purchases Eastern.

General Motors announces that it will close 11 plants as part of modernization program; Excel, small car built by Hyundai Corp. of South Korea, goes on sale in U.S.

Interstate Commerce Commission rejects proposed merger of Southern Pacific and Santa Fe railroads.

Pan Am begins shuttle service from La Guardia Airport in New York to Washington (D.C.) and Boston.

Last stretch of Interstate 80, a five-mile segment in Salt Lake City, is completed.

SCIENCE/MEDICINE

Space shuttle *Challenger*, with a crew of seven, explodes moments after liftoff, kills entire crew (January 28).

Voyager, an experimental plane piloted by Dick Rutan and Jeana Yeager, completes round-the-world nonstop flight without refueling, landing at Edwards AFB, a flight of nearly 26,000 miles in 9 days, 3 minutes, 44 seconds (December 23).

Dudley Herschbach and Yuan T. Lee share Nobel Prize in chemistry for helping create first detailed understanding of chemical reactions; Rita Levi-Montalcini and Stanley Cohen share Prize in physiology/medicine for major contributions to understanding substances that influence cell growth.

Surgeon General C. Everett Koop calls for widespread education, condom distribution, and antibody testing to prevent the spread of AIDS.

EDUCATION

Norfolk, Va., school board votes to end 15 years

of busing for racial balance, returns to neighborhood elementary schools.

Barbara A. Black becomes dean of Columbia Law School, first woman to head major private law school.

Carnegie Foundation for the Advancement of Teaching urges overhaul of undergraduate education, including dropping of standardized admission tests.

Carnegie Corporation to establish nation's first system of certifying elementary and high school teachers.

RELIGION

United Methodist Council of Bishops calls for "clear and unconditional" opposition to use of nuclear weapons.

ART/MUSIC

John Harbison composes *The Flight into Egypt.*

Jeff Koons completes the sculpture *Statuary.*

SONGS (popular): "Addicted to Love," "How Will I Know?" "Kiss," "On My Own," "Rock Me Amadeus," "That's What Friends Are For," "West End Girls."

LITERATURE/JOURNALISM

Robert Penn Warren is named first official U.S. poet laureate.

Supreme Court overturns several statutes that put burden of proof on news organizations in libel cases.

BOOKS *Bearing the Cross* by David J. Garrow, *Thomas and Beulah* by Rita Dove, *The Counterlife* by Philip Roth, *Wanderlust* by Danielle Steel, *A Summons to Memphis* by Peter Taylor.

DEATH Theodore H. White, author of "making of the president" books.

ENTERTAINMENT

PLAY August Wilson writes *Fences.*

MOVIES *Top Gun* with Tom Cruise, *Crocodile Dundee* with Paul Hogan, *Platoon* with Charlie Sheen, *Hoosiers* with Gene Hackman, *Heartburn* with Meryl Streep, *Delta Force* with Chuck Norris.

A Lockheed employee at the Kennedy Space Center in Cape Canaveral, Fla., watches as the space shuttle *Challenger* explodes in the air, January 28, 1986. UPI/CORBIS-BETTMANN

L.A. Law appears on television.

DEATHS Screen actors Ray Milland and Jimmy Cagney; Desi Arnaz of *I Love Lucy* show; Marlin Perkins, zoo director and television personality; Otto Preminger, movie director.

SPORTS

Supreme Court upholds move of Oakland Raiders to Los Angeles.

NCAA adopts three-point field goal in men's basketball.

Federal jury awards $1 in damages to U.S. Football League in its $1.7 million suit against NFL; USFL cancels its fall season, hopes to start larger, stronger league in 1987.

NFL increases drug testing of players; repeat users to be suspended for life.

Angelo Bart Giamatti, Yale University president, is named president of National (baseball) League.

Jackie Joyner sets women's heptathlon record with 7,158 points.

WINNERS *Auto racing* — Bobby Rahal, Indianapolis 500; Dale Earnhardt, NASCAR; *Baseball* — New York Mets, World Series; *Basketball* — Ohio State, NIT; Louisville, NCAA; Texas, NCAA (women); Boston, NBA; *Bowling* — Tom Crites, PBA; *Boxing* — Michael Spinks, heavyweight; Lloyd Moneghan, welterweight; *Figure skating* — Brian Boitano, U.S. and world men's titles; Debi Thomas, U.S. and world women's titles; *Football (bowls)* — UCLA, Rose; Oklahoma, Orange; Tennessee, Sugar; Texas A&M, Cotton; Chicago, Super Bowl XX; *Golf* — Ray Floyd, U.S. Open; Bob Tway, PGA; Jack Nicklaus, Masters; Jane Geddes, U.S. Women's Open; Pat Bradley, LPGA; *Harness racing* — Nuclear Kosmos, Hambletonian; *Hockey* — Montreal, Stanley Cup; *Horse racing* — Ferdinand, Kentucky Derby; Snow Chief, Preakness Stakes; Danzig Connection, Belmont Stakes; *Tennis* — Ivan Lendl, U.S. Open (men); Martina Navratilova, U.S. Open (women).

DEATH Billy Haughton, all-time great harness-race driver.

MISCELLANEOUS

Fire in DuPont Plaza Hotel in Puerto Rico kills 96.

1987

INTERNATIONAL

U.S. and Soviet Union resolve differences in treaty to ban medium- and shorter-range missiles; Soviet President Mikhail Gorbachev comes to Washington to sign treaty (December 9).

U.S. and Canada agree on free trade that will eliminate all tariffs by 1999; must be approved by ational legislatures (October 3).

Four U.S. citizens are kidnapped in Beirut: Charles Glass, television reporter who is released two months later, Robert Polhill, Jonathan Turner, and Alan Steen.

An Iraqi missile strikes the USS *Stark* in the Persian Gulf; kills 37 sailors.

NATIONAL

President Ronald Reagan signs bill ratifying international genocide treaty, drafted 40 years ago; victory for Wisconsin Sen. William Proxmire who made 3,300 daily speeches over 19 years urging ratification.

President Reagan nominates Robert H. Bork for the Supreme Court; is not confirmed.

President Reagan submits the first trillion-dollar budget.

Iran-Contra hearings by Congress continue for three months to try to get facts about diversion of Iran arms-sales profits to Nicaraguan Contras.

Former Labor Secretary Raymond J. Donovan is acquitted of grand larceny and fraud charges in actions prior to his government service.

Supreme Court rules that states may force Rotary clubs to admit women to membership; Kiwanis International ends 77-year-old men-only policy.

Former Sen. Gary Hart drops out of race for Democratic presidential nomination after publicity about his affair with a model.

First Lady Nancy Reagan undergoes successful mastectomy.

Great Basin (Nev.) National Park is dedicated.

DEATHS Commerce Secretary Malcolm Baldrige;

two World War II generals, Maxwell D. Taylor and L. Lawton Collins; Bayard Rustin, civil rights leader.

BUSINESS/INDUSTRY/INVENTIONS

Stock market shows great activity: Dow-Jones industrial average closes above 2,000 for first time (January 23) and daily trading volume exceeds 300 million shares for first time; then in steady climb passes 2,300 and 2,400 early in spring, 2,500 and 2,700 in the summer; turnaround comes when average drops 91.55 points (October 6); 10 days later 338.4 million shares change hands and average falls 108.36 points (October 16), falls 508 points two weeks later.

Robert M. Solow is awarded Nobel Prize in economics for seminal contributions to theory of economic growth.

Mergers and new combinations in year include Standard Oil and British Petroleum, Dome Petroleum and Amoco, Chesebrough-Ponds and Unilever NV, Celanese and American Hoechst.

Bank failures for year reach 184.

TRANSPORTATION

Chrysler Corp. buys American Motors Co. from France's Renault for $1.5 billion; Ford announces purchase of a British luxury carmaker.

Conrail is sold to private investors for $1.65 billion after decade of federal operation.

Texaco files for bankruptcy; Texaco and Penzoil sign settlement of $10.3 billion suit.

Continental Airlines absorbs People's Express, USAir takes over Piedmont Aviation.

Senate gives states right to raise speed limit to 65 miles per hour.

Volkswagen announces that it will close its New Stanton, Pa., plant in 1988.

Interstate highway bridge on New York Thruway near Amsterdam collapses; 10 are killed.

DEATH Henry Ford II, chief executive officer, Ford Motor Co. (1945–1980).

Oliver North's first appearance before the Senate Iran-Contra Committee. Senator Daniel Inouye (back to camera) administers the oath to the lieutenant colonel. UPI/Corbis-Bettmann

1987

The AIDS quilt, brainchild of gay activist Cleve Jones, displays the names of thousands of people who have died of the disease. It is displayed in the Washington Mall in 1987. REUTERS/CORBIS-BETTMANN

As the Third International AIDS Conference meets in Washington, D.C., 36,000 cases have been diagnosed, with 21,000 deaths.

EDUCATION

Three lower-court rulings are reversed: Alabama law banning 31 textbooks for promoting "religion of secular humanitarianism," Louisiana law requiring equal time for teaching of evolution theory and divine creation as a science; Hawkins County, Tenn., law excusing children from classes using textbooks that are offensive to parents' religious beliefs.

Los Angeles puts its 618 schools and 592,000 pupils on a year-round schedule.

RELIGION

Rev. Pat Robertson resigns leadership of his religious broadcasting empire to run for Republican presidential nomination.

ART/MUSIC

William Bolcom composes *12 New Etudes for Piano*; John Conigliaro composes the opera *A Figaro for Antonia*.

DEATHS Jascha Heifetz, concert violinist; Sammy Kaye, orchestra leader; Andy Warhol, pop-art painter.

SCIENCE/MEDICINE

Donald J. Cram and Charles J. Pedersen share Nobel Prize in chemistry for wide-ranging research, including creation of artificial molecules.

IBM announces production of ceramic material capable of handling much greater amounts of electric current.

LITERATURE/JOURNALISM

Joseph Brodsky, exiled Soviet-born poet, is awarded Nobel Prize in literature.

Richard Wilbur is second U.S. poet laureate.

BOOKS *Beloved* by Toni Morrison, *Look Homeward* by David H. Donald, *Breathing the Water* (poetry) by Denise Levertov, *Fine Things* and *Kaleidoscope* by Danielle Steel.

ENTERTAINMENT

PLAYS Alfred Uhry writes *Driving Miss Daisy*; Terrence McNally, *Frankie and Johnny in the Clair de Lune*; Tina Howe, *Coastal Disturbances*.

MOVIES *The Predator* with Arnold Schwarzenegger, *Wall Street* with Michael Douglas, *Moonstruck* with Cher, *Tin Men* with Richard Dreyfuss, *Good Morning, Vietnam* with Robin Williams, *The Last Emperor* directed by Bernardo Bertolucci.

DEATHS Dancers Ray Bolger and Fred Astaire; Liberace, pianist; actors Danny Kaye and Robert Preston; actresses Mary Astor and Rita Hayworth; Clare Boothe Luce, playwright; Jackie Gleason, actor and entertainer; director and choreographer Bob Fosse; screen directors John Huston and Mervyn Leroy; David Susskind, producer and talk-show host; Bill Baird, puppeteer.

SPORTS

NBA awards four new franchises: Miami and Orlando, Fla.; Charlotte, N.C., Minneapolis.

NFL players strike for three weeks.

WINNERS *Auto racing*—Al Unser, Indianapolis 500; Dale Earnhardt, NASCAR; *Baseball*—Minnesota Twins, World Series; *Basketball*—Southern Mississippi, NIT; Indiana, NCAA; Tennessee, NCAA (women); Los Angeles Lakers, NBA; *Bowling*—Randy Pedersen, PBA; American women, world title; *Boxing*—Mike Tyson, heavyweight; Sugar Ray Leonard, middleweight; *Figure skating*—Brian Boitano, U.S. men; Jill Trenary, U.S. women; *Football* (bowls)—Arizona State, Rose; Oklahoma, Orange; Nebraska, Sugar; Ohio State, Cotton; New York Giants, Super Bowl XXI; *Golf*—Scott Simpson, U.S. Open; Larry Nelson, PGA; Larry Mize, Masters; Laura Davies, U.S. Women's Open; Jane Geddes, LPGA; *Harness racing*—Mack Lobell, Hambletonian; *Hockey*—Edmonton, Stanley Cup; *Horse racing*—Alysheba, Kentucky Derby and Preakness Stakes; Bet Twice, Belmont Stakes; *Tennis*—Ivan Lendl, U.S. Open (men); Martina Navratilova, U.S. Open (women); *Yachting*—U.S. boat *Stars and Stripes* regains America's Cup.

MISCELLANEOUS

Tornado wipes out Saragosa, Tex., a town of 350; 30 are killed, 121 are injured.

Northwest airliner crashes after takeoff in Romulus, Mich.; 156 die.

1988

INTERNATIONAL

U.S. naval gunners mistakenly shoot down an Iranian passenger plane over the Persian Gulf thinking it was a warplane; all 290 aboard die (July 3).

Senate approves free-trade agreement with Canada.

President Ronald Reagan authorizes "a substantive dialogue" with Palestine Liberation Organization.

Senate ratifies Intermediate Range Nuclear Forces Treaty between U.S. and Soviet Union.

Car bomb kills U.S. military attaché in Athens, Navy Capt. William E. Nordeen.

NATIONAL

Vice President George Bush, Republican, is elected president, receives 48,881,221 popular and 426 electoral votes against 41,805,422 popular and 111 electoral votes for his Democratic challenger Michael S. Dukakis.

President Reagan vetoes civil rights bill; it passes over his veto (March 22).

Reparations bill is signed, gives $20,000 to each of about 60,000 surviving Japanese Americans interned during World War II.

New York State declares Love Canal area in

1988

Niagara Falls safe to live in; declared disaster area (1978) because of chemical contamination.

Veterans Administration becomes 14th cabinet department; effective 1989.

President Reagan signs $3.9 billion drought-relief bill.

Supreme Court rules that children in sexual abuse cases must confront their alleged abusers.

First-class postage increases by 3 cents to 25 cents.

DEATH Stuart Symington, senator, first secretary of Air Force.

BUSINESS/INDUSTRY/INVENTIONS

Securities and Exchange Commission accuses Drexel Burnham Lambert Group and junk-bond leader Michael Milken of extensive fraud.

Toni Morrison, who wins the Pulitzer Prize for Literature in 1988 for her 1987 novel *Beloved*. AP PHOTO/CHARLES REX ARBOGAST

Most of nation suffers severe drought, with half of the agricultural counties designated disaster areas; fire destroys about 4 million acres of forest.

Reported bank failures are at a record high, 221 in year.

Important mergers and takeovers during year: Kohlberg Kravis Roberts acquires RJR Nabisco for $24.9 billion; Philip Morris acquires Kraft for $11.5 billion; Campeau acquires Federated Department Stores for $7.4 billion; Pillsbury becomes part of Grand Metropolitan; Bridgestone acquires 75% of Firestone Tire for $1 billion.

TRANSPORTATION

Smoking is banned on Long Island and Metro-North Commuter railroads (N.Y.) and all Northwest Airlines flights in North America.

Chrysler Corp. closes its 5,500-worker Kenosha, Wis., plant.

Texaco agrees to pay $1.25 billion to settle overcharge complaints.

Transportation Department orders drug testing for 4 million transportation workers.

Donald Trump buys Eastern Airlines Northeast shuttle; Interstate Commerce Commission approves purchase of Southern Pacific Railroad for $1.2 billion by Rio Grande Industries.

SCIENCE/MEDICINE

Leon M. Lederman, Melvin Schwartz, and Jack Steinberger share Nobel Prize in physics for research that improved understanding of elementary particles and forces; Gertrude B. Elion and George H. Hitchings share prize in physiology/medicine for discovering principles for drug treatment.

Senate by 87–4 vote approves a $1 billion program for prevention and treatment of AIDS.

Space shuttle *Discovery* is first U.S. space shot since the *Challenger* disaster (1986).

DEATHS Walter H. Brattain, co-inventor of transistor; Luis W. Alvarez, codeveloper of ground-controlled radar.

EDUCATION

Education Secretary William Bennett resigns;

Lauro F. Cavazos, first Hispanic cabinet member, succeeds him.

Supreme Court rules that public school officials have right to censor school newspapers and plays.

Dade County, Fla., turns over management of 32 schools to teams including teachers and parents; Illinois legislature restructures Chicago public schools, shifting power to run schools mostly to parents.

NAACP drops 15-year desegregation suit against Los Angeles schools because of changes in school population composition.

RELIGION

Barbara Harris is elected suffragan bishop of Boston by Massachusetts Episcopal Diocese, first woman named by the Anglican Church in 450 years (September 24).

Mother Katharine Drexel, a Philadelphia nun, is beatified; born to wealth, she took vow of poverty, founded Sisters of the Blessed Sacrament; Rev. Junipero Serra, founder of California missions, is beatified.

Televangelist Jimmy Swaggart confesses sins to 8,000 of his Baton Rouge (La.) congregation, takes indefinite leave; Assemblies of God Church defrocks him when he refuses to stop preaching for a year; televangelist Jim Bakker is indicted on 24 federal charges of fraud and conspiracy.

Catholic Bishop Eugene A. Marino of Atlanta becomes first African American archbishop; two archbishops are elevated to cardinal: James A. Hickey of Washington, D.C., and Edmund C. Szoka of Detroit, Mich.

Merger of American Lutheran Church, Lutheran Church in America, and Association of Evangelical Lutheran Churches creates Evangelical Lutheran Church.

ART/MUSIC

Roger Reynolds composes *Whispers out of Time*.

Gala in Carnegie Hall celebrates Irving Berlin's 100th birthday; Smithsonian Institution stages exhibition on his life and works.

National Gallery (Washington, D.C.) constructs 23 new galleries in East Building to display twentieth-century art.

DEATH Frederick Loewe, musical comedy composer.

LITERATURE/JOURNALISM

Maxwell Communications acquires Macmillan Publishing Co.

BOOKS *New and Collected Poems* by Richard Wilbur, *A Bright Shining Lie* by Neil Sheehan, *The Bonfire of the Vanities* by Tom Wolfe, *Anything for Billy* by Larry McMurtry, *Greenlanders* by Jane Smiley.

DEATHS Milton Caniff, cartoonist; Robert A. Heinlein, science-fiction writer.

ENTERTAINMENT

PLAYS Michael Crawford stars in *The Phantom of the Opera*; Wendy Wasserstein writes *The Heidi Chronicles*.

MOVIES *Rain Man* with Tom Cruise and Dustin Hoffman, *Who Framed Roger Rabbit?* with Bob Hoskins, *Coming to America* with Eddie Murphy, *Twins* with Arnold Schwarzenegger.

Congress passes bill, limits number of commercials in children's television programs, is vetoed by President Reagan.

DEATH John Houseman, actor, director, and producer.

SPORTS

A. Bart Giamatti, National League president, becomes baseball commissioner; effective 1989.

First game is played under lights in Chicago's Wrigley Field (August 9).

St. Louis Cardinals football team moves to Phoenix.

Roosevelt Raceway in Westbury, N.Y., announces it will close.

WINNERS *Auto racing*—Rick Mears, Indianapolis 500; Bill Elliott, NASCAR; *Baseball*—Los Angeles Dodgers, World Series; *Basketball*—Connecticut, NIT; Kansas, NCAA; Louisiana Tech, NCAA (women); Los Angeles Lakers, NBA; *Bowling*—Brian Voss, PBA; *Boxing*—Mike Tyson, heavyweight; *Figure skating*—Brian Boitano, U.S., Olympic, and world titles; Debi Thomas, U.S. women's; *Football* (bowls)—Michigan State, Rose; Miami (Fla.), Orange; Syracuse–Auburn (tie), Sugar; Texas A&M, Cotton; Washington, Super Bowl XXII; *Golf*—Curtis Strange, U.S. Open; Jeff Shuman, PGA; Sandy Lyle, Masters; Liselotte Neumann, U.S. Women's Open; Sherri Turner, LPGA; *Harness racing*—Ambro Goal, Hambletonian; *Hockey*—Edmonton, Stanley Cup; *Horse racing*—Winning Colors, Kentucky Derby; Risen Star, Preakness Stakes and Belmont Stakes; *Tennis*—Mats Wilander, U.S. Open (men); Steffi Graf, U.S. Open (women); *Yachting*—U.S. boat *Stars and Stripes* retains America's Cup.

DEATHS Pete Maravich, basketball star; Jockey Mike Venezia in Belmont Park race; Hap (Leighton) Emms and Babe (Walter) Pratt, hockey greats; Carl Hubbell, Hall of Fame pitcher.

MISCELLANEOUS

Pan Am airliner en route to U.S. explodes over Lockerbie, Scotland, killing all 259 aboard, 11 on the ground; cause is determined to be bomb in a suitcase.

Diesel-fuel storage tank collapses, pours about 1 million gallons into Monongahela River at West Elizabeth, Pa.

INTERNATIONAL

U.S. troops (20,000) invade Panama, overthrow regime of Gen. Manuel A. Noriega (December 20); Noriega surrenders (January 3, 1990), flies to Miami to stand trial on drug charges; four days of fighting result in 23 U.S. and about 250 Panamanian deaths; Canal traffic closes for one day.

Two U.S. fighter planes shoot down two Libyan jets over Mediterranean, north of Tobruk (January 4).

U.S. warships are permitted to protect neutral shipping in Persian Gulf.

U.S. to return Iranian assets ($567 million) frozen since 1979 as result of hostage-taking.

Free-trade agreement between U.S. and Canada goes into effect (January 1); over a 10-year period, will create a largely free market of 270 million people.

Islamic militants announce that they killed U.S. hostage Lt. Col. William R. Higgins.

President George Bush becomes first U.S. president to address Hungarian parliament.

NATIONAL

Supreme Court leaves intact constitutional right to

1989

abortion but encourages states to set limits; upholds mandatory urine testing of railroad employees involved in accidents, Customs Service employees who seek drug enforcement jobs; rules alcoholism to be "willful misconduct," allows Veterans Administration to deny benefits to alcoholic veterans.

House Ethics Committee unanimously charges Speaker James C. Wright with 69 violations of House rules; Wright resigns (June 6); Thomas S. Foley succeeds him.

Largest oil spill in North American history occurs when Exxon tanker, *Exxon Valdez*, runs aground on reef near Valdez, Alaska; damages miles of beaches, destroys wildlife.

Explosion in gun turret of USS *Iowa* kills 47 crewmen.

Department of Veterans Affairs begins operations (March 15); Edward J. Derwinski is secretary.

Richard B. Cheney is named defense secretary after former Senator John Tower's nomination is rejected; Gen. Colin L. Powell becomes first African American chairman of Joint Chiefs of Staff.

Pennsylvania is first state to restrict abortions (November 18) since *Roe v. Wade* Supreme Court decision.

Rescue workers pull up a car that was perched over a collapsed section of the San Francisco Bay Bridge after the 1989 earthquake. UPI/CORBIS-BETTMANN

New Jersey Supreme Court finds surrogate mother agreements illegal in "Baby M" case.

U.S. Appeals Court Judge Robert Vance is killed by mail bomb at his home near Birmingham, Ala.; two days later, a civil rights lawyer, Robert Robinson, is killed by a mail bomb in Savannah, Ga.

David N. Dinkins is first African American mayor elected by New York City.

DEATH Gen. Albert C. Wedemeyer, World War II commander in China.

BUSINESS/INDUSTRY/INVENTIONS

Rescue package of $159 billion is set up for ailing savings and loan industry; Resolution Trust Corp. is created.

Minimum wage is raised to $4.25 an hour, effective 1991.

Mergers and takeovers include Warner Communications and *Time* magazine, Squibb and Bristol-Myers, Sony and Columbia Pictures.

Dow-Jones industrial average reaches record high of 2,734.64 (August 24).

Bank failures total 209 in year.

TRANSPORTATION

Eastern Airlines files for bankruptcy protection.

American Airlines and Delta Air Lines form partnership to operate global computer reservations system.

SCIENCE/MEDICINE

Space shuttle *Atlantis* launches *Magellan* space probe to map Venus (May 4); five months later *Atlantis* launches spacecraft *Galileo* to begin six-year journey to Jupiter; *Voyager II*, in space 12 years, passes planet Neptune (August 24).

Norman F. Ramsey and Hans G. Dehmelt share Nobel Prize in physics for developing methods of isolating atoms and subatomic particles; Thomas R. Cech and Sidney Altman share prize in chemistry for independent discoveries about active role of RNA in chemical cell reactions; J. Michael Bishop and Harold E. Varmus share prize in physiology/medicine for discovery of normal genes that can cause cancer when they go awry.

Government extends 20-month-old ban on federal financing of research using transplanted fetal tissue.

Congress repeals Medicare Catastrophic Coverage Act, including surtax to finance program.

Senate votes $1 billion anti-AIDS program.

DEATH William B. Shockley, co-inventor of transistor.

EDUCATION

Annual federal assessment finds student performance "merely average" and "stagnant" with no improvement despite increased spending.

RELIGION

American Episcopal bishops approve election of Barbara Harris, first women bishop in church, consecrate her as suffragan bishop of Boston (February 11); Episcopal Synod of America is formed by Episcopalians upset by the consecration (June 2).

Televangelist Jim Bakker is sentenced to 45 years and $500,000 fine for fraud and conspiracy.

Catholic Archdiocese of Detroit closes 43 of 112 churches because of dwindling membership and high operating costs.

Moral Majority, religious right-wing political lobby, disbands.

ART/MUSIC

Senate votes to bar National Endowment for the Arts from supporting "obscene or indecent" works; House refuses to concur.

Mel Powell composes *Duplicates*.

SONGS (popular): "Wind Beneath My Wings," "Look Away."

DEATHS Irving Berlin, composer of 800+ songs ("White Christmas," "God Bless America"); Alvin Ailey, ballet dancer and choreographer; Vladimir Horowitz, pianist.

LITERATURE/JOURNALISM

BOOKS *In Our Image* by Stanley Karnow, *All I Really Need to Know I Learned in Kindergarten* by Robert Fulghum, *Star* by Danielle Steel, *Swan Lake* by Mark Helprin.

Walden Books and other chains remove Salman Rushdie's *The Satanic Verses* from shelves after threats by Iran; Walden later changes its mind.

DEATHS Robert Penn Warren, first U.S. poet laureate; authors Irving Stone, Barbara W. Tuchman, and Mary McCarthy.

ENTERTAINMENT

PLAYS August Wilson writes *The Piano Lesson*; Jerome Robbins produces *Jerome Robbins' Broadway*.

Kirk Kerkorian sells MGM/UA Communications Co., including United Artists studio and 4,000-film library, to Quintex Group of Australia for $1 billion.

MOVIES *Driving Miss Daisy* with Jessica Tandy, *Dead Poets' Society* with Robin Williams, *Steel Magnolias* with Julia Roberts, *Born on the Fourth of July* with Tom Cruise, *Mississippi Burning* with Gene Hackman.

DEATHS Laurence Olivier, actor; Bette Davis and Lucille Ball, actresses.

SPORTS

A. Bart Giamatti becomes seventh baseball commissioner (April 1); dies suddenly (September 1); Fay Vincent, deputy commissioner, is elevated to commissioner; William D. White becomes National League president.

Pete Rozelle resigns as NFL commissioner after 30 years (March 22), is succeeded by Paul Tagliabue (October 26).

Sky Dome, home of Toronto baseball team, opens; San Francisco voters reject $115 million bond issue for downtown baseball stadium.

New York Supreme Court rules that U.S. boat *Stars and Stripes* violated spirit of race in winning 1988 America's Cup; decision is appealed.

Art Shell is named coach of Los Angeles Raiders; first African American coach in NFL.

Four golfers shoot hole-in-one on same hole in less than two hours during U.S. Open tournament; there had only been 21 aces in previous 94 Opens.

Pete Rose is banished from baseball for gambling activities.

Michael Chang becomes first U.S. tennis player to win French Open in 34 years.

Steve Largent catches 100th touchdown pass to set career record; Wayne Gretzky sets hockey-career scoring record with 1,851 points.

Greg LeMond wins Tour de France bicycle race by 8 seconds for second win.

Driver Hervé Filion becomes first harness-race driver to win 800 races in a year.

National Hockey League votes to expand league from 21 to 28 teams by year 2000; first teams will join 1992–1993.

Nolan Ryan of Houston Astros records 5,000th strikeout.

Randy Barnes sets world indoor record for shot-put with toss of 74 feet, $4\frac{1}{4}$ inches.

WINNERS *Auto racing*—Emerson Fittipaldi, Indianapolis 500; Rusty Wallace, NASCAR; *Baseball*—Oakland Athletics, World Series; *Basketball*—St. Johns, NIT; Michigan, NCAA; Tennessee, NCAA (women); Detroit, NBA; *Bowling*—Peter Weber, PBA; *Boxing*—Mike Tyson, heavyweight; Sugar Ray Leonard, middleweight;

Figure skating—Christopher Bowman, U.S. men; Jill Trenary, U.S. women; *Football* (bowls)—Michigan State, Rose; Miami (Fla.), Orange; Florida State, Sugar; UCLA, Cotton; San Francisco, Super Bowl XXIII; *Golf*—Curtis Strange, U.S. Open; Payne Stewart, PGA; Nick Faldo, Masters; Betsy King, U.S. Women's Open; Nancy Lopez, LPGA; *Harness racing*—Park Avenue Joe, Hambletonian; *Hockey*—Calgary, Stanley Cup; *Horse racing*—Sunday Silence, Kentucky Derby and Preakness Stakes; Easy Goer, Belmont Stakes; *Tennis*—Boris Becker, U.S. Open (men); Steffi Graf, U.S. Open (women).

DEATHS Larry Fleisher, organizer, NBA Players Assn.; Lee Calhoun, Olympic hurdler; Claude Harmon, golfer; Billy Martin, baseball player and manager, in truck accident; Doug Harvey, hockey great; Sugar Ray Robinson, boxing champion.

MISCELLANEOUS

Severe earthquake hits northern California (October 17); more than 60 are killed, several thousand are injured, 100,000 homes are damaged; hardest hit are San Francisco, Oakland; quake occurs at 5:04 P.M. during rush hour and minutes before start of World Series game in Candlestick Park; park is not damaged, no spectators are hurt.

Hurricane Hugo hits Caribbean and southeastern U.S.; 504 die.

Truck hits school bus in Alton, Tex., killing 16 students, injuring 64; hurricane-force winds blow down cafeteria wall at Newburgh, N.Y., school during lunch hour, killing 7.

United DC-10 crashes during emergency landing at Sioux City, Iowa; 111 are killed.

1990

INTERNATIONAL

U.N. approves resolutions condemning Iraq's occupation of Kuwait; U.N. forces begin air attacks on Iraq to force withdrawal.

Soviet President Gorbachev and President George Bush hold summit meeting in Washington, agree to reduce long-range nuclear weapons by about a third over seven years.

Two U.S. hostages kidnapped in Lebanon are freed: Robert Polhill after more than three years, Robert Reed after nearly five years.

Congress increases annual immigration limit from 500,000 to 700,000 in 1992–1994 period.

NATIONAL

President Bush signs Americans with Disabilities Act to prevent discrimination against the handicapped.

Proposed constitutional amendment to permit prosecution of flag burners or desecrators fails to pass either house of Congress.

Former National Security Advisor John Poindexter is found guilty of five felony counts in Iran-Contra case, is sentenced to six months; Appeals Court suspends three felony convictions of Oliver North.

Senate Ethics Committee studies five senators' involvement with Charles Keating, head of a failed California savings and loan; find "credible evidence" of misconduct by Sen. Alan Cranston of California.

Supreme Court Justice William Brennan Jr. retires after nearly 34 years; Appeals Court Judge David Souter succeeds him.

Twenty-first census reports national population of 249,632,692.

Washington Mayor Marion Barry is found guilty on one charge of drug possession, is sentenced to six months.

Congress passes clean air and deficit reduction legislation, President Bush signs it but vetoes a civil rights bill, arguing that it would require quotas for hiring and promotion.

Mrs. Imelda Marcos, widow of former Philippines president, is found not guilty on charges of racketeering, fraud, and obstruction of justice.

DEATH Ralph B. Abernathy, civil rights leader.

BUSINESS/INDUSTRY/INVENTIONS

Drexel Burnham Lambert Group, a securities firm, files for bankruptcy; Michael Milken, former "junk bond" king, pleads guilty to securities fraud, agrees to pay $600 million in fines, restitution, is sentenced to 10 years in prison.

Harry M. Markowitz, William F. Sharpe, and Merton H. Miller share Nobel Prize in economics for work in providing new tools to weigh risks and rewards of different investments and valuing stocks and bonds.

Joseph Hazelwood, captain of the *Exxon Valdez*, which spilled millions of gallons of oil in Alaskan waters, is found guilty of negligence.

Contel and GTE, communications firms, merge.

Allied/Federal Stores and Ames Department Stores file for bankruptcy; year's bank failures total 169.

Dow-Jones industrial average reaches an all-time high of 2,999.75 (July 16–17).

DEATHS Joseph Schumpeter, economist; Lewis Mumford, architectural and urban design critic; Harry Bridges, West Coast longshoremen's union president; Gordon Bunshaft, architect; Halston, designer.

TRANSPORTATION

Three Chrysler Corp. engineers develop first fully electronic force-fed automatic transmission.

Space shuttle *Discovery* deploys the $1.5-billion Hubble telescope; soon after launch, it is learned that serious design flaws will mar many of its experiments; *Magellan* space probe sends back image strips taken in its $1\frac{1}{2}$ orbits of the planet Venus.

Joseph E. Murray and E. Donnell Thomas share Nobel Prize in physiology/medicine for pioneering work in organ transplantations; Jerome I. Friedman and Henry W. Kendall share prize in physics for experiments confirming existence of quarks, fundamental to all matter; Elias J. Corey is awarded prize in chemistry for new ways to synthesize complex molecules.

Supreme Court rules that a person whose wishes are clearly known has right to refuse life-sustaining medical treatment.

Four-year-old girl becomes first human recipient of gene therapy when she is infused with white blood cells containing copies of the gene she lacked.

DEATH Karl Menninger, psychiatrist.

EDUCATION

DEATH Bruno Bettelheim, psychoanalyst specializing in autistic children.

ART/MUSIC

Twelve artworks valued at about $100 million are stolen from Gardner Museum in Boston.

Record price for a painting is set when Vincent Van Gogh's *Portrait of Dr. Gachet* sells for $82.5 million.

William S. Paley bequeaths major collection of art to Museum of Modern Art.

Kurt Masur is named musical director of New York Philharmonic Orchestra, succeeding Zubin Mehta.

SONGS (popular): "Blaze of Glory," "Knockin' Boots," "Hold On," "Step by Step," "All Around the World."

DEATHS Jimmy Van Heusen and David Rose, popular song-

writers; Kurt Weill, composer; Buddy DeSylva, lyricist; Sarah Vaughan and Pearl Bailey, singers; Leonard Bernstein and Aaron Copland, composers and conductors.

LITERATURE/JOURNALISM

St. Louis Sun folds after only seven months of publication.

Mark Strand is fourth U.S. poet laureate.

Supreme Court rules that First Amendment does not automatically shield opinions in newspaper columns from being found libelous.

BOOKS *Hocus Pocus* by Kurt Vonnegut Jr., *The Witching House* by Anne Rice, *Deception* and *Patrimony* by Philip Roth, *Clear and Present Danger* by Tom Clancy.

DEATHS Malcom Forbes, magazine publisher; Marquis Childs, columnist; Laurence J. Peter, developer of the Peter Principle.

ENTERTAINMENT

A Chorus Line closes (March 31) after 6,104 performances.

PLAYS Maggie Smith stars in *Lettice and Lovage*; *Six Degrees of Separation* by John Guare.

MOVIES *Pretty Woman* with Julia Roberts, *Home*

Pete Sampras volleys with Andre Agassi during the second set of their final U.S. Open tennis match, 1990. REUTERS/CORBIS-BETTMANN

1990

Alone with Macauley Culkin, *Dances with Wolves* with Kevin Costner, *Kindergarten Cop* with Arnold Schwarzenegger.

DEATHS Five noted screen actresses, Paulette Goddard, Barbara Stanwyck, Ava Gardner, Irene Dunne, and Greta Garbo; Rex Harrison, actor; Mary Martin, actress; Sammy Davis Jr., entertainer and actor; William S. Paley, CBS head; three radio/television celebrities: Jim Henson, creator of the Muppets; Bill Cullen, game-show host; and Ray Goulding, of Bob and Ray comedy team.

SPORTS

Baseball Commissioner Fay Vincent forces George Steinbrenner to resign as New York Yankees managing general partner for associating with a "known gambler."

Oakland, Calif., and Al Davis agree on $602-million, 15-year deal to bring the football Raiders back to Oakland; popular referendum rejects the deal.

Baseball owners and players agree on settlement of claims for free-agent violations: $280 million in damages.

New York Court of Appeals upholds awarding 1988 America's Cup to *Stars and Stripes* (see 1989).

Pete Rose, barred from baseball, pleads guilty to filing false income tax returns, is sentenced to five-month prison term, is fined $50,000.

Greg LeMond wins Tour de France bicycle race for third time in five years.

Willy Shoemaker, 58, rides final race (February 3); won 8,833 races in 40,350 starts.

CBS fires sportscaster Brent Musburger after 15 years (April 10); he signs with ABC (May 2).

Cleveland voters approve higher taxes for downtown stadium/arena.

Rickey Henderson of Oakland Athetics sets new American League career stolen-base record (893); Nolan Ryan of Houston Astros pitches record sixth no-hit game, wins 300th game.

Comiskey Park in Chicago closes after 80 seasons; new baseball stadium to open in Spring 1991.

Wayne Gretzky of Los Angeles becomes first NHL player to score 2,000 points.

WINNERS *Auto racing*—Ariel Luyendyk, Indianapolis 500; Dale Earnhardt, NASCAR; *Baseball*—Cincinnati Reds, World Series; *Basketball*—Vanderbilt, NIT; UNLV, NCAA; Stanford, NCAA (women); Detroit, NBA; *Bowling*—Jim Pencak, PBA; *Boxing*—Evander Holyfield, heavyweight; Pernell Whittaker, lightweight; *Figure skating*—Jill Trenary, U.S. and world women's titles; Todd Eldredge, U.S. men's; *Football* (bowls)—Southern California, Rose; Notre Dame, Orange; Miami, Sugar; Tennessee, Cotton; San Francisco, Super Bowl XXIV; *Golf*—Hale Irwin, U.S. Open; Wayne Grady, PGA; Nick Faldo, Masters; Betsy King, U.S. Women's Open; Beth Daniel, LPGA; *Harness racing*—Harmonious, Hambletonian; *Hockey*—Edmonton, Stanley Cup; *Horse racing*—Unbridled, Kentucky Derby; Summer Squall, Preakness Stakes; Go and Go, Belmont Stakes; *Tennis*—Pete Sampras, U.S. Open (men); Gabriele Sabatini, U.S. Open (women).

DEATHS Hap Day, hockey great; Fortune Gordien, Olympic discus thrower; Bronko Nagurski, football star (University of Minnesota, Chicago Bears); Lawrence O'Brien, former NBA commissioner.

MISCELLANEOUS

Colombian jet liner crashes on Long Island, N.Y., kills 73.

Social club fire in New York City claims 87 lives.

Mt. Kilauea in Hawaii and Mt. Redoubt in Alaska erupt.

NASA reports that the average global temperature in year is 59.81 degrees, the warmest since 1880.

1991

INTERNATIONAL

GULF WAR Operation Desert Storm (the war in Iraq) begins (January 17) with U.S.-led air units striking Iraqi targets; ground-war fighting begins (February 24), virtually ends in five days.

Queen Elizabeth of Great Britain makes two-week visit to U.S., addresses Congress (May 16); first by a British monarch.

President George Bush lifts economic sanctions against South Africa.

President Bush and Soviet President Mikhail Gorbachev sign treaty to reduce nuclear-weapons stockpile.

American Edward Tracy, a hostage since 1986, released in Lebanon.

Philippines Senate rejects renewal of lease for Subic Bay Naval Station; U.S. to withdraw within three years; eruption of Mt. Pinatubo forces the evacuation and eventual abandonment of Clark Air Force Base, 10 miles from volcano.

NATIONAL

Commission recommends that 34 U.S. military bases be closed, 48 be realigned; Congress approves (July 30).

Senate votes 52 to 48 to confirm Clarence Thomas as Supreme Court associate justice (October 15), succeeding retiring Thurgood Marshall; action comes after controversial hearings.

Special prosecutor drops charges against Oliver North in Iran-Contra investigation.

Trial of Gen. Manuel Noriega, former Panama leader, on drug trafficking and money laundering charges begins in Miami.

First-class postage rises to 29 cents an ounce (February 3).

Bank that served House of Representatives to close at year's end after revelations that members had written 8,331 bad checks in one year.

Supreme Court lets stand New York City's prohibition of begging in subways; rules police can search trunk of a car and its contents without a warrant; rejects challenge to punitive damage awards, leaving juries with historic broad discretion.

Remains of President Zachary Taylor are exhumed at request of a historical novelist who thought he may have died of arsenic poisoning rather than acute gastrointestinal illness; study shows no trace of arsenic.

DEATHS Senator John Heinz of Pennsylvania and former Senator John Tower of Texas in separate plane crashes.

BUSINESS/INDUSTRY/INVENTIONS

Ronald H. Coase is awarded Nobel Prize in economics for work on role of institutions in the economy.

Supreme Court rules that employers cannot bar women from jobs where they might be exposed to materials hazardous to developing fetuses.

Three major bank mergers occur: Chemical Banking Corp. and Manufacturers Hanover, NCNB Corp. and C. & S. Sovran to form Nations Bank, and Bank America Corp. and Security Pacific Corp.; ATT and NCR complete their merger.

Federal regulators take over Bank of New England Corp. after huge fourth-quarter loss and run on bank.

Minimum wage increases to $4.25 an hour (January 1).

Five-millionth patent is given by Patent Office, to researchers at University of Florida for a genetically engineered microbe; other patents issued include one for a machine to measure fats, oils, and moisture in baked goods as they come off assembly line, and a magnetic hammer to make it easier to drive nails without hitting one's fingers.

1991

U.S. Marines look over a wall in the U.S Embassy in Kuwait City, looking for snipers, February 1991. REUTERS/CORBIS-BETTMANN

TRANSPORTATION

Pan American World Airways files for bankruptcy, sells most of its remaining assets to Delta; Eastern Airlines stops flying, sells most of its assets; bankrupt Midway Airlines ceases operating.

Nissan Motors plans to build second U.S. plant at Decherd, Tenn.

General Motors announces it will close 21 of 125 assembly and parts plants in North America over the next few years, eliminating more than 70,000 jobs.

General Motors begins building first commercially available electric car in modern times in Lansing, Mich.

SCIENCE/MEDICINE

National Association of Health Commissioners selects nine private health-insurance policies as supplements to Medicare, replacing the large number now available.

Federal government announces new nationwide fee schedule under which family doctors and general practitioners will receive more (but less than expected), specialists will receive less.

NASA reports that a satellite above Antarctica found ozone level in the atmosphere to be lowest on record.

AIDS spreads rapidly among the poor, African Americans and Hispanic Americans, and women and children. A variety of drugs are available to patients, who often live ten or more years with the disease.

EDUCATION

Supreme Court rules that school desegregation busing could end if school districts have done everything "practicable" to eliminate "vestiges" of past discrimination.

President Bush calls for national education tests and for redirecting federal money to help disadvantaged students who choose to go to private schools or parochial schools.

RELIGION

Survey shows that 90% of Americans identify with some church.

Southern Baptists who are unhappy with conservative leadership create 6,000-member Cooperative Baptist Fellowship.

Catholic archbishops Roger M. Mahoney and Anthony J. Bevilacqua are elevated to cardinal; Bishop Daniel A. Cronin is named archbishop of Hartford, Conn.

ART/MUSIC

Supreme Court rules 5–4 that while nude dancing is entitled to protection under the First Amendment's freedom of expression, states may ban it in the "interest of protecting order and morality."

Carnegie Hall celebrates 100th birthday with two gala concerts (May 5).

Walter H. Annenberg bequeaths about $1 billion worth of impressionist and postimpressionist art to Metropolitan Museum of Art; also donates $10 million to Los Angeles County Museum of Art.

Willie Nelson releases special recording designed to raise $15 million owed in back taxes to Internal Revenue Service.

DEATHS Robert Motherwell, abstract expressionist painter; Miles Davis, jazz trumpeter.

1991

LITERATURE/JOURNALISM

Joseph Brodsky becomes fifth U.S. poet laureate.

Rupert Murdoch, faced with huge debt burden, sells nine magazines (including *Racing Form*, *New Woman*, *Seventeen*, *New York*) for more than $600 million to K-III Holdings.

Robert Maxwell, British publisher, agrees to buy *New York Daily News* after reaching agreement with 13 labor unions.

Supreme Court reverses New York State law that prohibits criminals from profiting from stories sold to publishers.

Dallas Times Herald folds.

BOOKS *A Soldier of the Great War* by Mark Helprin, *Sliver* by Ira Levin, *Pinocchio in Venice* by Robert Coover, *Harlot's Ghost* by Norman Mailer, *Scarlett* by Alexandra Ripley.

DEATHS Isaac Bashevis Singer and Dr. Seuss (Theodore Seuss Geisel), authors.

ENTERTAINMENT

FCC votes to relax but not eliminate rule that prohibits television networks from owning and selling reruns of shows they broadcast.

New television shows include *America's Most Wanted*, *Beverly Hills 90210*, *Thirtysomething*.

MOVIES *Cape Fear* with Nick Nolte, *Field of Dreams* with Kevin Costner, *Bugsy* with Warren Beatty, *Thelma and Louise* with Susan Sarandon and Geena Davis, Disney's *Beauty and the Beast*.

DEATHS Frank Capra, movie director; Eva Le Gallienne and Colleen Dewhurst, actresses; Joseph Papp, theatrical producer; Redd Foxx, television entertainer.

SPORTS

Dennis Martinez of Montreal Expos pitches perfect game (13th to do so); Rickey Henderson of Oakland Athletics sets new career stolen-base record (939).

Mike Powell breaks 23-year-old long-jump record with leap of 29 feet, $4\frac{1}{4}$ inches; Carl Lewis sets world 100-meter record of 9.86 seconds.

The National, first sports daily, folds after 18 months.

Don Shula, coach of Miami Dolphins, coaches his 300th career football-game victory.

WINNERS *Auto racing* — Rick Mears, Indianapolis 500; Dale Earnhardt, NASCAR; *Baseball* — Minnesota Twins, World Series; *Basketball* — Duke, NCAA; Stanford, NIT; Tennessee, NCAA (women); Chicago, NBA; *Bowling* — Mike Miller, PBA; *Boxing* — Evander Holyfield, heavyweight; *Figure skating* — Kristi Yamaguchi, world women's title; Todd Eldredge, U.S. men's; Tonya Harding, U.S. women's; *Football* (bowls) — Washington, Rose; Colorado, Orange; Tennessee, Sugar; Miami (Fla.), Cotton; New York Giants, Super Bowl

Oklahoma law professor Anita Hill testifies before the Senate judiciary committee, claiming she was harassed sexually by Supreme Court nominee Clarence Thomas. Her testimony stimulates discussions across the nation of the meaning of sexual harassment. REUTERS/CORBIS-BETTMANN

1992

XXV; *Golf* — U.S., Walker and Ryder cups; Payne Stewart, U.S. Open; Ian Woosnam, Masters; John Daly, PGA; Meg Mallon, U.S. Open (women); *Harness racing* — Giant Victory, Hambletonian; *Hockey* — Pittsburgh, Stanley Cup; *Horse racing* — Strike the Gold, Kentucky Derby; Hansel, Preakness Stakes and Belmont Stakes; *Tennis* — Stefan Edberg, U.S. Open (men); Monica Seles, U.S. Open (women).

DEATH Lyle Alzado, football player.

★ ★ ★ ★ ★ ★ ★ ★

1992

INTERNATIONAL

President George Bush and Russian President Boris Yeltsin announce (December 30) agreement on a nuclear arms reduction treaty that would reduce their countries' strategic arms by two-thirds, eliminate land-based multiple-warhead missiles by 2003; the agreement, to be signed January 3, 1993, in Moscow, must be ratified by the Senate and the legislatures of Russia and three other Soviet republics.

U.S. forces land in Somalia (December 3) to protect food shipments for the starving populace; for many months, shipments were looted by native gangs; U.N. forces join U.S. in securing airports and towns, protecting relief centers.

U.S. planes shoot down an Iraqi jet when it violates U.N.-created no-fly zone in southern Iraq (December 27).

U.S., one of 178 nations attending the U.N. Environment and Development Conference in Rio de Janeiro, does not sign the international treaty designed to preserve the world's plants, animals, and natural resources; argues that treaty is "seriously flawed" by not protecting U.S. patents on biological inventions; U.S. does sign a treaty to try to halt global warming.

Representatives from Canada, Mexico, and the U.S. approve (August 12) draft agreement that establishes free trade among the three in 15 years; treaty is signed by the nations' leaders (December 17), must be ratified by legislatures of the nations.

President Bush visits Australia, Singapore, South Korea, and Japan to improve U.S. international trade, collapses during a state dinner in Japan, recovers quickly, diagnosed as having had intestinal flu.

Bush Administration lifts sanctions against China's transfer of high technology after China pledges to abide by restrictions on missile sales to Mideast.

Supreme Court lifts injunction that bars U.S. from returning Haitian refugees held at base at Guantanamo Bay, Cuba.

NATIONAL

Democratic Gov. Bill (William J.) Clinton of Arkansas is elected president, defeats President Bush and independent candidate H. Ross Perot; Clinton receives 370 electoral and 43,682,624 popular votes; Bush, 168 and 38,117,331; Perot, no electoral votes and 19,217,213 popular votes; Tennessee Senator Albert Gore is elected vice president. Carol M. Braun becomes first African American woman senator, wins in Illinois; California fills both Senate seats with women, San Francisco Mayor Diane Feinstein and Rep. Barbara Boxer.

Supreme Court upholds part of Pennsylvania law that imposes strict limits on a woman's right to abortion (June 29), but its 5–4 vote also upholds "essence" of constitutional right to abortion. Bush Administration rules that doctors in federally funded family-planning clinics may give limited advice on abortion but nurses and counselors may not.

Rioting sweeps through south central Los Angeles (April 29) after a jury acquits four white police officers on all but one count in the beating of Rodney King, a black man; 52 are killed in riots that go on for several days.

House Ethics Committee reports (March 5) that 329 present and former House members wrote almost 20,000 overdrafts on their accounts in the

Los Angeles police officers train their guns on a looter in south central Los Angeles during the riots that follow the Rodney King verdict, April 1992. REUTERS/LEE CELANO/ARCHIVE PHOTOS

House bank in nearly three years; the private bank serves only House members.

Twenty-seventh Amendment to Constitution, approved by Congress in 1789, is finally ratified (May 7) when Michigan legislature acts favorably; amendment, proposed by James Madison, provides that congressional pay raises cannot take effect until a new Congress takes office.

President Bush pardons former Defense Secretary Caspar Weinberger and five other former Reagan administration executives accused of lying to Congress about Iran-Contra acts.

Congress approves bill to extend benefit payments for 13 weeks to long-term unemployed persons during a recession; president signs it.

Former Panama military ruler Manuel Noriega is convicted for racketeering, drug trafficking, and money laundering.

Sweeping law that requires businesses to give equal access to disabled Americans goes into effect (January 27).

California Insurance Commissioner, in first case since voter-approved rollback of auto insurance, orders 20th Century Insurance Co. to refund more than $100 million to 650,000 policyholders; California, where legislature and governor cannot agree on a budget, runs short of cash, begins to pay bills with IOUs.

More than a million votes are cast to select a portrait of the late Elvis Presley to be used on a postage stamp.

DEATHS Philip Habib, Mideast negotiator; Wilbur Mills, head of House Ways & Means Committee 17 years; George Murphy, screen actor, California senator; John J. Sirica, judge who presided at Watergate trials.

BUSINESS/INDUSTRY/INVENTIONS

Gary S. Becker is awarded Nobel Prize in economics for extending economic theory to human behavior dealt with by other social sciences.

R. H. Macy & Co., owner of 251 retail stores; Wang Laboratories, computer maker; and Zale department stores file for bankruptcy.

Economic depression in defense industry leads to layoffs and consolidations: General Dynamics sells its jet-fighter division to Lockheed, its missile division to Hughes Aircraft; Martin Marietta buys

1992

General Electric's aerospace division; LTV Corp. sells aircraft and missile divisions.

President Bush directs U.S. manufacturers to stop producing virtually all ozone-destroying chemicals by end of 1995.

First food irradiation plant in U.S. (Mulberry, Fla.) ready for service, begins to irradiate strawberries for shipment, other produce follows.

Charlotte Beers becomes first woman chairman of a major advertising group (Ogilvy & Mather).

Dow-Jones industrial average hits record high of 3,280.64 (February 20).

Federal Communications Commission proposes opening many radio frequencies for "emerging technologies."

DEATHS William McGowan, former MCI head whose antitrust suit against ATT led to competition in telecommunications; Sam Walton, founder of Wal-Mart stores; George J. Stigler, Nobel Prize economist.

TRANSPORTATION

"Big Three" automakers report huge losses for year: Chrysler, $895 million; Ford, $2.26 billion; General Motors, $4.5 billion. Ford announces investment of $3 billion in new machinery and plant, some to be used for new minivan in late 1993; GM announces first stage of three-year plan to close 21 plants in U.S. and Canada.

Trans World Airlines (TWA) files for bankruptcy.

Chrysler Corp. selects Robert G. Eaton, a GM executive, to succeed Lee A. Iacocca as chief executive January 1993; GM replaces its chairman, Robert C. Stempel, with John G. Smale as head of executive committee.

Federal officials estimate (December 29) that 1992 traffic deaths will drop below 40,000 for first time in 30 years.

President Bush signs bill to end strike that shut down nation's freight lines; calls for 20-day cooling-off period, then (if needed) binding arbitration.

British Airways and USAir plan to form world's largest airline partnership with British Airways buying 44% of USAir; deal falls through when Britain refuses to open more air space to U.S. carriers; Northwest Airlines and KLM Royal

Dutch Airlines combine operations; Air Canada buys Continental Airlines.

Senate passes energy bill to encourage development of alternative-fuel vehicles.

SCIENCE/MEDICINE

Edmond H. Fischer and Edwin G. Krebs share Nobel Prize in physiology/medicine for discovering a regulatory mechanism affecting most cells; Rudolph A. Marcus is awarded prize in chemistry for finding way to predict certain interactions between molecules in solution.

NASA reports that danger of ozone depletion over northeastern U.S. and eastern Canada has increased as chemicals harmful to ozone reach record levels.

Three space-shuttle crew members, working more than eight hours outside the spacecraft, succeed in capturing a communications satellite that went off course; after repairs, the satellite returns to proper orbit; Richard H. Truly resigns as head of NASA after long battle with White House over direction of space program; Daniel S. Goldin succeeds him.

Food & Drug Administration orders moratorium on sale and implantation of silica gel breast implants while safety of implant operations is studied.

Scientists discover what could be oldest, largest living organism on Earth: a giant fungus, possibly 10,000 years old, that covers more than 30 acres near Crystal Falls, Mich.; Washington scientists dispute claim, saying that a fungus near Mt. Adams, N.H., is 40 times as large.

DEATHS Barbara McClintock, Nobel Prize scientist; Robert M. Page, physicist who helped develop radar.

EDUCATION

Supreme Court rules that nonsectarian prayers at a public high-school graduation in Providence, R.I., were unconstitutional.

Supreme Court rules that Mississippi failed to prove that it erased segregation in its state university system; also rules that students can sue schools and colleges for sexual harassment and other forms of sex discrimination.

Yale University President Benno C. Schmidt Jr. resigns (effective January 1, 1993) to head a project to create a national private school system; Whittle Communications funds project with $60 million; Michael I. Sovran to step down June 1993 as president of Columbia University; other 1992 resignations are Hannah H. Gray of University of Chicago, H. Keith Brodie of Duke University, and Donald Kennedy of Stanford University.

RELIGION

Harvey W. Wood, longtime chairman of Christian Science Church, resigns amid bitter dispute over church's direction and finances.

Center for Christian-Jewish Understanding is created at Sacred Heart University in Fairfield, Conn.

DEATH Frederick W. Franz, president, Jehovah's Witnesses (1977–1992).

ART/MUSIC

President Bush dismisses John E. Frohnman as chairman of National Endowment for the Arts after criticism of some grants made by agency.

J. Carter Brown retires after 27 years as director of National Gallery of Art.

Philip Glass's opera *The Voyage* is produced to commemorate Christopher Columbus's trip; Lyric Opera of Chicago presents William Bolcom's opera *McTeague*.

SONGS (popular): "Here Comes the Hammer," "Justify My Love," "I Do It for You," "Ropin' the Wind," "Unforgettable," "End of the Road," "Baby Go Back."

Many New Yorkers switch to country music as alternative to hip-hop and rap; WYNY–FM claims largest country-music audience in world.

DEATHS John Cage, experimental music composer; William Schuman, composer, founding director of Juilliard School; Lawrence Welk, orchestra leader.

LITERATURE/JOURNALISM

Mona Van Duyn becomes sixth U.S. poet laureate; first woman so honored.

BOOKS *Memories of the Ford Administration* by John

Updike, *Women of Sand and Myrrh* by Hanan el-Shaykh, *The First Dissident* by William Safire, *The Way Things Ought to Be* by Rush Limbaugh.

Two new magazines begin publication: *Worth* by Fidelity Investments and *Smart Money* by Hearst Corp. and Dow Jones; former *Vanity Fair* editor Tina Brown edits *The New Yorker*.

Arthur Ochs Sulzberger, publisher of the *New York Times* for 29 years, steps down, is succeeded by son, Arthur O. Jr.

DEATHS William Shawn, editor, *The New Yorker* (1957–1992); author Isaac Asimov (468 books), Alex Haley (*Roots*), and Frank Yerby, novelist; CBS newsman Eric Sevareid.

ENTERTAINMENT

Johnny Carson retires after 29 years as emcee of *The Tonight Show*, succeeded by Jay Leno.

Federal Communications Commission allows television networks to buy local cable systems.

MOVIES *A Few Good Men* with Tom Cruise, *Hoffa* with Jack Nicholson, *Home Alone 2* with Macauley Culkin, *Batman Returns* with Michael Keaton, *Sister Act* with Whoopi Goldberg, Disney's *Aladdin*, *Malcolm X* with Denzel Washington.

PLAYS Alan Alda stars in *Jake's Women* by Neil Simon, Judd Hirsch in *Conversations with My Father*, Gregory Hines in *Jelly's Last Jam*, Brid Brennan in *Dancing at Lughnasa*; Wendy Wasserstein writes *The Sisters Rosensweig*.

DEATHS Stage/screen/TV actors Shirley Booth, Judith Anderson, Ralph Bellamy, Sandy Dennis, Marlene Dietrich, Jose Ferrer, Allan Jones, Fred MacMurray, Gene Tierney, Molly Picon; Hal Roach, pioneer screen comedy writer and producer; Mark Goodson, TV game-show producer (*The Price Is Right*, *What's My Line?*); country-music greats Roy Acuff, Tennessee Ernie Ford, Roger Miller.

SPORTS

Fay Vincent resigns as baseball commissioner after majority of owners ask him to step down; John Ziegler quits as National Hockey League president after 15 years.

Magic Johnson, basketball star who contracted AIDS virus, resigns for second time; Hall of Fame

1993

Jockey Angel Cordaro Jr. retires after racing accident; Larry Bird, Boston Celtics star, retires.

Winter Olympics are held in Albertville, France; U.S. wins 5 golds, with Bonnie Blair winning 2 in speed skating; Summer Games held in Barcelona, Spain; U.S. wins 37 golds.

Former heavyweight boxing champion Mike Tyson is convicted of rape in Indianapolis, is sentenced to six-year prison term.

National Hockey League players begin first strike (April 2) after rejecting contract proposal; return 10 days later with new contract.

Baseball club owners approve sale of Seattle Mariners to group of investors including Nintendo Co. of Japan as a minority stockholder.

WINNERS *Auto racing* — Al Unser, Indianapolis 500; Alan Kulwicki, NASCAR; *Baseball* — Toronto Blue Jays, World Series; *Basketball* — Virginia, NIT; Duke, NCAA; Stanford, NCAA (women); Chicago, NBA; *Boxing* — Evander Holyfield, heavyweight; Virgil Hill, light heavyweight; Reggie Johnson, middleweight; *Figure skating* — Kristi Yamaguchi, Olympics, world, U.S. singles, women; Christoper Bowman, U.S. singles, men; *Football* (bowls) — Washington, Rose; Miami (Fla.), Orange; Notre Dame, Sugar; Florida State, Cotton; Washington, Super Bowl XXVI; *Golf* — Tom Kite, U.S. Open; Nick Price, PGA; Fred Couples, Masters; Patty Sheehan, U.S. Women's Open; Betsy King, LPGA; *Harness racing* — Alf Palema,

Hambletonian; *Hockey* — Pittsburgh, Stanley Cup; *Horse racing* — Lil E. Tee, Kentucky Derby; Pine Bluff, Preakness Stakes; A. P. Indy, Belmont Stakes; *Tennis* — Stefan Edberg, U.S. Open (men); Monica Seles, U.S. Open (women); *Yachting* — U.S. retains America's Cup.

DEATHS Carl Stotz, founder of Little League baseball; baseball players Billy Herman, Ken Keltner, Eddie Lopat; football players Buck Buchanan, Mel Hein; Red (Walter H.) Barber, baseball announcer; Samuel Reshevsky, U.S. chess champion.

MISCELLANEOUS

Hurricane Andrew devastates part of southern Florida and Louisiana (August 24); 30 are killed, 85,000 homes are destroyed or damaged, leaving 250,000 homeless; estimated loss of $7.3 billion; Hurricane Iniki strikes Hawaii (September 11), kills 3, causes about $1 billion in damage.

Most powerful earthquake in California in 40 years strikes 125 miles east of Los Angeles, near Landers, followed by another three hours later; one death, numerous injuries, much property damage.

About 250 million gallons of water from Chicago River flood into downtown tunnels, basements in Chicago; forces evacuation of 200,000 people for several days.

INTERNATIONAL

United States and 116 other countries agree to GATT (General Agreement on Tariffs and Trades), remove export barriers, tariffs on thousands of manufactured products, include agriculture and service industries in world trade rules; to be signed April 1994 in Morocco; must be approved by nations' legislatures; effective 1995.

Congress approves NAFTA (North American Free Trade Agreement), the House by 234–200, the Senate by 61–38, to phase out tariffs between U.S., Canada, and Mexico in 15 years.

U.S. is one of more than 120 countries that sign agreement not to manufacture, stockpile, or use chemical weapons.

U.S. hands control of relief efforts in Somalia to U.N. after six-month effort to remove weapons in the streets, safeguard food distribution. Twenty U.S. soldiers killed in Mogadishu, Somalia, in

1993

fierce clash with Somali warlord forces. Incident leads to increasing U.S. military presence and the decision to bring U.S. troops home by March 31, 1994.

U.S., French, and British planes bomb missile sites in southern Iraq when Iraq defies terms ending Persian Gulf war; another strike at Baghdad suburb when Iraq refuses to guarantee safety of U.N. inspectors.

President Bush and Russian President Boris Yeltsin sign second Strategic Arms Reduction Treaty; later in year, President Bill Clinton meets with Yeltsin to arrange aid to Russia.

U.S. naval forces patrol waters around Haiti to enforce U.N. sanctions imposed when Haitian military leaders refuse to let elected president return.

President Clinton attends economic summit of major industrial nations in Tokyo; reaches accord with Japan to resolve trade disputes; later, U.S. is host to APEC (Asia Pacific Economic Cooperation) forum designed to reduce or eliminate trade disputes.

President Clinton announces U.S. will sign international treaty protecting rare and endangered species, follow timetable to reduce threat of global warming; both items were rejected by President Bush.

NATIONAL

President Clinton proposes plan to assure health insurance for all Americans and to lower health-care costs.

House (218–216) and Senate (51–50) approve bill to reduce federal budget deficit by $496 billion over five years.

Congress passes Family Leave Act to permit employees of government and companies of 50 or more workers to take up to 12 weeks of unpaid annual leave to deal with family problems.

Janet Reno is confirmed as first woman U.S. Attorney General; Ruth Bader Ginsburg becomes second woman Supreme Court justice, succeeds retiring Byron White.

Women become eligible to pilot combat aircraft and serve on fighter and bomber crews in all services.

Michael Jordan of the Chicago Bulls, shown here scoring against the New York Knicks in Madison Square Garden, is called "Air Jordan" because of his ability to appear as if he can defy gravity. Jordan will retire—as it turns out, temporarily—from basketball in 1993. UPI/CORBIS-BETTMANN

1993

Defense Base Closure and Realignment Commission recommends closure of 33 major military bases, 100 smaller facilities, realignment of 45 others; President Clinton and Congress approve.

President Clinton dismisses FBI Director William Sessions after probe of alleged use of FBI funds for personal purposes; Louis J. Freeh succeeds him. Gen. Colin Powell resigns as joint chiefs of staff chairman; Gen. John Shalishkashvili succeeds him; Defense Secretary Les Aspin resigns; Retired Admiral Bobby Ray Inman is nominated as successor.

Administration announces program to streamline federal government, designed to save $108 billion over five years, lower federal employment by 252,000 jobs.

Supreme Court rules 6–3 that federal judges may not bar protestors from blockading abortion clinics; President Clinton signs order repealing ban on abortion counseling at U.S.-funded clinics.

Majority of Puerto Rican residents vote to remain a U.S. commonwealth, turning down proposal to become a state.

U.S. Holocaust Museum in Washington, D.C., is dedicated by President Clinton.

DEATHS Thurgood Marshall, Supreme Court justice; Gen. Matthew B. Ridgway, led American troops in Normandy, U.N. forces in Korea; John B. Connally, Texas governor wounded when President Kennedy was assassinated; former First Lady Pat Nixon (1969–1974).

BUSINESS/INDUSTRY/INVENTIONS

Robert W. Fogel and Douglass C. North share Nobel Prize in economics for leadership in field of "new economic history."

IBM announces $4.97 billion loss in 1992, largest one-year loss by an American firm; also announces first employee layoffs.

Sears to stop publishing annual catalogs, a marketing tool since 1896; will close 113 of 859 stores, eliminate 50,000 jobs. Other announced layoffs include McDonnell Douglas 8,700, Boeing 20,000, Pratt & Whitney 6,700, Procter & Gamble 13,000 jobs and closure of 30 factories.

Bell Atlantic Corp. and Tele-Communications Inc. announce plans to merge, will create company able to develop, deliver many types of new programming. Primamerica proposes acquisition of Travelers' Insurance; Amax Inc. and Cyprus Minerals Co. to merge into one of largest mining companies.

Supreme Court upholds law allowing banks to sell insurance nationwide.

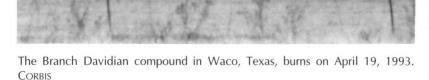

The Branch Davidian compound in Waco, Texas, burns on April 19, 1993. CORBIS

DEATHS Thomas J. Watson, former IBM head; Cesar Chavez, farmworkers labor leader; Julio Gallo, winemaker.

TRANSPORTATION

Los Angeles opens 4.4-mile portion of its first subway.

General Motors to build 20,000 cars annually in U.S. for sale in Japan under Toyota name.

GM, Ford, and Chrysler consider joint building of electric car to meet requirements of clean-air acts in California and elsewhere.

Greyhound Lines Inc. and drivers union settle three-year-old strike.

DEATH Olive A. Beech, cofounder and chairwoman, Beech Aircraft Co.

SCIENCE/MEDICINE

Princeton University researchers produce strongest controlled-nuclear-fusion reaction on record: 3 million watts of energy, later 5.6 million; may eventually lead to inexhaustible supply of energy.

Kary B. Mullis shares Nobel Prize in chemistry for work on amplifying (or copying) DNA; Joseph H. Taylor and Russell A. Halse share physics prize for discovering first known binary pulsar; Philip S. Sharp and Richard J. Roberts share prize in physiology/medicine for independent discovery of split genes.

Mars Observer spacecraft, $980-million craft launched in September 1992, ceases communication as it approaches Mars; NASA space crew repairs Hubble space telescope launched in 1991; repairs are expected to give telescope ability to provide new space views.

Four men and four women emerge from glass-enclosed "Biosphere 2" in desert near Tucson, Ariz., after two-year experiment in enclosed ecosystem.

DEATHS Robert W. Holley, Nobel biologist; Vincent J. Schaefer, chemist who developed cloud "seeding"; Polykarp Kusch, Nobel physicist.

EDUCATION

George E. Rupp is named president of Columbia University; Richard C. Levin as Yale University president.

President Clinton's plan to give students help for tuition, living allowances for college and vocational training in return for two years of community service is enacted by Congress.

DEATH Dr. Jean Mayer, Tufts University chancellor.

RELIGION

Pope John Paul II visits U.S. to participate in youth festival in Colorado.

Supreme Court rules unanimously that schools must allow church groups the same after-hours access to facilities as secular community groups.

Supreme Court rules that ban by Hialeah, Fla., of a ritual animal sacrifice violates religious freedom of Santeria religion followers. Later, Court passes law overturning 1990 decision that made it easier for government to pass laws that infringe on religious beliefs.

DEATH Norman Vincent Peale, minister, noted author.

ART/MUSIC

Cezanne painting *Still Life with Apples* sells for $28.6 million at Sotheby's auction.

New York Philharmonic celebrates 150th anniversary with year-long observances.

DEATHS Richard Diebenkorn, premier postwar U.S. abstractionist painter; Rudolf Nureyev, ballet dancer; Sammy Cahn, popular songwriter; Bob Crosby, bandleader; Billy Eckstine, popular singer; Dizzy Gillespie, jazz trumpeter; Marian Anderson, world-renowned contralto; Agnes de Mille, choreographer; Conway Twitty, country-music star.

LITERATURE/JOURNALISM

Rita Dove becomes seventh U.S. poet laureate, first African American so honored.

Toni Morrison becomes first African American writer (*Songs of Solomon, Beloved, Jazz*) to win Nobel Prize in literature.

BOOKS *Feather Crowns* by Bobbie Ann Mason, *Remembering Babylon* by David Malouf, *Lenin's*

1993

Tomb by David Remnick, *See, I Told You So* by Rush Limbaugh, *Without Remorse* by Tom Clancy.

The *New York Times* acquires *Boston Globe* over five years in $1.1-billion merger; Mortimer B. Zuckerman purchases *New York Daily News*.

Federal Appeals Court upholds 1991 ruling that regional Bell telephone companies may own information services.

DEATHS Authors Kay Boyle, John Hersey (*Hiroshima*), and William Golding (*Lord of the Flies*); newspaper publishers William R. Hearst Jr. and Joseph Pulitzer Jr.; Vincent T. Hamlin, creator of "Alley Oop" comic strip; Harrison E. Salisbury and William Shirer, foreign correspondents and authors.

ENTERTAINMENT

Federal Communications Commission orders cuts in cable TV rates that could total $1.2 billion annually nationwide; six months later, state and federal investigations begin study into the rates that increased rather than decreased.

David Letterman moves late-night show from NBC to CBS; Chevy Chase begins and quickly ends late-night TV show.

MOVIES *Jurassic Park* sets record of $18.2 million for opening-day gross ticket sales; *Sleepless in Seattle* with Tom Hanks and Meg Ryan, *Falling Down* with Michael Douglas, *The Firm* with Tom Cruise, *Schindler's List* with Ralph Fiennes, *The Remains of the Day* with Anthony Hopkins, *Philadelphia* with Tom Hanks, *The Fugitive* with Harrison Ford.

THEATER *Putting It Together* with Julie Andrews, *Kiss of the Spider Woman* with Chita Rivera, *The Who's Tommy*, *Angels in America* with Ron Liebman.

DEATHS Actresses Lillian Gish (last of the silent-film stars), Helen Hayes ("first lady" of American theater), Audrey Hepburn, Eugenie Leontovich, Ruby Keeler; Joseph Mankiewicz, film director and producer; Raymond Burr, actor; Carlton E. Morse, radio writer (*One Man's Family*).

SPORT

Marge Schott, baseball-team owner (Cincinnati Reds), is suspended for year for racist remarks.

Michael Jordan (Chicago Bulls) retires from basketball.

National Football League and players agree on seven-year contract that allows players freedom to move to other teams.

Monica Seles, top-ranked tennis star, is stabbed by a spectator at a German match; muscle tear sidelines her for a time.

Madison Square Garden presents final boxing match (July 8), ending almost 70 years of boxing.

WINNERS *Auto racing* — Emerson Fitipaldi, Indianapolis 500; Dale Earnhardt, NASCAR; *Baseball* — Toronto Blue Jays, World Series; *Basketball* — Chicago Bulls, NBA; North Carolina, NCAA; Texas Tech, NCAA (women); Minnesota, NIT; *Bowling* — Norm Duke, ABC Masters; George Branham 3rd, Tournament of Champions; *Boxing* — Riddick Bowe, Evander Holyfield, heavyweight; Gerald McClellan, light heavyweight; Pernell Whittaker, welterweight; Julio Chavez, lightweight; *Figure skating* — Scott Davis, U.S. men's title; Nancy Kerrigan, U.S. women's; *Football* (bowls) — Alabama, Sugar; Michigan, Rose; Notre Dame, Cotton; Florida State, Orange; Dallas, Super Bowl XXVII; *Golf* — Bernhard Langer, Masters; Lee Janzen, U.S. Open; Lauri Merten, U.S. Women's Open; Paul Azinger, PGA; Patty Sheehan, LPGA; *Harness racing* — American Winner, Hambletonian; *Hockey* — Montreal, Stanley Cup; Maine, NCAA; *Horse racing* — Sea Hero, Kentucky Derby; Prairie Bayou, Preakness Stakes; Colonial Affair, Belmont Stakes; *Tennis* — Pete Sampras, U.S. Open (men); Steffi Graf, U.S. Open (women).

DEATHS Arthur Ashe, former tennis champion; Baseball Hall of Famers Charley Gehringer, Bill Dickey, Johnny Mize, Roy Campanella, Don Drysdale; Hank Iba, basketball coach; auto racer Alan Kulwicki and Davey Allison in separate plane crashes; Willie Mosconi, billiards champion.

MISCELLANEOUS

Explosion in underground parking garage at World Trade Center in New York City kills six, forces temporary closing of complex; seven men are arrested. FBI uncovers second bomb plot, arrests nine men; Sheikh Omar Abdel Rahman, whose followers were arrested in both plots, is detained.

Four agents of Bureau of Alcohol, Tobacco & Firearms are killed in shootout with members of Branch Davidian religious cult, outside Waco, Tex., when Bureau tries to arrest leader David Koresh; group holds out until government use of force ends standoff two months later (April 19), killing 55 adults and 17 children.

March blizzard in eastern U.S. causes 200 deaths; summer flooding in nine midwestern states results in about 50 deaths, more than 700,000 homeless, $12 billion in property damage.

In Amtrak's deadliest wreck, 47 die as train plunges into Alabama bayou when bridge collapses after being struck by a barge.

Bagels become country's latest food craze.

1994

INTERNATIONAL

U.S. and North Korea agree in principle (January 5) on inspection of nuclear facilities; talks break down. Former President Carter convinces North Korea to resume discussions (June 22); two nations sign agreement (August 6) that allows U.N. inspections of nuclear plants. Late in year, a U.S. helicopter accidentally flies into North Korean territory and is shot down; one airman is killed, the other is held prisoner briefly.

President Clinton lifts 19-year-old trade embargo against Vietnam (February 3).

President and Mrs. Clinton participate in 50th-anniversary commemoration of D-Day (June 6) in France. President attends meeting of industrial nations in Naples; then becomes first U.S. president to visit Baltic nations.

Former President Carter, Georgia Sen. Sam Nunn, and Retired Gen. Colin Powell negotiate peaceful end (September 18) to Haiti's military rule, return of deposed president, Jean-Bertrand Aristide. U.S. troops arrive to keep peace until restored government is in place.

Special session of Congress in December ratifies GATT (General Agreement on Tariffs and Trade), which is designed to lower tariffs on manufactured and agricultural products among 117 nations.

NATIONAL

Final report on Iran-Contra scandal is issued (January 18) by Lawrence Walsh, independent counsel who headed 6½-year investigation.

Supreme Court Justice Harry A. Blackmun resigns after 24 years of service; Circuit Court Judge Stephen Breyer succeeds him.

President Clinton's proposed health plan is not voted on by Congress and is withdrawn.

Congress approves (August 28) $30.2 billion crime bill, providing funds for hiring 100,000 police, helping to establish new prisons, and banning some automatic weapons.

Social Security Administration, part of Health and Human Services Department, is scheduled to become an independent agency March 31, 1995.

Republicans win control of Congress (November 8) for first time since 1952.

Small plane crashes (September 12) on White House lawn, skids against building; pilot is killed; presidential family not at home. Gunman sprays White House with bullets from an assault rifle (October 29); no one is injured; the gunman is captured.

Several Administration officials resign: Agriculture Secretary Michael Espy (succeeded by former Kansas congressman Dan Glickman); Treasury Secretary Lloyd Bentsen (succeeded by Robert Rubin); Surgeon General Dr. Jocelyn Elders; and CIA Director R. James Woolsey.

Letter from former President Reagan (November 5) discloses that he suffers from Alzheimer's disease.

DEATHS Former President Richard M. Nixon; former First Lady Jacqueline Kennedy Onassis.

1994

BUSINESS/INDUSTRY/INVENTIONS

Dow-Jones industrial average passes 3,800 mark for first time (January 6); two weeks later (January 21), it closes at more than 3,900.

Viacom Inc. gains control of Paramount Communications for about $10 billion, after it agrees to buy Blockbuster Entertainment Corp. for $8.4 billion. Lockheed and Martin Marietta agree to merge, creating Lockheed Marietta, the largest U.S. defense contractor.

John C. Harsanyi and John F. Nash share Nobel Prize in economics for pioneering work in the field of game theory.

Orange County, Calif., declares bankruptcy when its $7.8 billion investment fund covering 180 cities and agencies suffers a more than $2 billion loss.

Federal legislation permits banks to operate branches across the nation.

DEATHS William Levitt, developer ("Levittowns"); Dave Beck, Teamsters Union president.

TRANSPORTATION

Federal court in Anchorage, Alaska, orders Exxon to pay $5 billion to more than 34,000 persons for damages resulting from the oil spill from the *Exxon Valdez* tanker in 1989.

Three plane crashes occur during year: a commuter plane near Gary, Ind., killing all 68 aboard; a USAir jet on approach to Pittsburgh, killing 132; and a USAir jet near Charlotte, N.C., killing 37 of 67 aboard.

SCIENCE/MEDICINE

First Russian astronaut flies as crew member on U.S. shuttle *Discovery* (February 3–11).

Space shuttle *Endeavor* carries first space radar laboratory, maps Earth's surface in three dimensions.

A doctor who performed abortions and his escort are shot to death outside a Pensacola, Fla., abortion clinic; two workers are shot to death in two Brookline, Mass., clinics.

George A. Olah wins Nobel Prize in chemistry for his contributions to hydrocarbon research; Clifford G. Shull shares prize in physics with Bertram N. Brockhouse of Canada for techniques to use neutron probes into atomic structure of matter; Alfred G. Gilman and Martin Rodbell share prize in physiology/medicine for research in natural substances that help cells control fundamental life processes.

DEATH Linus Pauling, winner of Nobel Prizes in chemistry and peace.

EDUCATION

A court orders The Citadel, state-financed military college in Charleston, S.C., to admit female students, holding school in violation of constitutional equal protection provisions; school appeals ruling.

RELIGION

DEATHS Ezra Taft Benson, head of Mormon Church (1985–1994); Menachem M. Schneerson, leader of a Jewish Hassidic sect.

ART/MUSIC

Concerts (August 12–14) at Saugerties, N.Y., mark 25th anniversary of the Woodstock concert in Bethel, N.Y., which was attended by about 500,000; about 350,000 attend Saugerties concerts.

POPULAR MUSIC Albums: *Waymore's Blues, Part II* with Waylon Jennings; *Turbulent Indigo* with Joni Mitchell; *Natural Ingredients* with Luscious Jackson; *Let the Picture Paint Itself* with Rodney Crowell. Songs: "Lost in America," Alice Cooper; "Dignity," Bob Dylan; "The Farmer's Daughter," Vince Gill; "California Dreamin'," American Music Club.

DEATHS Cab Calloway, orchestra leader and singer; singers Dinah Shore, Dorothy Collins, and Carmen McRae; composers Henry Mancini ("Moon River," "Days of Wine and Roses") and Jule Styne.

LITERATURE/JOURNALISM

BOOKS *The Shipping News* by E. Annie Proulx; *The Hot Zone* by Richard Preston; *No Ordinary Time* by Doris K. Goodwin; *A Map of the World* by Jane Hamilton; *The Celestine Prophecy* by James Redfield; *Gal* by Ruthie Bolton.

DEATHS Ralph Ellison, author (*Invisible Man*); Lawrence Spivak, originator and first moderator, *Meet the Press.*

O. J. Simpson flees from police in his white Bronco, while the news media record the drama and fans cheer him on, 1994. (See 1995, 1996, "Misc."). GAMMA

ENTERTAINMENT

MOVIES *The Lion King* with the voice of Jeremy Irons; *Forrest Gump* with Tom Hanks; *Nobody's Fool* with Paul Newman; *Pulp Fiction* with John Travolta; *Speed* with Keanu Reeves; *The Santa Clause* with Tim Allen.

PLAYS *Passion* by Stephen Sondheim with Donna Murphy; *Angels in America: Perestroika* with Stephen Spinella; *Any Given Day* by Frank D. Gilroy with Sada Thompson; *Laughter on the 23d Floor* by Neil Simon.

DEATHS Actors Cesar Romero, Telly Savalas, Joseph Cotten, Vincent Price, Martha Raye, Burt Lancaster, Don Ameche, Myrna Loy, Jessica Tandy; Henry Morgan, television comedian; Harriet Nelson of *Ozzie and Harriet* show; Garry Moore, television host.

SPORTS

Winter Olympics are held in Lillehammer, Norway; U.S. wins 13 medals, the most it has won in a single winter games.

U.S. plays host for first time to World Soccer tournament; Brazil wins title.

New York Rangers win hockey's Stanley Cup for first time in 54 years; defeat Vancouver 4 games to 3.

Labor disputes affect two major sports: baseball players strike (August 12), force cancellation of remainder of season and World Series; hockey players and owners fail to reach agreement, force delay of season (October 1). Neither dispute is resolved at year's end.

George Foreman becomes oldest heavyweight boxing champion at 45, knocks out Michael Moore (November 5) to regain title he lost to Muhammad Ali 20 years earlier.

WINNERS *Auto racing* — Al Unser Jr., Indianapolis 500; Dale Earnhardt, NASCAR; *Basketball* — Houston Rockets, NBA; Arkansas, NCAA; North Carolina, NCAA (women); Villanova, NIT; *Bowling* — Steve Fehr, ABC Masters; Norm Duke, Tournament of Champions; *Boxing* — George Foreman, heavyweight (WBA, IBF); Oliver McCall, heavyweight (WBC); *Figure skating* — Scott

1995

Davis, U.S. men; *Football* (bowls)—Wisconsin, Rose; Florida State, Orange; Florida, Sugar; Notre Dame, Cotton; Dallas, Super Bowl XXVIII; *Golf*—Ernie Els, U.S. Men's Open; Nick Price, PGA; Jose Maria Olazabal, Masters; Patty Sheehan, U.S. Women's Open; Laura Davies, LPGA; *Harness racing*—Victory Dream, Hambletonian; *Hockey*—New York Rangers, Stanley Cup; *Horse racing*—Go for Gin, Kentucky Derby; Tabasco Cat, Preakness Stakes and Belmont Stakes; *Tennis*—Andre Agassi, U.S. Open (men); Arantxa Sanchez Vicario, U.S. Open (women).

DEATHS Charles Feeney, president, National (baseball) League; Wilma Rudolph, track star; Jersey Joe Walcott and Jack Sharkey, boxing champions; Vitas Gerulaitis, tennis star; Allie Reynolds, baseball pitcher; Julius Boros, golfer.

MISCELLANEOUS

Predawn earthquake in Los Angeles area kills 61, injures more than 9,300, damages or destroys 45,000 residences; damage is estimated at $13–$20 billion.

Series of tornadoes in Alabama, Tennessee, and North and South Carolina kills 52; flooding in Georgia and Alabama results in 32 deaths.

Four men are convicted of bombing the World Trade Center in New York City in 1993; each is sentenced to prison for 240 years.

INTERNATIONAL

U.S. leads United Nations effort to end 3½ years of fighting in Bosnia; agreement is reached (November 21) by Balkan leaders in Dayton, Ohio, calling for a U.N. force, including 20,000 U.S. troops, to maintain peace; U.S. troops arrive in December.

U.S. also is principal backer of Israeli-Palestinian peace talks; agreement is signed in Washington, D.C., in October.

Nobel Peace Prize is awarded to British physicist Joseph Rotblat, who was a member of the Manhattan Project that developed the U.S. atomic bomb, but resigned when it was clear Germany was not working on a nuclear weapon.

U.S. announces plan to place 100% tariff on Japanese-made luxury cars because Japanese markets are closed to U.S. cars. Japanese automakers agree to buy more U.S. parts; tariff plan is dropped.

U.S. eases trade embargo against North Korea in effect since Korean War. Vietnam and U.S. exchange low-level diplomats in July.

U.S. peace-keeping forces in Haiti are replaced (March 31) by a U.N. mission.

NATIONAL

First Republican-controlled Congress since 1953 convenes (January 4); adopts "Contract with America" to be accomplished in year. Session is marked by Clinton-Congress fights over budget and deficit, which lead to two government shutdowns—one very brief, the second in 17th day at year's end.

Oklahoma City federal building is bombed (April 19); 160 people killed. Two men with ties to right-wing U.S. militia group are charged.

An unidentified terrorist, the Unabomber, believed responsible for 17 deaths, demands publication of 35,000-word manifesto calling for revolt against industrial-technological society. He threatens to bomb an airliner if it is not published; The *New York Times* and *Washington Post* print it in September.

United Nations observes 50th anniversary in October, with nearly 140 heads of state attending ceremonies in New York City.

National 55-mile speed limit is repealed, effective December 8; some states set maximum at 75, Montana sets no daytime limit.

Supreme Court in 5–4 decision invalidates a

The north side of the Alfred Murrah Federal Building in Oklahoma City shows the devastation caused by the car bomb that was detonated early on April 19, 1995. CORBIS-BETTMANN

Georgia congressional district whose boundary lines were drawn with race as a "predominant factor."

NAACP, faced with a $4-million debt, names Rep. Keisi Mfume of Maryland as its new head. Nation of Islam leader Louis Farrakhan organizes "Million Man March" (October 16) in Washington, D.C., to create unity among African American men.

General Colin Powell, a potential Republican 1996 presidential candidate, announces he will not run.

Cost of first-class postage rises to 32 cents per ounce (January 1).

A number of congressmen announce they will not seek reelection in 1996, including Senators Bill Bradley (N.J.), Sam Nunn (Ga.), Mark Hatfield (Oreg.), Alan Simpson (Wy.), and Nancy Kassebaum (Kans.).

Senator Robert Packwood (Oreg.) retires (September 7) after Ethics Committee recommends his expulsion because of sexual misconduct and influence peddling.

Defense Base Closure Commission's recommen-dations to close 79 bases and consolidate 26 others are approved.

DEATHS Warren E. Burger, former Supreme Court chief justice; Dean Rusk, former Secretary of State; Oveta Culp Hobby, first director of WAC, first HEW secretary; Margaret Chase Smith, first woman elected to both houses of Congress; Orval Faubus, Arkansas governor.

BUSINESS/INDUSTRY/INVENTIONS

Acquisitions and mergers mark the year, including combinations of Time Warner and Turner Broadcasting, Disney Co. and Capital Cities/ABC, Westinghouse Electric and CBS; Seagram acquires MCA, Kimberly Clark acquires Scott Paper; Martin Marietta and Lockheed merge; Rite Aid and Revco join, forming a 4,500-drugstore chain; Chase Manhattan and Chemical Bank merge under Chase name to form $297-billion-assets bank.

Dow-Jones industrial average, which began July 3, 1884, when Charles Dow published first averages, passes the 4,000 mark (February 23) and 5,000 (November 21).

Three large industrial unions, auto workers, steel-workers, and machinists, vote to merge by year

2000. AFL-CIO President Lane Kirkland retires in August after 16 years.

Nobel Prize in economics is awarded to Robert E. Lucas, the fifth Nobel prize–winning economist at University of Chicago in six years; selected for his mathematical critiques of activist governmental policies.

Congress for first time overrides a President Clinton veto (December 22), thereby approving legislation that limits stockholders' ability to sue for fraud; opponents argue that small investors will suffer.

DEATHS John V. Atanasoff, electronic computer inventor; Edward Bernays, public relations pioneer; J. Peter Grace, corporation head; Orville Redenbacher, agricultural scientist, popcorn manufacturer; George Romney, president, American Motors.

TRANSPORTATION

DEATH Douglas (Wrong Way) Corrigan, transatlantic flier, who said he thought he was flying to California when he landed in Ireland (July 1938).

SCIENCE/MEDICINE

Galileo spacecraft, launched October 1989, reaches within 130,000 miles of Jupiter; launches probe into Jupiter's orbit (December 7), diving into planet's atmosphere, collecting atmospheric data. Spacecraft begins first of 11 orbits around Jupiter that will last until November 1997.

Swiss scientists report discovery of new planet in constellation Pegasus; American astronomers Geoffrey March and Paul Butler confirm the findings.

F. Sherwood Rowland shares Nobel Prize in chemistry with Paul Chutzen of Netherlands and Mario Molina of Mexico for warning of ozone depletion; Martin Perl and Frederick Raines share physics prize for discovery of subatomic particles; Edward B. Lewis and Eric F. Wieschaus share medicine/physiology prize for research into fruit flies.

U.S. shuttle *Atlantis* and Russian space station *Mir* join in space (June 29) for six days.

American Museum of Natural History in New York City opens largest, most scientifically ambitious dinosaur exhibit in the world.

DEATHS Jonas Salk, developer of first polio vaccine; Nobel prize–winning physicists Eugene Wigner and Subrahmanyan Chandrasekhar; Astronaut Stuart A. Roosa, third man on the moon.

EDUCATION

Shannon Faulkner, after long legal battle, is admitted as a cadet at The Citadel (August 11); she resigns after four days of training. Legal efforts to change all-male admission policy at the state-supported Virginia Military Institute begin, reach Supreme Court where a decision is expected by mid-1996.

DEATH Former Arkansas Senator J. William Fulbright, whose fellowship legislation aided higher education.

RELIGION

Pope John Paul II issues his 11th encyclical, opposes abortion, birth control, and euthanasia; makes his fourth visit to U.S. in October.

Supreme Court rules 5–4 that a student-run religious publication must be funded by University of Virginia just as any other student publication.

Billy Graham, 77-year-old evangelist, reduces his activities after he suffers a fall; designates his son, Franklin, as his eventual successor.

DEATH Howard W. Hunter, Mormon Church leader.

ART/MUSIC

Private funds enable opening of long-awaited Vermeer art exhibit at National Gallery of Art, closed because of a federal government shutdown.

Barnes Foundation, renowned private art collection in Merion, Pa., reopens after 30-month renovation.

The Grateful Dead, a rock-and-roll group, folds after its founder, Jerry Garcia, dies. Selena, the queen of Tejano music, is murdered; event creates quick popularity rise in her music and Latin pop music.

MUSIC Albums include *The Ghost of Tom Joad* by Bruce Springsteen, *To Bring You My Love* by P. J. Harvey, *The Hits* by Garth Brooks, *Any Man of Mine* by Shania Twain, *Thinkin' About You* by Trisha Yearwood.

DEATHS Band leaders Phil Harris, Lee Elgart, and Jerry Garcia; jazz trumpeter Don Cherry; singers Burl Ives, Charlie Rich, and Maxene Andrews; Eazy-E, cofounder of "gangsta" rap group.

1995

LITERATURE/JOURNALISM

Mergers and acquisitions continue in television field as Cable News Network launches a 12-hour daily financial news service (CNNfn); Microsoft and NBC team up to develop 24-hour cable news and Internet service, expects to begin operations in mid-1996.

Robert Haas is named the eighth U.S. poet laureate.

Robert MacNeil, co-anchor of *MacNeil-Lehrer News Hour* for 20 years, retires.

BOOKS *Stories* by Vladimir Nabokov, *Familiar Heat* by Mary Hood, *Collected Short Fiction* by Bruce Jay Friedman, *The Road Ahead* by Bill Gates.

DEATHS Ian Ballantine, publisher; Alfred Eisenstadt, *Life* photographer; John Cameron Swayze, early TV newsman; James (Scotty) Reston, *New York Times* reporter.

ENTERTAINMENT

Carol Channing, who first starred in *Hello, Dolly!* in 1964 through nearly 4,500 performances, starts a revival in October.

MOVIES *Apollo 13* with Tom Hanks, *Bridges of Madison County* with Meryl Streep and Clint Eastwood, *Star Trek* with William Shatner, *Toy Story*, first entirely computer-animated full-length feature.

Television programs include *ER* (a medical drama), *Friends*, *Murder One*, and *The Single Guy*.

DEATHS George Abbott, playwright and director; actors Eva Gabor, Ida Lupino, Ginger Rogers, Lana Turner, and Dean Martin; Jerry Lester, early television host.

SPORTS

Cal Ripken Jr., Baltimore Orioles shortstop, breaks (September 6) Lou Gehrig's consecutive-game streak of 2,130 games, set in 1939.

Michael Jordan returns to the Chicago Bulls basketball team.

Baseball strike ends after NLRB and federal court action; sides agree to 144-game season, instead of usual 162. National Hockey League and players agree on new contract and 48-game season, instead of usual 84.

Cleveland Browns football team announces move to Baltimore in 1996; Houston Oilers to move to Nashville soon. Local opposition arises and Browns face lawsuits before moving.

Serge Grinkov, who with his wife, Yekaterina Gordeyeva, won Olympic gold medals (1988, 1994) for pairs skating, dies of a heart attack while practicing in Lake Placid, N.Y.

Mike Tyson completes three-year prison term, wins his first fight with an 89-second TKO of Peter McNeely.

WINNERS *Auto racing*—Jacques Villeneuve, Indianapolis 500; Jeff Gordon, NASCAR; *Baseball*—Atlanta Braves, World Series; *Basketball*—Houston Rockets, NBA; UCLA, NCAA; University of Connecticut, NCAA (women); Virginia Tech, NIT; *Bowling*—Mike Aulby, ABC Masters and Tournament of Champions; *Football* (bowls)—Penn State, Rose; Nebraska, Orange; Florida State, Sugar; Southern California, Cotton; San Francisco, Super Bowl XXIX; *Golf*—Corey Pavin, U.S. Men's Open; Steve Elkington, PGA; Ben Crenshaw, Masters; Anika Sorenstam, U.S. Women's Open; Kelly Robbins, LPGA; *Harness racing*—Tagliabue, Hambletonian; *Hockey*—New Jersey, Stanley Cup; *Horse racing*—Thunder Gulch, Kentucky Derby and Belmont Stakes; Timber Country, Preakness Stakes; *Tennis*—Pete Sampras, Wimbledon and U.S. Open (men); Steffi Graf, Wimbledon and U.S. Open (women).

DEATHS Sportscasters Howard Cosell and Lindsey Nelson; baseball players Leon Day and Mickey Mantle; auto racer Juan Manuel Fangio; tennis stars Pancho Gonzales, Bobby Riggs, and Fred Perry; basketball player and coach Nat Holman.

MISCELLANEOUS

Heavy March rains in California cause 15 deaths and $2 billion damage; 1,001 tornadoes in Midwest create second-most-active season, and 8 tropical storms and 11 hurricanes make for worst season since 1933.

July heat wave causes more than 800 deaths in Midwest and Northeast.

O. J. Simpson, football star, after a 16-month trial, is found not guilty of murdering his former wife and her friend.

1996

INTERNATIONAL

A bomb explodes at military complex near Dhahran, Saudi Arabia, 19 U.S. servicemen die, several hundred are wounded.

Troops from U.S. and other countries monitor peace accord among the three warring factions in Bosnia-Herzegovina.

Senate approves (January 26) the Second Strategic Arms Reduction Treaty, which was signed three years earlier by presidents Bush and Yeltsin.

President Clinton announces that he will authorize renewal of most-favored-nation trade status for China, which would provide lower export tariffs on trade to U.S.; many oppose action because of Chinese human-rights violations.

President Clinton visits Japan and South Korea, signs agreements on joint security.

Cuban jets shoot down two unarmed planes carrying four Cuban exiles based in Miami ((February 24); U.S. says planes were shot down over international waters. Economic embargo against Cuba is strengthened by President Clinton (March 12).

NATIONAL

President Clinton is re-elected, the first Democratic president re-elected since Franklin D. Roosevelt. The president receives 47,401,185 popular votes and 379 electoral votes while Sen. Robert Dole, the Republican candidate, receives 39,197,469 popular and 159 electoral votes and the Reform Party candidate Ross Perot draws 8,085,294 popular votes but no electoral votes.

President nominates Madeleine Albright, U.S. representative to United Nations, to become secretary of state, the first woman in that post.

Legislative battle of 1995 ends (January 26) when President Clinton signs stopgap bill to keep government operating into March. Later (September 30), another bill takes care of rest of fiscal year and funds for fiscal year 1997.

Federal agents in Montana seize Theodore Kaczynski, former mathematics professor, for possession of bomb-making materials. He is believed to be the Unabomber, the object of a search since 1978 for sending mail bombs that killed 3, injured 23.

Montana is also the scene of FBI confrontation with the Freemen, an antigovernment group (March 25). Group surrenders without incident (June 13), is charged with defrauding businesses of $1.8 billion, conducting seminars on how to defraud. A plot to bomb seven government buildings is thwarted when a 12-man paramilitary group is arrested in Phoenix, Ariz., area.

President Clinton signs legislation that changes welfare program to state programs using federal funds. Other enacted legislation includes line-item veto by president of parts of spending and tax bills, $1 billion to fight terrorism over four-year period, and gradual elimination of farm-subsidy program.

A commission recommends changes in how to determine Consumer Price Index, which could result in reducing inflation rate and cost-of-living raises tied to CPI.

Supreme Court holds a Colorado law unconstitutional for excluding homosexuals from civil rights protection; upholds right of law-enforcement officials to seek criminal penalties against a defendant and seize the defendant's property.

DEATHS Spiro T. Agnew, former Vice President (1969–1973) and Maryland governor; Ronald Brown, Commerce Secretary killed in plane crash (April 3); Edmund S. Muskie, secretary of state (1980) and Maine governor, senator; Quentin Burdick, North Dakota senator for 32 years; Edmund G. (Pat) Brown, California governor; William E. Colby, CIA director (1973–1976); McGeorge Bundy, former national security advisor; Carl B. Stokes, first African American mayor of major city (Cleveland, 1967–1971); Barbara Jordan, Texas legislator; Alger Hiss, former official accused of spying.

BUSINESS/INDUSTRY/INVENTIONS

Dow-Jones industrial average passes 6,000 mark for first time (October 14); ends year at 6,448.27, a 26% gain over 1995.

President Clinton signs (February 8) Telecommunications Reform Act deregulating in large measure telephone, mobile phone, and cable television service.

President Clinton approves regulations to curb sale of tobacco products to young persons. A major tobacco company, Liggett Group Inc., breaks with industry, agrees to a settlement in a class-action suit.

Boeing Co. buys McDonnell Douglas for $13.3 billion and Rockwell aerospace and defense operations; several mergers are made, including Pacific Telesis Group and SBC Communications, Continental Cablevision and U.S. West Media Group, and Nation's Bank and Boatmen's Bancshares.

Minimum wage increases from $4.25 an hour to $4.75 (October 1) and set to rise to $5.15 on September 1, 1997. President Clinton signs bill that allows workers changing jobs to maintain their health insurance.

Two corporations settle actions against them:

Archer Daniels Midland agrees to pay $100 million fine for conspiring to fix prices on two products; Texaco agrees to pay $520 million to settle employees' racial-bias suit.

DEATHS Canadian-born American William Vickery, shares 1996 Nobel Prize in economics, dies suddenly three days later (October 11); James W. Rouse, developer of malls, "cities"; Max Factor, cosmetics manufacturer; David Packard, electronics industry pioneer.

TRANSPORTATION

Valujet DC-9 crashes (May 11) into Florida Everglades, kills all 110 aboard; accident caused by fire in cargo hold. TWA jetliner traveling from New York to Paris explodes, crashes shortly after takeoff, kills all 230 people aboard (July 17).

SCIENCE/MEDICINE

NASA Administrator Daniel Goldin says that evidence found in a small meteorite points to possible existence of life beyond Earth. Meteorite reportedly originated on Mars $4\frac{1}{2}$ billion years ago.

Mars Environmental Survey *Pathfinder* space

Blizzard blankets the Capitol in a rare snow, 1996. TERRY ASHE/THE GAMMA LIAISON NETWORK

1996

shuttle, first of 13 Mars flights, is successfully launched.

David M. Lee, Robert C. Richardson, and Douglas C. Osheroff share Nobel Prize in physics; Robert F. Curl Jr. and Richard Smalley share chemistry prize.

President Clinton vetoes bill that would ban late-term abortions, which, he says, are few but often important to save life; efforts to override fail.

Dr. Jack Kevorkian, retired pathologist who was present at 27 suicides, is acquitted of violating Michigan law against assisted suicide.

DEATHS Carl Sagan, astronomer who popularized space study; Mary Leakey, anthropologist; Roger Tory Peterson, author and illustrator of bird books; Paul Erdos, founder of discrete mathematics.

EDUCATION

Supreme Court rules (June 26) that Virginia Military Institute, state-supported school, may not bar women from admission. The Citadel, a South Carolina state-supported school, which began admitting women in previous year, admits four women (August 24).

DEATH Arthur S. Flemming, University of Oregon president, HEW secretary.

RELIGION

DEATHS Two Catholic cardinals and archbishops: Joseph Bernardin of Chicago (1982–1996) and John J. Krol of Philadelphia (1961–1988); a Catholic priest, Lawrence M. Jenco, who had been a hostage in Lebanon for 18 months.

ART/MUSIC

Songs and recordings include "Unchained" by Johnny Cash, "Because You Loved Me" by Diane Warren, "Mystery Box" by Mickey Hart, "Blue" by LeAnn Rimes, "Give Me One Reason" by Tracy Chapman; *25th Anniversary Metropolitan Opera Gala* by James Levine.

DEATHS Henry Lewis, first African American conductor of major U.S. orchestra (New Jersey Symphony); Morton Gould, composer and conductor; Lincoln Kirstein, cofounder New York City Ballet; Juliet Prowse, dancer; Gerry Mulligan, saxophonist and band leader; Ella Fitzgerald, singer; Bill Monroe, founder of bluegrass music; Tiny Tim, falsetto singer; Tupac Shakur, rap superstar.

LITERATURE/JOURNALISM

BOOKS *The First Man* by Albert Camus, *All the Days and Nights* by William Maxwell, *The Body Is Water* by Julie Schumacher, *The Tailor of Panama* by John le Carré, *Lily White* by Susan Isaacs, *Executive Orders* by Tom Clancy, *The Christmas Box* by Richard P. Evans.

DEATHS John Chancellor, television newsman; Erma Bombeck, author and humorist; Joseph Brodsky, exiled Soviet poet who became U.S. poet laureate and Nobel prize-winner in literature.

ENTERTAINMENT

Television executives agree to implement use of v-chip (*v* for violence) that can be installed in sets to block out programs. At year's end, industry adopts six-tier rating system for sex and violence of its shows, similar to system used by movies.

MOVIES *Grumpier Old Men* with Jack Lemmon and Walter Matthau, *Fargo* with Frances McDormand, *The Crucible* with Daniel Day-Lewis and Winona Ryder, *Shine* with Geoffrey Rush, *Secrets and Lies* with Brenda Blethyn.

PLAYS *State Fair* with John Davidson and Kathryn Crosby, *Big* with Daniel Jenkins and Crista Moore, *Rent* with Adam Pascal, Anthony Rapp, and Daphne Rubin-Vega.

DEATHS Movie actors Dorothy Lamour, Claudette Colbert, Greer Garson, Martin Balsam, Lew Ayres; television actors Audrey Meadows of *The Honeymooners*; Vince Edwards, who played Dr. Ben Casey on television; Morey Amsterdam; singer and dancer Gene Kelly; veteran comic George Burns, almost 100; country-music star Minnie Pearl.

SPORTS

Summer Olympic Games open in Atlanta (July 19); eight days later a pipe-bomb explodes in Centennial Park in downtown Atlanta, kills one person; does not affect the games.

Evander Holyfield, former heavyweight champion, upsets Mike Tyson to regain WBA boxing title that Tyson retook earlier in year.

Baseball club owners approve five-year agreement with players, calling for revenue sharing by clubs and interleague play; owners turn down pact (November 6), then reverse themselves (December 9).

National Football League owners approve moves of Cleveland Browns to Baltimore for 1996–1997 season and Houston Oilers to Nashville in 1998.

Twenty-year-old Eldrick "Tiger" Woods wins U.S. amateur golf title for record third year, turns pro.

Eddie Murray of Baltimore Orioles hits 500th home run, the 15th player to hit that many.

New York Jets Nick Lowery kicks field goal (October 13) to become all-time career field goal kicker with 346.

Major League Soccer (MLS) debuts with 31,683 watching San Jose Clash beat DC United 1–0.

WINNERS *Auto racing*—Buddy Lazier, Indianapolis 500; Terry Labonte, NASCAR; *Baseball*—New York Yankees, World Series; *Basketball*—Chicago, NBA; Kentucky, NCAA; Tennessee, NCAA (women); Nebraska, NIT; *Bowling*—Ernie Schliegel, ABC Masters; Dave D'Entremont, Tournament of Champions; *Figure skating* (world)—Todd Eldredge, men; Michelle Kwan, women; *Football* (bowls)—Southern California, Rose; Florida State, Orange; Virginia Tech, Sugar; Colorado, Cotton; Dallas, Super Bowl XXX; *Golf*—Nick Faldo, Masters; Steve Jones, U.S. Men's Open; Mark Brooks, PGA; Annika Sorenstam, U.S. Women's Open; Laura Davies, LPGA; *Harness racing*—Continentalvictory, Hambletonian; *Hockey*—Colorado, Stanley Cup; *Horse racing*—Grindstone, Kentucky Derby; Louis Quatorze, Preakness Stakes; Editor's Note, Belmont Stakes;

Tennis—Richard Krajcek, Wimbledon (men), Pete Sampras, U.S. Open (men); Steffi Graf, U.S. Open and Wimbledon (women).

DEATHS Pete Rozelle, NFL commissioner (1960–1989); Charles O. Finley, baseball club owner (Kansas City, Oakland); Mel Allen, baseball sportscaster; Roger Crozier, hockey goalie; Minnesota Fats (Rudolf Wanderone), legendary pool hustler; Jimmy ("the Greek") Snyder, oddsmaker and sportscaster.

MISCELLANEOUS

Blizzard deposits up to three feet of snow on mid-Atlantic and New England states (January 7–8), causing more than $1 billion in damage; tornadoes (March 28–29) cause 52 deaths in Alabama, Tennessee, Georgia, and the Carolinas.

Hurricane Bertha arrives (July 5) near Jacksonville, N.C., causes $270 million in damage; Hurricane Fran comes ashore (September 6) at Cape Fear, N.C., causes 34 deaths, $3.2 billion in damage.

A seven-year-old girl, trying to become the youngest to pilot a plane across the U.S., is killed along with her father and flight instructor in crash in Wyoming.

Four-day auction of about 5,900 items owned by the late Jacqueline Kennedy Onassis brings in more than $34 million.

99% of approximately 97 million homes in U.S. have a color television; 82% have a videocassette recorder (VCR).

Civil trial against O. J. Simpson, former football star, begins; Simpson was acquitted (1995) of murdering his wife and her friend, now is being sued for damages.

1997

INTERNATIONAL

Iraqi President Saddam Hussein refuses in October to allow United Nations arms inspections to continue unless American members are removed; U.N. Security Council orders inspections to continue; Iraq orders U.S. inspectors to leave; entire U.N. team leaves (October 29). U.S. begins military buildup; Russia leads move to end impasse; inspectors return after three-week absence, but haggling over inspection sites continues.

Global warming conference in Tokyo reaches tentative agreement (December 11) to reduce fossil fuels in the future, marking first historic steps to binding reductions in industrial gases.

Iranian President Muhammad Khatami (December 14) calls for talks with U.S., changing his nation's nearly 20-year-old anti-American attitude.

Seventy countries in World Trade Organization agree to open banking, insurance, and securities markets to outside firms; open policy is already in effect in U.S.

Although U.S. opposes immediate ban of land mines, the international banning group and its coordinator, Jody Williams of Poultney, Vt., convince many nations to sign ban. The group and Williams are awarded Nobel Peace Prize.

U.S. and Russia are among 146 nations to sign Comprehensive Test Ban Treaty; only eight countries have ratified pact (U.S. and Russia have not). Senate ratifies Chemical Weapons Treaty in April, making U.S. 75th nation to approve elimination of such weapons by 2007.

President Jiang Zomin of China visits U.S. in November; signs nuclear proliferation treaty, agrees to end nuclear assistance to Iran.

U.S. and Mexico agree on broader efforts to fight drug trafficking.

President Clinton visits U.S. troops in Bosnia at Christmastime, tells them of decision to extend their stay.

The Spice Girls, a popular singing group. From left to right, Sporty (Melanie Jane Chisholm), Baby (Emma Lee Burton), Scary (Melanie Janine Brown), Posh (Victoria Caroline Addams), and Ginger (Geri Halliwell). CORBIS

NATIONAL

Senate (March 4) defeats for third time in three years a proposed constitutional amendment requiring a balanced federal budget. White House and Congress agree in May to balance federal budget by 2002.

Line Item Veto bill, which would allow president to veto individual expenditures in large spending bills, is held to be unconstitutional (April 19) by a district judge; Supreme Court (June 26) dismisses challenge. President Clinton uses new veto power (August 11) on three specific items.

Timothy McVeigh is found guilty of 1995 bombing of Oklahoma City federal building that killed 168 people; death penalty is imposed. Terry Nichols, his alleged accomplice, is found guilty in December of conspiracy and involuntary manslaughter.

Jury is selected in December to try Theodore Kaczynski, the alleged Unabomber, in January 1998.

Four major tobacco companies and several state attorneys general agree on a settlement costing the companies $368.5 billion; approval is needed from president, Congress, and health community. Florida becomes second state, after Mississippi, to settle claims with tobacco industry in August.

California law bars state from race- or gender-based preferences in school admission, public hiring, or contracting (August 28).

President Clinton suffers serious knee injury (March 14) in Palm Beach, Fla.

Arizona Gov. Fife Symington resigns (September 5) after federal jury finds him guilty of fraud in actions prior to his election.

DEATHS William J. Brennan Jr., former Supreme Court justice; Pamela Harriman, ambassador to France; Robert C. Weaver, first African American cabinet member, first HUD secretary.

BUSINESS/INDUSTRY/INVENTIONS

United Parcel Service (UPS) and Teamsters Union settle 15-day strike (August 19) that costs UPS an estimated $600 million in revenues. Federal official orders new election of Teamsters president (August 22) after investigation finds that Ron Carey received illegal contributions to his campaign.

In August, Dow-Jones average reaches all-time high of 8,259.31; economic problems in southeast Asia cause drop of 554 points (October 27), biggest single-day drop. Year closes at 7,908, the

third consecutive year with more than a 20% increase.

Justice Department files complaint against Microsoft Corp. for allegedly forcing computer companies to use its browser program; court (December 11) orders Microsoft to stop practice.

Federal minimum wage rises to $5.15 an hour (September 1) from $4.75; unemployment rate for year is 4.6%, a 24-year low.

Morgan Stanley Group Inc. reports that it will merge with Dean Witter, Discover & Co., creating largest U.S. securities group. Three other mergers are announced: NYNEX and Bell Atlantic, Northrup Grumman and Lockheed, Hughes Aircraft and Raytheon.

U.S. trade deficit for 1996 is reported at $114.23 billion, up 8.7% from 1995.

DEATHS Robert Goizueta, Coca-Cola president; Robert W. Sarnoff of RCA; James A. Ryder, pioneer in truck leasing.

TRANSPORTATION

A British racing team breaks sound barrier on land (October 15) when a jet-powered Thrust SSC reaches 763.035 miles per hour on Black Rock Desert in Nevada.

FBI completes its investigation of TWA Flight 800 crash, states there is no evidence of any criminal action.

SCIENCE/MEDICINE

American spacecraft, the Mars *Pathfinder*, lands (July 4) on planet Mars; sends back pictures.

President Clinton (March 4) bans use of federal funds for human embryo research in wake of successful cloning of adult sheep in Scotland.

Immense Hale-Bopp comet with a 25-mile wide icy core reaches its point closest to Earth, about 122 million miles; first appearance near Earth in 4,200 years.

Paul D. Boyers shares Nobel Prize in chemistry with John E. Walker of Great Britain and Jens C. Skou; Steven Chu and William D. Phillips share prize in physics, and Stanley B. Prusiner is awarded prize in physiology/medicine.

1997

The view from the Pathfinder on Mars shows the small rover "Sojourner," in the foreground. The white items on either side of the rover are airbags used to absorb the shock of landing on Mars. AGENCE FRANCE PRESSE/CORBIS-BETTMANN

In June, Supreme Court upholds Washington and New York state laws that make it a crime for doctors to help patients end their lives.

DEATHS Biochemists Melvin Calvin, John C. Kendrew, and George Wald; physicists Robert Dicke and Edward Purcell; surgeons Alfred D. Hershey and Charles B. Huggins; astronomer Clyde V. Tombaugh.

EDUCATION

George Bush Memorial Library opens in College Station, Tex.

RELIGION

Promise Keepers, an evangelical group, organizes a rally (October 4) in Washington, D.C., for Christian men to reaffirm their faith and to help restore and preserve the nation and families.

DEATH Ruffin Bridgeforth, first African American Mormon high priest.

ART/MUSIC

Performing arts center opens in downtown Newark, N.J.; Los Angeles opens a new Getty art museum.

Songs of the year include "Candle in the Wind," Elton John's eulogy for Princess Diana.

DEATHS Rudolph Bing, Metropolitan Opera manager (1950–1972); Helen Jepson, opera singer; John Denver, singer and composer, in plane crash; songwriter Irving Caesar; orchestra conductor Georg Solti; artists Willem de Kooning and Roy Lichtenstein.

LITERATURE/JOURNALISM

Supreme Court rules 7–2 in June to extend right of free speech to the Internet.

Robert Pinsky is named the ninth U.S. poet laureate.

Some books of the year are *Cold Mountain* by Charles Frazier, *The God of Small Things* by Arundhati Roy, *Midnight in the Garden of Good and Evil* by John Berendt, *Angela's Ashes* by Frank McCourt, *Into Thin Air* by Jon Krakauer.

DEATHS Poets James Dickey and Allen Ginsberg; columnists Mike Royko, Murray Kempton, and Herb Caen; TV performer and author Charles Kuralt of *On the Road* fame; authors James Michener, Harold Robbins, Leon Edel, Vance Packard, Leo Rosten.

ENTERTAINMENT

Major television networks, except NBC, agree (July 9) to revised, expanded TV rating system; revision expands contents ratings of January.

The musical *Cats* becomes longest-running show in Broadway history (June 19) with its 6,138th performance, passes *A Chorus Line*.

The year's movies include *LA Confidential*, *Titanic*, *Amistad*, *As Good as It Gets*, *The Ice Storm*, *Men in Black*.

Plays of the year include *The Lion King*, *Ragtime* with Brian Stokes Mitchell, and *A Doll's House* with Janet McTeer.

DEATHS Screen actors Burgess Meredith, Robert Mitchum, Jimmy Stewart; TV and film comic Red Skelton; pioneer TV announcer and game-show host Dennis James; Brandon Tartikoff, NBC executive; screen director Fred Zinneman.

SPORTS

Tiger Woods set new record (270 strokes) in winning Masters golf tournament (April 13); also youngest (21) event winner and first African American to win major tourney.

Tara Lipinski becomes youngest (14) U.S. figure-skating champion (February 16).

Evander Holyfield retains WBA heavyweight boxing title (June 28) when Mike Tyson is disqualified after biting Holyfield's ear several times.

Retirees in sports world include Dean Smith, University of North Carolina basketball coach for 36 years with a record 879 wins, and Eddie Robinson, Grambling College football coach for 56 years with 408 wins.

Baseball salaries hit new high when Boston Red Sox sign pitcher Pedro Martinez (December 10) to six-year $75 million contract. Baseball also enters new era (June 12) with start of regular season interleague play.

Detroit hockey coach Scotty Bowman becomes (February 8) first NHL coach to achieve 1,000 wins; later (June 7) his Red Wings win Stanley Cup for first time in 43 years.

WINNERS *Auto racing*—Ariel Luyendyk, Indianapolis 500; Jeff Gordon, NASCAR; *Baseball*—Florida Marlins, World Series; *Basketball*—Chicago, NBA; Houston, WNBA (women), Columbus, ABL (women); Kentucky, NCAA; Tennessee, NCAA (women); Michigan, NIT; *Bowling*—John Gant, Tournament of Champions; Jason Queen, Masters; *Figure skating*—Tara Lipinski, U.S., world women's title, Todd Eldredge, U.S. men's title; *Football* (bowls)—Ohio State, Rose; Nebraska, Orange; Florida, Sugar; Brigham Young, Cotton; Green Bay, Super Bowl XXXI; *Golf*—Ernie Els, U.S. Men's Open; Davis Love III, PGA; Tiger Woods, Masters; Allison Nicholas, U.S. Women's Open; Chris Johnson, LPGA; *Harness racing*—Malabar Man, Hambletonian; *Horse racing*—Silver Charm, Kentucky Derby, Preakness Stakes; Touch Gold, Belmont Stakes; *Tennis*—Patrick Rafter, U.S. Open (men); Pete Sampras, Wimbledon (men); Martina Hingis, U.S. Open, Wimbledon (women).

DEATHS Pro football club owners Jack Kent Cooke and Robert Irsay; golfer Ben Hogan; baseball players Johnny Vander Meer, Buck Leonard, and Curt Flood; football star Don Hutson; Eddie Arcaro, only jockey to ride two Triple Crown winners; tennis star Helen Jacobs; boxer Tony Zale.

1997

MISCELLANEOUS

Bobbi McCaughey of Carlisle, Iowa, gives birth to first set of living septuplets (October 26) in nearby Des Moines; all seven doing well at year's end.

Flood-swollen rivers force about 100,000 persons in upper Midwest from their homes in April; a month earlier, floods in Ohio River Valley claim 35 lives.

Tornadoes in central Arkansas (March 1) kill 26; six tornadoes rip through central Texas; one kills 27 persons in Jarrell.

Ted Turner, media and sports leader, announces donation of $1 billion over 10 years to United Nations agencies.

Approximately 41% of U.S. homes have a personal computer.

INDEX

Numbers in **boldface** indicate years; each year is followed by a colon and the corresponding page number.
Page numbers in *italics* indicate illustrations. Roman numbers indicate pre-Independence entries.

volcanic eruptions, **1912**:260, **1990**:486
Alaska Airlines, **1971**:432
Alaska-Yukon-Pacific Exposition, **1909**:252
Albanese, Licia, **1940**:342
Albany (N.Y.)
  fires set by rebel slaves, **1793**:27
  New York State Library School, **1887**:199
  slave rebellion, **1793**:27
  as state capital, **1797**:33
Albany Argus (newspaper), **1813**:55
Albany Evening Journal (newspaper), **1830**:80
Alba Settlement House (Cleveland), **1900**:231
Albee, Edward, **1974**:441
Albers, Josef, **1950**:373
Albert, Eddie, **1965**:414
Albert, Stephen, **1984**:467
Albertson, Jack, **1972**:434
Alice Adams (book), **1921**:287
Albertville (France), **1992**:494
Albion (N.Y.), **1937**:335
Albright, Jacob, **1800**:37, **1808**:47
Albright, Madeleine, **1996**:506
Albright, Tenley, **1952**:380, **1953**:382, **1955**:389, **1956**:391
Albright Art Gallery (Buffalo, N.Y.), **1862**:144
Albuquerque (N. Mex.), **1957**:393
Alcan Highway, **1942**:348
Alcoa Building (Pittsburgh), **1953**:381
Alcoa Corp., **1888**:201
alcoholic beverages
  ban on sales to Native Americans, **1892**:209
  distillation prohibitions, **1777**:4
  distilled liquor taxes, **1791**:23, **1802**:39
  distiller fraud conspiracy, **1875**:173
  interstate commerce limits, **1913**:262
  state prohibition laws, **1908**:249, **1909**:251, **1913**:262
  Whiskey Rebellion, **1794**:27, **1794**:*28*
  See also Prohibition; temperance movement
Alcoholics Anonymous, **1935**:329
alcoholism, **1989**:480
Alcorn University, **1871**:165
Alcott, Amy, **1980**:457
Alcott, Louisa May, **1868**:158, **1871**:166, **1888**:202
Alda, Alan, **1972**:432, **1992**:493
Alda, Robert, **1950**:375
Alden, Henry M., **1919**:281
Aldrich, Bess Streeter, **1928**:305
Aldrich, Thomas B., **1870**:164, **1873**:170, **1880**:185
Aldrich Family (television program), **1949**:371
Aldrich Family, The (radio program), **1939**:340
Aldrich-Vreeland Act, **1908**:248
Aldrin, Edwin E., **1969**:424, **1969**:*424*
Alemany, Jose S., **1853**:124, **1888**:201

Alex, Janet, **1982**:463
Alexander, Franz, **1963**:408
Alexander, John W., **1915**:269
Alexander Hamilton (painting), **1792**:25
Alexander Smith Carpet Co., **1876**:176
Alexanderson, Ernst F. W., **1906**:243, **1916**:272, **1924**:293
"Alexander's Ragtime Band" (song), **1911**:258
"Alfie" (song), **1966**:416
Alfred University, **1836**:91
Alger, Cyrus, **1827**:74, **1834**:86, **1856**:130
Alger, Horatio, Jr., **1867**:156, **1869**:161, **1899**:228
Algerine Captive, The (book), **1797**:32
Algiers (movie), **1938**:337
Algiers, peace treaty, **1795**:29, **1815**:57
Algren, Nelson, **1949**:370
Alhambra, The (book), **1832**:84
Alias Jimmy Valentine (play), **1910**:256
Alice Adams (book), **1921**:287
"Alice Blue Gown" (song), **1919**:281
Alien and Sedition Acts, **1798**:34, **1799**:34
Alien Corn (play), **1933**:322
Alien Registration Act, **1940**:341
aliens
  deportations, **1919**:280
  Johnson Act limiting, **1921**:285
  public schooling rights, **1980**:456, **1982**:461
  wartime registration of, **1917**:274, **1940**:341
Ali, Muhammad, **1964**:411, **1965**:414, **1966**:417, **1994**:501
  conviction overturned, **1971**:431
  heavyweight title, **1974**:441, **1975**:444, **1976**:447, **1977**:449, **1978**:451
  sentenced for refusing military service, **1967**:420
Alin, John M., **1974**:440
All About Eve (movie), **1950**:375
Allaire Works, **1816**:59
"All Alone" (song), **1924**:294
"All Around the World" (song), **1990**:485
Allée (painting), **1914**:266
Allegheny Athletics Assn., **1893**:211
Allegheny College, **1815**:57
Allen, Aaron H., **1854**:126
Allen, Ethan, **1789**:21
Allen, Florence E., **1922**:288, **1934**:323
Allen, Fred, **1932**:319, **1956**:391
Allen, Gracie, **1932**:319, **1950**:374, **1964**:411
Allen, Hervey, **1924**:295, **1933**:322, **1949**:371
Allen, James L., **1894**:216, **1897**:223
Allen, John, **1851**:120
Allen, Mel, **1996**:509
Allen, Paul (Microsoft co-founder), **1977**:447
Allen, Paul (poet), **1801**:39
Allen, Richard, **1831**:82
Allen, Robert, **1932**:319

Allen, Scott, **1964**:411, **1966**:417
Allen, Steve, **1950**:374, **1954**:385
Allen, Ted, **1955**:388
Allen, Tim, **1994**:501
Allen, Tom, 1869, **1869**:161, **1873**:170
Allen, Woody, **1969**:426
Allen, Zachariah, **1821**:66
Allentown (Pa.), **1777**:4
Allerton, Samuel, **1914**:265
Alliance for Progress, **1961**:402, **1966**:415
Allied Chemical Co., **1899**:226
Allied Stores, **1986**:472, **1990**:484
All in the Family (television program), **1971**:431
All I Really Need to Know I Learned in Kindergarten (book), **1989**:482
Allison, Bobby, **1983**:465
Allison, Davy, **1993**:498
Allison, Wilmer, **1935**:329
"All I Want for Christmas" (song), **1946**:361
All My Sons (play), **1947**:364
"All Night Long" (song), **1983**:465
"All of Me" (song), **1931**:316
All Quiet on the Western Front (movie), **1930**:313
All-State Insurance Co., **1931**:314
Allston, Washington, **1804**:42, **1817**:60, **1819**:63, **1843**:104
All the Days and Nights (book), **1996**:508
"All the Gold in California" (song), **1980**:457
All the King's Men (book), **1946**:362
All the King's Men (movie), **1949**:371
All the President's Men (movie), **1976**:446
"All the Things You Are" (song), **1939**:339, **1940**:342
"Almost Like Being in Love" (song), **1947**:364
Almy, Brown & Slater, **1793**:26
"Aloha Oe" (song), **1878**:181
"Alone Again" (song), **1972**:434
Alone at Last (musical), **1915**:269
Along the Erie Canal (painting), **1890**:207
"Alouette" (song), **1879**:183
Alpha Kappa Alpha, **1908**:250
Alphonsa, Mother (Rose Hawthorne), **1901**:233
Alston, Walter, **1984**:468
Altair (microcomputer kit), **1975**:442
alternative-fuel vehicles, **1992**:492
alternator, **1906**:243
Altman, Benjamin, **1865**:151
Altman, Sidney, **1989**:482
Alton (Tex.), **1989**:483
aluminum, **1886**:197, **1888**:201, **1889**:203, **1958**:395
Aluminum Co. of America, **1886**:197
alum works, first, **1811**:51
Alvarado (Calif.), **1870**:163
Alvarez, Luis W., **1968**:421, **1988**:478
"Always" (song), **1925**:297
Alzado, Lyle, **1991**:490
Alzheimer's disease, **1994**:499
Amahl and the Night Visitors (opera),

Army Engineer Corps, **1802:**39
Army Medical Corps, **1818:**62
Army Nurse Corps, **1901:**233
Army School of Nursing, **1918:**277
Army War College, **1901:**232, **1907:**245
Arnaz, Desi, **1950:***373*, **1986:**473
Arness, James, **1955:**388
Arno, Peter, **1925:**297, **1933:**321
Arnold, Benedict, **1778:**4-5, **1780:**7, **1781:**8, **1801:**38
Arnold, Billy, **1930:**313
Arnold, Henry H. (Hap), **1949:**369, **1950:**372
Arnold, Thurmond, **1969:**424
Around the World in 80 Days (book), **1890:**205
Around the World in 80 Days (movie), **1956:**391
Arp, Bill (pseud. of Charles B. Smith), **1903:**237
Arrangement, An (painting), **1901:**233
Arrangement, The (book), **1966:**416
Arrow, Kenneth J., **1972:**432–33
Arrowsmith (book), **1924:**295
arsenal, **1796:**30
Arsenic and Old Lace (play), **1941:**345
art
    Armory Show (N.Y.C.), **1913:**263
    auction prices, **1979:**453, **1990:**485, **1993:**497
    first Ashcan School exhibit, **1908:**249
    first museum, **1786:**16
    Hudson River School, **1825:**72
    museum thefts, **1990:**485
    See also specific artists, artworks, and museums
Arthur, Bea, **1972:**432
Arthur, Chester A., **1871:**164, **1878:**181, **1880:**184, **1881:**186, **1882:**188, **1886:**196
Arthur, Ellen L., **1880:**184
Arthur, Jean, **1936:**331, **1938:**337
Arthur, Timothy S., **1850:**119, **1854:**127
Arthur Kill Cantilever Bridge (Staten Island-N.J.), **1928:**304
Arthur Mervyn (book), **1800:**37
Arthur's Home Gazette (magazine), **1850:**119
Articles of Confederation
    adopted, **1777:**4
    amended, **1786:**16
    drafted, **1776:**2
    Maryland ratifies, **1781:**8
    Massachusetts calls for revision, **1785:**14
    South Carolina ratifies, **1778:**4
artificial heart, **1969:**425, **1982:**461
Art Institute of Chicago, **1879:**183
Artist in His Museum, The (painting), **1822:**67
art museums. *See specific names*
Arundel (book), **1930:**312
Arver v. United States, **1918:**277
Aryan, The (movie), **1916:**272
Asbury, Francis, **1782:**11, **1784:**14, **1786:**16, **1816:**59

Asbury Park (N.J.), **1934:**326
ASCAP (American Society of Composers, Authors, and Publishers), **1914:**266
Ascent (painting), **1958:**396
Asch, Sholem, **1939:**339, **1943:**352, **1949:**370, **1957:**394
As Good as It Gets (movie), **1997:**513
Ashburner, Charles E., **1908:**248, **1932:**317
Ashcan School (art), **1908:**249
Ashe, Arthur, **1968:**423, **1993:**498
Ashfield Reservoir, **1874:**172
Ashtabula (Ohio), **1876:**177
Asimov, Isaac, **1950:**374, **1992:**493
"Asleep in the Deep" (song), **1897:**222
Asphalt Jungle, The (movie), **1950:**375
asphalt pavement, **1877:**179
Aspin, Les, **1993:**496
assassinations and assassination attempts
    Cermak fatally shot, **1933:**320
    Evers (Medgar) fatally shot, **1963:**407
    Ford (G.) unharmed, **1975:**442
    Garfield fatally shot, **1881:**186, **1882:**188
    Jackson (A.) fails, **1835:**88, **1835:***89*
    Kennedy (J. F.) fatally shot (Dallas), **1963:**407, **1964:**409
    Kennedy (R. F.) fatally shot (Los Angeles), **1968:**421
    King (M. L., Jr.) fatally shot, **1968:**421
    Long (Huey) fatally shot, **1935:**327
    Malcolm X fatally shot, **1965:**412
    McKinley fatally shot, **1901:**232
    Reagan seriously wounded, **1981:**458, **1982:**460
    Roosevelt (F. D.) unharmed, **1933:**320
    Roosevelt (T.) unharmed, **1912:**260
    Truman unharmed, **1950:**372
    Wallace (G.) paralyzed, **1972:**432
Assemblies of God Church, **1914:**264, **1988:**479
assembly line, conveyor-belt, **1913:**263, **1914:**265
assisted suicide, **1996:**508, **1997:**512
Associated Bill Posters and Distributors, **1891:**208
Associated Press, **1848:**115, **1893:**213
Association of American Advertisers, **1914:**266
Association of American Physicians, **1950:**373
Association of Collegiate Alumnae, **1882:**189
Association of Evangelical Lutheran Churches, **1982:**462, **1988:**479
Astaire, Adele, **1924:**295, **1927:**303, **1931:**316
    Broadway debut, **1917:**275
Astaire, Fred, **1924:**295, **1927:**303, **1931:**316, **1932:**319, **1933:**322, **1934:**326, **1935:**329, **1936:**331, **1948:**368, **1953:**382
    Broadway debut, **1917:**275
    death of, **1987:**477

As Thousands Cheer (play), **1933:**322
Astor, John Jacob, **1789:**21, **1808:**47, **1811:**50
Astor, Mary, death of, **1987:**477
Astoria settlement (Ore.), **1811:**50, **1811:***51*
Astor Place Opera House (N.Y.C.), **1847:**113
Astor Place riot (N.Y.C.), **1849:**117
astronauts. *See* space program
astronomy
    first expedition, **1780:**8
    first woman's honorary doctorate, **1925:**296
    Hale-Bopp comet, **1997:**511
    Halley's Comet, **1910:**255
    Jupiter moons discovered, **1914:**264
    Mars satellites discovered, **1877:**179
    Milky Way distances, **1917:**274
    new planet discovered, **1995:**504
    observatories, **1888:**201, **1894:**215, **1897:**221, **1906:**243, **1908:**249, **1921:**287, **1930:**311
    photography of nebulae, **1880:**184
    Pluto discovered, **1930:**311
    radio waves source, **1932:**318
    Saturn-related discoveries, **1886:**197, **1892:**210, **1898:**225
    spectroheliograph, **1888:**201, **1891:**208
    star distances, **1914:**264
Astrophysical Journal (journal), **1895:**217
Asylum, The (book), **1811:**51
Atanasoff, John V., **1995:**504
Atchison, Topeka & Santa Fe Railroad, **1859:**135
"At Dawning" (song), **1906:**244
At Heaven's Gate (book), **1943:**352
Atherton, Gertrude, **1923:**292, **1948:**368
"A-Tisket, A-Tasket" (song), **1938:**337
Atkinson, Brooks, **1925:**297, **1984:**468
Atlanta (Ga.)
    African American mayor, **1973:**436
    Carter Memorial Library, **1986:**472
    fire, **1917:**275
    first Episcopal bishop, **1907:**247
    Olympic Games pipe-bomb explosion, **1996:**508
    Roman Catholic archbishop, **1988:**479
    Union troops capture, **1864:**147, **1864:***148*
Atlanta Compromise, **1895:**218
Atlanta Constitution (newspaper), **1868:**158
Atlanta University System, formed, **1929:**308
Atlantic & Pacific Tea Co., **1859:**135
Atlantic Charter, **1941:**344, **1942:**347
Atlantic City (N.J.), **1882:**190, **1898:**225
    boardwalk opens, **1870:**164
    dirigible explosion over, **1912:**261
Atlantic Greyhound Co., **1924:**293
Atlantic Monthly (magazine), **1857:**132
Atlantis (newspaper), **1894:**216

oldest heavyweight champion, **1994:**501
Sullivan death, **1918:**279
superwelterweight title, **1984:**468
Tyson rape conviction, **1992:**494
See also under SPORTS *in text for specific yearly title winners*
Boyd, Alan S., **1967:**419
Boyd, Glenn R., **1914:**267
Boyd, James, **1821:**66
Boyd, William, **1949:**371
Boyden, Seth, **1819:**63
Boyden, Uriah A., **1844:**106
Boyer, Charles, **1938:**337, **1944:**355
Boyer, Ernest L., **1977:**448
Boyer, Joe, **1924:**295
Boyers, Paul D., **1997:**511
Boyertown, (Pa.), **1908:**250
Boyle, Kay, **1993:**498
Boylston, Zabdiel, xi
"Boy Named Sue, A" (song), **1969:**425
Boy Scouts of America, **1910:**256, **1911:**259, **1912:***260*
Boys from Brazil, The (book), **1976:**446
Boys' Life (magazine), **1911:**259
Boys Town, founding, **1917:**275
Boys Town (movie), **1938:**337
Bracebridge Hall (book), **1822:**67
Brace, Charles Loring, **1853:**125
Brackenridge, Hugh H., **1792:**26
Bradbury, Ray, **1953:**382
Braddock, Jim, **1935:**329
Brademas, John, **1981:**459
Bradford, Barbara T., **1983:**465
Bradford, Gamaliel, **1912:**261
Bradford, Roark, **1931:**316
Bradley, Bill, **1995:**503
Bradley, Milton, **1911:**257
Bradley, Omar N., **1949:**369, **1979:**452
Bradley, Pat, **1981:**460, **1986:**474
Brady, Alice, **1915:**269, **1939:**340
Brady, James, **1981:**458
Brady, James B. ("Diamond Jim"), **1917:**274
Brady, Mathew, **1844:**106, **1865:**151, **1877:***178*, **1896:**219
Brady, William A., **1950:**375
Brady Bunch, The (television program), **1969:**426
Bramble, Livingston, **1984:**468
Branch, Arnold, **1939:**339
Branch Davidian cult (Waco, Tex.), **1993:***496*, **1993:**499
Brandeis, Louis D., **1916:**270
Brandeis University, **1947:**364
Brando, Marlon, **1947:**364, **1951:**377, **1952:**379, **1954:**385
Godfather, **1972:***433*, **1972:**434
Brandywine (Pa.), **1777:**3
Branham, George III, **1993:**498
Braniff Airways, **1930:**311, **1982:**461
Brattain, Walter H., **1948:**366, **1956:**390, **1988:**478
Braun, Carol M. *See* Moseley-Braun, Carol
Brave Men (book), **1944:**354

Brazil, **1824:**69, **1828:**75, **1914:**265, **1939:**338
"Brazil" (song), **1939:**339
Breakfast at Tiffany's (book), **1958:**396
Breakfast at Tiffany's (movie), **1961:**404
Breakfast Club (radio program), **1933:**322
Breaking Point, The (book), **1922:**289
Break the Bank (radio program), **1945:**358
Breasted, James H., **1919:**281
breast implants, **1992:**492
Breathing the Water (book), **1987:**476–77
Breathless (movie), **1983:**465
Breck, John H., **1908:**249
Breckenridge, John C., **1860:**137, **1875:**173
Bremen Glass Manufactory, **1784:**13
Bremer, Arthur, **1972:**432
Brennan, Andrew J., **1926:**299
Brennan, Brid, **1992:**493
Brennan, Francis, **1969:**425
Brennan, William J., Jr., **1990:**484, **1997:**511
Brent, Charles H., **1929:**308
Brewer, Gary Jr., **1967:**420
Breyer, Stephen, **1994:**499
Brezhnev, Leonid, **1974:**439
Briar Cliff (play), **1826:**74
Brice, Fanny, **1910:**256, **1928:**306, **1936:**331
brick, insulating, **1913:**262
Brico, Antonia, **1935:**328
Bride-Elect, The (opera), **1897:**222
bridge (game), **1925:**298
Bridge, The (painting), **1911:**258, **1939:**339
bridge disasters, **1876:**177, **1980:**457, **1983:**464, **1987:**475
Bridgeforth, Ruffin, **1997:**512
Bridge of San Luis Rey, The (book), **1927:**302
Bridge on the River Kwai, The (movie), **1957:**394
"Bridge Over Troubled Water" (song), **1970:**428
Bridger, James, **1824:**70, **1824:***70*
bridges
    cantilevered, **1877:**179
    Delaware River, **1806:**44
    first iron railroad, **1845:**107
    first iron truss, **1840:**98
    first iron-wire suspension, **1816:**59
    first railroad over Mississippi, **1854:**127
    first stone-arch railroad, **1829:**78
    first suspension, **1796:**31
    Glasgow (Mo.), **1879:**182
    Harrodsburg (Ky.), **1877:**179
    Idaho, **1971:**430
    Louisiana, **1983:**464
    Maryland, **1977:**448
    Merrimack River, **1792:**25
    New York City, **1903:**237, **1909:**252, **1917:**274, **1931:**314, **1961:**403
    New York City tolls imposed, **1977:**447
    Niagara River, **1883:**191

    Ohio River Railroad Bridge, **1870:**163
    over Niagara Falls gorge, **1855:**128
    over Ohio River at Cincinnati, **1867:**156
    Pennsylvania, **1974:**440
    St. Louis, **1874:**172
    several completed, **1929:**308
    Staten Island (N.Y.), **1928:**304
    Virginia, **1928:**304
    wire suspension (Ky.), **1851:**120
    wire suspension across Monongahela, **1846:**110
    wire suspension across Niagara River, **1847:**112
    world's longest opens, **1849:**116
    See also bridge disasters; *specific bridges*
Bridges, Harry, **1990:**484
Bridges, Jeff, **1971:**431
Bridges at Toko-Ri, The (book), **1953:**382
Bridges of Madison County (movie), **1995:**505
Bridgestone Tires, **1988:**478
Bridge World (magazine), **1929:**309
Bridgman, Elijah C., **1861:**141
Bridgman, Percy W., **1946:**360
Brigands, The (play), **1889:**204
Briggs, Charles A., **1893:**213
Briggs, Clare A., **1930:**313
Brigham Young University, **1875:**173
Bright and Shining Lie (book), **1988:**479
"Brighten the Corner Where You Are" (song), **1913:**264
Brighton Beach Memoirs (play), **1983:**465
Brill, Abraham A., **1948:**367
Brimmer, Andrew F., **1966:**415
Brimming Cup, The (book), **1921:**287
Brinks, Inc., **1918:**277
Brisbane, Arthur, **1917:**275, **1936:**331
Bristol-Myers, **1989:**481
Bristow, George F., **1850:**119
Britain. *See* Great Britain
British Airways, **1992:**492
British Petroleum, **1987:**475
"British Prison Ship, The" (poem), **1781:**9
British West Indies, **1830:**79
Britton, Jack, **1919:**282
Britz, Jerilyn, **1979:**454
broadcasting. *See* radio broadcasting; television
Broadway (play), **1926:**300
Broadway Tabernacle, **1834:**88
Broca's Brain (book), **1979:**453
Brock, Lou, **1974:**441, **1977:**449, **1979:**454
Brockhouse, Bertram N., **1994:**500
Brockport Bridge (Paducah, Ky.), **1929:**308
Brodie, H. Keith, **1992:**492
Brodsky, Harold, **1987:**476
Brodsky, Joseph, **1991:**488, **1996:**508
Broken Blossoms (play), **1919:**282
Broker of Bogota, The (play), **1834:**88
bromine, **1889:**203
Bronk, Detlev, **1953:**382, **1975:**442

cancer
first isolation of virus, **1910**:255
National Cancer Institute formed,
1937:334
pap smear detection, **1928**:305
relief organizations, **1901**:233
Candidate, The (movie), **1972**:434
Candid Camera (television program),
1948:368
Candide (opera), **1956**:391
"Candle in the Wind" (song), **1997**:512
Candler, Asa G., **1887**:199
Candlestick Park (San Francisco),
1989:483
Candy (book), **1955**:388
"Candy Man, The" (song), **1972**:434
Cane (book), **1923**:292
Canham, Erwin, **1982**:462
Caniff, Milton, **1934**:325, **1988**:479
can-making machine, **1885**:195
Cannery Row (book), **1945**:357
Cannery Row (movie), **1982**:462
Cannon, Annie Jump, **1925**:296
Cannon, Harriet S., **1865**:152
Cannon, Joseph G., **1910**:254
Cannonball Express (train), **1901**:233
cannons, **1877**:178
Canteline, Anita, **1956**:391
Canterbury Pilgrims, The (opera), **1917**:275
"Can't Fight This Feeling" (song),
1985:470
"Can't Get Used to Losing You" (song),
1963:408
"Can't Help Falling in Love" (song),
1961:404
Canticle of the Sun (music), **1945**:357
Canti del Sole (musical composition),
1983:465
cantilever plane, **1927**:301
Canton (Ohio), **1963**:409
Cantor, Eddie, **1923**:292, **1928**:306,
1930:313, **1964**:411
"Can't Take My Eyes Off of You" (song),
1967:419
Cantwell v. Connecticut, **1940**:342
Canyonland National Park (Utah),
1964:410
Can You Top This? (radio program),
1942:349
Canzoneri, Tony, **1930**:313, **1935**:329
Cape Canaveral (Fla.), **1962**:405
Cape Cod (Mass.), **1898**:225
hurricanes, **1938**:337, **1944**:355
"Cape Cod Girls" (song), **1830**:80
Cape Fear (movie), **1991**:489
Capital Cities/ABC, **1995**:503
Capital Cities Communications Inc.,
1985:470
capital punishment
of Cermak's assassin, **1933**:320
first electrocution, **1890**:207
first public execution, xiv
first state to abolish, **1846**:110
first state to use lethal gas, **1921**:286
of McKinley's assassin, **1901**:232
New Jersey reinstates, **1982**:460

of Rosenbergs, **1953**:380
of Sacco and Vanzetti, **1927**:303
Supreme Court rulings, **1972**:432,
1976:445
Capitan, El (opera), **1896**:220
Capitol, U.S., **1800**:*36*
British burn, **1814**:55
cornerstone laid, **1793**:26
gas lighting, **1847**:113
National Statuary Hall, **1864**:149
new House chamber, **1857**:131
new Senate chamber, **1859**:135
Weather Underground bombing of,
1971:430
Capitol Brush Co., **1906**:243
Capone, Al, **1931**:314, **1947**:364
Caponi, Donna, **1969**:426, **1970**:429,
1979:454, **1981**:460
Capote, Truman, **1948**:368, **1958**:396,
1965:413, **1984**:468
Capp, Al, **1934**:325, **1979**:453
Capra, Frank, **1991**:489
Captain Craig (book), **1902**:236
Captain from Castile (book), **1945**:357
"Captain Marvel" (comic strip), **1940**:342
Captains Courageous (movie), **1937**:334
Capt. Jinks of the Horse Marines (play),
1901:234
Capture of Major André, The (painting),
1833:86
Caracole (book), **1985**:470
Caraway, Hattie W., **1932**:317
carbon, trivalent, **1910**:255
carbon dating, **1947**:364, **1960**:400
Cardinal, The (book), **1950**:374
Care and Feeding of Children, The (book),
1894:215
"Careless Whisper" (song), **1985**:470
Carew, Rod, **1985**:471
Carey & Hart, **1829**:78
Carey Stewart & Company, **1790**:22
Carib (ship), **1915**:267
Carlile, John S., **1878**:181
Carlisle (Pa.), **1879**:183
Carlisle (Pa.) Trust Co., **1909**:253
Carlisle Indian School, **1879**:183,
1912:262
Carlson, Charles F., **1957**:393
Carlson, Chester, **1940**:342, **1968**:421
Carmer, Carl, **1934**:326
Carmichael, Oliver C., **1946**:360
Carnation Co., **1899**:226, **1984**:466
Carnegie, Andrew, **1865**:151, **1889**:203,
1901:233, **1903**:237
Carnegie, Dale, **1936**:331, **1955**:388
Carnegie, Hattie, **1956**:389
Carnegie Commission on Higher Educa-
tion, **1968**:422
Carnegie Corporation, **1911**:258
Carnegie Endowment for International
Peace, **1910**:256
Carnegie Foundation for the Advance-
ment of Teaching, **1905**:242,
1946:360, **1986**:473
Carnegie Hall (N.Y.C.), **1891**:208,
1938:337

celebrates 100th anniversary,
1991:488
gala for Irving Berlin's 100th birth-
day, **1988**:479
Heifetz debut, **1917**:274
Carnegie Hero Fund Commission,
1904:241
Carnegie Institute of Technology,
1900:230
Carnegie Institution, **1902**:234
Carnegie Mellon University, **1900**:230
Carnegie Steel Corp., **1889**:203,
1892:209
Carnera, Primo, **1933**:322, **1933**:323
Carner, Jo Anne, **1971**:432, **1976**:447
Carnes, Peter, **1784**:13
Carney, Art, **1955**:388, **1965**:414,
1974:441
Carnival (play), **1920**:285
Carnival, The (painting), **1877**:179
"Carnival of Venice" (song), **1854**:127
Caro, Robert A., **1974**:440
"Carolina in the Morning" (song),
1922:289
Carolina Low Country (painting), **1939**:339
Caron, Leslie, **1958**:396
Carothers, Wallace H., **1934**:324,
1937:333
Carousel (play), **1945**:357
carousels, **1896**:220
Carpenter, John A., **1926**:299
Carpenter, William, **1779**:7
Carpenter's Union, **1882**:189
Carpentier, Georges, **1920**:285
Carpetbaggers, The (book), **1961**:404
carpets, **1876**:176
carpet sweeper, **1876**:176
Carr, Benjamin, **1796**:31, **1800**:37
Carr, Joe E., **1921**:287, **1939**:340
Carr, Sabin, **1927**:303
Carrel, Alexis, **1912**:261
Carrere, John M., **1911**:257
carriages, first two-wheeled, **1780**:8
Carrier, Willis H., **1915**:268
Carrier Corp., **1915**:268
Carrillo, Leo, **1917**:275
Carroll, John, **1776**:1, **1784**:14, **1789**:21,
1790:22, **1815**:57
Carry, Luther, **1891**:209
"Carry Me Back to Old Virginny" (song),
1875:174
cars. *See* automobiles
Carslbad (N.Mex.), **1930**:310
Carson, Johnny, **1962**:407, **1992**:493
Carson, Kit, **1868**:157
Carson, Rachel, **1951**:376, **1955**:388,
1962:406, **1964**:411
Carter, Don, **1953**:382, **1954**:386,
1958:396, **1960**:402
Carter, Elliott, **1959**:398, **1972**:433
Carter, Jimmy
Alaskan public lands, **1978**:450
Camp David Mideast peace talks,
1978:449
elected president, **1976**:444
gasoline price controls, **1977**:447

1870:163

Color Purple, The (book), **1982:**462

Color Purple, The (movie), **1985:**471

color television, **1940:**343, **1950:**374

    Bell Lab demonstration, **1929:**308

    number of sets owned, **1996:**509

Colt, Samuel, **1830:**79, **1835:**89, **1836:**91, **1842:**102

Col. Thomas H. Perkins (painting), **1832:**84

Columbia (newspaper), **1852:**123

Columbia (ship), round-the-world trip, **1787:**18, **1790:**22

Columbia (steamer), **1918:**279

Columbia (yacht), **1871:**166, **1901:**234

Columbia Broadcasting System. *See* CBS

Columbian (ship), **1916:**270

Columbian Exposition (Chicago), **1893:**213, **1894:**216

Columbian Magazine, **1786:**17

Columbia Pictures, **1924:**295, **1989:**481

Columbia Records, **1948:**367

Columbia River Treaty, **1961:**402

Columbia University

    Barnard College, **1883:**192

    Butler presidency, **1902:**235

    College of Physicians and Surgeons, **1807:**46

    Eisenhower presidency, **1947:**364

    first African American PhD recipient, **1912:**262

    first full-time U.S. nursing professor, **1907:**246

    first president, **1787:**18

    first Pulitzer Prize awards, **1917:**275

    football, **1873:**170

    founding, xii

    Graduate School of Journalism, **1903:**237, **1912:**261

    law lectures, **1797:**32

    law school, **1858:**134, **1986:**473

    library school, **1887:**199

    Moore as president, **1801:**39

    optics and optometry courses, **1910:**255

    rowing, **1878:**182

    Rupp presidency, **1993:**497

    School of Architecture, **1881:**186

    Sovran resigns presidency, **1992:**493

Columbus (N. Mex.), **1916:**270

Columbus (Ohio), **1886:**196

Columbus, Christopher, **1992:**493

Columbus Day, three-day weekend, **1971:**430

Columbus Monument, **1792:**25

Column (sculpture), **1923:**292

Colwell, Paul, **1976:**447

Come Back, Little Sheba (play), **1950:**375

"Come Back to Erin" (song), **1866:**154

Come Blow Your Horn (play), **1961:**404

Comedy Overture on Negro Themes (musical composition), **1905:**242

"Come, Josephine, in My Flying Machine" (song), **1910:**256

comets, **1843:**103, **1910:**255

"Come Where My Love Lies Dreaming" (song), **1855:**129

comic books, color, **1904:**240

comic strips, **1902:**236

    "Blondie," **1930:**312

    "Captain Marvel," **1940:**342

    "Dick Tracy," **1931:**316

    first color, **1894:**216

    first daily, **1907:**247

    forerunner, **1892:**211

    "Gasoline Alley," **1919:**281

    "Hogan Alley," **1894:**216

    "Katzenjammer Kids," **1897:**222

    "L'il Abner," **1934:**325

    "Little Orphan Annie," **1924:**295

    "Peanuts," **1950:**374

    "Terry and the Pirates," **1934:**325

    See also cartoons

Coming of Age in Samoa (book), **1928:**305

Coming to America (movie), **1988:**479

Comiskey, Charles A., **1931:**317

Comiskey Park (Chicago), **1910:**256, **1990:**486

Commentaries on American Law (book), **1830:**80

Commerce and Labor Department

    established, **1903:**236

    separated, **1913:**262

Commerce Department

    civil aviation jurisdiction, **1926:**298

    formed, **1913:**262

    Hoover (H.) as Secretary, **1921:**285–86

Commerce of the Prairies (book), **1844:**107

Commercial Cable Co., **1883:**191, **1928:**304

Commercial Carriers Inc., **1930:**311

commission (governmental form), **1901:**232

commission-city manager government, **1914:**265

Commissioner of Indian Affairs, **1832:**83

Commission for Relief in Belgium, **1915:**267

Committee of Industrial Organization. *See* Congress of Industrial Organizations

Committee on Public Information, **1917:**273

Commodity Credit Corp., **1933:**321

Commodore Barry Bridge (Chester, Pa.), **1974:**440

Common Law, The (book), **1881:**188

Common School Journal, **1838:**94

Common Sense (book), **1776:**2, **1783:**12

Commonwealth Edison Co., **1906:**243

Communications Satellite Corp., **1962:**405

Communism, **1935:**328, **1953:**380, **1957:**392

    conspiracy convictions, **1949:**369

    Hiss-Chambers confrontation, **1948:**366, **1950:**372

    McCarran Act, **1950:**372

    McCarthy hearings, **1954:**383

    See also Communist Party of America

Communism and Christianity (book), **1925:**297

Communist Labor Party, **1919:**280

Communist Party of America

    founding, **1919:**280

    leaders convicted, **1949:**369

    leaders' conviction upheld, **1951:**376

    registration of members mandated, **1950:**372

Como, Perry, **1944:**355, **1948:**368

compact discs (CDs), **1983:**464

Company (play), **1970:**428

Compendious Dictionary of the English Language (book), **1806:**44

Compendium of Various Sects (book), **1784:**14

Complete Poems (Sandburg book), **1950:**374

Composition (painting), **1942:**349

Comprehensive Test Ban Treaty, **1997:**510

Compromise of 1850, **1850:**118

comptometers, **1884:**193

Compton, Albert A., **1927:**301

Compton, Arthur H., **1923:**292, **1942:**348, **1962:**405

Compton effects (X-ray scattering), **1927:**301

Compton, Karl T., **1930:**311

Comptroller General, office established, **1921:**285–86

Comptroller of the Currency, **1863:**146

Comptroller of the Treasury, **1802:**39

computers

    airline reservation system, **1989:**481

    Altair kit, **1975:**442

    animation, **1995:**505

    Apple I desk-top, **1976:**445, **1977:**447, **1982:**460

    Apple introduces "mouse," **1983:**463

    digital, **1945:**357

    early analog, **1928:**304

    electronic, **1951:**376

    ENIAC, **1946:***361*

    first large-scale digital, **1944:**353

    home ownership numbers, **1997:**514

    IBM introduces personal computer, **1981:**458

    Internet, **1995:**505, **1997:**513

    mainframe, **1970:**427

    memory chips, **1970:**427

    memory development, **1977:**448

    Microsoft antitrust suit, **1997:**511

    Microsoft founding, **1977:**447

    screen icons, **1983:**463

Computing-Tabulating Recording Co., **1911:**257, **1914:**265

"Comrades" (song), **1887:**200

Comstock, Ada Louise, **1973:**437

Comstock, Anthony, **1915:**268

Comstock Lode, **1859:**135

Conable, Barber B., **1985:**469

Conant, James Bryant, **1933:**322, **1978:**450

Conception of God, The (book), **1897:**222

Concerto for Orchestra (musical composition), **1981:**459

Concert Singer, The (painting), **1892:**211

Concord (Mass.), **1875:**174
Concord, Battle of, x
Concorde SST
    service begins, **1976:**445
    Supreme Court limitations, **1977:**447
condensed milk, **1857:**132
Condominiums (book), **1977:**448
condoms, **1986:**472
Condon, Eddie, **1976:**446
Condon, Richard, **1982:**462
Conduct of Life, The (book), **1860:**138
Coney Island (N.Y.), **1903:**238
Confederacy. *See* Civil War
Confessions of Nat Turner, The (book),
    1967:419
Congo and Other Poems, The, **1914:**266
Congregational Christian church,
    1948:367, **1957:**393
Congregational Church, xiii, **1887:**200
Congregationalist, The (newspaper),
    1889:204
Congress
    African slave trade ban, **1892:**209
    Alaskan delegate, **1906:**243
    American Revolution veterans pen-
        sions, **1818:**61
    annexation of Texas, **1845:**107
    antipolygamy act, **1862:**142
    antislavery petitions to, **1790:**22
    antitrust legislation, **1890:***205*
    balanced-budget amendment defeat,
        1997:510
    budget dispute with Clinton,
        1995:502
    censures, **1873:**169, **1954:**383
    Chrysler loan bailout, **1979:**452
    civil rights bills, **1875:**173
    creates army, **1789:**21
    creates militia, **1797:**32
    creates navy, **1794:**27
    crime bill approved, **1994:**499
    Electoral Count Act, **1887:**198
    embargos, **1807:**45, **1808:**46,
        1809:47, **1809:***48*
    Equal Rights Amendment failure,
        1923:290
    federal salaries set, **1789:**20
    first, **1789:**20
    first address by British monarch,
        1991:487
    first African American members,
        1870:163, **1874:**172
    first African American woman
        member, **1968:**421
    first game law, **1796:**30
    first override of Clinton veto,
        1995:504
    first presidential annual message to,
        1801:38
    first presidential appearance before
        since J. Adams, **1913:**262
    first Republican control since 1952,
        1994:499, **1995:**502
    first Socialist elected to, **1910:**254–55
    flag-burning prosecution amendment
        fails, **1990:**484

GATT ratified, **1994:**499
    general embargo, **1812:**52
    Hayes-Tilden electoral dispute,
        1876:175
    immigration limit increased,
        1990:484
    imprisonment of debtors abolished,
        1798:33
    international slave trade ban, **1794:**27
    interstate shipment of liquor limits,
        1913:262
    Iran-Contra hearings, **1987:**474,
        1992:491
    MacArthur addresses joint session,
        1951:376
    Medicare Catastrophic Coverage Act
        repeal, **1989:**482
    Mother's Day, **1914:**265
    NAFTA approval, **1993:**494
    National Endowment for the Arts
        funding, **1989:**482
    naval appropriations, **1886:**196
    naval authorization, **1883:**190
    Nineteenth Amendment approval,
        1919:280
    overrides presidential veto for first
        time, **1845:**107
    pay raises, **1992:**491
    polygamy laws, **1882:**188
    presidential salary approval,
        1873:169, **1874:**171
    presidential widow's pension,
        1870:163, **1882:**188
    public lands sale, **1800:**36
    Second Bank of the United States,
        1816:58
    Sherman Silver Purchase Act repeal,
        1893:212
    student-aid program passed,
        1993:497
    tax-reform law, **1986:**472
    Twelfth Amendment approval,
        1803:40–41
    Twenty-seventh Amendment
        approval, **1992:**491
    Washington (D.C.) set as capital,
        1800:36, **1801:**38
    World War I declarations, **1917:**272,
        1917:273
    World War I termination and treaties
        ratifications, **1921:**285
    World War II declaration, **1941:**343
    See also Continental Congress; House
        of Representatives, Senate; *specific*
        legislation and members
Congressional Union for Woman Suf-
    frage, **1913:**262, **1917:**274
Congress of Industrial Organizations,
    1937:333, **1940:**342, **1950:**372,
    1952:378
    Committee of Industrial Organiza-
        tion, **1935:**327
    merges with AFL, **1955:**386
Congress of National Black Churches,
    1982:462
Congress of Racial Equality (CORE),

1942:350
Conigliaro, John, **1982:**462, **1985:**470,
    1987:476
Conjure Woman, The (book), **1899:**228
Conn, Billy, **1939:**340
Conn, Charles G., **1888:**202
Connally, John B., **1963:**407, **1993:**496
Connecticut, **1818:**61
    agricultural experiment station,
        1875:173
    American Revolution, **1777:**3, **1779:**6
    chaise introduction, **1780:**8
    clock manufacture, **1794:**28
    copyright law, **1783:**11
    county government abolished,
        1960:400
    Goodspeed Opera House, **1876:**177
    mints copper cents, **1785:**14
    newspapers, **1784:**14
    new state constitution, **1818:**61
    prohibition law, **1854:**126
    ratifies Constitution, **1788:**18
    religious persecution, xiii
    voter property qualifications
        removed, **1818:**61
Connecticut Society for Mental Hygiene,
    1908:249
Connecticut Turnpike, bridge collapse,
    1983:464
Connecticut Yankee in King Arthur's Court
    (book), **1889:**204
Connelly, Cornelia, **1846:**111
Connelly, Marc, **1929:**308, **1980:**457
"Conning Tower, The" (FPA column),
    1913:264
Connolly, James B., **1896:**220
Connolly, Maureen, **1951:**377, **1952:**380,
    1953:382, **1954:**386
Connor, Roger, **1881:**188
Connors, Jimmy, **1974:**441, **1976:**447,
    1978:451, **1982:**463, **1983:**466
Conoco Oil Co., **1981:**458
Conqueror, The (play), **1898:**225
Conquest of Mexico (book), **1843:**104
Conquest of Peru (book), **1847:**113
Conquistador (book), **1932:**319
Conrad, Robert, **1959:**398
Conrad, Robert T., **1835:**90
Conrail, **1985:**469, **1987:**475
Conroy, Sara A. M., **1928:**304
conscientious objection, **1918:**277,
    1971:431
conscription. *See* draft
conservatism, **1908:**248, **1909:**252,
    1910:254
Conservative Baptist Association of
    America, **1947:**364
Constance Latimer (book), **1838:**95
Constellation (carrier), **1960:**402
Constellation (ship), **1799:***35*
Constitution (ship), **1797:***32*, **1812:***52*
    launched, **1797:**32
    reconditioned, **1930:**310
Constitution
    adopted, **1788:**18
    Bill of Rights, **1789:***20*

onship, **1924**:295
Corning, Erastus, **1872**:168
Corn Is Green, The (play), **1942**:349
Cornish, Samuel, **1827**:75
corn production, **1860**:138
Cornwallis, Charles, **1781**:8
Corporation for Public Broadcasting, **1967**:420
Corregidor, **1942**:346
Corrigan, Douglas ("Wrong Way"), **1938**:336, **1995**:504
Corrigan, Michael A., **1886**:197
corrugated paper, **1871**:164
Corrupt Election Practices Law, **1907**:245
corsets, **1914**:267
Corson, Juliet, **1874**:172
Cortelyou, George B., **1903**:236
Corum, L. L., **1924**:295
Cosby, Bill, **1965**:414
Cosell, Howard, **1995**:505
cosmetics, **1910**:255
cosmic microwave background radiation, **1978**:450
cosmic rays, **1925**:296
Costain, Thomas B., **1945**:357, **1948**:368, **1952**:379
Costello, Lou, **1959**:398
Costner, Kevin, **1990**:486, **1991**:489
Cost of Living Council, **1971**:430
cotton
    cotton gin, **1793**:26, **1793**:*26*
    mechanical picker, **1927**:301
    plantation, **1820**:*64*
    production, **1830**:79, **1850**:119, **1859**:135
    See also textile industry
Cotton, Joseph, **1994**:501
Cotton Belt Railroad, **1871**:164
Cotton Bowl
    first played, **1937**:335
    See also under SPORTS *in text for subsequent years*
cotton gin, **1793**:26, **1793**:*26*
Cotton, Henry, **1948**:368
Cotton Pickers (painting), **1932**:319
Coughlin, Charles E., **1934**:323, **1942**:348
Council of Economic Advisors, **1946**:360
Council of Environmental Quality, **1970**:427
Council of National Defense, **1916**:270
Counsellor-at-Law (play), **1931**:316
Counterlife, The (book), **1986**:473
Counterpoise (painting), **1959**:398
Country Girl, The (movie), **1954**:385
Country Girl, The (play), **1950**:375
country music, **1925**:297, **1992**:493
Country of the Pointed Firs (book), **1896**:220
County Builder's Assistant (book), **1796**:31
County Fair, The (painting), **1810**:*49*
Coup, The (book), **1978**:450
coupler, railway, **1873**:170
Couples (book), **1968**:422
Couples, Fred, **1992**:494

Courageous (yacht), **1974**:441, **1977**:449
Courier de Boston (magazine), **1789**:21
Cournand, Andre F., **1956**:390
Court, Margaret, **1969**:426, **1970**:429, **1973**:438
court-martial
    first, **1778**:4
    of Mitchell (B.), **1925**:296
Court of Appeals
    established, **1780**:8
    first African American judge, **1949**:369
Court of Claims, **1855**:128
Court of Commerce, **1910**:255
courts. *See* judiciary; Supreme Court
Courtship of Miles Standish, The (book), **1858**:134
Cousins, Norman, **1940**:342
Covered Wagon, The (book), **1922**:289
Covered Wagon, The (movie), **1923**:292
Cover Girl (movie), **1944**:354
Cowan, Joshua L., **1900**:230, **1965**:412
Cowans Ford Dam, **1971**:430
Coward, Noel, **1933**:322
"Coward of the County" (song), **1980**:457
cowboy museum, **1979**:454
Cowl, Jane, **1912**:261, **1950**:375
Cowles, E. H. and A. H., **1885**:195
Cowles, Gardner, **1935**:328
Cowpens, Battle of, **1781**:8
Cow's Skull (painting), **1931**:316
Cox, Archibald, **1973**:435, **1973**:435–36
Cox, James M., **1920**:28
Cox, William D., **1943**:352
Coxey, Jacob S., **1984**:214
Coxey's army, **1894**:*215*
Cozzens, James G., **1948**:368, **1957**:394
Crabtree, Charlotte (Lotta), **1867**:156, **1877**:179
cracker bakery, first, **1792**:25
Cram, Donald J., **1987**:476
Cram, Ralph, **1942**:348
Crane, Stephen, **1895**:218, **1896**:220, **1898**:225
cranes, **1883**:191
Cranston, Alan, **1990**:484
Crater Lake (Ore.) National Park, **1902**:234
Crater, Joseph F., **1930**:313
Craven, Frank, **1914**:266, **1917**:275
Crawford, Broderick, **1937**:334, **1949**:371
Crawford, Joan, **1928**:306, **1977**:449
Crawford, Michael, **1988**:479
Crawford, Thomas, **1857**:132
Crawford, William H., **1825**:71
creationism, **1925**:296, **1982**:462, **1987**:476
Creavy, Tom, **1931**:317
credit
    automobile financing, **1924**:293
    Chrysler bailout, **1979**:452
    debtor prison abolished, **1798**:33
    debtor's court, **1913**:262
    farm, **1916**:270, **1923**:291

    first automobile finance company, **1915**:268
    first rating organization, **1841**:99
    installment buying, **1910**:255
credit cards, **1951**:376
Crédit Mobilier, **1872**:167, **1873**:169
Creek Nation, **1813**:54, **1814**:55, **1832**:83
Crehorne, Benjamin, **1803**:41
Creighton University (Omaha), **1878**:181
Creole mutiny, **1841**:99
Crescendo (painting), **1910**:256
Crèvecoeur, J. H. St. John de, **1782**:11
Cribb, Tom, **1805**:43
Crick, Francis, **1953**:381, **1962**:405
cricket, xiv
    Boston club, **1809**:48
    club founded, **1832**:84
    international tournament (Hoboken), **1859**:136
    Pennsylvania club, **1843**:104
    University of Michigan team, **1860**:139
Crile, George W., **1921**:287
Crile Hospital (Cleveland), **1929**:309
crime
    anti-crime organizations, **1878**:182
    criminals' sale rights to own stories upheld, **1991**:489
    federal bill approved, **1994**:499
    lie detector, **1921**:286
    See also capital punishment; *specific crimes*
Crimes of the Heart (play), **1981**:459
Crimmins, John, **1941**:346
Crippen, Robert L., **1981**:458
Crisco (shortening), **1911**:257
Crisis, The (book), **1901**:234
Cristofer, Michael, **1977**:449
Crites, Tom, **1986**:474
Criticism and Fiction (book), **1891**:208
Crittenden, John J., **1860**:137
Croce, Jim, **1973**:438
Crocker, Fay, **1955**:389
Crockett, Davy, **1821**:*66*
Crocodile Dundee (movie), **1986**:473
Croly, Herbert D., **1914**:266
Cronin, A. J., **1941**:345
Cronin, Daniel A., **1991**:488
Cronin, James W., **1980**:456
Cronin, Joe, **1934**:326, **1959**:398, **1965**:414
Cronkite, Walter, **1950**:374
Cronyn, Hume, **1977**:449
croquet, **1860**:139
    U.S., **1976**:447
Crosby, Bing, **1927**:302, **1932**:319, **1940**:343, **1942**:349, **1944**:354, **1945**:358, **1947**:365, **1977**:448
Crosby, Bob, **1993**:497
Crosby, Frances J., **1915**:269
Crosby, Kathryn, **1996**:508
Crosby, Percy L., **1964**:411
Crosley Corp., **1921**:286
Crosman, Henrietta, **1891**:208, **1900**:231, **1903**:238

1997:511
wartime labor dispute mediation, **1941**:345
Defense Mediation Board, **1942**:347
deficit, federal
reduction bill, **1990**:484, **1993**:495
reduction policy, **1802**:39
De Forest, J. W., **1867**:156
De Forest, Lee, **1906**:243, **1907**:247, **1923**:292, **1961**:403
Deformed, The (play), **1830**:80
DeGraff, Robert F., **1981**:459
Dehmelt, Hans G., **1989**:482
Déjà Vu for Percussion and Orchestra (musical composition), **1977**:448
de Kooning, Willem, **1955**:388, **1997**:513
De Koven, Reginald, **1891**:208, **1917**:275, **1920**:284
de Kruif, Paul, **1926**:299
Delafield, Edward, **1875**:173
Delafield, Francis, **1915**:268
Delahanty, Thomas, **1981**:458
Delano, Jane, **1919**:281
Delaware (ship), **1910**:255
Delaware, **1776**:2, **1897**:221
Delaware Memorial Bridge, **1951**:376
first state to ratify Constitution, **1787**:17
state constitution, **1776**:2, **1832**:83, **1897**:221
Swedish colonists, ix
votes against secession, **1861**:139
Delaware and Hudson Canal, **1823**:69
Delaware Indians, *x*, **1778**:5
Delaware River, **1787**:*17*
bridges, **1926**:299
canal, **1829**:78
Washington crossing of, **1776**:1
Delaware Water Gap (painting), **1861**:141
Delbruck, Max, **1969**:424
Delcambre, Adrien, **1841**:100
Delco (co.), **1910**:255, **1925**:296
DeLee, Joseph B., **1895**:217
Delehanty, Ed, **1903**:238
Delicate Balance, A (play), **1966**:417
delivery services, **1907**:246
Dello Joio, Norman, **1956**:390
Delmonico, Lorenzo, **1881**:186
Delta Air Lines, **1973**:438, **1986**:472, **1989**:481, **1991**:488
"Delta Dawn" (song), **1973**:438
Delta Force (movie), **1986**:473
Delta Wedding (book), **1946**:362
Del Tredici, David, **1979**:453
De Mar, Clarence, **1930**:313, **1958**:396
Demaret, Jimmy, **1950**:375
de Mille, Agnes, **1993**:497
DeMille, Cecil B., **1913**:264, **1959**:398
DeMille, Henry, **1887**:200, **1889**:204
Democracy and Education (book), **1916**:271
Democratic Party
donkey symbol, **1870**:*162*, **1870**:163
first convention, **1832**:82
national headquarters break-in, **1972**:432

Dempsey, Jack, **1919**:282, **1920**:285, **1921**:288, **1923**:293, **1950**:375, **1983**:466
Dempsey, Tom, **1970**:429
Dempster, Arthur J., **1935**:328, **1950**:373
Demuth, Charles, **1935**:328
Denali National Park (Alaska), **1917**:274, **1980**:456
dendrochronology, **1920**:283
DeNiro, Robert, **1976**:446, **1978**:451, **1980**:457, **1984**:468
Denishawn School of Dance, **1915**:269
Denmark, **1949**:369
recognizes American independence, **1783**:11
treaty with, **1826**:72
U.S. pledges Iceland and Greenland defense, **1941**:344
Virgin Islands sale, **1900**:229, **1916**:270, **1917**:274
World War II, **1941**:344, **1942**:346
Dennis, Sandy, **1992**:493
Dennison, Aaron L., **1812**:53
Dennis v. United States, **1951**:376
Denny, George H., **1955**:388
Dental Art, The (book), **1839**:97
Dent Bridge (Idaho), **1971**:430
dentistry
Army Dental Corps, **1901**:233
drills, **1875**:173
early American dentist, **1782**:11
equipment, **1871**:165, **1875**:173
gold inlay fillings, **1907**:247
Naval Dental Corps, **1912**:261
novocain, **1905**:241
orthodontist society, **1900**:230
orthodontia, **1895**:217
professional founding, **1876**:177
D'Entremont, Dave, **1996**:509
Denver (Colo.)
Art Museum, **1923**:292
juvenile court opens, **1899**:226
library system, **1894**:216
National Jewish Hospital, **1899**:226
school desegregation plan, **1973**:437
theaters, **1890**:207
Denver, James W., **1892**:209
Denver, John, **1997**:512
Denver Post (newspaper), **1895**:218
De Palma, Ralph, **1915**:269
DePaolo, Peter, **1925**:298
departments and agencies, U.S. *See key word, e.g.,* Education Department
department stores. *See* retailing
DePauw University, **1837**:93, **1870**:164
deportations, **1919**:280
depression (economic). *See* Great Depression; panics and depressions
deregulation
intercity bus industry, **1982**:461
interstate trucking, **1980**:456
Dere Mabel (book), **1918**:279
Derwinski, Edward J., **1989**:480
Descendant, The (book), **1897**:222
Deserter, The (ballet), **1827**:75
Desert Song, The (movie), **1953**:382

Desert Song, The (operetta), **1926**:299
De Seversky, Alexander P., **1974**:440
Design for Living (play), **1933**:322
Desire Under the Elms (play), **1924**:295
Desjardins, Peter, **1928**:306, **1985**:471
Des Moines (Iowa), **1872**:167, **1948**:367
Des Moines Register (newspaper), **1860**:138
Des Moines River, flood, **1903**:238
Destroyer, The (book), **1841**:100
DeSylva, Buddy, **1950**:374, **1990**:485
Detective, The (movie), **1968**:423
Detective Story (play), **1949**:371
Detroit (Mich.), **1967**:418-19, **1967**:*418*
Ambassador Bridge, **1929**:308
court-ordered school integration, **1975**:443, **1977**:448
fire, **1805**:43
first archbishop, **1937**:334
markets, **1880**:184
race riots, **1967**:418-19, **1967**:*418*
Roman Catholic archbishop elevated to cardinal, **1988**:479
Roman Catholic church closures, **1989**:482
Temple of Islam opens, **1931**:317
Tiger Stadium, **1912**:261
Detroit Evening News (newspaper), **1873**:170
Detroit Free Press (newspaper), **1835**:90, **1901**:234
Detroit Gazette (newspaper), **1817**:61
Detroit Institute of Arts, **1927**:302
Detroit Lions, **1975**:444
Detroit Nationals (baseball), **1887**:200
Detroit Red Wings, **1997**:513
Detroit Tigers, **1968**:423, **1984**:468
Detroit-Windsor Tunnel, **1930**:311
Detroit Zoological Park, **1928**:306
deuterium, **1931**:314-15
Deutsch, Babette, **1919**:281
Devers, Jacob L., **1979**:452
Devery, Bill, **1903**:238
Device Circle (painting), **1959**:398
Devil and Daniel Webster, The (opera), **1939**:339
DeVilbiss, Allen, Jr., **1900**:230
DeVilbiss Co., **1909**:252
Devil's Dictionary, The (book), **1906**:244
Devil's Disciple, The (play), **1897**:223
Devils Tower (Wyo.), **1906**:243
De Voto, Bernard, **1947**:364
DeVries, Peter, **1954**:385, **1964**:411
Dewey, George, **1898**:223
Dewey, John, **1896**:219, **1899**:227, **1916**:271, **1952**:378
Dewey, Melvil, **1876**:177, **1887**:199, **1890**:206, **1931**:315
Dewey, Thomas E., **1944**:353, **1948**:365, **1971**:430
Dewey decimal system, **1876**:177
Dewhurst, Colleen, **1991**:489
Dewing, Thomas W., **1891**:208
Dexter, Henry M., **1856**:130
Dharma Bums, The (book), **1958**:396
Dial (painting), **1956**:390

patents electric iron and toaster, **1908**:249

produces bazooka, **1942**:348

researchers make synthetic diamonds, **1955**:387

General Electric Theater (television program), **1953**:382

General Federation of Women's Clubs, **1890**:205

General Foods, **1986**:472

General Land Office, **1812**:52

General Motors, **1930**:311, **1936**:330, **1945**:357, **1954**:384, **1970**:427

  employment discrimination suit settled, **1983**:463

  first modern electric car, **1991**:488

  incorporates, **1908**:249

  laboratories, **1925**:296

  major losses, **1992**:492

  mergers, **1984**:466, **1985**:469

  plant closures, **1986**:472, **1991**:488, **1992**:492

  Research Corp. formed, **1925**:296

  Smale as executive committee head, **1992**:492

  subcompact car with Toyota, **1983**:464

  Toyota association, **1983**:464, **1993**:497

  UAW as bargaining agent, **1937**:333

General Munitions Board, **1917**:273

General Services Administration, **1949**:369

General Slocum (steamer), **1904**:241

general strike, first American, **1919**:280

General Trades Council, **1833**:85

"General William Booth Enters into Heaven" (poem), **1913**:264

Generation of Vipers (book), **1942**:349

generator, electrostatic, **1931**:314

Genet, Edmond, **1793**:26

gene therapy, **1990**:485

genetic engineering, **1991**:487, **1997**:511

genetics

  biological organisms patents, **1980**:456, **1991**:487

  chromosome role in heredity, **1933**:321

  gene split discovery, **1993**:497

  plant, **1983**:464

  See also DNA

Geneva arms control talks, **1982**:460, **1985**:469

genocide treaty, **1986**:472

Gentleman from Mississippi (play), **1908**:250

Gentleman's Agreement (book and movie), **1947**:364

Gentlemen from Indiana, The (book), **1899**:228

Gentlemen Prefer Blondes (book), **1925**:297

Gentlemen Prefer Blondes (play), **1949**:371

geodesic dome, **1954**:384

Geodesics Inc., **1954**:384

Geographical Dictionary (book), **1817**:60

Geography Made Easy (book), **1784**:14

geological survey, first official state, **1825**:72

Geological Survey, U.S., **1879**:182

Geometric Statue (sculpture), **1913**:263

George, Grace, **1906**:245, **1909**:253, **1934**:326

George, Henry, **1879**:183, **1897**:221

George, Milton, **1880**:184

George VI, King of Great Britain, **1939**:338

George A. Hormel & Co., **1892**:209

George Bush Memorial Library (College Station, Tex.), **1997**:511

Georgetown University, **1789**:21, **1791**:24, **1815**:57

George Washington (book), **1954**:385

George Washington (submarine), **1959**:397

George Washington Bridge (N.Y.C.-N.J.), **1931**:314

George Washington University, **1821**:66, **1898**:225

Georgia, **1777**:4, **1789**:21, **1868**:157

  abolishes slavery, **1866**:153

  American Revolution, **1778**:4, **1779**:6, **1782**:10

  Carter elected governor, **1971**:430

  Carter Memorial Library, **1986**:472

  first woman U.S. senator, **1922**:288

  Institute of Technology, **1885**:195

  racially drawn congressional district disallowed, **1995**:503

  ratifies Constitution, **1788**:18

  readmitted, **1868**:157, **1870**:163

  secedes, **1861**:139

  state constitution, **1777**:4, **1789**:21, **1868**:157

  tornadoes, **1936**:332, **1996**:509

  Union troops march through, **1864**:147

Georgia Female (later Wesleyan) College, **1839**:97, **1840**:99

"Georgia on My Mind" (song), **1930**:312

Georgia School for the Deaf, **1848**:115

Georgia University, **1785**:15

"Georgy Girl" (song), **1966**:416

Gerald R. Ford Library (Ann Arbor, Mich.), **1981**:458

Gere, Richard, **1983**:465

German Männerchor, **1835**:89

Germantown (Pa.), **1777**:3

  Cricket Club, **1928**:306

Germany, **1952**:378, **1955**:386

  reparations, **1924**:293, **1929**:306

  Versailles treaty signing, **1919**:279

  World War I, **1915**:267, **1916**:270, **1918**:276–77

  World War II, **1941**:343, **1941**:344, **1945**:355–56

Geronimo, **1886**:196, **1909**:252

Gerry, Elbridge, **1812**:52, **1814**:56

"gerrymandering," **1812**:52

Gershe, Leonard, **1969**:426

Gershwin, George, **1918**:278, **1924**:294, **1924**:*294*, **1924**:295, **1926**:300, **1927**:303, **1935**:329, **1937**:334

Gershwin, Ira, **1983**:465

Gerulaitis, Vitas, **1994**:502

Gesner, Abraham, **1855**:128, **1856**:130

Gessell, Arnold L., **1911**:257

Get-Rich-Quick Wallingford (book), **1908**:250

Get-Rich-Quick-Wallingford (musical), **1910**:256

"Getting to Know You" (song), **1951**:376

Getty, Harold, **1931**:314

Getty, J. Paul, **1950**:372, **1976**:445

Getty Oil Co., **1916**:271, **1956**:389, **1984**:466

Gettysburg, Battle of, **1863**:144, **1872**:167

Ghezzi, Victor, **1941**:346

"Ghostbusters" (song), **1984**:467

Ghost City, The (painting), **1936**:331

Ghost of Tom Joad, The (album), **1995**:504

Giaever, Ivar, **1973**:437

Giamatti, Angelo Bart, **1986**:474, **1988**:479, **1989**:482

Giannini, A. P., **1904**:239

Giant (book), **1950**:374

Giant (movie), **1956**:391

Giants in the Earth (opera), **1951**:376

Giauque, William F., **1949**:369

Gibbons, James, **1877**:179, **1886**:197, **1889**:204

Gibbons, Joseph, **1840**:98

Gibbons v. Ogden, **1824**:70

Gibbs, James E. A., **1857**:132

Gibbs, Josiah Willard, **1903**:237

Gibbs, Oliver W., **1865**:151

Gibbs, William F., **1967**:419

Gibbstown (N.J.), **1902**:235

GI Bill of Rights, **1944**:353

Gibson, Althea, **1957**:394, **1958**:396

Gibson, Charles Dana, **1899**:*227*

Gibson girls, **1899**:227

Gideon (play), **1961**:404

Gideon Bible, **1908**:249

Gideons International, **1899**:227

Gideon v. Wainwright, **1963**:408

Gielgud, John, **1947**:364

Gigi (movie), **1958**:396

"Gigi" (song), **1958**:396

Gigot (movie), **1962**:407

Gila (N. Mex.) National Forest, **1924**:293

Gilbert, Alfred C., **1912**:260, **1961**:403

Gilbert, Cass, **1934**:324

Gilbert, Henry F. B., **1905**:242, **1928**:305

Gilbert, John, **1925**:297, **1936**:332

Gilbert, Walter, **1980**:456

Gilbert Islands, **1942**:346

Giles, Warren C., **1951**:377, **1979**:454

Giles Goat-Boy (book), **1966**:416

Gill, Vince, **1994**:500

Gillespie, Dizzy, **1944**:353, **1993**:497

Gillette, King C., **1895**:217, **1901**:*233*, **1932**:318

Gillette, William, **1881**:188, **1886**:198, **1888**:202, **1894**:216, **1896**:220, **1899**:228

Gillette Safety Razor Co., **1901**:232

Gilman, Alfred G., **1994**:500

Gilman, Arthur, **1909**:252

1939:340
Gulflight (ship), **1915:**267
Gulf Oil Co., **1913:**263, **1984:**466
Gulf Railroad, **1972:**433
Gulf Stream, The (painting), **1899:**227
Gulf War, **1991:**487, **1993:**495
Gulick, Charlotte V., **1910:**256
Gulick, Luther H., **1910:**256, **1918:**277
guns. *See* weapons; *specific types*
Gunsmoke (television program), **1955:**388
Guns of August, The (book), **1962:**406
Gunterville Dan, **1939:**338
Gunther, John, **1936:**331
Gurney, Dan, **1967:**420
Guston, Philip, **1956:**390, **1957:**393,
　1961:404
Guthrie, A. B., **1947:**364
Guthrie, Janet, **1977:**449
Guthrie, Samuel, **1831:**81
Guthrie, Woody, **1967:**419
Guys and Dolls (book), **1931:**316
Guys and Dolls (play), **1950:**375
Gwenn, Edmund, **1947:**365
Gwinnett, Button, **1777:**4
gymnastics, **1897:**223, **1931:**317,
　1940:343
　　AAU all-around title, **1925:**298
　　first national organization, **1850:**119
　　first Olympics all-around winner,
　　　1984:*467*, **1984:**468
　　first organization, **1848:**115
Gymnastics for Youth (book), **1802:**40
Gypsy (play), **1959:**398
"Gypsy Love Song" (song), **1898:**225
gyroscope, **1910:**255

H

Haas, Robert, **1995:**505
Haatanen, Alfred, **1922:**289
Habberton, John, **1876:**177
Habib, Philip, **1992:**491
Hackett, James H., **1826:**74, **1829:**78
Hackman, Gene, **1971:**431, **1972:**434,
　1986:473, **1989:**482
Hadassah, **1916:**272
Hadaway, William S. Jr., **1896:**219
Hadden, Briton, **1923:**292
Haddix, Harvey, **1959:**398
Hadley, Arthur T., **1930:**311
Hadley, Henry K., **1909:**252, **1920:**284
Hagasake (Japan), **1945:**355
Hagen, Uta, **1950:**375, **1962:**407
Hagen, Walter, **1914:**267, **1919:**282,
　1924:295, **1925:**298, **1926:**300,
　1927:303, **1969:**426
Hagge, Marlene, **1956:**391
Hagler, Marvin, **1980:**457, **1984:**468,
　1985:471
Hagman, Larry, **1965:**414, **1978:**451
Hague Conferences, **1899:**226, **1907:**245
Hague v. CIO, **1939:**338
Hahnemann Society, **1833:**85
Haig, Alexander M., **1982:**460
"Hail Columbia" (song), **1798:**34
Hailey, Arthur, **1965:**413, **1968:**422,
　1971:431

Hair (musical), **1967:**420
"Hair" (song), **1969:**426
hairpins, **1913:**263
hair styles
　accessories, **1913:**263
　bobbed, **1915:**268
　care products, **1908:**249
　children's curls, **1800:**37
　hair-straightener treatment,
　　1905:243
　male pomade use, **1900:**232
　male powdered hair out, **1794:**28
　male slicked, parted in middle,
　　1921:288
　permanent wave, **1908:**250
　powdered hair, **1796:***31*
　ringlets, **1881:**188
　women's piled high, **1830:**80,
　　1871:166
Hairy Ape, The (play), **1931:**316
Haiti
　Marine occupation, **1915:**267
　refugees at Guantanamo Bay base,
　　1992:490
　treaty for U.S. control, **1916:**270
　U.N. sanctions, **1993:**495
　U.S. negotiators end military rule,
　　1994:499
　U.S. peace-keeping forces replaced,
　　1995:502
Halas, George, **1983:**466
Haldeman, H. R., **1973:**435, **1974:**439
Haldeman-Julius, Emanuel, **1919:**281,
　1951:377
Hale, Edward Everett, **1863:**146
Hale, George E., **1888:**201, **1891:**208,
　1895:217
Hale, Irving, **1930:**310-11
Hale, Lucretia P., **1880:**185, **1886:**198
Hale, Nathan, **1776:**2
Hale, Sarah J., **1830:**80
Hale, Sarah J. B., **1837:**93
Hale-Bopp comet, **1997:**511
Haley, Alex, **1976:**446, **1992:**493
Haley, Jack, **1929:**308
Halimi, Alphonse, **1957:**394
Hall, Asaph, **1877:**179
Hall, Charles M., **1886:**197, **1889:**203
Hall, Granville Stanley, **1888:**201,
　1892:210
Hall, Henry, **1859:**136
Hall, James, **1932:**319
Hall, John, **1819:**63
Hall, Joyce C., **1910:**255
Hall, Thomas S., **1880:**184
Hall Brothers, **1916:**279
Halley's Comet, **1910:**255
Hallidie, Andrew S., **1900:**230
Hallinan, Paul J., **1962:**405
Hallmark Cards, **1910:**255, **1916:**270
Hall of Fame
　baseball, **1939:**340
　basketball, **1972:**435, **1985:**471
　bowling, **1941:**346
　college football, **1978:**451
　golf, **1974:**441

hockey, **1973:**438
Hall of Fame, The (play), **1902:**236
Haloid Corp., **1948:**366, **1957:**393
Haloid-Xerox Co., **1959:**397
Halper, Albert, **1937:**334
Halpert, Samuel, **1921:**287
Halsam, John, **1803:**41
Halse, Russell A., **1993:**497
Halsey, William F., **1959:**397
Halsted, William S., **1881:**186, **1885:**195,
　1890:206
Halston, **1990:**484
Hambletonian
　first, **1926:**300
　See also under SPORTS *in text for subse-
　quent games played*
Hamill, Dorothy, **1974:**441, **1975:**444,
　1976:447
Hamill, Mark, **1977:**449, **1980:**457,
　1983:465
Hamilton (Mo.), **1924:**293
Hamilton, Alexander
　Federalist Papers, **1787:**17
　as first Treasury Department secre-
　　tary, **1789:**20
　killed in duel with Burr, **1804:**42
Hamilton, Bob, **1944:**355
Hamilton, Edith, **1963:**408
Hamilton, Jane, **1994:**500
Hamilton, Scott, **1981:**459, **1982:**463,
　1983:465, **1984:**468
Hamilton College, **1793:**27, **1812:**53
Hamilton Watch Co., **1957:**393
Hamlin, Cyrus, **1899:**227
Hamlin, Emmons, **1885:**195
Hamlin, Hannibal, **1891:**208
Hamlin, Vincent T., **1993:**498
Hamlisch, Marvin, **1975:**444
Hammerstein, Oscar I, **1883:**191,
　1919:281
Hammerstein, Oscar II, **1959:**398,
　1960:402
hammer-throw, records, **1897:**223,
　1910:256, **1913:**264
Hammett, Dashiell, **1930:**312, **1934:**326,
　1961:404
Hammond, George H., **1886:**197
Hammond, John B., **1880:**184
Hammond, Laurens, **1934:**325
Hampden, Walter, **1909:**253, **1916:**272,
　1923:292, **1955:**388
Hampton Institute, **1868:**158
Hampton Roads (Va.), **1907:**245
Hanby, Benjamin, **1856:**130
Hanchet, M. Waldo, **1848:**115
Hancock, George W., **1887:**200
Hancock, Winfield S., **1880:**184
Handball (painting), **1939:**339
handball, **1897:**223, **1920:**285
Handel and Haydn Society, **1815:**57
handicaps. *See* disabilities
Hands Across America, **1986:**472
"Hand That Rocks the Cradle, The"
　(song), **1895:**218
Handy, W. C., **1958:**396
Hanks, Benjamin, **1783:**11

Hanks, Rodney and Horatio, **1819:**62
Hanks, Sam, **1957:**394
Hanks, Tom, **1993:**498, **1994:**501, **1995:**505
Hanlon, Lorraine, **1963:**409
Hanna, Edward J., **1944:**353
Hannan, John, **1780:**8
Hannon, Edward J., **1919:**281
Hansberry, Lorraine, **1959:**398
Hans Brinker, of the Silver Skates (book), **1865:**152
Hans Christian Andersen (movie), **1952:**379
Hansel and Gretel (opera), **1931:**316, **1943:**351
Hanson, Beverly, **1955:**389
Hanson, Howard, **1924:**294, **1934:**325, **1943:**351
Hanson, John, **1783:**11
Happy Birthday (play), **1946:**362
Happy Days (television program), **1974:**441
Happy Hypocrite, The (ballet), **1925:**297
Harbert, Melvin, **1954:**386
Harbison, John, **1986:**473
Harbor, The (book), **1915:**269
Harcourt, Brace (co.), **1919:**281
Hard, Darlene, **1960:**402, **1961:**404
Harder, D. S., **1946:**362
Harding, Ann, **1927:**303
Harding, Chester, **1828:**76
Harding, Florence, **1924:**293
Harding, Tonya, **1991:**489
Harding, Warren G.
    death of, **1923:**290
    elected president, **1920:**283
    Teapot Dome, **1922:**288
    as U.S. senator from Ohio, **1915:**267
Hard Times (book), **1960:**401, **1970:**428
"Hard Times Come Again No More" (song), **1854:**127
Hardwick, Billy, **1963:**409
Hardy, Oliver, **1957:**394
Hare, David, **1951:**376, **1955:**388
Hare, Robert, **1801:**39
Harlem Globetrotters, **1927:**303
Harlem Heights, Battle of, **1776:**1
Harlem River (N.Y.C.), bridge tolls imposed, **1977:**447
Harlot's Ghost (book), **991:**489
Harlow, Jean, **1930:**313, **1933:**322, **1937:**335
Harmon, Claude, **1989:**483
Harmonia Americana (book), **1791:**24
Harmonists, **1805:**43
Harnden, William F., **1839:**96
Harned, Virginia, **1895:**218
harness racing
    Dan Patch (horse) dies, **1916:**272
    first driver to win 800 races in one year, **1989:**483
    first U.S. Trotting Derby, **1908:**250
    Meadowlands track (N.J.), **1975:**444
    See also Hambletonian
Harnett, William, **1885:**195, **1892:**211
Harper, Chandler, **1950:**375

Harper, John, **1875:**174
Harper, William Rainey, **1891:**208
Harper Bros., **1875:**174
Harper's (magazine), **1900:**231
Harper's Bazaar (magazine), **1867:**156
Harpers Ferry (Va.), **1796:**30, **1861:**140
    Brown's raid on arsenal, **1859:**135
Harper's New Monthly Magazine, **1850:**119
Harper's Weekly (magazine), **1857:**132, **1870:**163, **1874:**171
"Harper Valley PTA" (song), **1968:**422
Harper Valley PTA (television program), **1981:**459
Harridge, William (Will), **1931:**316, **1959:**398, **1971:**432
"Harrigan" (song), **1907:**247
Harriman, Herbert M., **1899:**228
Harriman, Pamela, **1997:**511
Harrington, George F., **1866:**154
Harrington, Michael, **1963:**409
Harris, Barbara, **1988:**479, **1989:**482
Harris, Chapin A., **1839:**97
Harris, Joel Chandler, **1879:**183, **1880:**185, **1904:**240, **1906:**244
Harris, Julie, **1950:**375, **1951:**377
Harris, Patricia R., **1979:**452
Harris, Paul P., **1905:**240
Harris, Phil, **1995:**504
Harris, Roy E., **1949:**370
Harrisburg (Pa.), **1897:**223
Harrison, Anna T., **1864:**148
Harrison, Benjamin, **1881:**186, **1888:**200, **1892:**209, **1893:**212, **1901:**232
Harrison, Elizabeth, **1927:**301
Harrison, George, **1964:***410*
Harrison, John, **1793:**26
Harrison, Mary S. L., **1948:**366
Harrison, Rex, **1948:**368, **1956:**390, **1964:**411, **1990:**486
Harrison, Wallace K., **1981:**458
Harrison, William Henry
    battle of Tippecanoe, **1811:**51
    dies in office, **1841:**99
    elected president, **1840:**98, **1840:***98*
    first presidential widow pension, **1841:**99
    Indian treaty, **1809:**47
    leads army in West, **1812:**52
    message from Perry, **1813:**53
Harrodsburg (Ky.), **1877:**179
Harroun, Ray, **1911:**259
Harry and Son (movie), **1984:**468
Harry and Tonto (movie), **1974:**441
Harsanyi, John C., **1994:**500
Hart, Doris, **1954:**386, **1955:**389
Hart, Gary, **1987:**474
Hart, Marvin, **1905:**243
Hart, Mickey, **1996:**508
Hart, Moss, **1943:**352, **1961:**404
Hart, William A., **1824:**70
Hart, William S., **1899:**228, **1916:**272, **1946:**362
Harte, Bret, **1869**, **1869:**161, **1870:**164, **1877:**179
Hartford (Conn.)

fires, **1944:**355
first extra-inning baseball game, **1876:**177
insurance business, **1794:**28, **1879:**182
Roman Catholic archbishop, **1991:**488
Wadsworth Atheneum opens, **1844:**106
Hartford, George H., **1917:**274
Hartford Convention, **1814:**56
Hartford Female Seminary, **1824:**70
Hartford Woolen Manufactory, **1788:**18
Hartley, Marsden, **1917:**275, **1940:**342
Hartline, Haldan K., **1967:**419
Hart-Parr Co., **1906:**243
Hart to Hart (television program), **1979:**454
Harvard Classics "five-foot shelf," **1909:**252
Harvard Observatory, **1839:**96, **1877:**179, **1921:**287
Harvard University, **1782:**10, **1871:**165, **1882:**189, **1894:**216, **1933:**322, **1944:**353, **1953:**382
    Andover Theological Seminary, **1908:**249
    astronomical expedition, **1780:**8
    Baker's "47 Workshop," **1904:**240
    becomes university, **1780:**8
    chemistry lab, **1858:**134
    divinity school, **1816:**59
    Doriot manufacturing course, **1926:**298
    Eliot death, **1926:**299
    first climatology professor, **1910:**255
    football, **1873:**170, **1874:**172, **1875:**175, **1920:**285
    founding, xii
    Graduate School of Design, **1938:**336
    Henley Cup win, **1914:**267
    Jackson (A.) honorary degree, **1833:**85
    Lawrence Scientific School, **1847:**112
    Law School, **1817:**60
    Lowell presidency, **1909:**252
    medical jurisprudence department, **1876:**177
    Medical School, **1782:**10
    obstetrics department, **1876:**177
    orchestra, **1808:**47
    School of Dental Medicine, **1867:**156
    tercentenary, **1938:**336
    Washington (G.) honorary degree, **1776:**2
Harvester, The (book), **1911:**259
Harvey (movie), **1950:**375
Harvey (play), **1944:**354
Harvey, Doug, **1989:**483
Harvey, Fred, **1876:**176
Harvey, P. J., **1995:**504
Hassam, Childe, **1890:**207, **1892:**211, **1905:**242, **1906:**244, **1910:**256, **1922:**289, **1935:**328
Hastie, William H., **1937:**332, **1946:**360, **1949:**369

Hastings (Colo.), **1917:**275
Hasty Pudding, The (poem), **1796:**31
Hatch Act, **1887:**198, **1939:**338
Hatcher, Richard, **1967:**419
"Hat Father Wore, The" (song), **1876:**177
Hatfield, Mark, **1995:**503
Hatfield family feud, **1880:***185*, **1880:**186
Hat Finishers Union, **1854:**126
Hatlo, Jimmy, **1963:**409
hats
    fashion importance of, **1900:**232
    soft felt, **1851:**121
    women's fashions, **1908:**259, **1921:**288
Haughton, Billy, **1986:**474
Hauptman, Herbert A., **1985:**469–70
Hauptmann, Bruno, **1932:**320
Have a Heart (musical), **1916:**272
Have Gun, Will Travel (television program), **1957:**394
"Have I Told You Lately That I Love You?" (song), **1945:**357
Haverstraw (N.Y.), **1780:**7
"Have You Ever Been Lonely?" (song), **1932:**319
"Have You Never Been Mellow" (song), **1975:**443
"Having My Baby" (song), **1974:**440
Hawaii (book), **1959:**398
Hawaii 5-0 (television program), **1968:**423
Hawaii
    commercial treaty, **1875:**173
    Congress formally annexes, **1898:**224
    declared U.S. protectorate, **1893:**211
    discovery of, **1778:**4
    first written constitution, **1840:**98
    hurricanes, **1992:**494
    Mt. Kilauea eruption, **1990:**486
    New England missionaries arrive, **1820:**64
    protectorate status, **1893:**211
    republic established, **1984:**214
    territorial status, **1900:**230
    volcanoes, **1961:**403
Hawaiian Eye (television program), **1959:**398
Hawaiian Reciprocity Treaty, **1887:**198
Hawthorne, Nathaniel, **1828:**76, **1837:**93, **1842:**102, **1846:**111, **1850:**119, **1851:**121, **1860:**138, **1864:**149
Hay, John, **1890:**207
Hay-Buneau-Varilla Treaty, **1903:**236
Hayden, Charles, **1937:**334
Hayden, Sterling, **1950:**375
Hayes, Elvin, **1984:**468
Hayes, Helen, **1917:**275, **1918:**279, **1922:**290, **1924:**295, **1927:**303, **1931:**316, **1932:**319, **1935:**329, **1946:**362, **1958:**396, **1970:**429, **1993:**498
Hayes, John J., **1908:**250
Hayes, Lucy W., **1898:**224
Hayes, Mary Ludwig. *See* Pitcher, Molly

Hayes, Patrick J., **1919:**281, **1924:**294, **1938:**336
Hayes, Rutherford B.
    Chinese immigration bill veto, **1879:**182
    death of, **1893:**212
    disputed presidential election, **1876:**175, **1877:**178
    free silver coinage veto, **1878:**180
    as governor of Ohio, **1868:**157, **1875:**173
    White House Easter-egg roll, **1878:**181
Hay-Herran Treaty, **1903:**236
Haymarket Massacre, **1886:**196, **1887:**199
Haynes, Elwood, **1894:**215, **1925:**296
Haynes, George H., **1912:**262
Haynie, Sandra, **1965:**414, **1974:**441
Hay-Pauncefote Treaty, **1900:**229, **1901:**232
Hays, Arthur Garfield, **1954:**383
Hays, Will R., **1922:**290
Hayward, DuBose, **1925:**297
Haywood, M. A., **1973:**438
Hayworth, Rita, **1944:**354, **1987:**477
Hazard, Erskine, **1816:**59
Hazel (television program), **1961:**404
Hazel Kirke (play), **1880:**185
Hazelwood, Joseph, **1990:**484
Hazzard, Shirley, **1980:**457
Head of a Woman (sculpture), **1916:**271
Heald, Henry T., **1952:**378
Health and Human Services Department, **1979:**452, **1994:**499
health board, first local, **1792:**25
health departments. *See* public health
Health, Education, and Welfare Department, **1953:**380
    children with disabilities protections, **1977:**448
    division into two departments, **1979:**452
health insurance
    Blue Cross, **1948:**366
    Clinton plan, **1993:**495, **1994:**499
    fee schedules, **1991:**488
    first important group policy, **1912:**260
    group hospitalization plan, **1929:**308
    job-change legislation, **1996:**507
    Medicare, **1966:**416, **1989:**482, **1991:**488
Healy, James A., **1875:**174
Heap o'Livin', A (book), **1916:**272
"Hear Dem Bells" (song), **1880:**185
hearing aids, **1901:**233
hearing loss
    American Association for the Hard of Hearing, **1919:**281
    school facilities, **1823:**69, **1857:**132
Hearn, Lafcadio, **1890:**207, **1904:**240
Hearns, Thomas, **1984:**468
Hearst, William Randolph, **1887:**200, **1895:**218, **1951:** 376
Hearst, William R., Jr., **1993:**498

Hearst Corp., **1992:**493
heart
    catheterization, **1956:**390
    first artificial implant, **1969:**425
    first permanent artificial implant, **1982:**461
    first successful transplant, **1968:**422
    surgery, **1893:**213
"Heartbreak Express" (song), **1982:**462
Heartburn (movie), **1986:**473
Heart Is a Lonely Hunter, The (book), **1940:**342
Heart of Maryland, The (play), **1895:**218
Heart of the Andes (painting), **1855:**129
"Hearts and Flowers" (song), **1899:**227
Hearts of Oak (play), **1879:**183
"Hearts of Stone" (song), **1955:**388
Heath, John E., **1850:**118
Heatter, Gabriel, **1972:**434
heat wave, **1995:**505
Heaven's My Destination (book), **1934:**326
Hebert, Jay, **1960:**402
Hebert, Lionel, **1957:**394
Hebrew Union College, **1875:**174, **1883:**192
Hecht, Ben, **1921:**287, **1964:**411
Heck, Barbara, **1804:**42
Hecker, Isaac T., **1858:**134
Hee Haw! (television program), **1969:**426
Heenan, Tom, **1858:**134
Heffelfinger, Pudge, **1892:**211
Hefner, Hugh, **1953:**382
Hegenberger, Albert, **1927:**301
Heiden, Eric, **1980:**457
Heidi (movie), **1937:**334
Heidi Chronicles, The (play), **1988:**479
Heifetz, Jascha, **1917:**274, **1987:**476
Heikes, Rollo O., **1900:**231
Hein, Mel, **1992:**494
Heinlein, Robert A., **1947:**364, **1988:**479
Heinrich, Anthony P., **1861:**141
Heinz, John, **1991:**487
Heiss, Carol, **1957:**394, **1958:**396, **1959:**399, **1960:**402
Heiss, Michael, **1868:**158
Held, Anna, **1901:**234, **1906:**245, **1908:**250
Held, John Jr., **1958:**396
Held by the Enemy (play), **1886:**198
"Helderberg War," **1839:**96
Helen's Babies (book), **1876:**177
helicopters, **1940:**342, **1942:**349, **1946:**360
    demonstrated, **1922:**289
    first flight, **1928:**304
    first nonstop transcontinental flight, **1956:**390
    first successful fully controlled flight, **1939:**338, **1940:***341*
    first transcontinental flight (with stops), **1931:**314
    service between New York City airports begins, **1953:**381
helium plant, **1920:**283
Heller, Joseph, **1961:**404
Hell Gate Bridge (N.Y.C.), **1917:**274

Johnson, Magic, **1992**:493
Johnson, Reggie, **1992**:494
Johnson, Richard, **1916**:272
Johnson, Richard M., **1836**:90, **1850**:118
Johnson, Thomas, **1777**:4
Johnson, Tom L., **1869**:159, **1911**:257
Johnson, Walter, **1920**:285, **1946**:362, **1983**:465
Johnson, William S., **1787**:18
Johnson & Johnson Co., **1886**:197
Johnson Act, **1921**:285
Johnston, Albert S., **1862**:142
Johnston, Joseph E., **1891**:208
Johnston, Mary, **1900**:231
Johnston, William, **1915**:269, **1919**:282
Johnstown (Pa.)
    flood, **1889**:*203*, **1889**:204
    mine disaster, **1902**:236
Joint Chiefs of Staff, **1947**:363, **1949**:369
    Powell as first African-American chairman, **1989**:480
    Shalishkashvili succeeds Powell, **1993**:496
Jolson, Al, **1913**:264, **1914**:266, **1918**:279, **1921**:287, **1927**:303, **1928**:306, **1950**:375
Jonathan Bradford (play), **1849**:117
Jonathan Livingston Seagull (book), **1970**:428
Jones, Albert L., **1871**:164
Jones, Allan, **1992**:493
Jones, Bobby, **1923**:293, **1926**:300, **1929**:309, **1930**:313, **1934**:326, **1971**:432
Jones, Casey, **1901**:233
Jones, Cleve, **1987**:*476*
Jones, Dean, **1970**:428
Jones, Edward D., **1882**:189
Jones, George, **1891**:208
Jones, Harold S., **1972**:433
Jones, James, **1951**:376
Jones, James Earl, **1968**:423
Jones, Jennifer, **1943**:352
Jones, Jesse H., **1956**:389
Jones, John, **1791**:24
Jones, John B., **1866**:154
Jones, John Paul, **1776**:1, **1778**:4, **1779**:*6*, **1779**:*6*, **1792**:25
Jones, Joseph S., **1839**:97, **1852**:123
Jones, Parnelli, **1963**:409
Jones, Paul, **1920**:285
Jones, Shirley, **1970**:429
Jones, Spike, **1965**:413
Jones, Steve, **1996**:509
Jones, Thomas H., **1969**:426
Jong, Erica, **1973**:438
Joplin, Janis, **1968**:*423*, **1970**:428
Joplin, Scott, **1899**:227, **1911**:258, **1917**:275
Jordan, Barbara, **1996**:506
Jordan, David Starr, **1891**:208
Jordan, Michael, **1993**:*495*, **1993**:498, **1995**:505
Jordon, Don, **1958**:396
Joseph, Chief, **1877**:178
Josephine Baker (wire sculpture), **1926**:300

Josephson, Brian, **1973**:437
Jouglard, Lee, **1951**:377
journalism
    press freedom, xiii, **1805**:43
    source protection ruling, **1972**:434
    women allowed in sports locker rooms, **1972**:435
    See also newspapers; *specific publications*
Journal of Allergy, **1929**:308
Journal of Geology, **1893**:213
Journal of Music, **1852**:123
Journal of Negro History, **1916**:272
Journeyman Stone Cutters Assn., **1855**:128
Joyce, James, **1918**:278-79, **1921**:287, **1933**:322
Joyner, Jackie, **1986**:474
"Joy to the World" (song), **1971**:431
J. P. Morgan & Co. financiers, **1864**:148
Jud, Sylvester, **1845**:109
Judaism
    American Jewish Historical Society, **1892**:211
    B'nai Brith founded, **1843**:103
    colonial era, xiii
    Congregation Rodeph Shalom opens, **1802**:40
    first congregation in Missouri, **1836**:91
    first rabbinical conference, **1855**:129
    first Supreme Court justice, **1916**:270
    first woman Conservative rabbi, **1985**:470
    first woman Reform rabbi, **1972**:433
    Free Synagogue (N.Y.C.), **1907**:247
    Hebrew Union College, **1875**:174, **1883**:192
    Jewish Center (N.Y.C.), **1916**:271
    Jewish Daily Forward (newspaper), **1897**:222
    Jewish Institute of Religion, **1922**:289
    Jewish Messenger, **1857**:132
    Jewish Theological Seminary, **1887**:200
    Museum of American Jewish History (Phila.), **1976**:447
    National Council of Jewish Women, **1894**:216
    Pennsylvania ban on public office-holding ends, **1783**:11
    Union of American Hebrew Congregations, **1873**:170, **1946**:360
    Union of Orthodox Rabbis, **1940**:342
    United Synagogue of America, **1913**:263
    Yeshiva College (N.Y.C.) chartered, **1928**:305
    Young Men's Hebrew Association, **1874**:172
    Zionism, **1897**:223, **1898**:225, **1916**:272
Judd, Max, **1890**:207
judicial review, **1803**:41
judiciary
    Court of Appeals established, **1780**:8

first court-martial, **1778**:4
first domestic relations court, **1910**:254
first impeached member, **1804**:42
first night court, **1907**:245
first woman Circuit Court of Appeals justice, **1922**:288
first woman state Supreme Court justice, **1922**:288
small municipal courts, **1913**:262
See also Supreme Court
Judiciary Act, **1801**:38, **1802**:39, **1837**:93
Judith (lyric drama), **1901**:233
Judson, Adoniram, **1850**:119
Judson, Edward Z. C., **1886**:198
Judson, Egbert P., **1893**:213
Judson, Whitcomb, **1896**:219
Juilliard, Augustus D., **1919**:281
Juilliard School of Music (N.Y.C.), **1905**:242, **1969**:425
Juleo, El (painting), **1882**:190
Julia, or the Wanderer (play), **1806**:45
Julius Rosenwald Foundation, **1917**:274
July Hay (painting), **1943**:351
Jumbo (elephant), **1882**:190
"Jump" (song), **1984**:467
Juneau (Alaska), **1971**:432
Juneau, Solomon L., **1846**:110
"June in January" (song), **1934**:325
"June Is Bustin' Out All Over" (song), **1945**:357
Jungle, The (book), **1906**:243
Junior Chamber of Commerce, **1915**:267, **1920**:283
junior high school, first, **1909**:252
junk bonds, **1988**:478, **1990**:484
Jupiter (planet)
    moons discoverd, **1914**:264
    space probes, **1972**:433, **1974**:440, **1989**:482, **1995**:504
Jupiter (ship), **1922**:288
Jurassic Park (movie), **1993**:498
Jurgen (book), **1919**:281
jury duty, **1875**:173, **1880**:184
Jusserand, J. J., **1917**:275
Just, Ward, **1984**:467
"Just a-Wearying' for You" (song), **1901**:233
"Just Before the Battle, Mother" (song), **1863**:146
Just Folks (book), **1917**:275
Justice Department
    first woman District Attorney, **1918**:277
    founding, **1870**:162
    Reno as first woman Attorney General, **1993**:495
    See also antitrust
"Justify My Love" (song), **1992**:493
"Just One Girl" (song), **1898**:225
"Just One of Those Things" (song), **1935**:328
"Just Tell Them That You Saw Me" (song), **1895**:218
Juvenile Miscellany (magazine), **1826**:74

Keogh, John W., **1960:**401
Keokuk Dam, **1913:**262
Keough, Francis P., **1947:**364
Kepley, Ada H., **1870:**163
Keppel, Francis, **1962:**406
Kerfoot, John B., **1866:**154
Kerkorian, Kirk, **1989:**482
Kermit the Frog (fictional character), **1955:**88
Kern, Jerome, **1912:**261, **1916:**272, **1945:**357
Kerouac, Jack, **1957:**394, **1958:**396, **1969:**426
Kerr, Deborah, **1953:**382
Kerr, George, **1889:**204
Kerrigan, Nancy, **1993:**498
Kerslake, Bill, **1953:**383
Kesey, Ken, **1962:**406
Ketchel, Stanley, **1908:**250, **1910:**256
Kettering, Charles F., **1910:**255, **1911:**257, **1925:**296, **1958:**395
Kevorkian, Jack, **1996:**508
Kewpie dolls, **1910:**256
Key, Francis Scott, **1814:**55, **1922:**288
Key Largo (play), **1948:**368
Keys of the Kingdom (book), **1941:**345
Keystone Co., **1912:**261
Khatami, Muhammad, **1997:**510
Khorana, H. Gobind, **1968:**421
Khruschev, Nikita, **1955:**386, **1959:**397
Kick In (play), **1914:**266
Kid, The (movie), **1921:**287
Kid Boots (play), **1923:**292
kidnapping
    of Lindbergh baby, **1932:***318*, **1932:**320. *See also* hostages; terrorism
kidney transplants, **1950:**373
Kienholz, Edward, **1982:**462
Kier, Samuel M., **1855:**128
Kiesling, Walt, **1962:**407
Kiewe, Frederick, **1988:**479
Kilbane, Johnny, **1912:**262
Kiley, Richard, **1965:**414
"Killing Me Softly with His Song" (song), **1973:**438
Kilmer, Joyce, **1914:**266, **1918:**279
Kimball, Jacob, **1793:**27
Kimball, Judy, **1962:**407
Kimball, Spencer W., **1973:**438
Kimberly Clark (co.), **1995:**503
kindergarten
    for blind children, **1887:**199
    first English-type, **1860:**138
    first German-type, **1855:**128
    free, **1876:**177
    public school (St. Louis), **1873:**170
Kindergarten Cop (movie), **1990:**486
Kindred Spirits (painting), **1849:**116
kinetoscopes, **1893:**213, **1894:**216
King, Betsy, **1989:**483, **1990:**486, **1992:**494
King, Billie Jean, **1967:**420, **1971:**432, **1972:**435, **1974:**441
King, Charles Brady, **1896:**219
King, Clarence, **1879:**182

King, Ernest J., **1941:**343, **1956:**389
King, Frank, **1919:**281
King, Franklin H., **1911:**257
King, Martin Luther, Jr., **1957:**392
    assassinated, **1968:**421
    birthday made national holiday, **1983:**463
    "I have a dream ..." speech, **1963:**408
    Nobel Peace Prize, **1965:**412
    Selma to Montgomery (Ala.) march, **1965:***413*
King, Richard, **1852:**122, **1885:**195
King, Rodney, **1992:**490, **1992:***491*
King, Rufus, **1816:**58
King, Wayne, **1985:**470
King, William, **1852:**122
King, William R. de Vane, **1853:**124
King and I, The (movie), **1956:**391
King and I, The (play), **1951:**377
King Coal (book), **1917:**275
King Dome (Seattle), **1977:**449
Kingdom of God (play), **1928:**306
King George's War, ix
King Kong (movie), **1933:**322
King of Kings, The (movie), **1927:**303
"King of the Road" (song), **1965:**413
Kings College. *See* Columbia University
King's Henchmen, The (opera), **1927:**301
King's Island (Ohio), **1978:**451
Kingsland (N.J.), **1917:**274
Kingsley, Ben, **1982:**462
Kingsley, Elizabeth S., **1957:**394
Kings Mountain, Battle of, **1780:**7
Kings Point (N.Y.), **1943:**351
Kingston (N.Y.), **1777:**3
Kingston, Maxine Hong, **1980:**457
King William's War, ix
Kinsey, Alfred C., **1948:**366, **1956:**390
Kiplinger Washington Newsletter, **1923:**292
Kirby, Fred M., **1887:**199, **1912:**260
Kirkland, Caroline, **1839:**97
Kirkland, Lane, **1995:**504
Kirstein, Lincoln, **1934:**325, **1996:**508
Kismet (play), **1911:**259
"Kiss" (song), **1986:**473
"Kisses Sweeter Than Wine" (song), **1951:**376
Kissinger, Henry, **1973:**436
"Kiss Me Again" (song), **1905:**242
Kiss Me, Kate (play), **1948:**368
Kiss of the Spider Woman (play), **1993:**498
Kiss/Panic (painting), **1984:**467
Kite, Tom, **1992:**494
"Kitten on the Keys" (song), **1921:**287
Kittinger, Joe, **1984:**466
Kitty Hawk (N.C.), **1903:**237
Kiwanis International, **1915:**269, **1987:**474
Kizer, Caroline, **1984:**468
"K-K-K-Katy" (song), **1918:**278
KKR (Kohlberg Kravis Roberts), **1986:**472, **1988:**478
Klein, Lawrence, **1980:**456
Kleindienst, Richard, **1973:**435-36
Kline, Franz, **1953:**382, **1958:**396
KLM Royal Dutch Airlines, **1992:**492

Klondike gold rush, **1896:**219
Klugman, Jack, **1970:**429
Klute (movie), **1971:**431
Knapp, James H., **1850:**118
Knapp, Seaman A., **1911:**257
Kneeling Woman (painting), **1938:**337
Knerr, Richard, **1958:**395
Knickerbocker Holiday (play), **1938:**337
Knickerbocker Magazine, **1833:**86
Knickerbocker Theater (Wash., D.C.), **1922:**290
Knight, Arthur F., **1910:**256
Knight, John S., **1981:**459
Knights of Columbus, **1882:**190
Knights of Labor, **1869:**159, **1879:**182, **1885:**195
Knights of Pythias, **1864:**149
"Knockin' Boots" (song), **1990:**485
Knock, Knock (play), **1976:**446
"Knock Three Times" (song), **1971:**431
Knopf, Alfred A., **1915:**269
Knopf, S. Adolphus, **1940:**342
Knorr, Nathan H., **1942:**349
Knot's Landing (television program), **1979:**454
Knowlton v. Moore, **1900:**230
Knox, Henry, **1785:**14, **1789:**20, **1806:**44
Knox, Philander C., **1921:**286
Knox College, **1837:**93
Knoxville (Tenn.) World's Fair, **1982:**460
Knoxville Gazette (newspaper), **1791:**24
Knoxville Road, **1791:**23
Knudsen, William S., **1948:**366
Koch, Bill, **1976:**446
Kohlberg Kravis Roberts, **1986:**472, **1988:**478
Kohut, Alexander, **1887:**200
Kojak (television program), **1973:**438
Kokomo (Ind.), **1894:**215
Kollege of Musical Knowledge (radio program), **1938:**337
Koller, Carl, **1884:**194
Koningsmark (book), **1823:**69
Kon-Tiki (book), **1950:**374
Koons, Jeff, **1986:**473
Koop, C. Everett, **1986:**472
Koopmans, Tjalling, **1975:**442
Kopit, Arthur, **1982:**462
Kopsky, Doris, **1937:**335
Korean Airlines, **1983:**463
Korean War, **1950:**372, **1950:***374*, **1951:**375, **1952:**378, **1953:**380
Koresh, David, **1993:**499
Kornberg, Arthur, **1957:**393, **1959:**398
Kosciusko, Thaddeus, **1777:**3
Kostelanetz, André, **1980:**457
Kosygin, Aleksei, **1967:**418
Kouros (sculpture), **1945:**357
Koussevitsky, Serge, **1924:**294
Kovacs, Ernie, **1952:**380, **1956:**391
Kraft, Charles H., **1952:**378
Kraft Foods, **1909:**252, **1988:**474
Kraft Music Hall (radio program), **1933:**322
Kraft Music Hall (television program), **1967:**420

Life Is Worth Living (television program), **1952:**379
Life of George Washington (book), **1800:**37
Life of Mrs. Jemison, The (book), **1824:**70
Life of Reason, The (book), **1905:**242
Life of Riley (radio program), **1943:**352
Life of Riley (television program), **1949:**371
Life of Washington (book), **1839:**97
Life on the Mississippi (book), **1883:**192
life-saving station, first, **1807:**46
Life with Father (book), **1935:**328
Life with Father (movie), **1947:**364
Life With Father (play), **1939:**340
Liggett, Louis K., **1946:**360
Liggett Group Inc., **1996:**507
Light, Earth, and Blue (painting), **1954:**385
lighting
    arc searchlight, **1918:**277
    electric, **1879:**182
    first in stores, **1879:**182
    first streetlights, **1806:**45
    first theater lighted by gas, **1825:**72
    incandescent, **1879:**182, **1880:**184
    lamps in trains, **1905:**241
    locomotive headlights, **1881:**186
    mercury vapor lamp, **1901:**232
    street, **1806:**45, **1880:**184, **1890:**206
    theater, **1882:**190
Lights Out (radio program), **1935:**329
Lights Out (television program), **1949:**371
Ligowsky, George, **1880:**185
"L'il Abner" (comic strip), **1934:**325
Liliom (play), **1921:**287
Lillard, Bill, **1956:**391
Lillehammer (Norway), **1994:**501
Lilly, Eli, **1977:**448
Lily (newspaper), **1849:**116
Lily White (book), **1996:**508
Limbaugh, Rush, **1992:**493, **1993:**498
"Limehouse Blues" (song), **1922:**289
Limelight (movie), **1952:**379
Lincoln, Abraham
    antislavery speeches, **1854:**126, **1858:**133
    assassinated, **1865:**150, **1865:***150*
    assassination trial, **1865:**150
    Civil War, **1861:**139
    Civil War powers, **1861:**140
    as congressman from Illinois, **1847:**112
    elected president, **1860:**137, **1860:***137*
    Emancipation Proclamation, **1863:**145
    Gettysburg Address, **1863:**145
    inflatable cylinders patent, **1849:**117
    as postmaster of New Salem (Ill.), **1833:**84
    reelected president, **1864:**147
    requests additional powers, **1861:**140
    statues of, **1887:**200, **1922:**289
    vetoes radical reconstruction bill, **1864:**147
Lincoln, Mary Todd, **1882:**189

Lincoln Center (N.Y.C.), **1962:**406, **1966:**416, **1969:**425
Lincoln Highway Assn., **1913:**262
Lincoln Institute, **1866:**154
Lincoln Memorial (Wash., D.C.), **1922:**289
Lincoln Motor Co., **1922:**289
Lincoln Park (Ill.), **1875:**175
Lincoln penny, **1909:**251
Lincoln Portrait (music), **1942:**349
Lincoln Tunnel (N.Y.C.-N.J.), **1937:**333, **1945:**357, **1957:**393
Lind, Jenny, **1850:**119
Lindbergh, Charles A.
    death of, **1974:**439
    first solo transatlantic flight, **1927:**301, **1927:***302*
    kidnapping of baby, **1932:***318*, **1932:**320
Lindbergh, Pelle, **1985:**471
Linden, Hal, **1975:**444
Lindsay, Howard, **1939:**340
Lindsay, Vachel, **1913:**264, **1914:**266, **1931:**316
Lindsey, Ben, **1899:**226, **1939:**338
Lindstrom, Marie, **1962:**407
line-item veto, **1997:**511
Lineup, The (television program), **1954:**385
"Linger Awhile" (song), **1923:**292
linguistics, **1933:**322
Linkletter, Art, **1954:**385
linoleum, **1873:**170
    embossed inlaid, **1925:**296
linotype, Mergenthaler, **1886:**198
Lionel Lincoln (book), **1825:**72
Lion in Winter, The (movie), **1968:**423
Lion King, The (movie), **1994:**501
Lion King, The (musical), **1997:**513
Lion of the West, The (book), **1830:**80
Lions International, **1917:**275
Lipchitz, Jacques, **1925:**297
Lipinski, Tara, **1997:**513
Lipman, Lyman L., **1858:**134
Lipmann, Fritz A., **1953:**381
Lippard, George, **1833:**86, **1844:**106
Lippincott's Magazine, **1868:**158
Lippmann, Walter, **1913:**264, **1931:**316, **1974:**441
Lipscomb, Eugene ("Big Daddy"), **1963:**409
Lipscomb, William N., **1976:**446
Lipton, Seymour, **1957:**393
liquor. *See* alcoholic beverages
"Listen to the Mocking Bird" (song), **1855:**129
Liston, Sonny, **1962:**407, **1963:**409
Litchfield law school, **1784:**14
literacy test, **1887:**198, **1917:**274
Literary and Scientific Circle of Chautauqua Institution, **1878:**182
Literary Digest (magazine), **1890:**207
Literary Guild, **1926:**300
Litle Caesar (movie), **1930:**313
Little, Arthur D., **1886:**197, **1902:**235
Little, Lawson, **1940:**343

Little, Sally, **1980:**457
"Little Annie Roonie" (song), **1890:**207
Little Bighorn, Battle of, **1876:**176
Little Blue Books, **1919:**281
"Little Boy Blue" (song), **1891:**208
Little, Brown (publisher), **1847:**113
"Little Brown Church in the Vale" (song), **1865:**152
"Little Brown Jug" (song), 1869, **1869:**161
Little Colonel, The (movie), **1935:**329
"Little Darlin'" (song), **1957:**393
Little Duchess, The (play), **1901:**234
Little Falls (N.Y.), **1796:**31
Littlefield Ballet, **1935:**328
Little Foxes, The (play), **1939:**340, **1959:**398
Little Giant Still-Life (painting), **1950:**374
Little Girl in White, The (painting), **1863:**146
"Little Help From My Friends, A" (song), **1967:**419
Little House on the Prairie (television program), **1974:**441
Littlejohn, Abram N., 1869, **1869:**161
Little Johnny Jones (play), **1904:**240
Little League, exclusion of girls ruled illegal (N.J.), **1974:**441
Little Lord Fauntleroy (book), **1886:**198
Little Madonna, The (painting), **1907:**247
Little Men (book), **1871:**166
Little Millionaire, The (play), **1911:**259
Little Minister, The (play), **1897:**223
Little Nell and the Marchioness (play), **1867:**156
"Little Nemo" (cartoon movie), **1910:**256
Little Night Music, A (musical), **1973:**438
"Little Orphan Annie" (comic strip), **1924:**295
Little Review (magazine)
    founding, **1914:**266
    moves to Paris, **1921:**287
    serializes Joyce's *Ulysses*, **1918:**278–79
Littler, Gene, **1961:**404
Little Rock (Ark.), **1957:***392*, **1957:**393
Little Shepherd of Kingdom Come, The (book), **1903:**237
"Little Sir Echo" (song), **1939:**339
Littleton (Ala.), **1911:**259
"Little White Lies" (song), **1930:**312
Little Women (book), **1868:**158
Litz, Tommy, **1963:**408
Liveright, Horace B., **1933:**322
livestock
    annual production, **1870:**163
    colonial, xi
    Packers and Stockyards Act, **1921:**286
    protective association, **1877:**179
    stockyards, **1871:**164, **1872:**168, **1874:**172
    See also meat
Livingston, Robert R., **1781:**8, **1783:**11
Livingston, David, **1871:**166
Lizana, Anita, **1937:**335
Lloyd, Harold, **1923:**292, **1925:**297
Lloyd, Henry D., **1895:**217

Lloyd Webber, Andrew, **1971**:431, **1982**:462

loans. *See* credit

Lobell, Steve, **1976**:447

lobotomy, **1956**:390

"Loch Lomond" (song), **1881**:188

Locke, Alain L., **1907**:247, **1954**:385

Locke, Bobby, **1949**:371

Locke, David R., **1888**:202

locker, coin-operated, **1911**:257

Lockerbie (Scotland), **1988**:480

Lockhart, Frank, **1926**:300

Lockheed, Malcolm, **1958**:395

Lockheed Aircraft Corp., **1932**:318, **1992**:491

    founding, **1927**:301

    mergers, **1994**:500, **1995**:503, **1997**:511

Lockheed Marietta, **1994**:500

Lockport (N.Y.), **1892**:209

locks, timed, **1874**:172

Lockwood, Belva A. B., **1879**:182

locomotives

    diesel electric, **1924**:293

    first American-built, **1830**:79, **1830**:*80*

    first experimental steam, **1824**:70

    first to operate in U.S., **1829**:78

    first with cab, **1836**:91

    headlights, **1881**:186

    See also railroads

Lodge, Henry Cabot, Jr., **1985**:469

Lodge, Henry Cabot, Sr., **1923**:291

Loeb Classical Library of Greek and Latin Literature, **1910**:256

Loesser, Frank, **1956**:391, **1969**:426

Loewi, Otto, **1936**:330

Loew, Marcus, **1922**:290

Loew v. Lawler, **1908**:248

Lofting, Hugh, **1920**:284, **1947**:364

Logan Airport (Boston), **1973**:438

Logan, Ella, **1947**:364

Lolita (book), **1955**:388

lollipops, **1908**:249

Lolly Willowes (book), **1926**:300

Lomax, John A., **1948**:366

Lombard, Carole, **1936**:331, **1941**:346

Lombardi, Vincent, **1970**:429

Lombardo, Guy, **1920**:284, **1977**:448

Lombards Ltd. (play), **1917**:275

London (Eng.)

    Concorde SST service, **1976**:445

    transatlantic service, **1927**:301

London, Jack, **1903**:237, **1904**:240, **1909**:252

"Londonderry Air" (song), **1855**:129

London Naval Conference, **1930**:310

Londos, Jim, **1934**:326, **1975**:444

"Lonely Boy" (song), **1959**:398

Lone Ranger, The (radio program), **1933**:322

Lonesome Cities (book), **1968**:422

Lonesome Dove (book), **1985**:470

Long, Huey P., **1935**:327

Long Beach (Calif.), **1900**:231, **1933**:323

Longfellow, Henry Wadsworth, **1847**:113, **1849**:116, **1855**:129, **1858**:134, **1860**:138, **1863**:146, **1875**:174, **1882**:190

Long Island, Battle of, **1776**:1

Long Island Railroad, smoking ban, **1988**:478

long-jump

    first African American gold medal winner, **1924**:295

    Gourdin record, **1921**:288

    Powell breaks record, **1991**:489

Long Valley, The (book), **1938**:337

Longview Bridge (Wash.), **1930**:311

Longworth, Nicholas, **1906**:243

Look (magazine), **1937**:334, **1971**:431

"Look Away" (song), **1989**:482

"Look for the Silver Lining" (song), **1921**:287

Look Homeward (book), **1987**:476

Look Homeward, Angel (book), **1929**:308

Look Homeward, Angel (play), **1957**:394

Looking Backward 2000–1887 (book), **1888**:202

Looking East from Leicester Hills (painting), **1800**:37

Looking for Mr. Goodbar (book), **1975**:444

looms

    first successful power, **1837**:93

    powered carpet, **1876**:176

Loon Lake (book), **1980**:457

Loos, Anita, **1925**:297, **1981**:459

Loose Ends (play), **1979**:454

Lopat, Eddie, **1992**:494

Lopez, Nancy, **1978**:451, **1985**:471, **1989**:483

Lopez, Narciso, **1851**:120

Lopez, Vincent, **1975**:443

Lord, Bradley, **1961**:404

Lord, Jack, **1968**:423

Lord, Pauline, **1921**:287

Lord, Royal B., **1963**:408

Lord Weary's Castle (book), **1946**:361

Lorimer, George H., **1900**:231

Los Alamos (N. Mex.), **1942**:347

Los Angeles (Calif.)

    Buddhist Temple, **1904**:240

    earthquake, **1992**:494, **1994**:502

    first aviation meet, **1910**:256

    first movie theater, **1902**:236

    founding, **1781**:9

    new Getty art museum, **1997**:512

    race riots, **1871**:164, **1965**:412, **1992**:490, **1992**:*491*

    school desegregation suit dropped, **1988**:479

    subway portion opens, **1993**:497

    trackless trolley system, **1910**:255

    year-round schools schedule, **1987**:476

Los Angeles Coliseum, **1983**:465

Los Angeles County (Calif.), public defender's office, **1913**:262

Los Angeles County Museum of Art

    Annenberg bequest, **1991**:488

    founding, **1911**:258

Los Angeles Dodgers, **1963**:409, **1981**:459, **1988**:479

Los Angeles Raiders (formerly Oakland Raiders), **1982**:462

    antitrust damage payments, **1983**:465

    Oakland rejects return bid, **1990**:486

    Supreme Court upholds move, **1986**:473

Los Angeles Symphony Orchestra, **1896**:220, **1936**:331

Los Angeles Times (newspaper), **1882**:190

    explosion in building, **1910**:256

"Lost Colony" (N.C.), ix

Lost Horizon (movie), **1937**:334

Lost Hunter, The (book), **1856**:131

"Lost in America" (song), **1994**:500

Lost Lady, A (book), **1923**:292

Lost Paradise, The (play), **1891**:208

Lost Weekend, The (book), **1944**:354

Lost Weekend, The (movie), **1945**:358

Lotbinier, Louis E., **1776**:2

Lothrop, Harriet, 1880:185

lottery

    American Revolution, **1776**:2

    Louisiana, **1868**:158, **1892**:209

    mail prohibition, **1903**:236

    Massachusetts prohibition, **1833**:86

    Pennsylvania prohibition, **1833**:89

    Washington (D.C.) improvements, **1793**:26

Lottery, The (book), **1949**:370

Lottery of Love, The (play), **1888**:202

Loud, John J., **1888**:201

Loughran, Tommy, **1927**:303

Louis, Joe, **1937**:335, **1938**:337, **1939**:340, **1940**:343, **1941**:346, **1942**:349, **1946**:362, **1947**:365, **1948**:368, **1981**:460

Louis Harris & Associates, **1956**:389

Louisiana, **1812**:52, **1852**:122, **1864**:148, **1867**:155, **1879**:182, **1898**:224, **1901**:232

    Baton Rouge as capital, **1879**:182

    Caddo oil pool, **1909**:252

    hurricanes, **1957**:394, **1965**:414, **1992**:494

    Mississippi River Bridge opens, **1983**:464

    offshore oil port, **1977**:447, **1981**:458

    plane crash, **1982**:463

    readmitted, **1868**:157

    secedes, **1861**:139

    Spain returns to France, **1800**:36

    Spanish holdings, **1779**:6

    state constitutions, **1812**:52, **1852**:122, **1864**:148, **1867**:155, **1879**:182, **1898**:224, **1901**:232

    statehood, **1812**:52

    state lottery, **1868**:158, **1892**:209

    sulphur deposits, **1869**:159, **1902**:235

    teaching of creationism with evolution mandate reversed, **1987**:476

    territorial governor, **1804**:42

    Territory established, **1805**:43

Louisiana Leper Home, **1894**:215

Louisiana Offshore Oil Port, **1977**:447, **1981**:458

Florida annexation, **1810:**49
reelected president, **1812:**52
Remonstrances Against Religious Assessments, **1784:**13
as Secretary of State, **1801:**38
sister's marriage, **1812:**53
as University of Virginia rector, **1826:**73
War of 1812, **1812:**52
Madison, James (clergyman), **1777:**4, **1790:**23, **1812:**53
Madison Square Garden (N.Y.C.)
bicycle race, **1899:**228
final boxing match, **1993:**498
first auto show, **1900:**230, **1910:**255
first color movies exhibited, **1909:**253
ice-skating rink, **1879:**183
national horse show, **1883:**192
new facility completed, **1890:**207
new facility opens, **1925:**298, **1968:**423
Madison Square Theater (N.Y.C.), **1879:**183
Mafia, **1890:**206
magazines and journals. *See* publishing; *specific titles*
Magda (play), **1903:**237
Magellan (spacecraft), **1989:**481, **1990:**485
Maggie, a Girl of the Streets (book), **1896:**220
"Magic" (song), **1980:**457
Magic (yacht), **1870:**164
"Magic Melody, The" (song), **1915:**269
Magic Show, The (play), **1974:**441
Magnani, Anna, **1955:**388
Magnificent Ambersons, The (book), **1918:**279
Magnificent Obsession (book), **1929:**308
Magnificent Obsession (movie), **1935:**329
Magnificent Seven, The (movie), **1960:**402
Magnolia (steamer), **1917:**272
Magnum P.I. (television program), **1980:**457
Magruder, Patrick, **1807:**45
Mahaffey, John, **1978:**451
Mahan, Alfred T., **1886:**196
Maher, Stephen T., **1930:**311
"Ma, He's Making Eyes at Me" (song), **1921:**287
mah-jongg, **1922:**290
Mahoney, Roger M., **1991:**488
Mahre, Phil, **1981:**459, **1983:**466
Maid of Cashmere, The (ballet), **1837:**94
Maier, Walter A., **1930:**311
mail bombs, **1989:**481, **1996:**506
mail boxes, drive-up, **1927:**301
mail chutes, **1883:**192
mail delivery
balloons, **1859:**135
first route west of Missouri, **1850:**118
free city delivery, **1863:**145, **1887:**198
letter carriers, **1794:**27
letter carrier uniforms, **1868:**157
Pony Express, **1860:**137, **1860:***138,* **1861:**140, **1872:**167

reduced to one-a-day, **1950:**372
rural free delivery, **1893:**212, **1896:**219
special-delivery service, **1885:**195
See also airmail; Post Office; stamps, postal
Mailer, Norman, **1948:**368, **1965:**413, **1967:**419, **1979:**453, **1991:**489
mail-order business, **1886:**196
Maiman, Theodore, **1960:**400
Maimonides College, **1927:**301
Maine, **1819:**62
Acadia National Park, **1946:**362
antitrust laws, **1889:**203
Aroostook "war" with Canada, **1839:**96
first newspaper, **1785:**15
first statewide prohibition law, **1846:**110
fish hatcheries, **1872:**167
newspapers, **1785:**15
separates from Massachusetts, **1787:**17
state constitution, **1819:**62
statehood, **1820:**64
Maine Woods, The (book), **1864:**149
Main Street (book), **1920:**284
Main-Traveled Roads (book), **1891:**208
Maitland, Lester J., **1927:**301
Major, Charles, **1899:**227
Major Bowes' Original Amateur Hour (radio program), **1935:**329
Major League Soccer, **1996:**509
Majors and Minors (book), **1895:**218
Making of an American, The (book), **1901:**234
Malaeska (book), **1860:**138
Malamud, Bernard, **1952:**379, **1966:**416
Malcolm X, **1963:**408, **1965:**412
Malcolm X (movie), **1992:**493
Mallon, Meg, **1991:**490
Mallory, Molla, **1926:**300, **1959:**399
Malouf, David, **1993:**497
Maloy, Francis E., **1976:**444
malted milk, **1883:**191
Maltese Falcon, The (book), **1930:**312
Maltese Falcon, The (movie), **1941:**346
Mamba's Daughters (play), **1938:**337
Mambo (dance), **1954:**385
Mamet, David, **1983:**465
Mammoth Cave National Park (Ky.), **1941:**345
Mammoth Hunters, The (book), **1985:**470
Man at the Crossroads (painting), **1933:**322
Man Called Peter, A (book), **1951:**376
Mancini, Henry, **1994:**500
Mandell, Sammy, **1926:**300
Mandlikova, Hana, **1985:**471
Mandrell, Barbara, **1980:**457
"Mandy" (song), **1975:**443
Manero, Tony, **1936:**332
Man for All Seasons, A (movie), **1966:**417
Man from U.N.C.L.E., The (television program), **1964:**411
Mangrum, Lloyd, **1946:**362
Manhattan Bridge (N.Y.C.), **1909:**252

Manhattan College, **1853:**124
Manhattan Project, **1942:**347, **1995:**502
"Manhattan Serenade" (song), **1942:**349
Manhattan Theater (N.Y.C.), **1901:**234
Manila Conference, **1966:**415
Man in Lower Ten, The (book), **1909:**252
Man in the Grey Flannel Suit, The (book), **1955:**388
Mankiewicz, Joseph, **1993:**498
Manley, Robert, **1917:**274
Mann, Carol, **1965:**414
Mann, Horace, **1837:**93, **1838:**94, **1853:**124, **1859:**135
Mann, William, **1800:**37
Mann-Elkins Act, **1910:**255
Manners and Social Usage (book), 1884
Manners, Customs, and Conditions of the North American Indians, The (book), **1841:**100
Manning, John, **1791:**24
Manning, William T., **1921:**287, **1950:**373
Man Nobody Knew, The (book), **1925:**297
Man of La Mancha (play), **1965:**414
Man o' War (horse), **1920:**285
Mansfield, Richard, **1882:**190, **1886:**198, **1890:**207, **1895:**218, **1897:**223, **1898:**225, **1901:**234, **1907:**247
Manship, Paul, **1965:**413
"Man That Broke the Bank at Monte Carlo, The" (song), **1892:**211
Mantle, Burns, **1949:**371
Mantle, Mickey, **1967:**420, **1995:**505
Manual of Bacteriology, A (book), **1892:**210
Manual of Geology (book), **1862:**144
Manual of the Railroads of the United States (book), **1868:**157
Manufacturers Hanover Trust, **1991:**487
Manufacturers Mutual Fire Insurance Co., **1835:**88–89
Man Who Came to Dinner, The (play), **1939:**340
"Man Without a Country, The" (story), **1863:**146
Man with Owl (painting), **1960:**401
Man with the Golden Arm, The (book), **1949:**370
"Man with the Hoe, The" (poem), **1899:**227
Map (painting), **1961:**404
"Maple Leaf Rag" (song), **1899:**227
Map of the World, The (book), **1994:**500
Mapp v. Ohio, **1961:**403
maps
first geological, **1809:**47
first of independent United States, **1784:**14
first road map, **1789:**21
Mara, Tim, **1925:**298, **1959:**399
Marathon Man (movie), **1976:**446
Marathon Oil Co., **1981:**458
marathon running, **1896:**220, **1897:**223, **1900:**231, **1930:**313, **1970:**429
marathons, dance, **1923:***291,* **1923:**292
Maravich, Pete, **1988:**480

Marble, Alice, **1936:**332, **1938:**337, **1939:**340, **1940:**343
Marble Collegiate Church (N.Y.C.), **1932:**319, **1982:**462
Marble Faun, The (book), **1860:**138
Marbury v. Madison, **1803:**41
March, Charles W., **1858:**134
March, Fredric, **1931:**316, **1935:**329, **1942:**349, **1961:**404, **1975:**444
March, Geoffrey, **1995:**504
March, Hal, **1955:**388
"Marching Through Georgia" (song), **1865:**152
"March of Time" (newsreel), **1934:**326
March of Time (radio program), **1928:**306
March on Washington, **1963:**408
Marciano, Rocky, **1952:**380, **1953:**382, **1954:**386, **1955:**388, **1969:**426
Marco Millions (play), **1928:**306
Marcos, Imelda, **1990:**484
Marcus, Rudolph A., **1992:**492
Marcus Welby, M.D. (television program), **1969:**426
Mardi (book), **1849:**117
Mardi Gras, **1827:**75, **1857:**132
Marechal, Ambrose, **1817:**60, **1821:**66
Margaret (book), **1845:**109
"Margie" (song), **1920:**284
"Maria" (song), **1957:**393
"Maria Elena" (song), **1933:**322
Marianna (Pa.), **1908:**250
"Marie" (song), **1928:**305
"Marie of Sunny Italy" (song), **1907:**247
Marietta College, **1835:**89
Marine Band, **1880:**184
Marine Biological Laboratory (Woods Hole), **1888:**201, **1930:**311
Marine Corps, **1893:**211, **1898:**223, **1933:**320, **1950:**372, **1958:**395
 Beirut base bombed by terrorists, **1983:**463, **1983:***464*
 Beirut withdrawal, **1984:**466
 in China, **1927:**301
 Cuban occupation, **1903:**236
 Dominican Republic occupation, **1915:**267
 founding, **1798:**34
 Honduras occupation, **1907:**245
 Nicaragua occupation, **1912:**259
 Nicaragua withdrawal and reoccupation, **1924:**293
 in Veracruz (Mexico), **1914:**265
Mariner 2 (space satellite), **1962:**405
Mariner 4 (space satellite), **1964:**410
Mariners Church, **1820:**65
marine stations, **1873:**170
Marino, Eugene A., **1988:**479
Marion, Francis, **1795:**29
Maris, Roger, **1961:**404, **1985:**471
Maritime Administration, **1930:**311, **1950:**372
Maritime Commission, **1936:**330
maritime workers, **1915:**268
"Mairzy Doats" (song), **1943:**351
Marjorie Daw and Other People (book), **1873:**170

Marjorie Morningstar (book), **1955:**388
Markey, Enid, **1916:**272
Markham, Edwin, **1899:**227, **1940:**343
Mark I computer, **1944:**353
Mark of Zorro, The (movie), **1920:**284
Markowitz, Harry M., **1990:**484
Mark Saber (television program), **1951:**377
Marks, Johnny, **1985:**470
Marland, Sidney P., Jr., **1971:**431
Marlowe, Julia, **1899:**228, **1901:**234, **1950:**375
Marne, Battle of the, **1918:**276
Marquand, John P., **1937:**334, **1939:**339, **1941:**345, **1960:**401
Marquette, Jacques, ix
Marquis, Don(ald), **1913:**264
Marquis of Queensberry rules (boxing), **1892:**211
Marr, Dave, **1965:**414
marriage
 Episcopal service, **1922:**289
 See also polygamy
Marriott, J. Willard, **1928:**304, **1986:**472
Mars (planet)
 space probes, **1993:**497, **1996:**507–8, **1997:**511, **1997:***512*
 two satellites discovered, **1877:**179
Marsh, Othniel C., **1866:**154
Marshall, Catharine, **1951:**376
Marshall, Frank, **1909:**253
Marshall, George C., **1947:**362, **1953:**380, **1959:**397
Marshall, Humphry, **1785:**15
Marshall, James, **1848:**114
Marshall, John, **1801:**38, **1835:**88
Marshall, Penny, **1976:**446
Marshall, Thomas R., **1925:**296
Marshall, Thurgood, **1967:**418, **1991:**487, **1993:**496
Marshall Islands, **1942:**346
Marshall Plan, **1947:**362
"Marshes of Glynn, The" (poem), **1878:**181
Marshfield, Edwin H., **1936:**331
Mars Observer (spacecraft), **1993:**497
Martell, Belle, **1940:**343
Martha Washington Hotel (N.Y.C.), **1903:**238
Martin, Billy, **1989:**483
Martin, David, **1807:***45*
Martin, Dean, **1905:**505
Martin, Dick, **1968:**423
Martin, Franklin H., **1935:**328
Martin, Glenn L., **1912:**262, **1955:**387
Martin, Mary, **1943:**352, **1949:**371, **1990:**486
Martin, "Plugger Bill," **1891:**209
Martin, Steve, **1982:**462
Martin, Sylvia, **1955:**388
Martin, William McC., **1938:**335
Martin Eden (book), **1909:**252
Martinez, Dennis, **1991:**489
Martinez, Pedro, **1997:**513
Martin Faber (book), **1833:**86
Martin Marietta, **1992:**491–92,

 1994:500, **1995:**503
Martino, Donald, **1973:**438
Martinsburg (W. Va.), **1877:**179
Martin v. Mott, **1827:**74
Marty (movie), **1955:**388
Marty (play), **1953:**382
Marvin, Lee, **1965:**414, **1967:**420
Marx, Groucho, **1931:***316*, **1977:**449
Marx Brothers, **1926:**300, **1927:**303, **1931:**316, **1931:***316*, **1938:**337
"Mary Had a Little Lamb" (song), **1867:**156
Maryknoll Sisters, **1955:**388
Maryland, **1851:**120, **1867:**155
 cedes land for District of Columbia, **1788:**18
 Chesapeake Bay Bridge, **1952:**378
 early newspapers., xiii, **1796:**31
 Episcopal bishops, **1911:**258
 first governor, **1777:**4
 first state workmen's compensation law, **1902:**235
 new constitution, **1867:**155
 property requirement for voting removed, **1810:**49
 ratifies Articles of Confederation, **1781:**8
 ratifies Constitution, **1788:**18
 removes religious voting qualifications, **1826:**72
 state constitution, **1776:**2, **1851:**120
 Toleration Act, xiii
 votes against secession, **1861:**139
Maryland College of Medicine, **1807:**46
"Maryland, My Maryland" (song), **1861:**141
Mary Margaret McBride (radio program), **1937:**334
Mary Poppins (movie), **1964:**411
"Mary's a Grand Old Name" (song), **1905:**242
*M*A*S*H* (television program), **1972:**432
Masked Ball, The (play), **1892:**211
Mason, Bobbie Ann, **1993:**497
Mason, George, **1776:**2, **1791:**23
Mason, James (actor), **1954:**385
Mason, James (chess champion), **1876:**177
Mason, James M. (Confederate commissioner), **1861:**139
Mason, John M., **1804:**42
Mason, Lowell, **1822:**67, **1833:**86, **1838:**95
Mason, Stewart T., **1843:**103
Mason & Hamlin Organ Co., **1854:**127
Masons, **1778:**5, **1871:**166
Masque of Pandora, The (book), **1875:**174
Mass (musical work), **1971:**431
Massachusetts, **1779:**6, **1780:**8
 American Revolution, **1777:**4
 antilottery law, **1833:**86
 Articles of Confederation revision, **1785:**14
 Board of Public Health, **1869:**160
 Board of Railroad Commissioners,

McDowell, Malcolm, **1971**:431
McEnroe, John, **1979**:454, **1980**:457, **1981**:460, **1984**:468
McFingal (Trumbull), **1776**:2
McGaughey, Janie, **1967**:419
McGill University, **1874**:172
McGinley, Phyllis, **1960**:401, **1978**:451
McGovern, George, **1972**:432
McGowan, William, **1992**:492
McGrath, Earl J., **1949**:369
McGrath, Mike, **1969**:426, **1970**:429
McGraw, Ali, **1970**:429
McGraw, James H., **1948**:368
McGraw, John, **1902**:236, **1917**:275, **1932**:319, **1934**:326
McGraw Electric Co., **1926**:298
McGraw-Hill Publishing Co., **1916**:272
McGuffey, Ives W., 1869, **1869**:159
McGuffey, James, **1891**:208
McGuffey, William H., **1836**:91, **1839**:97, **1873**:170
McGuire, George, **1921**:287
McGuire, Peter J., **1882**:189
McHale's Navy (television program), **1962**:407
McIlwaine, Charles P., **1832**:84
McIntire, Rufus, **1839**:96
McIntosh, Caroline C., **1858**:134
McIntyre, James F., **1948**:367, **1953**:382, **1979**:453
McIntyre, O. O., **1938**:337
McKay, David O., **1951**:376, **1970**:428
McKay, Donald, **1850**:119, **1880**:184
McKay, Gordon, **1903**:237
McKeen, Joseph, **1802**:40
McKellen, Gordon, Jr., **1973**:438, **1974**:441, **1975**:444
McKenna's Flirtation (play), **1889**:204
McKenzie, George, **1880**:185
McKim, Mead & White, **1878**:181
McKinley, Ida S., **1907**:245
McKinley, William
    assassinated, **1901**:232
    as congressman from Ohio, **1877**:178
    elected governor of Ohio, **1891**:208, **1892**:209
    elected president, **1896**:219
    reelected president, **1900**:229
    as representative from Ohio, **1885**:195
    Spanish-American War, **1898**:223
McKinley Tariff, **1890**:205
McKinney, Guy, **1926**:300
McKinney, Tamara, **1983**:466
McKuen, Rod, **1968**:422
McLaglen, Victor, **1935**:329, **1959**:398
McLaren, William E., **1874**:172
McLarnin, Jimmy, **1933**:323, **1934**:326
McLaughlin, Maurice, **1912**:262, **1913**:264
McLean, John, **1836**:90
McLean, William L., **1931**:316
McLeod, Fred, **1908**:250
McLeod, Gavin, **1977**:449
McMahon, Junie, **1950**:375
McManus, George, **1954**:385

McMillan, Edwin M., **1940**:342, **1951**:376
McMurrin, Sterling M., **1961**:403
McMurtry, Larry, **1985**:470, **1988**:479
McNally, Terrence, **1987**:477
McNamara, Robert S., **1960**:400
"McNamara's Band" (song), **1917**:275
McNamee, Graham, **1942**:349
McNary Dam (Wash.), **1953**:381
McNeeley, Peter, **1995**:505
McNeill, Don, **1933**:322, **1940**:343
McNichols, John T., **1925**:297
McPherson, Aimee Semple, **1918**:278, **1944**:353
McPherson, James B., **1864**:147
McQuaid, Bernard J., **1868**:158
McQueen, Steve, **1970**:429, **1980**:457
McRae, Carmen, **1994**:500
McSorley's Bar (painting), **1912**:261
McTammany, John, **1876**:177, **1881**:188, **1892**:210, **1915**:268
McTeague (opera), **1992**:493
McTeer, Janet, **1997**:513
McTigue, Mik, **1923**:293
McVeigh, Timothy, **1997**:511
Mead, George H., **1900**:231
Mead, Johnson & Co., **1928**:305
Mead, Margaret, **1928**:305, **1978**:450
Meade, George G., **1872**:167
Meade, William, **1841**:100
Meadowlands Harness Track (N.J.), **1975**:444
Meadows, Audrey, **1955**:388, **1996**:508
Means, Jacqueline, **1977**:448
"Mean to Me" (song), **1929**:308
Meany, George, **1940**:342, **1952**:378, **1955**:386, **1980**:456
Mears, Rick, **1979**:454, **1984**:468, **1988**:479, **1991**:489
meat
    antiprice-fixing measures, **1921**:286
    first packer, **1788**:19
    inspection, **1884**:193, **1890**:206
    Inspection Act, **1906**:243
    packers' trust breakup, **1905**:241
    Roman Catholic abstinence rules softened, **1966**:416
    slicer machine, **1873**:170
    stockyards, **1871**:164, **1872**:168, **1874**:172, **1884**:193, **1886**:197
Meat Inspection Act, **1906**:243
Mechanics Free Press (newspaper), **1828**:76
Mechanics Library opens, **1820**:65
Meddoff, Mark, **1980**:457
Medea (play), **1947**:364
Medeiros, Humberto S., **1970**:428, **1973**:438
Mediation and Conciliation Board, **1913**:262
Mediation Board, **1934**:323
Medical Center (television program), **1969**:426
medical insurance. *See* health insurance
medical jurisprudence, **1876**:177
Medical Respository (magazine), **1797**:32
Medical Society of Massachusetts, **1781**:9

Medicare, **1966**:416, **1991**:488
Medicare Catastrophic Coverage Act, **1989**:482
Medicine Man (sculpture), **1899**:227
Medill, Joseph, **1851**:121, **1874**:172, **1899**:228
Medium, The (opera), **1946**:361
Meet Corliss Archer (radio program), **1937**:334
Meet Me in St. Louis (movie), **1944**:354
"Meet Me in St. Louis, Louis" (song), **1904**:240
Meet the Press (radio program), **1945**:358
Meet the Press (television program), **1947**:364
Mehta, Zubin, **1990**:485
Melchior, Lauritz, **1973**:438
Melin, Arthur, **1958**:395
Mellichampe (book), **1836**:92
Mellon, Andrew W., **1921**:285–86, **1937**:332, **1937**:334
Mellon Institute of Industrial Research, **1913**:262
Melville, David, **1806**:45, **1814**:56
Melville, Herman, **1846**:111, **1847**:113, **1849**:117, **1850**:119, **1851**:121, **1851**:*121*, **1852**:123, **1856**:131, **1891**:208
Member of the Wedding, The (book), **1946**:361
Member of the Wedding, The (play), **1950**:375
Memorial Day, three-day weekend, **1971**:430
"Memories" (song), **1915**:269
"Memories Are Made of This" (song), **1956**:390
Memories of New York (painting), **1917**:275
Memories of the Ford Administration (book), **1992**:493
Memphis (Tenn.), **1893**:213, **1896**:219
    first Holiday Inn, **1952**:378
    race riot, **1866**:153
"Memphis Blues" (song), **1911**:258
Memphis State University, **1912**:261
Men and Women (play), **1890**:207
Mencken, H. L., **1914**:266, **1919**:281, **1956**:390
    American Mercury founding, **1924**:294
mendelevium, **1955**:387
Mendelssohn Quintet Club, **1849**:116
Mendez, Antonio, **1791**:23
Men in Black (movie), **1997**:513
Menken, Adah, **1861**:141
Menken, Helen, **1918**:279, **1922**:290
Menlo Park (N.J.), **1876**:176, **1880**:184
Mennen, William G., **1916**:2709
Menninger, Karl A., **1920**:283, **1990**:485
Menninger Clinic, **1920**:283
Menotti, Gian Carlo, **1937**:334, **1942**:349, **1946**:361, **1947**:364, **1950**:373, **1951**:376, **1954**:385, **1963**:408
mental health
    American Foundation for Mental Hygiene, **1928**:305

society founding, **1786:**16

See also opera; *specific composers, compositions, performers and song titles*

Musical Fund Society, **1825:**72, **1848:**115

Musical Journal, **1800:**37

Musical Society of Stoughton (Mass.), **1786:**16

"Music Goes Round and Round, The" (song), **1935:**328

"Music, Maestro, Please" (song), **1938:**337

Music Man, The (movie), **1962:**407

Music Man, The (play), **1957:**394

Music Master, The (play), **1904:**240

Muskie, Edmund S., **1996:**506

Mussolini, Benito, **1938:**335

Muth, Johann C. F., **1802:**40

Mutiny on the Bounty (book), **1932:**319

Mutiny on the Bounty (movie), **1935:**329

"Mutt and Jeff" (comic strip), **1907:**247

Mutual Assurance Company, **1784:**13

Mutual Fund Society, **1820:**65

Mutual Life Insurance Co. of New York, **1843:**103

Muybridge, Eadweard, **1872:**168

MX missile, **1979:**452

My Antonía (book), **1918:**279

My Best Girl (movie), **1927:**303

"My Blue Heaven" (song), **1927:**302

My Bondage, My Freedom (book), **1855:**129

"My Bonnie Lies Over the Ocean" (song), **1881:**188

"My Buddy" (song), **1922:**289

Myers, Jerome, **1905:**242

My Fair Lady (movie), **1964:**411

My Fair Lady (play), **1956:**390

My Favorite Martian (television program), **1963:**409

"My Favorite Things" (song), **1959:**398

"My Funny Valentine" (song), **1937:**334

"My Gal Is a High Born Lady" (song), **1896:**220

"My Gal Sal" (song), **1905:**242

"My Grandfather's Clock" (song), **1876:**177

"My Guy" (song), **1964:**410

"My Heart Belongs to Daddy" (song), **1938:**337

My Lady Pokahontas (book), **1885:**196

My Life and Hard Times (book), **1933:**322

"My Love" (song), **1966:**416, **1973:**438

My Man (movie), **1928:**306

"My Man" (song), **1921:**287

My Man Godfrey (movie), **1936:**331

"My Melancholy Baby" (song), **1912:**261

"My Melody of Love" (song), **1974:**440

My Name Is Aram (book), **1940:**342

"My Nellie's Blue Eyes" (song), **1883:**192

"My Old Kentucky Home" (song), **1853:**125

"My Pony Boys" (song), **1909:**252

Myra Breckenridge (book), **1968:**422

My Sister Eileen (movie), **1942:**349

"Mystery Box" (song), **1996:**508

Mystic Shrine of the Masonic Order, **1871:**166

"My Sweetheart's the Man in the Moon" (song), **1892:**211

My Three Sons (television program), **1960:**402

"My Wild Irish Rose" (song), **1899:**227

N

NAACP. *See* National Association for the Advancement of Colored People

Nabisco Co., **1985:**469

Nabokov, Vladimir, **1955:**388, **1995:**505

Nader, Ralph, **1965:**412

NAFTA. *See* North American Free Trade Agreement

Nagel, Conrad, **1918:**279

Nagurski, Bronko, **1990:**486

Nagy, Steve, **1952:**380, **1955:**388

Naismith, James, **1892:**211, **1939:**340

Naked and the Dead, The (book), **1948:**368

Name That Tune (television program), **1953:**382

Nantucket Island (Mass.), **1976:**447

Napoleon III, Emperor of France, **1867:**155

Napoles, Jose, **1969:**426, **1971:**432

"Narcissus" (song), **1891:**208

Narváez, Pánfilo de, ix

NASA. *See* National Aeronautics and Space Administration

Nasby, Petroleum V. (David R. Locke), **1861:**141, **1888:**202

NASCAR. *See* National Association for Stock Car Auto Racing

Nash, Charles W., **1948:**366

Nash, John F., **1994:**500

Nash, Ogden, **1938:**337, **1971:**431

Nash, Thomas, **1902:**235

Nashville (Tenn.)
  Centennial Exposition, **1897:**223
  first settlers, **1780:**8

Nash Motor Co., **1916:**271

Nast, Condé, **1942:**349

Nast, Thomas, **1862:**144, **1870:***162*, **1870:**163, **1874:**171

Nastase, Ilie, **1972:**435

Natchez (Miss.), fires, **1940:**343

Natchez (steamboat), **1870:**163

Nathan, George Jean, **1924:**294, **1958:**396

Nathans, Daniel, **1978:**450

Nation, Carry A., **1901:**232, **1911:**257

Nation, The (magazine), **1865:**152

National, The (sports daily), **1991:**489

National Academy of Design, **1826:**73

National Academy of Sciences, **1863:**146

National Advisory Committee for Aeronautics, **1931:**315

National Aeronautics and Space Administration, **1958:**395, **1992:**492
  forerunner, **1915:**267

National Aircraft Board, **1925:**296

National Airport (Washington, D.C.), **1940:**342, **1982:**463

National Air Transport Inc., **1925:**296

National Archery Assn., **1879:**183

National Association for Stock Car Auto

Racing, **1947:**365, **1949:**371. *See also under* SPORTS *in text for subsequent races*

National Association for the Advancement of Colored People, **1909:**251, **1988:**479, **1995:**503

National Association of Amateur Oarsmen, **1873:**170

National Association of Base-Ball Players, **1871:**166

National Association of Cotton Manufacturers, **1921:***286*

National Association of Finance Companies, **1924:**293

National Association of Health Commissioners, **1991:**488

National Association of Manufacturers, **1895:**217

National Association of Professional Baseball Leagues, **1901:**234

National Association of Retail Druggists, **1883:**191

National Association of Scientific Angling Clubs, **1906:**245

National Association of Social Workers, **1955:**386

National Audubon Society, **1885:**196

National Baptist Convention of the U.S.A., **1895:**218

National Barn Dance (radio program), **1933:**322

National Basketball Assn.
  American Basketball Assn. team mergers, **1976:**446
  comprehensive player contract, **1973:**438
  four new franchises, **1987:**477
  Minneapolis wins, **1949:**371
  O'Brien named commissioner, **1975:**444
  See also under SPORTS *in text for annual winners*

National Birth Control League, **1914:**265

National Biscuit Co., **1898:**224

National Board of Censorshp of Motion Pictures, founding, **1909:**253

National Board of Fire Underwriters, **1866:**153

National Boot and Shoe Manufacturers Assn., **1905:**241

National Bowling Assn., **1875:**175

National Boxing Assn., **1942:**349

National Broadcasting Co. *See* NBC

National Bureau of Economic Research, **1920:**283

National Bureau of Standards, **1901:**232

National Cancer Institute, **1937:**334

National Cash Register Co., **1884:**193

National Cathedral (Wash., D.C.), 75th anniversary, **1982:**462

National Catholic Welfare Council, **1919:**281

National Cattle & Horse Growers Assn, **1884:**193

National Cemetery (Arlington, Va.)

NBC (National Broadcasting Co.)
  baseball television broadcasting
    rights, **1983**:465
  first commercial television license,
    1941:345
  first major symphonic concert broad-
    cast, **1926**:299
  initiates broadcasting, **1926**:300
  Microsoft 24-hour cable news service,
    1995:505
  mobile television units, **1937**:334
  refuses rating system, **1997**:513
  station affiliates, **1926**:300
NBC Symphony Orchestra, **1937**:334
N by E (book), **1930**:312
NCAA. *See* National Collegiate Athletic
  Assn.
NCNB Corp., **1991**:487
NCR (co.), **1991**:487
Neal, Frankie, **1903**:238
Nebraska
  first Arbor Day, **1872**:167
  legislature, **1934**:323
  ratifies Prohibition Amendment,
    1919:279
  statehood, **1867**:155
  territory created, **1854**:126
  woman suffrage, **1917**:274
Nebraskan (ship), **1915**:267
Nebraska Palladium (newspaper),
  1854:127
Negri, Pola, **1924**:295
Negro Digest (magazine), **1942**:349
Neighborhood Playhouse (N.Y.C.),
  1915:269
Neiman Marcus, in-store fashion shows,
  1926:298
"Nelly Bly" (song), **1849**:116
"Nelly Was a Lady" (song), **1849**:116
Nelson, Byron, **1937**:335, **1939**:340,
  1940:343, **1942**:350, **1945**:358
Nelson, Christian K., 1921, **1921**:287
Nelson, Cleland K., **1907**:247
Nelson, Harriet, **1994**:501
Nelson, Larry, **1981**:460, **1983**:465,
  1987:477
Nelson, Lindsey, **1995**:505
Nelson, Rick, **1985**:470
Nelson, Warren, **1978**:451
Nelson, Willie, **1991**:488
Nemerov, Howard, **1977**:448
neoprene, **1931**:314
Neptune (planet), **1989**:482
neptunium, **1940**:342
Nestle Co., **1984**:466
Netherlands, **1942**:346, **1949**:369
  colonial settlements, ix
  large U.S. loan, **1781**:8
  recognizes American independence,
    1782:10
  war with France, **1793**:26
Network (movie), **1976**:446
Neuberger, Leah Thall, **1957**:394
Neumann, John, **1963**:408
Neumann, John H., **1852**:123
Neumann, Liselotte, **1988**:480

Neutra, Richard J., **1970**:427
Neutrality Act, **1794**:27, **1941**:344
Nevada
  capital punishment by lethal gas,
    1921:286
  Comstock Lode, **1859**:135
  Great Basin National Park, **1987**:474
  old-age pension, **1923**:290
  prohibition law, **1918**:277
  state constitution, **1859**:135
  statehood, **1864**:147
  territory established, **1861**:140
  woman suffrage, **1914**:265
Nevelson, Louise, **1958**:396, **1959**:398
Nevers, Ernie, **1929**:309
Nevin, Ethelbert, **1901**:233
New American Practical Navigator (book),
  1802:39
New Amsterdam, ix
New Amsterdam Theater (N.Y.C.),
  1903:237
New and Collected Poems (Wilbur book),
  1988:479
Newark (N.J.)
  performing arts center opens,
    1997:512
  race riots, **1967**:418
Newark Airport (N.J.)
  completed, **1928**:305
  new passenger terminal, **1973**:437
New Astronomy, The (book), **1888**:201
Newberry, Walter L., **1868**:158
Newbold, Charles, **1797**:32
New Brunswick (N.J.), **1886**:197
Newburgh (N.Y.), **1888**:201, **1989**:483
New Church (Swedenborgian), **1817**:60
New Church Theological School,
  1881:187
Newcombe, John, **1967**:420, **1973**:438
New Deal, **1932**:317, **1933**:320,
  1934:323, **1937**:332
*New Dictionary of Medical Sciences and Lit-
  erature* (book), **1833**:85
New England Association Football
  League, **1887**:200
New England Conservatory of Music,
  1867:156
New England Country Schoolhouse (paint-
  ing), **1871**:165
New England Farmer, The (book), **1790**:23
New England Female Medical College
  (Boston), **1873**:170
New England Idylls (musical composition),
  1902:236
New England Mutual Life Insurance
  Co., **1835**:89
New England Restraining Act, x
New England Watch, **1878**:182
New Found Land (book), **1930**:312
Newfoundland, **1782**:10, **1909**:251,
  1910:254
New Granada. *See* Colombia
New Guinea, **1943**:350
New Hampshire (book), **1923**:292
New Hampshire
  American Revolution, **1776**:2

library system, **1893**:213
limits workday to 10 hours, **1847**:112
prohibiton law, **1855**:128
ratifies Constitution, **1788**:18
state constitution, **1776**:2, **1783**:11
state lottery, **1964**:410
New Hampshire Patriot (newspaper),
  1809:48
Newhart, Bob, **1972**:432
New Haven (Conn.), **1878**:181,
  1880:184, **1882**:190
New Haven (Conn.) Gazette, **1784**:14
New Home, A (book), **1839**:97
Newhouse, Sewell, **1855**:128
Newhouse newspaper chain, **1921**:287
New Jersey
  American Revolution, **1776**:1,
    1777:3, **1778**:4, **1778**:5, **1779**:6,
    1780:7
  bridges to Staten Island, **1928**:304
  death penalty reinstated, **1982**:460
  first newspaper, **1777**:4
  Garden State Parkway, **1954**:384
  gradual emancipation law, **1804**:42
  Little League inclusion of girls man-
    dated, **1974**:441
  Meadowlands sports complex,
    1975:444
  Port Authority, **1921**:286
  ratifies Constitution, **1787**:17
  removes property requirements for
    voting, **1807**:45
  restricts voting, **1844**:105
  signs crime pact with New York,
    1833:84
  state constitution, **1776**:2, **1945**:357
  surrogate motherhood ruled illegal,
    1989:481
  tunnel to New York, **1907**:246
  Wilson (W.) elected as governor,
    1910:254
  woman suffrage, **1776**:2
  workmen's compensation law,
    1911:257
New Jersey Gazette (newspaper), **1777**:4
New Jersey Society for Promotion of
  Agriculture, Commerce, and the
  Arts, **1781**:9
Newlands Act, **1913**:262
New London (Conn.), Coast Guard
  Academy, **1876**:176
New London (Tex.), **1937**:335
Newlywed Game, The (television program),
  1967:420
Newman, Barnett, **1966**:416
Newman, Larry, **1978**:450, **1981**:458
Newman, Paul, **1960**:401–2, **1963**:409,
  1969:426, **1973**:438, **1974**:441,
  1984:468, **1994**:501
New Mexico
  Carlsbad National Park, **1930**:310
  constitutional convention, **1910**:254
  declared part of U.S., **1846**:109
  first Protestant church, **1854**:127
  gasoline tax, **1919**:281
  Gila National Forest, **1924**:293

Mexican cession, **1853**:124, **1854**:126
Native American revolt, ix
statehood, **1912**:259
State University, **1888**:201
territorial government formed, **1850**:118
New Mexico State Prison, riot, **1980**:457
New Moon, The (operetta), **1928**:305
New Orleans (La.), **1803**:*41*
cholera outbreak, **1832**:83
fire, **1788**:18
incorporated, **1805**:43
Isaac Delgado Museum of Art, **1911**:258
Mardi Gras, **1827**:75, **1857**:132
Mississippi River Bridge, **1958**:395
opera house built, **1808**:47
race riot, **1866**:153
Spanish control, **1803**:40
state capital moved from, **1879**:182
Superdome, **1975**:444
yellow fever epidemics, **1853**:124, **1905**:241
New Orleans, Battle of, **1815**:57, **1815**:*58*
Newport (R.I.), **1778**:4, **1884**:193
Newport Jazz Festival, **1954**:385
New Republic (magazine), **1914**:266
New School of Social Research (N.Y.C.), **1919**:281
Newspaper Enterprise Assn., **1902**:236
newspapers
automatic stereotype plate-casting machine, **1900**:231
cartoons, **1903**:237, **1918**:279
colonial-era, xiii
columnist libel liability ruling, **1990**:485
columnists, **1913**:264, **1917**:275, **1919**:281, **1921**:287, **1925**:297
comic strips, **1902**:236, **1907**:247, **1919**:281, **1924**:295
feature syndicates, **1902**:236, **1920**:283
first abolitionist, **1817**:61
first African American, **1827**:74
first Arizona, **1859**:136
first Arkansas, **1819**:64
first Army weekly, **1918**:277
first business weekly, **1795**:29
first California, **1846**:111
first Catholic, **1822**:67
first Colorado, **1859**:136
first crossword puzzle, **1913**:264
first daily comic strip, **1907**:247
first daily in Maine, **1829**:78
first English-language in Texas, **1819**:64
first European edition of U.S., **1848**:115
first German-language, **1834**:88
first Hawaii, **1834**:88
first Iowa, **1836**:92
first Kansas, **1835**:90
first labor, **1828**:76
first Minnesota, **1849**:116

first Montana, **1864**:149
first Native American, **1828**:76
first Nebraska, **1854**:127
first Nevada, **1858**:134
first New Mexico, **1868**:158
first North Dakota, **1864**:149
first Oklahoma, **1844**:107
first Oregon, **1846**:111
first published on Sunday, **1796**:31
first rotogravure sections, **1914**:266
first successful daily, **1784**:14
first successful penny daily, **1833**:86
first syndicate, **1861**:141
first Washington State, **1852**:123
first west of Mississippi River, **1808**:47
first Wisconsin, **1833**:86
first Wisconsin daily, **1837**:94
first Wyoming, **1863**:146
foreign-language, **1904**:240, **1913**:262
libel statutes, **1986**:473
mergers and acquisitions, **1991**:489, **1993**:498
Montana, **1864**:149
Munsey chain, **1901**:233
Newhouse chain, **1921**:287
press freedom guarantees, **1805**:43
printing-and-folding machine, **1876**:177
Scripps-Howard chain, **1876**:177, **1922**:289
Winchell gossip column, **1924**:294–95
See also specific publications; *under individual states*
newsreels
first, **1910**:256
"March of Time," **1934**:326
theater opens (N.Y.C.), **1929**:308
Newsweek (magazine), **1933**:322
New Testament, first U.S. publication, **1777**:4
New Testament: An American Translation (book), **1923**:292
Newton, Huey, **1966**:417
Newton, Isaac (American), **1862**:142
New York (painting), **1953**:382
New York (state), **1888**:202
Adirondack Mountains, **1885**:196
American Revolution, **1777**:3, **1778**:4, **1779**:6
Attica prison uprising, **1971**:430
automobile speed limits, **1904**:239
bans imprisonment for debt, **1832**:84
capital moved to Albany, **1797**:33
Catskills resorts, **1914**:265
Chautauqua Movement, **1874**:171
Cleveland elected governor, **1882**:188
Cold Spring Harbor Biological Laboratory, **1890**:206
Commission Against Discrimination, **1945**:357
crime pact with New Jersey, **1833**:84
early newspapers, **1776**:2, **1783**:12, **1785**:15, **1795**:29, **1801**:39
Episcopal bishop, **1972**:433
Erie Canal authorized, **1817**:60

fire escape law, **1860**:137
first African American Episcopal bishop, **1974**:440
first Episcopal bishop, **1786**:16
first public school, **1791**:24
first seat-belt requirements, **1984**:467
free public education system, **1867**:156
gradual emancipation statute, **1799**:34, **1817**:59, **1827**:74
high school graduation requirements stiffened, **1984**:467
Hudson-Fulton Celebration, **1909**:252
illegal wage raise attempts, **1835**:89
interracial boxing ban, **1913**:264
Lake Champlain Bridge, **1929**:308
license plates, **1901**:232
lotteries, **1830**:80
Love Canal chemical contamination, **1980**:455–56, **1988**:477–78
Manning as Episcopal bishop, **1921**:287
parochial school aid held unconstitutional, **1973**:437
perpetual leases eliminated, **1846**:109–10
press freedom guarantee, **1805**:43
public schools, **1791**:24, **1805**:43
racetrack betting, **1887**:200
railroad charter, **1826**:73
ratifies Constitution, **1788**:18, **1788**:*19*
removes voting property qualifications, **1821**:66
Roosevelt (F.D.) as governor, **1928**:303
Roosevelt (F.D.) elected to state Senate, **1910**:254
school building disaster, **1989**:483
State College of Agriculture, **1890**:206
state constitution, **1777**:4, **1805**:43, **1869**:159
State Library School, **1887**:199
state university founding, **1784**:14
New York & Harlem Railway, **1831**:81
New York Academy of Music, **1852**:123
New York Academy of Science, **1817**:60
New York American (newspaper), **1819**:64, **1919**:281
New York Arbeiter Zeitung (newspaper), **1881**:188
New York Argus (newspaper), **1795**:30
New York Athletic Club, **1868**:158, **1879**:183, **1896**:220
New York Caledonian Curling Club, **1855**:129
New York Cancer Institute, **1923**:292
New York Canoe Club, **1871**:166
New York Central Railroad, **1853**:124, **1869**:160, **1872**:168, **1891**:208, **1895**:217, **1966**:416, **1968**:421
New York City
air shuttle to Boston and Washington (D.C.), **1986**:472

Northrup Grumman, **1997**:511
North Star (publication), **1847**:113
Northwest Airlines, **1986**:472, **1987**:478,
    1992:492
Northwestern University, **1851**:120
Northwest Ordinance, **1787**:17, **1788**:18
Northwest Passage (book), **1937**:334
North Wind (painting), **1919**:281
Norton, Maria, **1931**:314
Norton Co., **1890**:206
Norway, **1905**:241
"No Sugar Tonight" (song), **1970**:428
"no summer" year, **1816**:59
Notes on Virginia (book), **1782**:11
Nothing But the Truth (play), **1916**:272
Notre Dame of Maryland College,
    1895:218
Notre Dame University. *See* University of
    Notre Dame
Not So Long Ago (play), **1920**:285
Nott, Eliphalet, **1804**:42
Notturno (musical composition), **1973**:438
Not Yet (sculpture), **1940**:342
Nourse, Edwin G., **1974**:440
Novarro, Ramon, **1926**:300
Nova Scotia fishing rights, **1782**:10
novel, first American, **1789**:21
novocain, **1905**:241
NOW (National Organization for
    Women), **1966**:415
Now and Then Poems (book), **1978**:450
"Now I Lay Me Down to Sleep" (song),
    1866:154
"Now the Day Is Over" (song), 1869,
    1869:161
Noyes, Harry A., **1970**:427
Noyes, John H., **1837**:93
nuclear energy, **1941**:345, **1953**:381,
    1954:383, **1958**:395, **1960**:400
    "atoms for peace" program, **1953**:380
    controlled-fusion reaction, **1993**:497
    first electric power from, **1951**:376
    Three Mile Island (Pa.) accident,
        1979:452, **1979**:*453*
nuclear fission, **1939**:338, **1942**:348
nuclear reactors, **1941**:345, **1953**:381,
    1954:383
Nuclear Regulatory Agency, **1975**:442
Nuclear Test Ban Treaty, **1963**:407
nuclear weapons
    Catholic Bishops condemn, **1983**:465
    hydrogen bomb, **1950**:372, **1952**:378,
        1954:383
    Methodist bishops oppose, **1986**:473
    neutron bomb deferral, **1979**:452
    North Korean inspection dispute,
        1994:499
    See also arms control; atomic bomb
nude dancing, **1991**:488
Nugent, Maud, **1896**:220
Nunn, Sam, **1994**:499, **1995**:503
Nureyev, Rudolf, **1993**:497
Nursery and Child's Hospital, **1854**:127
nursery school, first, **1827**:74
nursing
    Army Nurse Corps, **1901**:233

army school, **1918**:277
first full-time professor, **1907**:246
first school nurse, **1902**:235
monthly magazine, **1886**:197
Navy Nurses Corp, **1909**:252
public health, **1912**:261
schools of, **1873**:170, **1908**:249
yellow fever epidemic, **1878**:*180*
Nuttall, Betty, **1930**:313
Nutting, Mary A., **1907**:246
nylon, **1938**:335
nylon stockings, **1939**:338
NYNEX, **1997**:511

O

Oakland (Calif.)
    earthquake, **1989**:483
    Raiders' return rejected, **1990**:486
Oakland Athletics, **1972**:435, **1973**:438,
    1974:441, **1989**:483
Oakland Raiders. *See* Los Angeles
    Raiders
Oakley, Annie, **1926**:300
Oak Ridge (Tenn.), **1942**:347, **1949**:369
Oates, Joyce Carol, **1971**:431
Oberon, Merle, **1939**:340, **1979**:454
O'Boyle, Patrick A., **1948**:367, **1967**:419
O'Brien, Edward J.H., **1941**:345
O'Brien, Jack, **1905**:243
O'Brien, Lawrence R., **1975**:444,
    1990:486
O'Brien, Parry, **1954**:385
O'Brien, Pat, **1983**:465
obscenity
    National Endowment of the Arts
        charges, **1989**:482
    Supreme Court definition, **1957**:392
    Ulysses (Joyce) case, **1918**:279,
        1921:287, **1933**:322
*Observations on the Geology of the United
    States* (book), **1809**:47
Occidental Petroleum, **1982**:460
Occupational Safety and Health Act,
    1970:427
oceanography, first modern book,
    1855:128
Ochoa, Severo, **1959**:398
Ochs, Adolph S., **1878**:181, **1896**:220,
    1935:328
O'Connell, William H., **1907**:247
O'Connor, Carroll, **1971**:431
O'Connor, Edwin G., **1956**:390,
    1968:422
O'Connor, John J., **1984**:467, **1985**:470
O'Connor, Michael, **1843**:103
O'Connor, Sandra Day, **1981**:458
Octopus, The (book), **1901**:234
Octoroon, The (play), **1859**:136
Odd Couple, The (play), **1965**:414
Odd Couple, The (television program),
    1970:429
Odd Fellows lodge, first, **1819**:64
"Ode to Billy Joe" (song), **1967**:419
Odin, John M., **1848**:115, **1857**:132
O'Donnell, Rosey (Emmett), **1971**:430
Oerter, Al, **1962**:407

Office of Censorship, **1941**:344
Office of Civil Defense, **1941**:344,
    1942:347, **1945**:357
Office of Defense Transportation,
    1941:344
Office of Economic Opportunity,
    1964:410
Office of Economic Stabilization,
    1942:347
Office of Emergency Management,
    1939:338
Office of Price Administration, **1941**:344,
    1942:347
Office of Production Management,
    1941:344
Office of Scientific Research and Devel-
    opment, **1940**:341
Office of Strategic Services, **1942**:347
Office of War Information, **1942**:347
Office of War Mobilization, **1943**:351
Office of War Mobilization and Recon-
    version, **1944**:353
Officers Reserve Training Corps, found-
    ing, **1916**:270
Official Baseball Guide (book), **1878**:182
Of Human Bondage (movie), **1934**:326
Of Mice and Men (book), **1937**:334
Of Mice and Men (play), **1937**:334
Of Time and the River (book), **1935**:328
Ogden, William B., **1837**:93
Ogilvy & Mather (advertising), **1992**:492
Oglala Sioux, **1868**:157
Oglethorpe University, **1835**:89
O'Hara, John, **1934**:326, **1935**:328,
    1940:342, **1949**:370, **1958**:396
O'Hara, John F., **1951**:376, **1958**:395,
    1960:401
O'Hare Airport (Chicago), jet takeoff
    crash, **1979**:454
Oh, Calcutta (play), **1969**:426
"Oh, Dem Golden Slippers" (song),
    1879:183
Oh, God! (movie), **1977**:449
"Oh, How I Hate to Get Up in the Morn-
    ing" (song), **1918**:278
Ohio
    early newspaper, **1793**:27
    first woman state Supreme Court jus-
        tice, **1922**:288
    floods, **1913**:264
    Harding as U.S. senator, **1915**:267
    Hayes as governor, **1875**:173.173
    Honda assembly plant, **1980**:456
    Honda Motors plant, **1985**:469
    Indian treaty, **1795**:29
    Kent State shootings, **1970**:427,
        1970:*428*, **1975**:442
    oil discovered, **1882**:189
    Standard Oil Co. incorporated,
        1870:163
    state constitution, **1802**:39, **1851**:120,
        1902:39, **1912**:259
    statehood, **1803**:41
    10-hour workday, **1852**:122
    tornadoes, **1953**:383
    woman suffrage amendment defeat,

1922:289

Open Boat, The (book), **1898**:225

Open-Door Policy (China), **1900**:229, **1908**:248

Opening a Chestnut Burr (book), **1874**:172

"Open the Door, Richard" (song), **1947**:364

"Open Thy Lattice, Love" (song), **1844**:106

Open Wall (painting), **1953**:382

opera

first American, **1794**:28, **1910**:255–56

first house in North America, **1791**:24

first presented in America, xiii

first regular series of radio program broadcasts, **1927**:302

Safie composed, **1909**:252

See also Metropolitan Opera; *specific singers, other opera companies, and titles of works*

Operation Desert Storm, **1991**:487

ophthalmology book, first, **1823**:69

O Pioneers! (book), **1913**:264

Oppenheimer, J. Robert, **1954**:383, **1967**:419

Optic, Oliver (pseud. of William T. Adams), **1907**:247

optics, **1910**:255

Optimist's Daughter, The (book), **1972**:434

"optimum allocation of resources" theory, **1975**:442

optometry, **1910**:255

Oralloosa (play), **1832**:84

Orange Bars (painting), **1919**:281

Orange Bowl

first game played, **1935**:329

See also under SPORTS *in text for subsequent games played*

Orange County (Calif.), **1994**:500

Orantes, Manuel, **1975**:444

Oratorio Society of New York, **1873**:170

Orbach, Jerry, **1968**:423

Orchestra Hall (Chicago, Ill.), **1904**:240

Order of Carmelite Sisters, **1790**:22

Order of DeMolay, founding, **1919**:282

ordination of women

Episcopal bishops approve, **1976**:446

first Conservative rabbi, **1985**:470

first Episcopal priest, **1977**:448

first Episcopal priests (irregular), **1972**:433

first Presbyterian minister, **1956**:390

first rabbi (Conservative), **1985**:470

first rabbi (Reform), **1972**:433

Methodist Church, **1956**:390

Mormon rejection of, **1980**:456

Presbyterian Church, **1964**:410

Reformed Church allows, **1979**:453

Oregon

Crater Lake National Park, **1902**:234

direct primaries, **1904**:239

first settlement, **1811**:50

first settlement in north, **1836**:90

as first state to pass gasoline tax, **1919**:281

northern boundary set, **1846**:109

prohibition law, **1915**:267

state constitution, **1843**:103, **1857**:131

statehood, **1859**:135

territorial government, **1841**:99

territory established, **1848**:114

U.S.-British occupation agreement, **1827**:74

woman suffrage, **1912**:259

women's workday law, **1903**:237

Oregon City (Ore.), **1878**:181

Oregon State University, **1868**:158

Oregon Trail, The (book), **1849**:116

organ

electric, **1876**:177

pipeless, **1934**:325

organisms

patenting of, 487, 1991, **1980**:456

possibly oldest and largest discovered, **1992**:492

Organization of American States, **1948**:365

organized crime, **1890**:206, **1950**:372

organ transplantation, **1969**:425, **1982**:461, **1990**:485

Oriental Institute (Chicago), **1919**:281

Original Poems, Serious and Entertaining, **1801**:39

"Original Rag" (song), **1899**:227

Oriskany, Battle of, **1777**:3

Orlando (Fla.), NBA franchise, **1987**:477

Orleans Territory, **1804**:42

Ormandy, Eugene, **1980**:456, **1985**:470

O'Rourke, Jim, **1876**:177

Orphans of the Storm (movie), **1921**:287

Orr, Hugh, **1786**:16

orthodontia, **1895**:217

Ortiz, Carlos, **1962**:407, **1965**:414

Osage Indians, **1808**:46, **1808**:*46*

Osborn, Henry Fairfield, **1908**:249, **1935**:328

Oscar awards. *See* Academy of Motion Picture Arts and Sciences

Oscar Mayer & Co., **1888**:201

Osgood, Samuel, **1789**:20

Osheroff, Douglas C., **1996**:508

Osler, William, **1892**:210

Osmond (book), **1799**:35

Osmond, Donny and Marie, **1976**:446

Osnam, G. Bromley, **1944**:353, **1948**:367

"O Sole Mio" (song), **1899**:227

osteopathy, **1875**:173

O'Sullivan, Humphrey, **1899**:226

Osuna, Rafael, **1963**:409

Oswald, Lee Harvey, **1963**:407, **1964**:409

Oswego (N.Y.), **1777**:3

Oswego Training School for Primary Teachers, **1861**:141

Otey, James H., **1834**:88

Other America, The (book), **1963**:409

Other Girl, The (play), **1903**:238

Other Voices, Other Rooms (book), **1948**:368

Otis, Elisha G., **1852**:122, **1853**:124, **1857**:132, **1861**:141

Otis, Harrison G., **1882**:190, **1917**:275

Otis, James, **1783**:11

Otis, William S., **1839**:96

Otis Brothers, **1889**:203

Otis Elevator Co., **1900**:230

Otis Skinner as Colonel Bridan (painting), **1919**:281

O'Toole, Peter, **1962**:407

Ott, Mel, **1958**:396

Otterbein, Philip, **1789**:21, **1800**:37

Otterbein College, **1847**:113

Ouimet, Francis, **1913**:264, **1967**:420

Our American Cousin (play), **1858**:134

Our Boarding House (play), **1877**:179

Our Burden and Our Strength (book), **1864**:149

Our Country (book), **1885**:196

Our Dancing Daughters (movie), **1928**:306

"Our Day Will Come" (song), **1963**:408

Our Gang (book), **1971**:431

Our Miss Brooks (radio program), **1948**:368

Our Town (play), **1938**:*336*, **1938**:337

outboard motor, **1909**:253

Outcasts of Poker Flat, The (book), 1869, **1869**:161

Outcault, Richard, **1894**:216, **1902**:236

Outdoor Advertising Assn., **1891**:208

Outerbridge, Mary E., **1874**:172

Outlook, The (newspaper), **1870**:163

Out of Africa (movie), **1985**:470–71

"Over and Over" (song), **1965**:413

Overland Automobile Co., **1907**:246

"Over the Rainbow" (song), **1939**:339

"Over There" (song), **1917**:275

Over the Top (musical), **1917**:275

Ovington, Earl L., **1911**:259

Owen, John, **1890**:207

Owen, Laurence, **1961**:404

Owen, Robert, **1825**:71

Owen, Ruth Bryan, **1933**:320

Owen, Steve, **1964**:411

Owens, Jesse, **1936**:*331*, **1936**:332

Owens, Michael J., **1895**:217, **1943**:351

Owens-Illinois Glass Co., **1936**:330

Ox-Bow Incident, The (book), **1940**:342

Oxford University, first woman's honorary doctorate, **1925**:296

Oxnam, G. Bromley, **1963**:408

Oyster Gatherers of Cancale, The (painting), **1878**:181

ozone level depletion, **1991**:488, **1992**:492, **1995**:504

Ozzie and Harriet (radio program), **1944**:355

P

Paar, Jack, **1957**:394

Pacific (steamer), **1875**:175

Pacific Act, **1862**:143

Pacific Coast Borax Co., **1872**:167

Pacific Coast Intercollegiate Athletic Conference, **1915**:269

Pacific Island, cable, **1903**:236

Pacific Ocean

first nonstop balloon crossing, **1981**:458

first yachting race, **1906**:245

Pink Panther, The (movie), **1963**:409
Pinocchio (movie), **1940**:343
Pinocchio in Venice (book), **1991**:489
Pinsky, Robert, **1997**:513
Pin-Up Girl (movie), **1944**:355
Pinza, Ezio, **1949**:371, **1954**:385
Pioneer 5 (spacecraft), **1960**:400
Pioneer 10 (spacecraft), **1972**:433
Pioneer 11 (spacecraft), **1974**:440
Pioneers, The (book), **1823**:69
Pipe Dance, The (painting), **1879**:183
Pipe of Desire, The (opera), **1910**:256
Piper, William T., **1970**:427
pipe smoking, **1900**:232, **1977**:447
Pipes 'o' Pan at Zekesbury (book), **1888**:202
Pippin (musical), **1972**:434
Pique (play), **1875**:174
piracy, **1786**:16, **1793**:26, **1795**:29,
    1797:32
pistol
    automatic, **1911**:257
    revolving breech, **1835**:89, **1835**:*89*
"Pistol Packing Mama" (song), **1943**:351
Piston, Walter, **1928**:305, **1930**:312,
    1934:325, **1936**:331, **1938**:336,
    1944:353, **1947**:364, **1958**:396,
    1965:413, **1968**:422
Pit, The (book), **1903**:237
Pit, The (painting), **1946**:361
Pitcairn Field (Pa.), **1928**:304
Pitcher, Molly, **1778**:5, **1832**:83
Pitkin, Walter B., **1932**:319, **1953**:382
Pitts, John A. and Hiram A., **1837**:93
Pittsburgh (Pa.)
    Alcoa Building, **1953**:381
    almost destroyed by fire, **1845**:109
    first atomic power plant, **1954**:383
    first drive-in gas station, **1913**:263
    first national volleyball title, **1922**:290
    Forbes Field stadium, **1908**:250
    labor riots, **1877**:178–79
    nickelodeon, **1905**:242
    plane crash, **1994**:500
Pittsburgh Coal Consolidation Co.,
    1951:376
Pittsburgh Courier (newspaper), **1910**:256
Pittsburgh Gazette (newspaper), **1786**:17
Pittsburgh Pirates, **1894**:216, **1909**:253,
    1925:298, **1971**:432, **1979**:454
Pittsburgh Plate Glass Co., **1883**:191
Pittsburgh Reduction Co., **1888**:201
Pittsburgh Winter (painting), **1908**:249
Pittsfield (Mass.), **1903**:237
Pius VI, Pope, **1784**:14
plane crashes. *See* air disasters
"Plane Crazy" (animated cartoon),
    1928:306
Planned Parenthood Foundation,
    1914:265
Plant Forms (painting), **1915**:269
plastic, **1909**:252
Platoon (movie), **1986**:473
Plattsburgh (N.Y.), **1915**:267, **1946**:360
Playboy (magazine), **1953**:382
Player, Gary, **1961**:404, **1962**:407,
    1965:414, **1972**:435, **1974**:441,

1978:451
player-piano, **1876**:177, **1881**:188,
    1897:222
    music rolls, **1916**:271
    pneumatic, **1900**:231
Players Club (N.Y.C.), **1888**:202
Playground Association of America,
    1906:243
Play It Again Sam (play), **1969**:426
"Playmates" (song), **1889**:204
plays. *See* specific titles
Plaza Suite (play), **1968**:423
"Please Don't Go" (song), **1979**:453
"Please, Mister Postman" (song),
    1961:404
Pleasure of His Company, The (play),
    1958:396
"Pledge of Allegiance," **1892**:209
Plessy v. Ferguson, **1896**:219
Plimpton, James L., **1863**:146
PLO. *See* Palestinian Liberation Organi-
    zation
plow
    cast-iron, **1869**:159
    first with interchangeable parts,
        1819:62
    steel, **1837**:*93*
plug tobacco, **1900**:232
Plums on a Plate (painting), **1926**:299–300
plural marriage. *See* polygamy
Pluto (planet), discovered, **1930**:311
plutonium, **1940**:342, **1941**:345,
    1942:348
Plymouth (Mass.), ix
    first public execution, xiv
plywood, Douglas-fir, **1905**:241
pneumatic hammers, **1984**:214
Pocahontas (play), **1855**:129
Pocket Books, **1939**:339
pocket veto, **1929**:306
Poe, Edgar Allan
    "Cask of the Amontillado, The,"
        1846:111
    death of, **1849**:117
    edits *Southern Literary Messenger*,
        1835:89
    "Fall of the House of Usher, The,"
        1839:97
    "Masque of the Red Death, The,"
        1841:100
    "Murders in the Rue Morgue, The,"
        1841:100
    "Pit and the Pendulum, The,"
        1842:102
    "Purloined Letter, The," **1844**:106
    Raven and Other Poems, The, **1845**:109
    Tales, **1843**:104
    Tales of the Grotesque and Arabesque,
        1840:99
    Tamerlane and Other Poems, **1829**:78
Poems (book), **1836**:92, **1849**:116,
    1890:207, **1953**:382
Poems (Emerson book), **1847**:113
Poems (Moore collection), **1921**:287
Poems 1923–54 (book), **1954**:385
Poems for Our Children (book), **1830**:80

poet laureate, **1987**:476, **1990**:485,
    1991:488, **1992**:493, **1995**:505,
    1997:513
    first African American, **1993**:497
    first official U.S., **1986**:473
Poetry (magazine), **1913**:264, **1914**:266
    founding, **1912**:261
Poets and Poetry of America (book),
    1842:102
"Pogo" (comics), **1948**:367
Poindexter, John M., **1986**:471,
    1990:484
poinsettia plant, **1829**:78
Poinsett, Joel R., **1825**:71, **1829**:78
Point Four program, **1949**:369
Poitier, Sidney, **1959**:398
Poland, Reagan sanctions, **1981**:458
Polaroid camera, **1937**:333, **1947**:364,
    1963:408
Polaroid Corp., **1937**:333
pole vault, **1904**:240, **1912**:261,
    1927:303, **1963**:409, **1976**:447
Polhill, Robert, **1987**:474, **1990**:484
police
    Boston strike, **1919**:280
    Chicago identification bureau, 1884
    federal-law power, **1903**:236
    first uniforms, **1853**:125
    Gastonia (N.C.) strike violence,
        1929:307
    Los Angeles brutality charges,
        1992:490, **1992**:*491*
    random stoppage of motorists disal-
        lowed, **1979**:452
    St. Louis fingerprinting, **1904**:241
polio (infantile paralysis)
    case numbers, **1952**:378
    epidemic, **1916**:271, **1943**:351
    iron lung used, **1928**:305
    National Foundation for Infantile
        Paralysis formed, **1937**:334
    Roosevelt (F. D.) stricken, **1921**:286
    Sabin vaccine, **1957**:393
    Salk vaccine, **1953**:381, **1954**:384,
        1954:*385*
    vaccine effectiveness, **1964**:410
    virus isolated, **1914**:266
Polish National Catholic Church of
    America (Scranton), **1897**:222
political parties
    symbols, **1870**:*162*, **1870**:163,
        1874:171
    Washington warns against, **1796**:30
    See also specific parties
political scientist, **1858**:134
Politician Outwitted, The (play), **1789**:21
"Polka Dots and Moonbeams" (song),
    1940:342
Polk, James K.
    claims Oregon for U.S., **1845**:107
    death of, **1849**:116
    delivers war message re Mexico,
        1846:109
    elected House Speaker, **1835**:88
    elected president, **1844**:105
    governor of Tennessee, **1839**:96

Reagan proposes constitutional amendment allowing, **1982**:462

Senate rejects proposed constitutional amendment, **1984**:467

"silent contemplation" bill (N.J.), **1982**:462

"silent contemplation" ruled uncon-stitutional, **1983**:465, **1985**:470

student meetings disallowed, **1980**:456

unconstitutionality decisions, **1962**:405–6, **1963**:408

unconstitutionality reaffirmed, **1984**:467, **1985**:470, **1992**:492

Preakness Stakes, **1873**:170 (*see also under* SPORTS *in text for subsequent years*)

Predator, The (movie), **1987**:477

predestination, **1877**:179

Preface to Politics, A (book), **1913**:264

Prefontaine, Steve, **1975**:444

pregnancy and childbirth

fetal hazards ruling, **1991**:487

first successful cesarean, **1794**:28

maternity leave ruling, **1974**:440

surrogate motherhood case, **1989**:481

Prejudices (book), **1919**:281

Preminger, Otto, **1986**:473

Prendergast, Maurice, **1899**:227, **1910**:256

Preparedness (painting), **1968**:422

Preparedness Day Parade (San Fran-cisco), **1916**:270

Presbyterian Church, **1891**:208, **1892**:209

African American named moderator, **1973**:437

African American woman named moderator, **1976**:446

in Confederacy, **1861**:141

conservatives form National Presby-terian Church, **1973**:438

doctrinal schism, **1922**:289

first, xiii

first general assembly, **1789**:21

first ordained woman minister, **1956**:390

first woman named moderator, **1967**:419

Fosdick heresy charges, **1924**:294, **1925**:296

mergers, **1958**:395, **1982**:462, **1983**:465

Presbyterian Church in the U.S.A., **1982**:462, **1983**:465

Presbyterian Church of America, **1936**:331

preschool

in Boston schools, **1816**:59

first nursery school, **1827**:74

Prescott, Samuel, **1777**:4

Prescott, Samuel C., **1962**:405

Prescott, William, **1795**:29

Prescott, William H., **1843**:104, **1847**:113, **1859**:136

presidency

damages exemption, **1982**:460

first annual message to Congress, **1801**:38

first commission, **1794**:27

first regular news conference, **1913**:262

first third-term, **1940**:341

first to address Hungarian parlia-ment, **1989**:480

first to leave country while in office, **1906**:243

pocket veto, **1929**:306

salary, **1873**:169, **1874**:171, **1909**:251

succession, **1792**:25

widow's pension, **1870**:163

presidential elections

Adams (J.Q.)-Jackson lack of electoral majority, **1824**:69

biggest landslide of century, **1964**:409

electors cast ballots, **1789**:20

first radio program broadcast of returns, **1920**:283

first woman candidate, **1872**:167

first woman vice-presidential candi-date of major party, **1984**:466

Hayes-Tilden dispute, **176**:175

House decides deadlocked election, **1824**:69, **1825**:71

Jefferson-Burr tie, **1800**:36

Jefferson selected by House, **1801**:38

separate candidates for president and vice president, **1800**:36, **1803**:41

Presidential Succession Act, **1792**:25, **1886**:196, **1947**:363

Presidio of San Francisco, **1776**:2

Presley, Elvis, **1954**:385, **1956**:*390*, **1977**:448

commemorative postage stamp, **1992**:491

press. *See* newspapers; *specific publications*

press freedom, xiii, **1805**:43

pressing machine, steam-operated, **1909**:252

Preston, Richard, **1994**:500

Preston, Robert, **1957**:394, **1962**:407, **1987**:477

Preston, Samuel, **1833**:85

"Pretty Baby" (song), **1916**:272

"Pretty Girl Is Like a Melody, A" (song), **1919**:281

Pretty Woman (movie), **1990**:485

Primerica, **1993**:496

Price, Leontyne, **1957**:393

Price, Nick, **1992**:494, **1994**:502

Price, Vincent, **1994**:501

price controls, **1971**:430, **1973**:436

American Revolution, **1776**:2

crude oil decontrolled, **1979**:452

domestic oil and gasoline lifted, **1981**:458

ended, **1974**:439

restored on gasoline, **1977**:447

price fixing, **1921**:286, **1996**:507

Price Is Right, The (television program), **1957**:394

Priesand, Sally J., **1972**:433

primary elections

direct, **1900**:230, **1903**:236, **1904**:239

first statewide (Wis.), **1906**:254

Prince and the Pauper, The (book), **1882**:190

Prince Karl (play), **1886**:198

Prince of the House of David, The (book), **1855**:129

Princess Pat (musical), **1915**:269

Princeton (N.J.), **1783**:11

Princeton, Battle of, **1777**:3

Princeton Review (magazine), **1825**:72

Princeton University

first chemistry chair, **1795**:29

first indoor collegiate polo title, **1922**:290

football, **1869**:161, **1873**:170, **1875**:*174*

founding, xii

Institute for Advanced Study, **1930**:311, **1939**:338

nuclear-fusion research, **1993**:497

reopens, **1782**:11

theological seminary, **1812**:53

track and field, **1876**:177

Wilson (W.) presidency, **1902**:235

Principles and Practice of Medicine, The (book), **1892**:210

Principles of Psychology, The (book), **1890**:206

printing-and-folding machine, **1876**:177

printing press

automatic stereotype plate-casting machine, **1900**:231

cylinder and flatbed, **1844**:106

manufacturer, **1823**:69

Prioress (Horse), **1857**:132

Prisoner of Second Avenue, The (play), **1971**:431

Prisoner of Zenda, The (book), **1895**:218

Prisoners from the Front (painting), **1866**:154

prison riots

Attica (N.Y.), **1971**:430

New Mexico State Prison, **1980**:457

prisons

debtor abolished, **1798**:33

Leavenworth (Kans.), **1891**:207

reform, **1870**:164

Pritchett, Henry S., **1939**:339

Pritzer, Abram N., **1986**:472

privateers, **1793**:26

private schools

federal aid advocacy, **1991**:488

nondiscrimination mandated, **1976**:446

tax exemptions linked with racial integration, **1983**:456

See also parochial schools

Prizzi's Honor (book), **1982**:462

"procaine" (novocain), **1905**:241

Procter, William C., **1934**:324

Procter & Gamble Co., **1837**:93, **1878**:181, **1893**:212

Crisco shortening, **1911**:257

layoffs and closures, **1993**:496

Professional Air Traffic Controllers Assn., strike, **1981**:458, **1982**:461

Professional Bowlers Association. *See* SPORTS *in text for yearly titles*

Professional Golfers Assn.
    organized, **1916**:272
    tournament, **1922**:290
    See also under SPORTS *in text for subsequent years*

"Professor Tigwissel's Burglar Alarm" (cartoon), **1875**:174

Progress and Poverty (book), **1879**:183

Progressive Party, **1911**:257, **1912**:259, **1924**:293

Progress of Civilization (book), **1936**:331

Progresso, Il (newspaper), **1880**:185

prohibition
    Eighteenth Amendment, **1917**:274, **1918**:277, **1919**:279, **1920**:283, **1931**:314
    Eighteenth Amendment repeal, **1933**:320
    interstate commerce restrictions, **1913**:262
    state laws, **1881**:186, **1884**:193, **1889**:202, **1908**:249, **1909**:251, **1913**:262, **1914**:265, **1915**:267, **1916**:270, **1918**:277
    Treasury Department bureau, **1927**:301

Promenade (painting), **1926**:299

Promise Keepers, **1997**:512

Promises (book), **1957**:394

Promises, Promises (play), **1968**:423

Promontory Point (Utah), **1869**

property tax, **1798**:33, **1799**:34

Pro Rodeo Hall of Champions (Colorado Springs), **1979**:454

proteins, **1984**:467

Protestant Episcopal Church of America. *See* Episcopal Church

protons, **1943**:351

Proulx, E. Annie, **1994**:500

Providence (R.I.), **1872**:168, **1878**:182, **1882**:190, **1888**:201
    streetcar service, **1873**:170
    Vose Art Gallery, **1841**:100

Providence Journal (newspaper), **1820**:65

Provincetown (Mass.) Players, **1915**:269

Provoost, Samuel, **1786**:16

Provo University (Utah), **1875**:173

Prowse, Juliet, **1996**:508

Proxmire, William, **1987**:474

Prudden, T. Mitchell, **1924**:294

Prudential Friendly Society, **1875**:173

Prudential Insurance Co., **1875**:173

Prusiner, Stanley B., **1997**:511

"P.S. I Love You" (song), **1934**:325

Public Credit Act, **1869**:159

public defender, **1913**:262

public employees
    eight-hour day, **1906**:243, **1912**:260
    federal cutbacks, **1993**:496
    federal government shutdowns, **1995**:502
    loyalty oath upheld, **1947**:363

minimum wage, **1906**:243

Social Security amendment, **1983**:463

suits and claims against, **1982**:460

public health
    Centers for Disease Control, **1975**:442
    compulsory vaccination, **1905**:241
    county departments, **1911**:258
    first local health board, **1792**:25
    Massachusetts board, **1869**:160
    nurses, **1912**:261
    plant quarantine law, **1912**:260
    U.S. service, **1912**:261
    See also epidemics

Public Health Service, **1798**:34, **1912**:261

public land
    Alaskan national park system, **1978**:449, **1980**:456
    congressional sale of, **1800**:36
    Homestead Act repealed, **1976**:445
    Reclamation Act, **1902**:234
    Teapot Dome scandal, **1924**:293, **1927**:301, **1928**:303, **1929**:306
    See also national parks

Public Lands Act, **1820**:65

Public Occurrences (newspaper), xiii

public radio, first broadcast, **1920**:285

Public Utility Holding Company Act, **1935**:328

Public Works Administration, **1933**:320

Publishers Weekly (magazine), **1872**:168

publishing
    booksellers association, **1801**:39
    criminals' sales of own stories upheld, **1991**:489
    first book fair, **1802**:40
    first Book-of-the-Month Club selection, **1926**:300
    first books, xiv
    first business periodical, **1839**:96
    first children's magazine, **1789**:21
    first cookbook, **1796**:31
    first crossword puzzle book, **1924**:295
    first dental journal, **1839**:97
    first dictionary, **1788**:19
    first illustrated weekly, **1842**:102
    first magazine, xiv
    first newspapers, xiii
    first novel, **1789**:21
    first popular monthly, **1833**:86
    first radio broadcasting magazine, **1908**:250
    first specialized medical journal, **1844**:106
    Harvard Classics "five-foot shelf" of books, **1909**:252
    Literary Guild, **1926**:300
    Little Blue Books, **1919**:281
    mergers and acquisitions, **1988**:479, **1989**:481, **1991**:489
    Murdoch sales, **1991**:489
    music, **1790**:23
    personal finances magazines, **1992**:493
    reading primers, **1873**:170

speller, **1783**:12

See also newspapers; *specific titles*

Puccini, Giacomo, **1910**:256

Puck (magazine), **1877**:179

Pudd'n Head Wilson (book), **1894**:216

Pueblo (Colo.), **1920**:285

Pueblo (intelligence ship), **1968**:421

Puerto Rico, **1898**:224
    Commonwealth Act, **1950**:372
    commonwealth status, **1952**:378
    first elected governor, **1947**:363
    hotel fire, **1986**:474
    hurricane, **1900**:231
    as unorganized U.S. territory, **1900**:230
    as U.S. territory, **1917**:274
    vote to remain U.S. commonwealth, **1993**:496

"Puff the Magic Dragon" (song), **1963**:408

Pulaski, Casimir, **1779**:6

Pulitzer, Joseph, **1878**:181, **1880**:185, **1883**:192, **1911**:259, **1955**:388
    Columbia School of Journalism endowment, **1903**:237, **1912**:261

Pulitzer, Joseph, Jr., **1993**:498

Pulitzer Prizes
    first African American woman winner, **1950**:374
    first awards, **1917**:275
    Morrison as recipient, **1988**:*478*

Pullman, George M., **1858**:134, **1863**:146, **1864**:149, **1868**:157

Pullman Palace Car Co., **1867**:155

Pulp Fiction (movie), **1994**:501

Pumpelly, Raphael, **1866**:154

Pupin, Michael I., **1896**:219, **1984**:214

Purcell, Edward N., **1952**:378, **1997**:512

Purdue University, **1869**:160

Pure Food and Drug Act, **1848**:115, **1905**:241, **1906**:243

Puritan, The (sculpture), **1885**:195

Purple Heart medal, **1782**:11

"Purple People Eater, The" (song), **1958**:396

Pursley, Barbara, **1962**:407

Pusey, Nathan M., **1953**:382

Pussey, Joshua, **1892**:210

Putnam (play), **1844**:107

Putnam, George P., **1930**:313

Putnam, Herbert, **1899**:226, **1955**:388

Putnam, Rufus, **1788**:18

Putnam's Monthly (magazine), **1853**:125

"Put On Your Old Grey Bonnet" (song), **1909**:252

Putting It Together (play), **1993**:498

"Put Your Arms Around Me, Honey" (song), **1910**:256

"Put Your Hand in Mine" (song), **1971**:431

"Put Your Head on My Shoulder" (song), **1959**:398

Puzo, Mario, **1969**:426

Pyle, Charles C., **1926**:300

Pyle, Ernie, **1944**:354, **1945**:357

Pyle, Howard, **1911**:259

Pynchon, Thomas, **1973**:438
Pyrene Manufacturing Co., **1905**:241

Q

Quadrille (play), **1952**:379
Quaker Girl, The (play), **1911**:259
Quaker Oats Co., **1901**:232
Quakers, xiii
quantum mechanics, **1981**:458
quarks, **1990**:485
Quartering Act, ix
Queen, Ellery, **1929**:308
Queen, Jason, **1997**:513
Queen Anne's War, ix
Queen for a Day (radio program), **1945**:358
Queen High (play), **1926**:300
Queensborough Bridge (N.Y.C.), **1909**:252
"Que Será, Será" (song), **1956**:390
Quezon, Manuel, **1935**:327
Quidor, John, **1855**:129
Quiet Man, The (movie), **1952**:379
Quimby, Harriet, **1911**:259
Quincy (Ill.), **1878**:181
Quintet IV (musical composition), **1985**:470
Quintex Group, **1989**:482
Quiz Kids, The (radio program), **1940**:343
Quiz Kids, The (television program), **1949**:371
Quizon, Manuel, **1944**:353
quoit pitching, **1919**:282
quota system. *See* affirmative action

R

Rabbit Is Rich (book), **1981**:459
Rabbit Redux (book), **1971**:431
Rabbit, Run (book), **1960**:401
Rabe, David, **1976**:446
Rabi, Isidor I., **1937**:334, **1944**:353
race riots
    Birmingham (Ala.), **1963**:408
    Detroit, **1967**:418–19, **1967**:*418*
    East St. Louis (Ill.) riot, **1917**:274
    Los Angeles, **1871**:164, **1965**:412, **1992**:490, **1992**:*491*
    Memphis, **1866**:153
    Newark, **1967**:418
    New Orleans, **1866**:153
    Tulsa (Okla.), **1921**:288
Rachmaninoff, Sergei, **1943**:351
Racine (Wis.) Confectioner's Machinery Corp., **1908**:249
radar, **1930**:311, **1947**:364, **1954**:383
    first space laboratory, **1994**:500
    superheterodyne circuit, **1918**:278
    weather, **1945**:357
Radcliffe College, **1882**:189, **1894**:215
radio astronomy, **1932**:318
radio broadcasting
    baseball rights payment, **1983**:465
    Catholic Hour, **1930**:312
    Cities Service concerts, **1926**:300
    country music popularity (N.Y.C.), **1992**:493

family audience, **1930**:*312*
federal commission created, **1927**:302
first *Amos 'n Andy* show, **1928**:306
first Broadway show, **1922**:290
first coast-to-coast hookup, **1924**:295
first magazine about, **1908**:250
first major network, **1926**:300
first music program, **1907**:247
first news broadcasts, **1920**:284
first of voice and music, **1906**:244
first presidential election returns, **1920**:283
first presidential message, **1922**:288
first presidential message designed for, **1923**:291
first public radio program, **1920**:285
first radio minister, **1928**:305
first regular opera series, **1927**:302
first religious service, **1921**:287
first sports coverage, **1920**:285
first studio audience, **1922**:290
first World Series play-by-play bulletins, 287
FM, **1933**:322, **1940**:343
frequencies, **1937**:334, **1992**:492
"Grand Ole Opry," **1925**:297
networks, **1926**:300, **1927**:303
news commentary, **1929**:308
news programs, **1928**:306
New York Philharmonic regular Sunday program, **1929**:308
Nielsen ratings, **1941**:345
superheterodyne circuit, **1918**:278
symphony orchestras, **1926**:299, **1927**:302, **1929**:308
two-way (air-ground) contact, **1911**:257
War of the Worlds scare, **1938**:337
Radio City Music Hall (N.Y.C.), **1932**:319
Radio Corporation of America (RCA)
    founding, **1919**:280
    General Electric acquires, **1985**:469
    television sets, **1966**:415
radio immunoassay, **1977**:448
radio paging service, **1950**:375
radio sets
    installment buying, **1929**:307
    numbers owned, **1924**:295
    Sarnoff invention, **1915**:268
    tuning device, **1916**:272
radio telescopes, **1937**:334
radio waves, **1906**:243, **1932**:318
Raft, The (painting), **1830**:80
Rafter, Patrick, **1997**:513
Raftsmen Playing Cards (painting), **1847**:113
"Rag Doll" (song), **1964**:410
Rage to Live, A (book), **1949**:370
Ragged Dick (book), 1869, **1867**:156, **1869**:161
Raging Bull (movie), **1980**:457
ragtime, **1911**:258, **1912**:261
Ragtime (book), **1975**:444
Ragtime (musical), **1997**:513
"Ragtime Cowboy Joe" (song), **1912**:261
Rahal, Bobby, **1986**:474

Rahman, Sheikh Omar Abdel, **1993**:498
Raiders of the Lost Ark (movie), **1981**:459
railroad accidents, **1904**:241, **1918**:279, **1993**:499
    bridge collapses (Ohio), **1876**:177
    Cannonball Express crash, **1901**:233
    commuter train (Woodbridge, N.J.), **1951**:377
    first fatal, **1832**:83
Railroad Labor Board, **1920**:283, **1926**:298
Railroad of Love (play), **1887**:200
Railroad Retirement Act, **1935**:328
railroads
    Amtrak begins operations, **1971**:430
    antitrust, **1897**:221, **1902**:234, **1912**:261
    automatic signals, **1880**:184, **1882**:189
    Boston linked to Montreal/Great Lakes area, **1851**:120
    Buffalo to Chicago, **1882**:189
    chair cars, **1875**:173
    collective bargaining, **1939**:338
    collective freight rates denied, **1980**:456
    commuter lines smoking ban (N.Y.), **1988**:478
    Conrail initiated, **1985**:469
    Conrail sold to private investor, **1987**:475
    coupler patent, **1873**:170
    diesel, **1934**:324
    diesel electric locomotive, **1924**:293
    dining car introduced, **1868**:157
    electric, **1930**:311
    electric lamps in trains, **1905**:241
    elevated, **1878**:181, **1892**:210
    federal aid, **1976**:445
    federal control, **1917**:274, **1918**:277
    first American, **1830**:79
    first bridge across Mississippi, **1854**:127
    first chartered, **1826**:73
    first crossing over Mississippi, **1855**:128
    first East-to-Chicago through train, **1852**:122
    first experimental steam locomotive, **1824**:70
    first in Maine, **1833**:85
    first interstate, **1833**:85
    first inter-urban in New England, **1856**:130
    first iron bridge, **1845**:107
    first locomotive built in U.S., **1830**:79, **1830**:*80*
    first locomotive to operate in U.S., **1829**:78
    first locomotive with cab, **1836**:91
    first primitive, **1795**:29
    first Pullman car trip, **1859**:135
    first Pullman sleeping cars, **1858**:134
    first refrigerated car, **1866**:154
    first specially constructed sleeper, **1864**:149

Rhinemann Exchange, The (book), **1974**:441

"Rhinestone Cowboy" (song), **1975**:443

R. H. Macy & Co., bankruptcy filing, **1992**:491

Rhoads Theater (Boyertown, Pa.), **1908**:250

Rhode Island
  American Revolution, **1776**:2, **1777**:3, **1777**:4, **1778**:4
  emancipation statutes, **1784**:13
  Episcopal bishops, **1911**:258
  Mt. Hope Bridge, **1929**:308
  ratifies Constitution, **1790**:22
  rejects Constitution, **1788**:18
  religious freedom grant, xiii
  School of Design, **1880**:184
  wage and price controls, **1776**:2
  woman suffrage law, **1917**:274

Rhodes, John, **1975**:442

Rhodes scholarship, first African American recipient, **1907**:247

Rhythm Boys (musical group), **1927**:302

"Rhythm of the Rain" (song), **1963**:408

Rice, Alice Hegan, **1901**:234

Rice, Anne, **1990**:485

Rice, Dan, **1844**:107, **1900**:231

Rice, E. E., **1874**:172

Rice, Grantland, **1954**:386

Rice, Thomas D., **1828**:76, **1860**:139

Rice, Tim, **1971**:431

Rice, William M., **1912**:261

rice production, **1823**:68, **1861**:141

Rice University, **1912**:261

Rich, Charlie, **1995**:504

Richard Carvel (book), **1899**:227

Richard Carvel (play), **1900**:231

Richard Hurdis (book), **1838**:95

Richard III (play), **1849**:117

Richards, Dickinson W. Jr., **1956**:390

Richards, Laura E., **1917**:275

Richards, Theodore W., **1914**:266

Richards, Vincent, **1959**:399

Richards, Vinnie, **1926**:300

Richardson, Elliot, **1973**:436

Richardson, Henry H., **1886**:197

Richardson, Robert C., **1996**:508

Rich Man, Poor Man (book), **1970**:428

Richmond (Va.)
  British occupation, **1781**:8
  Civil War damage, **1865**:*151*
  Roman Catholic bishop, **1926**:299
  school desegregation plan ruled unconstitutional, **1973**:437
  streetcars, **1884**:194
  trolley system, **1887**:199

Richmond, Bill, **1805**:43

Richmond Whig (newspaper), **1824**:70

Richter, Burton, **1976**:446

Richter, Charles F., **1985**:470

Rickard, Tex, **1929**:309

Rickenbacker, Eddie
  death of, **1973**:436–37
  Indianapolis Speedway controlling interest, **1926**:300
  survives after forced down in Pacific,

1942:350
  World War I aviation feats, **1918**:276

Ricketts, Howard T., **1906**:243

Rickey, Branch, **1919**:282, **1959**:398

Rickover, Hyman, **1986**:472

Ride, Sally K., **1982**:461

Riders of the Purple Sage (book), **1912**:261

Ridgway, Matthew B., **1952**:378, **1993**:496

Ridgway, Robert, **1929**:308

Riegger, Wallingford, **1961**:404

rifles, repeating, **1884**:193

rifles tournaments, **1874**:172

Riggs, Bobby, **1939**:340, **1941**:346, **1995**:505

rights. *See* Bill of Rights; civil rights; *specific rights*

right-to-die cases, **1990**:485, **1996**:508

Riis, Jacob A., **1890**:207, **1892**:211, **1901**:234, **1903**:237

Riker, A. L., **1900**:231

Riley, James Whitcomb, **1883**:192, **1888**:202, **1900**:231

Rimes, LeAnn, **1996**:508

Rinehart, Mary Roberts, **1908**:250, **1909**:252, **1916**:272, **1917**:275, **1922**:289

Ring, The (book), **1980**:457

"Ring de Banjo" (song), **1851**:121

Ringling Bros., **1907**:247

Ringling Brothers Barnum & Bailey Circus, **1956**:390

Ringling Museum of Art (Sarasota), **1930**:312

Rinker, Al, **1927**:302

Rin Tin Tin (radio), **1930**:313

Rio Bravo (movie), **1959**:398

Rio de Janeiro Conference, **1942**:347, **1992**:490

Rio de Janeiro, Treaty of, **1947**:363

Rio Grande Industries, **1988**:478

riots
  anti-abolition, **1834**:86
  anti-British (N.Y.C.), **1849**:117
  anti-draft (N.Y.C.), **1863**:145
  labor, **1874**:171, **1877**:178–79
  Tompkins Square (N.Y.C.), **1874**:171
  See also prison riots; race riots

Riotte, C. C., **1904**:240

Ripken, Cal, Jr., **1995**:505

Ripley, Alexandra, **1991**:489

Ripley, Dan, **1976**:447

Ripley, Robert L., **1918**:279

Ripley's Believe It or Not (radio), **1930**:313

Rip Van Winkle (opera), **1850**:119, **1920**:284

Rip van Winkle (play), **1865**:152

"Rise" (song), **1979**:453

Rise and Fall of the Third Reich, The (book), **1960**:401

Rise of Silas Lapham, The (book), **1885**:196

Rise, Progress, and Termination of the American Revolution (book), **1805**:43

Rising of a Thunderstorm, The (painting), **1804**:42

Rising Sun, The (book), **1970**:428

Ritchard, Cyril, **1957**:394, **1958**:396

Ritchie, Lionel, **1985**:*470*

Ritchie, Willie, **1912**:262

Rite Aid, **1995**:503

Rittenhouse, David, **1785**:15, **1792**:25, **1796**:30

Ritter, Joseph E., **1946**:360, **1960**:401

Ritter, Tex, **1974**:441

Ritty, James and John, **1879**:182

Ritz, The (play), **1975**:444

River, The (painting), **1940**:342

Rivera, Chita, **1993**:498

Rivera, Diego, **1933**:322

Rivers, Larry, **1954**:385

Riverside Church (N.Y.C.), **1931**:315

Rivers to the Sea (book), **1915**:269

rivets, **1794**:28

R. J. Reynolds-Nabisco merger, **1985**:469

RJR Nabisco, **1988**:474

Roach, Hal, **1992**:493

Roach, John, **1887**:199

Road Ahead, The (book), **1995**:505

road map, first, **1789**:21

Road Roller (painting), **1909**:252

roads and highways
  Cumberland Road, **1806**:44, **1811**:51, **1818**:62
  Great National Pike, **1840**:98
  interstate highways, **1955**:387, **1956**:389
  Knoxville Road, **1791**:23
  last stretch of Interstate 80 completed, **1986**:472
  Philadelphia-Lancaster Turnpike, **1790**:22
  speed limit at 20 miles-per-hour, **1904**:239
  speed limit at 55 miles-per-hour, **1974**:440, **1995**:502
  speed limit at 65 miles-per-hour, **1987**:475
  transcontinental highway promoted, **1913**:262
  See also streets

Road to Rio, The (movie), **1947**:365

Road to Singapore, The (movie), **1940**:343

Roanoke Island (N.C.) Settlement, ix

Roan Stallion (book), **1925**:297

Robards, Jason, **1960**:401, **1962**:407, **1964**:411

robbery. *See* theft and robbery

Robbins, Betty, **1955**:388

Robbins, Frederic C., **1954**:384

Robbins, Harold, **1949**:370, **1961**:404, **1969**:426, **1971**:431, **1977**:448, **1997**:513

Robbins, Jerome, **1950**:373, **1958**:396, **1989**:482

Robbins, Kelly, **1995**:505

Robbins, Martin, **1983**:465

Robert, Henry M., **1876**:177

Robert, Kenneth, **1930**:312

Roberta (movie), **1935**:329

Robert E. Lee (steamboat), **1870**:163

Roberts, Benjamin T., **1860**:138

Roberts, Brigham A., **1900**:230

first session of National Council, **1852:**123
first Texas bishop, **1848:**115
first U.S.-born saint, **1975:**443
first U.S. citizen canonized, **1946:**360
forbids only priest in Congress to seek reelection, **1980:**456
liturgical calendar, **1969:**425
mass in English, **1963:**408, **1964:**410
meat abstinence rules softened, **1966:**416
missionaries, **1888:**201
Missionary Sisters of the Sacred Heart, **1880:**184
New York City archbishop, **1902:**235, **1939:**339, **1984:**467
papal encyclical, **1995:**504
papal U.S. visits, **1993:**497, **1995:**504
Paulist Fathers, **1858:**134
Philadelphia archbishop, **1918:**278
radio broadcast, **1930:**312
Richmond bishop, **1926:**299
St. Louis archbishop, **1903:**237
St. Patrick's Cathedral (N.Y.C.) begun, **1858:**134
St. Patrick's Cathedral (N.Y.C.) dedicated, **1910:**255
St. Paul (Minn.) Cathedral, **1907:**247
saints, **1969:**425
San Francisco archbishop, **1915:**269
Santa Fe (N.M.) archbishop, **1875:**174
Sisters of Charity, **1963:**408
Sisters of St. Francis, **1889:**204
Sisters of the Blessed Sacrament for Indians and Colored People, **1891:**208
Society of Jesus, **1889:**204
U.S. resumes Vatican relations, **1984:**466
See also specific orders
Romancing the Stone (movie), **1984:**468
Roman Hat Mystery, The (book), **1929:**308
Romberg, Sigmund, **1917:**274, **1921:**287, **1924:**294, **1926:**299, **1928:**305, **1945:**357
Rome Haul (book), **1929:**308
Romero, Cesar, **1994:**501
Romney, George, **1995:**504
Romulus (Mich.), **1987:**477
Room in Brooklyn (painting), **1932:**319
Room Service (movie), **1938:**337
Roosa, Stuart A., **1995:**504
Roosevelt, Alice Lee, **1906:**243
Roosevelt, Edith K. C., **1948:**366
Roosevelt, Eleanor, **1933:**320, **1939:**339, **1945:**357, **1946:**359, **1962:**405
Roosevelt, Franklin D., **1935:**327, **1936:**330, **1938:**335, **1939:**338, **1940:**341, **1941:**344, **1941:**345, **1942:**347, **1943:**350, **1943:**351, **1944:**353
as Assistant Secretary of the Navy, **1913:**262
dies suddenly (Warm Springs, Ga.), **1945:**355, **1945:**356

elected president, **1932:**317, **1932:***321*
fireside chat, **1933:**320
as governor of New York, **1928:**303
New Deal measures, **1933:**320
New York state senator, **1910:**254
100-days measures, **1933:**320
as polio patient, **1921:**286
Supreme-Court packing plan, **1937:**332
Roosevelt, Hilborne L., **1876:**177
Roosevelt, Theodore
antitrust, **1901:**232, **1902:**234
assassination attempt on, **1912:**260
as Assistant Secretary of Navy, **1897:**221
"big stick" cartoon, **1904:***239*
as Civil Service commissioner, **1889:**203
conservationism, **1908:**248
death of, **1919:**280
defeated for presidency, **1912:**259
elected to full presidential term, 239
invites African American B.T. Washington to White House, **1901:**234
Monroe Doctrine corollary, **1904:**239
Mt. Rushmore sculpture of, **1939:**339
Nobel Peace Prize, **1905:**243
Rough Riders command, **1898:**223, **1898:***224*
Russo-Japanese War mediation, **1905:**241
succeeds to presidency, **1901:**232
teddy bear as symbol, **1903:**238
Roosevelt Dam (Ariz.), **1911:**257
Roosevelt Raceway (Westbury, N.Y.), **1988:**479
Root, Elihu, **1912:**269
Root, George F., **1853:**125
Root, John W., **1873:**170
Roots (book), **1976:**446
Roots (television miniseries), **1977:**449
Root-Takahira agreement, **1908:**248
rope, wire, **1869:**159
"Ropin' the Wind" (song), **1992:**493
Rorem, Ned, **1975:**443
Rosalie (play), **1928:**306
"Rosalie" (song), **1937:**334
"Rosary, The" (song), **1898:**225
Rosburg, Bob, **1959:**399
Rose, Billy, **1966:**417
Rose, David, **1990:**485
Rose, Mauri, **1941:**346, **1947:**365, **1948:**368
Rose, Pete, **1978:**451, **1985:**471, **1989:**483, **1990:**486
Rose, Ralph, **1909:**253
Rose, Thomas, **1801:**39
Rose Bowl
first annual game, **1916:**272
first game played, **1902:**236
See also under SPORTS *in text for subsequent games played*
Rosebud River, Battle of, **1876:**176
Rosedale (play), **1863:**146
Rose Marie (operetta), **1924:**294

"Rose-Marie" (song), **1924:**294
Rosemary's Baby (book), **1967:**419
Rosenberg, Israel, **1940:**342
Rosenberg, Julius and Ethel, **1951:**376, **1953:**380, **1953:***381*
Rosenbloom, Maxie, **1930:**313
Rosenquist, James A., **1965:**413
Rosenwald, Julius, **1910:**255, **1932:**318
"Rose of Killarney, The" (song), **1876:**177
"Roses Are Red, My Love" (song), **1962:**406
"Roses of Picardy" (song), **1916:**272
Rose Tattoo, The (movie), **1955:**388
Rosewall, Ken, **1956:**391, **1970:**429
Ross, Alex, **1907:**247
Ross, Barney, **1933:**323, **1935:**329
Ross, Diana, **1972:**434
Ross, Harold W., **1925:**297
Ross, Nellie Tayloe, **1924:**293, **1933:**320
Rossini, Gioacchino, **1819:**63
Rossner, Judith L., **1975:**444
Rosten, Leo, **1997:**513
Rotary International, **1905:**240, **1987:**474
Rotblat, Joseph, **1995:**502
Roth, Philip, **1969:**426, **1971:**431, **1981:**459, **1986:**473, **1990:**485
Rothafel, Samuel L. (Roxy), **1936:**332
Rothko, Mark, **1945:**357, **1948:**367, **1954:**385, **1970:**428
Roth v. United States, **1957:**392
rotogravure sections, **1914:**266
Roughing It (book), **1872:**168
Rough Riders, **1898:**223, **1898:***224*
Rous, Peyton, **1910:**255, **1966:**416
Rouse, James W., **1996:**507
Route 66 (television program), **1960:**402
Routis, Andre, **1928:**306
Rowan, Dan, **1968:**423
Rowe, J., **1872:**168
rowing, **1879:**183, **1895:**218, **1899:**228, **1947:**365
Championship of America race, **1859:**136
Child's Cup race, **1879:**183
competitive, **1811:**51
first Blackwell Cup race, **1927:**303
first eight-oared shell race, **1900:**231
first intercollegiate race, **1852:**123
first intercollegiate regatta, **1859:**136
first regatta, **1848:**115
first U.S. Henley winner, **1914:**267
first woman coxswain of men's crew, **1936:**332
Harvard beats Yale, **1855:**129
Henley Regatta, **1878:**182
Men's and Women's Intercollegiate, **1985:**471
Rowing Association of American Colleges, **1871:**166
Rowland, F. Sherwood, **1995:**504
"Row, Row, Row Your Boat" (song), **1852:**123, **1912:**261
Rowson, Susanna H., **1791:**24, **1795:**30
Roxbury (Mass.), **1874:**172, **1887:**199

public kindergarten, **1873**:170
Roman Catholic archbishop,
   1903:237
school integration, **1980**:456
stockyards, **1872**:168
tornadoes, **1896**:221, **1927**:303
Wainwright Theater, **1890**:206
World's Fair, **1904**:239
zoo, **1921**:288
St. Louis Americans (baseball), **1886**:198
St. Louis Americans, **1885**:196, **1887**:200
St. Louis Art Museum, **1904**:240
"St. Louis Blues" (song), **1914**:266
St. Louis Cardinals (baseball)
   batting record, **1924**:295
   farm system, **1919**:282
   World Series wins, **1926**:300,
      1931:317, **1942**:349, **1982**:463
St. Louis Cardinals (football), **1988**:479
St. Louis Democrat (newspaper), **1875**:173
St. Louis Dispatch (newspaper), **1864**:149,
   1878:181
St. Louis Evening Chronicle (newspaper),
   1876:177
St. Louis Globe-Democrat (newspaper),
   1852:123
St. Louis Iron & Marine Works,
   1898:224
St. Louis Post and Dispatch (newspaper),
   1880:185
St. Louis Republican (newspaper), **1808**:47
St. Louis Sun (newspaper), **1990**:485
St. Louis University, **1819**:63
St. Louis Zoo, **1921**:288
St. Luke's Hospital (N.Y.C.), **1858**:134
St. Mary's Church (Phila.), **1782**:11
St. Mihiel, Battle of, **1918**:276
St. Moritz (Switz.), **1928**:306
St. Nicholas (magazine), **1873**:170
Saint of Bleeker Street, The (opera),
   1954:385
St. Patrick's Cathedral (N.Y.C.),
   1879:183, **1910**:255
St. Paul (Minn.), **1888**:201
   Cathedral, **1907**:247
St. Paul Pioneer Press (newspaper),
   1854:127
St. Paul's School, **1882**:190
St. Petersburg (Fla.) Kennel Club,
   1925:298
St. Valentine's Day massacre (Chicago),
   1929:309
St. Vincent's Hospital (New York City),
   1849:116
salaries. *See* wages and salaries
Salary Act, **1874**:171
Salem witchcraft trials, xiii
sales tax, **1933**:320
   first cigarette, **1921**:286
   first state, **1921**:286
   gasoline, **1919**:281
Salinger, J. D., **1951**:376, **1961**:404,
   1963:409
Salisbury, Harrison E., **1993**:498
Salk, Jonas E., **1953**:381, **1954**:384,
   1954:*385*, **1995**:504

Sallie Mae. *See* Student Loan Marketing
   Assn.
Sally (musical), **1920**:285
"Sally" (song), **1921**:287
Sally, Irene and Mary (play), **1922**:290
Salmagundi (book), **1807**:46
saloons, **1901**:232
Salsbury, Nate, **1879**:183
SALT I treaty, signed, **1972**:432
SALT II treaty, signed but not ratified,
   1979:452
salt
   manufacture begins, **1788**:18
   Michigan production, **1860**:137
   West Virginia production, **1797**:32
Salter, Susanna M., **1887**:198
Salt Lake City (Utah)
   last stretch of Interstate 80 com-
      pleted, **1986**:472
   Mormon 150th-anniversary obser-
      vance, **1980**:456
   sea gull monument, **1913**:264
saltworks, first, xi
Salvation Army, **1880**:186, **1896**:221,
   1904:241
Salvation Nell (play), **1908**:250
Salvino, Carmen, **1962**:407
Samba (dance), **1939**:340
Same Time, Next Year (play), **1975**:444
Samoan Islands, **1872**:167, **1878**:180,
   1889:202, **1899**:226
Sampras, Pete, **1990**:*485*, **1990**:486,
   1993:498, **1995**:505, **1996**:509
Samuelson, Paul A., **1970**:427
San Antonio (Tex.), **1968**:421
   first air-conditioned building,
      1928:304
   first Mexican-American mayor,
      1981:458
   flood, **1921**:287
"San Antonio Rose" (song), **1938**:337
Sanchez, Salvador, **1982**:463
Sanchez Vicario, Arantxa, **1994**:502
Sanctuary (book), **1931**:316
Sanctum Sanctorum (painting), **1962**:406
sand-blasting process, **1870**:163
Sandburg, Carl, **1914**:266, **1916**:272,
   1918:279, **1920**:284, **1928**:305,
   1936:331, **1939**:339, **1950**:374,
   1967:420
Sande, Earl, **1968**:423
Sanders, Millard, **1903**:238
Sanderson, Julia, **1905**:242, **1910**:256,
   1913:264
San Diego (Calif.)
   mid-air collision, **1978**:451
   Panama-California Exposition,
      1915:268
San Fernando Valley (Calif.), earthquake,
   1971:432
Sanford and Sun (television program),
   1972:432
San Francisco (Calif.)
   BART transit system opens, **1972**:433
   cable-car service, **1873**:*169*, **1873**:170
   DeYoung Memorial Museum,

      1897:222
   downtown baseball stadium rejected,
      1989:482
   earthquake, **1868**:158, **1906**:*244*,
      1989:*481*, **1989**:483
   Golden Gate Bridge, **1933**:321,
      1937:333
   Golden Gate Exposition, **1939**:340
   incorporated as city, **1850**:118
   major fire, **1851**:121
   Museum of Art, **1935**:328
   Preparedness Day parade explosion,
      1916:270
   Presidio founding, **1776**:2
   Roman Catholic archbishop,
      1915:269
   Russian Orthodox Church, **1872**:168,
      1905:242
   saloon/theater/gambling house,
      1849:117
   San Francisco-Oakland Bridge,
      1936:330
   theaters, **1869**:161, **1875**:174
   transcontinental airmail service,
      1920:283, **1928**:*304*
   War Memorial Opera House,
      1932:319
San Francisco Bay Bridge, **1989**:*481*
San Francisco Bulletin (newspaper),
   1855:129
San Francisco Chronicle (newspaper),
   1865:152
   first daily comic strip, **1907**:247
San Francisco Examiner (newspaper),
   1887:200, **1892**:211
San Francisco-Oakland Bridge, **1936**:330
San Francisco Stock & Exchange Board,
   1862:143
San Francisco Symphony Orchestra,
   1895:218
Sanger, Margaret, **1914**:265, **1916**:270,
   1966:415
Sanitas Food Co. *See* W. K. Kellogg Co.
San Jacinto, Battle of, **1836**:90
San Jose College, **1857**:132
San Juan Capistrano (Calif.), **1776**:2
Santa Anna, Antonio de, **1836**:90
Santa Barbara (Calif.), **1925**:298
Santa Clara University, **1851**:120
Santa Clause, The (movie), **1994**:501
"Santa Claus Is Coming to Town" (song),
   1934:325
Santa Fe (N. Mex.), **1875**:174
Santa Fe Railroad, **1876**:176, **1986**:472
Santa Fe Republican (newspaper),
   1847:113
Santa Fe trail, opens, **1821**:66
"Santa Lucia" (song), **1850**:119
Santana, Manuel, **1965**:414
Santayana, George, **1905**:242
Santee (S.C.), **1796**:31
Santee Canal (S.C.), **1793**:27, **1800**:37
Santeria, **1993**:497
Santo Domingo, **1870**:162
Sappho (yacht), **1871**:166
Saragosa (Tex.), **1987**:477

Sarah Lawrence College, **1945:**357
Sara Lee baked goods, **1976:***445*
Saranac Laboratory, **1894:**215
Saranac Lake (N.Y.), **1884:**194
Sarandon, Susan, **1991:**489
Sarasota (Fla.), **1930:**312
Saratoga (play), **1870:**164
Saratoga, Battle of, **1777:**3, **1777:**4
Saratoga Trunk (book), **1941:**345
Sarazen, Gene, **1922:**290, **1923:**293,
    1932:319, **1933:**323
Sarg, Tony, **1942:**349
Sargent, Aaron A., **1878:**181
Sargent, George, **1909:**253
Sargent, John Singer, 190, 1882,
    1878:181, **1879:**183, **1885:**195,
    1925:297
Sargent & Greenleaf, **1874:**172
Sarnoff, David, **1915:**268, **1919:**280,
    1930:311, **1997:**511
Saroyan, William, **1940:**342, **1981:**459
Satanic Verses, The (book), **1989:**482
satellites (artificial)
    commercial, **1965:**412
    communication, **1960:**400
    television, **1962:**406
    weather, **1960:**400
    See also space program; *specific satellites*
"Satin Doll" (song), **1958:**396
Satoll, Francesco, **1893:**213
Saturday Evening Post (magazine),
    1821:67, **1897:**222
    first Rockwell cover painting,
        1916:271
    Lorimer editorship, **1900:**231
Saturday Night Fever (movie), **1977:**449
Saturday Review of Literature (magazine),
    1924:294, **1940:**342
Saturday's Children (play), **1927:**303
Saturn (planet)
    composition of rings discovered,
        1886:197
    fifth satellite discovered, **1892:**210
    ninth satellite discovered, **1898:**225
    space probes, **1974:**440, **1980:**456
Saudi Arabia, **1957:**392
    oil exports ban, **1973:**435
    U.S. military complex bombing,
        1995:506
Saugerties (N.Y.), **1994:**500
Saunders, Clarence, **1916:**270
Savage Arms Co., **1895:**217
Savalas, Telly, **1973:**438, **1994:**501
Savannah (Ga.)
    American recapture attempts, **1779:**6
    British capture, **1778:**4
    British evacuate, **1782:**10
    Eugene Talmadge Memorial Bridge,
        1953:381
    first Girl Guide troop, **1902:**234
    hurricanes, **1893:**214
    mail bombing of civil rights lawyer,
        1989:481
Savannah (ship), **1959:**397
"Save the Last Dance for Me" (song),
    1960:401

savings and loans
    federal bailout, **1989:**481
    Keating misconduct charges,
        1990:484
savings banks, **1816:**58–59, **1819:**62
    postal savings, **1910:**254, **1911:**257
Savo Island, Battle of, **1942:**346
sawmill, xi
saxophone, **1849:**116, **1888:**202
Saxton, Johnny, **1954:**386
Saylor, David A., **1871:**164
Sayre, Lewis A., **1900:**230
"Say Say Say" (song), **1983:**465
Say, Thomas, **1824:**70, **1834:**87
"Say You, Say Me" (song), **1985:**470
SBC Communications, **1996:**507
scale, automatic computing, **1900:**230
Scanlan, W.J., **1891:**208
Scaramouche (book), **1921:**287
Scarface (movie), **1932:**319
Scarlet Feather (book), **1845:**109
scarlet fever, antitoxin, **1923:**292
Scarlet Letter, The (book), **1850:**119
Scarlet Letter, The (movie), **1926:**300
Scarlet Letter, The (opera), **1896:**220
Scarlet Pimpernel, The (movie), **1934:**326
Scarlet Sister (book), **1928:**305
Scarlett (book), **1991:**489
"Scenes That Are the Brightest" (song),
    1845:108
Schaaf, Ernie, **1933:**322
Schaalow, Arthur, **1981:**458
Schaefer, Jacob, **1883:**192
Schaefer, Vincent J., **1993:**497
Schaefer Brewing Co., **1891:**208
Schaff, Philip, **1888:**201, **1890:**207
Schally, Andrew V., **1977:**448
Schayes, Dolph, **1960:**402
Schecter, Solomon, **1913:**263
Schechter v. United States, **1935:**327
Scheel, Fritz, **1900:**231
Scheider, Roy, **1975:**444
Schenck v. United States, **1919:**280
Schenectady (N.Y.), **1900:**230
Scherman, Harry, **1969:**426
Schick, Bela, **1913:**263, **1967:**419
Schick, Jacob, **1924:**293, **1937:**333
Schick, Inc., **1931:**314
Schildkraut, Joseph, **1959:**398, **1964:**411
Schindler's List (movie), **1993:**498
Schirmer, Gustav, **1866:**154, **1893:**213
Schirra, Walter M., **1965:**412
Schlesinger, Arthur M., Jr., **1945:**357,
    1965:413
Schlesinger, James R., **1977:**447
Schliegel, Ernie, **1996:**509
Schmeling, Max, **1930:**313, **1931:**317
Schmidt, Benno C., Jr., **1992:**493
Schmucker, Samuel S., **1838:**95
Schneerson, Menachem, **1994:**500
Schneider, Louis, **1931:**317
Schnering, Otto Y., **1917:**274
Schoenberg, Arnold, **1934:**325
Schofield, Leonard, **1958:**396
Scholastic Magazine, founding, **1920:**284
Schollander, Don, **1964:**411

School and Society (book), **1899:**227
school board elections, **1970:**428
schoolbus accident (Alton, Tex.),
    1989:483
Schoolcraft, Henry, **1832:**83
"School Days" (song), **1907:**247
school desegregation
    Alabama state university, **1963:**408
    "all deliberate speed" mandate,
        1955:388
    Boston court-order, **1974:**440,
        1976:446
    busing, **1975:**443, **1979:**453
    busing upheld, **1971:**430
    busing violence, **1974:**439
    court-ordered upheld, **1977:**448
    Detroit court-order, **1975:**443
    federal aid program, **1972:**433
    "immediate" mandated, **1969:**425
    Little Rock (Ark.), **1957:***392*,
        1957:393
    NAACP drops Los Angeles suit,
        1988:479
    parochial schools, **1962:**405
    St. Louis program, **1980:**456
    Supreme Court rulings, **1954:**384,
        1955:388, **1968:**422, **1969:**425,
        1973:437, **1976:**446
    tax exemptions withheld, **1975:**443
    University of Mississippi, **1962:**405
    Virginia begins, **1959:**398
    Yonkers (N.Y.) "intentional" segrega-
        tion findings, **1985:**469, **1986:**472
*School District of Abington Township v.
    Schempp*, **1963:**408
school lunch program, **1908:**249
School of American Ballet, **1934:**325
School of Nursing of Philadelphia
    Woman's Hospital, **1861:**141
schools
    after-hours facilities availability,
        1993:497
    Akron model system, **1847:**112–13
    bars on children of illegal aliens disal-
        lowed, **1980:**456, **1982:**461
    for blind students, **1832:**83, **1887:**199
    called "mediocre," **1983:**465
    colonial, xii
    disabled student provisions, **1977:**448
    disasters, **1989:**483
    fire, **1908:**250
    first commercial high school,
        1858:158
    first for deaf, **1817:**60
    first for Native American boys,
        1823:69
    first high school, **1820:**65
    first junior high, **1909:**252
    first music, **1834:**88
    first nurse on staff, **1902:**235
    first parochial, **1782:**11
    first preparatory, **1778:**5
    first public, **1791:**24
    first public evening, **1833:**85
    first state for blind, **1837:**93
    first swimming, **1827:**75

Seghers, Charles J., **1878**:181
Segre, Emilio G., **1941**:345, **1955**:387, **1959**:398
segregation. *See* civil rights; school desegregation
Seiberling Rubber Co., **1921**:286
seismographs, **1930**:311
Seixas, Gershon M., **1783**:11
Seixas, Vic, **1954**:386
Selden, Edgar, **1889**:204
Selden, George B., **1895**:217, **1900**:230, **1922**:289
Selected Poems (Aiken book), **1929**:308
selective service. *See* draft
Selective Service Act, **1917**:273, **1918**:277
Selena (Tejano singer), **1995**:504
Seles, Monica, **1991**:490, **1992**:494
stabbed by spectator, **1993**:498
Self (play), **1856**:131
Selfridge, Thomas, **1908**:250
Selleck, Tom, **1980**:457
Sellers, Peter, **1963**:409, **1964**:411
Selma-Montgomery march (Ala.), **1965**:412
Selznick, David O., **1965**:414
semiconductors, **1973**:437
Seminole Wars, **1816**:58, **1817**:59, **1817**:*60*, **1835**:88, **1837**:93
"Semper Fidelis" (song), **1888**:202
Senate
    AIDS research program approved, **1988**:478, **1989**:482
    bank charter, **1811**:51
    bomb explosion, **1915**:267
    Canadian free-trade agreement approved, **1988**:477
    confirms Thomas's Supreme Court nomination, **1991**:487
    debates open to public, **1794**:27
    direct election of members, **1913**:262
    elects Johnson (R. M.) as vice president, **1836**:90
    failed efforts to unseat Smoot, **1907**:245
    fails to ratify League of Nations Covenant, **1920**:283
    first African American members, **1870**:163, **1874**:172
    first African American popularly elected, **1966**:415
    first African American woman member, **1992**:490
    first convening, **1789**:20
    first impeachment proceedings against member, **1799**:34
    first judicial impeachment, **1804**:42
    first rejection of cabinet appointee, **1834**:86
    first woman elected to, **1932**:317
    Jackson (A.) censure, **1834**:86
    Jackson censure expunged, **1837**:93
    Louisiana Purchase approved, **1803**:40
    number of member will not seek reelection, **1995**:503

ratifes UN treaty outlawing genocide, **1986**:472
ratifies Intermediate Range Nuclear Forces Treaty, **1988**:477
ratifies Kellogg-Briand Treaty, **1928**:303
ratifies Panama Canal treaties, **1978**:449
ratifies Pinckney's Treaty, **1796**:30
ratifies treaty with Tunis, **1800**:36
ratifies Virgin Islands purchase treaty, **1916**:270
ratifies War of 1812 peace treaty, **1815**:57
ratifies World War I debt-funding agreements, **1926**:298
rejects prayer-in-schools constitutional amendment, **1984**:467
rejects Texas annexation treaty, **1844**:105
savings and loan ethics investigation, **1990**:484
unprecedented number of women elected, **1992**:490
Watergate investigation, **1973**:435
See also Congress, House of Representatives
Senate Judiciary Committee, **1937**:332, **1950**:372
Senator, The (painting), **1941**:345
"Send in the Clowns" (song), **1973**:438
seniority systems, **1982**:460
Sennett, Mack, **1912**:261, **1960**:402
Sensible Etiquette of the Best Society (book), **1878**:182
"September in the Rain" (song), **1937**:334
septuplets, **1997**:514
Sequoia National Park (Calif.), **1890**:205
Serapis (ship), **1779**:6, **1779**:*6*
Sergeant York (movie), **1941**:346
Serling, Rod, **1959**:398, **1975**:444
Serpico (movie), **1973**:438
Serra, Junipero, ix, **1784**:14
    beatified, **1988**:479
Servant in the House, The (play), **1908**:250
Servants of Relief for Incurable Cancer, **1901**:233
Sesquicentennial Exposition (Phila.), **1926**:298
Sessions, Roger, **1923**:292, **1947**:364, **1964**:410, **1981**:459, **1985**:470
Sessions, William, **1993**:496
Seth Jones (book), **1860**:138
Seth Thomas Clock Co., **1853**:124
Seton, Elizabeth Ann, **1797**:33, **1809**:48, **1821**:67
    beatification, **1963**:408
    canonized, **1975**:443
Seton Hall and Seminary, **1857**:132
Seurati's Lunch (painting), **1939**:339
Seuss, Dr., **1957**:394, **1991**:489
Sevareid, Eric, **1992**:493
Seven Days (play), **1909**:253
Seven Keys to Baldpate (book), **1913**:264
Sevenoaks (book), **1875**:174

Seven Songs for the Harpsichord (music), **1788**:19
Seven-Story Mountain, The (book), **1948**:368
Seventeen (book), **1916**:272
Seventeenth Amendment, **1913**:262
Seventh Day Adventist Church, **1846**:111, **1863**:146
Seventh Heaven (movie), **1927**:303
Seventh Heaven (play), **1922**:290
77 Sunset Strip (television program), **1958**:396
"76 Trombones" (song), **1957**:393
Seven Year Itch, The (movie), **1955**:388
Seven Year Itch, The (play), **1952**:379
Seven Years' War, ix
Sevier, John, **1796**:30, **1815**:57
Seward, William H., **1866**:152, **1867**:*155*, **1872**:167
sewing machine, **1870**:163, **1889**:203
    chain-stitch single-thread, **1857**:132
    first practical, **1846**:110
    installment buying, **1929**:307
Sex (play), **1926**:300
sex discrimination. *See* equal employment opportunity; women's rights
sexual abuse, **1988**:478
Sexual Behavior in the Human Female (book), **1953**:382
sexual harassment, **1991**:*489*, **1992**:492, **1995**:503
Seybert, Adam, **1801**:39
Seymour, Horatio, **1868**:157
Seymour: An Introduction (book), **1963**:409
Shadow, The (radio), **1940**:343
Shadow Box, The (play), **1977**:449
"Shadow Dancing" (song), **1978**:450
"Shadow of Your Smile, The" (song), **1965**:413
Shadows on the Rock (book), **1931**:316
Shahn, Ben, **1933**:322, **1939**:339, **1946**:361, **1950**:374, **1960**:401, **1969**:426
"Shake, Rattle and Roll" (song), **1954**:385
Shaker Heights (Cleveland, Ohio), **1905**:240
Shakers, **1776**:2, **1788**:19
Shakur, Tupac, **1996**:508
Shalishkashvili, John, **1993**:496
Shallenberger, Oliver B., **1888**:201
Shame of the Cities, The (book), **1904**:240
Shampoo (movie), **1975**:444
Shane (movie), **1953**:382
Shapiro, Karl, **1944**:354, **1953**:382
Shapley, Harlow, **1917**:274, **1921**:287
Sharif, Omar, **1965**:414
Sharkey, Jack, **1932**:319, **1994**:502
Sharon Medical Society, **1779**:6
Sharp, Philip S., **1993**:497
Sharpe, William W., **1990**:484
Shatner, William, **1966**:*416*, **1966**:417, **1979**:454, **1995**:505
Shauhgran, The (play), **1874**:172
shaving
    beards fashionable, **1860**:139

banned with foreign nations, **1794**:27
federal importation ban, **1806**:44, **1808**:46
first imports, x-xi
Massachustts import ban, **1788**:18
Pennsylvania import ban, xi
South Carolina import ban, **1792**:25
U.S.-British suppression treaty, **1862**:142
Slave Trade Act, **1820**:64
"Sleepy Time Gal" (song), **1925**:297
"Slide, Kelly, Slide" (song), **1889**:204
Slidell, John, **1845**:107, **1861**:139
"Slip, Slidin' Away" (song), **1977**:448
Sliver (book), **1991**:489
S. L. Kraft Co., **1909**:252
Sloan, Alfred P., **1963**:408
Sloan, John, **1912**:261, **1914**:266
Sloan, John F., **1907**:247
Sloat, Jacob, **1839**:96
Sloat, John D., **1846**:109
Slumber (sculpture), **1948**:367
Smale, John G., **1992**:492
small claims court, **1913**:262
small debtor's court, **1913**:262
Smalley, Richard, **1996**:508
smallpox
epidemics, xi
inoculation, xi, **1800**:37
Smart Money (magazine), **1992**:493
Smart Set (magazine), **1890**:207, **1914**:266
"Smarty" (song), **1908**:249
Smet, Pierre Jean de, **1870**:163
"Smile" (song), **1954**:385
Smiley, Gordon, **1982**:463
Smiley, Jane, **1984**:467, **1988**:479
Smilin' Through (movie), **1932**:319
Smith, Alex, **1906**:245, **1910**:256
Smith, Alfred E., **1928**:303, **1944**:353
Smith, Bessie, **1923**:292, **1937**:334
Smith, Betty, **1943**:352
Smith, Charles B. (Bill Arp), **1903**:237
Smith, C. James, **1909**:253
Smith, Dean, **1997**:513
Smith, Elihu H., **1793**:27
Smith, Francis M., **1872**:167
Smith, George A., **1945**:357, **1951**:376
Smith, Hamilton L., **1856**:130
Smith, Hamilton O., **1978**:450
Smith, Henry, **1854**:127
Smith, Horton, **1936**:332
Smith, Hyrum, **1844**:106
Smith, John, xiv
Smith, John T., **1891**:208
Smith, Joseph (father), **1830**:80, **1831**:82, **1838**:95, **1839**:97, **1843**:103, **1844**:106
Smith, Joseph (son), **1860**:138, **1914**:262
Smith, Joseph Fielding, **1901**:233, **1970**:428, **1972**:433
Smith, Kate, **1930**:313
Smith, Lillian, **1944**:354
Smith, Maggie, **1990**:485
Smith, Margaret (tennis player), **1962**:407, **1965**:414

Smith, Margaret Chase (senator), **1995**:503
Smith, Martin C., **1981**:459
Smith, Nathan, **1829**:78
Smith, Red (Walter), **1945**:358, **1982**:463
Smith, Richard P., **1830**:80
Smith, Robert, **1935**:329
Smith, Robert Penn, **1829**:78, **1830**:80
Smith, Samuel F., **1831**:82
Smith, Seba, **1829**:78
Smith, Sidney, **1935**:328
Smith, Sophia, **1870**:163
Smith, Stan, **1971**:432
Smith, Tommie, **1966**:417
Smith, Walter B., **1961**:403
Smith, W. H., **1844**:107
Smith Act, **1951**:376
Smith College, **1875**:173, **1893**:214
Smith-Corona Inc., **1956**:389
Smith-Hughes Act, **1918**:278
Smithson, John, **1846**:110
Smithsonian Institution (Wash., D.C.), **1846**:110, **1847**:112, **1878**:181, **1988**:479
Smoke and Steel (book), **1920**:284
"Smoke Gets in Your Eyes" (song), **1933**:322
Smokey and the Bandit (movie), **1977**:449
smoking
airline ban on pipe and cigar, **1977**:447
airline bans, **1988**:478
cigar, **1900**:232, **1977**:447
cigarette advertising with health warnings, **1972**:433
cigarette push-up box, **1892**:210
cigarette-rolling machine, **1876**:176
cigarette television advertising banned, **1971**:430
cigar-rolling machine, **1883**:191
commuter railroad (N.Y.) bans, **1988**:478
first state cigarette tax, **1921**:286
illegality of women in public, **1908**:250
incidence of, **1889**:204
increases, **1921**:288
male fashions, **1900**:232
pipe, **1900**:232, **1977**:447
Surgeon General's warning, **1964**:410
See also tobacco
Smoot, Reed, **1907**:245
Smoot-Hawley Tariff, **1931**:314
Smyrna (Tenn.), **1980**:456
Snap the Whip (painting), **1872**:168
Snead, Sam, **1942**:350, **1946**:362, **1949**:371, **1951**:377, **1952**:380, **1954**:386
Snell, George, **1980**:456
Sneva, Tom, **1983**:465
Snow, Lorenzo, **1898**:225, **1901**:233
Snow-Bound (book), **1866**:154
snowstorms and blizzards, **1996**:509
eastern U.S. March blizzard, **1993**:499
Kansas blizzard, **1886**:198

New York and New England, **1888**:202
New York City, **1947**:365
Washington (D.C.), **1922**:290, **1996**:*507*
worst on East Coast in 36 years, **1983**:466
Snow White and the Seven Dwarfs (movie), **1937**:334
Snyder, Jimmy ("the Greek"), **1996**:509
soap, **1878**:181
So Big (book), **1924**:295
soccer
American Soccer League founding, **1921**:287
first U.S. game, **1886**:198
introduced in U.S., **1905**:243
Major League Soccer debuts, **1996**:509
North American League, **1972**:435
World Cup, **1950**:375
World Soccer tournament, **1994**:501
Soccer Football Assn. (U.S.), **1913**:264
social club fire (N.Y.C.), **1990**:486
Socialist Party, **1910**:254–55
Social Justice (book), **1942**:348
Social Security Act, **1935**:327
amendments, **1939**:338, **1983**:463
Social Security Administration, **1994**:499
social welfare. *See* welfare services
Society and Solitude (book), **1870**:164
Society for Alleviating the Miseries of Public Prisons, **1787**:18
Society for Ethical Culture, **1876**:177
Society for Independent Artists, **1917**:274
Society for the Prevention of Crime, **1878**:182
Society for the Promotion of Public Schools, **1827**:74
Society for the Relief of Poor Widows with Small Children, **1797**:33
Society for the Suppression of Vice, **1873**:170
Society of American Artists, **1877**:179
Society of Friends, **1790**:22
Society of Jesus. *See* Jesuits
Society of Saint Tammany, **1789**:21
Society of Spiritual Arts, **1931**:316
Society of the Cincinnati, **1783**:12
Society of Unitarian Christians, **1796**:31
Socony-Vacuum Oil Co., **1936**:330
soda fountain, marble, **1858**:134
Soglo, Otto, **1974**:441
Soil Conservation Service, **1935**:327
Sojourner (space rover), **1997**:*512*
solar eclipse, **1869**:160
solar energy, **1878**:181, **1957**:393
Soldier of the Great War, A (book), **1991**:489
soldiers' homes, national, **1867**:156
Soldiers of Fortune (book), **1897**:222–23
Soldier's Pay (book), **1926**:300
Soldier's Play, A (play), **1981**:459
"Solitude" (song), **1934**:325
Solomon Islands, **1942**:346, **1943**:350

independence, **1978**:449
Solow, Robert M., **1987**:475
Solti, Georg, **1997**:513
Somalia, U.S. troops in, **1992**:490, **1993**:494–95
"Somebody's Baby" (song), **1983**:465
"Somebody Stole My Gal" (song), **1918**:278
"Some Enchanted Evening" (song), **1949**:370
Some Like It Hot (movie), **1959**:398
"Some of These Days" (song), **1910**:256, **1911**:259
"Someone to Watch Over Me" (song), **1926**:300
"Something" (song), **1969**:426
Sometime (play), **1918**:279
sonar, **1932**:319
Sondheim, Stephen, **1973**:438, **1979**:454, **1984**:468, **1994**:501
Song and Dance Man, The (play), **1923**:292
"Song Is Ended, The" (song), **1927**:302
Song of Bernadette, The (movie), **1943**:352
Song of Hiawatha, The (book), **1855**:129
"Song of the Chattahoochee" (poem), **1877**:179
"Song of the Islands" (song), **1915**:269
Song of the Lark, The (book), **1915**:269
Songs of Experience (musical composition), **1982**:462
Songs of Innocence (musical composition), **1982**:462
"Song Sung Blue" (song), **1972**:434
sonic depth finder, **1922**:288
Sonnenberg, Gus, **1929**:309
Sonnets to Duse (book), **1907**:247
Sonny and Cher (television program), **1971**:431
"Sonny Boy" (song), **1928**:305
Son of the Middle Border, A (book), **1917**:275
Son of the Wolf, The (London), **1900**:231
Sons of Liberty, x, **1776**:*1*
Sons of the American Revolution, **1875**:175
Sony Pictures, **1989**:481
Soo Canals (Mich.), **1881**:186
Sophie's Choice (book), **1979**:453
Sophie's Choice (movie), **1982**:462
"Sophisticated Lady" (song), **1933**:322
Sorcerer (sculpture), **1957**:393
Sorenstam, Anika, **1995**:505, **1996**:509
Sorin, Edward F., **1893**:213
Sorokin, Pitrim A., **1931**:315
sororities
    first black, **1908**:250
    Kappa Alpha Theta, **1870**:164
Sorosis women's professional club, **1868**:158
Sothern, E. H., **1858**:134, **1885**:196, **1895**:218, **1933**:322
Soto, Hernando de, ix
Souders, George, **1927**:303
Soulé, Samuel W., **1867**:155, **1868**:157
Sound and the Fury, The (Faulkner), **1929**:308

sound barrier
    broken by jet-powered Thrust SSC, **1997**:511
    first to break on ground, **1979**:454
Sound of Music, The (movie), **1965**:414
Sound of Music, The (play), **1959**:398
Sousa, John Philip, **1880**:184, **1888**:202, **1889**:204, **1893**:213, **1896**:220, **1897**:222
Soutar, Dave, **1961**:404
Souter, David, **1990**:484
South
    American Revolution, **1776**:1–2, **1779**:6
    first African American mayor of major city, **1973**:436
    tornadoes, **1884**:194
South Africa, U.S. economic sanctions, **1986**:471, **1991**:87
South Carolina, **1865**:150, **1868**:157, **1896**:219
    abolishes slavery, **1865**:150
    American Revolution, **1776**:1, **1776**:2, **1780**:7, **1780**:7, **1781**:8
    Articles of Confederation, **1778**:4
    bans importation of slaves, **1792**:25
    canals, **1793**:27, **1800**:37
    earthquakes, **1886**:198
    Native Americans, **1777**:4
    prohibition law, **1915**:267
    ratifies Constitution, **1788**:18
    readmitted to Union, **1868**:157
    secedes, **1860**:137
    slave revolt, xiv
    state constitution, **1776**:2, **1778**:4, **1790**:22, **1865**:150, **1868**:157, **1896**:219
    tornadoes, **1994**:502, **1996**:509
South Carolina Canal & Railroad Co., **1830**:79
South Carolina College, **1801**:39
South Dakota
    Episcopal bishop, **1972**:433
    floods, **1972**:473
    Ft. Randall Dam, **1956**:389
    gold discovery, **1875**:173
    Mt. Rushmore, **1930**:312, **1936**:331, **1937**:334, **1939**:339
    state constitution, **1889**:202
    statehood, **1889**:202
    Wounded Knee battle, **1890**:206
Southeastern Conference, forerunner, **1921**:288
Southern, Terry, **1955**:388
Southern and Norfolk Western Railroad, **1980**:456
Southern Christian Leadership Conference, **1957**:392
Southern Commercial Convention, **1859**:135
Southern Illinois University, **1869**:160
Southern Intercollegiate Conference, **1921**:288
Southern Methodist University, **1911**:258
"Southern Nights" (song), **1977**:448

Southern Pacific Railroad, **1865**:151, **1881**:186, **1884**:194
    merger dissolved, **1912**:261
    proposed merger rejected, **1986**:472
    Rio Grande Industries acquires, **1988**:478
Southern Railway Co., **1894**:215, **1979**:452
Southern Rights Assn., **1850**:*118*
Southgate (Ky.), **1977**:449
South Holyoke (Mass.), **1875**:175
South Korea, **1996**:506
South Pacific (play), **1949**:371
South Pole, first flight over, **1929**:308
Southwestern Bell Telephone Co., **1946**:360
Southwest Intercollegiate Athletic Conference, **1914**:266
Southwest Wind (painting), **1905**:242
Southworth, Emma D., **1852**:123, **1859**:136, **1863**:146, **1864**:149
Soviet Union. *See* Russia
Sovran, Michael I., **1992**:493
Sowerby, Leo, **1945**:357
Spaatz, Carl, **1974**:439
Spacek, Sissy, **1980**:457
space program, **1972**:433, **1974**:440
    Apollo fire disaster, **1967**:419
    Apollo 13 problems/safe return, **1970**:427
    Atlantis joins Russian *Mir* in space, **1995**:504
    Atlantis launch, **1989**:481–82
    Challenger explodes after liftoff, **1986**:472, **1986**:*473*
    communications satellite repaired, **1992**:492
    damaged satellite repaired in space, **1984**:467
    Discovery, **1988**:478, **1990**:484, **1994**:500
    eighth successful flight, **1983**:464
    Endeavor, **1994**:500
    first African American astronaut in space, **1983**:464
    first American astronaut in space, **1961**:403
    first American to walk in space, **1984**:467
    first American woman astronaut, **1982**:461
    first American woman to walk in space, **1984**:467
    first astronaut to orbit Earth, **1962**:405
    first manned Earth orbits, **1981**:458
    first man on moon, **1969**:424, **1969**:*424*
    first Russian astronaut as U.S. crew member, **1994**:500
    first six-day moon flight, **1968**:421
    first space radar laboratory, **1994**:500
    first space walk, **1965**:412
    first space walk without ties to spacecraft, **1984**:467
    Galileo launched, **1995**:504

Galileo probe, **1989:**481–82

Hubble telescope, **1990:**484–85, **1993:**497

Magellan probe, **1989:**481, **1990:**485

Mariner 2, **1962:**405

Mars Environmental Survey, **1996:**507–8, **1997:**511, **1997:***512*

Mars Observer ceases communication, **1993:**497

moon program proposed, **1961:**402–3

Pathfinder launched, **1996:**507–8, **1997:**511, **1997:***512*

possibility of life beyond Earth raised, **1996:**507

satellite reaches moon, **1962:**403

Saturn probes, **1980:**456

space shuttle approved, **1972:**433

Truly resigns as NASA head, **1992:**492

U.S.-Russian spacecraft link in space, **1975:**442, **1995:**504

Spain

American Revolution, **1776:**1, **1779:**6, **1781:**8

explorers, ix

in Louisiana, **1779:**6, **1810:**49

Louisiana Purchase western limits set, **1819:**62

Mississippi River control, **1784:**12, **1785:**14

Mobile (Ala.) fort falls to Americans, **1813:**53

peace with Great Britain, **1783:**11

Pinckney's Treaty, **1795:**29, **1796:**30

recognizes American independence, **1783:**11

restores American access to New Orleans, **1803:**40

returns Louisiana to France, **1800:**36

U.S. military bases authorized, **1953:**380

Van Ness Convention settles claims, **1834:**86

war with France, **1793:**26

Spalding, Albert G., **1876:**177, **1878:**182

Spalding, James, **1876:**177

Spalding, Jim, **1957:**394

Spalding, Martin J., **1864:**149

Spalding's Official Baseball Guide (book), 1869

Spangenburg, August G., **1792:**25

Spanier, Muggsy, **1967:**419

Spanish-American War, **1898:**223–24

"Spanish Cavalier, The" (song), **1881:**188

Spanish Civil War, **1937:**332

Spanning the Continent (painting), **1935:**328

Sparks, Independence, **1835:**89

Sparks, Jared, **1834:**88, **1839:**97

sparrows, **1850:**119

Spartacus (movie), **1960:**402

Spaulding, H. H., **1836:**90

Speaker, Tris, **1925:**297–98

Speaks, Oley, **1948:**367

special-delivery service, **1885:**195

Special Prosecutor

Iran-Contra affair, **1991:**487, **1994:**499

Watergate affair, **1973:**435, **1973:**436

specie payments, **1874:**171, **1879:**182

Spectator, The (newspaper), **1846:**111

spectroheliograph, **1888:**201, **1891:**208

speech freedom. *See* free speech

Speed (movie), **1994:**501

speed limits, **1904:**239, **1974:**440, **1987:**475, **1995:**502

speed skating, gold medal winners, **1980:**457, **1992:**494

Spellbound (movie), **1945:**358

spelling bee, first national, **1925:**298

Spellman, Francis J., **1939:**339, **1946:**360

Spelman College, merger with Morehouse, **1929:**308

Spencer, Charles A., **1838:**94

Spencer, Christopher M., **1860:**137

Spencer, Platt R., **1864:**149

Sperry & Hutchinson, **1891:**208

Sperry, Roger W., **1981:**458

Sperry, Thomas A., **1891:**208

Sperry Co., **1986:**472

Sperry Electric Co., **1880:**184

Sperry, Elmer A., **1880:**184, **1918:**277, **1930:**311

Sperry Gyroscope Co., **1910:**255

Spice Girls, **1997:***510*

Spiegler, Caesar, **1878:**181

Spielberg, Steven, **1982:**462

Spindletop oil well (Tex.), **1901:**232

Spinella, Stephen, **1994:**501

Spingarn, Arthur B., **1971:**430

Spingarn, Joel, **1939:**338

Spink, Taylor, **1962:**407

Spinks, Michael, **1985:**471, **1986:**474

Spiral (sculpture), **1958:**396

Spirit of St. Louis (monoplane), **1927:***302*

Spirit of the Border, The (book), **1906:**244

spitball, **1919:**282

Spitz, Mark, **1972:**435

Spivak, Lawrence, **1994:**500

Spock, Benjamin, **1946:**360

Spofford, Ainsworth R., **1864:**148, **1908:**249

Spoilers, The (book), **1906:**244

Spokane (Wash.), Expo' 74, **1974:**439

Spokane (Wash.) Ministerial Assn, **1910:**256

Spooner, Eliakim, **1799:**35

Spoon River Anthology (book), **1915:**269

Sporting News, The (newspaper), **1886:**198

Sports Illustrated (magazine), **1954:**386

Sportsman's Companion, The (book), **1783:**12

Sprague, Frank J., **1887:**199, **1934:**324

Sprague, William P., **1791:**23

Sprague Electric Railway & Motor Co., **1884:**194

Spreckels, Claus, **1863:**146

Springer v. United States, **1881:**186

Springfield (Mass.), **1892:**210, **1892:**211

Armory, **1794:**27

Basketball Hall of Fame, **1985:**471

Springfield (N.J.), **1780:**7

Springfield Republican (newspaper), **1824:**70

Spring Hill College (Ala.), **1936:**330

"Spring Song" (song), **1844:**106

Springsteen, Bruce, **1995:**504

"Spring Will Be a Little Late This Year" (song), **1944:**354

sprinkler head, **1874:**172

Sproul, Robert G., **1930:**311, **1975:**443

Spruance, Raymond A., **1969:**424

Spy, The (book), **1821:**67

Spy, The (play), **1822:**67

spying. *See* espionage

Spy Who Came in from the Cold, The (movie), **1966:**417

Squalus (submarine), **1939:**340

squash (game), first national tournament, **1911:**259

Squaw Man, The (movie), **1913:**264

Squaw Man, The (play), **1905:**242

Squibb, Edward R., **1859:**135, **1900:**230

Squibb Co., **1989:**481

S. S. White Dental Manufacturing Co., **1867:**156

Staats-Zeitung (New York newspaper), **1834:**88

Stables (painting), **1932:**319

Stacy, Hollis, **1977:**449, **1978:**451, **1984:**468

Stafford, Thomas P., **1965:**412

Stag at Sharkey's (painting), **1907:**247

Stagecoach (movie), **1939:**340

stagecoaches, **1785:**14, **1785:***15*

colonial service, xi

first overland, **1857:**131

first overland-mail, **1858:**133

Stage Door Canteens, **1940:**343

Stagg, Amos Alonzo, **1892:**211, **1904:**240

stained glass, **1878:**181

Staircase Group, The (painting), **1795:**30

Stallone, Sylvester, **1976:**446, **1979:**454, **1985:**471

Stamm, John S., **1936:**331

Stamp Act, ix

stamps, postage

airmail, **1918:**277

eight-cent, **1971:**430

eighteen-cent, **1981:**458

first adhesive, **1842:**102

first general sale of adhesive, **1847:**111, **1847:***113*

issued in books, **1900:**230

mandated use of adhesive, **1856:**129

perforated in general use, **1857:**131

postage meters, **1920:**283

Presley commemorative, **1992:**491

ten-cent, **1974:**439

thirteen-cent, **1974:**439, **1975:**442

thirty-two cent, **1995:**503

three-cent, **1917:**274, **1932:**317

three-cent reduced to two cent, **1919:**280

twenty-cent, **1981:**458

twenty-five cent, **1988:**478

twenty-nine cent, **1991:**487

1990:486
Steinem, Gloria, **1972:**434
Steiner, Herman, **1948:**368
Steinitz, William, **1872:**168, **1900:**231
Steinmetz, Charles P., **1923:**291
Steinway, Henry E., **1871:**165
Steinway Hall, **1867:**156
Stella, Joseph, **1908:**249, **1919:**281, **1939:**339, **1940:**342
Stempel, Robert C., **1992:**492
Stenberg, George M., **1892:**210
Stengel, Casey, **1975:**444
    bird flies out from cap, **1918:**279
stenotype, **1876:**176
"Step by Step" (song), **1990:**485
Stephens, Alexander H., **1883:**190
Stephens, Ann S., **1860:**138
Stephenson, Benjamin F., **1866:**153
Stephenson, Jan, **1982:**463, **1983:**466
stereotype plate-casting machine, **1900:**231
Stern, Otto, **1943:**351
stethoscope, electric portable, **1924:**294
Stettinius, Edward R. Jr., **1949:**369
Stevens, Craig, **1958:**396
Stevens, Edwin A., **1868:**158
Stevens, Emily, **1913:**264
Stevens, James F., **1971:**431
Stevens, John, **1803:**41, **1813:**54, **1815:**57, **1823:**68, **1824:**70, **1826:**72, **1880:**184
Stevens, John C., **1851:**121
Stevens, John L., **1893:**211
Stevenson, Adlai, death of, **1914:**265
Stevenson, Adlai E.
    death of, **1965:**412
    named ambassador to U.N., **1961:**402
    presidential election defeats, **1952:**378, **1956:**389
Stevens, Robert L., **1830:**80, **856:**130
Stevens, Thaddeus, **1868:**157
Stevens, Uriah S., **1869:**159
Stevensville (Md.), **1981:**459
Stevenson, Robert Louis, **1885:**195
Stewart, James, **1939:**340, **1950:**375, **1954:**385, **1997:**513
Stewart, Payne, **1989:**483, **1991:**490
Stewart, William M., **1909:**252
Stieff, Richard, **1903:**238
Stieglitz, Alfred, **1902:**236, **1946:**361
Stigler, George J., **1992:**492
Stiles, Charles W., **1902:**235
Stiles, Ezra, **1795:**30
Still, Andrew T., **1875:**173, **1917:**274
Still, William G., **1936:**331
Still Life with Apples (painting), **1993:**497
Stillman, Alfred, **1911:**259
Stillness at Appomattox, A (book), **1953:**382
Stillson, Daniel C., **1876:**176
Stillwater Tragedy, The (book), **1880:**185
Stilwell, Joseph M. (Vinegar Joe), **1946:**360
Stimson, Henry L., **1950:**372
Stine, William H., **1972:**433
Sting, The (movie), **1973:**438

stock car racing. *See* National Association for Stock Car Auto Racing
Stockholm (liner), **1956:**391
stockings, fishnet, **1908:**259
stock market
    Babson Business Statistical Organization, **1904:**239
    biggest single-day drop, **1997:**511
    brokerage firms, **1914:**265
    crash, **1929:**307, **1929:***307*
    Dow industrial average, **1884:**193
    Dow Jones drops 86.61 points, **1986:**472
    falls 508 points, **1987:**475
    first Dow-Jones closing over 1,000, **1972:**433
    first Dow Jones closing over 2,000, **1987:**475
    first exchanges, **1791:**23, **1792:**25
    Philadelphia Clearing House, **1870:**163
    record highs, **1972:**433, **1987:**475, **1989:**481, **1990:**484, **1992:**492, **1994:**500, **1995:**503, **1996:**507, **1997:**511
    record shares traded, **1984:**466, **1986:**472
    Securities and Exchange Commission, **1934:**323, **1935:**328
    securities fraud, **1988:**478, **1990:**484, **1995:**504
    See also New York Stock Exchange; panics and depressions
Stockton (Tex.), world's deepest producing oil well, **1971:**430
Stockton, Dave, **1970:**429, **1976:**447
Stockton, Frank, **1879:**183, **1882:**190
stockyards, **1871:**164, **1872:**168, **1874:**172, **1884:**193, **1886:**197
Stoddard, Joshua C., **1855:**129
Stoddert, Benjamin, **1798:**34
Stokes, Carl B., **1967:**419, **1996:**506
Stokowski, Leopold, **1909:**252, **1912:**261, **1944:**353, **1947:**364, **1962:**406, **1977:**448
Stolle, Fred, **1966:**417
"Stompin' at the Savoy" (song), **1936:**331
Stone, Barton W., **1832:**83, **1844:**106
Stone, Edward Durrell, **1978:**450
Stone, Fred, **1920:**285
Stone, Harlan F., **1941:**345
Stone, Irving, **1934:**326, **1961:**404, **1989:**482
Stone, John A., **1829:**78
Stone, Lewis, **1912:**261
Stone, Lucy, **1870:**164
Stone, Marvin C., **1888:**201
Stone, Melville E., **1893:**213
Stono revolt (S.C.), xiv
Stony Point (N.Y.), **1779:**6
Stop the Music (television program), **1949:**371
Storck, Carl L., **1950:**375
Stories (Nabokov book), **1995:**505
Stormy Weather (movie), **1943:**352
"Stormy Weather" (song), **1933:**322

Story (magazine), **1931:**316
Story, William W., **1858:**134
Story of a Bad Boy, The (book), **1870:**164
Story of a Country Town, The (book), **1883:**192
Story of Dr. Doolittle, The (book), **1920:**284
Story of Philosophy, The (book), **1926:**300
Stotz, Carl, **1992:**494
Stout, Red, **1975:**444
Stover, Charles B., **1886:**198
Stowe, Harriet Beecher, **1851:**121, **1852:**123, **1853:**125, **1859:**136, **1869:**161, **1881:**187, **1896:**220
Stowel, Abel, **1809:**47
Strampee, Bob, **1964:**411
Strand, Mark, **1990:**485
Strange, Curtis, **1988:**480, **1989:**483
Strange Fruit (book), **1944:**354
Strange Interlude (play), **1928:**306
"Stranger on the Shore" (song), **1962:**406
"Strangers in the Night" (song), **1966:**416
Strang, James Jesse, **1844:**106, **1850:**119
Strasberg, Susan, **1955:**388
Strategic Arms Limitation Treaty I. *See* SALT I
Strategic Arms Reduction Treaty, **1992:**490, **1993:**495, **1995:**506
Stratemeyer, Edward, **1930:**313
Stratton, Dorothy C., **1942:**347
Straus, Isidor, **1888:**201
Straus, Nathan, **1888:**201
Strauss, Joseph B., **1938:**336
Strauss, Levi, **1902:**235
straw, drinking, **1888:**201
"Streak, The" (song), **1974:**440
"streaking" (fad), **1974:**441
Streamers (play), **1976:**446
Streep, Meryl, **1979:**454, **1982:**462, **1983:**465, **1985:**470–71, **1986:**473, **1995:**505
Streetcar Named Desire, A (movie), **1951:**377
Streetcar Named Desire, A (play), **1947:**364
streetcars, **1884:**194
    Cleveland-Shaker Heights line, **1905:**240
    first, **1864:**148
    gas-powered, **1873:**170
    See also trolley
Streeter, Edward, **1918:**279
streets
    first lights, **1806:**45
    first one-way, **1791:**24
Street Scene (movie), **1931:**316
Streisand, Barbra, **1964:**411, **1968:**423, **1973:**438
Strength of Fields, The (book), **1979:**453
Strictly from Hunger (book), **1937:**334
Strike It Rich (television program), **1951:**377
strikes, **1882:**189, **1885:**195, **1886:**196, **1888:**201, **1892:**209, **1894:**215, **1933:**321, **1933:**322, **1936:**330, **1945:**357, **1947:**364, **1948:**366,

Swaggart, Jimmy, **1988**:479
"Swan, The" (song), **1887**:200
"Swanee" (song), **1918**:278
Swan Lake (book), **1989**:482
Swanson, Gloria, **1983**:465
Swarthmore College, **1864**:149
Swayze, John Cameron, **1995**:505
Sweden
    colonial settlers, ix
    recognizes American independence,
      1783:11
    U.S. extradition treaty, **1905**:241
Swedenborgian (or New) Church,
    1800:37
Sweeney, John, **1818**:62
Sweeney Todd (musical), **1979**:454
Sweet Adeline (musical), **1929**:308
"Sweet Adeline" (song), **1903**:237
"Sweet Alice" (song), **1848**:115
"Sweet and Low" (song), **1863**:146
"Sweet Betsy from Pike" (song),
    1853:125
"Sweet By and By" (song), **1868**:158
Sweet Charity (play), **1966**:417
"Sweet Dreams" (song), **1983**:465
"Sweet Genevieve" (song), 1869,
    1869:161
"Sweet Georgia Brown" (song), **1925**:297
"Sweetheart of Sigma Chi" (song),
    1912:261
Sweethearts (operetta), **1913**:263
"Sweethearts" (song), **1913**:264
"Sweethearts on Parade" (song),
    1928:305
Sweet Iniscarra (play), **1897**:223
Sweet Kitty Bellaire (play), **1903**:238
"Sweet Leilani" (song), **1937**:334
"Sweet Rosie O'Grady" (song), **1896**:220
"Sweet Sue" (song), **1928**:305
"Sweet Violets" (song), **1908**:249
Sweezy v. New Hampshire, **1957**:392
Sweikert, Bob, **1955**:388
Swift, Gustavus F., **1903**:237
Swift & Co., **1877**:178, **1885**:195
Swilich, Ellen T., **1982**:462
Swim, R., **1868**:158
swimming
    English Channel feats, **1923**:292,
      1926:300
    first AAU national meet, **1916**:272
    first NCAA women's title, **1982**:463
    freestyle record, **1912**:262
    length records, 242
    Olympic gold medals, **1972**:435
    time records, **1906**:245
    Weismuller records, **1922**:290
"Swingin' on a Star" (song), **1944**:354
Swinnerton, Jimmy, **1892**:211
Swope, Gerard, **1957**:393
Swope, Herbert B., **1917**:275
Syllabus of a Course of Lectures on Chemistry,
    A (book), **1813**:54
Symington, Fife, **1997**:511
Symington, Stuart, **1947**:363, **1988**:478
Symphonic Piece (musical composition),
    1928:305

Symphony Concertante, **1951**:376
Symphony Orchestra (N.Y.C.), **1929**:308
Symphony, River Run (musical composi-
    tion), **1984**:467
synthesis, molecule, **1990**:485
synthesizer, electronic, **1962**:406
synthetics
    cellophane, **1924**:293
    coal gasification, **1974**:440
    dacron, **1941**:345
    rayon, **1910**:255
    rubber, **1913**:262
Syracuse University, **1870**:163
System of Anatomy, A (book), **1811**:51
System of Mineralogy (book), **1837**:93
Szell, George, **1970**:428
Szent-Györgyi, Albert, **1937**:334
Szilard, Leo, **1942**:348
Szoka, Edmund C., **1988**:479
Szold, Henrietta, **1916**:272

T

table tennis, **1931**:317, **1936**:332,
    1957:394
Tabulating Machine Co., **1896**:219
tabulating machines, **1889**:203
Taft, Helen H., **1943**:351
Taft, Lorado Z., **1920**:284, **1936**:331
Taft, Robert A., **1953**:381
Taft, William Howard
    Arizona statehood veto, **1911**:257
    begins tradition of throwing out first
      baseball of season, **1910**:256
    as Chief Justice of Supreme Court,
      1921:285–86
    dismissal of Pinchot, **1910**:254
    elected president, **1908**:248
    Philippines commission, **1900**:229,
      1901:232
    presidential reelection defeat,
      1912:259
    as Secretary of War, **1904**:239
    as Solicitor General, **1890**:206
    War Labor Board, **1918**:277
Taft-Hartley Act, **1947**:364, **1950**:372
Taggart, William H., **1907**:247
Tagliabue, Paul, **1989**:482
Tailor of Panama, The (book), **1996**:508
Tainter, Charles S., **1940**:342
Taipan (book), **1966**:417
Taiwan, **1979**:452
Takamine, Jokichi, **1901**:233
Take a Chance (play), **1932**:319
"Take Back Your Gold" (song), **1897**:222
"Take Me Home, Country Road" (song),
    1971:431
"Take Me Out to the Ball Game" (song),
    1908:249
"Takes Two to Tango" (song), **1952**:379
"Take the A Train" (song), **1941**:345
Tale, The (painting), **1961**:404
Talent Scouts (radio program), **1946**:362
Talent Scouts (television program),
    1948:368
Tales of a Traveler (book), **1824**:70
Tales of a Wayside Inn (book), **1863**:146

Tales of Peter Parley About America (book),
    1827:75
Tales of the Grotesque and Arabesque (book),
    1840:99
Tales of the South Pacific (book), **1947**:364
Talk of New York, The (musical), **1907**:247
Talledega, Battle of, **1813**:54
"Tall ships" parade (N.Y. Harbor),
    1976:444–45
Tally, Thomas L., **1902**:236
"Tamar and Other Poems" (book),
    1924:295
Tambourine, The (painting), **1905**:242
Tamerlane and Other Poems (book),
    1829:78
Taming of the Shrew, The (play), **1887**:200
Tammany Hall (N.Y.C.), **1871**:164,
    1872:167
Tammany, or the Indian Chief (opera),
    1794:28
"Tammy" (song), **1957**:393
Tampa (Fla.)
    bridge disaster, **1980**:457
    seasonal commercial passenger ser-
      vice to St. Augustine, **1914**:266
Tampico (Mexico), **1914**:265
Tan (magazine), **1950**:374
Tandy, Jessica, **1966**:417, **1977**:449,
    1989:482, **1994**:501
Taney, Roger B., **1834**:86, **1836**:90,
    1864:148
"Tangerine" (song), **1942**:349
Tanglewood Music Festival (Mass.),
    1934:325, **1937**:334
Tanguay, Eva, **1947**:365
Tannen, Harry H., **1895**:218
Tanner, Benjamin T., **1881**:187
Tanner, Henry O., **1931**:316
Tanner, Margaret Ellen, **1956**:390
tape recorder, **1948**:367, **1956**:390
Tappan, Arthur, **1833**:84
Tappan, Lewis, **1841**:99
Tappan Stove Co., **1955**:387
Tappan Zee Bridge (N.Y.), **1955**:387
"Taps" (music), **1862**:144
"Ta-ra-ra-boom-de-ay" (song), **1891**:208
Tar Baby, The (book), **1904**:240
Tarbell, Ida M., **1903**:237, **1944**:354
Tariff Act, **1870**:163, **1872**:167,
    1875:173, **1883**:190
Tariff Commission, **1882**:188, **1916**:270
tariffs
    acts of 1828 and 1832 amended,
      1833:84
    Canadian-U.S. reduction, **1911**:257
    cotton, **1824**:70
    cotton and woolens, **1818**:61
    emergency act, **1921**:286
    few commodities duty free, **1846**:109
    free commodity list, **1870**:163
    free-trade agreement, **1992**:490,
      1993:494
    GATT agreement, **1993**:494
    higher called for, **1827**:74
    rate rises, **1861**:140, **1922**:288
    reductions, **1872**:167, **1909**:251,

world's deepest producing oil well, **1971:**430

Texas A & M University, **1876:**177

Texas Air Corp., **1985:**469, **1986:**472

Texas & Pacific Railroad, **1871:**164

Texas Christian University, **1873:**170

Texas Republican (newspaper), **1819:**64

Texas Tech University, **1922:**289

textile industry

    card-making machine, **1777:**4

    cotton mills established, **1789:**21

    cotton promotion, **1921:***286*

    factory, **1813:**54

    import-limits bill vetoed, **1985:**469

    inception of, **1793:**26

    Lawrence (Mass.) mills., **1822:**67

    Slater's cotton mill, **1790:**22, **1790:***22*

    strikes, **1904:**239, **1912:**260, **1913:**262

Thaïs (opera), **1907:**247

Thalberg, Irving, **1936:**332

Thames, Battle of, **1813:**53

Thames, Battle of the, **1813:**53, **1813:***54*

"Thanatopsis" (poem), **1817:**60, **1878:**181

"Thank God, I'm a Country Boy" (song), **1975:**443

"Thanks for the Memories" (song), **1938:**337

Thanksgiving Day, American Revolution victories, **1777:**4

That Championship Season (play), **1972:**434

"That Old Black Magic" (song), **1942:**349

"That Old Feeling" (song), **1937:**334

"That Old Gang of Mine" (song), **1923:**292

"That's All Right, Mama" (song), **1954:**385

"That's Amore" (song), **1953:**382

"That's A-Plenty" (song), **1914:**266

"That's What Friends Are For" (song), **1986:**473

Thaw, Harry K., **1906:**245

Thayer, Abbott H., **1893:**213

Thayer, Ernest L., **1888:**202

Thayer, Frederick W., **1878:**182

Thayer, Sylvanus, **1817:**60

Theater Arts Magazine, **1916:**272

Theaterium (showboat), **1890:**207

theaters

    air-conditioning, **1848:**115

    Boston, **1796:**31

    colonial-era, xiv

    disasters, **1908:**250

    fires, **1903:**238

    first lighted by gas, **1825:**72

    first "little theater," **1900:**231

    first play opens, **1787:**18

    first radio broadcast of play, **1922:**290

    first summer, **1800:**37

    first ticket speculators, **1850:**119

    longest-running Broadway show to date, **1982:**462, **1997:**513

    opening of, **1794:**28

    San Francisco, **1869:**161

women ushers, **1903:**238

    See also movies; *specific cities and theaters*

Theater Syndicate, **1896:**220

Theatre Guild, **1919:**282

thefts and robbery

    artwork, **1990:**485

    bank, **1878:**182

    first bank, **1831:**82

    train, **1877:**179

Theiler, Max, **1937:**334, **1951:**376

Their Wedding Journey (book), **1872:**168

Thelma and Louise (movie), **1991:**489

Theobald, Samuel, **1930:**311

Theory of Business Enterprise, The (book), **1904:**239

Theory of the Gene, The (book), **1926:**299

Theory of the Leisure Class, The (book), **1899:**226

"There Goes My Baby" (song), **1959:**398

"There Is a Tavern in the Town" (song), **1883:**192

"There I've Said It Again" (song), **1941:**345, **1945:**357

"There'll Be Some Changes Made" (song), **1921:**287

"There's a Long, Long Trail" (song), **1913:**264

"There's a Rainbow 'Round My Shoulder" (song), **1928:**305

"There's a Small Hotel" (song), **1936:**331

There Shall Be No Night (play), **1940:**343

thermodynamics, chemical, **1949:**369

"These Foolish Things" (song), **1936:**331

"They Didn't Believe Me" (song), **1914:**266

They're Playing Our Song (play), **1979:**454

They Were Expendable (book), **1942:**349

thiamine, **1912:**261

Thief of Bagdad, The (movie), **1924:**295

"Thimble Theater" (cartoon), **1919:**281

Things of This World (book), **1956:**390

Thinker, The (painting), **1900:**231

Thinkin' About You (album), **1995:**504

Thin Man, The (book), **1934:**326

Thin Man, The (movie), **1934:**326

Third Congregational Unitarian Society (N.Y.C.), **1859:**135

Third International AIDS Conference, **1987:**476

13 Clocks, The (book), **1950:**374

Thirteenth Amendment, **1865:**150

Thirtysomething (television program), **1991:**489

"This Guy's in Love with You" (song), **1968:**422

This Is Your Life (television program), **1952:**380

"This Ole House" (song), **1954:**385

This Side of Innocence (book), **1946:**361

This Side of Paradise (book), **1920:**284

Thomas, Augustus, **1900:**231, **1907:**247

Thomas, Clarence, **1991:**487, **1991:***489*

Thomas, Danny, **1953:**382

Thomas, David, **1840:**98

Thomas, Debi, **1986:**474, **1988:**480

Thomas, E. Donnell, **1990:**485

Thomas, Herb, **1951:**377

Thomas, Isaiah, **1812:**53

Thomas, John, **1960:**402

Thomas, Lowell, **1930:**312, **1981:**459

Thomas, Martha C., **1884:**194

Thomas, Norman, **1968:**421

Thomas, Robert B., **1792:**26

Thomas, Seth, **1859:**135

Thomas, Theodore, **1861:**141

Thomas and Beulah (book), **1986:**473

Thomas Houston Electric Co., **1892:**209

Thomas-Morse MB-1 Scout, **1919:**280

Thomas Motor Co., **1908:**250

Thomas's Symphony Orchestra, **1868:**158

Thompson, Daniel T., **1839:**97

Thompson, Dorothy, **1961:**404

Thompson, Elihu, **1886:**197

Thompson, Eliza, **1873:**169

Thompson, John, **1864:**148

Thompson, John T., **1915:**268, **1940:**342

Thompson, J. Walter, **1878:**181

Thompson, Mary Harris, **1863:**146

Thompson, Sada, **1994:**501

Thompson, Will H., **1888:**202

Thomson, Bobby, **1951:**377

Thomson, Robert W., **1847:**112

Thomson, Virgil, **1934:**325

Thoreau, Henry David, **1849:**116, **1854:***126,* **1854:**127, **1862:**144, **1864:**149

Thorn Birds, The (book), **1977:**448

Thornton, William, **1793:**26, **1828:**76

Thoroughly Modern Millie (movie), **1967:**420

Thorpe, Jim, **1912:**261, **1953:**383

    American Professional Football Assn. presidency, **1920:**285

    posthumous restoration of Olympic medals, **1982:**463

    stripped of Olympic medals, **1913:**264

Thousand Clowns, A (play), **1962:**407

Thousand Days, A (book), **1965:**413

Thrasher (submarine), **1963:**408

Three Black Pennies (book), **1917:**275

Three Cheers (play), **1928:**306

Three Experiments of Living (book), **1837:**93

Three Faces of Eve, The (movie), **1957:**394

Three Hallucinations for Orchestra (musical composition), **1982:**462

"Three Litle Words" (song), **1930:**312

Three Mile Island (Pa.), nuclear accident, **1979:**452, **1979:***453*

Three Movements for Orchestra (musical composition), **1982:**462

Three Musketeers, The (movie), **1921:**287

Three Musketeers, The (operetta), **1928:**305

Threepenny Opera (opera), **1952:**379

Three Soldiers (book), **1921:**287

"Three Times a Lady" (song), **1978:**450

Three Wise Fools (play), **1918:**279

Throgs Neck Bridge (N.Y.), **1961:**403

"Throw Him Down, McCloskey" (song),

Willis, Nathaniel P., **1837:**94
Willkie, Wendell L., **1940:**341, **1944:**353
Wills, Helen, **1923:**293, **1927:**303, **1928:**306, **1929:**309
Wills, Nat, **1917:**275
Willson Aluminum Co., **1892:**209
Willson, Meredith, **1984:**467
Willys, John N., **1907:**246, **1935:**328
Willys-Overland Co., **1907:**246
Willys-Overland Dealers, **1915:**268
Wilman, Joseph, **1946:**362
Wilmer, Richard H., **1862:**144
Wilmington (Del.)
    DuPont plant explosion, **1915:**267
    DuPont research laboratory, **1928:**304
Wilmington (N.C.), American Revolution, **1776:**1, **1781:**8
Wilson, Alexander, **1813:**54
Wilson, Allen B., **1856:**130
Wilson, August, **1986:**473, **1989:**482
Wilson, Charles T. R., **1927:**301
Wilson, Earl, **1942:**349
Wilson, Edith (Gault), **1915:**267, **1961:**403
Wilson, Edmund, **1972:**434
Wilson, Ellen, **1914:**265
Wilson, Flip, **1970:**429
Wilson, Harry L., **1915:**269, **1922:**289
Wilson, Henry, **1875:**173
Wilson, Johnny, **1921:**288
Wilson, Kenneth G., **1982:**461
Wilson, Lanford, **1973:**438, **1981:**459, **1982:**462
Wilson, Robert, **1978:**450
Wilson, Sloan, **1955:**388
Wilson, William A., **1984:**466
Wilson, William B., **1913:**262, **1934:**323
Wilson, William G., **1935:**329
Wilson, William L., **1900:**230
Wilson, Woodrow
    death of, **1924:**293
    elected governor of New Jersey, **1910:**254
    elected president, **1912:**259
    first president to appear before Congress since J. Adams, **1913:**262
    Fourteen Points for peace program, **1918:**276
    League of Nations, **1919:**279
    marries Edith B. Galt, **1915:**267
    Mexican Expedition, **1916:**270
    National Research Council, **1918:**277
    neutrality proclamation, **1914:**265
    Nobel Peace Prize, **1919:**280
    Princeton presidency, **1902:**235
    reelected president, **1916:**270
    stroke, **1919:**279
    wife dies, **1914:**265
    World War I, **1915:**267, **1916:**270, **1917:**272, **1917:**273, **1917:**274
Wilson Dam (Ala.), **1925:**296
Wilson-Gorman tariff, **1984:**214
Wilson v. New, **1917:**274
Wimbledon, **1995:**505, **1996:**509, **1997:**513

Winchell, Walter, **1930:**313, **1972:**434
    begins gossip column, **1924:**294–95
Winchester, Oliver F., **1848:**115, **1857:**132, **1860:**137, **1886:**197
"Wind Beneath My Wings" (song), **1989:**482
windfall profits tax
    approved, **1979:**452
    ruled constitutional, **1983:**463
Window, The (painting), **1950:**374
Windows (musical composition), **1971:**431
Winds of War, The (book), **1971:**431
wind tunnels, **1931:**315
Winebrenner, John, **1830:**80, **1860:**138
Wine from These Grapes (book), **1934:**325
Winesburg, Ohio (book), **1919:**281
Wing-and-Wing (book), **1842:**102
Winged Victory (play), **1943:**352
Wings (movie), **1927:**303
Wings of the Dove (opera), **1961:**404
Wings of the Dove, The (book), **1902:**236
Winkler, Henry, **1974:**441
Winninger, Charles, **1925:**297, **1927:**303
Winning of Barbara Worth, The (book), **1911:**259
Winsor, Kathleen, **1944:**354
Winter, Allen, **1908:**250
Winter Garden Theater (N.Y.C.), **1911:**259
Winter Olympics. *See* Olympic Games, first winter
Winters, Jonathan, **1967:**420
Winterset (play), **1935:**329
Winter's Tale (book), **1983:**465
Winton, Alexander, **1897:**221
Winton Motor Carriage Co., **1897:**221
wireless transmitter
    ICC rate control, **1910:**255
    improved, **1901:**232
Wire Recording Corp., **1948:**367
wire rope, 1869
Wirt, William, **1832:**83, **1834:**86
Wisconsin
    constitution forbids slavery, **1848:**114
    direct primaries, **1903:**236
    first statewide primary, **1906:**243
    forest fires, **1871:**166
    Socialist congressional representative, **1910:**254–55
    statehood, **1848:**114
    territory established, **1836:**90
    unemployment insurance, **1932:**317
    University of Wisconsin, **1890:**206
    Woman Suffrage Assn., **1887:**200
Wisconsin Landscape (painting), **1940:**342
Wise, Isaac Mayer, **1873:**170, **1900:**231
Wise, John, **1835:**89, **1878:**181
Wise, Stephen S., **1898:**225, **1922:**289, **1949:**370
Wise, Stephen W., **1907:**247
Wish Tree, The (book), **1962:**406
Wistar, Caspar, **1811:**51
Wister, Owen, **1902:**236
Witchcraft (play), **1847:**113
witchcraft trials, xiii
Witching Hour, The (play), **1907:**247

Witching House, The (book), **1990:**485
"With a Little Luck" (song), **1978:**450
"With All Her Faults, I Love Her Still" (song), **1888:**202
"With a Song in My Heart" (song), **1929:**308
Witherspoon, John, **1782:**11, **1794:**28
Within the Law (play), **1912:**261
Without Remorse (book), **1993:**498
"Without You" (song), **1972:**434
With the Procession (book), **1895:**218
Witness Tree, A (book), **1942:**349
Wittemann, Charles R., **1918:**277
Wittenberg College, **1845:**108
Wittenmeyer, Anna, **1874:**171
Wittig, George, **1979:**452–53
Wizard of Oz, The (movie), **1939:***339,* **1939:**340
W. K. Kellogg Co., **1900:**230, **1906:**243
WMJ (Detroit radio station), **1920:**284
WNBT (N.Y.C. television station), **1941:**345
Wodehouse, P. G., **1916:**272, **1975:**444
Wolcott, Erastus B., **1861:**141
Wolfe, Richard, **1912:**261
Wolfe, Thomas, **1929:**308, **1935:**328, **1938:**337, **1939:**339, **1940:**342
Wolfe, Tom, **1988:**479
Wolgast, Ad, **1910:**256
Woman:Ochre (painting), **1955:**388
Woman of Andros, The (book), **1930:**313
Woman's Journal (magazine), 1869, **1870:**164
woman suffrage
    Arizona, **1912:**259
    bill fails Senate passage, **1878:**181
    California, **1911:**257
    California bill fails, **1878:**181
    Colorado, **1893:**12
    Congressional Union for Woman Suffrage, **1913:**262
    Fifth Avenue protest march, **1910:**254, **1910:***254*
    Idaho, **1896:**219
    in Illinois local election, **1913:**262
    Indiana, **1917:**275
    Kansas, **1912:**259
    march on Capitol, **1914:**265
    Michigan, **1917:**274
    Montana, **1914:**265
    National Woman Suffrage Assn., **1869:**159
    Nebraska, **1917:**274
    Nevada, **1914:**265
    New Jersey, **1776:**2
    Nineteenth Amendment, **1919:**280, **1920:**283
    Nineteenth Amendment upheld, **1922:**288
    North Dakota, **1917:**275
    Ohio, **1912:**259, **1917:**275
    Oregon, **1912:**259
    Rhode Island, **1917:**274
    state laws, **1910:**254
    Texas, **1917:**274
    Utah, **1896:**212